THE
FOREVER PRISONER

Also by Cathy Scott-Clark and Adrian Levy

The Exile: The Stunning Inside Story
of Osama bin Laden and Al Qaeda in Flight

The Siege: The Attack on the Taj

The Meadow: Kashmir 1995—Where the Terror Began

Deception: Pakistan, the United States, and the Global
Nuclear Weapons Conspiracy

The Amber Room: The Fate of the World's Greatest Lost Treasure

The Stone of Heaven: Unearthing the Secret History
of Imperial Green Jade

THE
FOREVER PRISONER

The Full and
Searing Account of
the CIA's Most
Controversial
Covert Program

Cathy Scott-Clark
and Adrian Levy

Atlantic Monthly Press
New York

FIRST EDITION

Published simultaneously in Canada
Printed in Canada

First Grove Atlantic hardcover edition: April 2022

Library of Congress Cataloging-in-Publication data is available for this title.

ISBN 978-0-8021-5892-5
eISBN 978-0-8021-5894-9

Atlantic Monthly Press
an imprint of Grove Atlantic
154 West 14th Street
New York, NY 10011

Distributed by Publishers Group West

groveatlantic.com

22 23 24 25   10 9 8 7 6 5 4 3 2 1

To all the victims of terror

CONTENTS

THE
FOREVER PRISONER

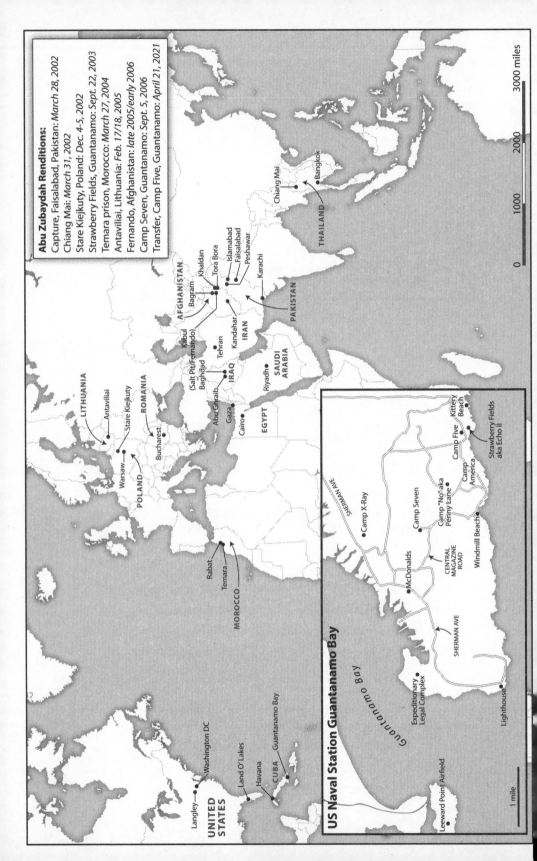

Abu Zubaydah Renditions:

Capture, Faisalabad, Pakistan: *March 28, 2002*
Chiang Mai: *March 31, 2002*
Stare Kiejkuty, Poland: *Dec. 4-5, 2002*
Strawberry Fields, Guantanamo: *Sept. 22, 2003*
Temara prison, Morocco: *March 27, 2004*
Antaviliai, Lithuania: *Feb. 17/18, 2005*
Fernando, Afghanistan: *late 2005/early 2006*
Camp Seven, Guantanamo: *Sept. 5, 2006*
Transfer, Camp Five, Guantanamo: *April 21, 2021*

0   1000   2000   3000 miles

UNITED
STATES

Langley
Washington DC
Land O' Lakes
Havana
CUBA   Guantanamo Bay

LITHUANIA
Antaviliai
Warsaw
Stare Kiejkuty
POLAND
ROMANIA
Bucharest

MOROCCO
Rabat
Temara

Gaza
EGYPT
Cairo
SAUDI
ARABIA
Riyadh

IRAQ
Baghdad
Abu Ghraib
(Salt Pit/Fernando)
Kabul
Tehran
Kandahar
IRAN
PAKISTAN

Khaldan
Bagram
Tora Bora
Islamabad
Faisalabad
Peshawar
Karachi
AFGHANISTAN

THAILAND
Chiang Mai
Bangkok

US Naval Station Guantanamo Bay

Guantanamo Bay

SHERMAN AVE

Camp X-Ray

Camp Seven

McDonalds

Expeditionary
Legal Complex

Leeward Point Airfield

Lighthouse

SHERMAN AVE

CENTRAL
MAGAZINE
ROAD

Camp "No" aka
Penny Lane
Camp
America
Camp Five
Kittery
Beach

Windmill Beach

Strawberry Fields
aka Echo II

1 mile

INTRODUCTION

M ore than twenty years after 9/11, we continue to wrestle with a paradox. Al Qaeda's much feared and anticipated "second wave" of attacks on the United States never materialized, which the CIA hails as a great success. But no "high value" detainees interrogated by the CIA have been sentenced for carrying out the 9/11 attacks that killed almost three thousand people, which makes for a monumental failure for the victims' families and also for the United States' justice system.

Central to this paradox is an experiment called "enhanced interrogation" by the CIA but dubbed torture by two US presidents, two former CIA directors, and two Senate committees. Successive US investigations into it have concluded that the CIA broke federal and international laws. The CIA inspector general reported that CIA detainees died during or after harsh interrogations. Official records show that at least thirty-nine CIA detainees were subjected to enhanced interrogation, while around twenty more were never properly documented, and disappeared. At the epicenter of this controversial program are two people: Abu Zubaydah, the first detainee subjected to enhanced interrogation; and Jim Mitchell, the CIA program's architect and Abu Zubaydah's primary interrogator. In this book, we explore their relationship, get back into the interrogation cell with them, and witness the secret program close-up. We hear from Abu Zubaydah, who was gagged by the CIA back in 2002 and has never spoken publicly; and Mitchell, who was exposed and trashed by the media, along with his interrogation partner, Bruce Jessen.

The CIA never wants the truth about enhanced interrogation to be told. Instead of fully investigating what went wrong, admitting the wide-ranging consequences, or prosecuting those who had committed abuse, the CIA ran

1

its own narrative, embracing Hollywood and Fox TV. Jack Bauer in *24* broke fingers and suffocated and electrocuted "bad guys," while in *Zero Dark Thirty*, a badly beaten Al Qaeda suspect gave up vital clues about Osama bin Laden's location, as if to say, as long as it was only the "good guys" doing the torturing, then it was justified—because it worked.

We began investigating enhanced interrogation in 2016 while finishing up a previous book, *The Exile*, about Osama bin Laden's last decade on the run, in which opposing views were regularly voiced about whether the CIA program had helped or hindered the hunt for the world's most wanted man. The story of Abu Zubaydah, who the CIA accused of being "Number Three" in Al Qaeda and a 9/11 planner and financier, consistently defied us. By the time *The Exile* was published in May 2017, he had been held in US government custody for fifteen years, although he was never charged. According to the Pentagon, he was still an "unlawful enemy combatant" and a danger to the world, even though the US government had by then conceded that he never fought American forces, did not have advance knowledge of any Al Qaeda attacks, and was not a member of Al Qaeda.

Only snippets of verifiable information about this "forever prisoner" were available, material that was overwhelmed by hundreds of best-selling "War on Terror" books, including several CIA memoirs. These memoirs told stories of diligence, valor, and success, in which Abu Zubaydah was a monster who had planned more attacks and who deserved to be treated harshly, while enhanced interrogation was legal, professional, and fully approved, all the way up to the president. They promoted the official CIA narrative that harsh techniques were tough but necessary, that enhanced interrogation had thwarted Abu Zubaydah's plans to kill countless more Americans.

However, the Senate Select Committee on Intelligence (SSCI) concluded otherwise. Its December 2014 CIA torture report stated that the case against him had been largely fabricated. Techniques trialed on him with devastating impact, and then used on others, amounted to torture. No actionable high-value intelligence was obtained through enhanced interrogation. The twenty most frequently cited and prominent examples of counterterrorism successes that the CIA attributed to its program were "wrong in fundamental respects." The CIA was guilty of murder, brutality, deception, withholding medical care, and allowing psychologists to approve abusive techniques, and then double up as interrogators, even though they had no experience or knowledge of Al Qaeda or Islam. The CIA had vastly inflated Abu Zubaydah's connections to Osama bin Laden, lied about his knowledge of future attacks, and then covered up its wrongdoings by destroying or hiding evidence of abuse. Senate investigators found no evidence that Abu Zubaydah had been trained to resist interrogation, as the CIA maintained when it presented its legal case for "hard approach measures" to senior administration lawyers in the spring of 2002.

Using contacts established over many years of reporting on terrorism, we delved deep, reaching out to Mitchell, Jessen, Abu Zubaydah, and many others. While the CIA was intent on keeping Abu Zubaydah "incommunicado" forever, he was able to speak to us via a circuitous route, although he did not authorize this book. The CIA also restricted access to the vast majority of the six-million-plus documents relating to Abu Zubaydah and its program, but Freedom of Information Act (FOIA) suits helped shake thousands of previously classified documents free.

Our primary motivation was to understand men whose lives changed forever after their eyes first met inside a secret CIA interrogation bunker in Thailand. What were the real reasons the US government was determined to keep Abu Zubaydah incommunicado forever? Was he really a danger to the world or an existential threat to the CIA? What had motivated Mitchell and Jessen, both stellar military psychologists with faultless careers to date, to invent the toxicity of enhanced interrogation? Money? Fame and respect? Or patriotism?

This book aims to tell these parallel stories through the key players' own recollections. We also sought out officers, contractors, lawyers, special agents, soldiers, and other detainees, who planned, designed, and lived through enhanced interrogation, to bring to life a story most often populated by inanimate objects with extraordinary resonance—waterboards, coffins, dog crates, "walling" walls, shackles, masks, diapers, and orange prison scrubs.

Mitchell threatened to have the FBI throw us off his property when we first approached him in February 2017. After he relented, he introduced us to his closest former colleagues, for which we are grateful. Many engaged with us, although a few, like Jessen, withdrew. Those who spoke revealed a complex picture of a program born out of genuine fears, and urgent national and political need, but sullied by xenophobia, nationalism, ignorance, suspicion, deception, aggression, and ambition. "Enhanced interrogation" entranced everyone connected to protecting America, then mutated like a virus, infecting everything and everyone who touched it. The consequences have been devastating.

So who was to blame? And who, if anyone, should face criminal charges? Who were the "good guys," and who were the "bad guys"? In the end, Mitchell told us one critical truth: that the binary Hollywood world the CIA liked to inhabit was irrelevant because humans were chameleons, always adapting to their circumstances. "Bad guys become good guys and vice versa," he said during one candid interview session at his home in Florida in June 2019. Who was he talking about? Himself or Abu Zubaydah?

January 18, 2020, 7:00 A.M., Andrews Air Force Base, Maryland

Just a few weeks prior to the onset of the COVID-19 pandemic, Jim Mitchell barrels into the overcrowded passenger service center, running the gauntlet of defense lawyers and media. Everyone is gathering for a flight down to Guantánamo Bay, Cuba, to attend a hearing of five men facing the death penalty for conspiring to kill almost three thousand Americans on September 11, 2001.[1] There have been more than forty "pretrial" hearings for "KSM et al.," Khalid Sheikh Mohammad, the self-confessed architect, and his co-conspirators.[2] But twenty years on from 9/11, the actual trial has not yet started because of what the Central Intelligence Agency paid Mitchell and his partner, Bruce Jessen, to do. This will be the first time Mitchell and Jessen take the stand, facing men they are accused of torturing, men they have not seen in more than a decade, and who now deny many of the confessions extracted from them.[3] It will be the last 9/11 pretrial hearing for twenty months.

Everyone arriving at Andrews on this chilly January morning is on tenterhooks about what Mitchell and Jessen will say. Most of the six-million-plus CIA documents related to the program remain classified, as does practically everything that happened inside the interrogation chamber.[4] Officially, only three CIA "detainees" died, but around twenty more were never registered, and disappeared.[5] Those who survived the program claim they suffered permanent mental and physical injuries, but no provably significant intelligence was gained from them, according to US Senate investigators.[6] Despite this, no CIA employee who worked in the program has ever been prosecuted.[7]

For many years, CIA insiders were gagged, although agency leadership publicly championed the program's success.[8] Those who spoke negatively, or briefed without authorization, were threatened with legal actions or jailed.[9] But in 2014, after the US Senate published a shocking summary of its six-year-long classified investigation—that reported the CIA had committed torture, brutality, cover-up, and murder—Mitchell was unleashed to tell folksy stories of "fireside chats" with detainees, sharing "tea and treats," movies and novels, playing ball games and doing calisthenics.[10] His stories were crafted with CIA public affairs officials and approved by CIA lawyers. But in the present book, Mitchell and those who worked closely with him speak frankly and describe the long march back to Guantánamo, as does Zayn-al-Abidin Abu Zubaydah, the first CIA detainee, whose physical and psychological injuries are the most extensive.

Back in 2002, before enhanced interrogation was started on him, the CIA extracted a promise from the US government that Abu Zubaydah would remain "incommunicado" for the rest of his life, irrespective of his level of guilt. His status as an "unlawful enemy combatant" would remain unchanged until the War on Terror was deemed to be over, a decision that rested with the president.[11] Twenty years on, Abu Zubaydah is still at Guantánamo, never charged. His chances of winning freedom remain microscopically small; while his lawyers say he is "not Hollywood innocent," new correspondence from him reveals an extraordinary story.[12]

———◆———

Mitchell weaves a rapid, deft path through suitcases, passing defense lawyers and NGO (nongovernmental organization) representatives who regard him as a war criminal. He winks at familiar faces before being ushered into the VIP waiting room by Brigadier General Mark Martins, the chief prosecutor, whose job is to make sure KSM et al. are "brought to justice"—although he will resign before the next hearing in September 2021.[13] Inside the VIP room, relatives of those who died in the attacks greet Mitchell warmly. They put their names into a lottery to attend hearings and catch a glimpse of the five men the government has accused of murdering their loved ones. Many call Mitchell a hero, and during this hearing one woman will propose marriage (he is already married).[14] The Guantánamo invitations in part promise restorative justice, though they attract a gallows crowd, and are a reminder of what has not been achieved. Following 9/11, President George W. Bush's War on Terror chipped away at Al Qaeda's sprawling network, killing or netting many of those connected to the attacks, including, eventually, in the succeeding administration, Osama bin Laden. However, the CIA's enthusiasm for "enhanced interrogation" meant that no conventional court could ever try those captured alive. Instead, after the program was exposed, the CIA detainees were rendered to an American corner of Cuba that the US government called the "endgame facility." Those who could be put in front of military commissions would be tried and executed. Those who could not would be held incommunicado until they died of natural causes. For extra security, the Bush administration passed laws to secure immunity from prosecution for itself, the CIA, and its agents and contractors, and to cut the detainees off from any legal recourse.

The coffee shop is closed, and tired, uncaffeinated people clump together. Defense attorneys debate what Mitchell might be persuaded to reveal, given that he has a self-confessed propensity to run his mouth off, and this is the first time he is being examined without a CIA chaperone.[15] If he can be goaded into revealing anything compromising, it could upend the government's 9/11 case, and might even be the first step on a long road to prosecuting some of the estimated two hundred CIA employees who worked in the program.[16] But Guantánamo's military commissions system, under which War on Terror detainees are tried outside the US judicial system, is designed to fail, and is part of the huge legal fortification constructed by the Bush administration so it could go to the dark side without fear of retribution. Only eight commissions, military courts run on Pentagon rules and controlled by military judges, have been completed, none of which relate to the 9/11 conspiracy or any of its principal characters.[17] Most of those judgments have been subsequently overturned. Fewer than 4 percent of the 779 detainees ever sent to Guantánamo have or will face charges, according to a former chief prosecutor.[18] In contrast, the US federal justice system has put more than six hundred people on trial for terrorism-related offenses since 9/11, including Ahmed Ghailani, a former CIA detainee, although only one of the 280 charges against him stuck.[19]

KSM et al. were originally charged based on confessions they gave to FBI interrogators after their transfer to Guantánamo in 2006. Allegedly, they gave them voluntarily, and the FBI "clean team" members who recorded them had no connection to the CIA program. Pledging in 2009 to close the facility,

President Barack Obama tried to shift the proceedings to a federal court in Manhattan, but his administration failed to see it through, and new military commission charges were brought in 2012.[20] Since then, progress has been glacial.[21] Hurricanes, "national security privilege," repeated CIA interference, and the pandemic have brought the 9/11 pretrial hearings to a standstill, as Guantánamo disintegrates.[22] Defense teams complain of moldy office space, interrupted Skype calls, blocked toilets, and flight cancellations. In 2015, one of the accused recognized a new interpreter assigned to his case as having previously worked at a CIA black site, an unacknowledged detention and interrogation facility in a third country.[23] Cells are searched, and privileged legal correspondence has been unlawfully photographed or confiscated.[24] Almost everything detainees request through their lawyers is declared contraband, including books and DVDs of Hollywood blockbusters to help while away the years. From a recent list, only the horror-comedy *Scary Movie* was approved.[25]

By spring 2021, the 9/11 case was into its ninth year of pretrial hearings and there had been seven turnovers among six military judges, four in the last year alone. US Air Force colonel Shane Cohen, the fifth judge, who took Mitchell's and Jessen's testimonies, retired just weeks afterward.[26] One of his successors lasted barely a month, while another recused himself after two weeks.[27] Evidence emerged that some FBI "clean team" members had previously interrogated detainees at CIA black sites.[28] One key defense counsel, at age seventy-five, took the hard decision to retire. Another, age seventy, took a back seat. The accused had not seen their lawyers in more than eighteen months.[29] Before departing, Cohen set a trial date for January 2021, but because of the pandemic, the next pretrial hearing was not set until September 2021. President Joe Biden renewed his promise to close the facility, but new charges announced on the day after his inauguration against three more former CIA detainees made that extremely unlikely.

The world might have forgotten Guantánamo, but the CIA never will. In rooms where detainees consult their lawyers, listening devices have been found hidden inside fire sprinklers.[30] When commissions were still in session, defense teams discovered the CIA had access to the white-noise button used to interrupt proceedings, obliterating defense accusations. Ahead of his hearing, Mitchell boned up on classified documents that the defense teams were not allowed to read. However, thousands of previously classified CIA and FBI pages have been released as a result of FOIA forays. Many are utilized in this book.[31]

Put up at the Ritz-Carlton in Tysons Corner, Virginia, Mitchell, who eschews flamboyance, spoke over piped Christmas carols a few weeks before giving his testimony. He said it was his moral duty to return to Guantánamo as a trial witness. "It's about preventing them from somehow managing to weasel out of the justice that they have coming to them for having killed nearly three thousand people and wanting to kill more," he said of KSM et al. "Justice has been denied to the survivors of 9/11 and the victims." He was unruffled at seeing again men he once took "to the verge of death."[32] He cared nothing about the arrangements. "I assume it's a little like an execution; all the important details have been taken care of for you," he joked. But unlike KSM et al., Mitchell was not facing execution. The closest he has come to prosecution was in 2015, when he and Bruce Jessen were sued by two former CIA detainees and the family of a CIA detainee who had died. The allegation was that all three were tortured in a program established by Mitchell and Jessen. Mitchell, who complains that he and Jessen are the only people not to be properly protected by the immunity legislation because they were contractors, was unhappy when the government settled for an undisclosed sum in 2017.[33]

At ten A.M., attorneys, NGO representatives, 9/11 victim families, and journalists flood onto the asphalt of Andrews, the home base for Air Force One, although we are flying in a decades-old charter from Atlas Air. Getting an entire war court's worth of staff "on island" for hearings is eye-wateringly expensive. Guantánamo is the costliest prison on earth, where a reported $13 million is spent annually on each detainee, compared with $78,000 at America's only federal super-maximum security prison, ADX Florence in Colorado, which holds terrorists convicted by the US judicial system.[34]

After more than two hours, the plane makes its final approach, following Guantánamo's pristine coastline to avoid entering Cuban airspace. The huge Camp Delta detention facility, which at its height held almost eight hundred detainees, unfurls below.[35] Camp Seven, the "endgame facility," where fourteen former CIA detainees including Khalid Sheikh Mohammad and Abu Zubaydah lived until their cells literally fell apart and they were transferred into the main camp in April 2021, is well hidden, its precise location still classified.

From Leeward Point airfield, new arrivals jostle for space on the ferry to Windward Point. As the ferry crosses Guantánamo Bay, where Christopher Columbus dropped anchor in 1494, the US naval station's infamous command tower comes into view.[36] At the ferry landing, visitors pile into courtesy buses that zip past baseball fields, open-air cinemas, a McDonald's, a Subway sandwich shop, and O'Reilly's Irish pub. The gift shop is filled with Joint Task Force Guantánamo T-shirts, shot glasses, and furry iguanas. The Navy Exchange sells Froot Loops alongside tactical gear. One third of Guantánamo's six thousand residents are Filipino or Jamaican guest workers, and reggae reverberates around their accommodations on Gold Hill. While the defense and prosecution teams, witnesses, and victim families are housed in the Navy Inns and Suites, with a sea view and American breakfast, the media is billeted (for free) in fiercely air-conditioned tents at the aptly named Camp Justice, right next to the Expeditionary Legal Complex (ELC). This is the Pentagon's eavesdrop-proof war court, when the military commissions take place, and it is swathed in razor wire, crash barriers, stadium lighting, and chain link fencing. Many of the eighteen hundred troops posted on-island (forty-five for every detainee) live in large, barrel-shaped military tents around its perimeter. When the court is not sitting, Camp Justice resembles an abandoned movie set. Banana rats nibble plastic sniper netting around unmanned checkpoints. Turkey vultures, harbingers of death, wait silently on fortified gateposts. Iguanas sleep under mechanical watchtowers.

With two days to go before Mitchell takes the stand, the media races around in courtesy buses, stocking up on Pop-Tarts, salty snacks, and whiskey. The MOC (Media Operations Center) springs to life. It is housed in a huge condemned aircraft hangar, where journalists can type up reports while watching a secure live feed from the courtroom (only old-fashioned pen and paper are allowed inside). Laid-back Mitchell chats with Hank Schulke, his civilian lawyer, under a banyan tree outside the Tiki Bar. On Monday evening, a handwritten notice appears on the MOC whiteboard: "TUESDAY JAN 18, 0805 DEPART TO COURT (fill out Subway order first), *10am: Mitchell testimony begins*"

———◆———

One person whose name is mentioned throughout Mitchell's testimony but who never appears is Zayn-al-Abidin Abu Zubaydah, the CIA's first detainee, a Palestinian born in Saudi Arabia, who was thirty-one when he was captured in Pakistan in March 2002. The CIA characterized him as the "the

Rosetta Stone of 9/11," and argued it needed to "enhance" his interrogation because he had authored an Al Qaeda resistance-to-interrogation training manual.[37] After the CIA convinced the National Security Council that Abu Zubaydah was also hiding crucial knowledge about a second wave of attacks against the United States, Mitchell was given legal authority to use psychological tools to get inside his head.

Rendered to a CIA black site in Thailand, Abu Zubaydah, who was recovering from severe gunshot wounds, first locked eyes with Mitchell on August 4, 2002. Strapped to a hospital gurney, he recalled the first gush of icy water hitting his face.[38] Mitchell held a sodden cloth down over Abu Zubaydah's nose and mouth, making it impossible for him to breathe. "One . . . two . . . three . . ." Mitchell counted in his southern drawl, as Bruce Jessen emptied several drinking-water bottles in quick succession.[39] "Four . . . five . . . six . . ." Water engulfed Abu Zubaydah's airway, evoking his dread of drowning.[40] He frantically tried to twist away, but a head clamp gripped his cheeks, forcing his lips open.[41] His heart galloped as the gurney's headrest was tilted farther backward, lining up his nostrils to Jessen's pour. "Seven . . . eight . . . nine . . ." Time was being counted out, just as it had been in the old nightmares. Each pour could last up to forty seconds and the number of pours was unlimited.[42] "I die, I die, I die," Abu Zubaydah gasped. "Need oxygen!"[43]

After his extremities started to spasm, written instructions authorized by the US attorney general stipulated that the gurney should be jolted upright. Mitchell and Jessen got in Abu Zubaydah's face and made breathing noises until he vomited water. Slamming the gurney back down, Jessen restarted the pours. In between pours, Mitchell claimed he told the detainee he had a "safe word" he could use anytime, an agreement to "tell us what Washington wants to know."[44] Abu Zubaydah was in charge of his own fate, not them. But enhanced interrogation took priority over everything, even medical need.[45] A CIA supervisor back at headquarters talked about wanting to cause a lot of pain. Abu Zubaydah needed to be treated like a laboratory dog repeatedly subjected to electric shocks until it learned there was no point in trying to help itself.[46] "Thirteen . . . fourteen . . ." In a vengeful program riddled with ignorance, brutality, and xenophobia, he was called everything from "motherfucker" to "Abu Butthead," and "Boo boo," as they broke him, dragging him down to a debilitating psychological state called learned helplessness.

The numbers faded as Abu Zubaydah took shelter in his past: his mother; her bedroom in Riyadh with its round mirror, perfume bottles, and floral bedcover; his younger brothers fighting over the Atari and scaring them-selves with American horror movies, and an all too brief "lovely period" of marriage.[47] Happy "Hani" they had all called him.[48] His father was a tough disciplinarian, but his mother had cooked special Palestinian treats.[49] Sinking into an ocean of memories, he never gave up on his determination to survive.

Nearly two decades later and, remarkably, still alive, he woke up on a plastic mattress at Camp Seven, shaken by the all too often occurring water-boarding nightmare, one of several signs that he was suffering from post-traumatic stress disorder (PTSD), although military psychiatrists still refused to make such a diagnosis.[50] Mitchell was long gone, Jessen too, but a pile of 9/11 books dominated his cell, and retold versions of the CIA story that Abu Zubaydah was a major Al Qaeda player.[51] No one cared about his life before jihad: his Palestinian heritage, family stories of loss and displacement, a controlling father, or the wrench of leaving home. No one mentioned his studying in India, touring the world, and playing the field. He made no secret of or apology for embracing jihad at the age of twenty, and he insisted his fight was a just one for his "own people," meaning persecuted Palestinians and oppressed Muslims in every other part of the world. Yes, he had run a *mujahideen* training camp where Muslim trainees learned guerrilla warfare, but he had never killed anyone. Yes, he had met Osama bin Laden, but only twice, not "on multiple occasions," as claimed by the CIA, and he had always been opposed to killing innocent civilians.[52] He did not plan 9/11, participate in it, fund it, or have any advance knowledge; he was not a member of Al Qaeda, nor did he hate America.[53]

However, now age fifty, the real Abu Zubaydah was reduced to a blur, with every genuine detail about his life covered up, lied about, classified, or redacted. For many years, he did not know that the man cage they kept him in after Thailand was inside a villa tucked away deep in Poland's northern forests. Only a "squiggly" signature etched into a wall confirmed he had spent time inside a secret CIA facility at Guantánamo called Strawberry Fields (forever).[54] After that, he was concealed inside a former riding school in Lithu-ania and sometimes fed only ketchup. He was also imprisoned at a Moroccan interrogation facility near Rabat, where local prisoners were beaten, raped with bottles, and electrocuted.[55] It had been a long and tortuous journey that he compared to passing through the rings of hell.[56]

Having survived twenty years of incarceration, he appreciated small comforts. He had a watch, a calendar, coffee candy and halvah, a pair of dress shoes, and a Palestinian scarf. He had reading glasses, pen and paper, and after years of waste buckets, coffins, dog crates, and diapers, a real toilet, soap, and a shower. He also had a collection of photographs—his lawyers, their families. Also, his own family, still living in Riyadh but too frightened of his notoriety to communicate regularly. Brothers and sisters he remembered as silly, squabbling kids were now parents themselves. He never forgot his family, but back in Saudi Arabia, some branches of the family changed their surname.[57] So did his younger brother, Hesham, who went to the United States before 9/11 to pursue an American dream that became a nightmare.[58]

Military generators and giant fans maintained a constant noise outside his cell. He lay on his right side to ease pressure on his left thigh, ripped up during his capture and atrophied after months of neglectful medical treatment. He had a ten-inch scar running down the left side of his torso, through which a significant section of his intestine had been removed.[59] He had lost a testicle and his left eye and accused CIA medics of performing an unnecessary vasectomy. In another life, he had been surrounded by female admirers and had devised a workaround that squared his libido with his faith by temporarily "marrying" a string of European and American girlfriends. Now, half his body was "no good."[60]

In the early years at Guantánamo, he smashed CCTV cameras that watched him 24/7, went on hunger strikes, and spent more time than anyone else in the "punishment cell."[61] During arguments with the "big shot" camp commander, Abu Zubaydah called him "big shit," and goaded, "Are you going to torture me like the CIA and the FBI?" He taunted inexperienced guards, saying, "I'm ready, bring the waterboard."[62] Later, he drew disturbing illustrations of his earlier experiences, berated his lawyers, and recorded everything that had happened in his diary.[63]

As the years bled away, daily life gradually improved. After guards were permitted to talk to detainees, they told him about life on the other side of Gold Hill, where they drank Guantánamo-themed cocktails and ate Guantánamo-themed burgers. He removed his prosthetic eye to shock a new legal intern and donned his famous black eye-patch like a pirate of the Caribbean, although in reality he was more like the Man in the Iron Mask.[64] He joked of having a bionic eye like the Six Million Dollar Man that enabled him to see through his female attorney's clothes, and he doodled cartoons of himself—a smiling skull and crossbones, with an eye patch.[65] On bad days, he still battled with fainting fits, panic attacks, stuttering, anger, and outrage at his extraordinary, unprecedented status as a forever prisoner, impossible to charge but impossible to release, because he was a witness to an atrocity, rather than a suspect. An avid reader of world history, he asked his military attorneys how that status squared with a country that championed "human rights, justice, and democracy."[66] They worked for the Pentagon's Office of Military Commissions—the website of which promises FAIRNESS ★ TRANSPARENCY ★ JUSTICE—but they had no answers for him.

Twenty years after 9/11, Abu Zubaydah still waited for a chance to plead his case. On his first day in office, President Obama admitted, "We tortured some folks," but no one in government ever apologized, while most of those involved in enhanced interrogation prospered. Gina Haspel, who interrogated Abu Zubaydah and witnessed waterboarding, became President Donald Trump's CIA director. CIA lawyer Jonathan Fredman, who sought legal justifications for waterboarding, and allegedly proclaimed, "If the detainee dies you're doing it wrong," became an agency associate general counsel.[67] Fredman's boss, John Rizzo, sold his story to Hollywood.[68] Alfreda Bikowsky, who supervised a damning "Zubaydah Biography," was promoted to the upper echelons of the agency's Counterterrorism Center. Michael Morell, who was deputy CIA director when Osama bin Laden was killed, wrote a memoir, saying only three people had been subjected to the waterboard, when evidence suggested there were many, and claiming there was absolutely no connection between the CIA program and the abuses at Abu Ghraib prison in Iraq. In January 2021, when President Biden considered Morell for the CIA directorship, many objected. However, Avril Haines, a former deputy CIA director, who refused to take action against CIA officials after they hacked the computers of the Senate Intelligence Committee investigators, still became Biden's director of national intelligence.

Every morning, as the dawn call filtered down the walkway of his block, Abu Zubaydah limped from his bed to his prayer rug. Outside, the velvety Cuban sky turned rose gold. In contrast, when he is at home in Land O' Lakes, Florida, Jim Mitchell wakes up in a luxurious $800,000 house. He pads barefoot around a lounge filled with souvenirs of his "temporary duty yonder" (TDY) years: antique Afghan muskets and Persian rugs and Taliban-hunter military badges. His mahogany library is filled with research papers on brainwashing and learned helplessness, debility, dependency, and dread, fossilized dinosaur eggs and a Neanderthal skull. Box files and shelves also contain an impressive display of military citations, certificates, and medallions.

However, Mitchell's studied sophistication masks an impoverished upbringing in the segregated Deep South, where a tobacco-chewing grandmother raised him. As a child, he bathed in pails in a condemned house and searched tree stumps for Confederate gold. Ragged, scrawny, jumpy, and with a mouthful of rotten teeth, he grew up an outsider. His father was buried in a pauper's grave, he tells friends, and in moments of black humor he jokes that his mother was "nearly cremated with Lassie" in a pet cemetery.[69] In his youth, he played in a "bad rock band," and then joined the military to bring order to his chaotic life and get an education. After defusing bombs and fighting bears in Alaska, he graduated into military psychology, becoming chief psychologist at the Survival, Evasion, Resistance, Escape (SERE) school at Fairchild Air Force Base in Spokane, Washington. He supervised the mock torture of students in pretend prisoner-of-war camps in a made-up country called Spokanistan.[70] Later, he became chief psychologist at the Twenty-Fourth Special Tactics Squadron at Pope Air Force Base, North Carolina, a classified special access program, where he befriended America's most senior military psychologists based at nearby Fort Bragg, and he taught "very, very high-speed ninja warrior types" how to survive being tortured by murderous regimes that disregarded the Geneva Conventions.[71]

Over twenty-one years, Mitchell became a leading figure in the US military's behavioral science scene. Commanders praised his "superb leadership," and those who graduated his courses felt permanently indebted for his help in teaching them to survive.[72] Deep bonds of brotherhood were forged. Mitchell was an air force hero, but unless you were an elite war fighter, you would never have heard of him, had 9/11 not happened. However, his CIA association transformed him into a household name.

After the atrocity, CIA director George Tenet faced intense criticism, an administration that was convinced a second wave of attacks was imminent, and a vice president determined to go to war with Iraq.[73] The US intelligence community needed to step up. Existing processes were outmoded, said the CIA leadership. Al Qaeda's murderous actions had changed the world forever, and it was time to embrace "the Israeli defense," whereby the pragmatic security services of a state in permanent war argued that the public would tolerate a prisoner being tortured to prevent another bus bombing in Jerusalem.[74] George Tenet told the head of Israeli intelligence that after 9/11: "We all became Israelis."[75]

Horrified by scenes of people jumping to their deaths from the Twin Towers, Mitchell, who had recently retired from the military, wanted to join the fight, and he provided a clear path forward. Al Qaeda operatives were trained to resist interrogation, he said, but repurposed SERE techniques could get them talking.[76] "My task was to take what we know about psychology and use it as a weapon against our enemies," he recalled.[77] The CIA described him and Jessen "as a weapons system." By 2002, they were globetrotting, doing "special things to special people in special places," protected by a legal opinion the CIA called a "golden shield."[78] Bush's third attorney general, Michael Mukasey, described this opinion as a "slovenly mistake," but Mitchell and Jessen still won a multimillion-dollar CIA contract based around its protections.[79] According to the agency, the waterboard was the "silver bullet." It had saved countless American lives.[80]

When glimpses of the program began leaking, Mitchell and Jessen were exposed. Those who were for them called them patriots and defended America's right to a muscular self-defense, while those against accused them of wrecking a rules-bound system that had kept the West united since the Marshall Plan rebuilt Europe after World War II. Mitchell complained of being "thrown under the bus."[81] Michael Morell recalled differently, saying that Mitchell took it upon himself to become the face of the program. "The real decision makers were George Tenet, the President and Condi Rice," said Morell.[82] "Any one of them could have said no."

What follows is not just a history of one of the most divisive clandestine operations in living memory, supported by a raft of new primary sources. CIA cable traffic, emails, reports, and candid interviews with the central players help piece together a large-scale road map of a top-secret project whose central role—to secure timely, reliable, actionable intelligence to stop the next attacks on the United States—was never provably achieved. Rules finessed in Washington were jettisoned in Afghanistan, Guantánamo, and

Iraq. Some black sites used Mitchell's techniques without permission or supervision. Unqualified instructors provided training, and trainee interrogators practiced "on the job." Nurses and medics were co-opted. Ambiguous guidelines approved in the White House Situation Room frayed in a dark world of reality where verbal trickery was key. How many water "pours" could be used without actually drowning a man? How many water "applications" to block his airway and make him think he was dying, but not actually kill him? What was the difference between "watering," "flicking," "hosing," "bathing," "dunking," and "waterboarding"? Which, if any, constituted full-blown "water torture"? How many times to "bounce" someone off a wall without causing permanent brain damage?[83] How cold was too cold? How far was too far? Was the wooden container they locked Abu Zubaydah in just an oversize crate, or a coffin?

In the 1980s, after CIA officers were found to have taught interrogation techniques bordering on torture to Honduran death squads, high officials were forced to admit to Congress that torture was illegal and dangerous, and did not work because prisoners always lied to make it stop, and some died.[84] But post-9/11, the CIA went even further. Internal correspondence warned that "underperforming officers, new, totally inexperienced officers or whomever seems to be willing and able to deploy at any given time" were eliciting "mediocre or, I dare say, useless intelligence" from brutal interrogations.[85]

The repercussions of a program that cost well over $300 million in non-personnel costs are wide-ranging, disastrous, and ongoing.[86] CIA detainees died, and enhanced interrogation leaked into the US military too, reinventing itself at Bagram, Guantánamo, and Abu Ghraib, where more detainees were abused and more died.[87] The unintended consequences were colossal: dozens of Americans captured, tortured, and murdered in retribution for America's War on Terror excesses, from Daniel Pearl in Pakistan in January 2002 to James Foley in Syria in 2014. Multiple countries mimicked the CIA's experiment: Brazil, India, Israel, the Philippines, and Saudi Arabia to name but a few. Abductions, renditions, dark prisons, torture, and death—acts that bypass judiciaries, parliaments, and the people—cost thousands of lives. According to the Senate investigation, "the program caused immeasurable damage to the United States' public standing, as well as to the United States' longstanding global leadership on human rights in general and the prevention of torture in particular."[88]

After Abu Zubaydah was rendered to Guantánamo's Camp Seven in 2006, the crimes committed against him were recognized outside US jurisdiction. Twice, he won compensation from the European Court of Human Rights for false imprisonment in CIA black sites in Poland and Lithuania.[89] The United Nations removed his name from the Al Qaeda sanctions list and in 2021 it was asked to intervene in his case.[90] A criminal investigation or an independent 9/11-style inquiry might have sorted out his real affiliations and could have recommended charges, if any were due. But his fate remained untouchable because of enhanced interrogation, and the US government's carefully constructed legal framework, which prevented anyone from reaching a proper determination about who actually acted more immorally—Abu Zubaydah or Mitchell and Jessen.

When they first met in the Thai bunker in August 2002, Abu Zubaydah had no way of knowing that the CIA had already decided he be kept in isolation "for the remainder of his life."[91] Mitchell never dreamed his spotless military career would be drowned out by the CIA program's notoriety. Twenty years after 9/11, the truth is only beginning to emerge from both of them, leaving much unfinished business to be dealt with. Thus, at six A.M., on January 21, 2020, law-abiding Mitchell, who is always early to bed and early to rise, ordered a modest coffee, fired up his MacBook, and settled down to scan emails from old friends at the agency before heading over to the Guantánamo war court to douse the dumpster fire left by enhanced interrogation.

CHAPTER 1

"MAI PEN RAI"

March 28, 2002, Faisalabad, Pakistan

We had rehearsed it," recalled a CIA officer. "In at 2:00 A.M., out by 2:20 A.M. at the very latest."[1] However, moments into the raid on Shahbaz Cottage, several Arabs made a break across the roof. Jittery Pakistani police officers opened fire from the street below as the suspects jumped ninja-style onto a neighboring house.[2] None of them had guns, but a Syrian wielding a fruit knife fell, fatally wounded. A clean-shaven Palestinian with wild corkscrew hair attempted a flying kick but was shot and was hauled into the street. A Pakistani policeman was shot dead. By the time it and simultaneous raids in a dozen other locations were over, fifty suspects were trussed up in cable ties.[3] A CIA officer, panicking that they had just killed their target, demanded: "Where is Abu Zubaydah?" A Pakistani intelligence official poked the clean-shaven Palestinian bleeding at his feet. "This is your man."[4]

FBI agents and CIA officers began arguing. According to an assessment given to the National Security Council in March 2001, Abu Zubaydah was a senior Al Qaeda operative working on attack plans.[5] On August 6, 2001, he was identified as a "bin Ladin [*sic*] lieutenant" in the Presidential Daily Brief.[6] Just before the March 2002 raid, the media reported that he was plotting a second wave of attacks on the United States.[7] The FBI team was sure they had the right man.[8] But the suspect at their feet looked nothing like the CIA's target photograph showing a trim, bespectacled bureaucrat.[9] "Honest to God, this guy's forty pounds heavier," estimated the CIA team leader. That they were also relying on computer-generated enhancements did not help. In one, Abu Zubaydah's black hair had been "dyed" blond, and another depicted him wearing a woolen beanie. A stash of passport photo-

18

graphs recovered from the safe house showed the real Abu Zubaydah was, indeed, a master of disguise.[10] But the other suspects captured with him all insisted his name was "Daood."[11] Someone called for a time-out. His eyes were rolling back. He wasn't going to make it.

The team rang Alejandro "Deuce" Martinez, a Latin America specialist who had been targeting Abu Zubaydah for two months, and was waiting at a nearby safe house to make the positive identification.[12] "What do we do?" Since the injured man was worth saving only if he was Abu Zubaydah, someone suggested a retinal scan. John Kiriakou, a CIA case officer from the Counterterrorist Center, said he shouted down: "Wake up! Open your eyes." No response. "So I got down and opened his eye with my thumb," he continued, although others on the operation later claimed Kiriakou was not even there.[13] "I pulled his eyelid out so we could steady his eyeball." Someone attempted the scan. "But the eyeball kept rolling back," said Kiriakou. "He was completely out of it."[14]

If the FBI had informed the CIA it already had Abu Zubaydah's younger brother Hesham and his cousin Maher in custody, DNA identification would have been far easier. Both Hesham and Maher had entered the United States to study at an English college long before 9/11. Both had failed to register for their courses and then overstayed their visas. They were now being accused of being among Abu Zubaydah's "army of sleepers," preparing for the second wave.[15] But relations between the FBI and the CIA were acrimonious post-9/11, as recriminations flew about who had hidden what in the run-up to 9/11. Before the Twin Towers collapsed, everyone had fought over the scraps of real intelligence to gain the upper hand, and they would also fight again over Abu Zubaydah and the much-disputed circumstances of the Faisalabad raid.

An evidence bag began trilling, said Kiriakou, claiming it was Abu Zubaydah's cell phone. An FBI agent snatched it away and yelled: "It's classified crime scene evidence." If Kiriakou was telling the truth, the desire to prosecute was clashing with the need to stop future Al Qaeda operations, as had occurred prior to 9/11. Someone called Martinez again. Previously, Martinez had tracked murderous Latin American drug cartels via digital means from CIA headquarters in Langley, Virginia. He offered a simple suggestion: take a photograph and email it to the technical experts.

A reply came back within minutes. Jennifer Matthews, a former imagery specialist who had been promoted post-9/11 to run the CIA Counterterrorist

Center's AZ (Abu Zubaydah) Task Force, was 85 percent sure they had a match.[16] "Unless you want to deliver a corpse to your director, we need to get him to the hospital," an FBI paramedic chipped in. The CIA had committed to pay Pakistani intelligence officials several million dollars for this tipoff.[17] Failure was not an option, so the Americans commandeered a Toyota pickup and heaved their prime suspect into the back.[18] But the truck would not start. Punjab Rangers pushed it down the road while the driver attempted a jump-start. Eventually, the engine sputtered and the truck roared off, with tooled-up Americans riding shotgun.[19]

It was 5:45 P.M. in Washington, and CIA director George Tenet was winding up his daily counterterrorism meeting. Alvin Bernard "Buzzy" Krongard, his executive director; Jim Pavitt, head of the National Clandestine Service; Cofer Black, the table-thumping chief of the Counterterrorist Center; and Jose Rodriguez, Black's wily, risk-taking deputy, were all there.[20] So was John Rizzo, who had been "surged" into the job of acting general counsel after his predecessor stepped down six weeks after 9/11, and described himself as "the skunk at the party."[21] Marty Martin, a hard-drinking veteran case officer, who characterized himself as a "jetfighter," and bragged of leading the "worldwide hunt for Al Qaeda," although he was just part of a much larger team, talked enthusiastically in his distinctive Cajun patois.[22] Chuck Frahm, a deputy assistant FBI director, who had been seconded to the CIA post-9/11 to improve interagency relations, leading some to joke that he had "gone over to the dark side," watched as CIA attorneys circulated a memo about the Geneva Conventions.[23] Michael Morell, President Bush's daily intelligence briefer on 9/11, noted every word.[24] Every day since 9/11, Morell had met Tenet in his downtown office at the Old Executive Office Building at 7:15 A.M. and walked with him to the West Wing of the White House to brief the president. "Every day on that walk over either I would say to George or he would say to me, 'is today the day we're going to get hit again?'"[25] If there was the smallest chance the suspect gunned down in Pakistan knew anything about Al Qaeda's future attack plans, he had to be thoroughly interrogated. What was the latest? Tenet fretted.

AZ Task Force chief Jennifer Matthews burst in trailed by "a gaggle of breathless trainees."[26] Their assessments—largely reliant on "terrorism open-source intelligence reports" (TOSRs, a.k.a. media reporting)—had placed Abu Zubaydah front and center of future attacks.[27] A prolific jihad networker, facilitator, and host of the House of Martyrs guesthouse in Peshawar, Pakistan, he was linked by key evidence to the so-called millennium plot, in which Al Qaeda was accused of planning to blow up Los Angeles International Airport, sites across Jordan, and other targets during the December 1999–January 2000 celebrations. By the summer of 2001, "the system was blinking red," and "AZ" appeared to be everywhere.[28] Without any assets inside Al Qaeda, and Osama bin Laden and Ayman al-Zawahiri both on the run, the task force had built a compelling case that Abu Zubaydah was the new mastermind of the group's killing machine.

Matthews, an evangelical Christian who had moved from Ohio to Washington, DC, in search of job that would enable her to "serve God and have an impact on the world," waved a piece of paper, an email from Bob Grenier, the chief of the CIA's station in Islamabad, Pakistan.[29] The Faisalabad raid was over, and they were reasonably confident they had their man. "It was the best—actually the first—piece of good news coming the Agency's way since 9/11," recalled Rizzo.[30] Tenet called the president, who later recalled that he "could hear the excitement in George Tenet's voice."[31] CIA chief spokesman Bill Harlow, one of Tenet's closest advisors, had already primed the media: *Time* announcing that Abu Zubaydah was Al Qaeda's de facto leader, controlling up to four thousand operatives "out there somewhere in the world right now."[32] Six months down the line from 9/11, the president could at last announce a major success. It was a seminal moment for Tenet, who had been repeatedly accused of making critical mistakes pre-9/11 that had cost thousands of American lives.

The discussion turned to "disposition," meaning where to take Abu Zubaydah in order to subject him to a "hard approach" interrogation outside US jurisdiction without observation or fear of prosecution.[33] Someone suggested putting him on a ship in international waters or sending him to Egypt, where local intelligence officials tortured terrorism suspects for the CIA, a discreet and illegal arrangement going back several years. They discussed Jordan, whose security services also had a cozy "rendition" relationship with the CIA. But the Jordanian security court had issued a death warrant for Abu Zubaydah over his alleged part in the millennium plot, and would want to put him on trial. Morocco, which also offered up its facilities to the CIA, including an out-of-the-way interrogation center located in a secluded forest near Rabat, was dismissed since local medical facilities were deemed not sophisticated enough to treat a dying man. Israel, another close partner, was far too risky, given Abu Zubaydah's Palestinian heritage and accusations he was plotting to attack Israel when he was caught. Krongard, who had the best foreign government contacts, hit the phones looking for new options, while Tenet went into a huddle with Rizzo.

Vice President Dick Cheney had given the CIA approval to use "any means at our disposal" to destroy Al Qaeda.[34] If Abu Zubaydah survived, Tenet wanted him interrogated hard by Americans. This was a CIA mission. There would be no sharing, with the FBI or a third country.[35] However, Tenet was overlooking a significant problem. Currently, the CIA did not have any interrogators, although two military psychologists had recently proposed a bold plan after advising the CIA that Al Qaeda operatives were trained to resist traditional methods.[36] Countermeasures based on mock torture techniques that were used in US military survival school could be "weaponized," they had said.[37] Previous agency forays into harsh interrogation had led to congressional investigations, so Rodriguez, whose job it was to assemble a team, was cautious. This mission needed to "stay clean."[38]

"Despite what Hollywood might have you believe, in situations like this you don't call in the tough guys; you call in the lawyers," explained Tenet. Since 9/11, the CIA's legal head count had tripled from three to nine people.[39] Luckily, the agency's chief counsel, John Rizzo, was a seasoned operator. His first covert action operation had been in 1979, when the Canadian government, assisted by the CIA, rescued US embassy staff from Tehran after convincing the Khomeini regime they wanted to make a sci-fi movie, *Argo*, in the Iranian desert. The story eventually became a real Hollywood movie, which won three Academy Awards including Best Picture and reaped over $230 million at the box office, although the Canadian government's role was dropped to enhance the CIA's reputation.[40]

After main five o'clock meeting broke up, Rizzo got together with Tenet and Tenet's closest advisors, including Michael Morell, for what they called a "rump" discussion, meaning the most sensitive matters were discussed off-record.[41] At the core of the interrogation proposal sat the psychological theory of learned helplessness, something US military survival school instructors avoided at all costs because students who fell into this state of despair gave up on everything.[42] If Abu Zubaydah could be kept alive and brought to a state of learned helplessness, he would give up everything he knew about future attacks.

To achieve this, the CIA intended to unleash its new secret weapon: "two PHD psychologists with a unique interrogation strategy based on science."[43] The fact that some of the most aggressive techniques used in training "overwhelms most people's ability to resist is precisely why [we] think this procedure would be effective," they recommended.[44] However, there were many legal hurdles, as pointed out by the Counterterrorist Center's chief attorney, Jonathan Fredman, who had spent the past six months studying the limits. A CIA operations handbook updated after 9/11 stated that agency officers could not engage in "human rights violations," which were defined as "torture, cruel, inhuman, degrading treatment or punishment."[45] It was current CIA policy to follow US Army field manuals that banned "interrogation which involves the use of force, mental or physical torture, extremely demeaning indignities or exposure to inhuman treatment of any kind." It had been this way since 1989, when the head of the clandestine service had been forced to admit to Congress: "Inhumane physical or psychological techniques are counterproductive because they do not produce intelligence and will probably result in false answers."[46] Before "we found ourselves in the prison business which we knew absolutely nothing about," the CIA needed top-down legal approval, recalled Morell.[47]

Rizzo called Condoleezza Rice's chief counsel, John Bellinger. They had captured Number Three in Al Qaeda, an "academically inclined psychopath."[48] He was "the most senior Al Qaeda member in US custody," and the CIA needed urgent permission to take the gloves off as the proposed interrogation techniques might overstep the legal line into torture.[49] Bellinger warned Rizzo the CIA would need the attorney general's approval. Rizzo wanted a more collective decision, all the way up to the president. "We would all be in this together, for better or worse," he recalled.[50] Luckily, Rizzo had known Bellinger since 1988, and David Addington, Vice President Cheney's counsel, had previously worked as Rizzo's subordinate at the CIA.[51] Tenet recalled: "Nothing else mattered here: it was the law."[52]

The following morning, Fredman's office sent an email with the subject line, "Torture Update," listing laws the CIA would need approval to circumvent prosecution.[53] The president had already dismissed Geneva Conventions rights for Al Qaeda and Taliban detainees back in February 2002 on the basis of a legal opinion drawn up by a young Department of Justice lawyer named John Yoo, someone Rizzo later characterized as "the Bush administration's designated go-to guy."[54] Yoo's legal skills were needed again now to find a path through a complex tangle of legislation, both federal and international, with the United Nations Convention against Torture and the criminal prohibition on torture being particularly worrisome.

In Pakistan, the team riding with Abu Zubaydah encountered more problems. At the nearest hospital, "the floors were awash with body fluids."[55] Pakistani doctors started pumping blood into the detainee, but he was leaking like a sieve. The number of bullets that had entered his body was still disputed twenty years later, but one had torn up his thigh, hit coins in his pants pocket, and blasted a fist-sized hole through his groin and into his guts.[56] "I've never seen a man this badly injured survive," muttered a surgeon. Station chief Bob Grenier rang Brigadier Azmat Hyat Khan, Pakistan's counterterrorism chief, who requested the Pakistan Air Force to evacuate the party to a secure military facility at Lahore airport.[57] The new location was no better. "It was just a clinic," recalled Kiriakou. "There was no theater, no surgeons." He called Grenier in Islamabad again. "If you want him alive he needs a Western-style medical facility." But headquarters had not yet established a secure place, so Kiriakou claimed he tied the suspect to his bed with a sheet and pulled up a chair. For the next twenty-four hours, Abu Zubaydah wavered between life and death while Buzzy Krongard zeroed in on a "plain sight" location where no one would ever think of looking for him.[58]

Tenet's executive director operated in the jet stream. In his youth, Krongard had been a clandestine CIA officer. A gilded career in investment banking followed, and he had become the richest man in Maryland. "Spying and banking, the only two professions where lying, cheating, and stealing are considered assets," he joked.[59] An accomplished networker, he had chaperoned the future King Abdullah of Jordan when he came to the United States to study and regarded Erik Prince, the founder of the private security company Blackwater, and Kevin Plank, the founder of sports apparel company Under Armor, as surrogate sons. In Maryland, where he owned a huge country estate and drove a 1986 Rolls-Royce Corniche, a 1998 Bentley Brooklands, and later a Tesla S 60, Krongard surrounded himself with high achievers, and he sat on the board of directors at Johns Hopkins Hospital in Baltimore. While working up a suitable interrogation location for Abu Zubaydah, he also called up senior medical friends. Whoever was willing to fly out to help keep Abu Zubaydah alive would be performing a patriotic duty, and an Agency Seal Medallion was on the table.

Kiriakou claimed he received orders to discharge Abu Zubaydah from the military clinic in the early hours of March 30. The detainee was wheeled across the asphalt at Lahore airport to a CIA-leased Gulfstream filled with security contractors dressed head to foot in black and carrying M4s.[60] They shackled Abu Zubaydah to a luggage rack at the back of the cabin, and a Johns Hopkins surgeon got working on him as the door was closed. The jet then waited, engines rolling, for several hours. "There was some problem with the flight plan," according to Kiriakou.[61] "They wanted to fly him around from A to B to C to D, and then leave him at D. But the people at D were not ready." After the plane took off, around 3:30 A.M. local time, Jennifer Hale Keenan, who led the FBI's Pakistan team, sorted through the wealth of evidence recovered from a battered briefcase hidden under a bed on the top floor of Shahbaz Cottage. It contained Abu Zubaydah's address book, fake identity papers, personal diaries going back a decade, a copy of a hand-written *mujahideen* camp training manual, and a deeply incriminating video recording.

The video had been filmed while Abu Zubaydah was hiding out on the Afghan-Pakistan border in January or February 2002, on the verge of leaving war-torn Afghanistan for good.[62] After dodging missiles and bullets; nearly dying when a bombed building collapsed on him in Kandahar; seeing count-less friends, acquaintances, and innocent Afghanis die; and burying many of them with his own bare hands, he was fired up, ready to deliver an angry message. After Keenan's team rigged up a way to watch the video at the FBI safe house in Lahore, they were stunned.[63] Unlike Osama bin Laden, he was not an experienced orator. "I am not among those in favor of these press interviews," he told the cameraman, after they recorded a test session in the dark that produced only a fuzzy night-vision Abu Zubaydah. They went outside and waited for the sun to come up, their murmurings caught on the camera's audio, their breath visible in the cold early morning air. Dressed in traditional Afghan robes, a heavy woolen waistcoat, shawl, and a black turban, Abu Zubaydah looked the part. "That's when we realized we had conducted a stunning operation," Keenan said. Abu Zubaydah made several failed attempts to deliver his message. When he screwed up, he threw a stone in frustration, tugged his beard and walked up to the camera, putting his finger on the lens to stop the recording, as his friend backed up.

It was clear to the FBI agents and CIA targeters watching this video that not all Abu Zubaydah's anger was directed at America. Bin Laden's actions had put everyone involved in jihad in danger. After his first mention of "the sheikh," he paused before adding, "bin Laden," with a look of disdain. The next take was smoother. "We and the sheikh are one," he said.[64] Now that the United States had invaded Afghanistan, and the Taliban regime had collapsed, the entire jihad community needed to regroup. "For the past ten years, God be praised, we have not been in the picture," Abu Zubaydah continued. "But, as I said before, the events that transpired forced us, with the advice of our brother advisors, to come into the picture." Describing the destruction of the World Trade Center as "truly magnificent," he said he supported it wholeheartedly. "But as to our participation . . . this is a matter between us and God." The video, which was never broadcast, had instead stayed in his briefcase, as he and his companions traveled on to Lahore and then Faisalabad, staying in safe houses provided by Lashkar-e-Taiba, a Pakistani jihad group closely associated with Pakistani intelligence. The consequences of it falling into CIA hands would be enormous for Abu Zubaydah.

His diary looked just as bad. He had composed a poem lauding 9/11 that began, "Today, your turn has come, America," written of "a general war, nonstop and without mercy," proclaimed a desire to "torture the enemies of God," and suggested that he and Al Qaeda had nuclear ambitions.[65] Other pages suggested his connections to bin Laden and 9/11 were less well established. "The Pakistani newspapers are saying that I am in Peshawar, trying to reorganize [the] Al-Qa'ida organization, for war against America, and that I am the heir of bin Laden," he wrote six weeks before he was captured.[66] Nevertheless, as the CIA and FBI team stormed the Faisalabad house, Abu Zubaydah ripped up diary pages that eulogized the 9/11 attacks and talked of wanting to attack Jewish targets, and taking revenge on America.[67]

When this material reached the United States and copies were shared with the CIA, Alec Station, the CIA unit dedicated to tracking bin Laden and his followers, quickly concluded that Abu Zubaydah had conspired in

9/11, had declared war on America, and was plotting more attacks. Jose Rodriguez said the video was "designed to rally supporters and solicit funds from backers of their evil jihad."[68] He was planning to release the video material after his second wave got underway, said Rodriguez. Although John Kiriakou did not enter Shahbaz Cottage, he fanned the flames by claiming the raid team had found a "still hot" soldering iron, parts for an improvised explosive device, and a prospectus for the British School in Lahore, suggesting that Abu Zubaydah personally planned to kill hundreds of children.[69] Although Kiriakou would be shunned by his former CIA colleagues, accused of inventing stories, and he was eventually jailed for naming two undercover CIA officers connected to Abu Zubaydah's capture—including Deuce Martinez—he was not the only one varnishing the truth.[70]

Keenan's inventory from Faisalabad listed "training manuals, fake passports, computer allegedly used to provide training and allegedly containing anti-American material, H-bomb plans, electronic parts, and an electronic gun."[71] Keenan believed Abu Zubaydah was a key jihad facilitator, but not a leading figure in Al Qaeda.[72] The CIA's Islamabad station chief Bob Grenier agreed, and wondered what headquarters intended to do with Abu Zubaydah, as unsubstantiated claims were thrown about, especially the much repeated mantra that he was Number Three in Al Qaeda, an allegation that came from a single, questionable CIA source.[73] Abu Zubaydah appeared to be the very epitome of who the president had in mind when he signed a critical Memorandum of Notification (MON) on September 17, 2001, which gave the CIA the lead to capture and detain senior Al Qaeda and Taliban suspects.[74] Grenier, who had tracked Abu Zubaydah for two years, was as determined as everyone else to crush Al Qaeda, but he disagreed with some headquarters assessments. "I did not believe [Abu Zubaydah] was a senior leader; he was merely a senior, and a very important one," Grenier explained. In his opinion, if Al Qaeda were an army, Abu Zubaydah would be a sergeant major. "He wasn't hatching plots and giving orders: he was the guy who got things done."[75]

Many of those inflating Abu Zubaydah's position and association with Al Qaeda knew Grenier was right. Among them was Jose Rodriguez, who later conceded, "Quite a few of the people taken down were described as the 'number three' person in Al Qaeda" when in truth it was "difficult to ascribe an exact pecking order position."[76] Mike Scheuer, an acerbic analyst who in 1995 had founded the Bin Laden Issue Station, Alec Station's forerunner, echoed Rodriguez. "Abu Zubaydah as far as I'm concerned was a gatekeeper, a comms guy, someone who knew who to call, when to call, and how to call," Scheuer reflected.[77] He knew this because pre-9/11, he and his team spent six years studying Al Qaeda's vast, amorphous network, compiling link charts and "most wanted" cards identifying everyone from bin Laden's driver to his real Number Three, Mohammed Atef, a.k.a. Abu Hafs al-Masri, a former Egyptian policeman. But post-9/11, the gloves were off; the CIA had to save its reputation and protect the American people. After Abu Hafs was killed in a missile strike on an Al Qaeda safe house in Kabul in November 2001, Abu Zubaydah became a primary candidate as the new Number Three, in part because he was tantalizingly visible. Naval Criminal Investigative Service agent Robert McFadden, who co-led the investigation into the October 2000 bombing of the USS *Cole* guided missile destroyer, explained that before Al Qaeda began targeting Americans: "We were all wondering whether OBL [Osama bin Laden] was just a big bullshitter, but Abu Zubaydah was a blabbermouth and stood out as a dangerous SOB, a *takfiri* warrior of God."[78] There was another more significant reason for the CIA insisting that Abu Zubaydah was Number Three in Al Qaeda. Only "persons who pose a continuing, serious threat of violence or death to US persons and interests or who are planning terrorist activities" were covered by the presidential MON.

———•———

Abu Zubaydah had been on Mike Scheuer's radar for years. For the first few years of his virtual station's existence, Scheuer and his female analyst squad were snubbed by macho CIA case officers, who did not think Al Qaeda posed any real danger. His terrifying reports of coming death and destruction were ignored; he was described as "Crazy Mike," and his station was located off-site in Tysons Corner, Virginia, meaning it had even less influence. But Ric Prado, Scheuer's deputy for the first eighteen months of the unit's existence, described him as "one of the smartest guys that ever walked this earth."[79] After Al Qaeda conducted its first attacks in August 1998, bombing the US embassies in Nairobi, Kenya, and Dar es Salaam, Tanzania, Scheuer was vindicated; his station was brought into headquarters, given a bigger budget, and renamed "Alec" (after Scheuer's son).

Being right turned Scheuer into "a bull in a china shop," said Prado, and he launched a bitter turf war with the FBI, clashing with its counterterrorism boss, John O'Neill, and his staff.[80] "Mike was a good American with all the right reasons, but he lost his bubble," reflected Prado.[81] Scheuer and O'Neill hid information from each other as they fought to dominate the hunt for Al Qaeda. Mark Rossini, one of several FBI agents assigned to Alec Station to improve relations, said that when he challenged Scheuer's favorite analyst, Alfreda Bikowsky, over not sharing information about two Saudi Al Qaeda suspects who had entered the United States and were attending flight school in San Diego, she turned on him. "It's not an FBI case," she yelled. "It's not an FBI matter. When we want the FBI to know, we'll let them know."[82] With the help of the Saudis, Alec Station wanted to turn the two suspects into assets. Prado, who was not a fan of Bikowsky, called her "a psycho."

The FBI-CIA standoff led to ugly exchanges, and George Tenet eventually fired Scheuer, replacing him with Rich Blee, who had worked for him on the staff of the Senate Select Committee on Intelligence. "[Mike Scheuer] was very hard to work with," Tenet recalled, although he had more time for Bikowsky, calling her "a very capable woman."[83] However, on 9/11, Bikowsky's two suspects were part of the team that crashed American Flight 77 into the Pentagon, killing 184 people.[84] O'Neill, who had also lost his job as a result of his fight with Scheuer, died too, in the Twin Towers, where he had just taken up the post of head of security. When evidence emerged that Alec Station had hidden intelligence that could have prevented the attacks, O'Neill's former FBI team, the I-49 Squad, blamed Scheuer's team in part for causing his death. Bikowsky was forced to testify before the 9/11 Commission.[85] But she kept her job, as did Jennifer Matthews, who was also accused of hiding evidence.[86]

Post-9/11, any knowledge of Al Qaeda was indispensible, and Scheuer, who later declared that the only good thing that happened on 9/11 was "that the building fell on [O'Neill]," also returned to the CIA as a special advisor.[87] He found the Counterterrorist Center to be a shocked and vengeful place, with some people weeping, while others were furious at the politicians.[88] "The idea that CIA was intentionally withholding information on the two hijackers is so not true," recalled Morell.[89] In this angry climate, everyone associated with Al Qaeda would be hunted down and made to pay for all the lives lost. Everyone talked of wanting to "get the bastards."[90] Scheuer did not "care" if torture happened or not.[91] Tenet was more diplomatic. Capture, detention, and interrogation of terror suspects was "not something we had a lot of experience with," he said. "But I felt an enormous responsibility to make sure it did not happen again."[92]

With Abu Zubaydah in custody, the CIA had to make sure he fulfilled the president's MON to the letter. He was concealing actionable intelligence that would prevent more Al Qaeda attacks, Tenet, Scheuer, Bikowsky, Matthews, and Alec Station colleagues, including Gina Haspel, assured.[93] Congressional leaders, who had failed to listen to their 9/11 warnings and then blamed them for missing vital clues, would be made to eat their words. Abu Zubaydah would be made "twelve feet tall," his fate sealed before he even opened his mouth, and the CIA would be vindicated.[94] As Marty Martin, the new head of Alec Station, put it: "Congratulations Abu Butthead, you're now the Number Three in Al Qaeda. Your career path is probably going to be shortened."[95] Tenet later characterized the moment: "We're off and running. The rest of the world is watching us. Boom, boom: check, check, check. The only discussion was, 'It's yours—go, go.'"[96]

March 29, 2002, early morning, Bangkok, Thailand

A few hours after Abu Zubaydah's capture, Bangkok's streets were deserted, except for sweepers and food vendors. Buzzy Krongard woke up Mike Winograd, chief of the CIA's Bangkok station. Fizzing with excitement down the line from Washington, Krongard laid out headquarters' requirements: They had caught a leading figure in Al Qaeda who was planning future attacks and needed to be interrogated in total secrecy. He was badly injured, so the team traveling with him needed access to sophisticated medical facilities. Would Thailand, America's greatest regional friend in Southeast Asia, help?

In free and easy Thailand, money could buy anything. The national credo was *mai pen rai*, which covered everything from "you got it" to "never mind." Krongard, who had spent part of the Vietnam War deep undercover there, knew this. During Vietnam, the United States had invested millions of dollars into developing Thailand's air force bases, and the CIA's Bangkok station had played a critical role in the secret Phoenix Program to destroy the Viet Cong through infiltration, torture, and assassination, another notorious CIA operation that had led to congressional hearings. But relations between Washington and Bangkok survived, the Phoenix Program ultimately enhanced the CIA's reputation, and Thailand felt safe, familiar, and accessible. Most important, it craved NATO ally status.

Winograd knew exactly who to call: General Tritot Ronnaritivichai, the head of the Thai Special Branch, the country's domestic intelligence agency, a man with an unpronounceable surname (for foreigners) but magic connections. He and Winograd were already working together on a suspected Al Qaeda cell operating out of Bangkok. Could they discuss another urgent situation? "Yes, of course," said Tritot, giggling, as was his habit.[97] Fluent in English and FBI-trained, Tritot was an atypical policeman. He was fast thinking, quick-witted, and sophisticated. An advocate for what he called "sabotage operations," he embraced the colorful extremes of intelligence work. He and Krongard lived by the same mantra: "If you ain't going over the edge, you ain't really living it."[98] After more than a decade at Special Branch, Tritot appreciated how Western countries conducted their dirty business in Thailand, and Winograd's request was just another opportunity for Thailand to benefit.

A man of secrets, Tritot was on first-name terms with intelligence chiefs the world over. Ambassadors courted him. His house was full of diplomatic thank-you notes. He stole from Saddam, threatened Putin, and seized suspicious diplomatic packages from the Israelis, telling the ambassador he was within his rights to do so because the pouch had not been delivered to the embassy directly from the airport. Doors were open whenever Tritot and his wife, Angelina, traveled abroad. He was also sufficiently cunning to avoid upsetting Thai establishment heavyweights.

As Abu Zubaydah zigzagged the skies, Winograd laid out the CIA's specific needs: a regular-looking, accessible but isolated place that could be cut off from the world and was big enough to build a small interrogation bunker inside. Tritot recalled the discussions: "Was it worth the risk for Thailand? At the time nobody knows this guy is a big fish. After he talked, then they realized he is like a whole command of militants of Al Qaeda."[99] Krongard expected the arrangements to involve the Thai military—an old hangar on a secure airbase, like the many the US military was now occupying in Afghanistan. What about Udon Thai, in the northeast, or U Tapao, southeast of Bangkok? Both were US-built facilities. Tritot advised against it. "We don't want the military involved, because if this leaks my life won't be worth living." The police and military both regularly went for the kill, and the deputy prime minister General Chavalit Yongchaiyudh was a former army chief. But Chavalit was also a seasoned political operator and would later claim he knew nothing of this operation.[100] "Don't put it in his face and he won't ask questions," recommended Tritot. "If he doesn't know officially, then *mai pen rai*."

Winograd returned to the question of location. What about somewhere remote on the Burmese or Laos border? "No," said Tritot. "You say he needs to be near a Western-standard medical facility. That means not far from a big city. Plus, the further he has to travel, the more likely he will die." Tritot had a much simpler solution. He owned a house outside Chiang Mai in the mountainous north of Thailand. It was pretty run-down and surrounded by overgrown jungle, said Tritot. But because everyone local knew it was owned by an influential police general, no one would dare stick their nose in. "You know in Thailand, Special Branch has authority above everyone else," Tritot explained. "They will not even know who is coming in and out," he said. "It will be secret." Tritot's wife was a senior Thai Airways official and could make arrangements for the CIA landing party to avoid immigration at the nearby international airport.

What about official authorization? asked Winograd. Surely the CIA couldn't smuggle a high-value detainee into Thailand without informing its prime minister? Tritot giggled: "*Mai pen rai*." The prime minister, Thaksin Shinawatra, was a former policeman. He came from Chiang Mai and Tritot outranked him. As head of Special Branch, Tritot briefed Thaksin daily, so he would bring it up at an appropriate moment. "Leave it with me," Tritot reassured. "If I recommend it, he will authorize it."[101] Tritot had the whole thing sewn up.

During Tenet's and Morell's daily intelligence briefing on the morning of March 29, Bush approved Abu Zubaydah's rendition to Thailand.[102] The CIA rendition pilots, who carried bundles of used $100 bills with which to bribe ground staff, set a new flight plan.[103] Back at headquarters, a senior counterterrorism official with a bad sense of humor gave their newly acquired facility a code name: CATSEYE.[104] General Tritot pulled through just in time. Thaksin was far twitchier than he had anticipated. Angry about losing face because his security chief had made a decision without telling him first, and worried about bringing unwanted attention to his home city and main political power base, Thaksin had set conditions, even though General Tritot outranked him: the Americans could have the facility for only three weeks, and would have to pay Thailand several million dollars in compensation.

March 29, 2002, 11:00 A.M., CIA headquarters, Langley, Virginia

It was Good Friday, but Jose Rodriguez gave his staff five hours' notice to assemble a fully equipped medical team. It was what he called a "short fuse" situation, because they needed to arrive in Thailand before Abu Zubaydah. Someone from the Counterterrorist Center's Renditions Group went up to the Office of Medical Services, a department buried inside Human Resources that did its best to avoid any contact with the stickier side of operations.[105] In contrast, the paramilitary-led Renditions Group handled the well-established but illegal third-party interrogation arrangement whereby terrorism suspects snatched off the world's streets were dispatched to handlers in Cairo, Amman, or Rabat who did not care a jot about Geneva Conventions rights. The renditions guy told Medical Services they needed a "sophisticated medical care" team to keep a high-value Al Qaeda suspect alive as supposedly he had "information on immediate future threats."[106] Everything needed to stay in-house so the CIA medical team would fly out with the CIA interrogators.

Terry DeMay, the Medical Services chief who handled the request, was surprised. As far as he knew, the agency did not have interrogators and had even banned use of the word "interrogation" since Congress admonished it for training Honduran death squads during the 1980s, replacing it with the more euphemistic, "human resource exploitation."[107] But DeMay was given only the most basic information because he was not "read-in," meaning he was not fully briefed about the unfolding plan, and so he had no choice but to comply with orders.

At noon, the renditions guy was back with an update: the destination was Chiang Mai and a leading trauma surgeon from Johns Hopkins Hospital was already traveling with the detainee.[108] A full CIA medical team needed to fly out to support the surgeon, and then take over. DeMay stripped out Langley's medical bay and sourced emergency-room supplies from a local hospital. Someone went to Tysons Corner to buy hot-weather clothes. They gathered that night at Dulles International Airport. An anesthetist, who had never worked for the CIA, was taken into a phone booth to sign a secrecy agreement. One of the "physician's assistants" had done a first aid course before joining the CIA, but was still in training.[109] DeMay, who in his spare time was a member of a magician's circle in Fairfax, had overcome limitations of it being the Easter holidays, with everything closed and many people away on vacation, to pull a rabbit from the hat.

Two FBI special agents joined the CIA team on the asphalt.[110] Both had interrogated Al Qaeda suspects before, and they had been warned not to read Abu Zubaydah his rights to remain silent or worry about inadmissibility of evidence in court. They were simply to observe and assist a CIA-led interrogation of a suspect who knew about future attacks.[111] If the "CIA began using techniques that gave the agents discomfort," they should simply leave.[112]

After two refueling stops, the team landed in Chiang Mai, and was then driven for under an hour to Tritot's compound, around which Special Branch checkpoints had been erected. From the outside, it looked like a tangle of uninhabited jungle. Led through vines to a building that someone joked looked like a "chicken coop," Ali Soufan, one of the two FBI agents, was shocked.[113] "Kind of like a small little house that nobody has been there for years," he recalled.[114] Surely, this was not a suitable place to interrogate a dying man?

It was not Soufan's job to question, so he and his partner, Steve Gaudin, got to work, battling mosquitoes and removing giant Thai *takab* centipedes and cobras from the house.[115] The detainee would be arriving shortly. Everyone was jetlagged and tension filled the air. They all knew someone who had died on 9/11. One New York–New Jersey Port Authority policeman on assignment to the FBI and involved in Abu Zubaydah's capture had been seriously injured in the first World Trade Center attacks of 1993 and had lost a close friend in the second.[116] Soufan, the only native Arabic-speaker, had lost his boss and friend, John O'Neill, in the Twin Towers. Born in Lebanon, Soufan had immigrated to the United States as a child, and he felt a strong sense of duty to his adopted homeland. After he won a coveted job on the FBI's Al Qaeda hunting squad, I-49, the first Muslim to wear an FBI badge rather than simply being a confidential informant, O'Neill took him under his wing and put him on several Al Qaeda–related investigations, including the 1998 US embassy attacks in Kenya and Tanzania, the millennium plot in Jordan, and the USS *Cole* bombing in Yemen.

Soufan had gained important insights into Al Qaeda. Having Arabic as his mother tongue also helped Soufan score far higher during Al Qaeda–

related interrogations than his white American partners did. But he was overly confident, and had already clashed with the CIA, particularly during the millennium plot investigation in Amman, where he shared an office inside the US embassy with Marty Martin, who was then the CIA's Amman station chief.[117] Soufan accused Martin of being jaded and not bothering to check important intelligence passed by the Jordanians. Soufan also disliked Martin's deputy, Albert El Gamil, an Egyptian Coptic Christian who ran "liaison" with the Jordanian security agency, the GID. Youthful, arrogant Soufan riled his older CIA colleagues, and he cozied up to the GID, enjoying *iftar* meals during Ramadan to which Martin and Gamil were not invited. "The CIA became uncomfortable with the relationship we had built with the Jordanians," said Soufan.[118] Martin referred to Al Qaeda–related suspects as "Abu Buttheads," and went around talking about "going to the battle stations," although he preferred hotel bars.

After 9/11, Marty Martin was recalled to the United States and put in charge of Alec Station. He was intent on getting aggressive. "We didn't ask for this; we didn't ask to get attacked," he reflected.[119] "If we can't make them uncomfortable in order to save lives, then we've missed the boat here." However, despite the fighting talk, six months on from 9/11 Abu Zubaydah was the CIA's first significant catch and some key arrangements still needed work, particularly around interrogation. After arriving in Thailand, Soufan learned that the CIA interrogators were supposed to have been on the plane with them.[120] Why had they had not shown up? Bangkok station chief Winograd had no idea. He had other pressing issues to worry about. For all Tritot's promises about secrecy, several high-ranking Thai officials appeared to know the CIA was in Chiang Mai. A local media channel with police connections was sniffing around.[121] Since this was Tritot's setup, Winograd could not chastise him, but he had to keep his friends away from the black site. He was also under pressure to convert Thaksin Shinawatra's deadline of three weeks into an open-ended arrangement.[122] Jose Rodriguez was flying over to inspect his first coveted "high-level Al Qaeda terrorist" and wanted to know how much more money the CIA needed to fork out to extend its invitation to work in the Land of Smiles.[123]

CHAPTER 2

"I AM THE HEAD MOTHERFUCKER-IN-CHARGE"

Still wearing a bloodied Pakistani medical smock, Abu Zubaydah arrived in Thailand in the early hours of March 31. He was cuffed to a hospital gurney and hooded, his body swaddled in bandages.[1] He had no idea where he was, whether it was day or night, or how long it had been since his capture. He was dosed up with Demerol and Valium, and everything that had happened to him was a blur: a door battered in, shouts in Urdu, footsteps on the stairs, jumping across a roof, and then shattering pain.[2] Flashlights and gun muzzles were thrust into his face as a thumb poked his eye followed by a metal object. "Wake up," ordered an American voice. Overwhelmed, he let his head fall back against the gurney. No one watching felt any pity. This suspect was going to pay for all the lives lost. "Please, God, help me," Abu Zubaydah whispered. He understood enough to know he was a world away from his old life of hanging out with his Palestinian school friends in Riyadh. They had called themselves the "fun and carelessness clique."[3] Now, he was dying at the bottom of the ocean.

He heard planes. They were commercial airliners landing at Chiang Mai International Airport, filled with frazzled passengers ready to embrace all that Thailand had to offer.[4] He had been to Thailand once before, as a nineteen-year-old, when he had come to learn Muay Thai boxing.[5] Now, he was the focus of urgent discussions at the White House about torture. President Bush "wanted to kill somebody."[6] Vice President Dick Cheney had promised to go to the dark side. Cofer Black intended to take the gloves off and declared that those who had attacked the United States and had knowledge of future attacks would be fully interrogated and then dumped in "prison cells and graves around the world."[7] Senior administration lawyers were debating how far CIA operatives could go without fearing prosecution. Everyone was agreed: no one outside this "highly classified and sensitive" operation could ever know anything about it.[8] All the team on the ground needed do now was to keep the detainee alive until the CIA interrogators could get approval and get started. Where were they?

Clues as to just how close to the legal "chalk line" the CIA was prepared to go with interrogation emerged five days after 9/11, when Vice President Cheney appeared on *Meet the Press* to declare war on the perverted "barbarians" surrounding Osama bin Laden.[9] "It is a mean, nasty, dangerous, dirty business out there, and we have to operate in that arena," he told Tim Russert.[10] The interview was beamed from Camp David, where the president was chairing a "war council" attended by George Tenet, Cofer Black, Condoleezza Rice, and other members of his national security team. Conflicting agendas were already emerging. Cheney was focused on Iraq. Defense Secretary Donald Rumsfeld warned it would take weeks if not months to prepare a battle plan for Afghanistan. Tenet needed to move on from the allegations of intelligence failure, and he and Black talked the president into giving the CIA a lead role to destroy Al Qaeda by "any means."

"Our plan was ready," Tenet said.[11] Black, who had "skin in the game," had been itching to send a CIA hit squad after Osama bin Laden since 1995, when, as the Khartoum station chief, he had discovered that bin Laden, also in Khartoum, was allegedly plotting to kill him.[12] The Clinton administration had been reluctant to act, but three days after 9/11, Congress voted 420–1 in the House and 98–0 in the Senate to give the president authority to use "all necessary and appropriate force" against those who had plotted 9/11 and those plotting the next wave.[13] The CIA had a clear mandate to prevent Al Qaeda's next attack, destroy Osama bin Laden, blow apart his insidious network, and pave the way for war against Saddam Hussein.

"Cofer spoke with such a passion that when the president looked at him, he went, 'Holy shit, this is my guy,'" recalled Ric Prado, who had been promoted from Mike Scheuer's Alec Station to become Black's operations chief.[14] What did the CIA need to get started? asked Cheney. "Covert action authorization," replied Tenet, handing over a document the CIA's most senior lawyer, John Rizzo, claimed to have written as he watched the Twin Towers burning.[15] Since Black was promising that "when we're through with them they will have flies walking across their eyeballs," legal immunity was a key feature.[16] To avoid war crimes, they had to neutralize the Convention against Torture, which criminalized torture and "other cruel, inhuman or degrading treatment or punishment." Cheney, who regarded bin Laden and his mob as subhuman, had no problem with this. Federal laws like the War Crimes Act that allowed the death penalty would also have to be circumvented. Cheney was talking things through with his chief lawyer, David Addington.[17] The biggest problem appeared to be Common Article 3 of the Geneva Conventions, which enshrined prisoner-of-war rights and prohibited torture, "cruel treatment," and "humiliating and degrading treatment." But Al Qaeda did not play by the Geneva rules, so its leaders and operatives did not deserve human rights, argued Cheney.[18] Since there was no statute of limitations on war crimes if death was involved, White House chief counsel Alberto Gonzales and Pentagon chief counsel William "Jim" Haynes were seeking a detailed legal opinion about that from the Department of Justice.[19]

On September 17, 2001, Bush signed his critical covert action Memorandum of Notification—the famous MON that gave the CIA lead authority to "capture and detain persons who pose a continuing, serious threat of violence or death to US persons and interests or who are planning terrorist activities."[20] The CIA later described it as a "key weapon in the War on Terror," and it placed the Pentagon on the back foot.[21] However, there was no mention of interrogation protocol. Three days later, the president launched his "War on Terror" in a speech to Congress, witnessed by families of 9/11 victims.[22] Out at Langley, Black was already war-gaming, Rizzo and Fredman were eviscerating the laws of war, and Prado sought out veterans willing to drop into Afghanistan.[23] This was no job for "piss and vinegar guys," said Prado.[24] The CIA was in charge.

Almost immediately, Prado ran into Jose Rodriguez in the CIA gym.[25] Cuban-born Prado and Puerto Rico–born Rodriguez had both spent their formative years in the CIA's Latin America Division. Rodriguez rode around El Salvador with a sawed-off shotgun, rescued the Salvadoran president's daughter from kidnappers, and put Panamanian general Manuel Noriega's witch doctor on the CIA payroll.[26] He loved the CIA and expected total loyalty from his officers. "For us it's a calling," he explained.[27] "It's like people who go and become nuns or priests." Prado was a young CIA paramilitary officer in 1981 when President Ronald Reagan had authorized the CIA to fund and train Contra rebels to fight the revolutionary anti-American Sandinista government of Nicaragua. Dispatched to set up jungle training camps in Honduras, he described it as the best job in the world. "There was no supervision," he reflected.[28] However, in the end, Latin America had gone bad, civilians had died, and Congress had launched an investigation. "They said, 'Off with your heads,'" Rodriguez recalled.[29] "You lose your jobs. A big political fight. . . . 'Interrogation' was one of those things they said no more." Prado and Rodriguez both returned to Langley, the former joining the Counterterrorist Center, while the latter became deputy head of the Crime and Narcotics Center, chasing down the likes of Pablo Escobar. Rodriguez was then promoted to run the entire Latin America Division, a poisoned chalice given the interrogation and death squad scandals, not to mention the Iran-Contra affair, which he had had no role in. But he did not last long, and was "essentially fired" for using his influence to save a friend falsely accused of being a drug dealer.[30] Cofer Black had joined the division as deputy director in his wake.

Before 9/11, Rodriguez, who after the drugs scandal was "unfired" and sent off to run the Mexico station, was at fifty-two dreaming of retirement, preferably somewhere by the ocean where he could indulge his passion for big-game fishing. Post-9/11, he was just the kind of person Black needed back in, for an "aggressive, relentless, worldwide pursuit of any terrorist who threatens us."[31] After meeting Rodriguez in the gym, Prado went downstairs to consult Black, who he called "the Hulkster."

"Holy shit, wouldn't Jose be a great addition?" Prado recalled saying.[32] "I love him," replied Black. "We need that kind of talent." But Rodriguez was cautious. "I'd had my fingers burnt before in Latin America, counterinsurgency and counternarcotics, across the board," he recalled. He relished a challenge but was not going to risk another crash and burn.[33] "This time we had to get it right. . . . Everyone from the president down, everybody had to approve this."[34] CIA director George Tenet recollected being in total agreement: "All the authorities were laid out with absolute clarity, they were fully briefed, they knew about the program in excruciating detail. There were no surprises here: the Justice Department had full access to everything we did. Central America, Iran-Contra, was totally different generationally, from legal framework, national security. . . . It was like the Wild West versus much more disciplined."[35]

When Rodriguez arrived ten days after 9/11, the Counterterrorist Center was being "surged" with new hires and retired officers.[36] He set up as chief operating officer in the only space available, a cubbyhole housing a Xerox machine, and he reassigned his favorite analysts from the Crime and Narcotics Center to become Al Qaeda "targeting officers."[37] Key among them was Alejandro "Deuce" Martinez, the thirty-six-year-old son of a former CIA technician. Martinez Jr. would be assigned to the Abu Zubaydah operation. A political-sciences graduate of James Madison University, Martinez was a data-sifting expert. Rodriguez told him that rebuilding the agency's reputation was foremost. "When it came out that there had been a planning meeting in Malaysia of 'bad guys' in January 2000, the shit really hit the fan," said Rodriguez, using a favorite CIA catchall phrase for anyone being hunted down by the "good guys," a.k.a. the CIA. "The politicians were saying the CIA better get its act together. You cannot allow this shit to happen again."[38] Al Qaeda and those perceived to be connected to it, had to be neutralized.

The counterattack began on September 26, 2001, when a unit of CIA paramilitary veterans of the Soviet-Afghan war dropped into the Panjshir Valley, north of Kabul. Black's mission priority was to "get bin Laden. . . . I want his head in a box. . . . I want to take it down and show the President."[39] There were no briefings about the Rome Statute of the International Criminal Court, which stated that the "degrading treatment" of dead bodies during armed conflict amounted to a war crime. America was going to put Al Qaeda's heads on sticks, Black warned the world.[40] "Cofer had just enough of that hubris to say, 'I am the head motherfucker-in-charge, and we're going to do this,'" recalled Prado.[41]

Among those encouraging Black's and Prado's aggressive approach was Billy Waugh, an Arabic-speaking Vietnam and Soviet-Afghan War veteran with eight Purple Hearts, a $23,000 Rolex, and a living room filled with military accolades and mementos. He had a ceremonial baseball bat, gifted by CIA officers, embossed: "Billy Waugh's interrogation tool." It was no joke. "If you beat a guy up and you get the information, who gives a fuck?" he said. "I put my shit on and do what I'm told to do."[42] During the 1990s, Waugh had worked for Black in Khartoum, jogging around Osama bin Laden's compound nightly, "conducting surveillance." He had helped the French grab Carlos the Jackal, who was also living in Khartoum.[43] Sitting in front of citations reading "We sleep safely at night only because rough men stand ready to do violence on our behalf," Waugh expressed uncompromising views about Arabs. They never listened and talked too much. "They jibber jabber till one A.M., then they are out." Despite his advanced age of seventy-one, Waugh put on his old *mujahideen* gear, grabbed an MP5 carbine, and happily joined the CIA's Afghan team. "[Bin Laden] was gloating, giggling, having a good time," he said. "He needed to be taken out, put on top of a vehicle, and driven all over the Arab world so they can see this dead SOB, see what happens to you." Waugh, Black, and Prado all felt the same way about bin Laden, his "barbarian" followers, and Afghanistan. It was a "shithole country," and they all had to be taught a lesson for sheltering Al Qaeda.[44]

The US military followed the CIA into Afghanistan on October 7, with instructions to rout Al Qaeda and destroy the Taliban. Since the Bush administration was heavily invested in the theory that Al Qaeda was linked to Saddam Hussein and that both had weapons of mass destruction (WMDs), detainees would have to be harshly interrogated to give up clues. The initial idea was that the CIA and Pentagon would work in tandem: detainees would be prescreened by the military, and anyone "high value" handed over to the CIA. A rudimentary processing facility was set up at Bagram: wire-mesh cells inside a disused aircraft hangar. It quickly filled up with men and boys who started out as "persons under control," then became "detainees" and/ or "illegal enemy combatants" or "enemy belligerents," but never "prisoners-of-war," to whom would have to be given human rights protections.[45] However, with US leaflets offering $5,000 rewards raining down on penniless Afghan villages, many turned out to be nobodies with nothing to say.

Rather than accept that US forces were simply picking up the wrong people, the Pentagon erected more wire pens at an old US naval station at Guantánamo Bay, Cuba, where it planned to push harder, away from the prying eyes of the International Committee of the Red Cross (ICRC). After Justice Department lawyer John Yoo issued a legal opinion stating that the laws of armed conflict did not apply to War on Terror detainees, hundreds were transferred to Cuba as Bush administration lawyers mined the legality of "hard approach" methods of interrogation. "If you want to deal only with sort of officially approved, certified 'good guys,' you're not going to find out what the 'bad guys' are doing," Cheney had warned.[46] "You need to be able to penetrate these organizations. You need to have on the payroll some very unsavory characters."

Hiring unsavory characters was nothing new to the CIA. Its Latin America Division had trained rebel armies that tortured and killed. Its Renditions Group routinely subcontracted torture to Cairo, Amman, and Rabat. Mike Scheuer, who established the renditions setup in the summer of 1995, told a later congressional hearing that there was a "kind of joking up our sleeves about what would happen to those people in Cairo, in Egyptian prisons."[47] The CIA merely "picked up the fruit the Egyptians had shaken from detainees." A key figure in Scheuer's covert arrangement was Egyptian-born Albert El Gamil, who went on to become Marty Martin's deputy at the CIA's Amman station. Originally employed by the FBI as a linguist in the New York office, Gamil had won a contract at the CIA after his application to become an FBI agent was rejected.[48] He was a divisive and controversial figure. Popular with Scheuer and Martin because of his Middle Eastern insights and security connections, he had a reputation for aggression and unpredictability.[49]

While CIA paramilitaries and the US military hunted for bin Laden, Alec Station veterans, assisted by computer-savvy targeting analysts like Deuce Martinez, worked through Scheuer's "suspect cards."[50] Link charts filled the Counterterrorist Center conference room's walls. Incoming hard-ass Marty Martin said those who had "sponsored" the hijackers and "blessed their training" would be shown no mercy.[51] But while Alec Station drew up achievable targets, and Ric Prado's paramilitaries scoured Afghanistan, interrogation kept getting shunted sideways. "I said, 'We've never run a prison. We don't have the languages. We don't have the interrogators,'" recalled Buzzy Krongard, Tenet's executive director.[52] One of Tenet's mentors, Porter Goss, the chairman of the House Permanent Select Committee on Intelligence and the leading Republican member of the Gang of Eight (the congressmen and women who received CIA briefings on classified intelligence issues), echoed Krongard's concerns: "CIA doesn't even have a chair to sit somebody down on and say, 'Can I talk to you?' This is totally new. Do we have somebody who speaks a language? No!"[53]

The issue came to a head in early January when George Tenet learned from media reports that the Pakistanis had handed "one of Osama bin Laden's top paramilitary trainers" to the US military, and the FBI was interrogating him.[54] "The information we have gotten has been very fruitful in many cases, and we think we have thwarted attacks," General Richard B. Myers, the chairman of the Defense Department's Joint Chiefs of Staff, told reporters. The suspect's name was Ibn Sheikh al-Libi, and he was the commander of Khaldan, the oldest and most important *mujahideen* training camp in Afghanistan. A close friend of Abu Zubaydah's, he had been captured fleeing Afghanistan the previous November.[55] He had never sworn *bay'at* (allegiance) to bin Laden, and Khaldan was not an Al Qaeda camp; but numerous Khaldan graduates had joined Al Qaeda, and several had carried out real terrorist attacks, including two 9/11 hijackers.[56] Furious at losing such an important source to the FBI, territorial Tenet ordered the Counterterrorist Center to grab al-Libi using any means possible.

With no trained CIA interrogators on hand, Marty Martin dispatched Albert El Gamil, with instructions to flash the CIA's "weapon"—the presidential MON—at the FBI and US military, take custody of al-Libi by running a "false flag" operation, in which he would pretend to be an Egyptian intelligence official, and dispatch al-Libi to Egypt. It was a familiar routine for Gamil, but to pull it off he would have to get past two FBI agents, Russ Fincher and George Crouch, who had both worked with Ali Soufan on the USS *Cole* investigation, and Marty Mahon, a New York City detective. All three were interrogating the Khaldan emir, who was being bounced between cells in Kandahar, on the USS *Bataan*, and at Bagram air base.

However, when Gamil turned up throwing his weight around at Bagram, the US military slung him out, and the incident was reported to FBI director Robert Mueller.[57] Fincher and Crouch, both Christians, claimed they had struck up a good rapport with al-Libi, and he had been declared to the International Committee of the Red Cross, so if he disappeared, there would be trouble.[58] Armed with a copy of Bush's MON, Tenet took his argument to the White House and got Gamil into al-Libi's cell, along with Rich Blee, who was now chief of the CIA's Kabul station.[59] Gamil threatened al-Libi as Fincher attempted to read him his rights. On February 9, 2002, Gamil won out. "Blee comes in, they backed a pickup truck in, it's got a cardboard thing in it that looks like a coffin, they're going to wheel him out," recalled Fincher's colleague Jack Cloonan.[60] Wrapped up like an Egyptian mummy in duct tape, al-Libi was driven to a waiting rendition aircraft. "You're going to Cairo," Gamil snarled. "Before you get there, I'm going to find your mother and I'm going to fuck her."[61]

In Cairo, al-Libi's treatment got worse.[62] Telling him that a "long list of methods could be used against him, which were extreme," Egyptian interrogators demanded information about Al Qaeda's nuclear capabilities and connections to Saddam Hussein.[63] When they didn't like his answers, they "placed him in a small box approximately 50 cm × 50 cm" (twenty by twenty inches) for seventeen hours, and then beat him. He was also reportedly waterboarded.[64] Eventually, al-Libi produced a story about two Al Qaeda scientists going to Iraq to learn about nuclear weapons; and then a story about Al Qaeda collaborating with Russian organized crime to import "canisters containing nuclear material" to New York.[65] This pleased his interrogators, who gave him food, although al-Libi later claimed he made the whole thing up.[66]

Al-Libi gave the CIA what it needed to hear: WMD connections between Al Qaeda and Saddam Hussein.[67] Tenet was electrified, although he later claimed the original nuclear threat information came from French intelligence.[68] The vice president needed evidence that warranted war with Iraq.[69] But when Cheney demanded more details, the CIA became worried. Al-Libi's claims did not stack up, and the CIA knew why. Because he had been declared to the ICRC, human rights investigators would soon be demanding information and talking of "ghost detainees."[70] Al-Libi was a wake-up call, and after Abu Zubaydah was captured, the CIA concluded the time for third-party interrogations was over, "not because we believe necessarily we can improve on [Egypt's] performance, but because the reasons for the lack of progress will be transparent and reportable up the line."[71] Tenet later blamed the flimsiness of al-Libi's nuclear stories on his resistance-to-interrogation training.[72] Rodriguez admitted, "The results that [Cairo] passed to us from his interrogation were problematic."[73]

While al-Libi was locked inside a box in Cairo, the CIA quickly shifted its focus to his close associate Abu Zubaydah, who had been Khaldan's "external" emir, responsible for fund-raising and for vetting all young Muslims going for training via the House of Martyrs jihad guesthouse he supervised in Peshawar. Since the death of Osama bin Laden's real Number Three, Abu Hafs al-Masri, in November 2001, Tenet had demanded the Counterterrorist Center find his replacement, and Abu Zubaydah filled the bill. "Time and again in our five o'clock meeting we discussed how to run Abu Zubaydah to the ground," Tenet recalled.[74] In February 2002, after a dressing-down from Tenet and a demand that the team had to work faster, Marty Martin formed the AZ Task Force, appointing Jennifer Matthews as team leader, assisted by a group of new-hire analysts who boned up on newspaper reports about Abu Zubaydah, some of which were informed by Tenet's chief spokesman, Bill Harlow, or CIA sources, like Marty Martin.[75] The AZ Task Force concluded it was "inconceivable" that Abu Zubaydah did not know about future operations.[76] Hundreds if not thousands of Khaldan graduates were out there in the world. He had met almost all of them, and some were certain to be priming attacks against the United States.[77] It was a convincing argument. Abu Zubaydah, installed in Shahbaz Cottage, Faisalabad, knew his luck was running out. "The shadow of Ibn Al-Sheikh is still around me," he wrote in his diary at the end of February 2002.[78] "*Time* is saying that I know [Al Qaeda] and those collaborating with [Al Qaeda] more than bin Laden himself," he noted.[79] "I wish they know I am not with Al Qaeda." But back at Langley that was a distinction without a difference.

Now that Abu Zubaydah was gunned down, Rodriguez, who described himself as "no expert in counterterrorism," swung into action.[80] "Believe me there was a lot of shit coming from the White House," he said.[81] At first, nobody was certain if the man dying out in Thailand was even Abu Zubaydah. Rodriguez thought he had time on his side, as the medics had suggested the injured detainee would not be capable of talking for several weeks.[82] While he was stabilized, and the FBI collected fingerprints, DNA, and a voice sample, Langley set out to assemble an interrogation team.[83] Since resistance to interrogation was the name of the game, the primary focus for Rodriguez, who "went to law school to get a job at the CIA," was obtaining legal approval for a proposed "hard approach" interrogation plan.[84]

March 31, 2002, Thailand

Where were the CIA interrogators, asked Ali Soufan and Steve Gaudin, who had been on the US embassy bombings investigation in Nairobi and had brought along a digitized FBI "photobook" of suspected Al Qaeda operatives. Abu Zubaydah was in bad shape. He could die any moment and they would be left with nothing except a corpse. Station chief Winograd shrugged. He had no idea. "I don't know anything about this guy, and neither do my guys," he said. "But I understand the FBI knows something about him, so why don't you do the interviews? We're all working for Uncle Sam."[85] Soufan and Gaudin grabbed their chance.

The first thing they noticed when they removed Abu Zubaydah's hood was how different he looked from his pre-9/11 photograph. His face was covered in bruises and scratches, as if he'd been in a car accident, and his left eye, where the CIA had attempted a retinal scan, was clouded with infection. His head hair was long, but his armpits, chest, and genital region were all shaved.[86] This was a worrying sign for Soufan and Gaudin, who knew that suicide bombers often shaved their own body hair to purify themselves for the afterlife, because there would be no burial rites. Maybe, Soufan thought, Abu Zubaydah *had* been preparing another attack when he was captured? Maybe the CIA was right?

Speaking Arabic, Soufan asked the suspect his name. "Mahmoud el-Meliguy," Abu Zubaydah replied, using the name of an Egyptian actor famous for his villainous roles. Despite his parlous state, he had not lost his sense of irony. "He knew it was game over," Gaudin recalled. "He said 'You guys know who I am.'" "OK, how about I call you Hani?" jousted Soufan. It was a flashy start, learned from Abu Zubaydah's diary, in which he called himself Hani, his family's pet name. When Ali Soufan saw the detainee's reaction, he knew they had the right man. "Who are you?" asked Abu Zubaydah—fearful he had been rendered to the Middle East. "I'm with the FBI," Soufan replied. "I don't believe you," murmured Abu Zubaydah. Soufan and Steve Gaudin produced their FBI cards. "The battle is up," Soufan continued, gaining confidence. "We know everything about you. So don't play games with me, *Zayn*." He used the detainee's given name, Zayn-al-Abidin. Gaudin, who reflected that he spoke only enough Arabic to order food off a menu, let Soufan take the lead.[87] What did the captive know about Al Qaeda's future plans? Incredibly, Abu Zubaydah began talking. Within an hour, he had confirmed plans for a USS *Cole*–style attack against Israel, something he had written about in the ripped up pages of his diary. The information was cabled back to Langley, as medics attended to his wounds.[88]

George Tenet was delighted and informed the president that the CIA's first "high-value detainee" was already revealing details about future attacks.

The CIA had gone from "not knowing if he would live or die" to getting real actionable intelligence within hours.[89] But when Tenet asked the Counterterrorist Center team about the CIA interrogators who got the information and was told it was the FBI yet again, he blew his stack.[90] The CIA interrogation team had not yet left Washington, explained Rodriguez. In fact it was still being assembled. Tenet was unimpressed. He had strong-armed the president for lead authority and now his people were not even ready when they were needed downrange. They should have been there "yesterday."[91] Tenet did not want to hear another word until the CIA interrogation team had landed in Thailand. "Get them there and have them take over," he reportedly ordered.[92] However, the CIA later played down this standoff, with Tenet recalling, "I never thought about it from the perspective of us stealing the FBI's role."[93] Rizzo also tamped down the tension.[94] No one at the CIA wanted to be accused of putting self-interest ahead of national security.

Over the next twenty-four hours, Rodriguez brainstormed. He watched a PowerPoint of "hard approach" strategies produced by the Office of Technical Service where the CIA's behavioral scientists worked.[95] Their stock in trade was profiling case officers, assets and enemies, but when the CIA had previously dabbled with interrogation, Technical Service had taken a leading role, employing psychologists, psychiatrists, and sociologists to conduct research and experiments.[96] It was Technical Service that in December 2001 had contracted Jim Mitchell and Bruce Jessen to assess whether Al Qaeda operatives were trained to resist interrogation. They had recommended "countermeasures," some of which were harsh.[97] These were now on the table for Abu Zubaydah, even though he was giving up actionable intelligence and showing no signs of resistance. Alec Station was all for it, but Rodriguez was not prepared to break the law. "You need to be backed by your government," he said.[98] He wanted highly trained professionals who had the maturity to stay within whatever guidelines the lawyers drew up. "You want people with experience, guys in their forties and fifties who have been round the block a few times. He's not going to risk going to prison for something the government, the country needs to stand behind," he later reflected.[99]

———— • ————

In the early hours of April 1, Thai time, Ali Soufan was sleeping outside Abu Zubaydah's makeshift cell when the on-duty medic woke him.[100] Earlier assessments about Abu Zubaydah's slim chances of survival appeared to be coming true. "Hey, Ali, how important is this guy?" asked the medic. "If you want anything from him, you'd better go and interview him now. In the morning I don't think he'll be alive." The fist-size hole in Abu Zubaydah's groin was suppurating. The ten-inch-long bullet wound in his left thigh was septic. He had chronic diarrhea, a racing pulse, and a high fever, and his blood pressure was dropping rapidly.[101] Soufan rang the rest of the team. Twenty minutes later everyone was reassembled, and bleary-eyed. The Johns Hopkins surgeon concurred, saying: "If we don't do something, he will be dead by morning." He needed to go to a proper hospital. Winograd, who had promised that Thailand's cooperation would be kept secret and was concerned about moving Abu Zubaydah out of the black site, cabled Langley.[102] Tenet shot back a reply: "Death is not an option."[103] The Pentagon was about to announce Abu Zubaydah's capture, the first good news the administration had had to share with the American people since 9/11, and the CIA interrogation team was incoming. Winograd called General Tritot: "I need another favor."[104]

CHAPTER 3

"HANI 1"

He had started writing his diary in June 1990, about two years after he left home and twelve years before he was caught. He was in India, studying computer engineering at a third-rate college in Karnataka, and he explained on the opening pages that he intended to use his diary as a substitute friend to confess all his secrets, worries, and misgivings, and to contemplate the future stages of his life. He was currently "Hani 1," nineteen years of age, unhappy, lonely, confused, and lost, but curious to know what lay in store for "Hani 2," who was a decade older, and the person to whom he addressed his diary entries. If and when he reached thirty, he would start writing to "Hani 3," who would have reached the unimaginable age of forty, and "so on and so forth."[1] Never happy in the moment, he was always writing to his hopefully happier and more centered older self.

"If only I could wipe out all my past . . . by God, I will not hesitate," he began, having stuck a picture of himself aged five or six on the inside cover. Had he always been so unhappy? While still in Abi Tammam High School in Riyadh, he and his friends had hung out on Wednesday evenings, which in Saudi Arabia were the equivalent to Friday nights out. Hani waited in his bedroom for the sound of his friend's car honking and then tiptoed down the fire escape. They went "roistering" around, which meant climbing onto apartment building roofs, doing push-ups, "tackling, karate, dancing and laughs."[2] On weekends, they drove to a friend's farm, armed with *ouds* and cigarettes. Sometimes they took along his little brother Hesham, riding on Hani's knee, and discussions ranged from the countries they would visit to arguments about politics, religion, girls, and jihad. But they could not alter their Palestinian birthright, which afforded them no passports, citizenship, or guarantees, and Palestine often dominated the conversation. "As an

Arab national, especially as a Palestinian," Hani 1 wrote, "I adore sadness forcibly." Sometimes, "I sense mental happiness hidden in the folds of my sorrows."[3] Bad luck was his shadow, an idea instilled by his domineering Gazan-born father.

Muhammad Abu Zubaydah had left Palestine as a teenager, to study medicine in Egypt. His son became fixated on the old homeland.[4] The old family belonged to al-Zubayd, a Bedouin tribe that had migrated from Saudi Arabia to Palestine during biblical times, and had been in conflict with Jews since forever.[5] Ancestors had settled near Jericho, the first town attacked by Israelites after they crossed the Jordan River, according to the Old Testament. By the nineteenth century, Ottomans occupied Jericho, followed in 1921 by the British. In 1948, Israel had seized the city, forcing most Palestinians into refugee camps. That year's crops rotted, livestock ran wild, and vines grew over Arab houses as cousins, aunts, and uncles took sanctuary in Amman, while other relatives built a new village, az-Zubeidat, on a West Bank bluff that was still Palestinian controlled.[6] Abu Zubaydah's grandfather ended up in Gaza, a thin desert strip running alongside the Mediterranean. Every displaced Palestinian kept the keys to their old home, believing one day they would return.

By the time Muhammad was born, Gaza was overflowing with refugees and policed by Egypt. The family lived in Khan Yunis, a densely packed town filled with anti-Israeli resentment and stories of the *nakhba* (catastrophe), as Palestinians called the 1948 Arab-Israeli war. Building a tin-roofed house a short stroll from the beach, the Abu Zubaydahs did better than some of the estimated two hundred thousand refugees who descended.[7] However, while his parents could never forget what they had lost, Muhammad wanted a better future. Some his age joined the emerging *fedayeen* massing in the hills of northern Jordan. Many enlisted to pursue the idea of "defensive jihad," a struggle both armed and intellectual to regain their homeland. In 1956, the Israel Defense Forces (IDF) overran Khan Yunis, breaking up *fedayeen* cells and leaving hundreds of bodies in the streets. While the slaughter bolstered the movement, Muhammad was repelled, and in his teens he went south to Cairo on a one-way *laissez-passer* issued by the Egyptian government. He enrolled at medical school with the intention of becoming an orthopedic surgeon.[8]

After war broke out between Egypt and Israel in 1967, the Gaza Strip was occupied by the Israelis, who also seized the West Bank.[9] Muhammad's childhood home in Khan Yunis, his father's old farm near Jericho, and homes of distant relatives in az-Zubeidat were now all occupied by Israel. Having lost all their land, his parents could no longer pay his medical college fees and so Muhammad had to give up on his dream career and retrain as an Arabic teacher. Because he was absent during a subsequent Israeli census, he could not return to his birthplace, and instead headed to the land of rising skyscrapers, Saudi Arabia. It needed teachers, and he secured a job at a primary school in Riyadh, rented a modest apartment in a low-income guest-worker district, and longed for a wife. When relatives in Jordan suggested their teenage daughter, he bought an American car and gold jewelry and drove to Amman, where they lived in a Palestinian refugee camp beside the international airport. The "rich" cousin dressed like a Saudi prince impressed the family, and Malika Abu Zubaydah agreed to marry him.

It was an incendiary match. In Jordan, Malika wore flowery open-necked blouses and a sultry pout and piled her long, curly black hair on top of her head with a zebra clip.[10] Dreaming of Saudi citizenship, hot-tempered Muhammad had already adopted a conservative outlook. Malika's world transformed as soon as she donned an obligatory black abaya and her new husband became her legal guardian. Stuck inside a cramped apartment in run-down Riyadh, she learned how to become a mother from neighboring wives. Her first son, Maher, was born in January 1970, the second on March 12, 1971. Muhammad named him after the fourth imam, Zayn-al-Abidin. But he was a mischievous baby, and Malika gave him a nickname, "Hani" (happy). Three girls quickly followed, Muhammad worked hard, and the growing family moved to a nicer apartment.[11] Muhammad bought a tape player and a television. The family hired an African maid who learned to make Palestinian food. "I believe that we were a happy family . . . perhaps because I was little . . . I didn't notice," Hani recalled in his diary.[12]

In reality, his father lived under a cloud. Craving respect, stability, and wealth, he queued up to renew his annual permit with all the other migrant workers—road sweepers, maids, and garbage collectors. Trying to improve the family's situation, he invested his wages in small Saudi businesses, and hosted banquets in smart Riyadh hotels, cutting a big hole in the family budget. Hani's priorities lay elsewhere. "Many have chased the essence looking for happiness, yet I don't believe that anyone found it there among the piles of gold," he reflected.[13]

Having been unable to complete his own studies, Muhammad aspired for his sons to become doctors, and he recorded a "what do you want to be when you grow up?" conversation with them when Hani was age four, and Maher, age five. "A doctor," said dutiful Maher. "An engineer?" wayward Hani squeaked. Muhammad scowled, and in school, Hani became a class clown and fell behind in his studies. At home, he crashed about, and goofed with his sisters. Muhammad took to calling him the "bad-luck son."[14] Hani was on a trajectory to trouble.

Family road trips to visit Malika's and Muhammad's families in Amman and Gaza began when Hani was about seven. On reaching Khan Yunis in their red Buick, Hani was shocked to see how much Palestinians struggled. Back home, his father barely ever talked about his homeland, although he had hand-painted an image of Jerusalem's al-Aqsa mosque on the wall of their formal living room.[15] After Hani became a teenager, the mammoth round-trips to Gaza and Amman took on more meaning. Malika had yet another new baby, Kamal, and on one trip, after Muhammad had upgraded the family car to a Chevrolet Suburban, they were pulled up by an Israel Defense Forces patrol on their way into the Gaza Strip. The soldiers had noted the family's apparent wealth, and threatened to confiscate Malika's jewelry. Muhammad had no choice but to submit to their abusive language and ridicule. It was a defining moment for the children, who finally understood what it meant to be Palestinian, and when they returned home, Hani and Hesham began agitating. Why had his father not stayed to fight for Palestine? they asked. Why did they live in a country that rejected them? At school, they fought with Saudi boys on the soccer field. "It's a matter of pride," Hani told Hesham.

Sensing danger, Muhammad banned all talk of Palestine from the house. "The Abu Zubaydahs of the West Bank and Mafraq were just *fellahin* [peasant farmers]," he lectured Hani and Hesham, who shared a bedroom as well as a sense of recklessness.[16] Muhammad dressed them in starched Saudi *thobe*s and marched them off to Friday prayers. Hani was fully committed to God, but Hesham "barely prayed." If anyone complained, they were whipped with the heavy black cord of Muhammad's headdress. "It was like being whacked by a hose," recalled Hesham. Whenever their father went to work, they played love songs by Abdel Halim Hafez, Egypt's "King of Music."[17] Hani also listened to Chris de Burgh, whose "soft and beautiful songs" soothed him when he could not sleep.[18] He played keyboard, smoked cigarettes, and flirted with a girl living upstairs. He took up bodybuilding and Thai boxing, read Agatha Christie, and studied everything from Palestinian history to parapsychology. In his mid-teens, he also started sneaking out. Going up to his room to "study," he listened for the honk of his friend's Nissan ZX before shimmying down the fire escape. Hesham covered for his absences.

Most of the time it was "fun and carelessness." But whenever the conversation turned to Palestine, they argued. Abu Zubaydah insisted it was the duty of Muslims to defend Palestine. "End of the discussion!" he yelled, storming out. He railed against Saudi society, threw aside his *thobe*, and wore jeans. "[Father] always asked me in a screaming, reprimanding, and mocking manner to fully integrate into the society I'm living," he wrote in his diary. His elder brother, Maher, who was now studying medicine in Faisalabad, Pakistan, the city where Abu Zubaydah would be hunted down by the CIA in years to come, was his opposite, the studious and obedient "good-luck son." With Maher on track to becoming a doctor, Muhammad's greatest dream, he refocused on Hani and Hesham, his troublesome black sheep.

Muhammad's careful investments in Saudi-owned grocery stores and barbershops eventually had made him modestly rich. The family moved into a palatial house with marble stairs, gilded pillars, and a huge formal lounge. But it did not bring happiness. One day, while watching a TV news report about addiction, Muhammad accused Hani of using drugs. "Nobody should be surprised, given the life I have had to live," his son snapped back. Muhammad was furious. Hani was spoiled rotten and knew nothing about real suffering. Muhammad threw him out, and he slept on an old mattress in a vacant apartment for a week.

When Hani moved back home, his father withdrew his allowance, so Hani donated blood at a local hospital to earn money and applied to study computer engineering in the United States. But when he received an offer, his father refused to give him the paperwork needed for a travel document. Muhammad would not sponsor a debauched American life. "A huge gap between my father and me was growing bigger over the days," Hani reflected. He became listless, believing there was "no need to work hard for nothing." He suffered debilitating dreams about a huge wave gathering in the ocean, before beating the rocks and shaking the earth. The wave was accompanied by a voice, "coming from the bottom of the sea," that counted out the seconds before impact, "one, two three . . . ," a horrible premonition of the waterboard.[19]

Hesham also became terrified of the night, suffering screaming nightmares that woke everyone in the house.[20] Worried this would put off potential suitors for his daughters, who needed to marry, Muhammad moved Hesham into the servants' quarters, while a neighbor confided in Malika that someone had once been murdered in their fancy new home and the *djinn* were exacting their revenge. Although she was not overtly religious, Malika felt compelled to bring in sheikhs to conduct an exorcism, when conventional medics failed to provide a solution. The sheikhs loomed in the dark, reciting special Koranic verses for a sizable donation. The youngest brothers, Kamal and Sultan, who had only ever seen this kind of thing in American horror movies, were mesmerized.

In March 1989, Hani turned eighteen. A friend had recently applied to study in India and won a place. He did the same, selecting computer engineering. It required less paperwork and far less money than any US school. When Hani was offered a place, Muhammad agreed. His bad-luck son was now an adult, and in the early summer, Hani said tearful goodbyes to his mother. Hesham rode with him to the airport, with Muhammad lecturing all the way. "He called Hani a loser and told him never to come back," recalled Hesham. This was his way of saying goodbye. The following day, Hani arrived at a filthy student hostel in Pune, Maharashtra. "I am lost," he wrote. What had he done?

April 1, 2002, 5:00 A.M., Thailand

The CIA had a full-blown medical emergency on its hands. Abu Zubaydah had developed acute respiratory distress syndrome. Ali Soufan and Steve Gaudin rode with him to the hospital.[21] En route, he stopped breathing; a CIA medic intubated him, and they took turns hand-pumping oxygen. General Tritot had made arrangements with a local military hospital, after dreaming up another clever story.[22] Special Branch had been conducting a joint exercise with the Americans, he explained. It had gone wrong after an Arab American went crazy and had to be shot. To back his story, all the Americans were dressed up in military fatigues, even Abu Zubaydah.

Thai doctors watched nervously as the bloodied "soldier" was wheeled in. He was anemic and septic, his pulse was weakening, and a fever burned.[23] They anesthetized him and opened up his left thigh. The Americans prayed no one would spot the stories about the capture of a high-ranking Al Qaeda operative, some of which carried Abu Zubaydah's old "businessman" picture. After surgery, he was wheeled into intensive care and hooked up to a ventilator. Gaudin drew a curtain, CIA contractor guards chained him to the bed, and everyone mounted a vigil, with Soufan recalling that he held the patient's hand.[24] Station chief Michael Winograd cabled headquarters: George Tenet's prize detainee was clinging to life.[25] What was the plan?

Inside the Counterterrorist Center at Langley, Jose Rodriguez was frantic. Everyone was talking up a "hard approach," but Fredman, Rizzo and other CIA lawyers were still debating whether it was legal. The CIA also still hadn't resolved the issue of who would actually conduct the interrogations, although Abu Zubaydah's identity had been confirmed by a DNA sample from Hesham, who had replaced Hani as his father's punching bag, had followed him out of Saudi Arabia in 1998, and had gone to the United States to make a new life. The FBI had caught up with Hesham two days after 9/11, and he was being questioned at an immigration detention center in Portland, Oregon.[26]

One of those mining down into interrogation options was Kirk Hubbard, the head of psychological research and development at the Office of Technical Service. Hubbard was a behavioral psychologist who, before joining the CIA, had worked at Walter Reed Medical Center with broken soldiers coming home from Middle Eastern conflicts. After the 1998 US embassy attacks, he began promoting behavioral science as a tool to fight terror.[27] The idea came from Jim Mitchell, a military psychologist and CIA contractor, who in December 2001 wrote a CIA paper, "Al Qaeda's Resistance-to-Interrogation Training Manual," an assessment that played a critical role in the birth of enhanced interrogation.

British anti-terrorism police had recovered the training manual in May 2000 during a raid on a suspected Al Qaeda safe house in Manchester, England. It consisted of hundreds of handwritten pages in a flower print binder and was an example of manuals used in *mujahideen* training camps all over Afghanistan that drew from multiple sources, from *Martyrdom Codes*, a pamphlet written by a Palestinian incarcerated in an Israeli jail during the 1980s, to copies of US Army field manuals stolen from the global home of US special operations forces in Fort Bragg, North Carolina.[28] Some manuals quoted Sun Tzu's *The Art of War*, written in the fifth century BCE. Others cited the *The Philosophy of Confrontation Behind Bars*, a collection of essays by Palestinian Arab prisoners, interrogated in Israeli jails, and a twelve-page distillation of this work by Ali Hattar, a Christian Arab socialist and political activist.[29] Yet more utilized *Memoirs of a Captured Commando*, a work based on the experiences of an Iranian communist imprisoned in Tehran.[30] During and after the Soviet-Afghan War, publishing houses associated with Al Qaeda, the Libyan Islamic Fighting Group, Makhtab al-Khidamat (Afghan Services Bureau), and Egyptian Islamic Jihad shared and photocopied manuals, adding their own logos, to use in their camps. Widely circulated among *mujahideen* fighters, translated manuals also later turned up in Bosnia, Chechnya, and Kosovo.[31] Only those with a deep understanding of the history and nature of jihad would know how the manuals, authored by many for use in multiple theaters of conflict, had come into being and who had contributed what to their writings. It was *The Anarchist Cookbook* of the jihad world.

The version recovered from Manchester had a strip of masking tape across the front cover instructing: "It is forbidden to remove this from the house."[32] On the first page was a hand-drawn picture of a globe with a sword thrusting through it. Scrawled across the globe in Arabic was the title "Military Studies in the Jihad against the Tyrants," and inside, it included everything from how to blow up an Israeli defensive position to how to survive being hung upside down and tortured in a prison cell in Cairo. In early 2001, the FBI had presented it as evidence against four men accused of plotting the US embassy attacks, claiming that it was written by Ali Mohamed, a former Egyptian special forces officer turned Al Qaeda operative and trainer, who had assisted those charged by conducting initial surveillance of the embassies in Nairobi and Dar es Salaam and then turned double agent, informing for the FBI.[33] The manual proved its value as an evidential tool as all four suspects were convicted.[34] When the CIA took it off the shelf post-9/11, Langley dubbed it the "Manchester manual."[35]

In their assessment, Mitchell and his survival-school partner Bruce Jessen recommended "countermeasures" to get those trained to resist interrogation talking. These were based around mock torture techniques used in US military Survival, Evasion, Resistance, and Escape (SERE) schools.[36] Later Mitchell reflected, "My task is to take what we know about psychology and use it as a weapon against our enemies." He said at the time he and Jessen were only talking hypothetically, but that after the CIA captured Abu Zubaydah, counterterrorism officials decided to "reverse engineer" their suggested countermeasures and use them for real.[37] "Too many people have these romantic notions that for an effective interrogation you give him four beers and a packet of cigarettes and somehow he's going to give you everything," explained Jose Rodriguez, who knew they were sailing into choppy waters that had cost the CIA dearly before.[38]

At the end of the Korean War, during which more than two-thirds of American prisoners of war had signed statements urging the United States to quit the conflict or had "confessed" to war crimes, the CIA had commissioned studies about the brainwashing capabilities developed in the Communist Bloc.[39] Using bogus academic foundations to conceal the CIA's role, agency chemist Sidney Gottlieb paid American psychiatric institutions handsome research grants for access to real patients, who were subjected to hypnosis, isolation, verbal and sexual abuse, stress positions, sensory deprivation, threats, electric shocks, and mind-altering drugs. Starting in 1959, gangster Whitey Bulger, who was serving his first prison sentence, was given LSD every day for eighteen months.[40] Author Ken Kesey and poet Allen Ginsberg both got their LSD from Gottlieb.[41] The secret program was code-named MK-ULTRA (*MK* was CIA code for "mind control") and resulted in a 1963 CIA interrogation manual code-named KUBARK (*KU* was code for the CIA) that recommended using drugs and psychological torture on recalcitrant prisoners to instill a state of "debility-dependency-dread."[42] By the mid-1960s, MK-ULTRA was over, and Gottlieb went on to develop poisons and make high-tech spy gadgets for the CIA. But in 1974, after the *New York Times* revealed the CIA had experimented on humans, Congress began investigating. The CIA had already destroyed most MK-ULTRA files, but it emerged later that several well-respected American medical institutes had been duped into helping, with the powerful American Psychological Association (APA) playing a critical supportive role. The CIA had also experimented on prisoners held in secret detention camps in Japan, the Philippines, and Germany, mimicking what it would later do at black sites.[43]

While MK-ULTRA was never revisited, in 1983 the CIA quietly revived KUBARK. Some of the more extreme recommendations were scored through (but still visible); it was given a new introduction, warning against the use of torture, renamed the *Human Resource Exploitation Training Manual*, because the CIA was banned from using the word "interrogation," and put to use training rebels in Latin America.[44] After a prisoner died and two CIA officers were found to have conducted real interrogations, which went against the rules, another congressional investigation resulted, forcing the CIA to concede that torture never worked. For one thing, it yielded unreliable results because prisoners lied to get it to stop. Second, it was illegal. Third, if uncovered it might "result in adverse publicity."[45] The agency pledged never to interrogate again.[46]

However, post-9/11, "any means" were at the CIA's disposal, according to Dick Cheney, and George Tenet needed to get Abu Zubaydah talking about future attacks on the United States. The "Mitchell paper," as Langley came to call his and Jessen's December 2001 assessment, provided a clear way forward, and on April 1, 2002, the Counterterrorist Center dispatched a cable to Thailand setting out the parameters for a new "hard approach." Abu Zubaydah's environment would be manipulated to "cause psychological disorientation," to establish "psychological dependence upon the interrogator," and ultimately to create "an increased sense of learned helplessness."[47] If that did not work, they could always resort to mock torture.

Although Rodriguez had not yet met "Doc Mitchell," as colleagues called him, Jim Mitchell had been building a power base inside the Office of Technical Service for several years. Around the time of the US embassy bombings in 1998, while Alec Station grappled with Al Qaeda's organizational structure, communication methods, and future plans, Mitchell, then chief psychologist at the Twenty-Fourth Special Tactics Squadron at Pope Air Force Base, was contracted by the Technical Service to help with "developing psychological profiles of terrorists who would likely employ WMDs."[48] He also delivered seminars on "psychological aspects of detention and resistance training." By 2000, he was also a consultant to the CIA's Professional Standards Advisory Board, a great honor, since several former APA presidents sat on it, including Joseph Matarazzo, a significant veteran heavyweight, who in the 1950s had laid the foundations for the study of medical psychology in America, and was a proponent of learned helplessness. Matarazzo had known

Mitchell since the 1980s and was a keen supporter of SERE psychologists stepping up to the national security need.[49] In the summer of 2001, Matarazzo gave the keynote speech at a SERE conference, saying that if the government ever asked him to use his skills to help the nation, he would not hesitate. Three months later, Mitchell called the CIA as the Twin Towers burned.

Having retired from the air force on his fiftieth birthday in July 2001, Mitchell had recently signed a new CIA contract: $90,000 to advise on "conducting cross-cultural psychological assessments under dynamic conditions."[50] Post-9/11, it did not get much more dynamic than helping interrogators cross-examine unlawful enemy combatants at a secret CIA locations. Kirk Hubbard's deputy Judy Philipson, also a clinical psychologist and having some unspecified previous "interrogation experience," introduced Mitchell's work to the Counterterrorist Center through her husband, Jonathan Fredman, Jose Rodriguez's chief attorney.[51] Another Mitchell cheerleader was Mike McConnell, a senior operational psychologist, who had joined the Technical Service team in 1999.[52] Having previously worked in the SERE program at Fairchild, McConnell was a close friend of Mitchell's and both had worked in the "high-risk-of-capture course," a highly classified special access program run out of Spokane, in which students were hooded, stripped, subjected to a "body cavity check," humiliated, sleep-deprived, starved, and then put through a rigorous "enhanced" or "coercive" interrogation. After the nasty role-play was over, students were taken to the Resistance-Training Lab (RT Lab), where they were taught "bounce-back" skills and how to "return with honor."[53]

As the CIA sought to restore its reputation post-9/11, SERE, Mitchell, and his psychological weapons system became a rallying cry at Langley, championed by McConnell, Matarazzo, Philipson, and Hubbard. Clandestine officers all had experience of SERE since there was a mini survival school at "The Farm," the CIA's sprawling, wooded training campus at Camp Peary, Virginia.[54] Ric Prado, who had been a marine, had also attended the US Air Force survival school in Spokane. "They jumped us and hog-tied us," he recalled.[55] The training started with isolation, loud music, nudity, and sleep deprivation. Prado was then locked in a "confinement" box. "They take you into the interrogators. They do the good-guy, bad-guy routine. They are not allowed to punch you, but they are allowed to smack you around." Because it was only role-play, most students got through it. Prado, who before joining the CIA had allegedly worked as a mobster's enforcer in Miami, although he denied this, took it in his stride.[56] But some did not. "They told us about guys who had literally tried to commit suicide," Prado said, "or had nervous breakdowns."

The most aggressive part of the US Air Force SERE course took place inside a bunker at a mock prisoner-of-war camp hidden away on the edge of the huge Fairchild Air Force Base.[57] Mitchell and Jessen had both worked there during the 1980s and '90s. They trained survival instructors, tweaked "mock torture" routines, watched for signs of "abusive drift" during role-play, made sure students did not reach a state of "despair" or "helplessness," and ran the resistance-training classes. The course was built around research conducted by sociologist Albert Biderman, who had also worked in the MK-ULTRA program. Biderman had designed the mock-torture element of SERE training after interviewing Americans returning from Korea. One air force pilot described his psychological ordeal as the "slow, quiet and diabolical" destruction of his mind.[58] Biderman concluded that mind control was the most effective torture tactic because it induced hopelessness and despair. A perfect example was chaining prisoners into standing stress positions. "The immediate source of pain is not the interrogator but the victim," wrote Biderman.[59] Interrogators should also seek to establish "omnipotent power" to make prisoners compliant, Biderman recommended, controlling everything from light, heat, noise, and food to even bodily functions. If a prisoner came to see the interrogator as his "God," he could be persuaded to give up secrets in exchange for small rewards. Biderman drew up a "Chart of Coercion" that championed isolation, humiliation, degradation, and death threats. By the Vietnam War, the SERE school in Spokane was utilizing techniques learned from the Communist Bloc and tested out on real patients during MK-ULTRA. "Biderman was a brilliant man," reflected Bruce Jessen.[60] Now, the CIA was planning to unload it all on Abu Zubaydah.

However, not everyone "read-in" to the Abu Zubaydah operation was convinced by this radical plan. Scott Shumate, another senior CIA operational psychologist in the Office of Technical Service, was concerned about psychologists getting their hands dirty. His job, profiling assets and officers, was always done from outside the room: watching on CCTV or through a one-way mirror. Also, Mitchell's bold assurances that SERE techniques had been safely conducted on tens of thousands of US service personnel for over half a century without any significant injuries did not chime with widely published research.[61] There were rumors that cadets had died during or after attending SERE courses, but the Counterterrorist Center was in no hurry to check into them.[62] Mitchell's science was wonky, said Shumate. Some of his overconfidence appeared "off." But Jose Rodriguez did not listen to Shumate because he had a life-threatening "short-fuse" situation on his hands. He also did not consult Terry DeMay, who ran the Office of Medical Services and had been the CIA's chief psychologist for fifteen years, even though the evolving interrogation plan would be presented to administration lawyers as a science- and physician-led operation.[63]

"The CIA didn't read the science," said Susan Brandon, a senior research psychologist opposed to the SERE plan.[64] Putting a military psychologist at the forefront of CIA interrogation policy was crazy, she said. But although Brandon was consulted by Hubbard, she did not work for the CIA, so had no influence. Charles Morgan, a Yale University psychiatrist who was regarded as the leading expert in SERE-related stress studies, echoed her concerns. Long before 9/11, he had looked through Mitchell's data while testing blood and saliva samples from US military survival schools for the Pentagon and concluded it was "no good." Mitchell and his clique "had a reputation for being confident but not checking things," said Morgan.[65] "They were advocates, but they were not scientists. They just believed they were right and they thought they were saving the world." Putting torture role-players into real-world interrogations would lead to disaster, warned Morgan. But at the time Morgan worked for the Pentagon, not a CIA, so no one listened to him either.

Instead, Kirk Hubbard sought out Philip Zimbardo, who was also not CIA but the incoming APA president. In 1976, Zimbardo had conducted a groundbreaking experiment into interrogation psychology at Stanford University.[66] The US Navy had wanted to establish whether brutality reported among guards in naval brigs was due to sadistic personalities or simply bad prison environments.[67] Zimbardo was paid to build a mock-up prison in a university basement, where he employed psychology students to act as guards or prisoners, while acting as superintendent himself. "Prisoners" were strip-searched, hooded, shackled, and given numbers to replace names. "Guards" wore mirrored sunglasses to prevent eye contact and wielded baseball bats.

The experiment had to be abandoned after guards began showing signs of "abusive drift," such as subjecting their prisoners to psychological torture. The answer to the navy's question was that untrained humans could do terrible things when placed in an abusive real-world environment. However, Hubbard did not want to talk about Zimbardo's prison experiment, which became so notorious it was turned into a movie; he wanted to know whether the APA was willing to assist the CIA with psychological expertise, starting off with a lecture at Langley on the subject of "hate."[68] Zimbardo declined.[69]

Susan Brandon, who worked at the APA as a visiting scientist, caught a whiff of what the CIA was planning when she met Hubbard at Langley shortly after 9/11. She was willing to offer expertise, but Hubbard said he was unable to tell her what the CIA needed because she did not have proper clearances. "I saw this cluster of people including Joe Matarazzo, and I remember being told, 'You can't listen to them,'" Brandon recalled.[70] Eventually, Hubbard gave her a list of CIA requirements. She was shocked by its naivety. "It was the most innocuous list, like 'What is a terrorist?' I just sat and looked at it and said, 'Well, you could read a book.'" Brandon knew there was psychological research into terrorism and terrorist methodology going back to the 1980s, but the CIA was not interested. "They had already decided they wanted to hurt people and were looking for psychologists willing to approve it," she alleged. A later investigation found that during the six months prior to Abu Zubaydah's capture, the CIA did not conduct any significant research to identify effective interrogation practices, such as conferring with experienced US military or law enforcement interrogators.[71] There were no reviews of past practices or the lessons learned from MK-ULTRA, KUBARK, or the *Human Resource Exploitation Training Manual*. The only documented research was the December 2001 assessment of Al Qaeda's resistance-to-interrogation capabilities prepared by Mitchell and Jessen, who knew nothing about Al Qaeda.

A hint that the CIA commissioned the "Mitchell paper" to fit around a preconceived desire to use the harshest possible methods on Al Qaeda detainees appeared on November 7, 2001, when CIA lawyers drafted a twenty-eight-page summary of federal and international torture legislation, the result of two months of research.[72] On November 26, Tenet's chief lawyer, John Rizzo, circulated a draft legal memo citing the "Israeli example," meaning that "torture was necessary to prevent imminent, significant, physical harm to persons, where there is no other available means."[73] Jonathan Fredman, Rodriguez's chief attorney, was in the email chain. Foreign governments might be "very unwilling" to call the United States to task for torture "when it resulted in saving thousands of lives," Rizzo's office advised, knowing that Tenet had convinced the president and vice president that another Al Qaeda attack, possibly nuclear, was imminent.[74] The Bush administration was on the back foot, having been repeatedly attacked for having missed multiple warning signs before 9/11, including the crucial August 6, 2001, intelligence report stating, "Bin Laden determined to strike in US," which had incorrectly identified Abu Zubaydah as a key Bin Ladin [sic] lieutenant."[75]

Mitchell insisted he got the contract to review the Manchester manual by pure chance. "I was in headquarters doing a presentation to the advisory board; I'm standing there, and there's a female psychologist with a copy of the manual on her desk," he recalled.[76] "She said, 'How are we supposed to analyze this? We have been tasked to understand what it means and its implications, and I haven't a clue about it.'"[77] Mitchell told her he had already seen it in the special forces library at Fort Bragg, which was near to his office at Pope Air Force Base and where he spent much of his time. "You could do with having someone like me to go through it and tell you what the terrorists who wrote it would look like and behave like," he said.[78] Days later, he signed a contract to assist the CIA with "covert action/covert influence operations."[79] Hubbard handled Mitchell's contract.[80] Jessen's too. They were paid $16,000 each to review the manual and other materials inside a "sensitive compartmented information facility" at Langley—a soundproof and leakproof box. Their report took "a few days, maybe, probably not very long."[81] It was easy money, but the impact was enormous.

In their introduction, Mitchell and Jessen explained why they had been chosen: "We are familiar with how hostile countries approach interrogation and knowledgeable about how trained captives organize their resistance efforts." They had "32 years of combined experience in providing operational support to detained US personnel, training special operations personnel in resistance to interrogation, and debriefing hostages, peacetime governmental detainees and prisoners of war." They acknowledged they were not experts in Arab culture or Al Qaeda but did not regard this as a hindrance as they explained how to spot the signs of Al Qaeda suspects trained to resist. They would be "feigning confusion," "feigning injuries or disabilities," playacting or "exaggerating an existing injury," digressing into irrelevancies, "leading the interrogator away from sensitive information," and making contradicting, misleading, and inaccurate statements. They would stall and pause, use religious chants and phrases, and complain about translation. Overall they would "be misleading with the appearance of sincerity."[82] They would probably also "complain that any information given during the interrogation was provided under duress." Their conclusion: "A sophisticated level of resistance training is available to high risk Al Qaeda operatives."

It sounded authoritative, but the analysis was garbled, partial, and deeply flawed. Noting that the Manchester manual had been utilized to win convictions in the trial of several East Africa embassy bombers, other summaries of the manual stated that much of the resistance-training material in it came from "Ali Hatter," a "rabid anti-western/Zionist personality" who wanted to "help Palestinians counter Israeli interrogation techniques."[83] As well as misspelling the author's name and misrepresenting his activism, this assessment highlighted resistance techniques "Ali Hatter" and others had recommended, such as making false claims of torture "to invalidate information provided" and "self-inflict[ing] wounds to provide the appearance of torture." It concluded: "Allegations of torture are the most public examples of a counter-interrogation technique that impact both on-going and future interrogation operations."

The real Ali Hattar was a political activist, who had been repeatedly harassed by the CIA-friendly Jordanian security establishment. He had been arrested many times, and at one stage faced the death penalty simply for demanding "freedom of expression"; Human Rights Watch supported his claims of state harassment, and at times he fled to Syria to avoid ending up in Jordan's much-feared Special Security Court.[84] A Christian, an engineer by trade, and a member of the Union of Professional Associations, the largest civil society organization in Jordan, Hattar was falsely accused of supporting Islamists and planning to kill Israelis.[85] All this would have been familiar to Marty Martin, who was serving as the CIA's Amman station chief when Hattar came into focus.[86]

After giving advice on how to recognize when captured Al Qaeda operatives were resisting, Mitchell and Jessen provided "strategies for developing countermeasures." These were later redacted, but Mitchell later confirmed they were based on psychological and physical "pressures" employed at the Personnel Recovery Academy, the advanced SERE school at Fairchild Air Force Base where he had worked for many years and where Jessen was still chief psychologist.[87] According to training manuals, these pressures included "walling," whereby a student was bounced off a flexible wall; slaps to the face and abdomen; stress positions ("on his knees, arms fully extended over the head"); and a technique called "watering." This covered everything from flicking or spraying a student with cold water while he was "standing or lying on a bench on the floor" to the "water pit," in which a naked student was submerged up to, but not including, the head.[88] Students called it "water torture." The role-play was based on real torture methods employed by foreign regimes that did not adhere to the Geneva Conventions, but Mitchell and Jessen advised the CIA they could adapt them for use in the real world so that they did not violate the conventions.

Although they had never met an Islamist or a terrorist, they advised that Al Qaeda detainees would be adept at using cultural differences as an "interactive impediment to the interrogation process" and as a "psychological support mechanism behind which to hide from interrogation efforts." This commentary chimed with what the CIA and the Pentagon had observed of Ramzi Yousef, who had bombed the World Trade Center in 1993 and steadfastly refused to cooperate with anyone from his arrest to conviction. "The experience with Ramzi had taught US interrogators, mainly FBI, that hardened Islamists were tough nuts," explained Richard Shiffrin, a deputy general counsel at the Pentagon.[89]

Mitchell and Jessen explained that their techniques were carefully "crafted" and employing them would be "a dynamic process." What they were offering was not a "detailed cookbook" but simply a "flavor" of what could be achieved, based on their experience as SERE school psychologists. However, there were important caveats. In SERE school, instructors (who were called "interrogators") were let loose on real cadets only after they were trained, qualified, and certified to use these techniques, by psychologists, like Mitchell and Jessen. During "interrogations," instructors were always supervised by the psychologists, who were referred to as "controllers." "Interrogators" were subordinate to "controllers," whose main job during "interrogations" was to watch out for "learned helplessness," a psychological state SERE schools made strenuous efforts to avoid. Cadets who fell into learned helplessness gave up on everything. "I have learned I'm helpless and there is nothing I can do to get out of this situation," as Charles Morgan, the psychiatrist who led the field in SERE research, explained.[90] It was the psychologist's job to intervene to stop it from happening. And it was the psychologist's job to counsel any cadets who got too close to the edge.

Learned helplessness leapt out when the CIA first read the "Mitchell paper."[91] If important Al Qaeda detainees reached a state of learned helplessness through real psychological torture, maybe they would give up everything, said some who read the report. This alarmed the lawyers. If the interrogation process scarred detainees mentally or physically, then the CIA could rightly be accused of torture. There was a fine line between what was needed and playing it safe, and the CIA needed more refined advice. Shortly after Mitchell submitted the Al Qaeda resistance paper, the CIA sent him to meet the real expert behind the learned helplessness theory, Professor Martin Seligman. Kirk Hubbard accompanied Mitchell as his CIA chaperone.

The setting was benign, a two-day mini-conference at Seligman's mansion in Philadelphia, held on December 15 and 16, 2001. It had been arranged weeks earlier, with some of the most important psychologists in the country attending. They came together to discuss how psychologists could assist in the War on Terror.[92] Seligman, who was also a past APA president, agreed to be the host. Mitchell and Hubbard both secured invitations and were listed among the sixteen attendees as "CIA," although Seligman claimed he had no idea who invited them or that the CIA was considering deploying his theory for real on War on Terror detainees.[93] Had he known this at the time he would have been deeply alarmed, he reflected.

Seligman's experiments had been conducted on stray dogs at the University of Pennsylvania in 1967. A dog was placed in a six-foot-long run, one-half of which was electrified and delivered shocks every few seconds.[94] The other half, separated by a low barrier, was benign. If an "experimentally naïve" dog was placed in the electrified end of the box, it would always attempt to escape. "At the onset of the first painful electric shock, the dog runs frantically about defecating, urinating and howling, until it accidentally scrambles over the barrier," wrote Seligman. However, dogs previously subjected to shocks while held immobile in a rubber "Pavlovian hammock" did nothing to save themselves from trauma when given the choice in an electrified run.

Seligman observed similar results in humans subjected to incessant loud noise.[95] They had learned they were helpless.

Post-9/11, Seligman, who had become a world authority on treating depression, wanted to send recommendations on "how to counter Islamic extremism" to the White House.[96] He never received a reply, and after he was later accused of helping the CIA design a harsh interrogation policy for Abu Zubaydah, he did everything he could to distance himself from any involvement. Writing of the mini-conference, he insisted, "There was not a single mention of interrogation, torture or detainees."[97] The professor recalled that the only time Mitchell spoke was during a break when he came up and gushed about how much he respected Seligman's work.

Nothing of what, if anything, Mitchell and Hubbard reported back to Langley has ever been published. But a month after Seligman's mini-conference, treating detainees harshly was debated at the National Security Council. Afterward, the Justice Department was persuaded to issue a legal opinion recommending that War on Terror detainees should be denied Geneva Conventions rights. An unidentified CIA attorney stepped up the lobbying, arguing that the CIA would have "few alternatives to simply asking questions" if Common Article 3 of the conventions was not set aside.[98] "The optic becomes how legally defensible is a particular act that probably violates the convention, but ultimately saves lives," the attorney explained.[99] On February 7, 2002, President Bush complied.[100] One significant hurdle barring "hard approach" interrogations was eliminated, and the author of the legal opinion, John Yoo, would go on to play a leading role in CIA interrogation policy. Born in Seoul, raised in Philadelphia, educated at Harvard and Yale, and just thirty-four on 9/11, Yoo was exceptionally bright, Republican-leaning, capitalist-hungry, and ambitious. He was married to Elsa Arnett, the daughter of Pulitzer Prize–winning war reporter Peter, one of the few journalists to interview Osama bin Laden. Yoo also played squash with Jim Haynes, Donald Rumsfeld's chief lawyer.[101]

Days after Common Article 3 was ditched, Bruce Jessen also contacted Professor Seligman: an email asking Seligman to speak about learned helplessness at an upcoming conference organized by his employer, the Joint Personnel Recovery Agency (JPRA), which supervised all the US military survival schools, including the Personnel Recovery Academy in Spokane. The conference would be held at the naval survival school in San Diego, the only location where the most aggressive SERE technique, a form of mock drowning called "waterboarding," was authorized. "[Jessen] sent along a collection of papers on how our troops were trained to resist interrogation and survive captivity," Seligman recalled. "He asked to meet with me in April to discuss the contents of the talk," which would take place in May. Seligman thought JPRA was interested because of concerns that US military personnel might be captured and tortured by Al Qaeda in Afghanistan.[102]

Mitchell and Jessen spent the rest of February and most of March advising the US government on War on Terror interrogation policy. Mitchell joined Susan Brandon on February 28 at an APA-sponsored conference at the FBI Academy in Quantico, Virginia, entitled "Countering Terrorism: Integration of Practice and Theory." Mitchell also talked to military psychologist friends at Fort Bragg, and "possibly" gave them a copy of his Al Qaeda resistance-to-interrogation paper.[103] Jessen, who was a seven-hour flight away in Spokane, worked on detention and interrogation bids for the US military, assisted by Chris Wirts, JPRA's chief of operational planning.[104]

In the first months after 9/11, the CIA considered running its interrogations through the US military, which had numerous military intelligence brigades and a well-established training program at Fort Huachuca, Arizona. And like the CIA, post-9/11 the military sought to harshen up preexisting interrogation practices by embracing SERE. On December 17, 2001, the day after Professor Seligman's mini-conference in Philadelphia, the Pentagon asked to see SERE and JPRA training materials.[105] A formal request for help with interrogating Al Qaeda detainees landed on Jessen's desk in February, one month after Guantánamo opened. "Chris and I sat down at a console" and "draft[ed] out a—like, a straw-man protocol for what you would do if you were going to set up an interrogation captivity facility," Jessen recalled.[106] Their "Prisoner Handling Recommendations" included a detention and interrogation facility based around the "strictest baseline prison behavior policy possible," where punishment was tailored to "maximize cultural undesirability."[107] Wirts had no compunction about JPRA instructors and psychologists bidding to interrogate real detainees. "It was up to the customer to decide," he said.[108]

In early March 2002, Jessen and Joe Witsch, a senior SERE instructor, prepared slide presentations for Guantánamo-bound interrogators.[109] Most of them had already attended training courses at Fort Huachuca, but existing courses had been drawn up before 9/11 and were not Al Qaeda specific. One of Jessen's presentations was entitled "Al Qaeda Resistance Contingency Training Based on Recently Obtained Al Qaeda Documents," a rerun of his and Mitchell's CIA paper. The other presentation concerned "exploitation" (a.k.a. interrogation) and covered topics such as "isolation and degradation."[110] Interrogators should "establish absolute control, induce dependence to meet needs, elicit compliance, shape cooperation," wrote Jessen and Witsch. They suggested "how to exploit Al Qaeda detainees for intelligence within the confines of the Geneva Conventions," although Jessen later clarified that he would "not have known at the time if isolation, degradation, sensory deprivation, or other topics referenced in the slides would have been within the confines of the Geneva Conventions."[111]

Dan Baumgartner, JPRA's chief of staff, wrote in a July 2002 memo that Jessen and Witsch's exploitation methods "may be very effective in inducing learned helplessness and breaking the [War on Terror] detainees' willingness to resist." Baumgartner, who was not a psychologist or a training instructor, pitched his agency's unparalleled expertise, writing: "JPRA has arguably developed into the DoD's experts on exploitation."[112] Jessen and Witsch then participated in a video teleconference with Guantánamo interrogators. Jessen recalled making a "pitch," but later he tried to distance himself, saying the slides and supporting documents "turned into something that I had no control over or nothing to do with."[113] Other people revised and changed them multiple times, he recollected. "Eventually, a curriculum was made up that I would never have agreed with," he said, wary of the detainee abuse scandals at Guantánamo and Abu Ghraib, where US military and CIA interrogators trained in JPRA methods abused detainees, some of whom died. "But my name was still attached to it because I was the first one to get on the computer."

However, contemporary records suggested that Jessen's participation was far from reluctant. On March 12, 2002, he sent a copy of the CIA's "Mitchell paper" to Randy Moulton, the JPRA commander, who recommended forwarding it to the Joint Chiefs of Staff. "After over 30 years of training we have become quite proficient with both specialized resistance and the ways to defeat it," wrote Moulton.[114] It was one of several attempts by Moulton, Baumgartner, and other senior JPRA officials to promote SERE techniques for use in the real world. Jessen later said he could not recall sending the "Mitchell paper" to his boss. "I absolutely don't remember doing it. I don't think the CIA would have let me do that. It was their document."[115]

But Steven Kleinman, who worked as director of intelligence at the JPRA's SERE academy in Spokane, recalled some former colleagues being desperate to help destroy Al Qaeda. "It was an amazing thing to watch up front, up close, and then when I left, trying to keep tabs on it—un-freakin'-believable," he said.[116] It was a complex picture involving multiple requests for assistance fielded by multiple SERE and JPRA experts. As well as helping out Jessen with the Guantánamo request, Chris Wirts was also advising the CIA on SERE-style interrogation techniques. In December 2001, around the time Mitchell and Jessen were at Langley writing their Al Qaeda resistance-to-interrogation paper, Wirts was sharing interrogation role-play manuals with the CIA, including one that advocated "treating a person like an animal."[117] This led to a further four meetings at Langley, Wirts later recalled, although Mitchell insisted that Wirts had nothing to do with the official enhanced-interrogation program.[118]

Martin Seligman's learned helplessness theory was heading for Guantánamo as well as the CIA, whether the professor liked it or not. However, when Jessen's scheduled meeting to discuss the upcoming SERE conference with Seligman happened on April 1, the same day the CIA informed the team in Thailand they intended to force Abu Zubaydah into a state of learned helplessness, Jessen did not turn up. Instead, Seligman found Kirk Hubbard on his doorstep, accompanied by his deputy, Judy Philipson, and Elizabeth Vogt, an attorney who worked with Fredman in the Counterterrorist Center.[119] "They asked me at length about learned helplessness," Seligman recalled.[120] He "outlined procedures for inducing helplessness" and how to "do therapy to cure helplessness."[121] But someone was not playing straight. According to the professor, the discussions "were entirely about how captured Americans could resist and evade torture."[122] He still thought the CIA was concerned about US personnel being tortured by Al Qaeda. Seligman was being encouraged under false pretences to talk up a theory that the CIA intended to present to the National Security Council to win approval for use on Abu Zubaydah. Kirk Hubbard later conceded: "His 'learned helplessness theory' may have been considered in the formulation of the interrogation strategy, but, if true, Dr Seligman would not have been aware of that."[123]

Although Abu Zubaydah was on the verge of death in a Thai hospital, Langley was forging ahead with plans to subject him to an interrogation so aggressive that he would probably be permanently damaged, if he survived. Rizzo needed to dampen that message and also wanted advance declination of prosecution.[124] Although Seligman never discussed the interrogation of detainees with the CIA, the CIA told National Security Council lawyers that the author of the theory had told them learned helplessness "does not result in a permanent change in a subject's personality and that full recovery can be expected once the conditions inducing learned helplessness are removed."[125] SERE stress expert Charles Morgan, who reviewed a Department of Justice account of this conversation, said: "Some of the comments in here are just contrary to what we know in science, that it's reversible, it doesn't hurt people, that's scientifically wrong, so someone is lying to someone in this document when they say it doesn't hurt people."[126]

Condoleezza Rice's chief lawyer, John Bellinger, recollected that when Rizzo first called him about Abu Zubaydah in "the Spring of 2002," he asked for a declination "in advance of the interrogation because of concerns about the application of criminal laws, in particular the torture statute, to their actions."[127] The CIA wanted to brief Department of Justice attorneys about the laws and statutes it was most worried about. Bellinger arranged for the CIA to meet John Yoo and Michael Chertoff, the assistant attorney general. Bellinger recalled that "the CIA attorneys may have even brought a draft declination" with them.[128] Jack Goldsmith, another senior Justice Department attorney, later characterized it as the CIA demanding "get-out-of-jail-free cards."[129]

According to the record, the CIA attorneys, who included John Rizzo, had been researching the torture statue since September 17, 2001. They handed Yoo draft legal arguments in favor of harsh techniques.[130] Yoo, who had helped form a legal opinion to dismiss the Geneva Conventions for Al Qaeda and Taliban detainees, was warned by Rizzo to keep their discussion completely under wraps. The CIA had informed Bellinger that it was not even telling the State Department or the Pentagon about its plan, although there was a dangerous crossover between Mitchell, who until recently had worked for the Pentagon, and Jessen, who still worked for the Pentagon, and was promoting similar techniques in military circles.

Bellinger felt intense "pressure" coming from the CIA. Tenet characterized Abu Zubaydah as one of the "worst terrorists on the planet" and "the highest-ranking al-Qa'ida official captured to date."[131] Led by Rizzo, the CIA lobbied hard for the "necessity defense" that the agency knew further terrorist attacks would occur; it had a person in custody "who had information about terrorist attacks"; its proposed interrogation program was "safe and effective"; and "without the interrogation program and the use of the specific interrogation techniques, the CIA did not believe that they could get the information necessary to prevent the attacks and save American lives." Using an Israeli bus-bomb-style argument, the CIA had the White House, the National Security Council, and the Department of Justice "boxed in," making it impossible to reject its request for legal cover, Bellinger reflected.[132] Furthermore, an impression was given that this was a CIA Office of Medical Services–led interrogation plan, put together by caregivers and health professionals and based on real science, when in reality Medical Services had not even been consulted and the scientist behind the primary theory had been misquoted.[133] Dan Jones, who led the subsequent Senate inquiry into enhanced interrogation, accused the CIA of "constant exaggeration," and said the agency had "manipulated and misled" the White House, attorney general, National Security Council, and Department of Justice.[134]

One of those with a bird's-eye view of what was going on, at least internally, was Scott Shumate, the senior CIA psychologist from the Office of Technical Service. He had been "surged" into the Counterterrorist Center as chief operational psychologist and was now deeply involved in the Abu Zubaydah discussions.[135] Listening to talk about the "balance of harms" between subjecting the detainee to techniques bordering on torture versus saving American lives, Shumate tried to take the shine off, pointing to studies that suggested torture only produced lies. One study conducted on Japanese prisoners-of-war during World War II at Fort Hunt, in Alexandria, Virginia, had found rapport building worked far better than beatings.[136] But no one was listening to Shumate. "You'd have to knock hundreds of pounds' worth of dirt off that study because nobody ever read it," he said, echoing Susan Brandon's concerns about the CIA's indifference to research.[137] He was also deeply worried that the CIA's real behavioral science and medical experts were being kept out of key discussions.

Shumate also recited a revealing true story about a US naval aviator tortured by North Vietnamese interrogators, who wanted to know how US aircraft carriers could remain at sea for many months without coming into port to resupply. Every time the aviator told the truth, that they had refrigerators aboard filled with food, they tortured him more. "Eventually, he said the Americans had tiny farms in the bowels of their ships, stocked with miniature cows, sheep, and pigs," said Shumate.[138] "The North Vietnamese got the story they wanted because they had broken him." Rodriguez did not have time for smart-ass lectures, and he did not like Shumate, who towered over him physically and was prone to silent staring matches. Now that the FBI had knocked the CIA harsh approach off course by getting Abu Zubaydah talking without any signs he was resisting, Rodriguez was in a hurry. While he would have to make Shumate part of the team, his main focus was covering the SERE component. The CIA needed to someone who knew what they were talking about.

What about Mitchell? suggested Fredman.[139] Mitchell had a PhD in psychology and had spent most of his career inside the SERE program; his military performance scores were off the chart, and he already had CIA classifications. Furthermore, he was a contractor, which could offer some deniability if things went wrong. Fredman's wife, Judy Philipson, vouched for Mitchell, as did Joe Matarazzo, Kirk Hubbard, and Mike McConnell. He could go as an observer, fulfilling his August 2001 contract to offer psychological assessments in "dynamic conditions," while headquarters continued to work on the legal underpinnings of a learned-helplessness-based interrogation plan. It was good enough for Rodriguez. Mitchell was qualified, Rodriguez said, "because we needed to do something different than what had been done before."[140] He "had a tremendous expertise" and a "good vision for what needed to be done." As long as it could be made legal, Rodriguez was not interested in the science. "Frankly, my interest was in getting results, not in, you know, the psychological state of people," he said.[141] Without conducting any further vetting, Rodriguez "took it for granted" that Mitchell knew what he was doing.

All they had left to do was find actual interrogators, which after so many months of supposed agonizing seemed like an afterthought. The Office of Security, which administered the agency's clearances program, investigated security breaches, provided security guards, and supervised polygraphs on staff, contractors, and assets, put forward a polygraph expert. He was an authority on "detecting deception" and backed the Reid technique of rapport-based interrogation that the FBI used; his code name was "Bryan."[142] The second pick was a senior CIA operations officer of Egyptian origin, deep undercover for his entire CIA career, who had worked on previous Al Qaeda–related investigations, including those concerning the USS *Cole* and the US embassy bombings, and had interrogated detainees at Guantánamo. His wife worked in the Counterterrorist Center as a targeter and his code name was "Adil."[143]

Rodriguez's team was coming together nicely, and he asked to meet Mitchell. On April 1, Fredman asked his wife for Mitchell's cell-phone number.[144] Rodriguez was informed: "According to CTC/LGL [Counterterrorist Center/Legal] . . . [Mitchell] is currently in [redacted;] could be available tomorrow afternoon if anyone needs to talk to him."[145] Another person in the email chain asked: "Presume you/someone is calling Jim back for our 9am tomorrow?" An unequivocal message was sent to Ali Soufan and Steve Gaudin in Thailand. While they needed to stay on for continuity, "all conversations with subject should be strictly limited to the exchange of critical medical information."[146] No premature questioning, prompting, or manipulation of any kind could happen until the new headquarters team arrived. "Under no circumstances should preparations for interrogation commence at this time," Langley directed, ignoring the fact the Soufan and Gaudin had already begun interrogating Abu Zubaydah.

Alec Station also sent a summary of the "Mitchell paper" and signed off with a startling claim that would have dire consequences for Abu Zubaydah: he was the author of the Manchester manual and therefore the foremost Al Qaeda expert in resistance-to-interrogation training. This was pure extrapolation. Just like every other group with a camp, Khaldan trainers had printed out training materials available on the web or in book form under their own logo. But the manual found in Manchester and reviewed by Mitchell and Jessen had no specific connection to Khaldan or Abu Zubaydah. Mitchell later agreed with the FBI assessment that the manual contained "resistance-to-interrogation course materials" stolen from US special forces at Fort Bragg by Ali Mohamed, the former Egyptian army officer who had joined Al Qaeda and was close to Ayman al-Zawahiri, and had immigrated to the United States in 1984 and got a job as a Fort Bragg interpreter.[147] It was a complex and tangled story that only an Al Qaeda expert would fully understand.

In the early 1990s, Mohamed had taught Osama bin Laden and his real Number Three, Abu Hafs al-Masri, how to blow things up and resist torture.

If the CIA had genuinely wanted to understand the manual's background, it could have asked Mohamed, because he was sitting in a cell at the Metropolitan Correctional Center in Manhattan while Mitchell and Jessen were writing up their assessment of his materials. A CIA paramilitary officer working with Ric Prado and Billy Waugh had even visited Mohamed to seek advice on Al Qaeda's weaknesses shortly before deploying to Afghanistan in September 2001.[148] But Rodriguez sent no one, and the false authorship of the manual was slipped into Abu Zubaydah's weighty Alec Station biography with a note that "CIA psychologists" supported this assertion.[149]

CHAPTER 4

"DISGRACE IN THEIR FACE"

April 2, 2002

J im Mitchell drove north on I-95 from Washington to Philadelphia with
an eye on the speedometer. Bruce Jessen was beside him, Kirk Hubbard
was in the back, and they were heading from CIA headquarters, where
Mitchell had had a nine A.M. meeting with Counterterrorist Center officials.[1]
The CIA wanted Mitchell, Jessen and Hubbard to quiz Martin Seligman yet
again about "learned helplessness."[2] A key question on everyone's minds: Did
it cause permanent damage, in which case it would be illegal as an interrogation goal, or was it potentially reversible, in which case it could be a useful
tool? It was the CIA's second house call to Seligman in twenty-four hours
and at least the fourth time since 9/11 that Mitchell, Jessen, or CIA officials
had discussed his trademark theory with him.

It was a fast-moving situation. Abu Zubaydah was on a ventilator in a
Thai military hospital. The Pentagon had just announced his capture, and
the White House was describing him as part of "Osama bin Laden's inner
circle." Officials had considered sending Abu Zubaydah to Egypt or Jordan,
reported *ABC News*, but had dismissed it because "such a move would directly
raise a question of torture." Instead, Americans were interrogating him at
an undisclosed location. "Aggressive tools may be used," said a source, hinting at the discussions John Rizzo was having with the Department of Justice
and the National Security Council.[3]

Mitchell recalled the chief operational psychologist at the CIA's Office
of Technical Service calling en route with news that Jose Rodriguez wanted
to meet him. "You should be ready to leave the country immediately after
that," Mitchell was told.[4] Later, Mitchell claimed surprise, even though he

had been advising the CIA on "conducting cross-cultural psychological assessments under dynamic conditions" for nine months, had delivered the critical "Mitchell paper," had suggested countermeasures based on mock torture, and had "been at Langley earlier in the day for a meeting."[5] Furthermore, the team in Thailand had already been informed the CIA was going down the "learned helplessness" route.

"We spent the night in Philadelphia," Mitchell recalled.[6] They arrived at Seligman's mansion early the next morning, April 3. The professor did not remember this particular meeting, but he was still emphatic: he never discussed detainees, the interrogation of detainees, or the use of learned helplessness on detainees with the CIA. "Had they mentioned any of these at any time, alarm bells would have sounded, I would surely have remembered it, and the meeting would have stood out in my memory," Seligman insisted.[7] "My discussions with Hubbard and Mitchell were entirely about how captured Americans could resist and evade torture." Mitchell, Jessen, and Hubbard were back on the road to Langley by lunchtime, Mitchell's day having finally come.

———— • ————

Jim Mitchell had been born in "nowhere" Tennessee in July 1951, when schools were still segregated and chain gangs cut weeds beside the roads.[8] Both his parents had troubled backgrounds. His mother, Juanita, suffered from an "undiagnosed personality disorder."[9] Her grandfather "drove the Klan out of Tennessee," fought the Confederates, and shot dead his son-in-law, "a rich Irish drunk," who left his family penniless.[10] Without a father, Juanita had married rakish Elmer Mitchell at fourteen and spent World War II alone with her first baby, a daughter called Bonnie. After the war ended, Elmer returned home, having suffered spinal meningitis and having become addicted to barbiturates prescribed by a military doctor.

Elmer and Juanita were incapable of looking after their children, said Jim, recalling that he had come home one day to find an empty house. Even the cats and dogs were gone. For the next few years, his parents spun around the Deep South in a dilapidated truck, periodically checking Elmer into veterans' hospitals. They spent Christmases and Thanksgivings in cheap motels. Juanita wore silky dresses with socks and sandals in family photos. When Elmer's head was clear, he tried to make a living as a private detective, then a cabdriver. He was clever and funny. But from the age of four, Jim and two siblings lived mostly with Juanita's mother, Nancy, a formidable old woman who healed their scratches with snuff-spit and wielded an unlicensed shotgun.

They lived mostly on a derelict farm in Williamson, Georgia, where Jim recalled being attacked by a giant rooster and falling out of the hayloft. One time, his parents turned up, piled everyone into their truck, and drove them back to Tennessee. Jim, his mother, and his two sisters rode on top of boxes lashed with clothesline and rusty chains.[11] But after a couple of weeks, Elmer and Juanita disappeared again, and Nancy took the children back to the farm. She believed it was better to live poor and raise chickens than to take social security. Jim recalled money being so tight that one time they camped out in a condemned house. Nancy cooked on a potbellied stove, and they washed in well water decanted into a tin tub. Having raised fourteen children already (ten of her own and four inherited from others), Nancy knew how to survive. "Granny taught us to make do," recalled Jim.

Jim and his little brother, Robert, played cowboys and Indians in the long grass and "cow-pie dodgeball" in the yard. Jim created alternative worlds of ancient scrolls, lost adventures, secret societies, and treasure maps, and imagined following a dying man's directions written in blood.[12] But reality was sharp, and Nancy's dog, Teddy, taught him all he needed to know about being bitten. Jim's main role model was Nancy's wayward son Red, who had a thirst for women and moonshine. "He was a horrible influence," Jim recalled. They raided orchards, chased rats and squirrels. Neighbors called them the "little shits," and while Jim dreamed of catching monsters, Nancy, a disciplinarian, marched them down to the bookmobile so they could learn to read "big words." There was care but not much tenderness. There was government-issue peanut butter smeared with jelly or sprinkled with sugar, but absolutely no frills.

Occasionally, Elmer and Juanita rolled up to take their kids away. "My brother and I were kidnapped by our parents around the time JFK was killed," Jim recalled.[13] "I remember granny running down the road . . . my father shouting that they couldn't get state aid without kids in tow." After that, Jim didn't see Nancy again until he was an adult. His upbringing was chaotic, but some life lessons sank in. Nancy's takeaway was: "If you want something, you have to get off your ass to get it."[14] Bragging spoke of low moral character, hitting women was even worse, and life should be lived without weakness, especially alcohol. The most important lesson came from his father. "He was super-smart at word games," Jim recalled. "How far is far?" Elmer asked his son, and Jim inherited his father's love of verbal trickery.

Juanita got more unpredictable as she got older. When he was sixteen, Jim moved away, renting an apartment in Tampa, Florida. He grew his hair and started a rock band with Robert, the Lost Souls.[15] They played in bars and, on one occasion, MacDill Air Force Base, which got Jim thinking about the military. After such a disrupted childhood, he craved stability, uniformity, discipline, and an education. But his aspirations remained a pipe dream, until he played a gig at the Hullabaloo club in Tampa and met a skinny girl with ramrod-straight blond hair. Kathy Oaks was the most exotic thing Jim had ever encountered. She had a high school education and a no-nonsense attitude. Awkward and inexperienced, he asked for a date. When Jim was eighteen, he proposed to Kathy, who was nineteen. She agreed, so long as he got his teeth fixed (he had rarely visited a dentist, and they were rotten and crooked) and went back to school.

Both were teetotalers, atheists, tough, and pared-down. Jim's experiences of Uncle Red being so blind drunk he drove his Pontiac into a tree (more than once) were enough to last a lifetime.[16] His father Elmer's addiction had affected the whole family. By contrast, Kathy's father was a war hero who had been blown up at Iwo Jima, and survived to tell the tale. Jim moved into his in-laws' sun porch, Kathy bought a camper van and painted it with flowers, and they made a pact never to have children. Jim was so certain of it that shortly before his nineteenth birthday, he even had a vasectomy. Because he was still a minor, Kathy had to sign off on the surgery.[17] He enrolled in an adult high school program and worked in a car wash, dreaming of the day he could buy a real home.

After school, Jim joined the air force. As a kid, he had wanted to escape the rural Deep South, and go "off the chart, to places dangerous and unexplored," he wrote later.[18] He cast aside his torn-up Converse sneakers, cut his hair, and put on a uniform. He saved money and began to realize his ambitions. Deploying to Alaska as part of a bomb squad, he learned how to diffuse Cold War ordnance floating over from Soviet waters. One day, out on the beach, he faced off with a Kodiak bear.

Jim began believing in himself. Standing over Soviet-made devices, he wondered about the "bad guys" who had built them.[19] After attending stress-management courses, he decided to go deeper into the human mind. The military agreed to put him through college, and by 1986 he had earned a doctorate in clinical psychology from the University of South Florida, a transformative academic achievement. Nancy was no longer around, but Jim had Kathy, his "lioness." A confident "Doc Mitchell" emerged. He became "airman of the month," then "airman of the quarter." Later, he reflected on his intellect: "I typically think faster than most people do. It's fluid intelligence, it's inherited not learned."[20] Outside work, he and Kathy were unsociable. Uninterested in drinking in bars or eating out, they could not see the point of wasting money on such pursuits. They canoed, hiked, climbed, or stayed home, where he researched mind control, and she embroidered in her craft room. He was a talented cartoonist and artist; they reared parrots and welcomed feral cats into their home.

In 1987, Mitchell's father, Elmer, died and was buried in a pauper's grave.[21] The following year, Mitchell won a military psychologist posting at the US Air Force SERE school in Spokane, a frontier city built around huge, cascading waterfalls in the wilds of Washington. Before training others to survive, he had to experience it for himself, and soon after arriving, he was subjected to "water torture"—put into a fifty-five-gallon drum buried in the ground, which was then filled up to just below his nose. "It was dark and cold," he recalled.[22] "It was November. I was outside. My legs were crushed up in fetal position. The lid was on." He had found his life's mission, and his graduation certificate was signed by his new boss, Roger Aldrich, a jovial Vietnam veteran full of war stories.[23]

Aldrich's active service days had ended with him searching for Americans who never returned from the jungle. From Vietnam, Aldrich had gravitated into survival training, then a degree in psychology, and then a job at the air force SERE school in 1972 (the same year Ric Prado attended). Aldrich was kind and gregarious, a natural-born leader.[24] Mitchell would learn the ropes from Aldrich, and the officer he was replacing, an outdoorsman from small-town America, who like him had had a tough start in life. Military psychologist Bruce Jessen was moving up the ranks to the advanced SERE school where special operators were put through aggressive mock torture and resistance training. On the face of it, Mitchell and Jessen were polar opposites. Mitchell was outspoken where Jessen was circumspect. Mitchell never questioned difficult decisions while Jessen revisited them every day.[25]

Mitchell controlled his temper while Jessen lost his. Mitchell was slight, and Jessen was athletic. Mitchell was atheist while Jessen was a committed Mormon. Nonetheless, "Docs" Mitchell and Jessen hit it off straightaway.

Mitchell became so engaged that he worked through the first Thanksgiving, happy to lecture to his heart's content about pride and weakness. He punished sniggering new arrivals who swaggered into the survival school, thinking this was just two weeks of "bugs and berries." He met a navy commander who had been a prisoner-of-war. "He told me he felt horrible when he capitulated," Mitchell recalled. "I told him the lack of honor is not in capitulating, it is in not having the skills to bounce back." The survival courses were bonding experiences, and real war fighters began to respect Mitchell.

His new world was a huddle of low-slung buildings on Fairchild Air Force Base. The SERE school's main campus had a library with closed shelves for classified items including copies of MK-ULTRA files. Here were experimental studies conducted for the CIA and SERE by brainwashing expert Albert Biderman and accounts of Canadian hospital patients being drugged and shocked by Donald Cameron, a Scottish-born psychiatrist who had come to the attention of US intelligence after conducting a psychiatric evaluation of Rudolf Hess during the Nuremberg trials.[26] A copy of the CIA's banned KUBARK interrogation manual was here, along with its 1983 update, the *Human Resource Exploitation Training Manual*. There were harrowing prisoner-of-war accounts of surviving torture such as "waterboarding" by the Japanese during World War II or being placed in "standing sleep deprivation" by the North Koreans or the KGB. The SERE school library was a dark palace of the mind.

The action took place at Aldrich's hidden "POW compound," complete with a bunker fashioned from rebar and poured concrete. Aldrich called the imaginary enemy nation "Spokanistan," stuck fake "People's Democratic Republic" decals on a black pickup truck, and recorded "torture" sessions on CCTV.[27] Instructors pretending to be brutal foreign interrogators wore Red Army–style uniforms and bore fake names and ranks. Aldrich, Mitchell, and Jessen dressed up too. They monitored from the "control center," intervening if an instructor exhibited signs of "abusive drift," or students, who ranged from US military cadets to special operators heading out on classified missions, looked like they were slipping into learned helplessness. They were stripped, hooded, slapped, starved, and brutalized. Various forms of "water torture" were utilized, although they did not have authorization to strap a student to a board and pour water up his nostrils and down his throat, which was what happened in navy SERE school. It was all based around Biderman and his "Chart of Coercion." "If you're a nothing, an animal," explained Aldrich, "it's way easier to treat you crappy, than if I thought you were a person."[28] Aldrich called the experience "the pre-academic lab, which is a polite way of saying you drop them in at the deep end of the pool and have them go, 'Whoa.'"[29] But it was all make-believe and students were told in advance they could always stop the action by yelling the emergency code: "flight-surgeon!"[30] Besides, the nasty stuff only ever lasted two or three days.[31]

Mitchell's church was the post-academic lab, also called the Resistance-Training Laboratory, where he and Jessen taught students post "torture" the tools to survive. Mitchell and Jessen were rarely apart, said Aldrich, who called them "the odd couple." The RT Lab consisted of a booth with a one-way mirror. White noise played as each student "prisoner" was installed, "bag on the head" (hooded), chained and shackled, sleep-deprived, and very hungry. "Interrogators," whose faces were hidden behind masks and goggles, aggressively tag-teamed them. "Prisoners" were kept in a cell painted bright white, which was uncomfortably cold and blasted with noise and blinding light, creating a shadow barrier so the student could not see out.[32] This was "conditioning," said Mitchell. Other students watched the ghoulish peep show from beyond the barrier, waiting their turn. "They did threats of violence," said Aldrich. "Disgrace in their face." After the first interrogation they did "booth-with-tools" and then conducted more aggressive interrogation in the lab, invoking Zimbardo's famous Stanford prison experiment.

Mitchell, Jessen, and Aldrich trained the instructors and were always in charge, although they sometimes swapped roles. "We did not have an infinite number of people running these exercises," explained Aldrich.[33] "For example, I would be the senior bad guy, the commandant, Colonel Klink, for one shift, and then Bruce would come on and become the bad guy." Aldrich was always careful to avoid abusive drift, and above all learned helplessness. "I used to tell Bruce and Jim, you have to be 51 percent instructor and 49 percent interrogator," he recalled.[34] "You have to realize if you smell blood in the water, you're getting ready to take them over the cliff. If you trash them, someone has to go down there to where they are dangling and pull them back." Out of the three, Mitchell was the biggest "stickler for health and safety," while Jessen was the most frightening.[35] With his beard grown out, Jessen looked like an outlaw, according to Aldrich. "In his younger days he had a pretty quick temper."[36]

Every SERE course ended the same way, with what Aldrich described as "the neatest thing." It brought tears to his eyes just describing it. The senior "bad guy" got up and gave a hate speech in which he told the students they had no integrity, no fight left in them. Then he bellowed, "I want to show you what pride is all about!"—and ordered an about-face. "And there's the American flag as they play the national anthem," explained Aldrich. "Powerful."

At the end, all the students were in tears and permanently indebted to Mitchell and Jessen for teaching them how to survive. Some became friends for life. Before going home, many graduates got a SERE tattoo inked on their backsides in a Spokane tattoo parlor: a combat boot with wings.[37] Outside work, Mitchell, Jessen, and Aldrich also stuck together, running most days, ice climbing or hiking off-grid during vacations. A double tragedy at Fairchild in June 1994 brought them even closer together: a crazed soldier shot dead a psychologist and a psychiatrist in the base hospital, and just days later a B-52 bomber crashed during practice for an air show, killing everyone on board and injuring people on the ground. The doctors who had been shot were colleagues, the bomber crew too, and the three psychologists counseled friends, families, co-workers, and each other.

Mitchell lived for his job and hung out with the war fighters. "I never really viewed myself as a clinician, I always viewed myself as a bomb disposal guy who got some additional skills," he reflected.[38] Psychology was a weapon with which to protect oneself and fight the enemy, he lectured. By the early 1990s, he and Kathy were renting a house in a comfortable neighborhood and had money in the bank. He proudly kept a growing collection of academic and military citations in a box file. Books on manipulating human behavior, the anatomy of interrogation, and surviving extreme conditions lined his shelves. Jim and Kathy were strong and self-isolating. There were few photographs on their walls and never much to eat in the fridge. With their Spokane friends, they shared professional and extracurricular interests. Mitchell grew close to Don Hutchings, the stepbrother of his former commanding officer in the bomb squad.[39] The Mitchells went trekking in the wilds of Washington with Hutchings, a psychiatrist working with brain injury patients at a Spokane hospital, and his wife, Jane Schelly. But while Hutchings and Schelly traveled the globe, the Mitchells stayed inside the United States. For all his talk of wanting to find the blank spaces beyond the oceans, Jim Mitchell was a homebody who rejected the dangers that lay beyond the horizon. He had heard enough from those he counseled when they returned home, broken by life-changing foreign tours.

In 1997, Mitchell became chief of psychological applications at the Twenty-Fourth Special Tactics Squadron, a tier-one special missions unit, at Pope Air Force Base in North Carolina. Now, he befriended senior psychologists attached to SEAL Team Six, Delta Force, and "other ones we can't talk about because nobody really knows they exist."[40] With Joint Special Operations Command (JSOC) on his doorstep, Mitchell's career really took off, and his commander described him as "the most technically gifted clinical psychologist I've ever seen."[41] Two survivors of the 1993 Black Hawk Down incident in Mogadishu, Somalia, became his friends.[42]

A new audience required a new program, because of a paradox about risk and reward. "A marine recon is going to be dropped behind enemy lines, move no more than thirty yards a day, piss on themselves, sit tight, no noise," Mitchell later explained.[43] "A Stealth fighter pilot will fly off long distance, drop bombs, go home, kiss his kids goodnight. The person who is 'braver' is more likely to break."

———◆———

Mitchell enjoyed an unblemished air force career of twenty-one years. His last performance report read: "Gifted! Absolutely the best in the business! Most effective operations-oriented 'Doc' I've seen in 20 plus years!"[44] Two months after retiring, and with a new CIA contract under his belt, 9/11 happened. The entire SERE community was "aghast," recalled Roger Aldrich.[45] "Being attacked was a game-changer. We were offended, we were angry. . . . What can we do to take revenge?" Stuck on the training side, Aldrich hoped those who he, Mitchell, and Jessen had taught over the years would hammer Al Qaeda. But Mitchell did not want to stay on the sidelines. He was intent on joining the "tip of the spear."[46]

As he parked up at Langley on the afternoon of April 3, 2002, his second visit to CIA headquarters in just over twenty-four hours, Mitchell remembered the "blood fever" that had gripped him on 9/11 when he called the CIA as the Twin Towers burned. He still could not quite believe that men in caves had killed so many people at the heart of America. "It was the biggest [single-day] loss of American lives since the Second World War," he said over and over.[47] He also had a personal connection to the rising terrorism. His friend and hiking buddy Don Hutchings had gone trekking in Indian Kashmir with his wife, Jane, in 1995, only to be kidnapped by Pakistan-backed *mujahideen* fighters who were among the first wave of a new kind of religious insurgent.[48] Mitchell had been caring for Hutchings's dog and looking forward to explaining how he had fixed its incessant barking by fitting it with an electric-shock collar.[49] But Jane Schelly returned to the United States alone, and Hutchings and three other Western travelers were never seen again. Another hostage in the group was found beheaded.[50] Only one escaped. A seed of revulsion grew inside Mitchell. Seeking to understand Islam, he bought an English-language Koran and interpretations of Islamic texts. After 9/11, his opinions became more fine-tuned and his mantra became "Keep Muslims out."[51]

Mitchell, Jessen, and Hubbard entered the CIA Counterterrorist Center conference room. It was "crowded with analysts, operations officers, case officers, physicians, an agency operational psychologist assigned to CTC [Scott Shumate], and senior CTC personnel."[52] The "jetfighter" Marty Martin was there, along with Jennifer Matthews, "psycho" Alfreda Bikowsky, Gina Haspel, and a large cohort from Alec Station. Rodriguez's army of targeting analysts was led by Deuce Martinez. Mitchell winked at the welcoming faces as fast-paced Rodriguez took charge. This was all about making sure America did not get "whacked again."[53] He evoked agency outriders overcoming the odds with certainty, cunning, and brute force. "We *are* the dark side, that's what we do."[54] One of the 9/11 "mass murderers" had been captured alive and needed interrogating hard to spill the beans about the second wave.[55] Bikowsky and Matthews laid down the "op-sec" (operational security). This was a "highly compartmented" mission, and because Jessen was still a Department of Defense employee, he was asked to leave. "I had a sinking feeling that I was going to be on my own," Mitchell later wrote.[56]

Bikowsky and Matthews came out with some disturbing truths. Contrary to public claims from Donald Rumsfeld that Abu Zubaydah was healthy and cooperating, he was critically ill and might die.[57] If he regained consciousness, they probably had only a small window. Matthews walked everyone through the "Zubaydah Biography" that Alec Station was preparing for the attorney general and the National Security Council. Using "open source re-porting (a.k.a. media reports) and information from Al Qaeda suspects already in US detention, plus genuine intelligence disseminations, the docu-ment transformed Abu Zubayah from jihad facilitator and emir of the House of Martyrs to Number Three in Al Qaeda, a senior lieutenant to Osama bin Laden, and a planner of 9/11 and all other Al Qaeda attacks to date.[58] Most importantly, he was a font of information about the "ticking time bomb"—another CIA name for the second wave of attacks—so they had come up with a new way of getting him talking

Intelligence prepared by the Jordanians in 1999, material that had been shared with the CIA during the millennium plot investigation, appeared to back the CIA's assertion that Abu Zubaydah had written the Manchester manual.[59] Even though the "Zubaydah Biography" looked rushed and scrappy, and relied predominantly on newspaper reports, inaccurate assertions, and unnamed sources, it was all dispatched to the Justice Department. Internal CIA emails concerning its compilation—peppered with phrases like "How does this look?" and "background on AZ (somewhat dated)"—were not submitted.[60] But Rodriguez did not care about the small details. Whether Abu Zubaydah had sworn *bay'at* to Osama bin Laden was a "meaningless distinction."[61]

Mitchell and Jessen's December 2001 paper on Al Qaeda's "resistance-to-interrogation training" was waved about. All eyes turned to Mitchell, who was happy to be a central attraction. "I heard for the first of many times that 'the gloves are off,'" he recalled.[62] Jonathan Fredman and his CTC legal team explained how the Geneva Conventions article on prisoner-of-war rights had been set aside after considerable pressure from the CIA. In a few days' time, Fredman and John Rizzo would present an interrogation plan "devel-oped by CIA psychologists" to the National Security Council.[63] Rodriguez wanted a "golden shield" to protect against future prosecution.[64] Mitchell felt the "crackle of excitement."

Rodriguez turned his attention to the problems created by FBI agent Ali Soufan, who had interrogated Abu Zubaydah out in Thailand and was still with him. "We need everyone to understand there's a new sheriff in town," he said, eliciting cheers.[65] The incoming CIA team would take over. Shu-mate's named was called out, then Mitchell's. "I saw him, how he dealt with the Arab culture, and I thought, you know, this is a person who understands it and can deal with it," Rodriguez remembered of Mitchell.[66] The plan being submitted for legal approval "relied on the theory of learned helplessness," but Mitchell later claimed that the CIA misunderstood the term and misapplied it. "I'd call it self-efficacy, they'd call it acute learned helplessness," Mitchell said. "They liked that term, it was a sexy term. I just got tired of fighting that, it was like a wildfire."[67] Learned helplessness, he said, was "completely worthless when it comes to intelligence gathering," and while he "gave briefings about avoiding that," it "sometimes gets misconstrued as me advocating it."[68] However, John Rizzo challenged Mitchell's recollection: it was the "outside consultants" who sold learned helplessness to the CIA.[69]

Mitchell's initial job would be reporting back evidence of Abu Zubaydah's resistance training. "I also was asked to help the team brainstorm possible countermeasures if that became necessary," he recalled, referencing the SERE techniques he and Jessen had already proposed in their December 2001 paper. Rodriguez's legal team had verbal approval for a Biderman-based list of "conditioning" techniques, and hoped the attorney general would sign off on the rest.[70] "The thought of placing an Al Qaeda leader under some discomfort for a few days in order to save thousands of American lives didn't worry me," Mitchell said, still mischaracterizing Abu Zubaydah twenty years later.[71]

After the meeting finished, Mitchell had a one-on-one with Matthews, whose "eyes flashed" as she ran him through her link charts and ticking-time-bomb scenarios. "Jennifer was excited and talked fast."[72] The next attack could come any moment and may involve chemical, biological, or nuclear devices, as Abu Zubaydah had hinted in his diary. Mitchell chipped in that he knew how "bad guys think," and had multiple qualifications for his new job, from being a doctorate in psychology to a trained bomb-disposal operator.[73] Next, Mitchell presented himself to the Office of Medical Services for a prerequisite psychological evaluation. Chief psychologist Terry DeMay gave him a frostier reception. Although he was not fully "read-in," DeMay had been briefed enough to understand the interrogation plan was based around "learned helplessness," which was dangerous and probably illegal, in his opinion. DeMay had also studied Martin Seligman's famous theory and knew it was not necessarily reversible but could lead to permanent psychological damage. CIA lawyers were selling the complete opposite to the

Bush administration, and in his opinion, Mitchell was "crossing the line" in supporting them.[74] Mitchell brushed DeMay aside and ignored his concerns. He had approval all the way up the chain of command.[75]

Mitchell went over to his sanctuary, the Office of Technical Service, where he handwrote his new terms for Kirk Hubbard.[76] To provide "psychological consultation to CTC in debriefing and interrogation operations for Quick Response Tasking," he would charge $1,000 a day INCONUS (inside the continental United States) and $1,800 a day OCONUS (outside the continental United States). The rate was four times that of a standard interrogator, but significantly less than what he could earn from the Pentagon ($3,000 a day OCONUS). Besides, he was providing "unique psychological consultation."[77] With extra add-ons, including $17,000 for travel expenses, his contract for an expected two-week temporary duty yonder (TDY) totaled $101,600.[78] Released from Langley, he had just enough time for a quick trip to Tysons Corner for tactical gear and a rucksack, and a call to Kathy to say he wasn't coming home, although he could not tell her where he was going.

Alec Station dispatched another cable to Thailand, with inputs from Mitchell. Since Abu Zubaydah was "a senior Al Qaeda member . . . and has likely received some or a lot of counter-interrogation training," an effective interrogation could "take a considerable amount of time and resource [sic]." He might divulge information "in spurts," but there would be periods of slow progress "until another level of disclosure is obtained." He would assume that "we may resort to physical torture to get revelations."[79] But the CIA had devised a clever workaround to achieve maximum results without leaving any physical marks.

Out in Thailand, Ali Soufan was furious. Not only was he proud of getting Abu Zubaydah talking so quickly, but he seriously doubted Abu Zubaydah had anything to do with the Manchester manual. Soufan had been on the raid when it was recovered among a haul of documents belonging to Abu Anas al-Libi, a Libyan Al Qaeda suspect who had won asylum in the United Kingdom in 1994.[80] In 1995, MI6 (Britain's Secret Intelligence Service) had tried to recruit al-Libi to kill Mu'ammar Gaddhafi, but the plot failed, and British police arrested al-Libi on terrorism charges instead. Freed for lack of evidence, he remained living in Manchester until British anti-terrorism officers and the FBI came calling in May 2000. After the raid, the British authorities were forced to free al-Libi again, and he fled to

Afghanistan with his family, while Soufan brought a copy of the manual back to New York and briefed his boss, John O'Neill. "This teaches us how the terrorists are taught to think and prepare themselves for operations," Soufan told O'Neill. "It offers insight into their mind-set, and behavior patterns we need to watch for. So it should help us catch them and, when we catch them, understand how to interrogate them successfully."[81] This wasn't so very far from what Mitchell and Jessen had told the CIA, but Soufan's conclusions were more nuanced, and he had not gone on to suggest aggressive interrogation. He knew the manual was used by Al Qaeda and all *mujahideen* groups, but it had not been written by Al Qaeda, and contained no mention of Al Qaeda, suicide bombing, mass-casualty attacks, or a war against the West.[82]

Soufan reported to O'Neill that chapter seventeen of the manual contained lessons on how to withstand torture by a brutal regime. The basic advice was to stick to preplanned cover stories. Brothers should also request legal counsel, complain about their treatment and conditions, ask for medical attention, and report if they had been tortured. The manual characterized torture as, typically: hanging by the feet, beating with sticks, squeezing of genitals, nails being pulled out, cuts with glass and knives, burning, kicking and punching, attacks by vicious dogs, putting out of cigarettes on skin, and whipping with sticks and rubber belts. "Let no one think that the aforementioned techniques are fabrications of our imagination, or that we copied them from spy stories," wrote the unnamed author. These were all factual incidents recorded in Middle Eastern prisons.

However, Alec Station had drawn up link charts that showed Abu Zubaydah was the author. He had a similar manual in his possession when he was captured, and during the millennium plot investigation in Amman that Marty Martin had led for the CIA, Jordanian intelligence officials had produced a CD copy of another training manual entitled *Encyclopedia of Jihad*, which was similar in content. The Jordanians claimed to have found it in a plotter's safe house and accused Abu Zubaydah of creating it with assistance from Khalil Deek, a Palestinian American living in Peshawar.[83] Deek had been born on the West Bank, and his family dispossessed twice by the Arab-Israeli wars of 1948 and 1967. After studying computer engineering in Italy, he headed for the United States, where he settled in Dallas, married an Arab American, and became a computer whiz kid.

In truth, the CIA's analysis was all back to front. Abu Zubaydah and al-Libi had fallen out with several rival groups including Al Qaeda, which tried to seize control of Khaldan, and the Libyan Islamic Fighting Group, which accused the Khaldan co-emirs of training people for no reason because they never carried out operations. Abu Zubaydah and al-Libi had done their best to maintain distance from Al Qaeda, the Libyans, and the Algerian GIA.[84] The Arabs involved in Afghanistan's wars were not one amorphous mass, said Robert McFadden, of the Naval Criminal Investigative Service, who had worked with the CIA on the USS *Cole* investigation. "It was always kind of squishy as to who was who," said McFadden. "There were some analysts at CIA who had never been further than South Beach, New Jersey. "They were paraded as experts but were clueless."[85] Years later, even the CIA admitted Abu Zubaydah was not the author of the Manchester manual and concluded that the "CIA knew [little] despite considerable effort about Al Qaeda and its allies on 9/11."[86]

Soufan sent his analysis of Mitchell's and Jessen's Al Qaeda resistance report to Langley on April 4, 2002. "I have added my comments to the cable on countermeasures that I feel may be of relevance based on my access and discussions with AZ," he noted. He cautioned against a new team taking over, since he had established a rapport with Abu Zubaydah, who had already been "somewhat forthcoming."[87] Rodriguez ignored him. Alec Station wanted Abu Zubaydah to be the author of the Manchester manual because it significantly helped in making a solid case that the CIA needed to go the "dark side."

Later Rizzo, a veteran maneuverer around numerous knife-edge moments, claimed to have been worried when Alec Station members first piled into his office in "early to mid-April," telling him they wanted to take off the gloves. Their techniques ranged from a "Three Stooges slapstick routine" to "sadistic and terrifying."[88] When they revealed they wanted to bury Abu Zubaydah in a coffin, Rizzo claimed he was "gobsmacked."[89] Their proposal had "crisis" written all over it. "I mean, there was actually a technique they wanted to use that called for a mock burial," he said. Tricking Iran into thinking Hollywood was coming to film a sci-fi movie had been fun. This was something else and would get the agency into trouble somewhere down the road, Rizzo warned. Mitchell reflected that Rizzo "was a dick."[90] Always dressed to impress, Rizzo reminded Mitchell of the flamboyant American novelist Tom Wolfe. But shortly after Abu Zubaydah was captured, Rizzo called up John Bellinger nevertheless. "Once the director had made it clear he wanted to go down this route, it was my job to make it legal," Rizzo said.[91] A primary objective was obtaining a "golden shield" declination of prosecution.

Seeking immunity from prosecution was not unique to the CIA. In the United Kingdom, spies working for MI6 were in 1994 protected under Section 7 of the Intelligence Services Act, which offered immunity to agents involved in bugging, bribery, murder, kidnap, and torture, as long as their actions were authorized by the home secretary. Since the president had given the CIA the lead role in hunting down Al Qaeda's leaders and a mandate to collect actionable intelligence, the Bush administration should provide the same to CIA employees, Rizzo argued. The CIA wanted to go right up to the legal line without invoking the torture statute.[92] Could mock execution, for example, be made legal? Bellinger advised him that such controversial decisions could be made only by the attorney general, John Ashcroft, a staunch Bush administration loyalist. Previously a senator, Ashcroft had lost his seat during the previous election, and Bush had appointed him attorney general to keep him on the team. Ahead of a formal meeting between CIA lawyers and the National Security Council, Bellinger arranged for Department of Justice attorney John Yoo to brief Ashcroft.[93] Yoo's message was that it was doable as long as the CIA conducted proper due diligence.

CHAPTER 5

"THE HELL WITH CHRIS DE BURGH"

Scott Shumate went into his long-haul routine. He wore his suit casually, threw his hat down on the best seat inside the Gulfstream, and asked for a drink.[1] "Big guy. Ruddy-faced," was how Mitchell characterized him.[2] Shumate started up straightaway. "He told me he was against me coming along," recalled Mitchell.[3] "He made it clear that he would be making all the decisions and that any recommendations concerning the psychological aspects of the interrogation would be coming from him. I think he thought he could do what I did, and they didn't need me." Shumate called himself "the senior" on the mission, but Mitchell shrugged it off. He had spent a life "getting bit."[4] First it was his granny's dog, Teddy, then his own dog, Brownie. After that, it was feral cats, barn cats, house cats, rats, and squirrels, not to mention his cousins Glenda and Dinky, both his sisters, Bonnie and Lois, even his little brother, Robert. "I think granny would have bit me too, if she had teeth," he joked. He was, after all, a professional survivor and could handle Shumate just fine.

Although Shumate had resisted moving to the Counterterrorist Center, now that he was on the team, he regarded it as his mission. He had better qualifications than Mitchell, was a Middle East expert, had tons of operational experience, and plenty of arrogance. "The better one knows the substantive landscape . . . the better one is able to provide competent and useful consultation," he wrote.[5] But he also "had integrity" and believed that when facing an unprecedented scenario like the one they were about to fly into, CIA op-psychs should "plant their feet firmly in basic ethical principles."[6] Mitchell dismissed Shumate's swagger, asserting, "He was the only CTC psych, and that's why he was the chief psych, it's like being the night manager at 7-Eleven."[7] Shumate mocked Mitchell as a "schoolhouse psychologist," and sneered at his background in bomb disposal, joking that an expert in blowing things up was not appropriate on a sensitive compartmented mission.[8] Shumate did not doubt Mitchell's oft-mentioned patriotism but suspected money was also a primary motivation. The CIA was flush with cash, and Mitchell had bargained hard. In all regards, the two psychologists had nothing in common. A teetolar, online by five A.M. every day and always ready to spin up a lecture, Mitchell kept a library of searchable PDFs on his laptop and hard copies of his favorite texts, particularly Biderman's 1961 brainwashing anthology, *The Manipulation of Human Behavior*, to hand. When Shumate left the office, he had a thirst for "diet and Jack," and good conversation.

They fell silent, as the other passengers, including a relief team from Medical Services, got some sleep. "Adil," the Egyptian American case officer, would be both "primary interrogator" and "chief of base" at the black site. While there was "a lot of expertise on the ground," all personnel were to follow Adil, who was "in charge of and responsible for all aspects of the interrogation of AZ."[9] Adil did not have much sympathy for his fellow Arab but he was a decent-hearted, nonviolent man and wanted to get Abu Zubaydah talking before the CIA won approval for harsher methods.[10] "Bryan," the polygraph operator, was flying out separately.

Shumate spent the journey observing Mitchell, who readily expressed his loathing for Al Qaeda. "He's always on transmit," Shumate reflected of Mitchell. "He doesn't receive. How the hell do you assess someone else's intellect when you are always only on transmit?"[11] Shumate suspected Mitchell was just a willing dupe. With no real Al Qaeda leaders in custody, Alec Station had hyped Abu Zubaydah, and recruited Mitchell after he spun the Al Qaeda manual so hard it justified harsh tactics. What most upset Shumate was the association between violence and patriotism. "The US is a hell of country," he liked to say. "There's no better place on the face of the earth." But somehow, "taking the gloves off" was now a mantra for real patriots, when it sounded like human rights Luddism to him. Shumate would not be called out as un-American, but he would oppose the immoral, illegal, and ineffective.

Those staying at headquarters suspected Shumate would be unable to push back. Mitchell's plan had high-ranking supporters right up to the CIA's seventh-floor executive suite. Shumate's only significant backer, Terry DeMay, ran what was regarded as a necessary but politically inferior medical support service, the agency's "institutional conscience," that could for the most part be ignored.[12] Mitchell's contracts manager Kirk Hubbard dismissed Shumate's doubts as self-serving. "He simply wasn't a player," Hubbard said. "He was in way over his head."[13] Shumate wondered at the devotion Mitchell had won; reflecting that some people would continue to support him even if he "brutally killed their kids."[14] But Shumate did not appreciate that Mitchell's professional friendships were fostered out of a deep sense of duty, honor, and service shared among military psychologists who had worked in SERE, a tiny, isolated but interconnected community, backed by the thousands of warfighters they had taught to survive torture. Mitchell was also willing to stick his neck out for his country, which was one of the reasons Rodriguez hired him. If things got too messy, the CIA could blame "the contractors" and walk away. As the plane made its final approach over a vibrant patchwork of paddy, Shumate weighed his options. He was not about to trash his career over Mitchell. Better to be the eyes and ears, the voice of reason. As the wheels screeched onto the melting tarmac, he decided it was more important to learn something new and try to control the damage if it all went wrong.[15]

It was early morning in Chiang Mai. When they got to the accommodation General Tritot had arranged near the black site, Ali Soufan and Steve Gaudin were nowhere to be seen. They were staying nearer to the hospital where Abu Zubaydah lay unconscious and still on a ventilator. A couple of mornings back, he had coughed up his breathing tube and had to be reintubated.[16] His fever had returned, and a decision had been taken to cut away, or debride, more necrotic tissue from his wounded left thigh. The interrogation was on hold, but the FBI agents were pleased to hear that some familiar faces had arrived in town. Soufan and Adil had worked together on the USS *Cole* investigation. Gaudin and Adil had been together on the East African embassy bombings investigation. Shumate and Soufan had met at Guantánamo.[17] Soufan described Shumate as a "brilliant" behavioral analyst.[18] Shumate liked Soufan, although he suspected he oversold his knowledge of Islam, and he worried about the Sunni–Shia clash with Abu Zubaydah.[19] He preferred Gaudin, "a hell of a guy," who shared his eye for the good times.[20]

Soufan and Gaudin delivered a remote assessment. The detainee was street-smart, sneaky, and knowledgeable, "a successful independent facilitator, well known for smuggling people and raising money." He had been a key figure in the Afghan Arab community of Peshawar.[21] He was not a formal member of Al Qaeda, but he had readily helped the outfit with forged passports and travel documents. In Afghanistan, he had always been welcome at Al Qaeda guesthouses. The House of Martyrs guesthouse in Peshawar was the gateway to Khaldan, where a whole host of terrorists had trained, from Khalid Sheikh Mohammad's nephew Ramzi Yousef to two 9/11 hijackers.[22] Abu Zubaydah was "one of the most important cogs in the shadowy network that we were struggling to disrupt."[23] But as far as him having advance knowledge about 9/11, Soufan was unconvinced. Given that Osama bin Laden had not even informed Al Qaeda's *shura* about the "Planes Operation" until June 2001, and then gave them no say in the operation thereafter, it was inconceivable that Abu Zubaydah had known about 9/11—until it happened.[24] Soufan was also not convinced he knew anything about the second wave.

After more than twenty-four hours of traveling and now eleven hours ahead of Washington, the new arrivals were exhausted. When he got up to his room, Mitchell was unimpressed. After years in the military, he expected certain standards, but here was a "sad bed and a shabby dresser that wobbled and lurched," he recalled.[25] The bathroom had "leaky mismatched fixtures from another century." The bath had a V-shaped tub, which meant he could not shower standing up. It felt like "camping out in a mausoleum." Adil went to join Soufan and Gaudin at the hospital, taking along a spy camera from the Office of Technical Service. Mitchell had no interest in watching a guy who was just "fucking dying" and not exhibiting any signs of resistance.[26] He was itching to turn the "holding compound" into a psychologically disorienting space to help Abu Zubaydah on his way to the desired state of learned helplessness.[27]

The following morning, April 7, Abu Zubaydah woke up. According to Soufan, he opened his eyes, saw female nurses wearing uniforms and surgical masks, and thought he was in heaven. Later, Abu Zubaydah laughed this off as "ridiculous talk." He was chained to a hospital bed, on a plastic sheet smeared with blood, vomit, and disinfectant.[28] "I came to and found Ali Soufan, Steve Gaudin and Adil in my presence. I was naked and attached to medical monitoring equipment as well as IV equipment. My left leg and abdomen were bandaged, with significant quantities of muscle removed from my left leg. They were interrogating me as I became conscious."[29]

The bloodied sheet beneath him had a label spelling out in English, "Made in Thailand." Soufan, who Abu Zubaydah described as "cold," insisted he be respectful. They were saving his life. He should be thankful, and say "please."[30] But Abu Zubaydah was in no mood for politeness. Weaned off the ventilator, experiencing the daily debridement of his leg wound fully conscious was agonizing. However, he found himself powerless to resist Soufan's questions, which, he assumed, "was due to the lingering affects of anesthesia or to some additional drug given to induce my cooperation." When Thai nurses came to clean his wounds, he saw to his horror that he now had only one testicle. Later, he accused American doctors of subjecting him to unnecessary surgical procedures, including an unauthorized vasectomy. But his medical condition remained perilous. His liver was malfunctioning, his hemoglobin level was falling, his pancreas and an intra-abdominal mass near the site of a bullet fragment were both inflamed, and his left eye was clouded with infection.[31] Hani 1 was gone forever, and Hani 2's fate was worse than he could have possibly imagined.[32]

Glaring at his new "primary interrogator," Abu Zubaydah correctly identified him as Egyptian.[33] Was he being shipped off to Cairo? Soufan made it clear. "He is American, and he is my boss." Abu Zubaydah addressed the new interrogator directly. "Who are you?" The undercover CIA officer replied: "Call me Adil." Abu Zubaydah got that. "His name meant fair and he said they would treat me fairly if I was honest. But in the end he wasn't really fair."[34] Later, testing out Adil's promise, Abu Zubaydah asked what had happened to his left eye. He remembered going for an eye test in Faisalabad just two days before his capture, and his vision had been fine. Now, he could not see through it and it was weeping "blood and pus."[35] Adil had no idea. He knew nothing about the botched retinal scan, and the CIA would later determine that the circumstances around the loss of the eye were classified, so Abu Zubaydah never received an answer.[36]

He recalled the three interrogators bombarding him with questions. When he was still intubated, he could not speak, so Soufan wrote Arabic letters on a pad, telling him to nod or shake his head and point. While the Thai doctors requested Abu Zubaydah's shackles be loosened, because "the blood was stuck in my limbs and my hands' color became green," the interrogators accused Abu Zubaydah of lying.[37] The most volatile, he said, was Soufan, who became so angry at one point that he ripped out the IV drip.[38]

Adil listed the accusations laid out in Alec Station's "Zubaydah Biography." He was Number Three in Al Qaeda and senior lieutenant to bin Laden. Soufan later said he knew these claims to be false but they were repeated in reports sent back to FBI headquarters.[39] When Abu Zubaydah denied being in Al Qaeda, Soufan brought up the millennium plot in Jordan, something that he, Marty Martin, and Albert El-Gamil had all worked on. How could Abu Zubaydah talk his way out of that?

On November 30, 1999, sixteen Palestinians had been rounded up in Jordan, accused of conspiring to blow up tourist sites popular with Americans and Israelis during the forthcoming millennium celebrations.[40] Supposed targets included the Radisson SAS Hotel and the US embassy in Amman, a crossing point between Jordan and Israel, and a holy site on the Jordan River.[41] Local intelligence officials claimed they were tipped off when the mastermind, "Abu Zubaydah," called one of his subordinates from Peshawar and said that "the time for training is over."[42] Abu Zubaydah had arranged explosives training for the terrorist cell at Khaldan, according to Jordan's chief prosecutor. "We knew we could wait no longer," he said, and Abu Zubaydah was on the phone again when they raided the home of an Amman-based conspirator. A few days later, the police "found" fifty-two hundred pounds of nitric acid beneath the floor of another suspect's apartment. They also "recovered" several forged passports, and a digital copy of the *Encyclopedia of Jihad*. The Jordanians linked it back to Abu Zubaydah through his Palestinian friend Khalil Deek.[43] The CIA's Amman station chief, Marty Martin, fed everything back to the "boss" at Langley.

CIA director George Tenet warned the National Security Council that Jordan was the tip of a multiple-target operation to kill Americans the world over.[44] Abu Zubaydah was its linchpin, and some of the attacks might involve chemical weapons, said Tenet. On December 4, 1999, President Bill Clinton's counterterrorism coordinator, Richard Clarke, wrote: "If George's story about a planned series of UBL [Osama bin Laden] attacks at the Millennium is true, we will need to make some decisions NOW."[45] Abu Zubaydah was named in American newspapers as a senior Laden operative.

Tenet's warnings gained traction when the FBI arrested an Algerian exiting the car ferry at Port Angeles, Washington, on December 14, 1999, after explosives were found hidden in the trunk of his rental car.[46] After months of intense interrogation, Ahmed Ressam admitted he had been planning to blow up Los Angeles International Airport (LAX).[47] He had trained at Khaldan, had stayed with Abu Zubaydah at the House of Martyrs, and was charged on multiple counts of conspiring to commit terrorism.[48] According to the CIA, the two plots, LAX and Jordan, were deeply connected, and Abu Zubaydah was "the top guy."[49] Three days after Ressam's capture, Abu Zubaydah's friend Khalil Deek was arrested in Peshawar, extradited to Jordan, and accused of being a co-conspirator in the Jordan plot.[50] Hider Hanani, Abu Zubaydah's friend in London, who was also Algerian, was named as a co-conspirator in Ressam's LAX plot and was later arrested.[51]

Abu Zubaydah went into hiding. "About a week ago, my name was mentioned by a Washington radio station as the person in charge of communication and foreign affairs for bin Laden," he wrote in his diary.[52] "I don't know who gave them this wrong information; there is no relation between us and bin Laden except brotherhood in God." When Deek went on trial in Amman, charged along with sixteen others of coordinating the millennium plot, the *Chicago Tribune* reported that investigators in Amman were "absolutely" certain that Deek had had direct contact with bin Laden.[53] Al Qaeda was behind the LAX and Jordan plot. The main coordinator was Abu Zubaydah, all the reports said.[54]

Deek, who spoke to a journalist from his GID cell, hinted at a less streamlined story, claiming that all the accused had been tortured, and describing the charges as "hocus-pocus."[55] Nevertheless, the State Security Court sentenced six of the accused to death, including Abu Zubaydah, in absentia. "There is a political background behind these sentences," said Jawad Younis, one of the defense lawyers. "It's to serve the Americans and to prove that Jordan is pursuing what they call terrorists."[56] Deek was later released for lack of evidence, but he was silenced for good in 2005 when he was shot dead by mystery gunmen in Pakistan.[57] There was only more bad news for Abu Zubaydah, still hiding out in Pakistan. In January 2001, the *New York Times* reported a wiretapped conversation in which Abu Zubaydah allegedly said he was authorized to act in bin Laden's name "anywhere in jihad territories," although the original intelligence was not produced.[58]

When these allegations were raised again in Thailand, Abu Zubaydah protested. This was guilt by association. Thousands of *mujahideen* brothers had passed through his guesthouse. He couldn't be held responsible for everything every one of them did subsequently with their lives. He had only met

Ressam briefly and they never discussed terrorist operations. The Jordan plot was more "ridiculous talk" and propaganda, dreamed up by the GID, to keep the CIA happy, he claimed.[59] But what Abu Zubaydah failed to appreciate was that post-9/11 America's national security apparatus was operating under the "one percent doctrine," new rules set down by the vice president. "If there's just a one percent chance of the unimaginable coming due, act as if it is a certainty," Cheney had declared.[60] Abu Zubaydah could see that the CIA was intent on transforming him into a murderous monster, "worse even than Osama bin Laden," and the FBI was playing along.[61] The more he denied it, the angrier they got.

Abu Zubaydah's situation got even more unpleasant after Jennifer Matthews read all six volumes of his diary. Late-adolescent wrangling about family, his place in the world, and his sexual desires dominated the first volume. Only Paul Wolfowitz, Rumsfeld's deputy, took an interest. When told the diary contained "a young man's thoughts about life—and especially about what he wanted to do with women," Wolfowitz reportedly asked: "Well, what have you learned from that?" A female CIA debriefer replied: "That men are pigs!"[62] But the last volume, which started shortly after 9/11, contained what seemed like deeply incriminating statements. On the run, having buried the remains of Afghan and Arab children blown to bits by American missiles, and sure that the United States was intent on killing as many Muslims as possible, Abu Zubaydah knew Ibn Sheikh al-Libi and many other acquaintances he knew had been captured or killed, and likely he was next. He had nothing left to lose, and he railed against America, talking of wanting to wage war, possibly nuclear. "We might prepare, start, but not continue," he wrote.[63] "We might not start to begin with." Expressing such ideas was enough to condemn him, and Matthews' AZ Task Force reported that his real plotting was written on pages of his diary that he had ripped up moments before he was captured.

Mitchell later claimed Abu Zubaydah had tried to flush away compromising sections when cornered inside Shahbaz Cottage, including pages that contained information about building a nuclear bomb.[64] Twenty years later, Abu Zubaydah confirmed that he had ripped out pages and thrown them in the kitchen garbage. Other pages of his diary were missing, because they "became ruined and fell off due to the rain, snow, or gunpowder" during his time training and fighting jihad in Afghanistan.[65] He admitted to deliberately ripping out other pages after committing fully to jihad, because they contained stories of personal weakness that he wanted to hide from God.[66] Although he had not written his diary for an audience, he had signed his own death warrant by keeping it with him.

———•———

The first volume was scribbled in an Indian exercise book. It was June 1990, and Abu Zubaydah, age nineteen, was at the end of months of traveling, not just around India but all over Asia, Europe, and the United States, a huge trip, during which he had enjoyed countless girlfriends. Alone in student digs in Mysore, Karanataka, he wrote to his future self, Hani 2, noting that if anyone else ever read his diary they would think he was insane. "Whoever talks to himself or writes to himself—as I am doing now—is nothing but crazy." But, having been "stabbed in the back over and over," he had concluded that real "friendship is a fantasy." He could trust only himself. He knew it was just a literary device that he had created so he could speak freely to his diary about everything. "You are mere imagination," he wrote years later, looking back over thirty years of diary entries, "you basically don't exist."[67] On several pages he also doodled pictures—something that his father had always frowned upon even though he was also an artist. As well as his own rendition of Jerusalem's Al Aqsa mosque, Abu Zubaydah drew a hand holding an ink pen drawing a feminine eye crying tears of blood, cartoon figures, palm trees, desert views, and grotesque Daliesque creatures: lips walking on hands, eyes in chins.[68]

Abu Zubaydah had expected to find the exotic India portrayed in newspaper advertisements and on TV. Real India horrified him: thousands of sects and millions of Muslims but no true Islam, he complained in his diary. Everyone cheated and lied. India's true "gods" were Bollywood movie stars, alcohol, and cricket.[69] "Dominating" poverty sat side by side with the "filthy rich." Compared with Saudi Arabia's veneer of order, India appeared to be out of control. The college in Pune where he had been offered a place to study computer engineering was also a disappointment. It was cramped and filthy, and instead of computer engineering, college administrators tried to enroll him in a commerce course. He was vexed. His father had predicted he would come back begging for forgiveness, but pride prevented him from giving up. Instead, he went exploring.

Traveling by train, sleeping in Muslim student hostels, and hanging out in restaurants serving Arabic-style food, he absorbed the subcontinent like any budget-constrained gap-year student, surviving on money given for his studies. He was charming and curious, and chatted easily, starting off with Arabs and Indian Muslims before graduating to Western backpackers. For the first time in his life he was able to flirt without fear of being whipped, and with his striking looks, he attracted women by the dozen, making them laugh by waggling his head Indian-style as he ordered "chicken tandoori." Fastidious, funny, and with a splash of One Man Show aftershave on his neck, he stood out from the multitudes of wasted, unwashed travelers. At first, he just flirted, because Islam forbade sex before marriage. But then he hit upon a fix. "I would say to the girl that all I need is for you to say 'yes' when one of our friends . . . asks you, 'do you accept him as a husband?'"[70] After two friends witnessed this exchange, he and the woman could legitimately get intimate. "It was a game (God forgive me). In fact, the game actually begins once everyone leaves." He knew "marriage for sex only" was wrong but could not stop. "I gorged myself without any restrictions, limits or orders," he wrote later.

By the time he reached Mysore, an ancient city of sandalwood and silk in southern Karnataka, he had decided to knuckle down and he enrolled in a computer-language course at Sarada Vilas College, near Mysore Palace. He signed the register in July 1989, ratifying his entry with a black-and-white passport photo. He rented digs in a crowded Muslim quarter and hired a servant, a young Christian widow with three children. "She was familiar with some of our customs and religion, and she also knew how to cook," he recalled. Philomena had never encountered anyone like Abu Zubaydah before, and she stole glances.

Unwilling to call home for money, he began trading aloeswood, a dark and resinous timber that grew around Mysore, and was the source of *oud*, a rich fragrance hugely popular across the Persian Gulf region, with a tiny flask worth hundreds of dollars. Indians preferred sandalwood, for which Mysore was famous, so there was plenty of aloeswood going cheap, and he was soon coining it in. But inevitably, his *oud* business began interfering with his studies, and his tutor called him in.

It turned out to be an inspired conversation. The tutor told Abu Zubaydah he was wasting his time at Sarada Vilas, because the school was not recognized internationally. If he wanted more than a worthless degree, he should travel to the United States. Digital technology was booming there, he was bright, and if he impressed the right people, they might fund his studies—and give him a job. The tutor had once taught in Missouri and gave him contacts. But Abu Zubaydah was unsure about making another major transition to a place so far away, so decided to embark on a series of nearer explorations first. Flush with *oud* cash, he bought a stolen passport. He did not look much like its Kuwaiti owner, but it was filled with valid visas, including one for the United States. Trying to match the photo, he grew a goatee. "I bid my friends and lovers farewell, picked up my bags and set out roaming the world as a tourist not a terrorist."[71]

First, he went home to renew his Saudi residency permit and get copies of his "Egyptian papers for Palestinian refugees," a legacy of his father's decision to leave Gaza for Cairo in the 1960s.[72] It was a brief reunion, happy because he had a new baby sister, Inas, his tenth and final sibling, but unhappy because his younger brother Hesham was ill with as yet undiagnosed cancer. It was the last time Hesham ever saw "Hani." After bidding them all farewell, Abu Zubaydah flew to Bangkok, where he booked into an expensive hotel, intending to study Muay Thai boxing. There was another reason for wanting to stay off the streets. "I was determined to completely stay away from women there because that country was known for its tourism for sex and because I hate sex for money," he recalled.[73] But he was a "young adolescent who is driven by his testicles instead of his brain and heart," and the first person to knock on his hotel door was a pimp carrying a briefcase. "Without any introduction he offered me his sex services as a dealer," he recalled. "With disgust and rudeness I said to him, 'no.'" The pimp insisted, and whipped out albums filled with photographs of nearly naked women. "Which merchandise do you prefer?" he asked. When Abu Zubaydah asked whether the women were compelled to have sex, he was handed an album of men. He recoiled. "Do . . . do you also provide services of sex for women?" he asked, baffling the man, who then produced pictures of children. "I got him out of my room and moved to one of the foreign student unions," Abu Zubaydah recalled many years later. Thailand was morally repugnant (and totally exhilarating). Everything and everyone had a price.

He headed for Malaysia, the Philippines, exploring, flirting, and finding new girlfriends (including a nun) all the way.[74] Then Turkey, and on into

Europe, visiting potential colleges and tourist sites. He sought out religious scholars of all denominations, wanting to understand the many different incarnations of God, and curious to know more about the different rules and regulations, particularly regarding sex and marriage. France, Italy, Spain, Greece, Germany, and the United Kingdom, he saw them all, and not once was his passport questioned, even though he often made the mistake of saying "Hani" or "Zayn" when asked his name at immigration counters. Sometimes he told officials he was Palestinian, though his passport was Kuwaiti. But it was pre-9/11, and he always managed to talk his way out of trouble.

When he finally decided to tackle America, he flew to St. Louis, in Missouri. But his tutor's connections were out of date. Couch-surfing, he stayed with young Arabs, most of whom were working illegally and chasing unmarried American women for a green card. Abu Zubaydah would not settle for the immigrant margins but America was not ready for him. "I wasn't lucky with women/girls there perhaps because they prefer a one-night stand or a few, when I prefer marriage . . . even though it is a fly-by-night marriage," he reflected.[75] Most American women he met found his habits confusing. "I stop when I am at my wildest moment," he later explained with candor. "And I can see her also at her wildest moment. . . . I would repeat it for a second, third and fourth time in the same night or day, because I am not selfish and I want to make sure she gets what she deserves . . . and more." When he told one woman that the act of intercourse outside marriage was forbidden for Muslims, she laughed, saying he was deceiving himself and his God. He felt ashamed because "her words were true." Eventually, the wife of one of his Arab friends introduced him to an American divorcée who rented her guest room to female students. He talked his way in without signing a rental contract and ended up in bed with her too. But she was older and had three teenage children, and he was not ready for that.

Running low on money, and with no proper job or college offer on the horizon, he returned to India in early 1990, disenchanted. He went back to Sarada Vilas College. Back in student digs in a low-rent neighborhood, he was instantly lonely again. He wanted "someone to say good morning to," but his only friend was the cigarette. He wanted "an equal who will share my insanity with me; but where, how and when?" Would he be luckier in the future? "How about you, Hani 2? Are you still waiting?" How about Hani 3, 4, or 5?

In the end, he turned to his servant, Philomena. She was "dark, short, without feminine curves," more than ten years older, a widowed mother of three children, and looking for love. He wanted companionship, "touching, hugs and hot kisses," but did not want his life to become "a ridiculous Indian movie." At night, she stayed over: "Her kisses are hovering over my hot submissive body." But he refused to have full intercourse, driving her crazy and shocking himself with his harshness. He paraphrased Victor Hugo, "A man is the woman's toy and a woman is the devil's toy," but later described this period as Hani-1, or "sub-zero Hani."[76] Determined to turn his back on "fornication" and devote himself to his studies, he wrote in his diary: "I do not have sex for religious reasons, although, thank God, I am confident of my manhood."[77] No more fly-by-night marriages. It was time to grow up, give up sex and smoking, and get serious.

However, when final-year grades were posted on a college noticeboard, his name was not on the list of those who had passed. When he informed his parents, the letter back from Riyadh was "overwhelming." His father was cutting him off. To stay on, he would have to retake his courses, but he did not have the money. He was filled with self-doubt. Contemplating suicide, he latched onto a "crazy" solution. "A crazy thought is going through my mind but it's very tough to make a decision about it."[78] Over the border in Pakistan lay Peshawar—the gateway to the Afghan *mujahideen* camps. Every young man growing up in Saudi Arabia during the 1980s had heard apocryphal stories of older brothers leaving home to help Afghan Muslims fight Soviet occupation during the CIA's secret war. If they came back, they were welcomed as heroes. If they were killed, they became martyrs. Osama bin Laden, the seventeenth son of the kingdom's richest man, who had given up his life of luxury for a cave, was the most famous example.

However, the real hero for Palestinians was Abdullah Azzam, the leader of the Palestinian *fedayeen*, for whom he was "Sheikh al-Jihad." Born on the West Bank, Azzam in recent years had lived in exile in Peshawar, and was credited with having persuaded bin Laden to abandon his worldly possessions.[79] Azzam had been assassinated in November 1989, but his adherence to the Palestinian struggle still drew thousands of supporters and still vibrated around Peshawar. For many Palestinians, Azzam was more appealing than the much-hated Yasser Arafat, leader of the Palestinian Liberation Organization. As the idea of joining jihad coalesced, Abu Zubaydah wrote in his diary of how "the daily killing and maltreatment of [his] people" preyed on his mind.[80] An intifada had exploded in 1987, and his father's hometown of Khan Yunis was at the volatile epicenter. Abu Zubaydah felt ashamed about his philandering, self-obsession, and daydreaming. "The hell with Chris de Burgh," he wrote.[81] Palestinians were dying. It was his duty to help them. "I desire to be a martyr."

He ripped up pages about his sexual conquests, gave away his music tapes, and joined a Palestinian student friend for the journey to Afghanistan. They left on January 12, 1991, heading to Bangalore by bus, then to Delhi, two days north, by train, and across the Indian-Pakistan border. They would travel on by train to Peshawar, then somehow find a way to go "inside," as he said, whenever referring to Afghanistan. When he crossed into Pakistan on January 17, 1991, and heard that President George H. W. Bush had launched Operation Desert Storm, sending almost a million coalition troops to fight Saddam Hussein, he became convinced he was doing the right thing. There were "signs of a third world war around the corner . . . nothing is better than jihad for Almighty Allah's cause," he wrote soon after. But even now, his eyes still wandered. "We are on the train to Okara . . . with a Pakistani family and two beautiful girls," he noted. "Do you know that sometimes I feel that I am a devil? Now I'm on the way to train in jihad for Allah's cause, yet I am still looking at this one and that one and, and, and . . ."[82]

In Peshawar, he was directed to the House of Martyrs, one of several guesthouses run by Abdullah Azzam's Makhtab al-Khidamat (Afghan Services Bureau). Reality hit him squarely between the eyes. War-crippled veterans carried out clerical jobs. *Mujahideen* injured and evacuated from the front lines lay in a "patients" room. "I am actually scared," he wrote, before settling down in a room full of ripe-smelling men on his first night. The prospect of battle terrified him. What if he was injured? Who would take him to the bathroom? Who would marry a one-legged man if the "party is over and there is no more jihad in Afghanistan?"[83]

April 10, 2002, Chiang Mai, Thailand

Abu Zubaydah distrusted Ali Soufan and disliked Steve Gaudin, a rough-and-tumble Bostonian and former soldier, whose testimony had helped convict several US embassy bombers.[84] Polygraph operator "Bryan" had also shown up, but Abu Zubaydah dismissed him as a "fool" after he asked, when he offered a decent meal in return for information, "What does *halal* mean?" Only Egyptian-born Adil half-won Abu Zubaydah's respect. "He told me they knew I probably had nothing to give but they were just making sure," he recalled.[85]

Soufan was the most vocal, cold, and insistent.[86] "Is bin Laden planning any attacks?" he demanded. Abu Zubaydah winced. He was still hooked up to drips and machines, chained to his bed, falling in and out of consciousness, and in severe pain. Soufan repeated his question. Exhausted, Abu Zubaydah nodded. Soufan wrote it down. Yes, bin Laden had people working on plots. When the Thai doctors needed to conduct an MRI scan, Abu Zubaydah became terrorized as he was forced into its confined space. But they kept up the questioning.

Gaudin opened up his FBI photobook. "I want you to grab my arm when you see Saif al-Adel," he instructed, referring to Al Qaeda's military commander.[87] Abu Zubaydah had planned to join al-Adel in Iran, traveling overland west of Kandahar via Herat to the Iranian border.[88] But instead of identifying al-Adel, Abu Zubaydah grabbed Gaudin's arm when they reached a photograph of Khalid Sheikh Mohammad, who was also on the most wanted list, for conspiring with Ramzi Yousef to blow up US-bound flights in 1995."[89] Gaudin lost his cool. "I can't believe we just saved your life, cleaned up your shit. . . . Indulge me, who the fuck is this?" Abu Zubaydah could not take the screaming any longer. "Mokhtar," he murmured. "The guy who did the Planes Operation."[90]

Gaudin and Soufan were stunned. The FBI knew little about Mohammad other than he was Ramzi Yousef's uncle. They had never considered he could be the mastermind of 9/11. But Abu Zubaydah and Khalid Sheikh Mohammad knew each other from Peshawar, where the Afghan Arab brothers lived and worked in close proximity, often debating world events and tactics. Abu Zubaydah had primarily argued for "defensive" jihad against Israel that was attacking "my people, Palestinians," and other countries persecuting Muslims, like Serbia and Russia. Mohammad rallied hard for "offensive" jihad against America.[91] He wanted to blow up the United Nations building in New York, tall buildings on the West Coast, and gas stations and apartment buildings across the States, and to cut the cables on the Brooklyn Bridge. Sometimes, the brothers watched Hollywood blockbusters to relax, which gave Mohammad ideas. The Brooklyn Bridge idea had come to him after watching the 1998 movie *Godzilla*, in which the "king of monsters" becomes entangled in the bridge's cables, said Abu Zubaydah, who was quite possibly teasing Soufan.[92] While Mohammad may have taken inspiration from movies and a coffee-table book of America's tallest buildings, plotting to knock them off one by one, for Abu Zubaydah movies were simply an "escape" from reality. "I live the events of that movie as one of its characters, until that movie is over," he had written in his diary when he still lived in Mysore.[93]

However, according to Soufan, when Mohammad first began toying with flying planes into the World Trade Center, Abu Zubaydah was part of the initial discussion. "You will only break windows, why not put bombs inside the planes?" he allegedly suggested.[94] Soufan claimed Mohammad asked for his help with the plan, but Abu Zubaydah refused, telling him to present his idea to Osama bin Laden, who also had ambitions to attack the United States, and plenty of money.[95] Soufan claimed that Abu Zubaydah engineered Mohammad and bin Laden's first meeting. Abu Zubaydah later denied this, pointing out that he did not meet bin Laden himself until 2000.[96]

Soufan knew he had written himself into 9/11 history by eliciting the "Mokhtar" revelation. The name "Mokhtar" had already been noted on several Al Qaeda videos, but its owner was always behind the camera. The FBI now had confirmation Mokhtar was Khalid Sheikh Mohammad and that he was the architect of 9/11.[97] But when Soufan excitedly reported this back to the rest of the team, Mitchell tried to squash it. Scott Shumate had brought Mitchell over to the hotel where Soufan and Gaudin were staying. It was their first meeting, and a nasty face-off ensued in one of the guest rooms. Mitchell questioned Soufan's Mokhtar story, saying there was no camera footage of this exchange. "I never saw that," Mitchell said, "and neither did Jose."[98] Even official cables back to headquarters described it as a "throwaway" line and focused instead on Mitchell's message that the detainee was already exhibiting signs of resistance.[99] "Part or all of his statements below may be an attempt to mislead and/or misinform," the CIA team reported.[100]

It was the beginning of the slippery slope for Abu Zubaydah, with Mitchell equally focused on building up evidence of his resistance training, and neutering Ali Soufan. "Believe me, if [Abu Zubaydah] had given what the CIA needed, then the FBI would have continued with him," Mitchell said. "The CIA doesn't give a rat's ass where they get information. They will take it from good guys or bad guys."[101] But of course, it was in Mitchell's interests to belittle Soufan's achievements, so he could get approval for his own aggressive plan, which he now laid out for Soufan and Gaudin.

Abu Zubaydah, who Mitchell had not yet met, was withholding the "mother lode," a favorite George Tenet concept, and would not give it up without a fight.[102] Soufan sized up the contractor: no foreign-tour experience, no Arabic, and no knowledge of Al Qaeda or understanding of Muslims. Mitchell continued. He knew more about Sunni Arabs than Soufan because he had "sat down with an Islam expert at Agency," a Muslim from whom Abu Zubaydah would "accept a fatwa," (religious edict).[103] What was this magic method, Soufan interjected? Mitchell launched into an explanation of Albert Biderman's theory.[104] Soufan and Gaudin would withdraw. Abu Zubaydah would only see Adil, who would become a God who "controls his suffering."[105] Once everything was taken from him—sheets, clothes, medical care, food, even the choice of how, when, or where to defecate—Abu Zubaydah would become compliant and tell his God the truth to improve his own life. "This is science," Mitchell explained, casting aside the fact that Abu Zubaydah was a deeply committed Muslim. They had to role-play him, humiliate him, and make it clear they would not be jerked around. "He'll fold quickly. You'll see." Gaudin, who had attended SERE school when he was in the Army, recognized exactly where Mitchell was going.

If Mitchell had read the CIA's old KUBARK interrogation manual he would have learned that role-play was poor interrogation. "The interrogator who merely pretends, in his surface performance, to feel a given emotion or hold a given attitude towards the source is likely to be unconvincing; the source quickly senses the deception," it had advised. "Even children are very quick to feel this kind of pretense."[106] But Mitchell had never read this manual, he said.[107] He also took Alec Station's "Zubaydah Biography" at face value, saying, "It was not my job to question intelligence," and he was not concerned with Abu Zubaydah's life story or background, except where it connected to jihad. KUBARK would have informed him that "some of the most glaring blunders in interrogation have resulted from ignoring the source's background." A person's past was "always reflected, however dimly, in his present ethics and behavior. Old dogs can learn new tricks but not new ways of learning them." Mitchell did not care.

Soufan could not conceal his contempt. Later, Mitchell described him as "an arrogant Middle Eastern shit." In private, he went further. "Scratch the surface and he's a male chauvinist pig like the rest of them."[108] All Arabs were "smarmy." Arab men were "histrionic." After Mitchell left the hotel, Soufan took Scott Shumate aside. "Is this a joke?"[109] No.

The morning after this ugly standoff, Soufan and Gaudin returned to the hospital while Mitchell began re-creating a SERE school interrogation bunker at the black site. He sought advice from his best buddy Bruce Jessen, who had helped Roger Aldrich design the original mock-up prisoner-of-war camp at Fairchild Air Force Base. Jessen remembered Mitchell calling and asking for "good documentation about captivity facilities and how they're constructed."[110] Jessen helped without hesitation, even though he was not yet read-in to the CIA program. Later, he likened it to "building a barbecue pit" as if they were going to smoke the detainee. "There are certain elements that need to be there." Mitchell, who would soon be surrounded by young Abu Zubaydah "experts" who were flying over from Alec Station, belittled Ali Soufan's efforts down at the hospital. "We'd come back together and look at the tapes," he recalled.[111] A lot of the time it was "just a guy laying there with a tube sticking out of him."

For now Mitchell focused on the interrogation bunker that consisted of two small cells, side by side, inside an airtight outer shell similar to a shipping container. Anyone locked inside would have no clue whether they were in Amman, Cairo, or an Israeli detention center. At Fairchild, they called it "iso-stress."[112] The "holding cell" was painted bright white; it had three solid cement walls and a fourth wall of vertical steel bars. There were shackle points in the floor and in the ceiling. Access was through a three-foot-wide "vestibule" with two sets of double doors.[113] Outside the bunker in General Tritot's preexisting Thai building, a room on the first floor was turned into a CCTV "control center" for the psychologist "controllers," Mitchell and Shumate, while the upper floor was partitioned into workstations for the Alec Station "experts," guards, and medical staff. It was not Spokanistan or *Hogan's Heroes*, and there were no fake military decals on rusty pickups, no library of torture texts down the road, but to Scott Shumate, Mitchell still looked like he was playacting.[114] Mitchell later reflected: "The original Zubaydah cell looked like a Matt Dillon *Gunsmoke* cell."[115]

He never stopped inspecting every detail, from the brand of fluorescent light bulbs to the reflective quality of the paint. Important materials were shipped in from the United States. Other things were purchased from the market or Thai hardware stores. Specifications included "the installation of a white curtain to partition off the holding cell from the interrogation room."[116] Mitchell wanted to create a "shadow barrier," like the one he had once experienced at the Hullabaloo nightclub in Tampa, and modeled on the Resistance-Training Lab at Fairchild. Halogen lights on yellow metal stands positioned outside the cell bars would further blind the detainee.[117] Mitchell also wanted "short nap carpeting on the walls of the interrogation room to dampen sound." The cell bars should be sanded "to reduce AZ's ability to stimulate his sensorium."[118] Using Seligman's model, white noise or music and cold air would blast through the bars. Abu Zubaydah would be watched on CCTV 24/7, "to support/monitor psychological effectiveness of interrogations; to record interrogations; and to ensure physical security at all times."[119] Should he die, recorded footage would, it was hoped, provide evidence they had not intended to kill him.[120] In case of nonlethal injury, the medical team hid a fully kitted hospital crash cart outside the curtain. The primary intention of the entire setup was stated again and again in cables: Abu Zubaydah should develop "an increased sense of learned helplessness."[121]

As they prepared for Abu Zubaydah's arrival, schoolhouse shrink Mitchell coached senior CIA case officer Adil in "interrogation-style dialogue." To enhance Abu Zubaydah's sense of helplessness, he would never see Soufan, Gaudin, or Bryan again. Any medics or guards who needed to enter the cell would remain silent and be dressed in black jumpsuits, boots, balaclavas, gloves, and goggles.[122] Making a Hollywood joke, he called them the "men in black."[123] Scott Shumate had already worked out that ridiculing Mitchell was dangerous. The others realized it too, after Jose Rodriguez flew in for a site visit and took a particular interest in watching Mitchell working.[124] His main concern was keeping Mitchell happy, and he joined Mitchell in lamenting his Spartan accommodation, and was willing to do anything to help sideline Ali Soufan and the FBI.[125] "It was our prisoner, our site, our everything," Rodriguez said.[126]

CHAPTER 6

"OH MY GOD, I CAN BE HORRIBLE"

Former infantry captain Steve Gaudin was happy to roll with the punches. Working on the CIA's first high-value detainee was a career-changing opportunity. But proud, ambitious Ali Soufan, who would later deck his office in New York with medals, citations, and photographs of himself with high-ranking US officials and Middle Eastern dignitaries, refused to back down. He and Mitchell were similarly hotheaded, each determined to be top dog. Soufan called his FBI colleagues in New York to tell them about Abu Zubaydah's reference to "Mokhtar," and he cabled FBI headquarters in Washington to complain that Mitchell had already acquired "tremendous influence" and was forcing through a crazy, dangerous plan.

"It should be note [*sic*] that we have obtained critical information regarding AZ thus far and have now got him speaking about threat information," Soufan wrote. "Suddenly the psychiatric team here wants AZ to only interact with their [CIA officer] as being the best way to get the threat information." Several compromise solutions had been "declined without further discussion." Soufan was furious. "I have spent an un-calculable amount of hours at [Abu Zubaydah's] bedside assisting with medical help, holding his hand and comforting him through various medical procedures, even assisting him in going [to] the bathroom," he reported. "We have built tremendous report [*sic*] with AZ and now that we are on the eve of 'regular' interviews to get threat information, we have been 'written out' of future interviews."[1]

Abu Zubaydah later described Soufan's rapport as "cold," "calm," and "threatening." Unfortunately for Soufan, all his complaints were routed via

Langley because this was a CIA operation, and the CIA had no intention of conducting "regular" interviews. Years later, it was confirmed that many of Soufan's cabled complaints had gone missing.[2] When Counterterrorist Center lawyers also learned Soufan was conducting unauthorized communications with FBI officials, a warning was dispatched to Thailand. "Given the substantial legal equities here and the concomitant substantial risks to our personnel if there are any glitches, could you please be sure to route all traffic concerning interrogation methods through CTC/LGL for coordination," it read.[3] The CIA needed to be certain "that you, and the other members of the team, are fully protected." In other words, shut up.

Soufan was wasting his time. This was a CIA-led interrogation at a CIA-run black site. The FBI had no authority, while Mitchell had been hand-picked by Rodriguez.[4] On April 13, after Abu Zubaydah left intensive care and was transferred to a private hospital room, Soufan and Gaudin entered. Following Mitchell's script, Soufan told Abu Zubaydah through gritted teeth that they would not see him again. Adil then went in alone, to deliver Mitchell's message that Abu Zubaydah had "a most important secret that [we] needed to know." This was straight out of SERE school, where every student was given a secret to protect before being "tortured" until he or she gave it up.[5] Speaking English "by design," so Mitchell and other non-Arabic speakers could understand and also to place Abu Zubaydah at further disadvantage, Adil (a native Arabic speaker) explained to the detainee (also a native Arabic speaker) he had one chance to give up everything he knew about the second wave, or "bad things" would happen.[6] He should give a "thumbs-up" when he was ready.[7]

Abu Zubaydah had no idea what was going on. His English was "not that great," mainly because he had hated studying a language that reminded him of "the Balfour Promise to the Jews."[8] He called out hoarsely as Adil stormed out: "What do you want to know?"

The team reported the eleven-minute role-play act as a breakthrough moment. Abu Zubaydah had "feigned failure to understand English"—a resistance technique—attempted to divert the conversation by complaining of "medical discomfort"—another resistance technique—but "nodded in agreement" when told that he was concealing critical information.[9] "Morale here, never a problem, is quite high," the cable continued, before ending with a joke about Abu Zubaydah's gastric problems. A significant portion of his intestine had been ripped up when he was shot and had been removed. "We hope never to have to report on bowel sounds (or lack thereof) again."[10] At the black site there would be no more warm hospital meals, as his nutritional needs would be met with a "bare bones" diet of water and the nutrition drink Ensure. It would provide a daily intake of fourteen hundred calories and probably give him diarrhea.[11] Abu Zubaydah would then face "a far more precarious and uncomfortable situation," if the CIA secured approval from the National Security Council.[12]

On April 15, Adil returned alone to Abu Zubaydah's bedside for another Mitchell-scripted scene, "delivering the message" and "hit[ting] subject with the key question."[13] What was the secret he did not want them to know? "What do you want to know?" asked Abu Zubaydah, not comprehending the strange behavior. Adil ignored his question, took a photograph of him, and walked out.[14] "If he won't talk, don't hang out there talking about other shit," Mitchell lectured.[15] Outside the room, a CIA medic readied two vials of sedative.

Back in Washington, DC, on April 16, George Tenet, his acting general counsel John Rizzo, and the Counterterrorist Center's legal team met the National Security Council in the White House Situation Room. Rizzo recalled that enhanced interrogation meetings were typically chaired by Condoleezza Rice and with himself, Tenet, Donald Rumsfeld, Colin Powell, Dick Cheney, John Ashcroft, and the president's chief of staff, Andy Card, all expected to attend. Also often there were top-ranking administration lawyers: David Addington, Jim Haynes, Alberto Gonzales, and John Bellinger. According to Rizzo, Rice attended "about at a dozen Principals' meetings" to discuss enhanced interrogation, while Rumsfeld ducked as many meetings as he could.[16] At one meeting, where Rice introduced detainee issues as a last-minute issue, Rumsfeld got up to leave, declaring, "I don't do detainees."[17] But for Rizzo, the most interesting figure was Colin Powell. "At the end of each [enhanced interrogation] update session, Powell would bolt out of the Situation Room as fast as he could," Rizzo recalled, although Powell later denied any knowledge of the program.[18] Michael Morell backed Rizzo's version. "People think of this as a CIA program but let me tell you it was approved by President Bush's national security team, was approved by the Office of Legal Counsel and by the Attorney General on multiple occasions," he reflected.[19]

During the April 16 meeting, Tenet asked for permission to unfurl a plan "developed by CIA psychologists [that] relied on the theory of learned helplessness."[20] The condition created psychological dependence and instilled "a sense that because resistance is futile, cooperation is inevitable." To bring about this condition, the CIA wanted to "disorient Abu Zubaydah by rendering him unconscious through sedation, shaving his face and scalp, and moving him to the interrogation site."[21] He would then be placed in a "featureless white, brightly-lit room and prevented from sleeping for one or two days." Medical care and meals would be provided at unpredictable intervals, and he would be interrogated at random times. More aggressive techniques based on SERE training were also on the table. Someone produced a copy of the operating instructions used in the advanced SERE course, which included techniques such as "walling," "cramped confinement," the "body cavity check," and the "water pit."[22] How much of this could be made legal for use in the real world? John Yoo, who represented the Department of Justice, said that for any action to constitute torture, "an interrogator must have specific intent to cause severe physical or mental pain or suffering." Rizzo shot back: "That is clearly not our intent." Professor Martin Seligman had told the CIA that learned helplessness "does not result in a permanent change in a subject's personality." Full recovery could be expected once the conditions inducing learned helplessness were removed, the CIA lawyers reported. There was nothing to worry about.

After the meeting, Yoo briefed John Ashcroft and Alberto Gonzales. Bellinger also briefed Gonzales, and Condoleezza Rice. According to Rizzo, no one objected, and Yoo promised to write "a short anodyne memo" confirming legal approval.[23] Rizzo wrote: "I do not intend, and Bellinger/Yoo do not expect, that I will brief them on every new variation or technique that comes up. Based on the relatively bright legal lines we have drawn, we will brief them as necessary where and if it appears that we are approaching one of those lines."[24] The CIA had full clearance to proceed, although Mitchell later claimed not to know anything about the plan to drug Abu Zubaydah. "It was not me driving that train," he said.[25] Declassified cable traffic from the black site reported that "all concurred that AZ would be transported in a state of pharmaceutical unconsciousness."[26]

The underpinnings of an experiment based on a deliberate misinterpretation of Martin Seligman's famous theory had been spelled out in official

CIA correspondence. Roger Aldrich said of his SERE students: "They were taken to the edge of the cliff, and we made them look over. And then we pulled them back."[27] Abu Zubaydah was to be conditioned until he reached a "baseline, dependent state," and then if he still refused to comply, he would be pushed off the cliff without any SERE tools to haul himself back up. Whenever he listened to Mitchell speaking, Shumate was reminded of the apocryphal story about the captured US airman telling his North Vietnamese torturers that American warships carried miniature farms to raise food for their sailors.[28] A tortured detainee was likely to say anything to stop his mistreatment, reflected Shumate.

———◆———

Abu Zubaydah's transition to the black site was completed without incident, and at eleven P.M. on April 16, he woke up.[29] It was incredibly bright, like a "football stadium," he recollected. He was also freezing cold, and being pounded by earsplitting noise. "There was nothing except for three walls that reflected the lights as if they were lights," he recalled.[30] The IV drip was gone. His hair and beard were gone. His hospital smock was gone but he was still shackled to a gurney. This was "conditioning."[31] Straining to see behind him, he saw "metal bars" and nothing but blackness beyond them. "So I am in a prison and not in a hospital," he told himself. In his diary, he had written of his fear of "deadly isolation."[32] Now it was real, and he closed his eyes to escape it.[33] "Water was thrown in my face." It was icily cold and caused a shock reaction. When he recovered, Abu Zubaydah "saw a black object carrying a [bucket] and standing outside the bars." When he blinked to make sure he was not dreaming, another torrent of water hit him. "Hey, what is wrong with you?" he yelled at the black object, a human entirely clad in black. "Even his face, his nose and his mouth were all covered." The man, who wore a balaclava and tinted diving goggles, gestured, "as if he was telling me not to sleep." Abu Zubaydah tried to reply, but white noise drowned out his words. Every time his eyelids drooped, he was doused again. Mitchell was deploying the least invasive "watering" technique to "firmly roust" the detainee.[34] It seemed to have the desired effect. Shivering uncontrollably, Abu Zubaydah tried to warm himself by waggling his fingers and toes, the only bits of his body not tied down. Up in the control center, eagle-eyed Mitchell watched for signs of resistance.[35] When Abu Zubaydah made what appeared to be a thumbs-up, it was written down as a "a false ploy by subject in a continuing effort to resist."[36] Soufan, who had no idea about the "bright legal lines," concluded Mitchell was crazy.[37]

The noise stopped. Abu Zubaydah tensed. Was he about to meet his new jailers? Three padlocks unfastened, and the door swung open. Even before he got a chance to look at who or what was coming, he was hooded, "bag on the head," SERE-style. The hood came off, and he saw Adil. Relief. Followed by panic, as a team of huge, masked men in black clattered in. Tiny versions of his frightened face reflected in their tinted goggles. "Haven't I told you that things are going to change?" said Adil. Until he began cooperating, things would steadily get worse, he explained. Adil also explained that Abu Zubaydah controlled his own fate and environment. Like a SERE student screaming "flight-surgeon," he could stop the mistreatment anytime by revealing details of the second wave. Since Abu Zubaydah always had this "escape" option, the CIA was further protecting itself from allegations of abuse.[38]

"What is the secret you don't want us to know?" Abu Zubaydah's fear exploded. "I don't know what I said," he wrote later; he knew only that he was dopey, hungry, and confused.[39] A cable went back to headquarters, observing that Abu Zubaydah "became very angry and shouted that he had nothing to add and we could take him to [Egypt] if we wanted."[40] Mitchell, watching in the control center, added a celebratory note: "The circumstances subject now finds himself in are beginning to wear a little thin."[41] Soufan, who had no experience of SERE but could spot a charlatan from a mile off, accused Mitchell of experimentation. Year later, Mitchell was still adamant it was all science-based. "There's a difference between trial and error and experimentation," he recalled.[42]

There was no respite. "What is the secret you don't want us to know?" Abu Zubaydah was shivering so much that no one could understand his reply. "Even your friends that were captured along with you, their condition and treatment will depend on you," warned Adil. Until the detainee stopped being "duplicitous," his situation and that of his "friends" would only get worse. This was another classic SERE trick. "We had to show them that by not talking they would be hurting themselves and hurting their friends," Mitchell later explained.[43] And it worked, as Abu Zubaydah became deeply worried. What had they done to the brothers captured with him, including Syrian

Noor al-Deen, who was still only a teenager?[44] Abu Zubaydah had always put their welfare before his own, acting as a surrogate father, even helping them find wives, as jihad was a lonely business.[45] The brothers were Abu Zubaydah's adopted family.

His thoughts also flicked to his birth family, Palestinian refugees living on temporary Saudi residency cards who could be thrown out for any infraction. Then, where would they go? The consequences of his capture on those he loved were deep and wide. Adil said the CIA was sending a photograph of him in custody to his mother.[46] Abu Zubaydah was horrified. What about Hesham in America? Surely the FBI had caught up with him by now? Adil ignored his questions while Mitchell noted that family was an "exploitable vulnerability," and could be used like a "mind virus."[47] "What is the secret you don't want us to know?" Abu Zubaydah did not know. Adil stormed out. "The loud noise was back in the cell even before the guards left and closed the door behind them," Abu Zubaydah recalled.[48]

He had not given up any information for twenty-four hours, but according to Mitchell, the plan was working. The team sent a cable to Langley: "His resistance may be weakening."[49] Sleep deprivation had to be extended. They were heading into a "prolonged interrogation process."[50] After "conditioning," Mitchell wanted the latitude to explore "corrective" techniques (slaps, grabs, holds, pressing, and a lot of yelling) and then "coercion," the most frightening aspect of SERE torture training, which at Fairchild involved drums, vats, water, and walls. A cable was sent to Langley seeking permission to extend sleep deprivation, despite protestations from the medical team about it impairing physical recovery. The reply came back: they were still well within Rizzo's "bright legal lines" and had permission to extend Abu Zubaydah's sleep deprivation for another twenty-four hours.[51] Inside the bunker, "the subject" was like a fish on a marble slab. The only respite was closing his eyes. But that simply brought more ice-cold water.

A few days earlier, President Bush had talked up the nation's big Al Qaeda catch at a fund-raising event in Connecticut. "The other day we hauled in a guy named Abu Zubaydah," he told diners, who whooped and applauded.[52] "He's one of the top operatives plotting and planning death and destruction on the United States." At that very moment, said the president, the CIA was extracting details from him about the second wave. "He's not plotting and planning anymore," Bush said to a cheering crowd. "He's where he belongs."

———◆———

However, Abu Zubaydah's troubles had started because he had never belonged anywhere. Thrown off ancestral lands in Palestine, his family was rejected as refugees by Saudi Arabia, and he was further alienated by India. When he first reached Peshawar, in January 1991, he wasn't sure he belonged there either. The city was in the midst of seismic changes. American military contractors and CIA operatives who had once thronged the bar at the Pearl-Continental Hotel had gone home. The Soviet war was over, and Afghan warlords were now fighting one another, sending the region into a hideous civil conflict. Abu Zubaydah stayed close by the House of Martyrs, and concentrated on becoming less conspicuous as an outsider. While his beard grew long and he learned a little Urdu, Pashtun, and Dari, he also learned about the new face of jihad filling the vacuum left by Abdullah Azzam, who had been killed by a roadside bomb in November 1989, turning the famous "Sheikh al-Jihad" into a martyr and leaving the Afghan Arabs who thronged Peshawar orphaned.[53] Azzam's former protégé, Osama bin Laden, wanted to redirect rootless Arabs who had come to defend Muslims persecuted by the Soviets into fighting a war against the West. Some blamed bin Laden for Azzam's killing. Others said it was Ayman al-Zawahiri, the leader of Egyptian Islamic Jihad, who later became deputy leader of Al Qaeda, and who wanted a bigger share of bin Laden's famous wealth.

By the time Abu Zubaydah arrived, bin Laden was back home in Saudi Arabia fund-raising, but his influence in Peshawar was growing.[54] The French, who had fought a grueling domestic-terrorism war against former North African colonies, especially Algeria, were particularly worried. Operatives from the Armed Islamic Group of Algeria (a.k.a. Groupe Islamique Armé, or GIA) were also camped out in Peshawar, and France's foreign intelligence wing, the Direction Générale de la Sécurité Extérieure (DGSE), warned that if the GIA's capabilities met with bin Laden's ambitions, it would be bad news for everyone. The GIA signature was mass-casualty suicide attacks on civilian targets.[55]

The House of Martyrs was located in the heart of Peshawar's Arab quarter. Azzam's widow and surviving children (two sons had died with their father) were neighbors. Palestinian jihad theologians and firebrand Egyptian doctors turned sheikhs lived down the road. Around the corner was a house full of Libyan academics. Tajiks, Uzbeks, and Chechens provided neighborhood muscle, and the Algerians were known as "pit bulls." Every Friday, this disunited army of holy warriors descended on the Saba-e-Leil mosque off Arbat Road, close to where Azzam had been assassinated. Abu Zubaydah was mesmerized by all the debating over "defensive jihad," espoused by Azzam's followers, and "offensive jihad," promoted by bin Laden and al-Zawahiri's group, Al Qaeda. "The idea of settling here is enticing and I can't seem to control it," he wrote.[56] Just shy of his twentieth birthday, he knew he was on the cusp of making an enormous, life-changing decision.

The guesthouse emir told everyone to choose a *kunya* and hand over their identity papers. Abu Zubayadah chose "Abu Hurayrah," after a companion of the Prophet, whose name literally meant "father of the kitten." Departure to Khaldan neared. A few days later, he climbed into the back of a truck. Everything from their old lives was supposed to stay at the guesthouse, but he could not bear to be parted from his diary and hid it in his bag. The colonial-era Durand Line separating Pakistan and Afghanistan was an undefined perilous stretch of mountains, ravines, and desert, and they knew they had crossed over only when donkey carts replaced the painted lorries of Pakistan. Decanted into a rusting car, they swerved through Khost Province, passing Pashtun families on unpaved mountain roads. They stopped at Bari, a new training camp consisting of caverns cut into a hillside. The road to Khaldan was "muddy and bumpy," impassable for now. They would stay at Bari until it improved. Abu Zubaydah wore five layers of clothing. "The coldness is freezing everything," he wrote, thinking as usual about sex.[57] He now looked like a *mujahid* but still felt like a city kid. Comforts, like hot water, Nivea, and heating crept into his head. "Don't I sound like a spoiled child?" he asked his diary.

While they waited, a Palestinian instructor showed them how to disassemble a Kalashnikov (AK-47). Within an hour, Abu Zubaydah, who was smart, and a fast learner, could do it blind. They were taken to the range. "My first gunshot ever," he wrote excitedly. At night he was put on guard duty, standing next to a looted Soviet military truck with a Kalashnikov on his shoulder, teeth chattering. A few days later, the road to Khaldan became navigable, and they drove on, standing in the back of the Soviet truck like real holy warriors. When they arrived in Khaldan, Abu Zubaydah was ecstatic.

"I feel happiness . . . and oh God!" Over the next two weeks, he trained hard, "slept like a kid" in a tent at the bottom of a boulder-strewn hillside, quit smoking, and washed in an icy river. Abdullah Azzam's ethos percolated through the camp. Defending Muslims in peril was a religious duty. They were training to fight a just war. From Khaldan, the most dedicated graduated to its sister camp, Derunta, to train in explosives, mines, and poisons as well as primitive biological and chemical weapons. Once they had graduated as *mujahideen*, some went home but most joined armed groups, like Al Qaeda.

Abu Zubaydah decided to commit to jihad. He wrote home, asking for his father's consent and telling him he did not have to send any more money, as "God would provide." He posted the letter on a trip to Peshawar. "Are they going to answer me? Only God knows." Arriving back at Khaldan for an advanced weapons course, he was in for a shock. One of the brothers previously sharing his tent had died after a huge boulder fell on it. Now, he lay buried in a *mujahideen* graveyard on the mountain. Abu Zubaydah wrote that he was happy his friend, who had called him "the rowdy guy," had been martyred. But the death of his friend hit home. Jihad was no party. He ditched his frivolous nickname and asked to be called Abu Zubaydah. He wanted to join the "land of the blessed jihad" with full honesty.

At first, he faltered, the physical training pushing him to the limit. "During the morning exercise I am always at the end of the line," he confessed. Years of smoking and hanging out with his "fun and carelessness clique" had taken their toll. Those who could not keep up were told to "pack and go back to Peshawar," and so he exercised at night, desperate not to be seen as a "holiday jihadi." By the end of March, he was fit, but having nightmares about his family, in which they were angry about his decision to quit normal life. It was "a dark road in the night," and the more he weighed the loss of family, the more he became fixated on the prospect of becoming a martyr.[58]

On April 25, 1991, he heard back from his father, who was "accepting condolences" for the "death" of his son. His father also shared some terrible family news. Hesham, fourteen, was undergoing chemotherapy and was "a skeleton with no hair or eyelashes." Abu Zubaydah wrote a twenty-eight-page reply. "I explained that jihad is an individual duty . . . and the *mujahid* son has the right to leave without his father's approval." But he did not send it. Instead, he focused on training and prayed the cancer story was a ruse to get him home. A few days later, he was called out of mortar-firing class to be told someone had left a message for him. It was Maher, his older brother, who had come to Peshawar from Faisalabad, where he was still studying medicine. When Abu Zubaydah called back, he learned that Hesham really had been diagnosed with cancer and had been asking for "Hani" before falling into a coma. Things had got so bad that the oncologist had stopped all medication, suggesting they "let the poor kid live a little before he dies."[59] Frightened that if he met Maher, his resolve would crumble, Abu Zubaydah lied, saying he could not leave the camp. The next day, Maher arrived at Khaldan. Stunned, Abu Zubaydah took him down to the river to hear him out. "Hesham is dying," said Maher. "Your mother is ill." Abu Zubaydah announced that he would not return home. "Isn't it time for you to get back to God, Maher?" he suggested. Maher told him to rethink his decision and be more considerate of family. In fury, Abu Zubaydah ripped up the unsent twenty-eight-page family letter in front of his brother. A trainer passed by, joking that Abu Zubaydah was a loser. "Your brother is a doctor, and what are you?" he said, without realizing the impact of such an accusation. Abu Zubaydah exploded in anger. End of the discussion! Maher departed back to Peshawar the following morning.[60]

Abu Zubaydah redoubled his jihad efforts. "Kalashnikov, Degtyaryov, Bruno, heavy Girinov, English rifle, M17, Doshka, M16 machine gun, RPG launcher, 82 mm gun and on and on."[61] In July 1991, he was called up for active duty in Gardez, Afghanistan, where opposing *mujahideen* forces were dug in. Muslims killing Muslims was not what he had trained for, yet he had no choice but to fight. Planes bombed his camp, and the men sheltered in dugouts, "face down on the ground." He received a letter from his mother wrapped around a box of *ma'amoul* cookies. Dotting her letter with "tears in red ink," Malika was distraught. Her son had made her "swallow bitter sadness." But still, she waited in hope. "He is my son and he will definitely return." Fearing the pull of her words, he threw the letter on the fire, and walked off into the cold for his guard shift. "I worry about myself from a change of heart, so I ask God for martyrdom." Later, he savored the smell of wood smoke melded with dust and rain. He belonged here, in the blessed land of jihad. "I breathe and I breathe and I breathe."

They inched around embattled Gardez, with a line of enemy tanks ahead, planes dropping cluster bombs, shells and rounds whistling over their heads.

"Death walks with all persons here," he wrote. After one devastating aerial attack, he emerged from a dugout to find everyone on the outside bombed to bits. Someone pulled a bulletproof vest from a corpse and handed it to him. "It had blood that was still crimson red in color," he wrote. "It had an aromatic scent. Really, I smelled the scent myself." His old life, the "fun and carelessness clique," was never coming back, and for now, all thought of women was gone, too. "Where would she come from, outer space? Mars?" he joked later.[62] "An Afghani wearing an Afghani burka?" He ran and hid and fought, expecting to embrace death at any moment. In November 1991, he filled the last page of his diary. On the inside back cover were photographs of Sultan and Inas, his youngest siblings, who he barely knew. "I may not see them again," he wrote. He pulled himself together, gave money to a brother going back to Peshawar, asking him to buy another notebook, and when he received it, started Hani 2. He wrote the date, December 22, 1991, noting that the light of the oil lamp was fading, and addressed Hani 3, aged thirty, wondering where he would be in a decade, hoping and praying life would be better than now. A few pages later, the diary went blank.

April 2002, CIA headquarters, Langley, Virginia

Abu Zubaydah had been kept awake for forty-eight hours, with Adil robotically asking the same question, over and over, in English. Official cables reported no sign of fatigue, but Mitchell, watching from the control center, noted plenty of resistance. The detainee used a variety of "sophisticated techniques" that included "feigning memory loss" and other neurological and physical problems, while "completely discounting the Herculean medical efforts and resources devoted to his physical care."[63] Although he also reported Abu Zubaydah for feigning an inability to understand English, Mitchell later claimed they were videotaping because his English was so hard to understand.[64] Acts of extreme tiredness were "deceptive malingering," Mitchell concluded, citing an entry in Abu Zubaydah's diary in which he described once faking seizures after being arrested in Peshawar.[65] In reality, the detainee was "a caged cat," ready to pounce the moment his shackles were loosened, an archetypal resistance-trained Al Qaeda kingpin. Mitchell warned the guards to adopt defense procedures as laid out in SERE training manuals. If they gave him an inch, the "noble-warrior facade" would disappear and a "crude thug" would emerge.[66] He was a danger to the world.

Cables listed the "poker tells" that Mitchell identified as evidence of Abu Zubaydah holding back. He denied being in Al Qaeda but did "use the pronoun 'we' when talking about what Al Qaeda wants to accomplish." He "often shakes his head affirmatively when asked if there are going to be future attacks in America."[67] Abu Zubaydah was a targeted liar, recalled Mitchell.[68] Adil needed to ask himself, "What it is he is leading me away from?" Mitchell called it "following the vagueness." During the evening "hot wash," or review sessions, Mitchell lectured the team about moral disengagement. "Ordinary people can do inhuman things," he explained. "It starts with what appears to be justification for what you are doing and a euphemism for what you are doing, and then it develops into dehumanizing a person."[69] In SERE school, they called it "abusive drift."

Listening to Mitchell, Shumate became convinced that the CIA was intent on constructing a false narrative to get rough, irrespective of how Abu Zubaydah behaved. Shumate had read the "Mitchell paper," had seen the signs of resistance listed there and reported here in Thailand, and knew all about the psychological weaponization plan. He was also deeply concerned about how Mitchell regarded Muslims. "Muslim cultural DNA goes back to the Bedouins," the contractor generalized.[70] "They were raiders. If you wanted a woman you would steal her. The individual can be sacrificed for the tribe. Al Qaeda is the new tribe." When someone told him the Arabic words for "virgin" and "raisin" were similar, he joked: "So they go to heaven expecting seventy-two virgins and find raisins waiting for them!"[71] The primary motivation for jihad was "because it's the easiest way to get into paradise," according to Mitchell.[72]

KUBARK had warned CIA interrogators to be wary of "impaired objectivity," saying: "A failure to report it would be evidence of a lack of professionalism." But Mitchell never read KUBARK because he did not want to become "contaminated."[73] Instead, he took cultural lessons from *The Arab Mind*, a book by Raphael Patai, a Hungarian-Jewish anthropologist, written in 1973. One twenty-five-page chapter lingered over Arab attitudes to sex, and depicted Arab culture as crippled by shame and humiliation, governed by outmoded social rules like female bondage. Arabs were consumed by a belief that their failure as a society had been caused by Western repression, according to Patai. Many senior Bush administration officials read it, too, taking away the message that "the biggest weakness of Arabs is shame and humiliation."[74] Post-9/11, *The Arab Mind* was republished, with a forward by Colonel Norvell De Atkine, who for eighteen years was the "resident expert" on the Middle East at the Special Warfare School in Fort Bragg, where many of Mitchell's close friends and colleagues worked. De Atkine, who would later deploy to Iraq with a "psychological operations unit," also worked under contract for the CIA, as well as publishing his own work, such as the essay "Why Arabs Lose Wars."[75] De Atkine, Mitchell, Patai, and the CIA shared many views about the Arab world.

Mitchell flummoxed Shumate. CIA psychologists were supposed to "bring a degree of objectivity or cross-cultural insight," Shumate argued.[76] Reading beyond Patai and understanding Arabic was a first step, in his opinion. Understanding Arabic was a second. "Arabic is a conversational language," explained Shumate. It was steeped in ambiguity. He was concerned Abu Zubaydah's interrogations were still being conducted in English and that Mitchell appeared to have no interest in his background or pre-jihad life. But Scott Shumate also needed his job and so he did not report his concerns to headquarters.

Keeping Abu Zubaydah awake became a real struggle. They tried placing him in the "standing sleep-deprivation" position, suspended from the ceiling, but his injured leg could not bear his weight, and when he fell the shackles bit into his wrists. Eventually, he stopped responding to water dousing, so guards chained him upright to a plastic chair, which caused other problems. "Many times, I urinated all over myself and on the bandages that were still wrapped around my left wounded thigh," he recalled.[77] He jumped up and down in frustration. The chair legs splayed, and he fell over. When it happened a second time, Mitchell arranged for a stack of identical chairs to be piled up outside the cell. Mitchell had spotted a keen opponent in Abu Zubaydah. They could keep this game going forever.[78]

When Abu Zubaydah fell asleep on the chair and no amount of icy water could "roister" him, the guards stood him up and walked him around in circles. Again, he fell because of his weakened leg. Sometimes he slept "while they were dragging me."[79] Every day or so, he also had to undergo another debridement of the "gaping" wound. Mitchell later joked: "It looked like how you'd cut a lobster."[80] A medical recommendation to perform a skin graft was rejected because it would "impede" interrogation.[81] Because he vomited every time they gave him Ensure, he stopped drinking it.

Starved, sick, and dehydrated, he hallucinated about his family. "These persons, suddenly and without introduction, their images are rushing into my mind . . . their voices echo. . . . Memories of being together, the good ones and the bad, are undulating in my heart as if they were a tide drawn by the full moon," he had written in his diary.[82] He reran old family arguments. "Kamal desperate to copy Hesham on the Atari and making mistakes, saying, 'I know, I know.'" Sometimes he was transported back to Peshawar: "I am sitting on the revolving chair behind the office desk . . . being the emir of the house, the martyrs house, the center of terrorism, as it's called . . ." He relived the moment his jihad-fighting career had ended, in December 1991, when a mortar shell exploded in his battlefield camp. "The hot shrapnel flew into the depth of my skull." He imagined the other brothers captured in Faisalabad, caged and naked, "shivering from the cold." When he woke, he begged Adil for news. "The more you refuse to cooperate with us, or you try to play games," Adil replied, "the more we will keep them naked and cold." Abu Zubaydah felt crazed: "Half of what was happening to me was the result of a breakdown and the other half was the result of letting myself go."[83] Sometimes he woke: "screaming or cussing or trying to kick something or hit something." Every which way he turned, he hit a wall: "The humiliations, the terrorizing, the hunger, the pain, the tension, the nervousness, and the sleep deprivation," he recalled later.[84] There was no safe place.

To comply with legal requirements, daily psychological assessments needed to remain upbeat, and day after day there were "no signs of distress, agitation, violence, hallucinations, nor delusions." Abu Zubaydah was "a healthy young man given to some hypochrondriasis."[85] However, in truth, the on-site medics worried his mistreatment was severely impacting his health, and secretly they contacted Terry DeMay. Both Abu Zubaydah's ankles were swollen with edema from all the standing up.[86] Given that he was also hallucinating, this was a clear sign his circulatory system was compromised. If the edema was left untreated, it could lead to heart failure, even death. Bulky and muscled when he had been arrested, he had lost almost a quarter of his body weight thanks to his intestinal injury and bare-bones diet.[87] After sleep deprivation was extended beyond seventy hours, DeMay made an official complaint. As a result, Rizzo's office asked the Counterterrorist Center to seek clinical assurances they were not straying beyond John Yoo's anodyne note or the established bright legal lines. Needing to keep this compartmented and top-secret classified operation strictly in-house, Kirk Hubbard asked Joe Matarazzo, who was paid a small stipend to sit on the CIA's Professional Standards Advisory Board. Matarazzo concluded that sleep deprivation was not torture.[88] "I had covered the literature on this topic in an annual lecture to medical students and felt qualified to offer an opinion," he later reflected.[89] He also consulted "five prominent psychologists" who agreed with him, although he later said: "However, I do believe that sleep deprivation could be a form of torture when combined with multiple other techniques capable of breaking resistance."

Back out in Thailand, one psychologist needed to remain on-site 24/7 for legal reasons, and because the guards kept Abu Zubaydah awake around the clock. Most guards were former soldiers, police, or correctional officers. Some were "enormous," Mitchell reflected. He always volunteered for the night shift, and said he had compared sleep deprivation rules with the FBI's. "The FBI told me it was legal as long as the interrogator also stayed up," he recalled, although in reality it wasn't always the same interrogator.[90]

Surrounded by fizzing jungle, General Tritot's compound took on a menacing air in the darkness. Shumate became concerned about what might be going unnoted while most of the team was asleep at the hotel, and asked to see for himself. Mitchell tried to dissuade him: "I said, 'I've done a lot of this and things can get weird at night, so you need to rest up and come back in the morning when things are less strange.'"[91] Shumate took offense: "You think I can't handle it?" Mitchell asked him to consider what was likely to happen when Abu Zubaydah got sleepy. "The guards are going to get handsy to keep him awake," he warned. As well as "flicking water," they might use an object to beat on the bars, "not his head, not touching, but to startle him, to keep him awake." There might be "loud noises, and other kinds of things." Shumate dug his heels in and stayed over. The next morning, Mitchell said, Shumate was "just undone" and physically exhausted. "It was as if he had been part of Zimbardo's prison experiment, and he had just realized, 'Oh my God, I can be horrible,'" Mitchell said. "From then on, I did the nights and he did the days."

Abu Zubaydah was undone by the nights, too. Many years later, and still in custody, he tried to communicate what had happened by drawing pictures of himself: a shorn, stick man with protruding ribs, strapped to a plastic patio chair, his body contorted, blood dripping from his open leg wound, urine and diarrhea pooling on the floor. It looked like a scene from one of those scary movies the Abu Zubaydah boys had watched at home in Riyadh, but this was real American horror. "I had reached a certain level of psychological, nervous and physical exhaustion that if it were not for God's protection, I could have officially declared myself psychotic," he recalled.[92] But a totally different picture was painted in official cables. On April 17, 2002, headquarters was informed that he was "using a variety of resistance techniques" and was "extremely resilient."[93] On April 18, they were told of "considerable resistance."[94]

That night, the medical team forced an intervention. Abu Zubaydah had not slept for seventy-six hours, and he later recalled a medic entering his cell. "He examined me and then he started making signals to them without saying anything as if to he was trying to tell them: 'He needs sleep otherwise he would go crazy.'"[95] The medic was hauled out and reprimanded for "speaking" in front of the detainee. An argument broke out, with Soufan, Shumate, and the medical team demanding he be allowed to sleep, while Mitchell and the Alec Station experts lobbied to go further. "Like many medical students, the subject appears to handle 76 plus hours of limited sleep with few problems," Mitchell later reported.[96] After the team consulted headquarters, Abu Zubaydah was allowed to sleep for three hours, chained to a plastic chair. He claimed he was warned, "you're gonna have to pay" for this privilege, and on April 19, after he was woken up, he was subjected to "rectal fluid resuscitation."[97] Years later, when he had a pen and paper, he drew a picture of "mock rape"—several guards poking a detainee with a baseball bat. He was chained and on his hands and knees.

Mitchell vehemently denied any connection to detainees being hydrated or "fed" rectally, as the CIA was later accused of doing, by congressional investigators.[98] But in an unguarded conversation about detainees and their motivations, Mitchell once let something slip. "They thought they could mess with American psyche by mounting other attacks," he explained. "Until they realized that if you mess with Americans, they'll put food in your ass."[99]

On April 19, headquarters was informed that Abu Zubaydah was "using counter-interrogation techniques outlined in the Al Qaeda training manual."[100] But because intelligence reports coming from the black site had completely dried up, and senior officials at headquarters and in other government agencies wanted to know why, Mitchell temporarily lost the argument, and Ali Soufan and Steve Gaudin were sent back into the cell. Mitchell was furious.

Soufan claimed he gave Abu Zubaydah a blanket.[101] Abu Zubaydah recalled being shackled to a plastic chair, "fully naked, shaking because of cold and hunger."[102] Soufan was cold and haughty, said Abu Zubaydah, jumped out of his chair, "threatening me and pointing his finger in my face."[103] He accused Abu Zubaydah of lying, threatening to kill him and talking over him.[104] "What is up with you?" Abu Zubaydah snapped. "Listen." He tried to give some information. Soufan shouted over him: "You don't order me. You have to say please, 'please listen.'" Abu Zubaydah held his ground. "I won't say 'please' to you, never, while I'm in this situation." It was a relentless faceoff, Abu Zubaydah reflected, with "Ali Soufan, Shiite Muslim."[105]

Guards wheeled in a cartload of audiocassettes: three genuine recordings of Abu Zubaydah talking on his phone at the House of Martyrs—material the CIA had got from the French, who had tracked his number during the 1990s—surrounded by blank cassettes. After Soufan played a couple of the real recordings, and suggested they had dozens more, Abu Zubaydah gave information about the plot to blow up an American installation in Israel, something he had mentioned during the very first hour of his FBI interrogation on March 31, 2002, and more snippets about Mokhtar, who he had identified on April 10, but nothing about the second wave. Soufan brought in Abu Zubaydah's address book, recovered from Shahbaz Cottage. He said it contained codes next to the names of senior Al Qaeda members. "Admit it, you are Number Three," Gaudin demanded. "Admit you are a liar." Abu Zubaydah recalled laughing. Cables noted that he admitted to lying. "He stated he lied because he was tired and simply said 'yes' to some questions."[106] But rather than accept that sleep deprivation had produced false information, on April 20 Mitchell lobbied for permission to "step up the psychological pressure." Abu Zubaydah's unwillingness to provide information about the second wave was simply another sign of "resistance."[107]

Determined to keep Mitchell out, Soufan tried another trick, and produced copies of emails Abu Zubaydah had sent to Mokhtar about two brothers he was dispatching to Karachi, where Mohammad was located post-9/11. The emails were genuine; Abu Zubaydah recognized them right away and began talking. Two inexperienced brothers had turned up in Afghanistan shortly before 9/11, got caught up in the fighting, and fled to the Pakistan border, where Abu Zubaydah had taken pity. One was American; the other was an Ethiopian with "a very good fake British passport."[108] However, after he'd brought them to Faisalabad, they had worried him. In the house were different groups of brothers who did not know each other, and everyone was reliant on their host, Lashkar-e-Toiba, a Pakistani group with close links to the Inter-Services Intelligence (ISI), Pakistan's premier intelligence agency. Everyone was paranoid about betrayal.

The two young brothers kept looking things up on a computer, recalled Abu Zubaydah. After a few days, they had come to him and said "they had a plan to follow up on 9/11 and deal a devastating blow to America."[109] What was it, he asked? They planned to steal uranium from a hospital or a research facility and make a dirty bomb by swirling it around in a bucket like a homemade enrichment centrifuge. Abu Zubaydah laughed. Like almost everyone else he encountered, they were "fools." But when they showed him the white supremacist websites they had been reading online, he became furious. They were endangering the security of everyone in Shahbaz Cottage by searching such things. The ISI was trying to monitor everyone's communications, said Abu Zubaydah who contacted Mokhtar, and put the two brothers on a train to Karachi. They were more of a liability than terrorist masterminds, but their passports might be useful.

When this story was reported back to Langley, Alec Station leapt on it and reported it up the chain of command: the 9/11 mastermind was planning to attack the United States with a dirty bomb. Here was clear evidence of the second wave in motion. A genuine American citizen, a terrorist with British residency status, and Abu Zubaydah were all involved. Cheney's "one percent doctrine" kicked in, and Soufan and Gaudin were sent back in to get more details. The two brothers story was "full of holes," they told Abu Zubaydah. What were their names? He shook his head. He never knew their real names. Mitchell reported he was resisting again. Abu Zubaydah had caused himself a whole lot of trouble by telling this story and would have to be treated far more harshly to cough up the full details. It was time to bring in more aggressive SERE techniques, including locking him in a box that resembled a coffin.[110]

Soufan took Adil to one side. "Is this all approved?" Adil produced a letter from the Justice Department that suggested Alberto Gonzales, the president's lawyer, had sanctioned everything. Despite this, Adil told Soufan he was still keeping a record of every order they had received, "because one day this is going to be a bad thing."[111]

CHAPTER 7

"A Full-Size American Refrigerator, Only Taller"

April 24, 2002, Chiang Mai, Thailand

Scott Shumate was leaving. Nobody at headquarters had suggested extending his two-week duty, and he certainly wasn't volunteering for more. "It's not worth losing myself for this," he told Ali Soufan on the way to the airport.[1] Back at Langley, one of the senior CIA op-psychs being considered to replace him in Thailand was Mitchell's friend Mike McConnell, another advocate for SERE. "They pulled [Shumate] off and replaced him with another op-psych who was there for months and I'm not telling you his name," reflected Mitchell, who added that Shumate's replacement also doubled up as chief of base, sidestepping reasonable Adil.[2] Jose Rodriguez was also being promoted. George Tenet had asked Cofer Black to help him prepare for the 9/11 investigation into whether the CIA and other agencies had fouled up, and Rodriguez was taking Black's job as chief of the Counterterrorist Center.[3] Shumate feared for Abu Zubaydah. Mitchell was advocating locking him in a coffin and burying him, a death threat in no uncertain terms.[4] Confederates had put enslaved people in coffins during the US Civil War, and the North Vietnamese had used coffins to torture US airmen in the Hanoi Hilton. Surely the "greatest country in the world," a global defender of human rights, was not resorting to real torture? No one listened to Shumate, who later described Mitchell as "sadistic," "evil," and "insecure," and compared him to serial killer Ted Bundy, "exploiting the system to get to the top."[5]

With Shumate out of the way, the CIA moved ahead. One cable from Thailand discussed the "mock burial event" and explained: "[The] individual is moved to a prepared site where he hears digging. The site has a prepared hole, dug in such a way that the box can be lowered into the ground and shovels of dirt thrown in."[6] Since the US Constitution and federal law forbade using a "threat of imminent death," Fredman and Rizzo sought approval from the attorney general, citing the fact that SERE students were routinely put into oil drums, "cramped confinement" boxes, and water tanks. However, mock execution was not an approved SERE technique, and later, even Mitchell tried to distance himself, saying it had been a headquarters recommendation and "would probably violate the torture convention."[7] An official CIA overview of the program later reported that mock burial was "originally proposed by Mitchell and Jessen."[8] Mitchell also sought to blame Steve Gaudin. "Steve was concerned that because the FBI had had a role in the nudity and sleep deprivation they needed something new. . . . Bad FBI is going to bury him and good FBI is going to come and rescue him."[9] But if the CIA could not obtain legal permission to bury Abu Zubaydah in a coffin, they could still give him the impression he was going to die by using a coffin-shaped "confinement box."

The day Shumate left Thailand, April 24, the black site team was given permission to construct a wooden box, its dimensions thirty by twenty by eighty-five inches—the size of a large burial casket. Painted black inside and out, it resembled the "black box" device used in air force SERE school.[10] The SERE school box was kept in an upright position, but the CIA planned to have Abu Zubaydah "reclining."[11] According to his later pictures, it had padlocks on the lid and small lockable hatches at each end .[12] According to the lawyers, Abu Zubaydah could be locked inside for up to nine hours a day, and they issued approval to place hidden cameras and microphones inside so they could spy on Abu Zubaydah when he was laid out as if dead.[13] Someone in Kirk Hubbard's office emailing these details to senior officials wrote in the subject field: "torture info."[14] Abu Zubaydah's pictures suggested various other uses for the coffin.[15] In one, he lay prone with his ankles and wrists shackled to a chain at his groin, a pool of urine gathering beneath him, the lid secured with padlocks. In another, he lay with his arms chained behind him and his body arched as the coffin was filled up with water, via a hatch. In a third, the lid was open, and his legs were being pulled upward and out, causing his head and body to become submerged. In a fourth, he was facedown, with hands holding his head underwater. Little bubbles were coming out of his mouth. Official cables make no reference to filling the coffin with water, and there was no way to verify whether Abu Zubaydah actually experienced such things, but in SERE school, instructors regularly mixed up different forms of "torture" for maximum effect. Mitchell later tried to soften the image. The CIA box was more spacious than the "prototype" SERE box. "Coffin," he argued, was a loaded word, although it appeared in cables.[16] Mitchell called it a "crate," the kind in which you would transport "a full-size American refrigerator, only taller."[17]

What the CIA had put on the table went so far beyond John Rizzo's "bright legal lines" that John Yoo and his deputy, a recently hired lawyer, struggled to draw up a positive legal opinion. On April 24, the deputy complained to a friend by email about the long hours she was working and stated, "I would have said, 'no,' but it didn't seem like that was an option here."[18] The key problem was sidestepping the definition of "severe mental pain or suffering," which had been enshrined in the UN Convention against Torture, signed by President Reagan in 1988. Dangerous areas were prolonged mental harm caused by inflicting or threatening severe physical pain or harm, the threat or use of mind-altering substances, the "threat of imminent death" or the threat that another person would be subjected to death, and severe physical pain or suffering.[19] CIA lawyers repeatedly pushed Yoo to become bolder. The definition of severe mental and physical pain had been "written vaguely," and since Reagan had not agreed to sign the second part of the convention, which outlawed "cruel and unusual punishment," the CIA had "more license to use more controversial techniques," Jonathan Fredman allegedly reported.[20] None of the techniques currently under discussion constituted severe pain or suffering, CIA lawyers concluded in a cable sent to Thailand, adding that a more detailed response "with any necessary legal fine-tuning" would follow.[21] A "greater leeway" was also being mapped out for how far the team could go with the "confinement box," a.k.a. coffin.[22]

Conditions inside Abu Zubaydah's bunker intensified nevertheless.[23] He recalled lying immobilized on the concrete floor of his cell, naked, short-chained (a Bureau of Prisons technique and similar to hog-tying), and shivering uncontrollably. Observers reported that some days his skin was bluish.[24] One day, the guards carried in a boom box. Abu Zubaydah hoped it was a good sign, but after he was blasted with the same song at maximum volume for twenty-four hours, he concluded, "It was a sign of disaster approaching."[25]

The song was "Bodies," by Texan hard rockers Drowning Pool, and began with whispered lyrics, "Let the bodies hit the floor," which gradually got louder until ending in a long caterwauling scream. The official aim was "to enhance his sense of hopelessness," and it worked, as he recalled his brain was "going up and down, left and right."[26] He tried to plug his ears with toilet tissue but was caught and punished. "I finally found myself screaming along with it," he recalled, "like someone collapsing." Mitchell blamed the guards, even though cables showed that psychologists asked headquarters for permission to use music as a specific technique.[27] Guards being guards, "occasionally I'd hear 'I'm from Wisconsin, I got a big Johnson' wailing from the speakers," Mitchell commented.[28] Someone produced a SERE audio loop of a little girl screaming, "Daddy! Daddy! The bad man is hurting Mommy." When the loud music failed to elicit anything new, Mitchell announced they were using the "wrong kind of noise" and took delivery of a three-foot-tall white-noise machine. Soufan and Gaudin laughed that Mitchell could have just turned up the air-conditioners and got the same effect. He was crazy, and dangerous. Outside the soundproof bunker, the only sound of madness came from millions of cicadas.

Everyone focused on the "dirty bomb plot," citing it as clear evidence that the second wave was up and running. Several senior officials were investigating Al Qaeda's nuclear ambitions, including Rolf Mowatt-Larssen, who was appointed head of "WMD intelligence collection" shortly after 9/11, and Dr. John Phillips, the CIA's chief scientist, who had spent thirty years at Los Alamos National Laboratory in New Mexico, where the United States had designed the atom bomb. The Al Qaeda nuclear-threat scenario appeared even more real when Mowatt-Larssen reported that Osama bin Laden had met two Pakistani nuclear scientists before 9/11 and tried to buy fissile material.[29] US forces also recovered manuals from a training camp that suggested Al Qaeda was experimenting with anthrax and trying to construct a primitive WMD.[30]

Pressed day after day for more details about the two brothers who had wanted to enrich uranium in a bucket, Abu Zubaydah eventually named them as "Abu Ameriki" and "Talha al-Kini."[31] The latter was Binyam Mohamed; he was an Ethiopian with asylum status in the United Kingdom. Abu Ameriki was Jose Padilla, a thirty-one-year-old Brooklyn-born Puerto Rican who had peddled drugs before converting to Islam. Post-9/11, Arabs were being scrutinized at airports the world over, but Padilla was Latino, Mohamed was African, and their passports made them valuable. A cable read: "[AZ] thought Mokhtar would be able to use them for whatever 'missions' Mokhtar was planning," but as far as he knew, there was no "nuclear plan."[32] Padilla had "five-six ideas for operations in the United States, but they were all assessed as bad."[33] Abu Zubaydah insisted he had no idea what had happened after he sent them to Karachi in "mid-March."[34] All he knew was that Mokhtar had told him that no "sleepers" remained in the United States after 9/11. However, when judged against Cheney's "one percent doctrine," and Abu Zubaydah's diary mentions of nuclear attacks, his statements looked extremely worrying, and George Tenet warned the president that Jose Padilla was planning to bomb the United States.[35]

Binyam Mohamed was no longer a problem. He had been picked up at Karachi airport on April 12 while trying to fly back to the United Kingdom and was now being interrogated by FBI agents at an ISI safe house. He later claimed he was held in the strappado position, a popular torture technique used by the Nazis, whereby a prisoner is suspended from his arms behind his back, with his toes barely touching the floor.[36] US officials liaising with the British Secret Intelligence Services told them the raw intelligence about Mohamed had come from Abu Zubaydah, who was being subjected to harsh interrogation techniques that caused "98 per cent of US Special Forces" to break under pressure.[37] The British checked out Mohamed's background, along with a whole host of other British Al Qaeda suspects, and made no comment or complaint about CIA practices.[38]

Abu Zubaydah learned they had caught Mohamed when he was shown his photograph.[39] He also saw the state of his eye. "When I saw a picture of a black brother placed into clear plastic it turned into a mirror," he recalled.[40] "I could see my whole eye in the blackness." It was the first time he had seen himself in more than a month, and his left eye now looked like "a rotten grape." It had also occurred to him that his interrogators believed he was involved in Padilla's crazy plan. At the end of one "dirty bomb plot" session, when one of the interrogators reiterated that what they were after was intelligence about operations in motion prior to his detention, he panicked and clammed up. Over in the control center, Mitchell interpreted this as another sign of guilt, and recommended that Soufan and Gaudin walk out. "Bodies" or the white noise machine revved up, and "subject was put back into isolation mode."[41]

Alone in his cell, Abu Zubaydah tried to care for himself while his watchers noted it all down: "The subject spends a considerable amount of every day grooming and inspecting himself and taking care of his bodily function."[42] Mitchell was fascinated by the frequency with which he masturbated. "He jerked off as often as he could in full view of the cameras," he recalled.[43] An unidentified colleague later characterized him as going at it "like a monkey in the zoo."[44] Later, when they were inside the cell with him, Mitchell and Jessen ridiculed Abu Zubaydah's references to sex and girlfriends in his diary.[45] When Abu Zubaydah complained of blood in his ejaculate, he was told he had injured himself by too much masturbation, his concerns passed off as unnecessary fears about the "impending loss of 'manhood.'"[46] He found out about the lack of sperm later. "To this day I have not been provided with an explanation and I cannot produce sperm," he said.[47] However, Mitchell's and the base chief's psychological assessments reported no signs of emotional or psychological distress. "No signs of stress, agitation, violence, hallucinations, nor delusions was ever observed," stated one written on April 25.[48] "His resistance posture became more defiant as the interview progressed," stated another.[49]

Mitchell later reanalyzed Abu Zubaydah's resistance posture. "When he was cooperating . . . he sat in a relaxed position and spoke clearly and on topic with little hesitation."[50] When he was being evasive, he yawned, inspected his nails, complained of feeling sick or needing to use the toilet. Most responses that began "actually" were true, while those that started with "not really" contained lies, said Mitchell, mimicking Abu Zubaydah's voice.[51] The next time he "pretended to be ill," Adil stepped in and, following a "scripted maneuver," warned that if he remained unwilling to talk, he would be isolated again.[52] The team reported: "Shortly after the interrogators left the cell, subject sat up, quit pretending illness, and ate his food."[53] The following day was dominated by "a display in dramatics."[54] Lying on the floor under a towel, the detainee appeared confused, and mumbled that he was too cold to talk. It was all playacting, argued Mitchell, who knew how to handle troublesome SERE students. The team dispatched a cable headlined: "Turning Up the Heat in the AZ Interrogation."[55] No more lies, dead ends, or dead people. It was time to "ratchet up [the] psychological behavioral interrogation process."[56]

———————•———————

Langley wanted more "bad guy" interrogators, people who were unafraid to go up to the legal chalk line and lean over. Bob Lewis, another SERE-trained former marine, who worked in the Counterterrorist Center under Rodriguez, was coordinating that search and he flew the most promising candidates to Washington, wining and dining them in Tysons Corner.[57] Some had worked as SERE instructors or at the Joint Personnel Recovery Agency (JPRA), Jessen's employer. Others had worked as military interrogators during the Vietnam War. Bob Dussault, who had just retired as JPRA's deputy director and was a close friend of Roger Aldrich's, had done all three.

Dussault recalled meeting Lewis and a CIA colleague at a steak restaurant in Tysons Corner in early April 2002. "They told me they wanted to put a team together, people who would help them develop a more coercive interrogation program and maybe do some of the interrogating," he recalled.[58] "They were in a panic, and Tenet had ordered them to get the capability together 'yesterday.'" Dussault told Lewis about his work in Vietnam. "I could spend a week with a guy and get his entire story," he boasted. What about War on Terror detainees? Dussault replied: "I would do what the North Koreans had done to us."

Dussault cited the case of the captain of a US warship, the USS *Pueblo*, who in 1968 had confessed to spying in North Korean territorial waters. "They took him in a room where there was a live Korean hanging on a meat hook," Dussault explained. "He had the hook through his face, and one eye was out of the socket and down on the cheek. He was yelling and screaming. They said, 'See that man, he's not been telling us the truth. He's a South Korean spy. And if you don't sign this confession we are going to start with the youngest man on your crew and make him look just like that.'" Dussault's idea sounded completely unworkable until he explained he would mock it up rather than actually maiming another a detainee to get Abu Zubaydah talking. He had already primed Ahmed Habib, a SERE instructor of Lebanese descent, who would play the role of an injured Al Qaeda suspect with the assistance of a lot of stage makeup and a harness. Habib, a former work colleague of Mitchell's and Jessen's at Fairchild, was happy to "hang on a meat hook, look terrible, scream and holler," for $50,000. Dussault said he was asked by Lewis to submit a formal proposal.

Shortly after flying home to Anacortes, Washington, Dussault received an unexpected email that read: "Subject: Future Plans. Bob, Roger tells me you are considering putting together a training package. Please keep me in mind. Working with you again would be great. . . . Regards, Bruce."[59] Having been thrown out of the CIA planning meeting in early April, Jessen was still advising the US military about the benefits of SERE. Despite later claiming he was reluctant to get involved with JPRA training drawn up by Chris Wirts, JPRA's operational chief, he was now working with the group on an "exploitation plan," in which JPRA would run a detention facility for War on Terror detainees, and JPRA instructors and psychologists would conduct the interrogations.

The day before contacting Dussault, Jessen had discussed this plan with Randy Moulton, the JPRA commander.[60] Jessen sent a draft to Wirts, so he could "operationalize" it. The plan drew on Patai's *The Arab Mind* and recommended techniques specifically designed to shame and humiliate Muslims: dogs, female interrogators, baseline conditions and nudity. Moulton emailed Jessen the following day, April 17, asking him to craft a slide briefing. It should include: "What generated this requirement, why we (USG) need it, how it falls within our chartered responsibilities (or if not, why we should do it) and then make a recommendation."[61] Jessen wrote that the objective was to "hold, manage and exploit detainees to elicit critical information." The plan proposed an "exploitation facility be established at [redacted] off limits to non-essential personnel, press, ICRC [International Committee of the Red Cross], or foreign observers," a place not unlike Guantánamo, or Abu Zubaydah's bunker in Thailand.

Jessen's preferred option was that "JPRA fields and deploys core captivity/exploitation team. . . . This team directs the process under the lead of the JPRA Senior SERE Psychologist," which likely meant himself. JPRA should retain "the authority to direct the entire process or current mistakes will be repeated ([Guantánamo], lack of experience of in-theater interrogators, ineffective captivity handling and facility routine)."[62] Any non-JPRA staff or contractors would have to be trained by a JPRA cadre. It was a self-confident proposal from someone who claimed to be a reluctant party in spreading the word about SERE. A section of Jessen's proposal that laid out "critical operational principles" is mostly redacted, except for one key phrase: "The only restricting factor should be the Torture Convention."[63] When questioned later about this plan, Jessen said that he knew how to set up training programs, had observed numerous "interrogations" at SERE school, and thought that some JPRA instructors would make "excellent interrogators."[64] He also supported having SERE psychologists observe real interrogations.

As well as bidding for War on Terror contracts through JPRA, Jessen wanted to work for the CIA too, and he had learned of Bob Dussault's discussions from their mutual friend Roger Aldrich. JPRA was a small community, based mainly in Spokane, and the key players talked all the time, said Aldrich, who characterized their world as "incestuous."[65] Dussault was delighted to hear from Jessen. They had worked together for fifteen years. "I totally trusted the guy," he said.[66] "He was my number one." Dussault invited Jessen to spend a weekend discussing the proposal at Leavenworth, Washington, a mock-Bavarian mountain village equidistant from Anacortes and Spokane. They both brought along their wives, and Dussault outlined his "Al-Qaeda-on-a-meat-hook" idea over dinner. Jessen was enthusiastic—if the price was right. "Bruce wanted to know how much it was worth," Dussault recalled. "I said $160K a year for each person on the contract." Ahmed Habib, the SERE instructor who was going to hang off the meat hook, was an old running buddy of Jessen's and Mitchell's. Dussault was Aldrich's mentor, Aldrich was Jessen's mentor, and at the start of Mitchell's SERE career, Jessen had been his mentor. It was a neat idea to get Dussault, Jessen, Habib, and potentially Aldrich all in on a potentially lucrative CIA contract. "I said, 'Let's do it,'" said Dussault. "Bruce told me, 'I'll call you next week.'" But when Jessen called back, he had changed his mind, Dussault recalled. "Bruce said, 'Bob, forget it. I'm going in another way.'"[67] Jessen had been speaking to his best buddy Mitchell, who was in Thailand. "He had doubled his money by signing on with Jim, but I didn't know that at the time. The CIA knew what it was doing. Jim and Bruce together: that's a powerful team. Neither of them ever spoke to me again."

Territorial Mitchell did not want Bob Dussault invading his CIA deal, and he later accused the former JPRA deputy director of becoming sour, and leaking details of the program. He described Dussault as "very swampish."[68] In his heyday, Dussault had been hugely influential, Mitchell explained. "He could make a phone call and move a satellite." But by the time the CIA came calling, Dussault was at the end of his career, sneered Mitchell. He had succeeded in maneuvering his mentor, partner, and best buddy into the program as a consultant and keeping out the competition. For now, they would hang on to Wirts because they still needed JPRA's help with training, but Mitchell would be soon gunning for him too.

———•———

Jose Padilla flew into Chicago's O'Hare International Airport on May 8, 2002, and was arrested by the FBI. George Tenet's chief spokesman, Bill Harlow, ran with the story.[69] Padilla's mug shot was everywhere, along with the banner headline: "Dirty Bomber." Newspapers reported he had thousands of dollars in his pocket from Khalid Sheikh Mohammad, who had instructed him to blow up apartments heated with natural gas.[70] Even though Padilla's uranium-enrichment idea was laughable, the CIA characterized him as an "explosives expert and terrorist trainer at Qandahar [*sic*]."[71] Attorney General John Ashcroft described him as the mastermind of an "unfolding terrorist plot" to launch a dirty bomb in an American city.[72]

"This was not true," said Ali Soufan. While Padilla was indeed committed to trying to harm the United States, the land of his birth, he was "a brain transplant away from making a dirty bomb." There was no unfolding plot. "Padilla *was* the plot," Soufan argued.[73] From a tiny seed of information gained from a detainee placed under extreme pressure, a huge Al Qaeda conspiracy had bloomed under Cheney's "one percent doctrine." Ashcroft ramped up the CIA's "ticking time bomb" theory ahead of the presentation of John Yoo's latest legal opinion to the National Security Council.[74] "Ashcroft's statement was not only inaccurate, it also made us look foolish in the eyes of Al Qaeda," reflected Soufan.[75] "The message was that it was easy to fool the United States." Many years later, the CIA conceded that it had used "imprecise language or made errors in some of its representations" about Padilla and his "dirty bomb."[76] References to Padilla were deleted from official tallies of CIA success stories.[77]

Scott Shumate's fears about detainees saying anything to stop harsh treatment were coming true, and Mitchell was getting stronger. Jennifer Matthews was now at the black site and she supported Mitchell to the hilt.[78]

Other important analysts also turned up, including someone who "wrote the President's Daily Brief," recalled Mitchell.[79] In early May, Ali Soufan was again warned to back off. "This is not a law enforcement interrogation," insisted headquarters.[80] "The interrogation team is not limited to the use of traditional law enforcement methods," and Abu Zubaydah was "not entitled to the legal protections of the Geneva Conventions." Mitchell was fully permitted to use tactics "designed to maximize psychological pressure" and "validated by SERE." Removing clothing and solid food, subjecting Abu Zubaydah to incessant light and constant noise, threatening to turn him over to another country, and putting him in a coffin were all legal. Mitchell was also being assisted on-site by another "SERE trained psychologist," whose identity was later redacted from all CIA cables, reports, and emails.[81] It was not Bruce Jessen, because he was still in Spokane.

According to Mitchell's CIA contract folder, the day before Padilla's arrest, Mitchell received classified security briefings into five special access programs (SAPs) and signed a new secrecy agreement.[82] A week after Padilla's arrest, he renegotiated his CIA contract up to $162,600.[83] As well as extracting information from Abu Zubaydah, the CIA wanted Mitchell's help with training.[84] Anticipating the capture of more high-value detainees, the Office of Technical Service wanted an "advanced interrogation capability" consisting of at least two fully trained teams, although Bob Dussault would not be winning any contracts.

Noting that a "highly talented team" was currently interrogating Abu Zubaydah and providing the US government with a "unique opportunity to . . . disrupt Al Qaeda plans," Technical Service intended to use Mitchell's model as the template. If the CIA did not expand its interrogation capabilities, "we risk missing highly valuable, time sensitive intelligence that could prevent another disastrous terror attack against the Homeland." The recent apprehension of Padilla "validates the logic of our proposal." It was yet another circular CIA argument based on self-interest.

Mitchell, in Thailand, and Jessen, in Spokane, helped assemble the curriculum remotely. Successful applicants would be put through classic SERE training, "a classroom portion and a lab," and familiarized with specific resistance strategies drawn from "what we know from captured manuals and our experience here," wrote Mitchell. There would be lessons on "the influence of Arab culture on the employment of resistance techniques." *The Arab*

Mind by Ralph Patai was required reading. The focus yet again was exploiting Arab weaknesses, and the curriculum was practically identical to the slide presentation Jessen had prepared for Guantánamo-bound interrogators on behalf of JPRA (and that he later tried to distance himself from).[85]

The hierarchy of the new interrogation teams was designed to avoid conflicts between competing agencies and to make sure the CIA always came out on top. The CIA team chief was also the base chief and would be deputized by SERE psychologists, who would have full authority to "develop, direct, and monitor the psychological pressures placed upon the subject." Below them came interrogators, who could "make recommendations" but not control the plan. Below them was an FBI special agent, who was needed as "an impartial observer," and below the FBI were medical staff, who were needed for legal cover and to keep the detainee alive. At the very bottom were the interpreters, security officers, analysts, and guards, who had no authority at all.

Out in Thailand, Mitchell reported that Abu Zubaydah was getting physically and mentally stronger. The Justice Department needed to hurry with permission to ratchet up interrogation pressures. "You should just go home and leave me," Abu Zubaydah said one day, according to cables.[86] Mitchell reported this as a sign that the detainee believed "he would outlast the interrogation team."[87] But, as Roger Aldrich pointed out, few people outlasted Mitchell, who was becoming irritated by his "subject" and intended to deliver the message in person.[88]

On May 19, two days after John Yoo and his deputy finished a second draft legal opinion, Mitchell was given permission to threaten Abu Zubaydah, a role-play move normally followed at SERE school by an immediate ramping up of interrogation. First, they sent a female nurse into the cell. When Abu Zubaydah complained about being naked before a woman, she made a big play of asking the guards to bring in shorts and a T-shirt. "Praise God, I am finally able to cover my genitals," Abu Zubaydah recalled thinking, no matter that the clothes were orange, the color of Guantánamo.[89] But no sooner had he dressed himself than six masked guards charged in, stood him up, chained his hands over his head, and hooded him. "A man came in and started screaming loudly and shoving me violently," Abu Zubaydah recalled.[90] It was Mitchell.

Swearing and calling Abu Zubaydah a "motherfucker," Mitchell threw a plastic lawn chair against the wall and began ripping off Abu Zubaydah's orange clothes.[91] "I felt . . . he was cutting my skin," Abu Zubaydah recalled. "I felt that worse was coming, that he was going to beat me up and whip me." Mitchell whispered into Abu Zubaydah's ear: "Are you sure you want to go down this path? Later on, remember it was *you* who chose it."[92] Mitchell was doing what he had done best at SERE: Colonel Klink on steroids. "I was a new voice and a new bad guy," he recalled.[93] He then stormed out, leaving Abu Zubaydah slumped and "visibly shaken."[94] An hour later, the guards returned, chained him up to the ceiling, and hooded him again before Mitchell reentered, screaming and cursing. "You may have fooled these other guys," he growled in Abu Zubaydah's ear. "But you don't fool me. After they get tired of you jerking them around and leave, it will be just you and me."[95] Mitchell walked out, slamming the door; the white noise was switched on, and the team went for dinner. Shortly after they sat down, one of the guards called from the black site. Abu Zubaydah was "asking to talk to an interrogator," the first time he had ever done so.[96] When the team raced back to the bunker, he told them he had prayed the *istikharah* (a prayer seeking God's guidance) and was writing out "names of operatives" and "notes about potential plans."[97] Mitchell was delighted.

They got straight to it, with Mitchell back in the control center. Abu Zubaydah explained that he had last seen Mokhtar in Kandahar in October 2001, when Osama bin Laden had called an *ulema* (religious council) to discuss the American invasion of Afghanistan. It was the second and last time Abu Zubaydah met bin Laden, who had angered him by attacking innocent civilians in America, an act that no one had been warned was coming and that had turned the Taliban and all the jihad groups into targets. Many *mujahideen* brothers who attended the *ulema* were unhappy, Abu Zubaydah insisted. But they all felt compelled to rally around bin Laden now that war was declared.

The CIA only wanted to know about the second wave. He retold scraps of conversation from the *ulema*. As well as saying he had no more sleepers in the United States, Mokhtar had told him: "The White House remains in my head, and I will get to it sooner or later."[98] Abu Zubaydah later claimed he made up the entire *ishtikarah* and *ulema* story to win a break from the mistreatment but the interrogators wrote it down.[99] What else? On an earlier occasion in Peshawar, Mokhtar had talked of bringing down the Brooklyn Bridge, Godzilla style, maybe the Statue of Liberty, too. The CIA was desperate to hear anything about the real "king of monsters," and wrote it all down. Abu Zubaydah was willing to say anything to keep the bad guy away. Mitchell felt vindicated, and that night the detainee prayed loudly. Alec Station was delighted and dubbed May 19, 2002, the day of "revelation."[100] Gaudin recalled being shocked when some of these stories were leaked to the media. "We talked to Abu Zubaydah, theorizing about attacks—the Statue of Liberty or the Brooklyn Bridge—and the next day we'd see on CNN that the bridge was closed or the statue closed." Later, Mitchell reflected on the old movie evenings in Peshawar. "The brothers sat around and talked and daydreamed," he said. "It's almost like you had a meeting of directors for Hollywood films and somebody said, 'We ought to do a movie, *Die Hard*-on-a-ship,' and they'd just talk about these things and somebody will pick up the project and run with it."[101]

Jennifer Matthews and the other Abu Zubaydah "experts" juggled a flood of new intelligence requirements. Alec Station wanted to match names to faces across Al Qaeda's spectrum, from military commanders to drivers. Adil, Soufan, Gaudin, and Bryan took turns tag-teaming Abu Zubaydah while he sat in a padded office chair, with his left hand cuffed to the arm, his feet shackled and chained to the bars of his cell. Eagle-eyed Mitchell watched on CCTV, looking for signs of "backsliding."[102] On April 27, Abu Zubaydah gave vague answers, feigned difficulty to understand, used shifting and stretching to stall his answers, and displayed general evasiveness. He was "actively resisting" again.[103] The following day, his "extraordinary resistance to interrogation techniques" was again noted.[104] On April 29, he feigned illness, confusion, and neurological problems.[105] Mitchell's message was heard loud and clear at headquarters, and on April 30, cables discussed the "need to draw up the list" of more aggressive techniques.[106]

According to the unidentified operational-psychologist base chief, who conducted six "modified interviews" with Abu Zubaydah in preparation for a psychological profile that was needed by the lawyers, he was "sophisticated, articulate and compelling." He had a clear sense of his presence, "consistent with what one would expect given subject's role as a leader within a culture that appreciates and respects men who are persuasive, eloquent, and articulate."[107] Sometimes he was arrogant, other times witty and funny.[108] Later, Abu Zubaydah recalled a joke from the Middle East. "A competition is organized among the world's intelligence services to use their skills and technology in a race to be the first to catch a rabbit in a nature reserve," he began.[109] "The Americans come back with a rabbit, followed by the British, Russians and Indians." Eventually, every service catches a rabbit except the Arabs, who are later found holding a cat and repeatedly slapping it. "Say you're a rabbit," the Arab spies yelled. "Meow," said the cat. When he was irritated by "silly" questions, Abu Zubaydah took to answering his interrogators with a "meow." He returned to calling himself Mahmoud el-Meliguy, after the villainous Egyptian actor.[110]

The team dispatched intelligence reports as Abu Zubaydah talked. Al Qaeda would be busy fund-raising, so that if Mokhtar got another American operation ready, they could afford to move operatives around. Mokhtar was probably doing what Abu Zubaydah had been doing before his capture, helping Al Qaeda families escape Afghanistan.[111] Abu Zubaydah drew up an Al Qaeda organizational chart.[112] The CIA team rewarded him with a "hygiene night," during which he was allowed to clean himself and his cell.[113] He received real food, and a clean T-shirt and shorts that were not ripped off. But Abu Zubaydah had trapped himself in a vicious circle. The more he talked to keep the bad guy out, the deeper he incriminated himself, and the louder the drumbeat for harsh measures got inside Alec Station. However, Abu Zubaydah's newly reported cooperation placed the CIA in a bind. According to the cables, there was no obvious need to upgrade interrogations, unless of course Abu Zubaydah started misbehaving. To resolve this logjam Mitchell talked up a good-cop/bad-cop routine Soufan and Gaudin played one day on Abu Zubaydah, who was apparently not impressed. "He told them to get fucked and go home," Mitchell recalled. "Every time you went in there after, he would just sit there, holding his crotch."[114] This unprovable story enabled Mitchell to conclude that Abu Zubaydah had "just flat quit talking."[115]

One morning, Ali Soufan arrived and saw "a big coffin" leaning against a wall, even though mock burial had not been approved. He confronted Mitchell and threatened to have him arrested.[116] Mitchell told Soufan to back off. "He started bouncing his chest off mine, yelling threats," Mitchell claimed.[117] Soufan was almost two decades younger, but Mitchell held his ground. "Ali, you may be an FBI agent, but if you hit me I'm going to knock you on your ass," he sneered. According to Mitchell, Soufan apologized, saying: "I'm Arab, hot-blooded and quick to show my emotions." Soufan had a pithier version.

He called FBI headquarters: "Either I leave, or I arrest him." Mitchell's techniques were "borderline torture."[118] Headquarters ordered Soufan and Gaudin to leave the black site and cool off. FBI director Robert Mueller would have to be consulted. They checked in with CIA station chief Mike Winograd, who, according to Soufan, agreed that the situation was untenable. After Mueller concluded that the FBI should not get tangled up in anything resembling torture, both agents were called home. On May 25, Soufan returned to the US, but Gaudin called Chuck Frahm, the senior FBI official assigned to the Counterterrorist Center, who gave him permission to stay.[119] Gaudin did not have a "moral objection" to the techniques and said the CIA was acting professionally.[120] Mitchell said "the red-haired FBI agent" should get "the most valuable player award."[121]

After Soufan left Thailand, Mitchell also returned to the United States to formalize the hard measures everyone had talked about for so long.[122] "Every day," recalled Jose Rodriguez, "the president was asking George Tenet, 'What is Abu Zubaydah saying about the second wave of attacks and about all these other plots?' Well, he was not saying anything. We had to do something different."[123] Other reasons for the break in Abu Zubaydah's interrogation were, according to a cable from the black site, to allow the team members to "attend to personal matters," have "time off for a break," discuss "the endgame" for Abu Zubaydah and keep him "off-balance."[124]

Mitchell later claimed a variety of interrogation upgrade plans were bandied about, even though the lawyers had been focused on SERE for months. "All kinds of crazy shit like hanging people from meat hooks and putting cadavers into the cell," he recalled.[125] Someone suggested "putting Abu Zubaydah in a room full of human heads or naked women." A CIA dentist recommended more traditional torture. "If we put that electrical thing on your tooth you will feel an immense amount of pain," he explained, evoking the movie *Marathon Man*, in which Dustin Hoffman's character had his mouth drilled out by an on-the-run Nazi played by Laurence Olivier.[126] A physician recommended a drug that paralyzed the central nervous system so Abu Zubaydah could not breathe. The physician would remain on standby to administer an antidote when the victim signaled he would talk (assuming he was capable of signaling). "Some people were just suggesting sending the biggest guy in there and beating the shit out of him, do it over and over. 'Are you willing to talk? No?' Send this goon in," said Mitchell.

Even though Mitchell and Jessen had proposed SERE-style countermeasures to the CIA the previous December, and the National Security Council and the attorney general had been debating them since April 2002, he claimed that it was only now that he put forward a formal list, motivated primarily by a desire to knock sense into people.[127] "I said, 'If you going to do this, you ought to use the shit that's been used for fifty years by the SERE and hasn't produced injuries,'" he recalled. "'We use it against our own side; we use it against fucking astronauts." Given that SERE techniques, including waterboarding, had been used on thousands of US special forces with "no significant or lasting injuries," according to Mitchell, they were already three-quarters of the way to making it legal.[128]

How long would they have to do it until they were certain it had worked? asked Rodriguez. Thirty days, replied Mitchell.[129] He refused to use the word "broken," but that was what they were talking about. Mitchell admitted that thirty days was an "off-the-cuff" assessment.[130] It was also significantly longer than the "two to four days" SERE students endured "a mini experience of being detained by a hostile government." Rodriguez could work with it as long as the Justice Department approved it.[131] There was no mention of the significant body of research conducted by Mitchell's old adversary, psychiatrist Charles Morgan, an internationally recognized expert on SERE-related stress. His studies had concluded that SERE training could cause long-term harmful effects and had in some cases had even proved lethal, work that had appeared in leading scientific journals.[132] Because Rodriguez insisted on getting written legal approval from "everyone, from the president down," Abu Zubaydah would be put into isolation until everyone was ready.[133] Combined with baseline food and medical care, "AZ's impression of abandonment" would significantly help soften him up ahead of "Phase 2," recommended Mitchell.[134]

Later, Mitchell claimed he was expecting to continue working as a contract psychologist, advising interrogators on how to play Abu Zubaydah, but he said that after a second meeting on June 10, Rodriguez pulled him aside. "I was walking out of the room," Mitchell recalled.[135] "He said, 'You don't understand this is a compartmented program, you've been with the guy for months. We want you to do the techniques.'" Fredman chipped in, according to Jessen, who was also there. "An attorney in the room basically said, if you don't—if you won't do it, who's going to do it? Basically, are you willing to stand up and help or are you going to run away?"[136] The CIA wanted Mitchell to abandon his professional codes and step over the line from psychologist to interrogator.

Mitchell recalled being reluctant to commit, even though he had already played the "bad guy" role with Abu Zubaydah. "If I agreed, my life as I knew it would be over," he reflected.[137] At Fairchild, he, Jessen, and Roger Aldrich had frequently switched from playing "psychologist" to "interrogator."[138] But that was role-play. This was real. He consulted Jessen, who recalled, "I think he actually waited until the next day before he gave them his answer."[139] Mitchell claimed he became convinced only after an image of people falling from the Twin Towers came to him overnight. Whenever he talked about this tragic scene he teared up.[140] He said he would only do it if Jessen assisted him. "He was and still is my buddy and I trust him with my life," Mitchell said of his partner.[141] Rodriguez agreed without vetting Jessen, and after agreeing to terms and taking a polygraph, Mitchell returned to Thailand, where he needed to stage a "crisis precipitation" event to warn Abu Zubaydah that his cozy chitchatting with the FBI was over.[142]

CHAPTER 8

"CONTROLLED DEATH"

June 18, 2002, 4:00 P.M., Thailand

Six masked guards flew in, hooded him, hauled him upright, and cuffed him to the crossbar. Mitchell entered, swearing, kicking chairs, and tearing off Abu Zubaydah's clothes.[1] The detainee had already been shaved. When he was in role-play mode, Mitchell came across as possessed: a raging bully capable of ripping someone's head off. He yanked Abu Zubaydah forward with a "controlled attention grasp," a SERE "corrective" technique approved for real-life use by John Yoo's "anodyne note."[2] "From now on it's just you and me," Mitchell snarled.[3] Still hooded, Abu Zubaydah recognized the voice. It was the same "bad guy" who had threatened him four weeks earlier. For a moment, Abu Zubaydah hung naked from his chains in a heart-pumping daze. Mitchell then stormed out, the padlocks snapped shut, and the team went to lunch.

When the guards unchained Abu Zubaydah, he said he fell to the floor, where he was short-chained. "What I have, I give it all," he cried out as they departed.[4] No doctors or nurses or guards or bad guys, just a void of white light and earsplitting noise. Mitchell watched his reactions from the control center, reporting: "He was insulted that we would treat him that way and started to sulk."[5] For the first ten hours, Abu Zubaydah clutched his head. At two A.M., he curled up in a fetal position, facing the bars, suggesting to Mitchell that he was waiting for someone to come in.[6] But no one came, and no one spoke to him for the next forty-seven days, as his diet reverted to bare-bones nutrition.

Abu Zubaydah paced his cell as the black site emptied out. "I am in dire need to talk to someone, anyone," he once wrote in his diary. "Talk to that someone about nothing."[7] But now, there was no one at all. Adil and Bryan returned to the United States, along with all the subject-matter experts and nonessential medical staff. They took all notes and videos with them in case of a "rapid burn," CIA-speak for a sudden evacuation.[8] Journalists were sniffing around.

Langley circulated a firm message to the Justice Department, the National Security Council, and the attorney general: Abu Zubaydah had shut down—of his own volition. Only Mitchell, Steve Gaudin, the base chief, a team of guards, and a couple of medics stayed.[9] Beyond the overgrown compound, no one had any idea that one of George Tenet's "worst terrorists on the planet" was chained up inside a stinking CIA bunker. Medical attention was limited to twenty minutes a day, and dressing changes were done silently and sporadically, to emphasize a "reduction in care."[10] His waste bucket filled up. Prayer-time notifications, a "reward" for his opening up about Padilla, were withdrawn as punishment and to enhance the "impression of abandonment."[11] When Abu Zubaydah finally slept, his dreams transported him to other times and places.

Before being captured by the CIA, one of the most vivid moments of his life to date was when a mortar hit his camp while he was serving on the front lines in Gardez, Afghanistan, in December 1991. He remembered holding a water pitcher, readying to make his ablutions.[12] "It all went dark, I was no longer able to see anything." When he came around, Ibn Sheikh al-Libi was looking down at him with tears in his eyes. The two young jihadis had first met at Khaldan earlier in the year, with al-Libi graduating from training as Abu Zubaydah arrived. They had struck up a strong bond and now al-Libi padded Abu Zubaydah's head wound with cotton. "I don't know what's going on," Abu Zubaydah tried to stammer, but his tongue "couldn't carry the words out." Another brother produced a syringe and painkillers. "I didn't feel anything except darkness." Unconscious, he was evacuated by al-Libi to the Kuwaiti hospital in Peshawar; there, surgeons patched up a hole in his skull where shrapnel had entered his brain. It took weeks before he could remember his name, never mind say it. He forgot everything: the countries he had visited, the fly-by-night marriages, and even how to pray.

After several weeks, he was shifted to the House of Martyrs and faced the prospect of being a useless, crippled veteran. When he was finally able to hold a pen, he filled his diary with lists of world events and scientific discoveries, trying to put his brain back in order. A crucial day came when he was able to say "Czechoslovakia" and "Constantinople." Everyone cheered and threw cushions at his face. When he insisted on returning to Gardez, three months after being injured, al-Libi told him: "Now I know for sure you are a really crazy guy!"[13] After he returned from the front to Peshawar, he wrote to his family. He was "extremely, extremely sorry" for the long silence.[14] He talked to his older brother, Maher, who was still in Pakistan and tried again to persuade him to go home. Get a job. Marry. Start a family. Stubborn as always, Abu Zubaydah refused, although he still called Riyadh to hear everyone's voices. "My father, mother, Jilinar, Wafa, Ibtisam, Hesham and Inas also. All of them were telling me, 'Aren't you coming back to your family?'" In between the tearful pleadings was a scrap of good news. Hesham was recovering.

Abu Zubaydah wanted to repeat his training because the shrapnel injury had wiped out much of what he had learned at Khaldan, but no camp would have him. Instead, he joined a gym, but it was not enough. "By God, I didn't come to stay in Pakistan to sleep, eat and talk," he wrote in his diary.[15] Every night, he calculated how much time had passed "without digging a trench, without working on artillery guns or without attacking the enemy of God." He was ashamed. "Are you afraid of the frequent sounds of guns and bombs hovering around you in the fronts? Are you? Are you? Are you?"[16] In December 1992, Al Farouq, the Al Qaeda training camp near Kandahar, offered him a place. He did not support Al Qaeda's offensive jihad ideology, but it was the only way back into the action. Osama bin Laden was in Sudan, but his influence over global jihad was palpable. Because Abu Zubaydah could not fight, the camp commander gave him the job of kicking lazy *mujahideen* out of their tents in the morning. He slept in the kitchen to stop Tajik brothers from stealing food, jealously watching as everyone else became "angels of jihad."

While he was at Al Farouq, a terrorist attack on the other side of the world split the global jihad community. Khalid Sheikh Mohammad's nephew Ramzi Yousef detonated an explosives-laden truck in a parking garage beneath the North Tower of the World Trade Center in Manhattan on February 26, 1993. Six people died, although the tower remained standing. Yousef was a familiar face on the Peshawar scene, hanging out with Mohammad and convincing him that attacking America was the right way forward.[17] From Khartoum, bin Laden hailed the attack, enhancing the reputations of Yousef and Mohammad, and the bombing became a hot topic of conversation.

Bin Laden had already issued a fatwa calling for war against the United States, and Al Farouq instructors argued for more "offensive jihad."

Abu Zubaydah was torn. According to the Koran and the writings of Abdullah Azzam, the only justification for holy war was self-defense or defending other Muslims. The brothers did not need to remind him that he was Palestinian, and the United States backed Israel. As he engaged in fireside debates, a "crazy idea" hit him.[18] The focus of global jihad was changing, and he was already months behind in his jihad journey. Abdullah Azzam was long dead, and a lone *mujahid* without a group was useless. On September 27, 1993, he wrote in his diary: "I am thinking of joining Al Qaeda." However, the Al Farouq commander was reluctant to admit him because of his "memory loss problems and poor mental state." When he sought direction from bin Laden, Abu Zubaydah was officially turned away. Furious and embarrassed, he returned to Peshawar. "What should I tell you?" he wrote in November 1993. "I am fed up. . . . I feel hopeless and going nowhere in *my* jihad."

Ibn Sheikh al-Libi, who had recently taken over as Khaldan's emir came to his rescue. The young Palestinian needed a purpose, and the House of Martyrs guesthouse also needed an emir who could double up as Khaldan's fundraising chief. Abu Zubaydah was familiar with its operating procedures and took the job. Soon, he was busy facilitating an influx of recruits from Europe. The Balkans were disintegrating, Bosnia was bleeding, and Chechnya was descending into war. Defensive jihad camps like Khaldan filled up with European Muslims. Street-smart Abu Zubaydah knew he needed to watch his back. The hunt was on for Ramzi Yousef, who had returned to Pakistan, and anyone else connected to the World Trade Center bombing. In Brooklyn, the FBI was investigating the "Blind Sheikh," an Egyptian religious scholar who had been a student of Azzam and was linked to the attack.[19] Under intense pressure from the United States to find Yousef and clamp down on the Afghan Arabs, the Pakistani ISI carried out raids all over Peshawar, while foreign intelligence agencies tried to penetrate the camps.

Abu Zubaydah and al-Libi adopted tighter vetting procedures. European Muslims wishing to train in Khaldan were told to travel to London and obtain a recommendation from a respected jihad sheikh like Abu Muntasir al-Baluchi, an Iranian Baluchi who was related to Khalid Sheikh Mohammad and lived in Suffolk; or Abu Qatada, a Jordanian Palestinian who preached at the Four Feathers youth club in Marylebone, London.[20] They dispatched hundreds of young Muslims down what the French referred to as the "London Road," a dig at the laissez-faire attitude of the British authorities that gave fundamentalists refuge in the United Kingdom and allowed them to stream out across the globe.[21]

Abu Zubaydah met new arrivals at Islamabad airport and screened everyone again at the House of Martyrs, checking stories and connections, always searching for spies. Three kinds of Muslims came: "Fundamentalist, extremist and fanatical."[22] He regarded himself as fundamentalist and claimed he took care to avoid fanatics. The worst offenders were Algerians affiliated with the Armed Islamic Group of Algeria (GIA), he wrote, describing them as *takfiri*, Muslims who attacked other Muslims. They also killed civilians, which went completely against his agenda. After the GIA hijacked an Air France airbus with the intention of crashing it into the Eiffel Tower in December 1994, the French stepped up efforts to break the London Road, down which many GIA members traveled to the camps.[23] Abu Zubaydah banned GIA members from Khaldan, which led to the GIA issuing death threats against him.[24] But he could not stop Khaldan graduates from joining the GIA or Al Qaeda, which left him and al-Libi open to accusations that they too were connected. After the GIA attacked the Paris Métro, killing several people, the French seriously began monitoring Abu Zubaydah's communications.[25]

Aware he was under surveillance Abu Zubaydah still had to keep Khaldan and the House of Martyrs running, and he came up with inspired fund-raising ideas. Unlike other camps, Khaldan welcomed those coming for "holiday jihad," which was the equivalent of an Islamist summer retreat. Many came from rich Persian Gulf families and were put through less-intensive training that enabled them to "play with weapons" before returning home with war stories. Hassan Ghul, a Pakistani brother with Saudi papers, followed up with holiday jihadis when they got home, tapping them, their friends, and their families for funds on trips around the Gulf.[26] Treating everyone respectfully as he prepared them for the perilous crossing into Afghanistan, Abu Zubaydah told pale-skinned Chechens and Tajiks: "Go up on the roof to let the sun do its work." Smooth-faced Algerians had to stay back extra long to cultivate beards.[27] Overweight Saudis were given huge *shalwar*s to wear. Black brothers were dressed in abayas for crossing Pakistani checkpoints. Drug peddlers smuggled white converts from the United Kingdom, Sweden, and the United States. Choose a *kunya* and leave all identity documents here with me, Abu Zubaydah instructed, giving everyone a handwritten letter of introduction to Ibn Sheikh al-Libi, "the valiant brother leader of Camp Khaldan."[28]

While they were away, Abu Zubaydah studied their passports, examining the color and texture of visa stamps, the stitching, and how the holder's photograph was affixed. He paid a local forger to fashion replica stamps, hand-carved rubber glued onto blocks of wood. He wrote down passport number sequences and details of issuing authorities. He hired an artist, whose day job was selling winsome paintings in smart Islamabad hotels, to make fake passports or repurpose stolen ones, adding the finishing touches himself.[29] Abu Zubaydah was a proficient jack-of-all-trades. Although he insisted that he never discussed plots, he helped Khaldan graduates with onward travel and tickets, which further implicated him.[30] If someone wanted to reach Al Farouq, he arranged transport. Although he claimed he did not support bin Laden's desire to attack civilian targets, Abu Zubaydah's assistance was later marked against him as evidence that he supported Al Qaeda.

Under Abu Zubaydah's stewardship, the House of Martyrs became a mini United Nations for Arabs streaming to Afghanistan for jihad training from across the world, far more cohesive than the United "Infidel" Nations, as he derided the organization, which had an office down the road.[31] "Our main enemy is Israel," he told new arrivals. "We are wasting our time, efforts, souls and blood with fighting America—as done by Al Qaeda—or with fighting the rulers of the Arab countries as done by the Algerians, Libyans, Egyptians and others."[32] A credo he made sure everyone understood was that the "blood of a human, any human, it is not cheap."[33] If someone threatened your life, "you have the right to save yourself, your family, your country." But killing innocents and attacking a country that was not oppressing Muslims was *haram* (forbidden).[34]

Khaldan was open to Arab trainees approved by Abu Zubaydah without condition, but the Al Qaeda camps were dogmatic and run on rigid lines.[35] Training at Al Farouq was offered in exchange for recruitment, and new arrivals were expected to swear *bay'at* to Osama bin Laden. Once joined to bin Laden, there was no independence. Dogmatic rivalry was soothed by silly comparisons. Abu Zubaydah's Algerian friend Hider Hanani recalled how Khaldan brothers joked that Al Farouq brothers had it easy and were served cream and honey for breakfast. "At Khaldan you were lucky to get stale bread."[36] Hanani had won asylum in the United Kingdom, becoming a pivotal figure on the London Road, and used the *kunya* Abu Doha. When news about Khaldan's resurgence reached bin Laden, he vowed to seize control, and after he returned to Afghanistan in 1996, he turned up with a phalanx of Toyota pickups, lecturing al-Libi's trainees on the need to bring war to America.

The Afghan Arab circle was small, was tight-knit, and overlapped with those who advocated offensive jihad. They included Abu Muhammad al-Maqdisi, a Palestinian jihad scholar, who had previously lived in Peshawar and who had a "love-hate" relationship with the London-based Palestinian scholar Abu Qatada, who the French accused of being Al Qaeda's man in Europe.[37] Al-Maqdisi had been born in the West Bank, grew up in Kuwait, and caught bin Laden's attention with his jihad writings. Later, he became known as an ideological godfather of Al Qaeda.[38] While Abu Qatada, Abu Zubaydah, and al-Maqdisi disagreed over global strategy, they were unified about Palestine. However, the outside world was not interested in the different strains of thinking, and when the United States began to mobilize against the threat posed by bin Laden, helped by the British and the French, everyone was targeted.[39] "There are [*sic*] news about an extensive raid that will be launched by the Pakistani police in order to put pressure on Arab extremists," Abu Zubaydah wrote in his diary on May 18, 1994. His name was on a police list, and he sat in the gloom of the House of Martyrs, "waiting to be captured." Like his pet canary, he was a "prisoner inside the cage." Brothers questioned by the ISI warned him to be extra careful. "They told me the Pakistanis always felt the left sides of their heads to see if they had the 'Abu Zubaydah scar,'" he said, referencing his old war wound. But although his name was well known and his voice had been recorded, no one had his picture, so he went out dressed smartly, carrying his briefcase. The police were much less likely to pick up a Middle Eastern businessman than someone looking like an Afghan Arab," recalled Abu Zubaydah's friend Hider Hanani.[40]

"The difficulty and danger were outside where all the intelligence agencies were searching for the very poor and innocent me, when all I do is run a nursery for children," Abu Zubaydah reflected wryly.[41] "Although they were children with long beards, they were also tall, strong, most were married, and some possessed terrorists' ideologies. . . . Poor children, aren't they?" When the police first raided the House of Martyrs in 1994, missing him by minutes but snagging Ibn Sheikh al-Libi's passport, Abu Zubaydah knew he needed to get smarter. He charmed a UN official into issuing him an Afghan refugee card. "I say to myself if these people knew that they are now helping the emir of the martyrs' house they would drop dead with anger," he gloated.[42] Some of Mitchell's later intuitions about his arrogance and ability to deceive were well founded.

His family still sent letters. "My son you are a piece of my heart and the reason behind my existence," wrote his father, despite having rejected him earlier. His sisters had married, and some had children. Maher had qualified as a doctor, was married and working toward becoming a leading orthopedic surgeon.[43] Even Sultan, his youngest brother, had graduated high school and was planning to study medicine. Happy family news made him happy, and sad. "I miss my mother's smile, my father's laugh, the yelling of my younger siblings and the look of my sisters sitting at their study desk or arguing or kidding around as innocent little children," he wrote. "I also miss my mother's cooking."

Abu Zubaydah really wanted to marry and start a family but always held back. "I can't put my son in any school without papers," he asserted.[44] "What if my wife wants to travel to her country, I cannot go with her." Famous for supplying fake passports, Abu Zubaydah was too notorious to travel with one himself. To get out of Pakistan and make a fresh start, which he craved, he needed a real travel document. Palestinian Egyptian refugee papers were so useless he needed a visa even "to go to a bathroom," and his Saudi residency certificate was long out of date.[45] The stolen Kuwaiti passport from Mysore had also expired, and the fake Saudi papers he used these days were good enough to open bank accounts and get him "inside," meaning Afghanistan, but nowhere else. He called home again but did not recognize the voice that answered. "Who is this? Hesham! 'God almighty! You are a man with a deep voice.'" Hesham had recovered from cancer, but after several years out of school, he was listless and getting into trouble with the authorities. Their father was angry. Abu Zubaydah felt guilty at not being there for his brother.

Back in the House of Martyrs, he cut a dark figure "on the revolving chair behind the office desk." Although he called it "my room," he shared it with six other brothers, which meant no girlfriends. When he occasionally got time to himself, he brooded, sensing there was no way back from the choices he had made. "The time is 8.30 in the evening," he wrote in July 1994.

"The scene: a gloomy person wearing a black Afghan dress . . . he is sitting on the ground, writing in his diary notebook, leaning on a diplomatic brief-case, which is broken at one side." His darkness frightened new arrivals.[46] Aimen Dean, a seventeen-year-old Saudi whose family had migrated to the United Kingdom, recalled "an unsmiling man" with "menacing eyes" like a cobra.[47] Khalid Sheikh Mohammad, who had turned up in Bosnia in 1995, had given Dean details of how to get onto the London Road, and he arrived in Peshawar with a genuine British passport. Abu Zubaydah inspected it, suspicious but envious too. "Over the course of a very uncomfortable hour he grilled me," recalled Dean. Later, Abu Zubaydah took pity. Frail-looking, Dean soon fell ill with malaria, and Abu Zubaydah gave him his bank account details so Dean's brother could wire money for medicine. When Dean's condition worsened, Abu Zubaydah lent Dean his battered Nokia cell phone so he could call home. These acts of generosity would rebound on Abu Zubaydah after Dean joined Al Qaeda, and then agreed to spy for MI6.[48]

As Osama bin Laden advanced his cause, the ISI and the "backwards Pakistani police" began to press in.[49] In 1995, Abu Zubaydah hid for months among the Afghan refugees camped east of Peshawar at Pabbi, where Abdullah Azzam, Azzam's mother, and two of his sons were buried in the martyrs' graveyard. One day, Abu Zubaydah was arrested at a checkpoint. No charming words, UN refugee cards, or bribes could shake him free. He was an Afghan Arab, living suspiciously among refugees, and the police took him in. In his pockets were the rubber seals he used for stamping fake passports.

"I need to go to the bathroom," he insisted as he entered the police sta-tion.[50] "I will urinate in my pants." Inside a bathroom, he peeled the seals off their wooden blocks and flushed them away. He hid the blocks on a windowsill, before being taken to Safwat Ghayur, an officer with "a cunning smile." Ghayur searched Abu Zubaydah and found another seal.[51] "Are you one of those Afghani Arabs?" he asked. Abu Zubaydah tried to flash his UN refugee card. Ghayur flung it aside. The officer was wise to all such tricks.

Handcuffed to a constable, Abu Zubaydah was driven around the city, and paraded before police snitches. They were too scared to identify him, so the police demanded he take them to the "Arab *mujahideen*" house. In-stead, he directed them to an irrelevant address. Furious, they returned to

the station, where he was beaten. He feigned seizures. They kept him overnight in a stinking lockup, with his hands cuffed up above his head, his first
experience of standing sleep deprivation.

The following day, Ghayur produced the wooden blocks jettisoned in
the bathroom. Abu Zubaydah was brought blindfolded into a room filled
with American voices. "What do you know about the House of Martyrs?"
Ghayur demanded. "I heard about it," he murmured. A cane lashed his calf.
"What do you know about the emir of the house?" A pause. "I don't know
him." Another whack. Suspecting Ghayur would not stop until he gave him
something, Abu Zubaydah admitted he had trained at Al Farouq but was
wounded in battle. "Who was your trainer?" His response was sly. "Mahmoud el-Meliguy," he said, using his villainous Egyptian-actor alter ego.
"What nationality?" "Bangladesh." The police knew no better. "Good, what
kind of training?" He pointed to his head injury, with a shaking hand. "My
teacher said I was not fit for training because I am unable to comprehend."
The questioners circled back to the House of Martyrs. "Who was the person
in charge?" He gave the name of a character in an Arab play. "How did you
become emir?" He was not an emir. "Or anything else." He heard the Americans leaving.

When the blindfold came off, Ghayur was furious. "Why are you trying
to embarrass us?" As a doctor checked Abu Zubaydah over, he slipped into
righteous mode. "I am not an animal that you beat in the morning and feed
in the evening." He refused food and medication. Ghayur set in motion deportation proceedings and dispatched him to Peshawar Central Jail.

Three months later, Ghayur learned that his troublesome Arab was a
stateless Palestinian, so no country wanted him. Let him rot, said Ghayur.
Abu Zubaydah had one more trick up his sleeve. When an Italian UN official, Mr. Fernando, visited the prison looking for refugees wrongly jailed
by the police, Abu Zubaydah produced his UN refugee card. Fernando eyed
him nervously, asking if he was an Afghan Arab. "I am scared of them; they
are fundamentalists," Abu Zubaydah lied. "Good! Be aware of them," Fernando replied. "God forbid! I hate terrorism," Abu Zubaydah continued,
making a fearful face. "You look like a terrorist," Fernando said uncertainly.
Abu Zubaydah smiled. His long beard merely reflected how long he'd been
in the prison. In January 1996, Fernando got him released.

June 2002, CIA headquarters, Langley, Virginia

The CIA plan was coming together nicely. Jose Rodriguez took Jim Mitchell up to the executive floor to brief George Tenet. Mitchell could not give the exact date, because the CIA was "funny about dates," but it was early June 2002, and they met in the director's wood-paneled suite, which had a commanding view over the Potomac.[52] John Rizzo was there too.[53] Two months on from the first request to make harsh interrogations legal, Rizzo was still working things through with John Yoo, ahead of yet another National Security Council discussion. "By the summer, we were all collectively seized by this notion of, well, if this is the only thing that is going to work," Rizzo recalled. Mitchell, who wore his only decent suit (black and crumpled), demonstrated SERE techniques. Rizzo said Mitchell used his hands and got out of his seat. He reenacted walling and waterboarding, reassuring Tenet and Rizzo that "all the techniques we were discussing had been used on thousands of US military personnel" for fifty-plus years.[54] There had been no serious injuries, and no one had suffered any lasting mental harm. Nobody mentioned Charles Morgan's contradictory research.

Tenet and Rizzo retreated to the inner sanctum, leaving the door open. According to Mitchell, the CIA director made a show of rummaging around for cigars, while murmuring: "Make sure this is legal." Rizzo recalled: "Once the director made it clear he wanted it, I had to make it legal."[55] Since the Justice Department was unwilling to provide advance declination of prosecution, another way would have to be found to reach the "golden shield."[56] Rizzo knew the risks involved. After World War II, several Japanese generals had been executed for authorizing "water torture," and during the war in Vietnam, a US soldier had been court-martialed for waterboarding a prisoner.[57] In 1984, a Texas sheriff was given a ten-year sentence for using "water torture" on suspected criminals.[58] However, the latest draft of Yoo's opinion still did not meet necessary legal standards.

Around the time of the Tenet briefing, Bruce Jessen joined Mitchell at Langley.[59] In a "sensitive compartmented information facility," they and unidentified CIA staff formalized the final menu of techniques. Mitchell recalled being told not to hold back. "They were going to go right up to the line of what was legal, put their toes on it, and lean forward," he remembered.[60]

He claimed they wanted to call their techniques "coercive physical pressures," the same as at SERE school, but the CIA wanted a more palatable term. Someone came up with "enhanced interrogation techniques," or EITs. "It's a euphemism," Mitchell explained. "Takes the sting out of things. It's one thing to say we killed children. It's better to say collateral damage."[61]

Mitchell and Jessen's EITs were designed as a journey into the dark, leading the detainee through "a Pavlovian process to condition compliance" with twelve techniques that, if "effectively orchestrated," would "convey the feeling of helplessness."[62] It began with the "controlled attention grasp" that Mitchell had already tested out on Abu Zubaydah to good effect, then progressed to the "facial hold," "facial slap," and "wall standing." Other techniques were more difficult to tone down. "Walling" involved pulling the detainee forward by a collar and "bouncing" him off a prefabricated wall. Only the detainee's shoulder blades should make contact, otherwise the technique could "hurt his head."[63] In SERE school the "collar" was the student's uniform, but since Abu Zubaydah would be naked, they would fashion a "safety collar" from a rolled-up towel wrapped in duct tape.[64] "Cramped confinement" referred to the coffin. The promised "greater leeway" had come through, and it could be used for up to eighteen hours a day. They also had permission to use a much smaller box, the size of a dog kennel or crate.[65] The *Guinness Book of World Records* noted the record for voluntary sleep deprivation was 205 hours, while the CIA limit was eventually extended to 264 hours.[66] Playing on Abu Zubaydah's cultural sensitivities, extreme fastidiousness and fears, there was also "use of diapers" and "insects." Anything that could humiliate him could aid a process based on degrading and ultimately breaking US special operators during training.

Abu Zubaydah had written of terrifying nightmares he had had when he was a teenager about drowning, and made a reference in his diary to "swimming in devil's lake (drowning)."[67] Mitchell and Jessen's most controversial technique was the waterboard. Although they had never used it, Mitchell and Jessen were very familiar with it, describing it as "historically the most effective interrogation technique used by the US military."[68] At the navy survival school in San Diego, the only place in the country authorized to use it, regulations were strict. Before getting on the board, students were medically screened, then ordered to raise their heart rate by doing jumping jacks.[69] Once the subject was strapped down, only "two canteen cups (one pint each) of water may be slowly poured directly onto the student's face from a height of about twelve inches."[70] There should be no attempt "to direct the stream of water into the student's nostrils or mouth." If a cloth was placed across the student's face, it could be left for only twenty seconds, and the technique could be applied only twice. "A student may be threatened at a later time with the waterboard and may even be strapped to the board again but under no circumstances may water actually be applied." Before subjecting Abu Zubaydah to the waterboard Mitchell and Jessen would need official training in order to be "certified." They also wrote up "mock burial."

Mitchell went back to headquarters on July 1, 2002, to introduce his new "bad guy," Jessen, to the team.[71] Adil, Bryan, Steve Gaudin, Kirk Hubbard, Alfreda Bikowsky, Jose Rodriguez, Marty Martin, Jonathan Fredman, Jennifer Matthews, and Terry DeMay were all present.[72] Jessen would be "more combative" than Mitchell was as "bad guy" and was "well-versed in conducting SERE-type hostile interrogations."[73] According to Mitchell's nemesis Charles Morgan, some time before he signed his CIA contract, Jessen was called out at a SERE conference for being "unethical" because he wanted to play interrogator and psychologist roles simultaneously.[74] Asked to choose between the two, he had reregistered as an interrogator.[75] Mitchell told everyone his partner had the "one-of-a-kind" skill set this mission required.[76] He was an ice climber, marathon runner, and martial-arts aficionado. He had a "dark side," a quick temper and extraordinary stamina.[77] The only other person Abu Zubaydah would see from now on was "a medical expert with SERE experience" who had been employed by the Office of Technical Service since the Latin America interrogator-training program.[78] He has never been identified, but Abu Zubaydah called him the "bad doctor."[79] Jessen, like Mitchell, insisted their plan was carefully modulated. The aim of Phase 2 was "not to beast people and not to technique people," he stated.[80]

While Justice Department attorneys worked on making Mitchell and Jessen's EITs legal, CIA attorneys remained open to new ideas. "Rule out nothing whatsoever that you feel may be effective," they advised, then "come on back and we will get you the approvals."[81] The legal team was available "24/7." US law was "more permissive than, say, the comparable European or Israeli law," reported Fredman, referring to a Department of Justice analysis of famous torture test cases. In 1978, in a case brought against the British security services in Northern Ireland, the European Court of Human Rights had ruled that wall standing, hooding, subjection to continuous loud noise, deprivation of sleep, and deprivation of food and drink were not torture.[82] However, in 1999, the Supreme Court of Israel had ruled that "violently shaking suspects, forcing suspects to crouch on the tips of their toes for long intervals, excessively tightening handcuffs, depriving suspects of sleep, and placing suspects in the 'Shabach' position [strapped to a chair in a stress position]" were torture.[83] Just because the Israelis were prevented from using certain methods on Palestinian prisoners did not mean the CIA could not use them on its Palestinian detainee, reported Counterterrorist Center attorneys.

Mitchell took Jessen to the Office of Technical Service to "hammer out" his contract. "I hadn't done this before," Jessen stated. Like Mitchell, he wrote out his terms on yellow legal paper. The CIA reps said, "hurry, hurry"; they finished the contract, and he signed it.[84] He and Mitchell then attended a "bunch more meetings," and took part in training sessions run by JPRA survival instructors at an off-site facility. According to a later inquiry, on July 1 and 2, 2002, two Spokane-based SERE survival instructors, Joe Witsch and Gary Percival, conducted training sessions designed by Jessen and Chris Wirts.[85] Like Wirts, Witsch and Percival had worked with Mitchell and Jessen for years. Elsewhere, Percival described Mitchell as his mentor.[86] Earlier in the year, Jessen, Witsch, and Wirts, JPRA's chief of operations, had developed SERE-based training packages for military interrogators heading to Guantánamo and suggested an alternative detention and interrogation setup. Jessen had to get specific permission from his commander, Randy Moulton, to attend the CIA training course. Moulton in turn informed Donald Rumsfeld's general counsel, Jim Haynes.[87] There was clearly some nervousness involved. To "prevent compromise and inadvertent modification of JPRA's charter," Moulton was informed, "personnel will avoid linking JPRA directly to this training."[88] He was also advised that, since "JPRA may be called upon in extremis to actually participate in future exploitation of foreign prisoners," he would have to seek "[Secretary of Defense] policy determination," as "this request would clearly fall outside JPRA's chartered responsibilities."

Joe Witsch noted that most CIA participants on the July 1 and 2 training course had "little to no . . . experience" in interrogation, although a few personnel had "recently returned from conducting actual interrogations in

Afghanistan," where the Bagram Collection Point, a detention sorting facility at Bagram Air Base, was overflowing.[89] The SERE experts brought everyone up to speed on "deprivation techniques," "exploitation and questioning techniques," "developing countermeasures to resistance techniques," and covered the "full spectrum [of] exploitation." They role-played "body slaps, face slaps, hooding, stress positions, walling, immersion in water, stripping, isolation, and sleep deprivation, among others." Witsch acted as the "beater" while Percival played the "beatee."[90]

The trainers also "provided instruction" on waterboarding. Moulton reported that the CIA had asked for help "because of the urgent need to extract information from captured Al Qaeda operatives, and because JPRA has the sole repository of the required skill set."[91] The need was so urgent, in fact, that Abu Zubaydah, the only high-value detainee in CIA custody, was at that very moment sitting on the floor of his cell in Thailand not being interrogated by anyone. The JPRA course was entirely designed around Abu Zubaydah's next Phase 2 interrogation, which had waterboarding at its core. But the trouble was that Witsch and Percival had never officially done waterboarding, according to a subsequent inquiry, "and would not have been qualified to do so at SERE school."[92] Questioned by the Senate Armed Services Committee (SASC) in 2007 as part of an eighteen-month-long investigation into the handling of War on Terror detainees, Witsch was unable to recall the regulations stipulated by the US Navy SERE school, where the maximum pour time was twenty seconds and the maximum number of pours was two.[93] Chris Wirts provided more clarity years later when he explained that ahead of the CIA course, he had sought out a retired SERE instructor who still lived in Spokane and had taught waterboarding at Fairchild during the 1960s.[94]

The navy and CIA guidelines did not match up in several ways. Mitchell and Jessen, who also were coached by the retired instructor, stated that "once the cloth is saturated and completely covering the mouth and nose, subject would be exposed to 20 to 40 seconds of restricted airflow" by water being poured to "keep the cloth saturated."[95] There was no reference to a maximum number of pours or the navy stipulation that "no attempt will be made to direct the stream of water into the student's nostrils or mouth," but they did state that each waterboard "application" should last only up to twenty minutes.[96] When JPRA wrote up instructions ahead of another CIA waterboarding course in July 2002, it recommended one and half gallons rather than the navy's maximum of two pints.[97] In 2007, when questioned by Senate investigators, authorized US Navy SERE instructors vehemently disagreed with using the technique on real detainees. Malcolm Nance, an instructor at San Diego, who had used the procedure on hundreds of trainees, said that even when done properly it was "controlled death."[98] "Waterboarding is torture . . . period," he wrote.[99] It belonged in training. "Period." He described Mitchell and Jessen as "theoretical practitioners" and characterized the CIA approach as "Tom Clancy" procedures, the logic being, "if it works in the book, it must work in real life."[100]

As well as trainee interrogators, two unidentified CIA legal personnel attended the July 1 and 2 course. They requested permission to "outline the legal limits of physiological and psychological pressures." Later, Witsch reported that the unnamed lawyers gave significant advice to everyone attending the CIA course.[101] Under international law, torture was defined as a "capital crime" and could result in a death sentence for those convicted, so everyone had to make sure not to step over the line. "An eye opener to say the least," reflected Witsch, who wrote an after-action memo for Chris Wirts.[102]

Mitchell and Jessen returned to Langley on July 8 for an "all hands" meeting at which they outlined their EIT roadmap.[103] Mitchell would "kick off" by warning Abu Zubaydah worse was coming if he did not reveal details of future attacks, before locking him in his coffin for several hours.[104] Then, the second "bad guy," Jessen, would introduce himself with a "facial slap." Together, they would then conduct several "fear and despair rounds," followed by "threat and rescue," which included mock burial in a box "that resembles a coffin."[105] Care needed to be taken when shoveling dirt onto the box "without blocking the air holes or actually burying the individual."[106] Decisions about individual techniques would be "fluid" and tailored around Abu Zubaydah's reactions.[107]

Even though the open wound in Abu Zubaydah's leg still measured six inches by three inches, and contained a large blister filled with exudate, medical care would be set to the legal minimum.[108] "We must act in a way outside AZ's expectations and follow through on our threats," reported Mitchell, who was unhappy that previous deployment of his "bad guy role" had "lacked the promised repercussions."[109] This was not lost on Abu Zubaydah, who had finally "scored a victory" by getting the medical team in Thailand to examine "blood in his semen."[110] Pandering to Abu Zubaydah's hypochondria was a mistake. The plan was submitted to the seventh floor for approval.[111] John Rizzo and Jonathan Fredman were scheduled to meet with John Bellinger at the National Security Council on July 13, and George Tenet was scheduled to brief National Security Advisor Condoleezza Rice four days later.[112] Only one critical detail was outstanding: Would the FBI be participating?

On July 8, FBI director Robert Mueller also visited Langley. Mitchell and Steve Gaudin both attended the meeting, in George Tenet's office.[113] "EITs were discussed," recalled Mitchell. "Mueller said, 'We don't want to do it' and he left." Mitchell was disappointed. "I said to Steve I was sorry he wasn't going to be there because I liked him," he recalled. "He told me he was also sorry he wasn't going to participate."[114] The meeting marked the official end of the FBI's involvement in the secret CIA program, but special agents including Ali Soufan and Steve Gaudin continued to question detainees at CIA black sites.[115] Gaudin recalled of the Mueller meeting: "The other camp won. The only way we're going to get Abu Zubaydah to reveal the crown jewels is to send him to SERE school."[116]

After the July 8 "all hands" meeting, Jessen returned to the Office of Technical Service to sign a new nondisclosure agreement; he was "read-in" to relevant special access programs, and his contract was set at $135,000. Mitchell's salary jumped to $257,600.[117] "I don't remember exactly when, but we were on a plane leaving the country shortly after that," recalled Jessen.[118] Inside his bunker, Abu Zubaydah was going crazy. "I spent one month or more in the vertigo of noise and thoughts," he recalled. "I didn't know where I was. . . . I almost didn't know who I was."[119]

CHAPTER 9

"BOO BOO"

During the forty-seven days Abu Zubaydah spent alone in Thailand, he revisited his troubled relationship with Osama bin Laden, trying to understand how the CIA had reached the conclusions he was Number Three in Al Qaeda. Rather than being close, or "worse even than Osama bin Laden," as characterized by Mike Scheuer and Alec Station, Abu Zubaydah insisted that the only thing he and bin Laden had really shared was "brotherhood in God," and a mutual distrust and suspicion.[1] He had never forgiven bin Laden for refusing to admit him into Al Qaeda in 1993, according to Ali Soufan, and soon after that the Al Qaeda leader had ordered an investigation into the House of Martyrs' finances, distrustful of Abu Zubaydah because of his Palestinian heritage and suspecting him of stealing money.[2] Their next confrontation happened when the Al Qaeda leader returned to Afghanistan in 1996, after several years in Sudan. He had no cash, as his bank accounts in Khartoum were all frozen, and no army, because his *mujahideen* all had malaria.[3] In contrast, Khaldan was flowing with fighters and healthy streams of funding from Europe and holiday jihadis. Jealous, bin Laden offered al-Libi and Abu Zubaydah the opportunity to swear *bay'at* and hand over their camp, in return for Al Qaeda's protection. "The brothers inside [Afghanistan] requested me to deliberate the issue," Abu Zubaydah wrote his diary. He refused the offer, without even meeting bin Laden.

After Al Qaeda issued its famous fatwa against the "Jews and Crusaders" in February 1998, bin Laden reapplied pressure on Khaldan's joint emirs as he exhorted all jihadists to emulate World Trade Center bomber Ramzi Yousef and "bring the fighting to America."[4] He made good on his promise on August 7, 1998, when suicide bombers drove explosive-laden trucks into the US embassies in Nairobi and Dar es Salaam. "Forgive me, I just received a news item that made me halt speaking," wrote Abu Zubaydah in his diary, shocked that bin Laden had flung noble jihad into the mud by killing innocent civilians. On August 20, 1998, American cruise missiles slammed into targets in Sudan and Afghanistan. Bin Laden's Al Farouq camp was obliterated. Would-be jihadis flooded into Peshawar, and Khaldan was compelled to offer them training. "I can barely withstand the pressure on my nerves," Abu Zubaydah complained. Worried about being watched as he was dragged into bin Laden's war, he moved the House of Martyrs to Islamabad and hid his diary. "I am concerned that someone would read what I write you," he wrote in it. "There are issues I cannot tell you."

Stuck in Pakistan without a passport, Abu Zubaydah could see that bin Laden had Khaldan in his sights. More worrying, Abu Zubaydah was exposed. Bin Laden was holed up with Khalid Sheikh Mohammad in Kandahar, secretly discussing the "Planes Operation," the "Boats Operation," and other plots in the Al Qaeda playbook.[5] Many of those who had once populated Peshawar's Afghan Arab scene were gone. Abu Muhammad al-Maqdisi was in prison in Amman, plotting mayhem with a crazy young Jordanian acolyte called Abu Musab al-Zarqawi.[6] Ramzi Yousef had been captured in Islamabad trying to stuff explosives into a doll and was sold to the Americans for a multimillion-dollar bounty.[7] After years of welcoming all, Abu Zubaydah wandered streets late at night, afraid to return to his own guesthouse. "Do they know the [address]?" he wrote. "Will they search the house?" Whenever a brother flew out of Pakistan, he worried. "Will they be caught? Will they know his passport is not original?" He dyed his hair blond, shaved off his beard, and stayed inside, reading the newspaper "with a passion."[8] But because brothers always needed helping, he still had to use his phone and email accounts. "The clouds of trouble started to return quickly," he wrote, after some of those connected to the embassy bombings were linked to Khaldan.[9]

To relieve the tension, a friend bought him a copy of *Rambo III*, set during the Soviet-Afghan War. "I laughed . . . I laughed . . . my eyes became teary," he recalled.[10] But the laughing did not last long, as the pressure increased. He derided the American press for claiming the Al Farouq missile attacks were a sideshow to the Bill Clinton–Monica Lewinsky scandal. "They said: we don't need a war for the sake of Monica. How dumb the Americans are—people, nation and leaders."[11] He understood bin Laden's strategy of drawing in the United States, but his inside track would not save him, as the Al Qaeda leader and twenty others were indicted.[12] Abu Zubaydah knew many of them, and the indictment described Al Qaeda as an "organization that grew out of the Services Office," a reference to Abdullah Azzam's old Makhtab al-Khidamat. A $5 million reward was offered for information leading to bin Laden's arrest, and US newspapers identified Khaldan as the place where the embassy bombings were plotted and the 1993 World Trade Center attack too. Abu Zubaydah's connections to Khaldan meant he stood out like a homing beacon.

As the dragnet tightened, brothers he had once helped turned against him, among them Aimen Dean, the British Saudi recruit, who had sworn *bay'at* to bin Laden. He had been at Al Farouq when the missiles screamed down in August 1998, and wanted to go home. During a last supper in Peshawar, Khalid Sheikh Mohammad told Dean that jihad had come of age. "The attacks in Africa have energized the whole Muslim world. . . . Nairobi and Dar es Salaam was just the opening salvo, *insh'allah*."[13] Dean wanted out, but Abu Zubaydah still held the young man's passport. Scared to tell Abu Zubaydah he was bailing out, Dean made up a story about having a medical appointment in Qatar, and his guilt evaporated as soon as he shut the door on the House of Martyrs emir.

Arriving in Doha, Dean was stopped by Qatari security officials tipped off by the French, who had been watching Abu Zubaydah for years. Jean-Louis Bruguiere, France's leading investigating magistrate for counterterrorism, explained, "Abu Zubaydah was far from innocent, but he was always external, a bridge. He was not inside Al Qaeda or privy to their plots."[14] Bruguiere's focus was on shutting down the London Road, because so many jihadis from France's former North African colonies used it to seek training in Afghanistan, and he was frustrated by Britain's reluctance to act against Abu Qatada, whom he regarded as Al Qaeda's man in Europe. "The British had not yet been attacked and did not want to open a foreign front," Bruguiere said. "Later, they regretted this." Dean gave the Qataris details of Abu Zubaydah's account at Faysal Bank in Peshawar. The Qataris passed the information to the French, who strong-armed the bank into handing over a photograph Abu Zubaydah had used to open his account in 1998. It was the first confirmed image of the elusive Khaldan gatekeeper; he was wearing his businessman guise. Now they had his picture as well as his voice, and French intelligence shared the information with the CIA.

Back in the United Kingdom, Dean gave up more compromising and incorrect information. Abu Zubaydah's checkpoint passes and hospital access were all facilitated by the ISI, he said, a useful pressure point to use against Islamabad. He also explained the importance of Abu Zubaydah's holiday jihadis, and he named Hassan Ghul, the Pakistani with Saudi papers. Money also flowed from Britain, said Dean. Abu Qatada, the Palestinian jihad orator based at the Four Feathers youth club in London, was one conduit. Moazzam Begg, a British Pakistani who ran an Islamic bookshop in Birmingham, was another.[15] Dean estimated that Khaldan raised $1.5 million a year from the United Kingdom and that the camp leadership had issued fatwas to UK mosques, saying credit-card fraud and theft were permitted if a percentage of the proceeds went to jihad. Abu Qatada's money was delivered via a Costco warehouse in London, according to Dean. Moazzam Begg's cash arrived via an Islamic charity in Afghanistan. Begg's bookshop was later targeted by MI5 (Britain's domestic intelligence agency), which raided it several times in unsuccessful attempts to tie its owner to Al Qaeda.[16] The evidential case against alleged "terrorist mastermind" Abu Zubaydah was building.

———◆———

The other thing that preoccupied Abu Zubaydah while he was alone in his cell for forty-seven days during the summer of 2002 was a secret he had not even told his diary. In September 1999, he started the fifth volume of his diary, writing of his desire to fall in love and marry. It was a code for something he dared not write down, fearing his words could endanger the most important thing in his life: his secret Swedish wife.

He never said how or when he met her. But she was beautiful, had blue eyes, blond hair, and was a medical doctor, maybe working for a relief agency in one of the Afghan refugee camps. She converted to Islam, chose a Muslim name, and fell utterly in love with "Hani." He revealed her existence to his diary only twenty years later, remembering with profound sadness how she would throw "herself into my arms . . . as soon as she sees me."[17] He told her "everything," even about the fly-by-night marriages, which they both agreed to call his "sub-zero Hani" period, and she told him "everything," in return. They married in secret, with only two witnesses signing the paperwork, Ibn Sheikh al-Libi and his son, and then rented a house in Islamabad, which Abu Zubaydah called their "marriage nest," and a "little paradise." She was "my friend, love and my (real) wife," he reflected. It was a "lovely period of time." She was "the only person who made me abandon you," he wrote in Volume 13 of his diary, in his Guantánamo cell. They set about making "birds," meaning babies.

Between October and December 1999 he wrote nothing at all.[18] He knew she was taking inordinate risks in "being a terrorist's wife," and he hid her from everyone, even his family in Riyadh. When she became pregnant, they began making plans to leave Pakistan. He searched around for real passports, and listened to the baby moving about inside her. "I was hoping for a daughter (a girl) and she was hoping for a son (a boy)," he remembered.[19] "She was sure he is a boy because he was kicking inside her womb." Muting their excitement was a fear their unborn son might one day become a target for the Americans. "Surely they would say we must kill him to protect the national security of [the] US, and Israel and Mars, 'perhaps,'" he wrote. The life he had chosen impacted everyone close to him. They needed to find sanctuary somewhere where America could never reach them.

Since the baby's father was "a terrorist," and the much sought after House of Martyrs emir, his wife could not go to a Pakistani hospital to give birth. So her mother, who was also a doctor, flew over from Stockholm. She was alarmed as soon as she arrived, telling her extraordinary new son-in-law, "Your life is dangerous and so hard and my daughter, because she loves you, chooses to stay with you." Every time he left the house, her daughter became petrified. "She is worried, fears for you, and cries," said her mother, frightened by the strength of her daughter's feelings, and fearful that her daughter might lose the baby. "If you really love her, let her live her life peacefully (but away from you, please, my son)," she pleaded.

Her fears turned out to be well founded. One day, while Abu Zubaydah was out on House of Martyrs duties, Pakistani police commandos and ISI officials stormed their marital house. His wife and her mother were roughed up and interrogated. "She got a miscarriage because of (the horror)," Abu Zubaydah wrote more than twenty years later.[20] The raid left her in such a bad physical state that she returned to Sweden, and spent time in intensive care. He was devastated. But the experience was a huge wake-up call. This was "selfish love." His mother-in-law was right. He could not put the woman he loved through any more anguish, and he divorced her to protect her from the "danger, which is around me everywhere." He then went into hiding.

However, she would not give up on Hani, and later returned to Islamabad. For days, she paced outside their "little paradise," praying he would return. He was already there, watching from a car across the street with blacked out windows, wrestling with himself not to open the door. "I saw her there, walking around the place in circles," he recollected. He watched as she wiped away tears with a red handkerchief. "I was ready to pay all that I have to get that handkerchief . . . since I couldn't get its owner," he wrote years later. His heart beat so loudly, he worried she would hear it. "Imagine, if I was weak for a moment. . . . Imagine, I opened the car's door . . . and I call her with her original Swedish name, or the new name that she chooses for herself before our marriage." He knew she would rush straight into his arms.

Day after day she returned, "spinning around our marriage residence like a bee." He was always there, watching from inside the car, trying to keep himself together and not open the door. Eventually, she returned to Sweden. "Goodbye, you who owns the red handkerchief, go well and safe from Allah," he reflected. He had saved the love of his life from being eaten by himself, "the wolf," but he was heartbroken.

———◆———

On Christmas Eve 1999, Abu Zubaydah returned to his diary, noting that he had just called his family in Riyadh. He did not mention the trauma of his marriage, her miscarriage, or the raid, but he owed them an explanation, since his name was splashed all over newspapers because of the so-called millennium plots in Jordan and America. His parents also had bad news for him. Hesham was living illegally in the United States, oblivious to the mounting danger of being an Abu Zubaydah. "He bears the same family last name and this issue might affect him," Abu Zubaydah wrote.[21] Because several of those arrested in the millennium plot investigation in Jordan had worked or studied in America, Muslims across the States were under scrutiny. Hesham, who had entered the country on a student visa in July 1998, had failed to register for his English-language course in Florida, and overstayed his six-month visa, which made him look suspicious, although he was entirely innocent. When Abu Zubaydah tracked him down in Portland, Oregon, where he worked illegally in a gas station, Hesham was delighted to hear from him.[22] He did not read newspapers, and was solely focused on his American dream. He also had a pregnant girlfriend, a white American woman, who was supporting his application for a green card. But they were broke, fighting over money, and his immigration status. Abu Zubaydah promised to rustle up some cash, although he felt "obligated" to do more. He had been negligent about his real family far too long. "I am thinking of bringing [Hesham] here," he told his diary. But he knew jihad was not for his unpredictable younger brother. When they shared a bedroom as teenagers, Hesham had "barely prayed."

Abu Zubaydah called Wafa, their sister, in Riyadh. When she agreed to wire family money to tide Hesham over, he rang Portland to pass on the good news. Then, he refocused on his own security, hopping from Islamabad to Lahore to Karachi in search of a safer place to live, trying to put all the recent trauma behind him. When he learned that Osama bin Laden had persuaded the Taliban to close down Khaldan, he was infuriated, and set out to confront the Al Qaeda leader at his base in Kandahar, traveling via Quetta and crossing into Afghanistan at Chaman.[23] Better to focus on fighting repression and injustice than to wallow in private sadness. Back in Portland, Hesham, who spent the family's cash on a Mustang, remained ignorant about the dangers that his brother's chosen life—and the two phone calls—had put him in.[24]

Arriving in Afghanistan in July 2000, Abu Zubaydah trailed bin Laden for weeks. The Taliban's influence was so great that he barely recognized the country he had first visited a decade earlier. "I felt like a stranger . . . even to the brothers." The more he saw, the more he worried that "those who preach ignorance and lack experience" were taking over. "I feel frightened," he wrote in his diary, which was back to being his only friend now that his wife was gone.[25] As always when he went "inside," he lost track of time, "as time has no value there," and he wrote of being "depressed," although he did not tell his diary it was sadness for the loss of his wife and unborn son. "I cannot talk to you about everything," he explained.[26]

On October 12, 2000, Abu Zubaydah learned why bin Laden had been so hard to pin down.[27] "A suicide mission carried out by two brothers in a boat or a small yacht killing 17 Americans and injuring 33," he wrote after hearing of the USS *Cole* attack in Yemen. The "Boats Operation" had come to fruition. He met bin Laden the following month. By now, the sheikh was in hiding, and the CIA was plotting to assassinate him with a drone. Al Qaeda's real Number Three, Abu Hafs al-Masri, reportedly greeted Abu Zubaydah with sarcasm: "So this is the famous Abu Zubaydah who everyone is talking about."[28] When Abu Zubaydah asked to reopen Khaldan, bin Laden first asked him to swear *bay'at* to Al Qaeda. Abu Zubaydah refused, and reflected: "My camp, it was more famous."[29] Bin Laden was jealous and so Khaldan stayed shut.

It was time for Abu Zubaydah to get out of this particular "jihad arena."[30] After a decade in South Asia, having lost his camp and the love of his life, he sought a new beginning. He could never match bin Laden's power and he vehemently disagreed with Al Qaeda's trajectory against innocent civilians. Without Khaldan there was no need for a House of Martyrs. He would sneak into Iran, Israel's arch-enemy, and focus on the Palestinian struggle. With the help of his ex-wife, and Moazzam Begg, who had relocated from the United Kingdom to Afghanistan, he had already launched a news agency, the Global News Network (GNN), which promoted an anti-Israel agenda.[31] Now, he set out to establish a Palestine-focused jihad group based on the teachings of Abdullah Azzam, the original "Sheikh al-Jihad." Abu Zubaydah had saved $50,000, but now that Western intelligence agencies had his photograph, he needed a new identity as well as a passport, and while he was still in Afghanistan, he underwent plastic surgery. "I didn't care whether I looked handsomer or uglier because all I wanted was a change in looks," he said.[32] He asked the surgeon to make him look "East Asian," anything to disguise his Palestinian heritage. But afterward, his face was barely changed. "Unfortunately the surgeon failed to turn me into a Chinese person," he said.[33] Nevertheless, he was determined to do his bit to help as the Palestinian Intifada was becoming ever more intense.

After his capture, when the CIA learned about the plastic surgery, Alec Station pounced on it. Mitchell characterized Abu Zubaydah as "a super-villain, the face of terror on the internet, raising money to attack and kill innocent victims while living the high life safely, protected by a new face."[34] His "twisted ambition" had backfired on him because the surgery had been done by a "street vendor," and took place just a few weeks before Abu Zubaydah's capture in Faisalabad in March 2002, Mitchell said inaccurately.[35] The quack had infected his eye, said Mitchell, blaming the surgeon for what Americans had done. Abu Zubaydah later dismissed Mitchell's claims as just more "lies," but as with all of Mitchell's stories, at the core lay a kernel of truth.

In June 2001, Osama bin Laden informed the Al Qaeda *shura* about the "Planes Operation," which was so well advanced that his many dissenters on the ruling council could do nothing to stop it.[36] Until this point, only bin Laden, Khalid Sheikh Mohammad, and Abu Hafs al-Masri had known what was coming. Abu Zubaydah, who had gone to Kandahar in May or June 2001 to prepare for his relocation to Iran, noted in his diary of widespread rumors that the sheikh had a "new operation" underway. Knowing nothing specific, Abu Zubaydah focused on his own plans: asking various sheikhs around Kandahar to support his new Palestine venture with fatwas and funding.

When bin Laden got to hear about the Palestine plan, he suggested, via Abu Hafs al-Masri, that Abu Zubaydah should channel his funding via Al Qaeda for maximum impact. More people would support him if he had Al Qaeda's blessing, said al-Masri, thinking as usual about Al Qaeda's best interests. Trapped in a corner, Abu Zubaydah reluctantly handed over his hard-earned $50,000, unaware that Osama bin Laden intended to use it for 9/11.[37] Worse still, two future hijackers, Majed Moqed and Satam al-Suqami, had trained at Khaldan. They were probably among the last cadre to pass through before bin Laden shut it down. Abu Zubaydah was now tied to an operation he had no role in, but as far as the CIA was concerned these inadvertent links made him a planner and financier of the "Planes Operation."

After 9/11, an attack that Abu Zubaydah described in his diary as "unimaginable," US missiles obliterated the empty Khaldan camp. The *Los Angeles Times* filed an on-the-ground report, describing it as "the birthplace of deadly terrorist attacks and plots against the United States for nearly a decade."[38] It had provided training to a "generation of Al Qaeda suicide bombers, hijackers and saboteurs from around the world." Well aware he was now high up on the "most wanted" list, Abu Zubaydah crisscrossed Afghanistan, helping those fighting, dying, and fleeing.[39] He asked in vain for his $50,000 to be returned.[40] Khaldan was in the headlines again in December 2001, after Zacarias Moussaoui, a French Moroccan Al Qaeda suspect accused of being the missing twentieth hijacker, was indicted by a grand jury in Virginia, the document signed by assistant attorney general Michael Chertoff.[41] Moussaoui and Ahmed Ressam had trained in Khaldan at the same time—yet another nail in Abu Zubaydah's virtual coffin. By then, he was heading back toward Pakistan, having learned that his closest friend, Ibn Sheikh al-Libi, had been captured and sold to the Americans.

———•———

Just as National Security Council (NSC) discussions about enhanced interrogation came to a head in July 2002, Jonathan Fredman's office was advised that the source who had identified Abu Zubaydah as Number Three in Al Qaeda and claimed he knew about the second wave had recanted his entire statement.[42] The man, whose name was later redacted from all CIA documents, had been in US custody since before 9/11 and had given the information without knowing about the devastating attacks against the United States. This update was withheld from the Justice Department, which continued to assert the "Number Three" line. On July 11, John Yoo briefed Michael Chertoff about what he was now calling the "bad things opinion." He referred to Abu Zubaydah as "Boo boo."[43] Yoo's deputy went along with the joking, writing in one email, "I like the opinion's new title."[44] On July 12, Yoo and his deputy prepared to meet Alberto Gonzales. "Let's plan on going over [to the White House] at 3:30 to see some other folks about the bad things opinion," wrote Yoo. Vice President Cheney's chief counsel, David Addington, was "probably" present, along with the CIA and FBI, represented by Dan Levin, Mueller's chief of staff, who reported that the FBI was pulling the plug and would not participate in any future discussions about techniques that Mueller regarded as torture.[45]

On July 13, the National Security Council met to decide Abu Zubaydah's fate.[46] Rizzo recalled: "I emphasized that we didn't have the luxury of time. . . . Zubaydah was sitting in his cell with knowledge of another imminent attack potentially in his head, and basically he was giving his interrogators the finger."[47] Evidence found in his possession suggested he was planning to attack the US himself, the CIA warned, when in fact his diary said very clearly that his focus was Israel. Abu Zubaydah had authored "a seminal Al Qaeda manual on resistance to interrogation methods," and had displayed numerous signs of resistance training during nonaggressive interrogation, insisted Tenet and Rizzo, although the CIA later conceded it had "no information" to support these claims.[48] They focused on the necessity argument, warning that if the NSC failed to authorize the CIA's recommended course of action, "countless more Americans may die unless we can persuade AZ to tell us what he knows."[49]

Rizzo gave a full description of Mitchell and Jessen's proposed techniques, including waterboarding and mock burial. Only Condoleezza Rice pushed back, asking how the CIA could be so sure that Abu Zubaydah would not suffer permanent mental or physical harm—like a heart attack, stroke, or PTSD. Rizzo gave her the Mitchell assurance: no harm had come to thousands of US personnel subjected to these techniques every day in military survival school. After the meeting, Rizzo and Fredman submitted another "formal declination of prosecution from the Attorney General for any specific methods which the team believes would be effective, but which might not otherwise be permissible."[50] Later, Rizzo recalled feeling "a little grubby" asking for it.[51] Again, their written argument focused on the necessity argument: aggressive methods were needed to "safeguard the lives of innumerable innocent men, women and children."

A draft of this declination had been shared with Mitchell, who was en route to Thailand.[52] When he reached the black site, he learned Chertoff had rejected it, and the NSC had thrown out waterboarding and mock burial. The black site base chief pushed back, making an alternative suggestion. "We need to get reasonable assurance that AZ will remain in isolation and incommunicado for the remainder of his life," he wrote.[53] They would not proceed without protection. Mitchell later conceded, "I probably had a hand in this."[54] While he was happy to be deployed as "a weapons system," against Abu Zubaydah he was not willing to be "abandoned in the field," or go to prison.[55]

While they waited for a response, Mitchell and Jessen prepared their tools. US Navy waterboarding regulations called for "a specially rigged, flat, wooded surface about four by seven feet with quick release bindings which will neither chafe nor cut when the student is strapped [down]."[56] They adapted a hospital gurney with four ratchet straps and a hinged headboard that lowered to a forty-five-degree angle. Mitchell suggested the medics helped them design it. "He would already be on a gurney if something went wrong," he explained.[57]

Years later, Abu Zubaydah drew a picture of himself wearing a head clamp that gripped his cheeks, forcing his mouth open.[58] Mitchell and Jessen's written description of waterboarding did not mention any restraint but did include the instruction "the detainee's head is immobilized." One cable dated July 19 noted that the team in Thailand was trying to acquire a "head immobilizer."[59] Abu Zubaydah's head clamp was fashioned from two parallel blocks attached together by straps across his chin and forehead. The team also added hidden microphones to his black coffin and constructed the smaller "cramped confinement box."[60] They then "practiced, practiced, practiced."[61] Mitchell likened the sensation of being waterboarded to standing on top of a tall building and feeling you might fall off.[62] He wanted Abu Zubaydah to experience what the 9/11 falling man had gone through. "It sucked," he stated, after undergoing waterboarding himself. "I had a hard time controlling the apprehension of it." After practicing on each other, Mitchell and Jessen conducted a "walk-through rehearsal," with a guard playing Abu Zubaydah.[63]

Addressing Condoleezza Rice's concerns, the team drew up contingencies in case Abu Zubaydah had "a heart attack or another catastrophic type of condition."[64] The fully stocked crash cart and a medic would remain outside his cell during all enhanced sessions.[65] Mitchell and Jessen would stand down "if any member of the team raised a concern," although the base chief would have final decision-making authority.[66] They also tackled the grimmest possibility: "In the event that AZ dies, we need to be prepared to act accordingly, keeping in mind the liaison equities involving our hosts."[67] Abu Zubaydah's body would be cremated in accordance with Thai Buddhist tradition, rather than a Muslim burial. General Tritot could arrange this, and no compromising evidence would be left behind.[68] Back at Langley, Rizzo raised concerns about this last point. If they disposed of the body, the CIA would need some other evidence that they had not deliberately killed Abu Zubaydah. "We were just trying to ponder every worst-case scenario," Rizzo recalled.[69] For this reason, the black site was ordered to continue videotaping all sessions.

On July 15, Yoo warned Rizzo that the CIA had to do a better job of due diligence.[70] The agency needed to survey professional literature, consult with experts, and seek evidence gained from past experience. Headquarters passed this on to Mitchell and Jessen in Thailand, asking for statistics about the long-term mental health of those who had undergone SERE training. Six "modified interviews" with Abu Zubaydah conducted by the senior staff operational psychologist in May and June were reviewed, as a full psychological assessment was drawn up to show he was resilient enough to survive what was coming.

On July 17, George Tenet briefed Condoleezza Rice at the White House.[71] The CIA needed approval for all the proposed enhanced techniques in order to stop countless more Americans from dying.[72] The CIA wanted the waterboard and mock execution back on the list. Rice tried to block it. How could the agency square its plans with the fact the United States was a signatory of the UN Convention against Torture, and the Eighth Amendment to the Constitution banned "cruel and unusual punishments"? She demanded to know how the CIA could be so sure that Abu Zubaydah would not suffer "lasting and irreparable harm" and she asked to see "any available empirical data on the reactions and likelihood of prolonged mental harm from the use of the 'water board' and the staged burial."[73] Out in Thailand, Mitchell and Jessen got to work "drilling and cutting" plywood to construct a ready-made walling wall.[74]

The CIA responded on July 19, with a Mitchell statement: "In just one year, September 1992 to September 1993, out of the seven years I was at the Survival School, I worked with 133 people who were emotionally overwhelmed by the use of enhanced measures in resistance to interrogation training. I estimate similar numbers for the remaining six years I was there."[75] According to Mitchell, all subsequently recovered.[76] The CIA did not cite the large body of research published by Mitchell's rival Charles Morgan that showed SERE training caused serious mental health damage and that some students had died. The Counterterrorist Center sent a confidant cable to Thailand. "There is fairly unanimous sentiment within HQS that AZ will never be placed in a situation where he has any significant contact with others and/ or has the opportunity to be released."[77] All the major players were in concurrence that Abu Zubaydah should "remain incommunicado for the remainder of his life." If he could not talk, they could not be prosecuted.

Despite the extreme efforts being made to prove that Abu Zubaydah would not suffer any lasting harm, some of those out in Thailand were worried. On July 23, the base chief issued a strongly worded cable. The United States was "a nation of laws." Abu Zubaydah was "being held in solitary confinement, against his will," unlike SERE students, who volunteered and were medically screened before and after training.[78] Students knew it was only role-play, but Abu Zubaydah "will be made to believe this is the future course of the remainder of his life." Since Mitchell and Jessen needed to "overwhelm him" to make his interrogation "absolutely convincing," they could not rule out that he would not be "permanently physically or mentally harmed." They needed full legal protection.

On July 24, CIA lawyers called up Dan Baumgartner, the chief of staff at JPRA, who said they should speak to Mitchell, as he would know of any relevant data. Mitchell said he was not aware of any specific research. The Office of Technical Service reported back to John Yoo that while "the intention of the process is to make the subject very disturbed, "the presumption [is] that he will recover."[79] Charles Morgan later said that Mitchell and Jessen should have known there was plenty of publicly available research that showed this was not true. "It's hard to miss the literature if someone was looking in the field, and half my colleagues were psychologists publishing in the field of stress and stress studies, so I don't know why they would be unaware of it."[80] Morgan's research was "right in the backyard of what they do." But Mitchell knew where Morgan stood on the issue of using SERE techniques in the real world. "I think when you're creating either physical or psychological harm to people, yes, I think that crosses the line," Morgan reflected. "A technique that's specifically designed to terrify a person and frighten them or cause them what we know would not be good for them physically, psychologically, medically, I, personally, think is wrong."

Instead of calling Morgan, whose research was funded by the Pentagon, Baumgartner kept it in-house, calling Jerald Ogrisseg, the US Air Force's chief psychologist, a job Mitchell had once held.[81] Ogrisseg had seen waterboarding in action during a visit to US Navy SERE school in September 2001 and would "never recommend using it in training," because produced learned helplessness—"a training result we tried strenuously to avoid."[82] When asked about using it for real against the enemy, Ogrisseg replied: "Wouldn't that be illegal?" Baumgartner pressed him to write up something positive, as people "from above" were applying pressure. Feeling uncomfortable, Ogrisseg stuck to statistics, reporting that out of the 26,829 students who had gone through US Air Force SERE school since 1992, there had been only thirty-seven "psychological pulls" of students from training.[83]

On July 24, the CIA sent Abu Zubaydah's psychological assessment to the Justice Department.[84] It was based on "direct interviews with and observations of subject," extracts from Abu Zubaydah's diary, information obtained from intelligence and press reports, and was designed to prove that "no physical harm or prolonged mental harm would result from the use on him of the EITs, including the water board."[85] The first page stated that he was the "third or fourth man in Al Qaeda," was a "senior Usama bin Laden lieutenant," and had played a "key role" in 9/11.[86] "Agency psychologists assess that he wrote the Al Qaeda manual on resistance techniques" was a claim based on no evidence whatsoever.[87] Turning to mindset, they wrote that he was driven by "self-discipline, self-assurance, perfectionism, narcissism, skepticism, suspicion, resilience, resolve, calm and confidence." Much was made of his proclivity to deceive. "His job is to lie," they reported, stating that he had admitted to lying to "neighbors, shopkeepers, bankers, travel agents, airport personnel and many others" to protect his brothers and their activities. "He said: 'I lie, lie, lie, lie and lie.'" From his girlfriends to the United Nations, "he has learned that the combination of skillful deception and lying pays off," they concluded.[88]

The stick-thin shadow-man falling to pieces inside his bunker was just an act. He would be put under pressure only until he revealed his secrets. Then, he would bounce back, according to the CIA's enhanced interrogation experts. "Excellent, very useful. Thanks," wrote one recipient in the email chain.[89]

On July 26, the attorney general, John Ashcroft, verbally approved the use of ten enhanced techniques, excluding waterboarding and mock burial. The CIA was not satisfied. Waterboarding was "an absolutely convincing technique," without which the other techniques would constitute only "a 50% solution."[90] The black site team would not proceed without it. "The fact that the water board overwhelms most people's ability to resist is precisely why IC [independent contractor] SERE psychologists think this procedure would be effective," the base chief reported. The safety of it, or any other technique, "lies primarily in how it is applied and monitored."[91] Luckily, Mitchell and Jessen were "highly trained experts" with thirty-two years of experience between them. The CIA called up John Yoo, asking for written approval for all twelve techniques, "some sort of short letter that tells them that they have the go ahead."[92] Tenet explained, "We needed the authoritative lead with absolute clarity."[93]

After Yoo "talked to the White House," Ashcroft verbally approved waterboarding. While Yoo finessed the final paperwork, with input from Alberto Gonzales and David Addington, Fredman informed the black site team. "Of course, the use of the water board . . . may well be viewed by foreign nations as violating their own statutes and their own interpretation of international law," he wrote.[94] But "the risks that other nations may view our activities as unlawful are risks we must incur." Mock burial was thrown out, with Yoo later reflecting that it was "so clearly illegal that he never seriously considered approving its use."[95] But Mitchell and Jessen still had the coffin.

John Yoo worked right up to the line with Gonzales, Addington, Chertoff, and Jay Bybee, another assistant attorney general who would be required to sign the legal opinion. There were several last-minute tweaks, such as removing all references to the "Commander-in-Chief," taking out "diapering," and discussing anaphylaxis.[96] "Do we know if Boo boo is allergic to certain insects?"[97] Yoo asked on July 30. Rizzo referred to this technique as "bug in a box," but the final memo was more diplomatic: "You have informed us that you are not aware that Zubaydah has any allergies to insects."[98]

On July 31, the NSC discussed Abu Zubaydah's enhanced interrogation yet again. There were now three memos—one detailing the legal limits, one which detailed the techniques and why they were needed for Abu Zubaydah, and a letter from Yoo to Gonzales. The CIA wanted everything signed and dispatched by the following day. Condoleezza Rice, her deputy Stephen Hadley, and her chief counsel, John Bellinger, were at the meeting and were briefed by George Tenet and his chief of staff, John Moseman.[99] "Dr. Rice indicated that she would not object to employing the techniques if they were determined by the Attorney General to be legal," reported the CIA.[100] Rice then left the discussion.

All that was left was presidential approval, something Jose Rodriguez had demanded from the start. The CIA had written up talking points for a briefing, including a description of waterboarding, but Bellinger now informed Moseman that the NSC had decided not to inform the president.[101] Bellinger explained that because the Justice Department had determined enhanced techniques were legal, Gonzales and Rice had agreed that the CIA could decide whether or not to apply them in a given instance. Rice later informed Tenet "there would be no briefing of the President on this matter."[102]

Tenet had full policy approval to authorize Abu Zubaydah's enhanced inter-rogation. Rizzo took this to mean that Rice had briefed the president herself.[103]

However, Secretary of State Colin Powell and Defense Secretary Donald Rumsfeld, who were both National Security Council principals, were not briefed. The Senate Intelligence Committee was not informed. Although the CIA and Mitchell regularly cited presidential approval as a stamp of le-gitimacy, Tenet later told the CIA inspector general that "he had never spoken to the President regarding the detention and interrogation program or EITs."[104] A path was being laid to provide plausible deniability to those at the top.

President Bush told a different story in a later memoir, saying that Tenet had specifically asked him to approve the waterboarding of Abu Zubaydah. "I thought about my meeting with Danny Pearl's widow, who was pregnant with his son when he was murdered. I thought about the 2,971 people stolen from their families by Al Qaeda on 9/11. And I thought about my duty to protect my country from another act of terror." So would he approve it, asked Tenet? Bush said he turned and exclaimed, "Damn right."[105]

John Rizzo recalled being so surprised when he read Bush's memoir, published in 2010, that he emailed Tenet. The former CIA director stuck to his original story. "He told me he had never briefed the President on EITs," Rizzo recalled.[106] However, five years later, in 2015, Tenet backed the Presi-dent's version, saying during an interview that Bush had "looked at the techniques, and decided he was gonna take two techniques off the table himself."[107] Both these revisions came long after Bush had signed off on new laws that protected anyone involved in Abu Zubaydah's interrogation from being prosecuted.

Requested by the CIA, authored by Yoo, and addressed to John Rizzo, the final "bad things opinion" was signed by Jay Bybee, the head of the Office of Legal Counsel, on August 1, 2002 and dispatched to Thailand two days later. "As we understand it, Zubaydah is one of the highest-ranking members of the Al-Qaeda terrorist organization," it began.[108] As author of the Manchester manual, he would "draw on his vast knowledge of interroga-tion techniques" to remain silent. Number Three in Al Qaeda "continues to express his unabated desire to kill Americans and Jews." According to the CIA, "there is currently a level of 'chatter' equal to that which preceded the September 11 attacks." No reference was made to the forty-seven lost days.

On due diligence, three SERE experts were quoted, including Major Ogrisseg, who later complained of being misquoted, and Dan Baumgartner, a pilot by training, who according to a former colleague was a "paper pusher," not a cortisol expert.[109] The name of the third expert was redacted. Although the CIA presented its plan as being led by health professionals and backed by science, and it informed Yoo that it had sought advice from medical experts, the CIA's Office of Medical Services was not consulted.[110] Instead, the CIA's Office of Technical Service, famous for having run MK-ULTRA, submitted a report after speaking to "outside psychologists," probably those on its Professional Standards Advisory Board.[111] Contrary findings published by real SERE stress expert Charles Morgan were not mentioned. The Yoo-Bybee memo concluded that, "based on information that you have supplied to us," Mitchell and Jessen's techniques would not violate Section 2340A of the United States Code, which made it a criminal offense for any person "outside of the United States [to] commit or attempt to commit torture."

The legal opinion was extraordinary and went much further even than previously banned interrogation manuals, such as the updated KUBARK manual used in Honduras during the early 1980s. That manual had warned, "The use of force, mental torture, threats, insults, or exposure to unpleasant and inhumane treatment of any kind as an aid to interrogation is prohibited by law, both international and domestic." However, the CIA was unlikely to face any consequences for going against its own previous advice, because no cases had ever been brought under the torture statute, Yoo-Bybee advised— before adding a caveat to protect the Department of Justice and the National Security Council: if the "facts" as presented changed, "this advice would not necessarily apply." Jose Rodriguez was delighted. "Once they told us it was good to go, you are authorized to go, please protect us, use these, off we went," he recalled.[112]

CHAPTER 10

"FULL-BLOWN, FULL-TILT, BOZO WILD PERSON"

August 4, 2002, 11:00 A.M., Chiang Mai, Thailand

It was a lazy Sunday morning, and Thai families milled around noodle carts. Inside his bunker, Abu Zubaydah was eating frozen rice with his fingers.[1] He was holding up the last to the halogen lights to warm it, when six huge men in black (guards) charged in.[2] Flinging aside his food, they hauled him up, hooded him, and cuffed him to the cross bar.[3] He heard more footsteps, was then uncuffed and dragged on his haunches to the far wall, where the hood was ripped off. A gray-haired American man stood above him, screaming expletives.

Mitchell was not wearing a mask and his angry, screwed-up face was the first Abu Zubaydah had seen in almost seven weeks. Covering one's face "when you are going to do something bad, intimate with a person" was cowardly, Mitchell later reflected.[4] Abu Zubaydah would be made to "fear for his life," and succumb to "complete helplessness."[5] Showing his face also conveyed another message: that Mitchell had no fear of Abu Zubaydah ever "[being] able to come after us."[6]

Mitchell claimed Abu Zubaydah circled him "like a cat . . . making intense eye contact."[7] The contractor was ready for anything. "We didn't want Abu Zubaydah to think he could stop interrogations by aggressive acting out," he recalled.[8] Abu Zubaydah said he was short-chained, like a "hunchback."[9] Without warning, Mitchell grabbed his head and slammed it backward against the concrete wall. The plywood "walling wall" Mitchell and Jessen had constructed two weeks earlier was still stacked up outside. After repeated blows, Abu Zubaydah collapsed on the floor, blinded by pain. Mitchell stood over him, "slapping my face again and again," yelling incomprehensible words.[10] Mitchell later denied it had happened this way. "The notion that he was rammed headfirst into a concrete wall is an exaggeration," he said.[11] Mitchell had years of professional "walling" experience. "You don't want to move them with such velocity and intensity that you injure them," he explained during the 9/11 pretrial hearing.[12] Abu Zubaydah just shrugged, he recalled. "He seemed to be saying, 'So what?'" Mitchell knew how to knock the swagger out of cocky students, and this detainee was a resistance-trained terrorist.[13] Mitchell had flipped into what his former boss Roger Aldrich described as "full-blown, full-tilt, bozo wild person" role-play mode.[14] Only this was real.

Getting up close, Mitchell delivered a grave message: "Zayn, in every man's life there are moments of choice when the decision you make, forever changes what happens to you."[15] He then signaled for the guards to bring in "a large black wooden box that looked like a wooden casket."[16] Mitchell got even closer. "This is going to be your home," he growled.[17] Abu Zubaydah said Mitchell called it a "coffin," a word that frequently appeared in cables but that Mitchell denied ever using. To do so would have been a threat of imminent death, which was illegal. But as long as Mitchell informed the detainee he would not die, the lawyers were satisfied. The coffin was upended and chained to the bars before Abu Zubaydah was shoved in, with a waste bucket, drinking water, and Ensure. "I heard the sound of the lock and found myself in total darkness," he recalled.[18] Because he was short-chained, he wedged himself on the bucket and listened as footsteps came and went. It sounded like carpentry was going on. He said he suffered the first of more than three hundred seizures while inside the coffin, caused, he believed, because Mitchell's walling had dislodged shrapnel that had been inside his head since 1991.[19]

After he'd spent four hours in darkness, the box was unlocked, at 4:45 P.M.[20] Light flooded in, and he saw a more muscular man "twisting a thick towel which was wrapped with a plastic tape so it could be given the shape of a noose."[21] It was Bruce Jessen. To avoid any accusations they were hinting at a "mock execution," Mitchell and Jessen called the reinforced towel the "safety collar." Mitchell later explained: "We wanted the towel to become the thing they came to fear."[22] Once Abu Zubaydah associated the towel with walling, they would not need to get violent. It was like teaching a dog to drool in an experiment where the feeding light switched on, although no meat was in the end delivered.

Jessen put the noose towel over Abu Zubaydah's head and yanked him out, upturning the toilet bucket, which spilled over his gaping leg wound.[23] According to cables, the detainee "stumbled" over the bucket and his bandage fell off. As part of Phase 2, wound care had been reduced to the "absolute minimum," since "the interrogation process takes precedence over preventative medical procedures."[24] Abu Zubaydah was told that all the doctors and nurses had gone home, and he had to clean the wound himself, "Afghan style," with strips of gauze soaked in Betadine.[25] Jessen "dragged me on the floor by the noose towel . . . towards the wall," he recalled.[26] A plywood "walling wall" now covered the concrete. Another team member recalled being ordered to fit it in place because Abu Zubaydah had suffered visible injuries during the first walling round.[27]

SERE rules stipulated that only the subject's shoulder blades should "bounce" off the wall to avoid head impact.[28] In the schoolhouse, instructors were warned not to be "sloppy" with their hands, recalled Mitchell.[29] Abu Zubaydah said Jessen slammed his head so hard that he "fell down on the floor," lost his vision for a few seconds, and "then I resumed seeing a person about to push my head hard against the wall again."[30] The Yoo-Bybee memo had stated, "You have indicated that these acts will not be used with substantial repetition," but Abu Zubaydah recalled Jessen walling him so many times he became breathless.[31] It was a constant cycle of "darkness, bright light, darkness, bright light, then a long period of darkness."[32] Every time he tried to lift his arms to shield himself, he fell over, because his wrists were short-chained to his ankles. "I see you don't cover your face to avoid the beating," Jessen yelled, deliberately misinterpreting Abu Zubaydah's inability to defend himself. "You think you have pride? I will show you what pride is all about."[33] Mitchell later reflected on their style of enhanced interrogation. "If they gave a bullshit answer, you would go boom, boom, against the wall, controlling the neck, and say, 'Is what you told me going to stop operations inside the US?' And they would typically go, 'no,' and then, boom, boom."[34]

Eventually, Abu Zubaydah collapsed, his head swollen and bruised. Now there was only darkness. Jessen could not get him up, so slapped him on the floor.[35] The official cable sanitized events: "Subject was told to compose himself and behave in a more dignified manner."[36] The detainee "feigned helplessness" and had a "generally pathetic posture." However, according to Abu Zubaydah, Jessen became so frustrated he grabbed his head with both hands and started banging it against the wall. While the Justice Department had approved "rough handling," it had not approved the "infliction of severe physical pain," and Abu Zubaydah, who later depicted walling in several grim drawings, accused Jessen of deliberately targeting his old shrapnel injury.[37] Each blow felt like an electric shock, he recounted.[38] He could no longer see. In one picture, he drew himself being walled without any neck support. In another, both the interrogator's hands were on his face as the back of his head was slammed into the wall. He drew bloody abrasions on his shaved skull.

At 5:00 P.M., a smaller box was carried in. Abu Zubaydah called it the "dog box," and with the help of guards, Jessen tried to squash him in. "When the guards lifted me up, I saw blood on the floor where my head was and I saw a lot of vomit that stuck to the military boots of the guards," Abu Zubaydah wrote later.[39] Legal approval had stipulated the box could not be "so small as to require the individual to contort his body."[40] But this box "would nearly fit under a chair."[41] As the lid jammed on, Abu Zubaydah tried unsuccessfully to twist into a fetal position.[42] "The contractions in my muscles and nerves were increasing with every hour, every minute and every second that were passing by, especially in the wounds I already had in my belly and thigh, let alone the pain in my head."[43] Official cables noted that he sounded "distressed."[44]

At 6:09 P.M., guards reentered, the small box was opened, and according to the record, he "scooted out on his hind quarters."[45] Mitchell and Jessen backed him up to the plywood wall and warned him that, if he did not cooperate, he was going to "bring more misery onto himself."[46] Abu Zubaydah claimed they both punched him, competing to deliver the hardest blow. They demanded to be addressed as "Sir," an act played out a thousand times at Fairchild, and ridiculed him for the adolescent sex-talk in his old diary, sneering that he would never get a chance to defile a white woman again. "Thanks to Allah they didn't know about my friend, love and my (real) wife," he wrote later.[47] "Imagine (they) captured her at the time they captured me?" They accused him of being Number Three in Al Qaeda, one of the worst terrorists on the planet. Abu Zubaydah yelled back: "O stupid, I'm not Al Qaeda."[48] They punched him again, Mitchell later explaining that punching was "better" because slapping was "disrespectful."[49]

At 6:15 P.M., on August 4, 2002, the waterboard was wheeled in. It looked like a regular hospital gurney, so Abu Zubaydah lay down, thinking they were about to attend to his thigh wound, which was open and bleeding. As the guards strapped him, he realized his mistake. One strap cut into the wound, exposing "a large piece of red flesh."[50] The "head immobilizer" clamped his mouth and nose in position.[51] "I was unable to make any movement whatsoever," he recalled. A black cloth came down over his face. "I suddenly felt water being poured," he said. "It shocked me because it was very cold." They kept pouring. "I really felt I was drowning." Yoo and Bybee had warned, "the water board constitutes a threat of imminent death" and fulfilled the "predicate act requirement under the statute" to ratify torture. But to invoke the statute, "prolonged mental harm" also had to be proven, and that meant "mental harm lasting months or years," like PTSD.[52] As the CIA intended for Abu Zubaydah to remain incommunicado for the rest of his life, getting an independent brain specialist to examine him and provide the correct diagnosis would prove impossible.[53]

Jessen used plastic bottles chilled in a cooler, far more than the navy's two-pint maximum. Mitchell controlled the duration of each "pour" by lowering and lifting the cloth, while a guard counted off seconds with a "clicker."[54] Abu Zubaydah claimed there was also a third interrogator. "During these torture sessions, many guards were present, plus two interrogators who did the actual beating, still asking questions, while the main interrogator left to return after the beating was over."[55] This third person was not accounted for in most official cables, which raised doubts about the transparency and accuracy of CIA reporting. Mitchell recalled that "when [Shumate] left they sent over a SERE trained psych who stayed and was in charge of operational psychology the whole rest of the time up until they moved AZ." This third person also doubled up as base chief. Citing his CIA nondisclosure agreement, Mitchell would never confirm any names, but other sources claimed that both Deuce Martinez and Mike McConnell interrogated Abu Zubaydah in Thailand.[56]

Yoo-Bybee had given approval for pours of up to forty seconds' duration, but Mitchell said it became apparent this was too long, after Abu Zubaydah "seemed slow to expel the water from his sinuses" during one of the longer pours.[57] Abu Zubaydah's heart was racing, and his chest "was just about to explode from the lack of oxygen."[58] As a child, he had dreamed of enormous waves crashing down on the shore, and a voice calling up from deep down in the ocean. As a teenager, he had sung a maudlin Arabic love song whenever he was in the shower: "I am sinking, I am sinking, under water."[59] In his diary he had likened drowning to swimming in the devil's lake. Now he was actually drowning. When Mitchell eventually lifted the cloth, and guards pulled the gurney upright, Abu Zubaydah hung limp, like a crucified man, while Mitchell and Jessen made breathing noises in his face.[60] He felt they were calculating how far they could go without actually killing him.

After a few seconds, he vomited water, followed by rice and beans. "It was an ugly sight," Mitchell said.[61] Mitchell claimed they waited "what seemed like a long time" to see if the medics were going to intervene. After "one stuck his head in the door for a confirming glance," they got back to it, so the detainee "didn't get the idea that a dramatic display would stop the procedures."[62] They tweaked their technique to shorter, more frequent pours. "We did a lot of three-second pours," Mitchell said.[63] The number of pours was not limited by Yoo-Bybee.

Whenever they brought the gurney upright, the ratchet strap across Abu Zubaydah's leg wound bit deeper, making him vomit even more. He insisted his "dramatic display" was a genuine struggle for life. The first time he vomited, he said Mitchell looked momentarily afraid. But they began again. "I tried to speak or yell with my head covered, 'I don't know anything,' but I suddenly felt the water flowing again." Observers in the control center noted "involuntary spasms of the torso and extremities."[64] Mitchell claimed they stopped to give him a chance to tell them about the second wave. "He would say, 'no,'" recalled Mitchell, "and we would go back to waterboarding him."[65] They advised Abu Zubaydah he could "stop it any time" by telling them what "Washington" wanted to know.[66] Mitchell maintained that, like the SERE students who could always reveal their "secret" or call out the emergency code—"flight-surgeon"—Abu Zubaydah had full control of his situation.[67] However, an official description more brutally defined the process and showed just how far removed the CIA waterboarding was from the navy procedure. Each "watering cycle" was split into four stages:

1) Demands for information interspersed with the application of water just short of blocking his airway;
2) escalation of the amount of water applied until it blocked his airway and he started having involuntary spasms;
3) raising the waterboard to clear subject's airway;
4) lowering the waterboard and return to demands for information.[68]

Mitchell later claimed that "application" meant a complete cycle as distinct from a single "pour," but on paper the words seemed interchangeable.[69]

They conducted four cycles on the first day, emerging from the cell at 6:29 P.M., 7:15 P.M., and 8:01 P.M. to consult with other team members.[70] The number of pours per cycle was not reported but the base chief was at pains to report every other detail to headquarters. "They wanted headquarters to know exactly what they were doing," reflected Dan Jones, who led the Senate investigation into CIA interrogation.[71] After the last cycle finished, at 8:54 P.M., Abu Zubaydah was locked in the small box for ninety minutes (exceeding the sixty-minute limit set by the Justice Department). Addressing this specific point in a cable, the base chief wrote that they intended to use it "as often as necessary" but would not exceed two hours at any one time.[72] Fewer than twelve hours into Phase 2, multiple legal guidelines already had been broken, which should have invoked the ruling that the legal opinion would cease to function if the facts as presented by the CIA changed.[73] But Yoo and Bybee were not reading cable traffic and no one complained. The team locked Abu Zubaydah in his coffin with a bottle of water, warning that if he did not drink it, they would "force it into him," then went off to dinner.[74]

Langley sent a hero-gram: "HQS wishes to extend congratulations to all personnel on a job well done in the first day of Phase 2."[75] Mitchell and Jessen went for a long walk. "This would become our habit after sessions using EITs, especially the ones involving waterboarding," Mitchell said.[76] "We didn't like using EITs, and we used the walks to think about what we were being asked to do." It was good to get outside, as Abu Zubaydah and his cell stank. However, his physiological condition was reported as "close to normal given his present circumstances," so he got no respite.[77] To be effective, Phase 2 had to be 24/7, and the guards rocked, tilted, or banged his coffin every fifteen minutes through the night.[78] Later, Abu Zubaydah drew pictures of them wielding baseball bats.[79] Since he was short-chained, he eventually became wedged between the waste bucket and a corner.[80]

Already worried his medics were primarily being used to provide legal cover and that Mitchell and Jessen had "no real interest in acting as the mental health component of the interrogation team," Medical Services chief Terry DeMay felt boxed in.[81] Despite a requirement that a fully trained and registered medical officer be present, currently only a nurse was on duty, kept outside the curtain, as headquarters had agreed that only Mitchell and Jessen should have direct contact with the detainee. The nurse did not have authority to intervene unless the base chief and "the senior CTC officer" approved it.[82] A sense of how the nurse felt was recorded in regular email he sent to DeMay, outside official cable traffic. At the start he was upbeat: "I recognize that this is one of the most important 'ops' I've been involved in."[83] Twelve hours later, he was still on duty and Abu Zubaydah was inside his dog box, praying for mercy. "I will be here all night," wrote the nurse.[84]

The next morning, the nurse was still on duty: "More waterboard sessions this AM planned. Subject was up and moving all night so is sleep deprived, the medical team a little less so." By the afternoon, he was less confident. "This EVENT is going to take a long time."[85] He was worried about the leg wound, which had been uncovered for twenty-four hours. They also needed to get fluids into him. The nurse warned an incoming fully trained medic, the same man who had flown with Abu Zubaydah from Pakistan, to be prepared for a shock. "This is almost certainly not a place he's ever been before in his medical career." It was "visually and psychologically very uncomfortable."[86] DeMay, who had been against Mitchell's involvement from the start, wrote back: this was a "very unpleasant business."[87]

By Thursday morning, Abu Zubaydah had been waterboarded for four days straight. This was turning into something far more grueling than the "mini-captivity" experience SERE students were exposed to.[88] In between "the drownings" as Abu Zubaydah later called them, he was left strapped to the board with the wet cloth over his face.[89] When he was not on the board, they made sure he could still see it through the curtain.[90] When he was in the dog box or coffin waiting for the squeaking gurney routine to start up again, he could be heard "crying/whimpering/chanting."[91] Mitchell later blamed the report writers for being overly dramatic. "They were writing those reports in the most dramatic way to get the attention of the people back home, so they were exaggerating to some extent. They were telling the truth but they were doing it in the most salacious ways," he recalled. "You'd get this report about, 'he slobbered and cried and rocked and blah blah,' and he did cry sometimes, but it wasn't as dramatic as what was reported."[92]

Abu Zubaydah named it the "torture circuit."[93] He was terrified of Mitchell. When he commanded, "you know what to do," he crawled into the dog box.[94] Whenever Jessen entered, his "distress level increased."[95] He was completely compliant and had reached a weakened mental state. Everyone was shocked at how quickly the waterboarding overcame him. Like the stray dogs in Martin Seligman's electric-shock experiments, Abu Zubaydah was hurtling toward learned helplessness far faster than anyone had expected. However, according to Rodriguez's schedule, they were supposed to keep going for another twenty-six days. His medical condition was the most worrying. His "splayed lobster" thigh wound had not been attended in seventy-two hours, and it was "beefy raw" and "steadily deteriorating."[96] No one at the black site wanted him to die.[97]

The base chief had another problem. "Subject has not provided any new threat information," he wrote, day after day.[98] Abu Zubaydah was not elaborating on threats he had already talked about. Some days, he was not talking at all. But given the tug-of-war between a man who insisted he knew nothing about future attacks and a headquarters team that maintained he was holding back Tenet's "mother lode," Mitchell and Jessen needed to proceed carefully. Marty Martin, Alec Station, Jennifer Matthews, and Tenet's chief CIA spokesman, Bill Harlow, had all worked hard turning Abu Zubaydah into "the most senior Al Qaeda operative currently in USG custody."[99] He could not be allowed to keep his secrets, and the president of the United States could not be left with egg on his face. According to Mitchell, one of those pushing hardest was Alfreda Bikowsky, the deputy chief of Alec Station, who along with Matthews had been admonished for hiding evidence from the FBI pre-9/11.[100] Mitchell was agnostic about Bikowsky, but was fond of Matthews. Given Abu Zubaydah's "position in the Al Qaeda network," there was a "compelling case" that he had to know about future planning.[101] Alec Station had a "body of evidence" that proved he was withholding information. There was pressure on all sides. Mitchell and Jessen had convinced everyone that Abu Zubaydah was a master of deception, and they had won lucrative contracts by promising to break him with SERE.[102]

Everything came to a head on August 8. After thirteen minutes of wall-ing, Mitchell ordered Abu Zubaydah to get on the waterboard and lie down. Normally he complied, but this time he refused. Mitchell repeated his in-struction. Get on the board. The observers saw a "noticeable change in sub-ject's breathing," as the guards manhandled him. "I have nothing more," Abu Zubaydah cried, as they strapped him down. "I give you everything."[103] Mitchell lowered the cloth, and Jessen poured. Every inch of the detainee's body shook. Mitchell signaled for Jessen to keep going, pour after pour. "The first time, I felt like I might die," recalled Abu Zubaydah.[104] "The second time, I'm really dying. The third time, I'm dead." When Mitchell eventually lifted the cloth, the detainee was elevated and spewed. As they set the board back down and prepared to start up again, he whimpered, "I have no more."[105] Some of those watching CCTV in the main building began sobbing. The sight of a half dozen Americans bearing down on an emaciated and terrified man begging for his life was too much to bear, even if he was America's enemy number one.

Mitchell called him "motherfucker," Jessen called him "Zayn." Some-times, they used "Hani," which he most hated.[106] "Hani" belonged to his Swedish wife and their "little paradise" marriage nest in Islamabad. "Hani" belonged to his family: his mother's bedroom with its flowery coverlet, blue telephone, round mirror, and perfume bottles stacked high. "Hani" did not belong inside this hellhole. Mucus and vomit flew, as the gurney crashed back down, and Jessen restarted pouring. The scene was described in the cables; the subject manifested "despair and helplessness."[107] Everyone could see he could not tolerate much more. The guards unstrapped him, and Mitchell ordered him into the dog box. He crawled across the floor. They locked him up and turned the white noise on.

The base chief convened a team meeting. Mitchell and Jessen entered, soaked in water. As a kid living on the margins, Mitchell had sometimes felt the "sense of welcome conveyed by having a pack of mangy dogs sic'ed on me."[108] It wasn't that different now, although he later said he was indif-ferent to his peers watching him working. Things had gone too far, said some. Abu Zubaydah could not take much more. "Use of force is a poor technique, yields unreliable results, may damage subsequent collection efforts, and can induce the source to say what he thinks the interrogator wants to hear," the CIA's banned 1983 Human Resource Exploitation Training Manual had advised. Mitchell had insisted his and Jessen's approach was science-based. The same manual went on to advise: "The use of force is not to be confused with psychological ploys, verbal trickery, or other nonviolent and non-coercive ruses." Mitchell said he was just following orders and that the president, the National Security Council, Congress, the Justice Department, and the director of the CIA had all approved this course of action.[109] It wasn't his and Jessen's job to question the decision-makers or the experts, he said.[110] Abu Zubaydah was a master faker. At times, the base chief had come into the cell to congratulate him on his fake drooling, saying things like: "Good job, it adds realism. . . . I'm almost buying it. You wouldn't think a grown man would do that."[111]

Was Abu Zubaydah still faking? Some were not sure. The nurse, who was due to fly home, secretly emailed DeMay: "Today's first session . . . had a profound effect on all staff members present."[112] Some were asking for counseling. They wanted senior officials to "witness first-hand what we're experiencing." Abu Zubaydah's leg wound was degenerating fast, and he was vomiting off the board as well as on it. "We should not go much further," wrote the nurse. Some people were reduced to "tears and choking up." The nurse requested a written record of his communications.

With Yoo-Bybee in mind, a collective decision was taken "to place the subject on the water board but not apply any water." That afternoon, Abu Zubaydah was strapped down and asked about future attacks. "I try, I try," he cried, finding himself still able to speak, as no water came, and he offered up anything he could think of. Yes, he had helped operatives with their training, he said. Yes, he had given $50,000 to bin Laden. Yes, he'd had another "$100,000 ready for operations against Israel at the time of his arrest."[113] But he did not have anything about attacks in the United States. That was never his intention. He did not plan 9/11. He did not know that Khalid Sheikh Mohammad had chosen two Khaldan graduates for 9/11. Alec Station was unimpressed. Information about old attacks or broadsides against Israel would not satisfy George Tenet's need to deter a nuclear assault on the US homeland.[114] Headquarters ordered the aggressive pressures be stepped back up.[115] Mitchell and Jessen went for another long walk. They were both worried.[116] Only their faces were on the waterboarding tapes; the government had failed to provide them with a declination of prosecution and was pushing them to go further. When the inevitable investigation came, they would be in the frame, unless they took radical action.

———— • ————

"I don't scare easily," Mitchell wrote.[117] "I've been in dangerous situations, many of them." In other lives, at different times, he had served on a bomb squad disarming live munitions, been part of a hostage negotiation team, fought a bear, watched a B-52 bomber smash into asphalt at close quarters, and once wrestled a loaded gun off a suicidal cop. But nothing provoked as much fear and inspired such dread as the words he heard one day in second grade: "You'll be the only boy dancing with the girls, so, of course, you'll have to wear a leotard like they do." Jim was seven. It was his first day in a new school, the second school he had been enrolled in that year as a result of his unorthodox family life. He was living in a condemned house with his grandmother Nancy and two of his three siblings and was now standing in front of his new classmates, a sea of smirking faces. The school pageant was just a week away, and the teacher didn't want Jim, in his torn-up sneakers and stained jeans, to feel left out. "You can be a snake charmer and dance with the girls!" she declared, beaming. "You'll need to wear a pair of leotards." Mitchell explained the significance: "This was in the Deep South in the 1950s. Men in yoga pants and Lycra bike shorts with butt pads and codpieces wouldn't become acceptable for several decades. . . . The idea of wearing girls' underpants was . . . unthinkable."

Seven-year-old Jim tried to stammer, "I don't have any leotards . . ." Of course, replied the teacher. "Leotards are for girls." She asked the class if anyone could lend a pair of tights to the new boy. "What kind of hell was this?" Jim wondered. A hand shot up at the back, a cute girl called Patti. "He can wear mine." On the day of the pageant, "hoochie-coochie" music played out across the school's baseball diamond. Jim's dance ensemble consisted of four girls in red leotards and him in black. They held snakes crafted from nylon hose stuffed with moss. "Shimmying my hips to the music, I completely forgot my reluctance to appear in a leotard. . . . There might have even been some finger snapping." But as he got into his rhythm, the leggings began to slip. Patti was small, and his "ass-crack" began to show. By the time it was over, the tights were down to his mid-thigh. "I ran off the field.

Onlookers clapped and the little girls behind me sniggered." Jim heard none of it, as he was gone. "Wile E. Coyote in a puff of smoke." This was what real humiliation felt like, and more than four decades later, he was not ready to be humiliated again in Thailand.

On August 9, 2002, Mitchell, Jessen, and the base chief judged Abu Zubaydah's psychological state to be "fundamentally sound" and restarted waterboarding, going against the previous agreement to stop.[118] "When they say 'I have nothing for you,' that doesn't mean I don't know I'm just not going to tell you." Mitchell later reflected.[119] "I think it goes back to their religion, even if you read Aladdin or anything about the *djinns*, they celebrate telling you the truth but fucking you over." The first session progressed with grim familiarity. When Abu Zubaydah was elevated to clear his "sinuses," as Mitchell always described it, he gasped for air. When they laid him back down and blocked his airway with water, his feet and hands went into spasms. At the end of the session, he was told to choose. "The small box? The floor with your hands, held up high? Standing against the wall? Or stay where you are?"[120] His response was redacted, but he stayed on the board. Later, he was rotated from the dog box to the coffin and then made to stand or sit in various stress positions for five hours. When he said he knew nothing, he was walled. They told him to get back on the board. He whimpered: he had nothing. No one declared war on the United States without knowing what the war entailed, Mitchell said, as Jessen poured.[121]

Mitchell was referring to the videotaped recording Abu Zubaydah had made after the US invasion of Afghanistan. Abu Zubaydah's decision to keep this material and his compromising diary with him as he fled Afghanistan was "like a serial killer keeping a dead hooker in the trunk."[122] Mitchell called it "the stupid shit he had in his bag," and claimed Abu Zubaydah had made "lots of short videos of him claiming credit for attacks," even though it was only one tape consisting of several outtakes.[123] He recalled that it captivated Alec Station. "They were absolutely convinced he had something cooking."[124] Rodriguez characterized the single recording as "videotapes prerecorded to celebrate a contemplated successful second wave of attacks against the United States."[125]

Later, Mitchell backed Rodriguez's opinion, saying Abu Zubaydah told him he was trying to raise his profile and attract money before disappearing into Iran to plan future attacks—against America. Since bin Laden had spent his $50,000 on 9/11, he was starting from scratch and planned to sell the video to the highest bidder.[126] Scraps of truth bundled up in a web of lies, as usual.

Many years later, when asked about this story, Abu Zubaydah accused Mitchell of lying. The fund-raising was for war refugees, not more attacks, he claimed. Before 9/11: "All my time in Afghanistan and Pakistan I was raising money and making fake passports not fighting." Post-9/11: "I decided to return to Pakistan or travel to Iran to try to raise more money to help the people who nobody cared about."[127] The second claim was not entirely backed by the threats he wrote his post-9/11 diary entries.[128] The CIA's claim that he was declaring war on the United States through his video was ridiculous, he said later. "I never conducted nor financially supported nor helped in any operation against America," he told US investigators.[129] Mitchell and Jessen paraphrased Abu Zubaydah's words and threw them back at him. How could he champion 9/11 without knowing how it was done? If he had been working with bin Laden for years, how could he not have prior knowledge about 9/11? It was time to stop lying. What was he up to when he was captured? What was Mokhtar up to? They had discussed flying planes into buildings, talked of cutting the cables on the Brooklyn Bridge, and were in it together, two angels of death, plotting more attacks against America based on Hollywood blockbusters. When he denied everything, they cut him off with water. "The interrogators . . . told subject that they would not let subject drown," noted a cable. But unless he was willing to change his attitude, he had better get used to this routine, because it was going to continue for a very long time.[130] At the end of the session, as he was unstrapped, Mitchell said, "You know what to do."[131] Abu Zubaydah staggered off the board and crawled into the dog box.

That night, one of the medics secretly reported back to DeMay: "Two, perhaps three [personnel] likely to elect transfer" away from the black site if headquarters forced them to continue, he said.[132] Most people's minds were made up. "It is the team's collective preliminary assessment that it is unlikely that subject has actionable new information about current threats to the United States."[133] The past eight days had "produced strong feelings of futility (and legality) of escalating or even maintaining the pressure."[134] Senior managers needed to come out and see what was happening.[135] In the shorter term, headquarters needed to watch the footage.

Mitchell recalled becoming increasingly worried that he and Jessen had been set up.[136] Their faces were on the tapes, not the staffers in the United

States ordering them to go further or the medics urging them to roll back. At Mitchell's request, the base chief called up Mike Winograd, the Bangkok station chief. "My recollection is the Chief of Station invited us to come to the Station for dinner and chat about our concerns," Mitchell said.[137] Mitchell wanted Winograd to witness a waterboarding session, so there were "other CIA officers on that tape."[138] So far, it was just him, Bruce Jessen, and possibly the base chief. Everyone else was masked up. Winograd did not want to do it, for obvious reasons. Mitchell recalled: "[Winograd] told me that to him it seemed voyeuristic, unnecessary and demeaning to Abu Zubaydah's dignity."[139] The station chief said he would watch from Mitchell's control center. Mitchell circled back. "It was just too sterile, like watching a video game," he said. This was about culpability—officers and contractors in it together. "I knew if there were CIA staffers on those tapes, we had some wriggle room," he later said.[140] In the end, Winograd agreed to witness a session, masked up and dressed as a guard. It wasn't what Mitchell had wanted.

After this session on August 10 or 11, the team dispatched a forceful cable to Langley. It was "highly unlikely" Abu Zubaydah knew anything about future attacks.[141] The medics were worried for the subject's health, as he had undergone a "profound transformation."[142] When the interrogator "raised his eyebrow," Abu Zubaydah "slowly walked forward of his own accord to the side of the water board and waited for interrogator to place the collar around his neck."[143] When the interrogator "snapped his fingers twice," Abu Zubaydah lay flat on the board.[144] He had learned helplessness but to avoid "going beyond legal authorities," they did not want to escalate the pressure.[145]

Jose Rodriguez was alarmed at legal talk being spelled out in official traffic. "Any speculative language as to the legality of given activities" should be "refrained from in written traffic (email or cable traffic)," he wrote back, suggesting a lot more was being said in phone calls.[146] The base chief asked for an explanation as to how the CIA intended to keep Abu Zubaydah "incommunicado" for the remainder of his life. What was the "endgame"? Headquarters did not answer, stating: "Please stay the course, medical situation permitting, and be certain you have our support."[147] Headquarters applied counterpressures: "We know this is a very difficult assignment. Your task is unique, stressful on the participants, as well as terribly important and sensitive." Recognizing the waning enthusiasm out in the field, the message continued: "Don't let this distance lead you to think that you have anything but our complete support."[148] Mitchell had a more granular recollection: "Actually, they were assuring us every day we are not going to get done over for this. That this would never be released and no one would ever know, and we were going, 'That's bullshit.'"[149]

On August 11, Mitchell and Jessen told Abu Zubaydah that if he did not give them what Washington wanted, "the only way he was going out of that room was in the large box in the corner."[150] It was a clear death threat. What did it look like? He whispered, "A coffin." Squashed inside the dog box that afternoon, he could be heard sobbing and appealing to God. "During the prayer, subject was heard saying that he had nothing and asking God to help him remember anything else."[151] After two more waterboarding sessions, they locked him inside the coffin for the night. He turned to the side and slumped, "forehead first." The guards "closed the box at 1812 hours, and departed the room."[152]

In the dark, Abu Zubaydah drowned in helplessness, and could be heard praying. As a child, he had recited this prayer daily: "O my Lord! I seek refuge with Thee from Thy anger and Thy punishment and from the evil of Thy servants and from the suggestions of the evil ones and lest they should come near me."[153] Now, he prayed to be martyred, and he thanked God that his beloved Swedish ex-wife had escaped his dangerous life. "Please do not imagine that she lost one of her beautiful eyes as I lost mine," he wrote years later, "do not attempt to imagine . . . they did with her the same as they did with me . . . or maybe worse."[154] He would thank God every day for the rest of his life that she was not with him when he was captured.

CHAPTER 11

"LOST IN SPACE"

August 13, 2002, Chiang Mai, Thailand

The black site team edited a thirty-minute show reel. Mitchell suggested the clips include "me, Bruce and the chief of base" and hoped they would seem "quite graphic to some viewers."[1] The base chief asked for "HQS attendees at the VTC [videotape conference] to be limited to the absolute minimum."[2] No recording should be done at the Langley end, as this all needed to stay outside US jurisdiction. Again, the base chief asked for clarification about the "endgame" and was ignored.[3] The nurse, who had decided to stay to support the incoming medic, warned Terry DeMay that anyone planning to watch the show reel should "prepare themselves for something not seen previously."[4] Worried about the legal repercussions of what they were doing to Abu Zubaydah, "folks here are truly all professionals," he assured, but no one was "enjoying what they are doing or seeing."[5] Team members took turns to decompress in Thailand's soupy heart. Tonight, it was his turn on duty, which meant takeout arranged by Thai Special Branch. "I guess that means I get my government provided grub(s) tonight," he quipped. "I like 'em barbecued and crunchy." On his bare-bones diet, Abu Zubaydah would spend the night being knocked about inside his coffin.

Jose Rodriguez chaired the screening. Jim Pavitt, the CIA's deputy director of operations and head of the national clandestine service, represented George Tenet. Everyone in Thailand was on the phone call except the guards on duty in the bunker.[6] "The intensity of the ongoing interaction was graphically evident," DeMay wrote, shocked by the footage.[7] Alec Station remained unmoved, saying it was difficult to see any suffering because the footage was grainy. Abu Zubaydah had "detailed, time-perishable information which

200

warranted a continuation of the process."[8] Bikowsky and those who had supervised the compilation of the "Zubaydah Biography"—Jennifer Matthews and her team—had considerable support. In addition to Marty Martin, Mike Scheuer also wanted to keep up the pressure. Uncompromising Scheuer reflected that post 9/11, "a lot of people needed to die."[9]

Mitchell had some sympathy for those pushing hardest at headquarters. "[They] were the same people Congress had chewed out. . . . 9/11 was their fault, they were told."[10] In Mitchell's opinion, "some of the most senior folks treated the water board as if it were a tool that should and could be used more than I thought it should."[11] It had been sold as the "silver bullet," the magic weapon with which to kill the werewolf.[12] But some senior staffers, believed Mitchell had to accept responsibility.[13] Mitchell reflected that he was reluctant to "get sideways" with people like Bikowsky, who he described as the "crazy red-haired lady."[14] In contrast, he referred to Matthews affectionately as "Jen."[15]

"Middle management said, 'Remember you are at a CIA black site and you are there at our convenience,'" Mitchell recounted, using a catchall for the Alec Station people he did not like.[16] "There was a suggestion we might have to find our own way home if we left," he later said.[17] An expletives-laden standoff ensued. "Middle management" called those at the black site "pussies" and told them, "You've lost your spines."[18] Mitchell described the argument as a "food fight." If Abu Zubaydah kept withholding and another attack happened, the "blood will be on your hands," said middle management. "They insisted we continue waterboarding for at least thirty days," Mitchell recalled, saying he regretted plucking that number "from the air." He claimed that he and Jessen "refused" to continue and told the skeptics to take over. "Dr. Jessen and I just told them . . . they should bring their rubber boots and come on down."[19] At the end of the call between the two camps, Rodriguez made a concession. He would send out a team to observe an interrogation session. He chose Bikowsky, Fredman, a "Chief of Base," who Mitchell described as a "highly respected senior operations officer," and the head of Technical Service. Mitchell and Jessen agreed not to use the waterboard again until they arrived, so during their next session, they put Abu Zubaydah on the board but did not pour water. At the end of the session, Mitchell warned Abu Zubaydah to be sincere. "Insha'Allah, am [sic] sincere," the detainee replied. "I not have chance not to be sincere."[20]

Ahead of the headquarters team arriving, Alec Station sent an outline of its "compelling body of reporting."[21] Much of the CIA's case against Abu Zubaydah still relied on media reporting. Angry rants about the United States in his diary were cited as "proof" he knew "details of potential Al Qaeda plans to attack a variety of targets in CONUS [continental United States]."[22] His revelations about Jose Padilla were an admission that he had personally planned to attack the United States. The millennium plot was front and center. Even Abu Zubaydah's sojourn in Missouri, where he had dreamed of studying and bedded his landlady, had been probed, on the specific direction of Jim Pavitt, who came from St. Louis.[23] Following Cheney's "one percent doctrine," the CIA could not rule out the possibility that, at age twenty, Abu Zubaydah had seeded Al Qaeda sleeper cells in the United States, which made his brother Hesham's situation even more precarious. Being emir of the House of Martyrs and author of the "Al Qaeda resistance-to-interrogation manual" put the icing on the cake. Given the number of compromised operatives who had passed through Khaldan, it was "inconceivable" that Abu Zubaydah had not known what they were all up to.[24]

Langley delivered its official response to the video screening. Abu Zubaydah had the "inner personal strength and mental acumen to withstand any pressure we can put to bear against him." The black site team should "continue with the aggressive interrogation strategy for the next 2–3 weeks," the logic being that if he stuck to his story after thirty days of intense pressure, then he was probably telling the truth.[25] Abu Zubaydah would be in his grave if they kept going for thirty days, warned the medics.[26] But an order was an order, and on August 15, the day before the headquarters team arrived, Abu Zubaydah was judged to be "backsliding" again.[27] Mitchell and Jessen put him back on the waterboard, told him that the people they worked for had demanded it, and subjected him to five sessions.[28]

During the last session, in the early afternoon, something bad happened. Before Mitchell lowered the cloth, Abu Zubaydah had "frantically begged them to believe he had told the truth." Jessen poured anyway. "When subject recovered," the official record stated: "He moaned: 'I die, I die, I tell the truth.'"[29] According to the official report, Mitchell and Jessen told him they "weren't going to let him," before leaving the cell.[30] Large portions of that day's cables were later redacted, but an email sent by the nurse to DeMay reported that Abu Zubaydah gave a glimpse of what had happened: Abu Zubaydah had momentarily died on the board.

At 1:27 P.M., he had become "completely unresponsive, with bubbles rising through his open, full mouth."[31] On being righted, "he failed to respond." The nurse went on to reveal that the detainee stopped breathing for eight seconds, prompting Mitchell to give him a xiphoid thrust, "with our medical folks edging towards the room."[32] Later, Mitchell, played it down, claiming he waited only "a couple of heartbeats," before manhandling Abu Zubaydah. When he regained consciousness, Abu Zubaydah expelled "copious amounts of liquid." He had fluid around his lips that was "kind of thick," recalled Mitchell. It bubbled as he began breathing.[33] Even though "there were no apparent after-effects," it was a dangerous moment that Abu Zubaydah later described as being "lost in space."[34] Roger Aldrich, Mitchell's former boss and mentor, and one of his greatest champions, had always warned him and Jessen to be careful. "All those techniques, if not done correctly, could be considered torture in my opinion," he reflected many years later. "If you had to revive this person . . . you have crossed the line."[35]

After this incident, someone went into the locked guardroom where VHS tapes of all Abu Zubaydah's interrogation sessions were stored and removed the tapes of a twenty-one-hour period of waterboarding. Dan Jones, who led the subsequent Senate investigation, described it as "the first stage" of the entire tape collection's destruction.[36] Shortly after this incident, the team also requested headquarters' advice about using a medical "disinhibitor," or truth serum.[37] Maybe it was better to drug Abu Zubaydah than drown him?

Terry DeMay had heard enough. Kept out of almost all decision-making as enhanced interrogation had been explored, put together, and approved under the guise of being a Medical Services–led operation, the most senior psychologist in the agency was not even consulted when the government had demanded better due diligence.[38] The Mitchell-friendly Office of Technical Service had provided the necessary backup instead and was understandably defensive, with Mitchell's contracting officer Kirk Hubbard characterizing DeMay's complaints as a petty attempt to start a turf war.[39] DeMay fundamentally distrusted Mitchell, and the CIA's Office of the Inspector General later described Mitchell's decision to double up as a psychologist and interrogator as "unprofessional."[40]

After Abu Zubaydah's episode of unconsciousness, Medical Services recommended fitting a pulse oximeter to the detainee's finger to measure the saturation of oxygen in his blood.[41] DeMay wrote that "the intensity and duration of AZ's interrogation" had caught his team by surprise.[42] He began researching alternatives, in an endeavor code-named Project Medication, which promoted "the seemingly more benign alternative of drug-based interviews."[43] DeMay was well aware that drugs also had negative connotations, given the CIA's history with MK-ULTRA, when hospital patients and prisoners had been dosed with LSD, some without their consent. Nevertheless, he reported that Versed, a sedative benzodiazepine that Abu Zubaydah had been given before being transported from the military hospital to the black site, produced similar effects, and the detainee had suffered no long-term side effects. Jonathan Fredman blocked the recommendation, stating that the Counterterrorist Center "did not want to raise another issued [*sic*] with the Department of Justice."[44]

Instead, DeMay and his staff began examining Mitchell and Jessen's waterboarding technique. Medics at the black site said that while most of Jessen's pours were "very brief," with the longest being around twenty seconds, they were "sometimes quickly repeated," and there had been thirty to forty "significant applications" of water.[45] The vaguely defined "pours," "applications," and "cycles" allowed for fuzziness to creep in. DeMay sent his deputy to be waterboarded at the navy SERE school in San Diego and learned that Mitchell and Jessen's waterboarding technique "differed substantially." While all instructors and psychologists had to be waterboarded themselves, fewer than half of navy SERE students ever experienced it. Those who went on the board "received only one application of 20 to 30 seconds," and no one ever experienced more than two. DeMay concluded: "AZ was the only multiple-application case known to us. Since he had had a period of unresponsiveness then surely a limit on the number of applications was in order?"[46] It was not just the number of pours but also Mitchell and Jessen's methods that were troubling. At navy survival school, water was dribbled onto the upper lip, and "little if any water passed through the cloth into the mouth." In Thailand, Mitchell kept a saturated cloth on Abu Zubaydah's face for the full duration of each pour and sometimes after as well. Jessen poured so much water that Abu Zubaydah swallowed copious amounts.[47] The detainee later stated that the cloth was also put "in" his mouth.[48] Mitchell later told the CIA inspector general that his technique was different because it was "for real" and needed to be convincing.[49]

DeMay's conclusion was stark: "The experiences of AZ had been little more than an amateurish experiment, with no reason at the outset to believe it would either be safe or effective."[50] Senior administration lawyers had been misled. The CIA had "exaggerated" the sophistication of the technique, had "overstated" its power, lied about the potential dangers, and had handed everything over to two men who had no official experience, beyond having watched demonstrations by SERE instructors who were either not qualified to use the technique or long retired.[51] As worrying, Mitchell and Jessen had conducted the sessions while also assessing Abu Zubaydah's psychological ability to withstand further sessions. "[Office of Medical Services] psychologists objected to the use of on-site psychologists as interrogators and raised conflict of interest and ethical concerns," DeMay reported. Many years later, the CIA's own assessment of waterboarding acknowledged that "this technique was used with a frequency that exceeded CIA's representations to the Department of Justice's Office of Legal Counsel."[52] The CIA had also failed "to perform a comprehensive analysis off the effectiveness" of enhanced techniques.[53]

On August 16, Alfreda Bikowsky arrived in Thailand, accompanied by Jonathan Fredman, the mystery "Chief of Base," and the chief of the Office of Technical Service[54] The Chief of Base was a "he" and had a "deep knowledge of Abu Zubaydah," according to Mitchell, which could cover everyone from Marty Martin to Mike Scheuer or Rich Blee.[55] Mitchell did not identify Bikowsky, saying only the "crazy red-haired lady turned up," after he asked them to "send your most skeptical people out here."[56] As deputy chief of Alec Station, Bikowsky was responsible for the "Zubaydah Biography." The Office of Technical Service had sourced Mitchell's and Jessen's expertise in the first place, held their contracts, and had provided the due diligence that had helped the CIA make the legal case for enhanced interrogation. All four visitors were strong supporters of the program.

Mitchell, with his self-preservation antennae switched on, wanted them all in the room—unmasked—while the videotape was recording. Convincing them was "pretty easy," he recalled.[57] "I told them they would not be able to engage with the detainee unless he could see their faces." He was now sure that the CIA intended for him and Jessen to take the flak to save the agency's reputation should the program come under investigation later, and he had not signed up for that.

On their first day in Thailand, only Bikowsky and the Chief of Base went into the cell. Mitchell said they turned up with "a bunch of maps, charts, photos."[58] Before the visitors entered, Mitchell and Jessen warned Abu Zubaydah to be on his best behavior. Abu Zubaydah recalled lying on the floor covered in vomit and surrounded by guards when the message was delivered.[59] Mitchell ordered the guards to clean him up with his hood. When he was pulled to his feet and walked to the walling wall, it was put back on. "We have two individuals that came from Washington to talk to you and they know more about you than you know about yourself," Mitchell said. The more truthful he was, Mitchell said, "the more you will be able to save yourself from worse troubles."[60]

Abu Zubaydah heard footsteps. "The hood was lifted and I saw . . . a man and a woman in civilian clothes." Standing naked in front of a woman, he was desperate to cover himself. But he was chained, and so he just glared. Jessen shoved him against the wall and put the noose/safety collar around his neck. "Don't start getting angry again or we'll start again from zero. Understand?" Abu Zubaydah nodded, like a dog drooling for meat when the feeding light was illuminated. His head was still throbbing from the last walling session. Bikowsky began reading off questions. Abu Zubaydah noticed that her hands were trembling, and she was speaking fast, stumbling over her words. After years of building up an Al Qaeda monster, she had him here in front of her, naked, stinking, and angry. An ugly red scar ran from his chest to his naval, his debrided leg was a mess, and he had trouble even standing up.[61] As Mitchell had said, watching CCTV did not really cut it. You had to be in the room and see the "water and snot flying."[62] The detritus of enhanced interrogation littered the filthy cell, and according to Mitchell, "it was just unpleasant." It smelled "like sweat and kind of musky."[63]

Bikowsky had gone after Abu Zubaydah with vigor, supporting Alec Station's assertions that he had helped plan 9/11 and countless other attacks. As far as her champion Mike Scheuer was concerned, Abu Zubaydah should rot in hell. "He's exactly where he needs to be just because you can't charge him with probably blowing up anything or killing anyone," he said.[64] The hammering Bikowsky and Scheuer received post-9/11 was something they would never forget, and eventually it brought them together romantically.[65]

Abu Zubaydah could not understand what Bikowsky was saying. The Chief of Base interrupted. "Ask one question at a time."[66] She started over. Abu Zubaydah replied. "I will answer the questions while looking at this man," he said, motioning to her male companion. "It's not appropriate for me to look at you while I am naked." Jessen took offense, grabbed his noose, and bounced him off the wall. "You still have pride, right?" he growled.[67] It was manners, not pride, retorted Abu Zubaydah. "Regardless of the circumstance and regardless of the fact that this woman is an enemy and regardless that she is part of the team that is torturing and humiliating me in such a rude and inconsiderate manner," he said. Jessen reacted furiously. "My words were like putting fuel on fire," Abu Zubaydah said, wondering why his interrogator was so "immaturely angry."

After Jessen calmed down, official cables described "an intense four-hour session" of talking, during which the detainee was "very engaged and provided answers."[68] However, there was no new information about future attacks, and the following day Bikowsky went back in for a longer session. While she and the Chief of Base sat on chairs, Abu Zubaydah, who had spent the night in a continuous cycle of coffin, dog box, and standing stress positions, was up against the wall with the noose around his neck. "They used it as a warning," he recalled.[69] For six hours, he stood on one foot because of what cables described as "knee pain."[70] He was "cooperative and conversant," assured them he "would not lie," and stuck to his guns. He knew nothing about future attacks, and later he wondered at Bikowsky's "stupid" questions.[71] Mitchell was relieved. His most skeptical critics could finally see how hard it was to get Abu Zubaydah talking about something he insisted he did not know. At the end of the session, they asked him to write an Al Qaeda link chart, and he was permitted to sit on the floor, like a child in kindergarten—as long as he cooperated.[72]

After two days of cooperation, they redeployed the hard approach. First, Bikowsky and her colleague watched as Mitchell and Jessen walled Abu Zubaydah, before he was "repeatedly and aggressively pressed" for information. He "displayed acute stress when the subject of the water board was addressed."[73] The following day they intended to conduct "two intense waterings."[74] Whenever he was on the board, Abu Zubaydah suffered from involuntary ejaculation, so Bikowsky watched from Mitchell's control center, while Fredman and the Chief of Base went into the cell. When the waterboard was wheeled over, Abu Zubaydah "begged and cried."[75] When he failed to come up with anything new, "water was applied with a soaked, full face covering, resulting in immediate fluid intake and involuntary body (leg, chest and arm) spasms."[76] Mitchell later claimed that he didn't see the spasms, "as I was controlling the cloth."[77] They elevated Abu Zubaydah to clear his airway before asking about future attacks. "Subject continued to cry, and claim ignorance."

Abu Zubaydah described August 19, 2002, as a "really crazy day."[78] Mitchell warned him to "give them something or we will have to show people you have nothing left to give."[79] Despite the fact that he had previously stopped breathing, he was subjected to a second "full-face watering." Mitchell later said that day's waterboarding consisted of "two 20 second pours and one 40 second pour, with lots of three to six second pours in between."[80] According to cables, Abu Zubaydah was thrown into spasms. He became "hysterical" and so distressed that "he was unable to effectively communicate."[81] He "could not breathe for several minutes," even after the waterboarding ended.[82] It was as if "they killed me," he said later.[83]

Years later, Mitchell admitted: "It was ugly and hard to do."[84] He and Jessen had decided to go extra heavy to persuade the skeptics to call a halt to the process. "Some folks watching were tearful," Mitchell recalled.[85] Even he felt sorry for Abu Zubaydah. Characterizing himself as a "softie," who cried at "dog food commercials," he said Abu Zubaydah had "agreed to work with us apart from lying a couple of times and he'd held up his end of the bargain and he'd said, 'I'll be your man.'"[86] Afterward, Mitchell was happy. "Their decision after watching that is we don't need to do that again," he said.[87] In his book, he described bathing Abu Zubaydah with warm water.[88] According to the cables and the CIA inspector general, they locked him in the coffin and sent a cable to headquarters recommending his "indefinite incarceration" at the US Naval Station, Guantánamo Bay.[89] The official tally noted that Abu Zubaydah had been subjected to eighty-three waterboardings, eighty-one more than were used in navy survival school.[90] However, VHS tapes of other waterboarding sessions were later found to be missing, broken, or erased.[91]

Abu Zubaydah did not believe it was over. The following day, August 20, he was shackled naked to a plastic patio chair before Bikowsky and the Chief of Base walked back in. Guards pulled him upright; Jessen walled him and he was threatened with more waterboarding. He had had enough. He believed he would not survive another round, and he did exactly what they had been demanding for months: to tell Washington what it wanted to know. "I started to confess to them of my responsibility for things that I did not do, and do not know anything about," he reflected.[92] "I would create, fabricate, and invent terrorist operations for them from my imagination just to take a break from their torture and terror." Yes, he was a 9/11 plotter, he told them. Yes, he was Number Three in Al Qaeda.

Although none of these claims was actually true and Abu Zubaydah was just repeating back to his interrogators what they wanted to hear, everything was reported in cables verbatim and the headquarters team went home happy. They finally had what they wanted, reams of it. "They were thrilled," said Mitchell, who felt vindicated and forever after maintained that what Abu Zubaydah had told them was the truth, rather than desperate lies.[93] "It was fascinating watching these people give everything up," he said later, speaking of Abu Zubaydah and other captives he subjected to enhanced interrogation. "The truth fell out like an alligator settling to the bottom of a pond."[94] However, according to an Office of Medical Services assessment, "there was no evidence that the waterboard produced time-perishable information which otherwise would have been unobtainable."[95] According to a subsequent Senate investigation, Abu Zubaydah never gave any actionable intelligence that helped stop another attack.[96] But because so many legal hurdles had been overcome to give the CIA what it demanded—a legal opinion that was described by a later Bush administration attorney general as a "slovenly mistake"—and because so many high-ranking officials were involved in that process, a story had to be maintained in perpetuity that enhanced interrogation worked.[97] Confessions had glided out of Abu Zubaydah easily, naturally, and inevitably—according to Mitchell, as the CIA now turned its attention to obtaining permission to do the same to other high-value detainees.

After Abu Zubaydah's last waterboarding, everyone received plaudits for persisting with the "silver bullet," while a Mitchell and Jessen "hot-wash" got underway.[98] An August 20 cable described their Phase 2 interrogation as a total success. The team had "broken any will or ability of subject to resist or deny" by applying physical pressures to "induce complete helplessness, compliance and cooperation."[99] Embracing language and descriptions that had been previously given a wide berth, the cable notes that when the large confinement box had first been brought into Abu Zubaydah's cell on August 4, it had been "placed on the floor so as to appear as a coffin." Waterboarding had been applied two to four times a day, with "multiple iterations of the watering cycle during each application." The amount of water had been "escalated . . . until it blocked his airway and he started to have involuntary spasms of the torso and extremities." Abu Zubaydah had "cried, begged and pleaded; finally becoming hysterical." The main takeaway: Abu Zubaydah's enhanced interrogation "should be used as a *template* for future interrogation of high-value captives." So much for reluctance.

The team sent another cable on August 23: "We have successfully broken subject's willingness to withhold threat and intelligence information. He is presently in a state of complete subjugation and total compliance."[100] Noting that "the issue of whether subject in fact has specific threat information will always be open to some conjecture," the base chief reported that "High-Value Terrorist Interrogators" Mitchell and Jessen were always "available" if required to "revisit a second aggressive phase of interrogation." They were "committed to providing long term support as needed to this mission" and had "done an incredible—and unprecedented job."[101] But unless they pushed Abu Zubaydah even harder, nobody would ever know if he had more to give. "Whilst we have no pretense that this is the sum total of what AZ knows, believe we are making a dent in that knowledge," the base chief continued. "Our bottom line is that we don't know what we don't know. We can only operate on what we do know, and that intelligence so far is consistent with AZ's story." Given that he had finally admitted to having direct access to "operational planners"—cited as Osama bin Laden, Khalid Sheikh Mohammad, Ahmed Ressam, and Jose Padilla—"we correctly assumed he would have some knowledge of operational planning and he does, indeed, have this knowledge. He admits this even for 9/11." However, "he still insists that he has no knowledge of the big follow-on attack." There was never any acknowledgment from headquarters that he simply did not know.

Inside the bunker, the subject of all this self-congratulatory reporting was given rewards too. The waterboard was removed, then the coffin. Only the dog box remained, "outside in a way that I could still see it through the bars." Soon after, he had an intense dream. "I was immersed in my most saddest moments and I had lost hope except from God." Dragged out of his coffin by Jessen, he was short-chained on the floor, while Jessen stood over him, telling him in Arabic, "It's gonna be fine."[102] But it never would be fine again for Abu Zubaydah, because after getting over the horror of what they had witnessed in Thailand, the headquarters visitors had turned tables and decided that he still was not broken. Unnamed senior officers were certain he continued to hold on to a nugget that could only be dislodged by the "silver bullet."[103] The headquarters team had made this clear before leaving Thailand. "I knew they didn't want to rule out the water board," Mitchell said.[104]

Bob Dussault, Mitchell's and Jessen's former boss at JPRA, used to warn his survival-course students against telling interrogators what they wanted to hear, because it never made the pain go away.[105] He gave North Korean examples during his lectures, stories he had learned from interviewing former American prisoners-of-war. Confessing to anything was always a cue for interrogators to push deeper for the "truth." Now that Mitchell and Jessen had forced Abu Zubaydah into making false confessions by almost drowning him, and regardless of the improbable, unlikely, and unprovable nature of some of his claims (e.g., that he had helped plan 9/11), the CIA was already contemplating reengagement. Despite Mitchell's claims of warm baths and pushback, he and Jessen were on standby to "tune [AZ] up" as required. If they could prove he was lying, they believed, it was "well worth the risk to press him hard to get one nugget."[106] But if they went back to the waterboard without any provable lie, "it is likely he may simply move into a state where we come close to the thresholds established by CTC/LGL." Mitchell and Jessen were patriots, willing to do many harsh things for their country, but they would "not go to prison."[107]

⸺⸺⸺◆⸺⸺⸺

It was never over for Abu Zubaydah, and it was only just beginning for others. On August 30, Rizzo and Fredman met John Bellinger, the National Security Council legal advisor, to discuss the possibility of using Yoo-Bybee for other high-value detainees.[108] To keep Mitchell and Jessen on board, their contracts were extended to December 31, 2002.[109] On September 5, their salaries were increased by $52,500, taking Jessen to $187,500 and Mitchell to $310,100.[110] Everyone agreed to keep quiet about the disunity that had split the team over Abu Zubaydah's interrogation. But details would eventually leak out in the form of a report Terry DeMay of the CIA's Office of Medical Services had prepared for the agency leadership and an investigation by the CIA's inspector general.[111]

A senior CIA official in the Counterterrorist Center, later revealed that the argument for going further with Abu Zubaydah had been led by a young male analyst he described as a "cocky SOB." It centered on National Security Agency intercepts about a plot that Abu Zubaydah was allegedly implicated in. "They said AZ knew it was going to happen," the officer recalled.[112] "They said it's inconceivable that he doesn't know this, so we want you to go out there and hammer him. Well, it turned out it was translated wrong and had nothing to do with AZ knowing anything. There was *nothing* there." Official inquiries later reached similar conclusions. "The Agency lacked adequate linguists or subject matter experts and had very little hard knowledge of what particular AQ leaders—who later became detainees—knew," reported one inquiry.[113] This lack of knowledge, languages, and nuance led analysts to speculate about what a detainee "should know," instead of establishing what they "did know." Diverging priorities also played a part. For Alec Station, the risk was not getting the information required to prevent the "next big attack."[114] For the interrogators, the concerns were "a detainee's death" or causing him "permanent harm." "Sharon," a pseudonym for an Abu Zubaydah subject-matter expert who later retrained as an interrogator, saw both camps and recalled that this conflict "bugged the hell out of people."[115] She said: "I know that Bruce and Jim were always struck by it. I know that Alfreda was very forceful and said they know more than they are giving you and if we stop being nice to them, we'll get this information."

Later, even Mitchell confirmed that Alec Station's insistence on getting rougher had been based on erroneous intelligence and poor translation—although he maintained they got excellent actionable intelligence nevertheless. "Five different times AZ contradicted things they said, and he was right every time," he said.[116] One of these times was when Alec Station's insisted that Abu Zubaydah had already been to Iran at the time of his capture. Alec Station had demanded Mitchell and Jessen press Abu Zubaydah about something they had dubbed the "Lobster Plot," allegedly taken from an intercepted communication. When Abu Zubaydah pointed out there was no specific Arabic word for "lobster," the two "docs" had contacted Langley. "We wrote back saying, 'Why do you believe this?'" Mitchell recalled.[117] "This was all going on during the time the red-headed Alec woman was saying, 'You've lost your spine, you'll have the blood of Americans on your hands, you are pussies.'" According to the senior CTC officer, Bikowsky "got hammered a little bit" as a result of making mistakes with intelligence material.[118] Intense pressure from the seventh floor to get confirmation of Al Qaeda's nuclear plots caused everyone to reach for the silver bullet.

September 11, 2002, Karachi, Pakistan

Stunning news from Pakistan marked the first anniversary of 9/11: Ramzi bin al-Shibh, a thirty-year-old Yemeni, the right-hand man of Khalid Sheikh Mohammad, had been captured in Karachi. He had been a roommate of lead 9/11 hijacker Mohamed Atta, with whom he had established the famous terrorist cell in Hamburg, Germany, and video footage showed them together at bin Laden's headquarters camp in Kandahar. Atta had called bin al-Shibh less than two weeks before the attacks, giving him a coded date for 9/11. Evidence suggested that bin al-Shibh would have been a 9/11 hijacker himself had it not been for the vigilance of US embassy officials in Germany and Yemen, from where he made multiple unsuccessful visa applications.[119] Unable to enter the United States, he became a key 9/11 planner, sending money, exchanging messages, and meeting hijackers in the weeks and days before the attacks. Shortly before his capture, a taped interview of him and Khalid Sheikh Mohammad bragging to a reporter about masterminding the "Holy Tuesday" operation aired on *Al Jazeera* as part of a groundbreaking two-part documentary to commemorate the attacks.[120] Capturing bin al-Shibh alive was a huge success for Pakistan and the White House. It also brought the CIA one step closer to "KSM."

The scene in Karachi was dramatic. Spent cartridges littered the alleged Al Qaeda safe house on Commercial Street; there were policemen all over the roofs, and two of bin al-Shibh's associates were carried out dead.[121] Blindfolded and wearing a navy blue T-shirt, his back arched as he yelled and flung a fist into the air in defiance, bin al-Shibh was photographed surrounded by a phalanx of armed Pakistani police officers. Breathless sharpshooters described a three-hour siege and recounted that inside the building, one of the gunmen had written "Allahu akhbar" on a wall in blood.[122] But the scene was complete theatrics. Official documents showed bin al-Shibh had actually been captured more than twenty-four hours earlier at an apartment on Tariq Road, three miles away, along with two of Khalid Sheikh Mohammad's sons, aged seven and eight.[123] It was not even clear whether the blindfolded man really was bin al-Shibh or a body double, but a large CIA and FBI team was already on the ground, going through boxes of documents and laptops at the Tariq Road address.[124]

Three nights later, the real Ramzi bin al-Shibh was led out on the asphalt at Karachi airport. He had been fingerprinted, retina scanned, and subjected to a body-cavity search. He was hooded, manacled, and wearing an adult diaper. American security contractors, CIA officials, and six FBI agents surrounded him, including Ali Soufan, who had got Abu Zubaydah talking, and Mike Butsch, who had been investigating the Hamburg cell over the past year. Butsch identified bin al-Shibh when a guard pulled up his hood and pointed a flashlight in his face. The detainee was hauled up the steps of a CIA rendition plane, his reception committee clattering up behind him. Despite the FBI's expressed reluctance to do any more work inside the CIA's black site program, Soufan, Butsch, and a third FBI agent were accompanying bin al-Shibh to a new CIA black site in Afghanistan known as the Salt Pit.[125]

The day after bin al-Shibh's restaged capture September 12, 2002, Mitchell's contract went up by a further $100,000, taking it to $410,100.[126] Jessen's contract jumped to $267,500.[127] Mitchell would later claim credit for bin al-Shibh's capture, saying that Abu Zubaydah had led him to bin al-Shibh's location while discussing the jihad-holiday fund-raiser Hassan Ghul, something that a congressional investigation later disputed.[128] How the CIA saved the world was a compelling good-news story, even though the truth behind Ramzi bin al-Shibh's capture had much more to do with timing, Pakistani president Pervez Musharraf's political survival, the ISI's vast Karachi network of informers, bin al-Shibh's unwise decision to show off in an interview, and the huge CIA bounty on offer for his head than any gobbet spit out in a moment of sheer panic by Abu Zubaydah. According to Butsch, the real intelligence had come from a Saudi Al Qaeda suspect being interrogated by the FBI at Bagram, where bin al-Shibh's CIA rendition flight would soon be landing. Only one thing about his future was certain. If the CIA could get legal cover lined up, he was a prime candidate for enhanced interrogation. Khalid Sheikh Mohammad's sons had been left behind in Karachi with the FBI but they were later transferred in secret to the CIA, which held them in small boxes, and threatened them with insects.[129] They would not see their mother again for several years and their father never at all.

CHAPTER 12

"On-the-Job Training"

A fter Abu Zubaydah "confessed" to being Number Three in Al Qaeda and a 9/11 plotter, the CIA treated Mitchell "like a rock star."[1] Because the work was so unpleasant, he and Jessen, who described himself as "the guy with all the tricks," intended to get whatever they could from designing an interrogation template that the CIA director had invested in.[2] Days after Ramzi bin al-Shibh's capture was announced to the world, the CIA sought to reuse the Yoo-Bybee approval memo. "If we capture [redacted], we'd like to have Jim or Bruce, one of [redacted] psychologist interrogators fly to [redacted] meet the detainee," the agency proposed. "With the approvals in hand, they can immediately begin interrogations and take advantage of capture shock."[3] However, Mitchell and Jessen did not immediately interrogate bin al-Shibh, for reasons that were also later redacted. It was left instead to Ali Soufan, who questioned him, naked, chained, and sleep-deprived on the dirt floor of the Salt Pit, a makeshift CIA interrogation site on the outskirts of Kabul.[4]

Jose Rodriguez's focus was on getting bin al-Shibh talking and expanding the enhanced interrogation program quickly and effectively. "The secret prison/EIT program was growing like topsy," reflected John Rizzo.[5] Rodriguez wanted Mitchell and Jessen's "toolbox" to be made widely available. But that posed a significant problem. Mitchell and Jessen had thirty-two years of combined SERE experience, while the CIA needed more interrogators "in the shortest time possible."[6] The rock stars were paid extra to become consultants. In private correspondence with a CIA psychologist thinking of retraining as an interrogator, Mitchell explained how to work the waterboard. Repetition was the key. "As for our buddy, he capitulated the first time," he wrote of Abu Zubaydah.[7] "We chose to expose him over and over until we had a high degree of confidence he wouldn't hold back." The detainee had told them "he was ready to talk during the first exposure," meaning all the rest had been window dressing. Mitchell also advised his colleague to read a book, *Torture and Its Consequences*, "especially the chapters that deal with Pavlovian conditioning neurosis," a psychological disorder similar to learned helplessness. Correctly judging how far to push detainees (or students) took years of experience, Mitchell lectured. But the CIA intended to get its new enhanced interrogators up to speed in just weeks.

To roll out the expansion, Rodriguez hired "Gus," a SERE-trained Vietnam veteran previously working in the always reliable Office of Technical Service.[8] Gus specialized in eavesdropping and secure communications but had no experience of interrogation.[9] His job was to head up Special Missions, a new Counterterrorist Center department that would run the "Renditions, Detention and Interrogation Group," a supercharged reinvention of Mike Scheuer's rendition team. Rodriguez wanted control over everything from techniques to shackles (made by Hiatt Handcuffs in Birmingham, England): a full "rendition go-bag."[10] He envisaged teams of highly trained interrogators working the globe. But Mitchell and Jessen were busy doing "special things to special people in special places," so most of the training would have to be outsourced to their former colleagues at the Joint Personnel Recovery Agency (JPRA).[11] Gus was initially reluctant to take the job. "I said, 'Jesus, that's all the cats and dogs,'" he recalled.[12] "We knew it would come back and bite us in the ass." But like Scott Shumate, Gus did not really have a choice as he was "surged" into the Counterterrorist Center.

Gus hit the ground running, "around the time of getting legal approval" to enhance Abu Zubaydah's interrogation, and his budget was "huge, bigger even than Alec Station."[13] As well as training new interrogators, he was responsible for establishing new black sites. "We sent people out to talk to liaison services," he recalled, using CIA-speak for foreign intelligence agencies. "They would take our team around and say, 'What about here?' 'Or here?' 'Or here?'" CIA stations were told to compile "wish lists" of financial assistance and "think big" in terms of figures.[14] They looked at an island off Costa Rica and ships permanently sailing international waters and spoke to former Eastern Bloc countries "wanting to get into NATO and the EU." Because of the nature of the work, one of his closest advisors was the CIA's acting chief counsel, John Rizzo, who Gus called "my favorite pimp." Gus and Mitchell also bonded.[15] They were both happily married without children, proud of their no-frills upbringings, and disdainful of privilege and excess.

However, Gus inherited one thing that would cause him and the agency significant problems: the new CIA interrogation site in Kabul where Ali Soufan interrogated Ramzi bin al-Shibh in September 2002. Commissioned by the Kabul station chief, Rich Blee, it had been hastily built to handle detainees passed to the CIA by US military intelligence personnel working at Bagram Collection Point, which was forty miles up the Kabul-Bagram Airport Road. The Counterterrorist Center approved the budget of $200,000 but provided no oversight.[16] Matthew Zirbel, a first-tour officer with no experience of prisons or interrogation, beyond having attended a four-day SERE course, was appointed as site manager.[17] Inside the building—an abandoned brick factory—all the windows were blacked out, and twenty fetid-smelling open-top concrete cells stood in total darkness. The CIA called it the Salt Pit, and allegations of abuse began emerging as soon as it opened for business in August 2002.[18] Detainees called it the "dark prison."[19] One interrogator sent there dubbed it "Hotel California."[20]

Because the Salt Pit was not officially a Counterterrorist Center operation, Rodriguez and his Special Missions chief Gus took no notice of it. They focused on hunting down more high-value detainees, setting up more black sites and molding an interrogator training program based on Mitchell and Jessen's template.[21] The CIA wanted to own everything at the top end, and Rodriguez demanded: "well documented oversight," "quality control," and "aggressive training and mentoring."[22] New interrogators would be taught that Al Qaeda operatives had "received formal training in techniques to resist interrogations." They would study "a manual found at an Al Qaeda safe house in Manchester, England in May 2000," written by Abu Zubaydah, who had employed "refined counter-interrogation techniques" during his initial interrogation but had been persuaded to give up "outstanding" results. They would be taught how Al Qaeda detainees were "particularly adept at using cultural differences as both an interactive impediment . . . and as a psychological mechanism behind which to hide." A core-curriculum subject was "the influence of Arab culture on the employment of resistance techniques."[23] Training materials talked of "the Arab mind," a reference to Ralph Patai's seminal work.

Trainee interrogators had to learn the limits of the law: only high-value detainees trained to resist and hide time-sensitive intelligence were covered by the Yoo-Bybee memo. But that did not really matter because the CIA was not interested in the low-value detainees being sorted at Bagram. Trainees also had to learn how to protect themselves and the agency. While the CIA did not have any "specific intent" to kill or inflict "severe physical or mental pain or suffering," "documentation" was critical in case of accidents. All this was virgin territory to Gus, who was more accustomed to the James Bond–esque gadgetry of Technical Service. He really needed help. But Mitchell and Jessen were always down-range. "The CIA came to us and said we want more people like you," Mitchell recalled. "We said we are already busy."[24]

Gus struggled. "The government flooded us with money, thinking it would solve the problem, but we needed trained people," he explained.[25] "You can't expect us to go to work on Monday when you've been hired on Friday." Surrounded by "surged" old-timers and newcomers with no experience, he called in Charlie Wise, a former Latin America Division interrogator trainer, who in 1983 had updated the banned KUBARK interrogation manual and taught its lessons to rebels in the Honduran jungle.[26] Some at the agency regarded Wise as a hero; his most famous operation had been to persuade the Afghan *mujahideen* to sell Stinger missiles back to the US government at the end of the Soviet war by telling them they were faulty.[27] But he was so controversially linked to the disastrous results of the CIA's work in Latin America that even risk-taking Rodriguez had sidestepped him the first time around, hiring Mitchell and Jessen, both with clean sheets, instead.[28] "Charlie was kind of a cowboy," said Gus.

Wise's *Human Resource Exploitation Training Manual* talked of "destroying" a subject's ability to resist interrogation. It listed the old KUBARK manual's "coercive techniques," some of which Wise had struck through or rewritten, but the original instructions were still clearly legible, such as "sensory deprivation tanks," in which a person or "subject" was suspended in water and put in a blackout mask, "which enclosed the entire head and only allowed breathing."[29] It was all remarkably similar to the countermeasures contained in the "Mitchell paper" of December 2001, and the techniques used on Abu Zubaydah: threats, deprivation of sensory stimulation, interrogators assuming a God-like role, cutting of hair, imposition of stress positions and sleep deprivation, and focusing on the early hours of the morning, when a subject's "mental and physical resistance is at its lowest." Only the concept of learned helplessness was missing, since the original KUBARK manual was conceived four years before Professor Seligman had begun his dog experiments. In KUBARK, the key concept was taking prisoners to the "three Ds": debility, dependency, and dread.

However, Wise had some plus points. He was a blue-badger (a CIA staffer) with existing classification, was SERE-trained (he was an ex-marine), and had experience (in Honduras and also as a Vietnam veteran). "Charlie was really our only trained interrogator at the time," Gus said, and in the fall of 2002, he offered Wise the title "chief of interrogations," handed him Mitchell's reading list on brainwashing and a pile of JPRA-training materials supplied by Chris Wirts, and asked him to take charge of a training program based on the "DoD/JPRA's training MO." Wise needed to hurry, because "the big boys are saying we are not getting enough information," recalled Gus.[30]

Wise got on the phone to JPRA.[31] Earlier in the year, Chris Wirts had drawn up training courses for Guantánamo interrogators with Bruce Jessen; he had helped design the CIA training courses of June and July 2002, and now he helped design a bespoke course for trainee CIA interrogators. Assisting him were Gary Percival, who had replaced Jessen as JPRA's senior SERE psychologist; Joe Witsch, who with Percival had conducted CIA training in July; and Terry Russell, JPRA's head of research and development, who Mitchell had known since the 1990s.[32] Charlie Wise's pilot course would be based on the Guantánamo interrogator-training course, which had taken place at Fort Bragg, used Jessen's material, and would draw on everyone's experiences of working on the "high risk of capture" course at JPRA's Personnel Recovery Academy in Spokane.[33] The new plan involved JPRA instructors the CIA was already familiar with, all of whom had previously worked with Mitchell and Jessen. They had security clearances and were deemed to be safe and professional.

Techniques to be taught on the course included "invasion of personal space by a female," and were designed, like nudity, to be "culturally undesirable for Arab or Islamic detainees."[34] Students also studied "the Arab mind."[35] There was also "hitting in a way that was not injurious," "exposing detainees to cold until they shiver," and rough handling.[36] Witsch later explained how "rough handling" worked. "You would pull the person up to their feet, you would move them rapidly in the direction that you were going to take them," he said.[37] "Basically, they have no control. They would feel like the person that has them is in total control of them." Wise decided to split his course (at an off-site CIA training facility in Virginia) between a week of classroom and a week of "hands-on training in EITs," which would enable students to "obtain, and then retain certification."[38] The second part was referred to as "OJT" (on-the-job training).[39] This was another term borrowed from SERE school, but normally it involved role-play only, with one instructor playing the "beater" while another played the "beatee," as Witsch and Percival had previously demonstrated at Langley.[40]

While Wise explored on-the-job-training options, Gus interviewed prospective interrogators. Because people connected to enhanced interrogation were "getting pay raises, jumps in their rank and cash rewards," according to Mitchell, Gus was deluged with applications.[41] "Too many of them said, 'I can't wait to get my hands on these guys,'" Gus recalled.[42] Everyone was sent to Medical Services for a psychological evaluation. "There were two that came back," said Gus. "They said, 'We don't recommend you send these guys.' I didn't ask any questions." Despite Gus's assurances that he was on the lookout for bad apples, a subsequent investigation found that a number of personnel admitted to the program as interrogators had "notable derogatory information" in their records that would have been available to the CIA at the time. "This group of officers included individuals who, among other issues, had engaged in inappropriate detainee interrogations, had workplace anger-management issues, and had reportedly admitted to sexual assault," investigators later concluded.[43]

Gus was firing on multiple cylinders. In late October 2002, he had to assign a new base chief to Thailand. Mitchell, Jessen and their mysterious operational psychologist base chief friend were needed elsewhere at short notice. Gus chose a female officer in Alec Station whose dedication to the agency had come to Jose Rodriguez's attention. Born in Kentucky, Gina Haspel had grown up wherever the US Air Force happened to station her father, including several years in London during her teens. She had graduated with a degree in journalism, worked in a library, and was married at twenty. By the time she joined the CIA as a "reports officer" in 1985 she was divorced, although she kept her married name.[44] Posted overseas, she later described her work as "right out of a spy novel," and she had helped capture two suspected East Africa embassy bombers. As the fight against Al Qaeda heated up, Haspel asked to transfer into the Counterterrorist Center. Over the weeks following 9/11, she worked grueling hours and empathized with those accused of failing to stop the attacks. In her résumé, Haspel eulogized "the extraordinary sisterhood that brought their passion and drive to the fight to bring down Al Qaeda." Like Alfreda Bikowsky and Jennifer Matthews, she was on the "get the bastards" side of the road, one colleague recalled.[45]

Haspel arrived in Thailand on October 27, 2002. The local CIA station was on high alert. In early October, several embassies around the world had been closed because of security concerns, and a pair of snipers had killed ten people in the Washington, DC, area. On October 12, more than two hundred people, mostly Western holidaymakers, had been murdered in horrific bombings at nightclubs in Bali. Al Qaeda was pathological and unpredictable, and American citizens were in its sights. The CIA needed to get tougher and rougher, not "wimp out on the waterboard," as one of those familiar with the Bikowsky standoff had jokingly accused Mitchell of doing.[46] After Bali, for which Khalid Sheikh Mohammad was partly blamed, Alec Station revisited its opinion of Abu Zubaydah, concluding that he was still playing them.[47] Shortly before departing Thailand, Mitchell and Jessen discussed with Haspel putting him back on the waterboard. Tenet raised the idea in the President's Daily Brief on October 18, stating that Abu Zubaydah was still withholding "significant threat information" about operatives hiding in the United States.[48] However, Abu Zubaydah won a last-minute reprieve when Mitchell and Jessen were called elsewhere. He remembered them bringing Haspel into his cell and saying, "She can make your life good or bad," before they disappeared.[49] Mitchell went back to the United States "feeling good about what we had accomplished."[50] Jessen headed to Afghanistan, where Alec Station wanted him to assess Salt Pit detainees for enhanced interrogation.[51]

With Mitchell and Jessen gone, Haspel advised Abu Zubaydah to "take advantage of the opportunity to set the record straight on any issues about which he has either been less than forthcoming or has obfuscated."[52] He recalled discussing the so-called London Road network, his passport tricks, and Khaldan's finances.[53] Haspel was particularly interested in the United Kingdom, and she brought photographs of British Al Qaeda suspects supplied by MI6.[54] The only three Abu Zubaydah could identify were Binyam

Mohamed (Jose Padilla's sidekick), Birmingham bookshop owner Moazzam Begg, and Shaker Aamer, a Saudi-born British resident who had worked as a US Army translator during the Persian Gulf War of 1990–91.[55] All three were already in US detention, and the CIA was trying to connect them to Al Qaeda. Abu Zubaydah told her that as far as he knew, none of them was in Al Qaeda or involved in any terrorist operations. He knew Begg and Aamer through charity work they had done in Afghanistan prior to 9/11, and he had stayed with Begg after the bookshop owner relocated to Afghanistan in July 2001. Begg's Palestinian wife had served up meals that reminded Abu Zubaydah of home.[56]

Haspel rewarded Abu Zubaydah for his compliance. He was given a foam mattress and a towel "to cover my genitals," and later, "they gave me some very light clothes, short slacks and an orange shirt."[57] He was also given a Koran, a pen, and a pad of paper. Officially, it was for noting down English words he did not understand. When he started using it as a diary, recording what had happened over his months in CIA detention, he checked to see whether he would get into more trouble. "Their response was, 'No, none of the things we did to you was considered illegal,'" he recalled.[58] "I was surprised to hear that, for I had a different understanding." But he was thankful for Haspel's efforts. "Even with your enemies, you have to be fair," he reflected.[59]

Two weeks after Haspel arrived, Abu Zubaydah was moved to the "interrogation room," the other cell designed by Mitchell, but never used. He was told: "We need your cell for a new person." Mitchell, back in the United States, learned about the "new person" when Rodriguez asked him to pick up Abd al-Rahim al-Nashiri, a Saudi national accused of plotting the October 2000 bombing of the USS *Cole*. He had been captured in the United Arab Emirates and was being handed over for a sizable cash bounty.[60] Both the FBI and the US Naval Criminal Investigative Service (NCIS) wanted to interrogate al-Nashiri—FBI special agent Ali Soufan and Robert McFadden from NCIS had been joint lead case officers on the USS *Cole* investigation.[61] No one knew more about al-Nashiri than they did, and both were Arabic speakers. The CIA point-blank refused. All the high-value detainees belonged to them and Mitchell was ordered to collect al-Nashiri in Dubai.[62] The plan was to stop off in Afghanistan, where Jessen was busy assessing other potential high-value detainees at the Salt Pit, and then bring al-Nashiri and anyone else of particular interest to Thailand for enhanced interrogation. The CIA had by now found a legal pathway for Mitchell and Jessen to expand enhanced interrogation beyond Abu Zubaydah.[63] Mitchell shouldered his rendition go-bag and boarded another flight.

He flew into Bagram with al-Nashiri on November 11. Jessen came to meet them on the asphalt but was so tooled up Mitchell walked past without recognizing him. "He was kitted up with protective gear and weapons," Mitchell recalled.[64] Jessen's hair, usually short, was "scraggly." He also had a full beard and a headdress. "When [Jessen] grows a beard, he looks like a biker, and that could put the fear in you," mused Gus.[65] Guards manhandled al-Nashiri, who was hooded, chained, and diapered, into a military vehicle that took off down the Kabul-Bagram Airport Road. The Salt Pit was located on littered scrubland in the northern outskirts of the Afghan capital, surrounded by razor wire, sniper netting, crash barriers, guard towers, and a high brick wall.

It was Mitchell's first (and only) time in Afghanistan, and the contrast with Thailand could not have been starker. The Salt Pit was forbidding, and would later be depicted in the opening scene of the film *Zero Dark Thirty*, although the real scene as later described by detainees was far grimmer than the Hollywood depiction. Mitchell was given a headlamp to get around. "It was completely dark, I'm looking through a beam of light," he recalled.[66] The cells looked like "horse stalls." A raised walkway was being constructed so guards and interrogators could look down through metal grills into the cells. The Detroit rapper Eminem's "The Real Slim Shady"—"will the real Slim Shady, please stand up"—played at maximum volume.[67] The reason for this choice was obvious. Inside cells, stripped and shaved detainees were hanging naked or semi-naked from walls and overhead crossbars in the "standing sleep deprivation" position, the old KGB torture method the CIA had tried out on Abu Zubaydah.[68] The CIA had defined it as a "conditioning technique," so interrogators did not need prior authorization from headquarters to employ it.[69] It was coupled with a bare bones diet of water and Ensure, which meant the detainees endured the further humiliation of semipermanent diarrhea. The lucky ones were taped into adult diapers.

Mitchell later described the Salt Pit regime as "unsupervised brutality" and primarily blamed its site manager, Matthew Zirbel, a first-tour officer who was only briefed about his new responsibilities three days after arriving in Afghanistan in August 2002. Zirbel's first detainee arrived two weeks later, in the middle of the chaos of setting up an ad hoc facility with limited resources in the middle of a warzone. The cells were not yet built and the guard force not stood up, so the first detainee was "left hanging," with his toes barely touching the floor, naked except for a diaper.[70] This became the detention "model," and detainees could go for "days or weeks" without anyone looking at them.[71] One low-value detainee was left for seventeen days straight.[72] Some "looked like a dog that had been kenneled."[73] Those interrogating detainees were told by Zirbel to "do the job without harming or killing detainees."[74] One day, Zirbel came into the lunchroom and quipped, "I had two guys hanging at once," holding out his arms crucifixion style.[75] Beyond giving statements during an internal CIA inquiry and to the CIA Inspector General, Zirbel has never spoken about his time in Afghanistan. Working in a chaotic and dangerous environment where everyone was overstretched, Zirbel had not been not well assisted. No one was trained or had any relevant experience and no headquarters guidance was provided because it was not a headquarters facility. For most of them time, no CIA linguists, trained interrogators, psychologists, or medics were available.[76]

During the night, an untrained Afghan guard force was left in charge.[77] The Americans stayed at the Ariana Hotel in the heart of Kabul's "Green Zone," close to the US embassy and the Presidential Palace. The CIA had rented the whole hotel, once a Taliban hangout, and set up its Kabul station there, along with a bar named the Talibar.[78] The Salt Pit–Ariana setup was a recipe for disaster, and Majid Khan, who spent months hanging naked, recalled his American interrogators often smelled of alcohol when they arrived in the morning. "They would come in with a bag of tools and set them down next to Majid," said previously classified notes written by his attorneys.[79] "They would pull out a hammer and show it to Majid. One of them threatened to hammer Majid's head." Later, the CIA also pureed his food and fed it to him rectally.[80] At one stage, he became so scared he tried to bite through veins in his arm to kill himself.

Many Salt Pit interrogators were reservists called to active duty after 9/11 and dispatched to Afghanistan to do menial jobs like traffic patrol.[81] One of the few with any real CIA experience was Marty Martin's colleague, Albert El Gamil, who had rendered Ibn Sheikh al-Libi to Cairo in a coffin. Zirbel advocated "mock execution," involving the firing of a handgun, and he told "interior guards" (the Afghanis) that detainee well-being was their responsibility and arranged cells in descending order of harshness from "baseline" to a "luxury suite."[82] Clothes, blankets, earplugs, tea, and "exotic food" were "creature comforts" to be won through compliance.[83] There were no heaters in the cell block, despite "drastically dropping temperatures," and it smelled so bad, a "very earthy, kind of mildewy, unpleasant smell," according to Jessen, that guards asked for face masks.[84]

Visitors reported alarming conversations about "torture" and "war crimes," but Rodriguez later denied any responsibility, saying he had "other higher priorities."[85] The buck stopped with the Kabul station chief, according to Mitchell.[86] This was George Tenet's old friend from Capitol Hill, Rich Blee. After appointing Blee to replace Mike Scheuer at Alec Station prior to 9/11, Tenet called Blee his "top Al Qaeda guy," and he was considered an expert on Abu Zubaydah.[87] After 9/11, amid recriminations about having missed crucial signs before the attacks, Blee went off to Afghanistan to support the mission to kill bin Laden. A year on, he was still there, based inside the Ariana, overworked and under-resourced.[88] Even though Rodriguez and Mitchell tried to maintain distance, interrogation plans for the Salt Pit's early detainees were circulated to senior officers, including Rodriguez, as part of the "DCI Daily Update," and headquarters authorized these plans.[89] Zirbel later pointed the finger at Bruce Jessen, who arrived in late October 2002. Jessen was in charge of the Salt Pit, insisted Zirbel.[90] Jessen "did not like this" characterization, because "it was a lie." He reflected: "I think [Zirbel] got scared . . . he was worried. He didn't know what to do."[91] While he was at the Salt Pit, Jessen reported a much more positive scene than anyone else did. He described Zirbel as "very bright and motivated" and said he "did a great job" in setting it up. The atmosphere of the facility was "excellent," Jessen said, describing it as "nasty, but safe." He acknowledged it was "pretty darn cold," but he did not foresee any "hiccups."[92]

During a two-and-a-half-week stay, Jessen made numerous recommendations, including one that solved two critical problems facing the CIA. Since Zirbel was "completely snowed under, officers who were in training at headquarters in interrogation should go to [the Salt Pit] for OJT," or on-the-job training.[93] If the trainee interrogators processed real detainees, "we could have multiple people work on some of the [detainees] all the time," said Jessen. And if on-the-job training really was "on-the-job" instead of classroom role-play, the interrogators would be better prepared to face real high-value detainees without supervision, easing up the pressure on the trainers. Charlie Wise jumped on Jessen's "OJT" idea. Sixteen people were registered to attend his pilot course, which was being finalized with input from Witsch, Percival, Wirts, and Russell from JPRA. Most of the Salt Pit detainees were "low" or "medium value." Better to practice on them than mess things up with the CIA's precious trio of Abu Zubaydah, Ramzi bin al-Shibh, and Abd al-Rahim al-Nashiri.

Mitchell recalled being shown around. "There were hard points/chain points on the floor, buckets and a door," he said.[94] It was "dark, cold, lots of open space at the top, music playing." There was dust and filth everywhere. Luckily, Mitchell and Jessen were staying at the Ariana Hotel, and he later described the scene. "The place was crawling with CIA officers, and every spot where someone could sleep was crammed with personnel," he said.[95] They slept on cots in "a converted broom closet" close to the bar, while their linguist spent the night "under the pool table in the bar, which remained open until after midnight." The next day the linguist complained of no sleep, due to "loud music and people shouting all night." Mitchell and Bruce laughed at the idea of him lying under a pool table, "in one of the most popular bars in that region of the world, trying to sleep in all that racket while trained killers and intelligence officers from all over the world stepped on his fingers."[96] It was like a scene from *Rambo III*.

Their first job was assessing al-Nashiri, who according to Mitchell had been living with a Chechen "escort" and driving a high-end BMW when he was caught.[97] "He said he even put on a Speedo swimsuit and frequented a large water park as part of his disguise." They questioned him at the Salt Pit because he had been "captured in the act of putting together a terrorist attack," Mitchell later explained, and headquarters did not want to wait until they got him to Thailand.[98] Al-Nashiri was chained up against a makeshift wall, and halogen lamps on stands beamed light onto him to create a "shadow barrier."[99] Mitchell recalled taking off al-Nashiri's hood and folding and placing it around the detainee's neck "like a shawl"—a substitute for the "safety collar."[100] He said they "had no interest in getting rough if it was unnecessary," but if al-Nashiri refused to cooperate, he would "not like what was going to happen next."[101] At the end of the interrogation session, Mitchell said he checked that al-Nashiri's cuffs and shackles were not too tight, made sure he had "water and plenty of blankets," and left him in the care of "indigenous guards."[102]

Next, they examined another detainee who Jessen and Zirbel had been interrogating for five days, an Afghan called Gul Rahman. Arrested in Islamabad on October 29, he had been rendered to the Salt Pit on November 7.[103] Jessen later described Rahman as "too damn tough," and "one of the most fanatical interview resisters" he had ever met.[104] Prior to Mitchell's arrival, Rahman had been subjected to what Jessen described as a "hard takedown."[105] Jessen, who preferred the term "rough handling," said it was a "good technique," and he witnessed it but did not participate. It was designed to "instill fear and despair" and involved running into the cell, cutting off Rahman's clothes, hooding him, securing him with duct tape, and then running him up and down outside the cell. Rahman was slapped and punched several times, recalled Jessen. It was "pretty forceful." A couple of times the detainee stumbled, and they dragged him, causing "contusions" on his face, legs, and hands that "looked bad." Jessen said he "watched from behind the lights" while Zirbel conducted Rahman's first interrogation.[106] Over the next four days, they subjected Rahman to four more interrogation sessions as well as forty-eight hours of standing sleep deprivation, minimal food, auditory overload, and what another CIA officer described as "the shower from hell."[107]

Questioned later, Zirbel's and Jessen's responses were inconsistent; Zirbel stated the water heater had not been working, while Jessen said the cold shower had been a deliberate "deprivation technique."[108] After the shower, Jessen noticed early signs of hypothermia in the detainee.[109] Another officer said Rahman had been so cold he could "barely say his alias," but he was still "left shivering for hours . . . with his hand [sic] chained over his head."[110] Rahman requested a blanket, but Jessen could not recall whether any were given.[111] Even though Rahman "appeared somewhat incoherent," Jessen concluded that he was an appropriate candidate for enhanced interrogation because he was using "health and welfare" as a "major part of his resistance posture."[112] When an unidentified interrogator was asked later whether temperature manipulation was used at the Salt Pit, he responded rhetorically: "How cold is cold? How cold is life threatening?"[113] It sounded remarkably similar to Mitchell's father, Elmer, asking his young son to define "how far is far?"

Mitchell described Rahman as "the best at resistance out of all Al Qaeda prisoners." The main evidence was his refusal to admit to being Gul Rahman, despite having been captured with a driver's license showing his name and photograph.[114] After the session, Mitchell walked out and told Jessen, "I love that guy."[115] They judged he would not be "profoundly or permanently affected" if subjected to enhanced interrogation.[116] However, there was a problem. The Salt Pit was not an authorized EIT facility, so Rahman would have to be moved elsewhere before anyone could get "handsy."[117] But since he was not yet identified as a high-value detainee, and Mitchell and Jessen were already busy rendering a real high-value detainee—al-Nashiri—to Thailand, for now they would leave Rahman behind. After conducting a final "mental status exam" on Rahman, Jessen advised Zirbel to continue with "environmental deprivations" for another two weeks. Rahman should be given "adequate rest and nourishment so he remains coherent and capable of providing accurate information."[118] If he started talking, they could come back for him.

The Salt Pit was "not an EIT program facility."[119] But it soon would be, and it played a vital role in the rollout of the program, because Gus had taken up Jessen's suggestion that trainee interrogators should be sent there for "on-the-job training," after coursework in the United States. The CIA wanted to apply the SERE school definition of "role-play training" to the real world. The course was approved on November 12, 2002, while Mitchell and Jessen were still in Afghanistan, and was endorsed by the top military brass. The JPRA command at Fort Belvoir, Virginia; US Joint Forces Command at Norfolk, Virginia; the Joint Chiefs of Staff in the Pentagon; and the undersecretary of defense were all informed. Supervised by the CIA chief of interrogations, Charlie Wise, the course was run by a team of JPRA instructors, who included Gary Percival, Joe Witsch, and Terry Russell, and included instruction on two techniques—"finger press" and "abdominal slap"—that had not been approved by the Department of Justice.[120] Chris Wirts attended at least one session, although he insisted later that he had never visited a CIA black site.[121] Mitchell denied having anything to do with the pilot course. "We were still at the first site [Chiang Mai] when the course started," he recalled.[122] "They used papers I'd worked on at SERE, including things we'd written on learned helplessness for the SERE school. They did not seek my permission as those papers belong to the government. But I did not construct the program for them."[123]

Mitchell had every reason to distance himself from the CIA's pilot training course. During a subsequent inquiry, the JPRA instructors accused Charlie Wise of breaking multiple rules. Terry Russell said Wise suggested ways to "enhance . . . the pain threshold" of a detainee by inserting a broomstick behind the knees.[124] Percival described one session as a "fiasco."[125] But the JPRA instructors also went beyond their remit and demonstrated waterboarding, even though they were not authorized to do it at SERE school.[126] First they waterboarded each other and then the trainees, recalled Russell. Nobody endured it for "very long," he said. Trainees "stayed there five seconds, ten seconds, thirty seconds," but generally "hopped off" as soon as they could.[127] They just had to experience the sensation, not endure it, he said. Certification to use it for real would follow as and when necessary. Among the seven trainee interrogators who "qualified" on the course was Matthew Zirbel from the Salt Pit.

Mitchell complained to Kirk Hubbard. A summary of their discussion suggested he and Jessen had been intending to teach the psychological element of Wise's course but had been redirected at the last minute to take charge of al-Nashiri. Hubbard noted that the ten-day pilot course had been abbreviated "due to operational exigency."[128] As a result of certain people being absent, full "interrogation tradecraft" was not covered, and instructions about the "psychology of interrogation" had been insufficient. Due to "abbreviated" time, there had been insufficient instruction on the need for a "repetition of using enhanced interrogation measures on a detainee as well as the importance of planning and keeping with the plan once in the heat of the interrogation."[129] Without Mitchell and Jessen monitoring for "abusive drift," Wise had veered off-course, according to the JPRA instructors. In the advanced SERE school, psychologists were always present and always senior to the interrogators.[130] Mitchell and Jessen needed to play a full hands-on role in future CIA training. "I also plan to have Jim and/or Bruce in this next course," reported Hubbard.[131] There was not much time to get things up to speed, as Gus intended to run the next course "towards the end of January '03."

On November 20, 2002, two days after the pilot course ended, Afghan guards looked in on Gul Rahman at eight A.M. and saw him "alive in his cell . . . with his eyes open."[132] When "station personnel," meaning Americans, turned up after ten A.M., the guards told them that Rahman "was sleeping."[133] When the Americans went into the cell, they found Rahman had actually frozen to death sitting up. Outside temperatures had plummeted to thirty-one degrees, and it was "real freakin cold."[134] Rahman, who was short-chained on the concrete floor, naked from the waist down, had been "too immobilized to generate sufficient muscle activity to keep himself alive."[135] It was an unmitigated disaster. Jim Pavitt, the CIA's deputy director of operations had no choice but to inform the Office of the CIA Inspector General, who referred the case to the Department of Justice.[136]

The pathologist and CIA physician's assistant who performed the autopsy took no photographs. The cause of death was "hypothermia."[137] Mitchell described it as unfortunate, noting that "reports say [Rahman] died of exposure."[138] Mitchell pointed to "serious flaws in the performance of a junior CIA officer in charge of the detention site." In Mitchell's opinion, the primary fault lay with the "indigenous guards," who were the only ones on-site "when the prisoner froze to death."[139] Afghans were to blame for an experiment gone wrong while the Americans were enjoying the comforts of the Ariana Hotel. An internal investigation concluded that Rahman's resistance to interrogation had cost him his life.[140] He had thrown away his last meal and acted violently toward the guards, which meant he had to be short-chained.[141] The CIA inspector general opened an investigation, but the Department of Justice declined to prosecute any agency employees, even though Rahman had died "as a result of the way he was detained."[142] The Salt Pit was a weeping sore far too closely associated with the enhanced interrogation program for Mitchell's comfort.[143]

Abu Zubaydah, 1989.
COURTESY OF LAIQ A. KHAN.

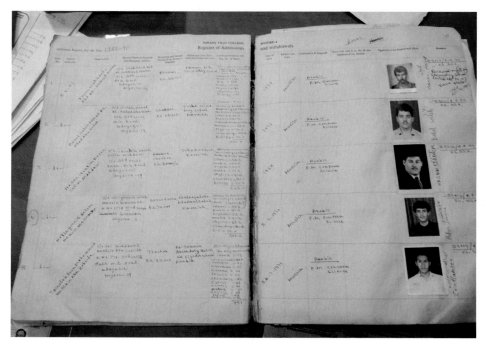

Abu Zubaydah's registration to study at Sarada Vilas College, Mysore, 1989.
COURTESY OF LAIQ A. KHAN.

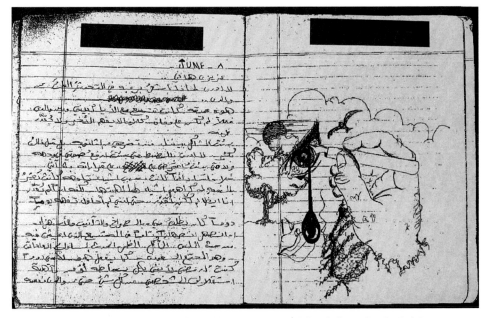

Abu Zubaydah's diary, 1990, recording old arguments with his father after he left home to study in India. AUTHOR COLLECTION.

After Abu Zubaydah was questioned by Pakistani police in 1995, he changed his appearance to look more like a student or businessman. U.S. CENTRAL COMMAND.

Jim Mitchell (L), with his brother Robert and "Granny Nancy," 1950s.
COURTESY OF JIM MITCHELL.

Jim Mitchell as a child, 1950s.
COURTESY OF JIM MITCHELL.

Jim and Kathy Mitchell's wedding, Tampa, FL, 1969. COURTESY OF JIM MITCHELL.

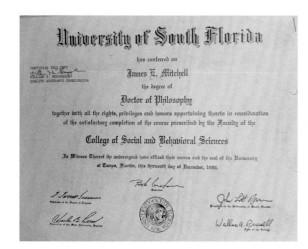

Jim Mitchell's psychology doctorate.
COURTESY OF JIM MITCHELL.

SERE School running team, Spokane, WA, 1980s: Standing: Bruce Jessen (L), Roger Aldrich (C), Ahmed Habib (R), Kneeling (R): Jim Mitchell.
COURTESY OF ROGER ALDRICH.

Jim Mitchell's medals. PHOTOGRAPH BY CATHY SCOTT-CLARK.

Still from Abu Zubaydah's post 9/11 video. AUTHOR COLLECTION.

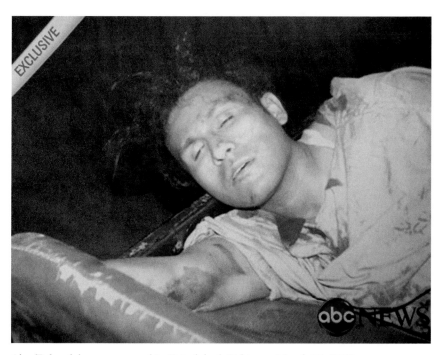

Abu Zubaydah was captured in Faisalabad, Pakistan, March 28, 2002. ABC NEWS.

Abu Zubaydah's fake identity documents, photographs, and bankcards.
FBI EVIDENCE PHOTOGRAPH.

To Tritot Ronnaritivichai
With Best Wishes,

General Tritot Ronnaritivichai, head of Thai Special Branch, lent his holiday home in Chiang Mai to the CIA for Abu Zubaydah's interrogation. With President George W. Bush, Bangkok, October 2003. COURTESY OF GENERAL TRITOT.

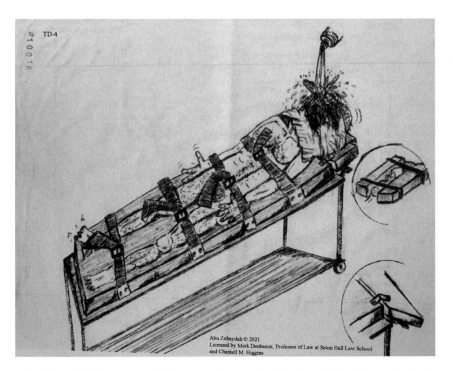

Abu Zubaydah's depiction of being waterboarded, with the additional use of a head vise. ABU ZUBAYDAH © 2021, LICENSED BY MARK DENBEAUX, PROFESSOR OF LAW AT SETON HALL LAW SCHOOL, AND CHANTELL M. HIGGINS.

After twenty years in detention without charge, Abu Zubaydah is still referred to by the Guantanamo authorities by his detainee number, 10016. He etches it onto his meagre possessions, like this pair of reading glasses.
PHOTOGRAPH BY CATHY SCOTT-CLARK.

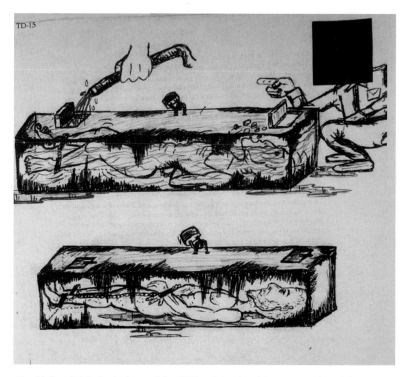

Abu Zubaydah's depiction of the CIA subjecting him to simulated drowning in a coffin. ABU ZUBAYDAH © 2021.

Two of Khalid Sheikh Mohammad's sons were captured in Karachi, Pakistan, in September 2002. Jim Mitchell threatened to slit their throats if Mohammad did not provide information about the second wave of attacks on the United States.

Jim Mitchell and Jose Rodriguez, former chief of the CIA's Counterterrorist Center.
PHOTOGRAPH BY CATHY SCOTT-CLARK.

Jim Mitchell and FBI Special Agent Fred Humphries. PHOTOGRAPH BY CATHY SCOTT-CLARK.

Abu Zubaydah's drawing of the CIA headquarters team that observed his enhanced interrogation in August 2002.
ABU ZUBAYDAH © 2021.

Abu Zubaydah depicting various types of enhanced interrogation.
ABU ZUBAYDAH © 2021.

John Rizzo, Acting General Counsel at the CIA, 2001-2002 and 2004-2009, Washington DC, October 2018.
PHOTOGRAPH BY CATHY SCOTT-CLARK.

Military contractor Billy Waugh with his baseball bat "interrogation tool," a retirement gift from his CIA colleagues, November 2018.
PHOTOGRAPH BY CATHY SCOTT-CLARK.

Porter Goss, former chairman of the House Intelligence Committee, and George Tenet's successor at the CIA, October 2018.
PHOTOGRAPH BY CATHY SCOTT-CLARK.

Gina Haspel, chief of staff to Jose Rodriguez during the enhanced interrogation years, served as CIA director in Donald Trump's administration.
OFFICIAL CIA PHOTOGRAPH.

Abu Zubaydah's depiction of his treatment at the second CIA black site, Stare Kiejkuty, Poland, 2002–2003.

ABU ZUBAYDAH © 2021.

Abu Zubaydah's drawing of "walling," an approved enhanced interrogation technique.

ABU ZUBAYDAH © 2021.

CIA director George Tenet at the Presidential Emergency Operations Center (PEOC) shortly after the 9/11 attacks. THE U.S. NATIONAL ARCHIVES.

From 2004 until 2009 the CIA's enhanced interrogation program was outsourced to a company formed by Mitchell and Jessen: Mitchell, Jessen and Associates. Here, staff and contractors enjoy an outing to Lake Coeur d'Alene, Idaho.
COURTESY OF ROGER ALDRICH.

The old airport hanger at Camp Justice, Guantanamo Bay, Cuba, January 2020.
PHOTOGRAPH BY CATHY SCOTT-CLARK.

Guantanamo Bay, Cuba, at dawn, January 2020. PHOTOGRAPH BY CATHY SCOTT-CLARK.

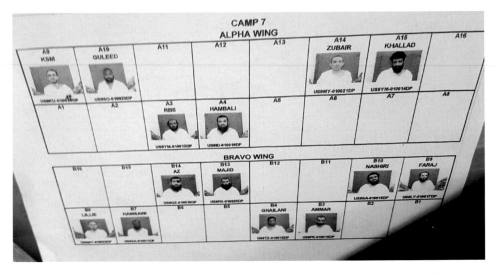

CAMP 7
ALPHA WING

The fourteen CIA high value detainees who were rendered to Guantanamo Bay, Cuba, in September 2006. COURTESY OF CAROL ROSENBERG.

Abu Zubaydah photographed at Guantanamo Bay, Cuba, in 2017. INTERNATIONAL COMMITTEE FOR THE RED CROSS.

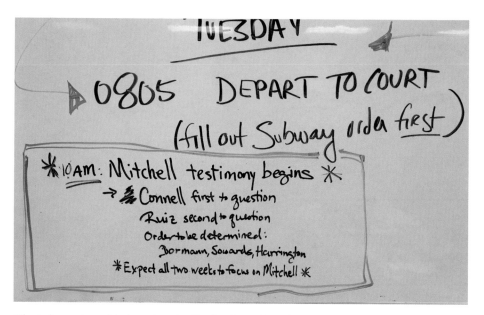

The information whiteboard at the Media Operations Center at Guantanamo Bay, Cuba, on the morning of Jim Mitchell's initial testimony to the 9/11 pretrial, January 2020. PHOTOGRAPH BY CATHY SCOTT-CLARK.

Abu Zubaydah depicts himself as being locked forever inside a CIA waterboarding bottle. ABU ZUBAYDAH © 2021.

CHAPTER 13

"ALLAH WILL LOOK INTO THEIR HEARTS AND KNOW"

November 15, 2002, Chiang Mai, Thailand

Before getting to work on al-Nashiri in Thailand, Mitchell said he and Jessen asked Abu Zubaydah for advice, because he was "the best source available to help us fully understand how Islamic terrorists were likely to respond to the water board."[1] Mitchell claimed they approached the topic with caution. "We told him we didn't like doing it," he recalled. Could he suggest other ways to get al-Nashiri talking? "No, no, you must do this for all the brothers," Abu Zubaydah apparently replied. Mitchell feigned surprise, saying, "This sounds like a justification for using 'hard times' on everyone." According to Mitchell, Abu Zubaydah then patiently explained that everyone had their breaking point and would not be sinning by answering questions if already pushed to the limit. "The line is different for each brother," Mitchell stated, supposedly quoting Abu Zubaydah. "Some brothers are incapable of withstanding any hard times. . . . Other brothers can stand a great deal to protect secrets. Allah will look into their hearts and know."[2] According to Mitchell, Abu Zubaydah was rooting for the waterboard just as the program was being expanded. It was a convenient justification for advancing enhanced interrogation, but a later psychological assessment done by Mitchell and Jessen stated that what Abu Zubaydah had actually told them was that he wanted to warn other captured brothers to cooperate with their interrogators so as "to avoid the 'hard times.'"[3] Nevertheless, the CIA would retell its version of this story several times, including to Condoleezza Rice and Dick Cheney.[4] The CIA Inspector General later reported that Abu

Zubaydah had given "interrogators information on how to induce other detainees to talk," but made no reference to any "waterboard" encouragement on the part of Abu Zubaydah.[5]

According to cables written by Thai base chief Gina Haspel, Mitchell and Jessen took al-Nashiri to his "limit" as quickly as possible. His interrogation started at 4:15 A.M. on November 15, just minutes after he was delivered to the bunker.[6] Wanting to re-create "capture shock," they began by telling him "he was now in the place they had warned him about."[7] According to the cables, they were verbally abusive, saying they would not "execute him," but if he refused to cooperate they would turn him over to "other people" who "would certainly kill him."[8] Mitchell reflected that there was every reason to treat al-Nashiri harshly, saying the Saudi detainee admitted to plotting marine attacks on tankers and warships moored at Dubai's Port Rashid, passing through the Strait of Hormuz, and at the Saudi port of Jeddah.[9] Alec Station claimed these were practice runs for another broadside against a US warship. Some insiders were unconvinced. "[Al-Nashiri] was an idiot," recalled one former US official. "He couldn't read or comprehend a comic book."[10] Robert McFadden, who led the USS *Cole* investigation with Ali Soufan, disagreed, saying: "He was emir of the Arabian Peninsular cell of Al Qaeda."[11]

Once again, headquarters demanded information about future operations. If al-Nashiri lied, "his life would become infinitely worse," Mitchell and Jessen warned him.[12] They "would stop at nothing." "Hulking, heavy muscled guards" ripped off his clothes, held him down on the floor, and forcibly shaved him.[13] He was walled multiple times and warned he would "suffer in ways he never thought possible."[14] Like schoolyard bullies, they called him "a little girl," "a spoiled little rich Saudi," and a "sissy."[15] When he asked for water to wash himself before prayers, they mocked him. "This is not—not—a hotel. We are not in the business of kissing your ass."[16] At the end of the first session, Abu Zubaydah's coffin was brought in. As the template suggested, it was al-Nashiri's "new home."[17]

It took twelve days to get legal approval for the waterboard, during which time Gul Rahman had died in Afghanistan. Everyone at CIA headquarters was twitchy about reintroducing the harshest technique, and Mitchell and Jessen needed to be careful.[18] Abu Zubaydah was tall and well muscled. Al-Nashiri "was a really small guy." Every time the guards stood the gurney upright, he almost slipped down through the ratchet straps.[19] After some tweaking of the waterboarding setup, they continued, telling him they would do so "for months if need be."[20] Haspel reported that al-Nashiri quickly became "compliant and cooperative."[21] However, Alec Station directed the field to stop making "sweeping statements." Al-Nashiri had to be treated harshly until he reached the magic "line." Hopefully, for all concerned, this was within the Justice Department–defined limits. Mitchell and Jessen warned al-Nashiri that he needed "tenderizing" like a "fine steak."[22] They told him the guards had all volunteered for duty when they heard the USS *Cole* bomber was coming, because they had "something to avenge."[23]

———————•———————

Halfway through al-Nashiri's enhanced interrogation, Haspel became distracted by a security crisis. Shortly before Thanksgiving 2002, headquarters learned that the *New York Times* knew the CIA was interrogating War on Terror detainees in Thailand. Tenet's spokesman Bill Harlow was doing his best to quash the reporting, citing national security concerns, but Jose Rodriguez told Haspel to prepare for a "rapid burn," meaning Abu Zubaydah and al-Nashiri would be rendered elsewhere while CATSEYE was demolished, so "as to leave no reminders of what had taken place there."[24] It was supposed to be a holiday weekend, and people in the Thailand operation had made plans for the beach or the mountains. All leave was canceled, as the men in black knocked down plywood cubicles and ripped link charts off walls. Chains, bars, padlocks, and cuffs were bundled into duffel bags.[25] Everything combustible was thrown in a pit and doused with petrol.[26] Medical staff packed their equipment, and the metal gurney was hosed down and stripped of its modifications. Haspel and a tech "geek" digitized paperwork.[27] General Tritot helped return his property to its original "chicken coop" state. "I had to move everything and everyone," he recalled. The last thing to be dismantled would be Mitchell's carefully crafted bunker, in which Abu Zubaydah and al-Nashiri had no idea about what was going on.

At headquarters, Gus, whose Special Missions was now running all Renditions, Detention, and Interrogation Group locations, including the Salt Pit, called in favors. He was already managing the Rahman fallout and fielding CIA inspector general inquiries. "Jose rang me and said, 'It's your responsibility now,'" he recalled.[28] Luckily, Poland had been persuaded to rent out an old villa with a large basement and a cabin in the garden. It was located inside a secure intelligence training facility three hours northeast of Warsaw. Hidden away in the northeastern lake district and serviced by a small private airport, Stare Kiejkuty was a restricted military area and in winter often became snowed in. During the Second World War, the Nazis had used it as an SS intelligence center. After the war, it was listed on maps as a holiday resort, although it was a Soviet-run intelligence facility, and in 1968 it was used during the Prague Spring uprisings.[29] Abu Zubaydah and al-Nashiri were moving from a Southeast Asian melting pot to a frozen Gulag. The Polish government received $15 million in cash, delivered in two large cardboard boxes.[30]

As in Thailand, protocols were drawn up for actions to be taken in the event of a detainee's death.[31] Gus spent $300,000 on security cameras, although he ruled out any more videotaping of actual interrogations. "I said absolutely not," he recalled.[32] The upper floor of the timber-framed villa, with its whitewashed walls and sharp-peaked red-tiled roof, consisted of mildewed bedrooms with Soviet-era wallpaper and nylon carpets. Some were turned into billets. On the ground floor was a traditional Polish kitchen with a tiled hearth and a dining room with a long wooden dining table.[33] Here members of the team would grab their breaks and mingle with locally hired contractors, although the CIA had to fly in food supplies after Americans were caught dumping Polish sausage over a fence.[34]

Detainees would be hidden away in the basement, another sealed and soundproofed bunker inside a building that looked nothing like a prison.[35] CIA contractors built three "holding units" connected by a walkway.[36] Each was fitted with "hard points," CCTV surveillance, and fluorescent tube lighting. The basement could be accessed through the main house or directly from outside. The "interrogation cell" (with no cameras) contained a walling wall and a waterboard. A new innovation was concealed behind a false wall at the end of the walkway, a hidden room containing "a metal cage of the size fitting a grown man."[37] The six-foot-square cage had been forged by a Polish metalworking company to CIA specifications and sat on a wooden platform mounted on half-inflated tires.[38] It was intended to make Abu Zubaydah feel permanently unstable. It was fitted out with CCTV surveillance, a boom box, a bank of freestanding fans, and air conditioners, even though thick snow fell outside.[39] Only the interrogators, guards, and medics would know he was in there. Code-named Quartz, the new black site was Gus's first tailor-made facility. "Poland was one of my favorites," he said.[40] Those who worked there described it as Spartan, but it was a step up from the pitch-black horse stalls of Afghanistan.

Mitchell and Jessen continued interrogating al-Nashiri in Thailand as everyone packed around them.[41] "You haven't given us anything that's helpful," they complained, backing him up against the walling wall with a noose around his neck.[42] Using the move to Poland as a threat that worse was coming, they warned him that his new inquisitors "will trash you." He was "headed for the inner ring of hell."[43] Someone went out to scout for cold-weather clothes, a challenge in a country where the temperature rarely fell below eighty-five degrees Fahrenheit. Mitchell had not yet told al-Nashiri he was going with him. "It's almost as if you want to get into more trouble," he and Jessen yelled. "Every time you open your mouth you make yourself sound like some stupid little helper, the shaykh's little errand boy."[44] Al-Nashiri could play stupid, but he would never win against him, Mitchell said. He would provide information, "but because of his own choices this would have to occur the hard way."[45] Conscious of the inspector general's inquiries, Mitchell and Jessen went easier on the waterboard, subjecting al-Nashiri to only three sessions. Haspel has also ordered that no permanent VHS tape record should be created for al-Nashiri, so tapes were erased and reused after each session was reported to headquarters.

Before leaving Thailand, there was one critical thing to dispose of—four boxes containing ninety-two videotapes of Abu Zubaydah's enhanced interrogation, including footage of eighty-three waterboarding sessions.[46] For the past three months, Jonathan Fredman and Rodriguez had been lobbying hard to destroy them. Even though the worst moments had already been deleted and the last two tapes were marked "use and rewind," Rodriguez, Fredman, and George Tenet regarded what remained as "an existential threat" to the CIA.[47] At least six senior staffers—Fredman, Bikowsky, the mystery Chief of Base, the Technical Service chief, the previous Thai base chief, and a masked-up Mike Winograd—were potentially on them, and they showed clear evidence of Abu Zubaydah being tortured. On one tape, Mitchell threatened: "If one child dies in America and I find out you knew something about it, I will personally cut your mother's throat."[48] Given that threats of death were illegal, was this permissible? "I met CTC attorney PJ1 and talked with him about what was legal," Mitchell later claimed, using the CIA's "unique functional identifier" code system to protect Fredman's identity. "If the threat was a threat of imminent harm, that would not be legal or right, but if it was conditional, it was legal."[49] But even as the CIA insisted nothing illegal had taken place, it sped to erase the physical evidence.

However, there was a significant problem. A headquarters meeting on September 5, 2002, just over two weeks after Abu Zubaydah's enhanced interrogation ended, had concluded that the tapes represented a "serious security risk," and that their preservation was "not required by law."[50] If they got out, they represented a "danger to all Americans." On October 25, another meeting discussed deploying a team to Thailand to destroy the tapes "completely." Mike Winograd flipped out, removed the tapes from the black site in Chiang Mai, and drove them to the embassy in Bangkok. "The chief of station was an asshole," recalled Gus.[51] "He should have been fired." A flurry of cables— later redacted—was exchanged between headquarters, the black site team, and the CIA station in Bangkok about the "destruction of magnetic media and hard drives."[52]

By the end of November, the inspector general was involved. No evidence of enhanced interrogation could be destroyed while his abuse inquiry was ongoing. Nevertheless, Rodriguez pushed forward and sent John McPherson, a senior agency lawyer, to watch the tapes in a sensitive compartmented information facility at the US embassy in Bangkok.[53] When McPherson reported back that the tapes and records were the same, Rodriguez tried to argue that the tapes were simply "copies" of the written record and could be destroyed.[54] John Rizzo issued a strong rebuke. Officers in the field had made a "mistake" in moving the tapes. Since they were not at the black site, they could not be destroyed as a legitimate part of the rapid burn. "I expect these [detailed instructions] to be followed without deviation," Rizzo wrote on December 3.[55] The tapes would have to stay locked in a safe in Winograd's office while the CIA figured out another way.

Mitchell, who had worked hard to record evidence of senior CIA officials—particularly a lawyer—in the room while Abu Zubaydah was being waterboarded, and therefore had no interest in the tapes being destroyed, invented a story to cover for Winograd's mistake. He claimed that as he was leaving the black site, he saw the tapes in the pit.[56] A guard was about to pour gasoline and burn them.[57] Mitchell claimed that he called out to base chief Haspel, "Don't forget to destroy the tapes," as he departed, but later learned that Haspel had ordered a sudden halt after receiving an urgent cable from Rizzo to "hold up on the tapes."[58] Had the message been delayed, even for a few minutes, Rodriguez said his life "in the years following would have been considerably easier."[59]

Rizzo, who claimed never to have watched the tapes, knew of the earlier deletions.[60] Eleven tapes were blank, two had only one or two minutes of recording on them, two more were broken, and a twenty-one-hour period of time that included two waterboarding sessions was missing.[61] When the inspector general's team later reviewed the tapes, they identified these anomalies and also concluded that Mitchell and Jessen's version of waterboarding, "continuously applied large volumes of water," did not comply with navy SERE-school rules, or even the technique as presented to the Justice Department. The tapes really were an existential threat to the CIA. Not only were they ugly and proved that the CIA had broken the law, but their current state also revealed someone had already tried to erase the worst moments.

———————◆———————

Gina Haspel informed Abu Zubaydah that he was moving on the evening of Eid al-Fitr, the breaking of the monthlong Ramadan fast, which that year fell on December 4. "They said, 'we will entirely leave this location for special reasons to us and you will go on a plane.'"[62] Because the trip would take over twenty-four hours, he would be placed in an adult diaper. Abu Zubaydah was horrified. "I said there was no way I would do it." Even if they forced him into it, "I would not use it." Slaps, punches, drowning, walling, rectal rehydration—his entire CIA experience had been a lengthy exercise in brutality. But being made to wear a diaper, "like the one they use for babies," tore into Abu Zubaydah's pride. Ignoring his pleas, guards pinned him down and secured a diaper on him with duct tape. He was dressed in sweatpants and a sweatshirt, its back slit open so chains could be threaded through. "Foamies" were shoved into his ears, and earmuffs followed, then a blindfold and opaque goggles, taped to his head so tightly they cut into his nose, leaving another permanent scar.[63] The rendition ritual was completed with a hood; it was sensory isolation on steroids. He was brought outside in the dead of night, with guards in rubber gloves gripping his forearms and shoulders.

It was the first time he had left the freezing air-conditioned bunker in nine months. He heard a door open, and hands squashed him down into the foot well of a vehicle. "I could feel the guards' feet on both the right and the left hand sides," he recalled.[64] Al-Nashiri was brought out in similar fashion.

At the airport, Abu Zubaydah was hauled up three steps into a room where his pants and diaper were removed. The hood, goggles, and earmuffs remained on, but he heard the faint snap of rubber gloves as he was bent over. "Somebody performed a cavity search on me," he said, disgusted.[65] It was the CIA medic who would also take the rendition flight, according to the standard operating procedure.[66] Mitchell explained, "There were cavity searches at both ends of the ride," to check for stashed objects that might be used as weapons.[67] Taken straight out of the advanced SERE school rulebook, cavity searches were, as far as Abu Zubaydah was concerned, just another excuse for humiliation.[68] Afterward, he was taped back into the diaper, redressed, and marched back outside. "I started going up some steps and it was clear I was boarding a plane." It was a Gulfstream leased from the American private military contractor DynCorp.[69] Abu Zubaydah was followed on board by al-Nashiri, five guards, and Mitchell, who carried a laptop containing intelligence files, cables, and other materials. Haspel was going home and handing over the reins to Mike Sealy, a senior CIA operations officer whom Gus had appointed base chief in Poland.

Abu Zubaydah spent most of the flight in an "indescribable state of pain."[70] Months after he had been shot, the wound in his left thigh was still red and raw. His guts churned, but he was determined not to use the diaper. After several hours, he felt the plane descending. Relief washed over him. Even a bucket would do at that point. But it was just a refueling stopover—Dubai—and the diaper stayed on. His abdomen was as tight as a drum as the pilots logged a bogus flight plan to Luton, England, via Vienna. In reality, they were heading for a private airstrip in northwestern Poland.

Szymany airport was normally closed in the winter months. But when the director received an urgent call about an "American aircraft" needing to land on December 5, he had the runway cleared and waited in the control tower, as instructed.[71] The airport was most famous for having once been used by the Luftwaffe. But this was something else, and he watched through gusts of snow as the Gulfstream landed just before three P.M. and stopped at the far end of the runway with its engines still rolling, as two Polish military vehicles sped toward it. Abu Zubaydah and al-Nashiri were bundled off, the rendition pilots paid the landing fee of seven thousand Polish zlotys ($1,850) in cash and took off again.

The Polish staff turned off the lights, locked up, and went home as the two vehicles headed off into the snow. Bypassing Stare Kiejkuty village, they passed a checkpoint, metal gates, and a guard tower, and then drove on through a slumbering forest. Ahead lay a red-roofed villa, its tiles obscured by thick snow. Icicles clung to its gables.[72] Frog-marched down a half dozen slippery steps, Abu Zubaydah entered a chilled void filled with deafening white noise. A door opened; he was pushed inside and made to sit down, his arms cuffed behind him, his ankles shackled to the floor. The air smelled of mildew, and as the Americans moved about, the floor beneath him tilted. When the hood eventually came off, he saw metal bars. "I realized I was in a cage," he recalled.[73] Although it had been snowing outside, inside air-conditioning roared. Naked save for a sheet, he eventually fell asleep.

———•———

After Mitchell arrived in Poland, he was accused of having stolen or made digitized copies of the compromising waterboarding tapes, insurance for the day that was surely coming when he and Jessen would be held accountable.[74] But pleased to have closed the door on Thailand, Mitchell concentrated on his trophy, Abu Zubaydah. "One of the most dangerous men on the planet" was now as compliant as a lapdog.[75] At one stage, Special Missions chief Gus flew in to meet Abu Zubaydah, introducing himself as "Paul." He was surprised to find "a handsome guy" who had simply gone down the wrong path.[76] "He just wanted a family. He wanted an education. Start a little business. But it went south." Abu Zubaydah was just a facilitator, said Gus, echoing everyone else at headquarters—when they were speaking candidly. "I don't think he ever killed anybody." However, Gus had no time to worry whether the CIA was interrogating the wrong people. He had too much on his plate at Langley, where everything was being sharpened up, from training manuals to death-in-custody protocols. He barely saw his wife. With Thailand shut, a maximum capacity of five detainees in Poland, and more than a dozen "medium value" detainees at the Salt Pit, where they had suffered abuse, he had no choice but to keep the Afghan facility open. Because the place was so tainted, no one wanted to run it, so Matthew Zirbel, who had been reprimanded for making "misstatements" and "omissions" about Rahman's demise, but avoided any criminal charges, remained in charge.[77] Several CIA employees asked to leave, including an interrogator who likened it to a Nazi prison camp.[78] However, not everyone saw Zirbel as the main problem. Post Gul Rahman, Jessen declared he would still work with Zirbel "anywhere, anytime" and recommended that since he was now "trained and qualified," he should be made part of the "lead [high-value terrorist] element."[79] Yes, the Salt Pit "looked dark and cold and crude," but it "didn't look like an old Nazi prison camp," said Jessen.[80] The CIA needed to hang on to anyone with experience, as back in the United States, Rizzo was busy briefing Gonzales, Bellinger, and other senior administration lawyers "on the scope and breadth of the CTC's Detention and Interrogation program."[81] All the talk was of expansion not contraction. Luckily for the CIA, concern about US abuses had shifted up the road to the military-run Bagram Collection Point, where two Afghans, named Habibullah and Dilawar, died within a few days of each other after undergoing prolonged standing sleep deprivation.[82]

On December 5, Mitchell met Charlie Wise, Gus's new chief of interrogations. They first came face-to-face in the dining room at Stare Kiejkuty.[83] Mitchell described a six-foot-four-inch-tall man in his mid-fifties, who had "the body of an aging special operator, hard at one time but starting to go soft." According to Mitchell, Wise called himself the "new sheriff in town" and told Mitchell his services as an interrogator were no longer needed, but they still needed him to play the psychologist role so they could legally conduct enhanced interrogations. "What a dick! I thought," Mitchell said, adding that Wise threw a trashy crime novel at him and told him to stay in the dining room while he got started on al-Nashiri in the basement.[84] When Mitchell protested that a psychologist actually needed to see an interrogation to authorize it, Wise backtracked: "You can watch, but don't interfere." Downstairs, Wise introduced Mitchell to three "newly minted interrogators" who had graduated from the CIA's pilot training course. "Until then I wasn't even aware there had been an interrogation course," Mitchell recalled.[85] He described them as Wise's "acolytes." They were in Poland to get "practical experience," part of Jessen's on-the-job training element. "What if EITs aren't needed?" Mitchell asked. "Oh, we're going to need them," Wise allegedly swaggered. Growing up in the Deep South, Mitchell was accustomed to people yelling at him, "Get the hell off my property."[86] He was tempted to yell the same thing to Wise. There could be only one winner in this dangerous face-off.

Everyone involved in the clandestine program was supposed to pull together, but Gus had caused himself a huge problem by putting Wise and Mitchell together. They were roughly the same age, equally aggressive, and territorial. The program had been designed by Mitchell and was formulated around his seminal paper about the Manchester manual. Mitchell had a direct line to Rodriguez and the seventh floor. He was close to the CIA lawyers who had made it legal. He had already fought hard to keep his turf, facing off Terry DeMay, Scott Shumate, and Ali Soufan. A year on, having broken Abu Zubaydah with the "silver bullet" and now helping Rodriguez realize his ambitions for a global program, he was being challenged by a former marine who had already caused potentially irreparable damage by teaching illegal techniques. But Wise was no pushover. He was a Vietnam veteran and had years of experience working in conflict zones from Latin America to the Middle East. After several years on the margins, he was not about to give up his new status as chief of interrogations.[87]

Wise subjected al-Nashiri to enhanced interrogation straightaway, including, according to Mitchell, several unauthorized techniques. Mitchell said he watched through a small observation window as Wise grabbed al-Nashiri and force him to kneel with a broomstick handle behind his knees, pushing him backward until his shoulder touched the floor. "He was screaming," Mitchell recalled.[88] Wise then put al-Nashiri into the strappado position, cinching his arms up behind him with a belt and lifting him off the floor. When al-Nashiri "squealed and struggled," Mitchell barged in and told Wise to stop.[89] "Get out," thundered the chief of interrogations, furious to be challenged in front of his acolytes.[90] A guard backed Mitchell out, and he watched the rest of the session through the door window. At the end, Wise came out yelling, "What the fuck is your malfunction?" If Mitchell interrupted again, the guards would remove him. "It got even uglier after that," Mitchell said. "He thought he'd been unleashed." He accused Wise of dousing al-Nashiri with cold water before "using a stiff-bristled brush to scrub his ass and balls and then his mouth." Another interrogator blew cigar smoke in al-Nashiri's face until he started retching, a technique tested out at the Salt Pit as a way to "purge" detainees.[91]

Mitchell threatened to call Rodriguez and Fredman. Wise told him he could not call anyone, "especially the fucking lawyers."[92] Mitchell said he wanted to email Kirk Hubbard. "He told me I couldn't." Mitchell decided to leave. "I would pay my own way back home. But Wise said I couldn't do that either." Mitchell characterized himself as being trapped in the snow-bound Polish forest with a dangerous sadist. Wise brought in the base chief, Mike Sealy, who also "chewed out" Mitchell. Wise had more news for the upstart contractor. He intended to restart enhanced interrogations on Abu Zubaydah too, and Mitchell would have to watch. Mitchell was furious. "I told him if he put AZ back [into EITs] he would quit providing intelligence and there would be a shit-storm," he recalled.[93] This was his program. Abu Zubaydah was his special project. But Mitchell was a contractor and Wise's staff position trumped all that.

Out on the walkway, the guards played songs from *Sesame Street*, like "Rubber Duckie": "Well, here I am in my tubby again, / And my tubby's all filled with water and nice fluffy suds, / And I've got my soap and washcloth to wash myself, / And I've got my nifty scrub brush." Guards sprayed cold water over Abu Zubaydah, chained up in his cage with his arms twisted behind his back, sending him into an uncontrollable fit of shivers and splashing blood, urine, and vomit across the platform.[94] He recollected that Wise and Mitchell interrogated him together, Bruce Jessen too. Wise was a "very white, tall and muscular man, with dark hair and dark eyes," he remembered.[95] Whenever they were around him, Mitchell and Jessen called Wise "boss." There wasn't ever much to eat, so Abu Zubaydah was driven to distraction by the smells wafting down from the kitchen, where American chefs cooked American food for the American team in a corner of US-controlled territory in the middle of a Polish forest. Abu Zubaydah was sheared again, and his new diary, permitted by Gina Haspel, was taken away. "That was a big deal for him," said Mitchell. "I felt bad about it."[96] The diary maintained his sanity and was a lifeline. "What they do on my body I will forget it," he said. But "I have these papers with me as my child."[97]

Ejected from al-Nashiri's cell, Mitchell told Wise he was leaving. "I am a US citizen," he thundered, "and as of right now you are holding me against my will in a foreign country. I will eventually get back home and report you." The official record stated that Mike Sealy sent home two interrogators in December 2002 because of "prolonged absences from family."[98] Wise and Mitchell were taking their argument to headquarters.

Mitchell burst into Gus's office shortly before Christmas Eve. Psychopath Wise, who had never studied the human mind, had been appointed to a position that far outranked his, and had then held him incommunicado and taken over his detainees.[99] After throwing his weight around, Mitchell stormed out, certain his CIA days were over. Before leaving Langley, he reported Wise for using unauthorized techniques and complained to Fredman.[100] Back in Poland, base chief Mike Sealy eased up on al-Nashiri, reporting that he was compliant and cooperative, an assessment that caused Alec Station to fire back another warning about not making "sweeping statements."[101] It was "inconceivable" that al-Nashiri did not have concrete leads, they said. His enhanced interrogation should continue. Sealy resisted. "Without tangible proof of lying or intentional withholding . . . we believe employing enhanced measures will accomplish nothing," he wrote back.[102] Go any further, and there was a danger he might "suffer the sort of permanent mental harm prohibited by the statute." It was Abu Zubaydah all over again.

Headquarters discussed the situation around Christmas Day. Alec Station wanted to dispatch its Egyptian attack dog—Albert El Gamil—to reassess al-Nashiri.[103] Gus objected. Gamil "had not been through the interrogation training," was not approved to use enhanced techniques, was "too confident, had a temper, and had some security issues."[104] Marty Martin overrode him. It was the holidays, and they were short of cover. Only the most dedicated officers had volunteered. Gus's base chief was being too lenient, and Gamil should "fix" the situation.[105]

Gamil arrived in Poland just as the *Washington Post* broke an explosive story about "stress and duress" tactics being used on terrorism suspects at secret CIA facilities in Afghanistan. "If you don't violate someone's human rights some of the time, you probably aren't doing your job," said an unnamed CIA official.[106] "A brass-knuckled quest for information, often in concert with allies of dubious human rights reputation, in which the traditional lines between right and wrong, legal and inhumane, are evolving and blurred," the newspaper reported. Those conducting the interrogations were described as "highly trained CIA officers." The first detainee to be subjected to these measures, Abu Zubaydah, was a "very clever" guy who had driven his interrogators "nuts." Al Qaeda detainees were not like normal people, said the source, who talked of "packaging" them for rendition and throwing them "into walls."

Sometime between December 28, 2002, and January 1, 2003, Gamil, who was not a trained interrogator so was referred to in cables as a "debriefer," ordered al-Nashiri to be strung up in the standing sleep-deprivation position and blindfolded. At the Salt Pit, Gamil had watched Zirbel conduct a "mock execution," and now he chambered a round in a sidearm next to al-Nashiri's head, suggesting he was about to be executed, just as Mitchell and Jessen had warned the detainee in Thailand.[107] Zirbel later told the CIA inspector general that he had conducted the mock execution "based on the concept, from SERE school, of showing something that looks real, but is not."[108] Gamil next produced a power drill and revved it up, the whirring motor whining and angry. He whispered in Arabic that if al-Nashiri refused to talk, "we could get your mother here," and "we can bring your family in here."[109] These echoed the threats he had issued to Ibn Sheikh al-Libi. "Nashiri responds well to harsh treatment," Gamil reported afterward.[110] Interrogators should continue "various degrees of mild punishment" but allow for "a small degree of 'hope,' by introducing some 'minute rewards.'" Someone reported Gamil for abuse.

Once again, Jim Pavitt had to refer an incident to the CIA inspector general.[111] Gamil and base chief Mike Sealy were both recalled to headquarters. Because Mike Sealy did not stop Gamil from using the gun and the drill, due to "the pressure he felt from headquarters to obtain imminent threat information from al-Nashiri on 9/11-style attacks," he received a two-year reprimand and a ten-day suspension without pay, and he chose to retire.[112] Gamil received a one-year reprimand and a five-day suspension and chose to stay on the team.[113] Mitchell denied any connection to Gamil, but he and Jessen had set the tone when they warned al-Nashiri in Thailand that he was "headed for the inner ring of hell." Abu Zubaydah, who was inside his cage behind the false wall, "heard a drill and someone screaming."[114]

CHAPTER 14

"ZAPPING THE DOG FOR
POOPING ON THE RUG"

January 2003, CIA headquarters, Langley, Virginia

B ecause of what was happening in Poland, Gus spent most of the holiday
season working. After Albert El Gamil returned to headquarters to be
investigated, Gus dispatched Bruce Jessen to "clean up the mess."[1] Jessen also
returned to the Salt Pit to tidy up Matthew Zirbel's regime, something he
could not later discuss, "because it would be classified."[2] Jessen had a lot of
time for Zirbel, reflecting that he "was capable, intelligent, enthusiastic."
Frantically busy, Gus did not have the time or inclination to question Jessen's
opinion. He had another training course to staff up, and the Office of the
Inspector General was already deep into the investigation of Gul Rahman's
death, plus other Salt Pit human rights violations.[3] For Gus, the most alarming prospect was the possibility of the whole program being wrapped up,
which could cost him his job. The American Psychological Association, which
controlled psychologists' licenses to practice, was considering a review of ethical codes to stop members from working with the CIA.[4] Joe Matarazzo, who
was still on the CIA's advisory board, was working all his connections to stop
this from happening.[5] Mitchell was focused solely on getting Charlie Wise
fired. He was "off the reservation and never coming back."[6] Gus was torn.
Mitchell was indispensable but the CIA was still so short of trained people
Gus could not afford to let Wise go. Besides, he felt Mitchell was overstating
the problem. The worst excesses, the "ball brushing, smoke blowing, and mock
execution," were not done by Wise, Gus said.[7] He wasn't even in Poland when
Gamil "screwed up by using a drill and racking a .45 next to Nashiri's ear."[8]

In the end, Gus agreed to admonish Wise for wedging a broomstick behind al-Nashiri's knees, but he warned Mitchell: "It's not a democracy in my office."[9] He was tired of the bickering. "Everyone wanted to be top dog." He was stressed out. "I told them, 'you can have my job if you want,'" he recalled. "No, they didn't want that." Mitchell, who reflected that he had earned $1,800 a day for the 279 days he was out of the US during 2002, relented after Gus offered him a new contract inside the Counterterrorist Center. As long as the CIA paid him what he was worth and everyone understood that he and Jessen were the experts with "a visceral, firsthand understanding of the motives of those attacking us," Mitchell would bide his time.[10]

On January 17, 2003, headquarters informed the Polish black site that three "psychologists/interrogators" approved to use the waterboard were inbound to help with interrogation and training: Mitchell and Jessen, who were both "certified" to use it without supervision, and a third, unidentified man, who was "qualified" to use it under their supervision. They would hold different responsibilities. Mitchell and Jessen would play an "active interrogation role," while the third man would provide "on the ground mentoring" for trainee interrogators going for "certification mode," meaning they needed to complete twenty hours of supervised hands-on practice.[11] Asked later to identify this third person, Mitchell gave the "unique functional identifier" NZ7, CIA code for a mystery figure never properly identified, who Mitchell called "the Preacher."[12] Previously a "seasoned intelligence officer," the Preacher was deeply religious and would put his hand on a detainee's forehead, raise his other arm in the air, and in a "deep southern drawl" say things like, "Can you feel it, son . . . can you feel the spirit moving down my arm, into your body."[13] Mitchell described him as a Southerner who "believed in learned helplessness" and was "totally unpredictable" and "the total opposite of me and Bruce."[14] He had been "handpicked" by Wise, suggesting he had trained in Wise's pilot course.

Several more fledgling interrogators from the pilot course were also en route to Poland seeking "certification," including Matthew Zirbel.[15] Everyone needed to see how the "rock stars" handled high-value detainees. Secluded inside a restricted military area, Stare Kiejkuty appeared to be the perfect location for on-the-job training.[16] Isolated and remote, it was remarkably similar to Mitchell's and Jessen's old working environment in Spokane, Washington. Senior CIA lawyer Jonathan Fredman set down new training requirements in a cable titled "Lessons for the Future."[17] He highlighted the need for the "entire range" of effective and lawful methods to be available to future interrogators. They should be constrained only by the most critical of considerations, "such as the prospective death of a detainee." Mitchell and Jessen, who were described as "high-value captive interrogation psychologists," would supervise the next generation of courses, while chief of interrogation Charlie Wise remained nominally in charge. Gus prayed he could hold it all together.[18]

One of those who undertook interrogator training in 2003 was Sharon, the interrogator who had previously been an Abu Zubaydah subject-matter expert. "[It] was clever and totally surprised me," she recalled.[19] "We thought we were flying to practice on strangers, working with volunteers, but then we got 'arrested' ourselves, as soon as we landed." This was a favorite Roger Aldrich trick. He was still dean at the Personnel Recovery Academy in Spokane and said people avoided him if they spotted him outside Fairchild. "They'd take off thinking, 'Oh god, this guy's coming after me again.'"[20] Aldrich and his team did follow-ups all over the world. "We would turn up without warning, take someone, and keep them for twelve hours to see if they remembered what they'd been taught in training."

Sharon remembered that her CIA training course had been terrifying, even though it was role-play. "They did everything to us except the last one [waterboarding]." She got to know Mitchell and Jessen, although her main trainers were JPRA contractors. "The interrogators didn't know us, and we didn't know them," she said. "They put hoods on us and screamed at us. They wanted to see how long we would last." As Mitchell and Jessen had done in Spokane, the CIA trainers subjected their students to the nasty stuff before bringing them into the classroom. They called it the "Pre-Academic Lab," the same as in Spokane, although this lab taught students how to break real War on Terror detainees.[21]

After qualification, Sharon became a star of the CIA program, the only interrogator who was also a subject-matter expert. She got on-the-job training with real detainees, including Abu Zubaydah, who remained in his wobbling cage behind the false wall. "We were super fortunate to have him," she reflected. "Jim called him a Jedi, and that's exactly what he was." A sly, charismatic chameleon, always preening, lying, and plotting, was how the CIA saw him. Sharon, who knew more about Abu Zubaydah's background than most people, knew he was far from being Al Qaeda's Number Three, as the rest of Alec Station still insisted. "He was a safe-house facilitator—at best," she recalled. Sharon got to interrogate other detainees. "I was at a house with a bunch of people in their early days. I spent hundreds of hours around some of them," she said. Being a woman had its advantages. "I wasn't full of testosterone, ready to kick some ass." Although she never certified to use the waterboard, she saw all the enhanced techniques at work and "had no problem with them." She called the Preacher, the third interrogator authorized to use waterboarding, "Dave" and got on fine with everyone, except for one male interrogator who told her, "You're going to freak out, you can't handle it." Sharon, who used what she described as "full-body techniques," proved him wrong.[22]

Wise was soon up to his old tricks, according to Mitchell, instructing students to put broomsticks behind detainees' knees. Mitchell, who was always quick to find fault in others, claimed that headquarters staff "came to the site, pulled the New Sheriff off and said, 'knock that shit off.'"[23] He and Jessen focused on al-Nashiri, whom they had previously threatened with "tenderizing" and execution.[24] Even though al-Nashiri had "cried," "whimpered," and "babbled" when Mitchell and Jessen had interrogated him, before he was subjected to a mock execution by Albert El Gamil, they judged he could handle more.[25] Jessen asked headquarters for "latitude to use the full range of enhanced exploitation and interrogation measures" on al-Nashiri, including waterboarding him again, to establish a "desired level of helplessness."

The CIA had mis-sold learned helplessness to the Bush administration, saying it had no long-term harmful effects. Mitchell blamed agency staffers, saying they did not understand the complex science behind Martin Seligman's concept. Jessen singled out Rodriguez, saying, "The term was catchy and I think it sounded okay to Jose so he used it." He was not denigrating his former employer; "he's a bright man . . . but I think it was a catch-all term."[26] It took years of study to understand it fully. But Mitchell and Jessen could not deny they had visited Seligman to ask him about learned helplessness just after Abu Zubaydah was captured.

To do a proper job on al-Nashiri, who was not yet helpless, according to Jessen's psychological assessment, the next stage would "require additional support" from Mitchell.[27] After he saw Jessen's forward planning, Wise wrote to headquarters that he was having "serious reservations with the continued use of enhanced techniques with [al-Nashiri] and its long-term impact on him."[28] Not sounding at all like the Wise whom Mitchell had characterized as a "twisted SOB," he warned: "It is the assessment of the prior interrogators that" more enhanced techniques would be "excessive and may cause him to cease cooperation on any level."

Wise also tried to head off Jessen, writing: "We note that [the proposed plan] contains a psychological interrogation assessment by psychologist [Jessen] which is to be carried out by interrogator [Jessen]. We have a problem with him conducting both roles simultaneously." It was the same issue Terry DeMay had complained about months earlier.[29] Working "both sides of the street" was ethically wrong and led to abusive drift.[30] Mitchell dismissed DeMay as "squawking" and "squealing." Others characterized the conflict as a fight over ownership of the waterboard. Wise had "a huge bias against the water board b/c he's not approved to use it," reported one CIA physician. "The reverse is true of the contract psy guys who have a vested interest in favor of it."[31] Asked at one point why he was so protective of it, Mitchell explained: "If misapplied it could cause prolonged mental harm."[32] Headquarters addressed the "dual role" conflict in a cable sent on January 30, 2002, saying that Mitchell and Jessen could continue as long as one of them played interrogator while the other played psychologist.[33] However, a later CIA reassessment acknowledged that allowing Mitchell and Jessen to play dual roles had been a serious mistake.[34]

Wise wanted out. He told colleagues he had "informed the front office" that he would "no longer be associated in any way with the interrogation program."[35] Having survived Latin America, he was not going risk prosecution for something he described as "a train wreak [sic] waiting to happen." He intended "to get the hell off the train before it happens." This time, Gus sided with Wise, writing: "Continued enhanced methods may push [al-Nashiri] over the edge psychologically." Fanning the flames, Wise reported Mitchell to the CIA inspector general, saying that waterboarding had been "overused" with Abu Zubaydah, and he formally accused Mitchell of stealing classified material from Thailand, including copies of videotapes of Abu Zubaydah's treatment[36] If this was true, then Mitchell had the CIA in a stranglehold.

To protect the CIA's reputation, George Tenet issued carefully worded interrogation guidelines on January 28, 2003, the first time any written guidelines were issued in a program that had been running for six months.[37] Standard techniques that did not "incorporate physical or substantial psychological pressure," and that had been used on Abu Zubaydah between April and

June 2002, included but were not limited to isolation, sleep deprivation for up to seventy-two hours, loud music, reduced caloric intake, and the wearing of diapers. Enhanced techniques that did "incorporate physical or psychological pressure" and started only after the CIA obtained the Yoo-Bybee memo of August 1, 2002, included but were not limited to "the attention grasp, walling, the facial hold, the facial slap, the abdominal slap, cramped confinement, wall standing, stress positions, sleep deprivation beyond 72 hours, the use of diapers for prolonged periods, the use of harmless insects, the waterboard." Enhanced techniques always required prior approval from headquarters, could be used only on high-value detainees to gain information about future attacks on the United States, and could be started only after a medical and psychological evaluation, and medical and psychological personnel had to be present. Standard techniques required no such conditions because they were covered under John Rizzo's "bright legal lines" of April 2002.

When the CIA inspector general, John Helgerson, reviewed these guidelines, he concluded that they were an improvement on having no guidelines, but "they still leave substantial room for misinterpretation."[38] No definition of "appropriate training" was given and the Directorate of Operations Handbook contained a "single paragraph" of guidance about detention and interrogation.[39] The ethical conflict of psychologists playing dual roles was not addressed. There was no reference to improvised techniques, like broomsticks behind knees, cinching up of arms, ice baths, water dousing, purging with cigar smoke, death threats, and mock execution. Terry DeMay, who also found the guidelines lacked clarity, wrote up supplementary guidelines to help his medical staff keep up with ever-changing interrogation rules.[40] His biggest problem was with standing sleep deprivation. If medical staff encountered a detainee strung up to an overhead bar, they should know that "arms can be elevated above the head (elbows not locked) for roughly two hours without great concern." There was no mention of seventeen days, as experienced by at least one low-value detainee at the Salt Pit. Tenet's final provision, titled "recordkeeping," required only a written record, meaning no more ugly interrogation videotapes.[41]

"Standard" was a word that belied danger. After Gul Rahman's death, a team from the US Federal Bureau of Prisons had visited the Salt Pit to conduct training sessions and reported back that they had been "WOWed" at how appalling it was.[42] Charlie Wise called the Salt Pit a "dungeon."[43]

In response, Tenet issued more guidelines, regarding "confinement conditions," but did not take much off the table.[44] Black sites need not conform to US prison standards. Medical care did not need to reach the standards in US medical facilities. Food and drink had to meet only "minimum medically appropriate nutritional and sanitary standards." Buckets "for the relief of personal waste" were not compulsory. When President Bush withdrew Geneva Conventions rights from War on Terror detainees in February 2002, he had pledged that they would be treated "humanely," and would receive clothes, shoes, *halal* meals, toilet articles, and "the opportunity to worship."[45] A year on, the CIA's goalposts had shifted significantly.

After Gus's intercession, al-Nashiri appeared to win a reprieve, when headquarters "took the further use of EITs off the table" for him.[46] Instead, he was stripped, shaved, and subjected to standing sleep deprivation, which was defined as a standard technique. Jessen described it as one of the best techniques, since when coupled with "fear of the unknown" and a "friendly approach," interrogators could "use this almost indefinitely and not hurt anyone."[47] However, this was not the conclusion the CIA had reached when it first studied standing sleep deprivation during the 1950s. Then, a Cornell Medical Center neurologist, Harold Wolff, had warned the CIA about the dangers of using it. Wolff, who worked with Mitchell and Jessen's favorite sociologist, Albert Biderman, described it as "a form of physical torture" and wrote that "many men can withstand the pain of long standing, but sooner or later all men succumb to the circulatory failure it produces."[48] They usually developed "a delirious state, characterized by disorientation, fear, delusions and visual hallucinations." The KGB kept prisoners in this fixed position until it "produces excruciating pain." The first sign of trouble was when a prisoner developed edema, or swelling, in the legs, warned Wolff. If left untreated, edema could prove fatal. Post-9/11, the CIA had recirculated this old study. Despite this, many Salt Pit detainees were hung up and subjected to standing sleep deprivation for days, not just hours. Some described being made to stand on prayer mats and never step off, further restricting their movement as well as offending religious sensitivities.[49]

---·---

A blizzard was howling at Szymany airstrip on February 8, 2003. The runway was buried beneath snow, so when the airport director was informed that another American plane was incoming, staff scrambled. The Gulfstream landed after midnight and, like the one before, stopped at the far end of the runway. This time, only one detainee was off-loaded, Ramzi bin al-Shibh. He was as close to a real 9/11 hijacker as the CIA had got to date and a tangible link to Khalid Sheikh Mohammad. For the previous five months, bin al-Shibh had been in "foreign government custody," held on the third floor of a GID prison located inside the heavily guarded GID headquarters in the Wadi Sir district of Amman, where Jordanian prisoners were threatened with snakes and dogs, beaten with sticks, and told "we will make you see death."[50] Bin al-Shibh was also rendered to a notorious Moroccan detention center outside Temara, a pretty coastal town south of Rabat. Temara prisoners claimed they were raped with bottles, burned with cigarettes, and electrocuted.[51] The CIA "guests" never entered the cell blocks but interrogated their detainees in a different building during daylight hours only. Tucked up in their hotels, the Americans could safely say they knew nothing about what happened to detainees at night. Moroccan jailers talked of taking prisoners out "to the desert."[52] CIA detainees complained of torture and hearing habitual "sobbing and yelling" from others.[53]

Around fifty intelligence reports were compiled while Ramzi bin al-Shibh was in Amman or Temara, including one about Khalid Sheikh Mohammad plotting to crash a plane into Heathrow Airport in London.[54] But Alec Station argued bin al-Shibh was still holding back vital clues about "upcoming attacks" that he would give up only if subjected to real American enhanced interrogation and after CIA lawyers got the go-ahead from John Yoo at the Department of Justice's Office of Legal Council (OLC) that the "1 August 2002 OLC opinion extends beyond the interrogation of Abu Zubaydah." The detainees being held in Poland were shuffled around to make room for him in the basement.[55]

Abu Zubaydah was moved upstairs to a real bedroom. It had Soviet-style central heating (switched off) and a worn synthetic carpet (which smelled of mildew) and was blasted 24/7 by "awful music with curse words."[56] Bin al-Shibh's entry treatment was eviscerating: psychological and medical assessments, a rectal examination, a retinal scan, shearing, stripping, and shackling, "hand and foot with arms outstretched over his head."[57] For the first three days, he was kept in a state of "sensory dislocation," with bright white light and "uncomfortably cool temperatures."[58] Like Abu Zubaydah, he was put on a bare bones diet and was hosed down with cold water to keep him chilled. Although Mitchell blamed "indigenous guards" for Gul Rahman's death at the Salt Pit, the team in Poland often strung up detainees, wet, naked, in freezing-cold cells for days on end, and called it "conditioning." Mitchell underplayed the severity, saying the guards "just wet them down with a hose."[59] It was just another form of the "water dousing" they had used without any problem in SERE school, which was authorized as long as the water tempera-ture was monitored and the detainee was checked for signs of hypothermia.[60] Only after the interrogators determined that bin al-Shibh's "initial resistance level [had] been diminished by the conditions" would they start the real rough stuff.[61] Until then, nobody talked to him.[62]

The plan had Mitchell's fingerprints all over it, but Charlie Wise, who was still on the team despite his written concerns, wrote it up, while his "aco-lyte" the Preacher administered the techniques. A later inquiry found bin al-Shibh's enhanced interrogation formed the template for all interrogations in Poland and was used on at least six other detainees, although Rizzo later denied the CIA used enhanced interrogation like a "cookie-cutter, one size fits all."[63] The requests for authorization were identical in all seven cases. Like Abu Zubaydah, bin al-Shibh was also threatened with rectal rehydration, which the CIA had determined was "an acceptable method of delivery" of liquids.[64] Bin al-Shibh's plan also utilized "behavior adjustment," which ac-cording to Mitchell was unauthorized. Enhanced techniques would be ad-ministered as "punishment" for actions perceived as disrespectful, such as failing to address an interrogator as "sir."[65]

Roger Aldrich, Mitchell's former boss, who later played a prominent role in CIA interrogator training, acknowledged that EITs were used as a punishment. "If you lie to me, I'm going to use them," he explained.[66] "Like zapping the dog for pooping on the rug." CIA cables also made reference to interrogators playing the Blues Brothers' version of "Rawhide" at the be-ginning of each of bin al-Shibh's sessions and to keep him awake while he was in the standing sleep-deprivation posture: "Keep them doggies movin', / rawhide, / don't try to understand 'em, / just rope 'em, throw, and brand 'em." One cable explained that music was a form of conditioning, since bin al-Shibh "knows when he hears the music where he is going to go and what is going to happen."[67] When Mitchell was later accused of using music as "an audible trigger like the Pavlovian buzzer," he blamed Wise and said the

Preacher wrote the cable.[68] CIA cables explained that the main purpose of bin al-Shibh's conditioning was to reduce him "to the state of infantile like dependence" so he would "respond appropriately to questions."[69] Abu Zubaydah had recalled "Bodies" being played over and over in Thailand to the point that he had screamed along. Gul Rahman had been subjected to standing sleep deprivation and endless repeats of "The Real Slim Shady" before he died. Others detained in Poland complained about "Rubber Duckie" playing on an endless, desperation-inducing loop as they were hosed down or scrubbed. Mitchell dismissed it all as "sound masking."[70]

Bin al-Shibh's conditioning and subsequent enhanced interrogation produced nothing new, frustrating Alec Station, which once again pushed the interrogation team to treat a detainee even more harshly. The team pushed back, demanding specific questions that Alec Station was "85 percent certain [bin al-Shibh] will be able to answer."[71] Someone went to talk to Abu Zubaydah. "He would help us with how to get the best out of [others]," recalled Sharon, who joked, "We could have put a green [contractor's] badge on him"— although of course he would not be paid for his expertise.[72]

Abu Zubaydah advised the CIA that bin al-Shibh would never have been given a new assignment or trusted with significant new information, given his close links to a high-profile attack that had already happened. Although bin al-Shibh had "achieved substantial notoriety after 11 September," he was still unproven in Al Qaeda circles and may have "been privy to information more as a bystander than as an active participant."[73] He was a foot soldier and would-be hijacker, never a planner. Alec Station disagreed. Since bin al-Shibh had spent extensive time with Khalid Sheikh Mohammad after 9/11, and had given a joint interview with Mohammad to *Al Jazeera* to commemorate the first anniversary of the attacks, it was "inconceivable" he did not know about future operations.[74] While the argument boiled, Bill Harlow, Tenet's chief spokesman and close advisor, used the media to promote the CIA's case for enhanced interrogation, leaking updates from black sites to exacerbate public fears and dampen political opposition to the program.[75]

Even though what was happening in Poland was top secret, and Mohammad remained at-large, bin al-Shibh's Heathrow story was leaked. Amid headlines such as "Warzone Heathrow" and "Heathrow Facing Twin Towers Hit," Tony Blair, the British prime minister, dispatched the British army, causing panic across the United Kingdom.[76] The CIA made sure Americans also understood the severity of threats. "US Braced for Nukes," reported one headline on February 12, four days after bin al-Shibh was rendered to Poland.[77] With both sides of the Atlantic primed, on February 13, Alec Station reported: "HQS strongly believes that Binalshibh [*sic*] was involved in efforts on behalf of KSM to identify and place operatives in the West."[78] The detainee was "uniquely positioned to give us much needed critical information to help us thwart large-scale attacks inside the United States, and we want to do our utmost to get it as soon as possible." But bin al-Shibh still was not talking. They needed something new.

On February 18, one of the two 24/7 overpowering light bulbs went out in his cell. "When security personnel arrived to replace the bulb, bin al-Shibh was cowering in the corner, shivering," reported a cable.[79] The CIA now knew the detainee's secret fear of darkness, and he spent the next month subjected to standing sleep deprivation, "with hands over his head, naked, in total darkness."[80] Still, he produced nothing about future attacks, forcing Alec Station to reluctantly conclude that Abu Zubaydah was probably telling the truth.[81] A later assessment stated that after coming into agency custody, bin al-Shibh's reporting had "steadily declined" to the point that "he has given us nothing on the Saudi hijackers or others who played a role"—things he actually knew about.[82] A CIA psychologist who examined bin al-Shibh in 2005 reported that he had developed severe psychotic disorders that included visions, paranoia, insomnia, and attempts at self-harm, similar to conditions Harold Wolff had observed in the 1950s. Bin al-Shibh's enhanced interrogation had had a "clear and escalating effect on his psychological functioning."[83] Given that he had been previously "a relatively high-functioning individual," his deterioration was "alarming."[84] The best intelligence obtained from him had come before he was sent to Poland, the review concluded.

During testimony he gave to the 9/11 pretrial in January 2020, seventeen years after Ramzi bin al-Shibh's enhanced interrogation in Poland, Mitchell was noticeably coy about his role and tried to lay all the blame on Wise and his "acolyte" the Preacher.[85] First, Mitchell claimed the Yemeni detainee had undergone enhanced interrogation in Afghanistan, where he was not present. "In my book I mistakenly wrote it was at [Poland]," he said. A couple of sessions later, he admitted it might have been Poland but that he had not witnessed bin al-Shibh's enhanced interrogation firsthand. Because this might imply that Tenet's guidelines had been, broken since a psychologist needed to attend all enhanced interrogation sessions, he corrected himself during a subsequent session, saying, "I think I observed EITs being applied to Ramzi." But it was the Preacher who was hands-on, he insisted. At one point, he also claimed to have seen the Preacher put a broomstick behind the detainee's knees, Charlie Wise–style. But since the Preacher was a "certified" interrogator, and this technique was illegal, he revised this statement too: "Originally I thought I was with him for EITs. But I didn't see EITs. Never saw the Preacher put the broomstick." Rules-bound Mitchell did not want to be associated with anything illegal.[86] When he was asked to clarify his interactions with bin al-Shibh, he claimed that most had been "maintenance visits." Asked what that meant, he characterized them as morale-boosting sessions: "How is it going, do you want a book, how his headache was, what are you thinking about." He said he did a lot of these over the years while working as a "debriefer," not an interrogator.

———————◆———————

After Ramzi bin al-Shibh was rendered to Poland, the same Gulfstream was used to render another detainee back into CIA custody, because information gained from him while he was held in "foreign government custody" was about to be used to start a war.[87] For the past year, Ibn Sheikh al-Libi had remained in the custody of Egyptian interrogators at an undisclosed location in Cairo. Now he was sent to the Salt Pit. He had made a key link between Al Qaeda and Saddam Hussein, and with the United States on the cusp of invading Iraq, the CIA wanted to reexamine his stories and make sure he did not talk to anyone else, especially the International Committee of the Red Cross (ICRC).

One February 4, 2003, four days prior to his rendition, al-Libi's dubious story connecting Al Qaeda to Saddam Hussein was cited in Colin Powell's world-changing address at the United Nations Security Council in New York.[88] The claims were so sketchy, they almost did not make it into the speech, according to Powell's former chief of staff, Larry Wilkerson.[89] He recalled Powell grabbing him a few days before the speech: "Powell said 'I'm really, really worried about the terrorist aspect of this intelligence.'" Wilkerson continued, "He said, 'This is not intelligence, this is bullshit. Take it out.'"

Wilkerson uncovered a deeply alarming story, one that began when the US Defense Intelligence Agency (DIA) queried the validity of al-Libi's claims almost as soon as they were reported to the CIA. The DIA stated that al-Libi might be "intentionally misleading the debriefers," giving them information "that he knows will retain their interest."[90] The DIA, considering it "unlikely" that Iraq had helped bin Laden, concluded that al-Libi's information was unreliable, was secondhand and not from his "personal experience." The CIA was advised to put a "burn notice" on the information, meaning to destroy it, but failed to follow through.[91]

Because of the Bush administration's determination to go to war with Saddam Hussein, the CIA revived al-Libi's unreliable testimony in the summer of 2002, using it in a briefing paper, "Iraq and al-Qa'ida: Interpreting a Murky Relationship."[92] Even though this document warned of the "questionable reliability of our sources," and reported that some analysts concurred there was "no conclusive evidence of cooperation on specific terrorist operations," it formed the basis for Powell's draft speech, and the CIA lobbied hard to keep the original al-Libi Al Qaeda–Saddam allegations in the text. Wilkerson described a rehearsal that Powell did in Tenet's office without al-Libi's material, during which Tenet abruptly got up and left the room.[93] Wilkerson was surprised, since in addition to Powell, Condoleezza Rice was there too. "Tenet came back minutes later, sat down next to the secretary, and said, 'We just learned from a high-level Al Qaeda operative of significant contacts between Saddam's secret police and Al Qaeda.'"[94] Tenet was citing al-Libi's claims yet again. "Powell turned to me and said, 'Put the intel back in,'" recalled Wilkerson. The following day, Powell did a final dress rehearsal with al-Libi's material placed front and center. Afterward, he asked Tenet: "You stand by every statement I just made, right?"[95] When Tenet said yes, Powell replied: "Good, George, because tomorrow you're going to be behind me on camera." Wilkerson described Tenet's eyes widening, "like saucers."

On the day of the televised UN hearing, Tenet sat behind the secretary, looking extremely awkward. He later said that the CIA had found "absolutely no linkage between Saddam and 9/11," but the Bush administration had boxed him in.[96] When Wilkerson subsequently asked Tenet's deputy John McLaughlin "why we had not been told about the burn notice," McLaughlin blamed a computer glitch. "Powell went through the ceiling," recalled Wilkerson. But by then, it was far too late.

CHAPTER 15

"MEOW"

March 1, 2003, 2:00 A.M., Rawalpindi, Pakistan

The Americans waited outside while Pakistani rangers charged in. "The boot that went through the door was always foreign," explained Gus. After months of skipping between safe houses, the game was finally up for Khalid Sheikh Mohammad. According to the CIA, he had taken sleeping pills before going to bed, was sleepy, and tried to make an unconvincing deal as the Pakistanis dragged him out in his underwear. But nothing he could offer could match the reported $25 million CIA bounty. Mohammad's traveling companion, a slim Saudi called Mustafa al-Hawsawi, who according to the CIA carried a laptop containing financial evidence connecting him to 9/11, gave up without protest. Alec station chief Marty Martin was personally overseeing the operation from headquarters and kept the "Boss," meaning Tenet, informed throughout, even though it was a weekend. Catching "KSM," as the CIA called him, was a huge coup. At last, the agency had the 9/11 mastermind, responsible for the death of almost three thousand innocent Americans, not to mention the Bali nightclub bombings and countless other attacks. Tenet's friend and advisor Porter Goss, the Republican chairman of the House Intelligence Committee, likened the moment to "the liberation of Paris in the Second World War."[1]

Goss and Bill Harlow worked the media into a frenzy, but Martin became furious when everyone started running Mohammad's picture from his FBI's Most Wanted poster. "They had him in a [*sic*] Arab yuppie outfit, looking very prim and proper," Martin complained. "I'm like, forget this."[2] Martin wanted to release photographs from the capture, showing Mohammad defeated and groggy.[3] "I want every guy downrange to know what their future is," he said. "This is their mack daddy. This is their chief gangster." Tenet gave permission and later flew to the US embassy in Abu Dhabi to hand over a reward to the Pakistani asset who had betrayed Mohammad—a nephew of Mohammad's relative Abu Muntasir al-Balochi in the United Kingdom.[4]

CIA station staff got working on Mohammad at an ISI safe house located in a luxury villa in Islamabad. Initially, he was "cocky," saying he would not talk until he got to New York and was assigned a lawyer, like his nephew Ramzi Yousef.[5] Asked about future attacks, he teased them, saying: "Soon you will see." Special Missions chief Gus tried to render him to Poland for enhanced interrogation, but the Polish government resisted.[6] Mohammad was too high profile, so he and al-Hawsawi were dispatched to the Salt Pit in Afghanistan.[7] Alec Station requested that Mitchell and Jessen lead the interrogation.[8] Mitchell regarded Mohammad as a "monster" and had no qualms about getting rough with him—but not at the Salt Pit.[9] He had built a firebreak between himself and Zirbel's "nasty, but safe" facility. Post Gul Rahman, not even Mohammad could tempt him back. "You would have had to put me in chains to go there," he asserted.[10] Instead, Mohammad's initial interrogation was done by Charlie Wise, who was still on the team and already at the Salt Pit, working his way through low- and medium-value detainees.[11] "Let's roll with the new guy," Wise wrote, requesting authorization to use enhanced measures.[12]

The CIA dispatched Mitchell's SERE-trained psychologist colleague Mike McConnell to check that Wise did not get too "handsy."[13] Diapered, cavity-searched, retina-scanned, photographed naked, and bristling after forty-eight hours without sleep, Mohammad recalled, he was now stripped, sheared, slapped, punched, and strung up in a horse stall "with my hands cuffed and chained to a bar above my head."[14] After an hour, Wise took him to the interrogation room, chaining him up so he stood on tiptoe. Mohammad counted thirteen people. As well as Wise and two female interrogators, there were ten masked "muscle guys." When he refused water, they grappled him to the floor and forcibly rehydrated him. Wise reported this was done to illustrate "total control over the detainee."[15] He was then repeatedly "water doused" with buckets.[16] The temperatures in Kabul were falling, and Mohammad was freezing. Mitchell later characterized Wise's efforts as a failed attempt to "break KSM's will," and anticipating that Gus would turn things around with the Polish authorities, he submitted an alternative plan, focusing on his and Jessen's exclusive use of the waterboard.[17] After the CIA paid another $9 million in bribes, raising Poland's CIA payments to $24 million, Mohammad was cavity-searched, re-diapered, re-hooded, trussed up, and put on a DynCorp-owned Gulfstream to Szymany.[18] Diminutive al-Hawsawi was left behind in the cold and dark with Charlie Wise, Matthew Zirbel, and a half dozen trainee interrogators.[19] "He was not high on my radar," said Mitchell.[20]

Huge, muscle-bound guards carried Mohammad into the Stare Kiejkuty villa at six P.M. on March 6, 2003. Rubber-gloved hands gripped his shoulders and forearms. He was only five feet two inches tall, and his feet barely touched the floor. Mohammad later called them "Planet X" people, an alien guard force.[21] He caught a glimpse of snow as he was maneuvered into the basement, where he was stripped again, given another cavity search and a retina scan, and then placed, "bag on the head," into the standing sleep-deprivation position.[22] In another cell, Ramzi bin al-Shibh was still strung up naked in total darkness and bombarded by "Rawhide." Upstairs, Abu Zubaydah and al-Nashiri were locked up in mildewed bedrooms like naughty children, oblivious to the scuffling arrival of "Mokhtar." Mitchell described Mohammad as a "hooded troll" with a "grotesque potbelly" and finger-length body hair that he shed "like a cat losing its winter coat."[23] The psychologist was full of zoomorphisms when it came to describing detainees, and he characterized Abu Zubaydah as constantly groping his crotch as if he were a bad monkey.[24] Back in SERE school, Roger Aldrich advised students that torturers found it much easier to conduct their work on people they regarded as subhuman.[25] Two worlds were set to collide.

Like Abu Zubaydah, Mohammad remembered three "experienced CIA interrogators . . . all strong and well-trained."[26] He said they never used the word "torture" but made it clear that was what they intended to do: "I was told that they would not allow me to die, but that I would be brought to the 'verge of death and back again.'"[27] A new waterboard, smaller than the Thai gurney, waited. Because everyone was charged up, and the CIA was concerned that nothing untoward should happen to its most prized detainee, the medics had instructions to monitor the frequency of the "pours" as well as the number of "applications." They also had a pulse oximeter, having finally heeded Terry DeMay's warnings about blacking-out episodes.[28] Mike McConnell, who had flown with Mohammad from Kabul, would conduct the prerequisite psychological assessment and monitor the detainee for signs of "severe physical or mental suffering." DeMay reported: "As with AZ, the interrogation was handled by psychologist/interrogators Jessen and Mitchell, and monitored by the OTS psychologist who had worked with AZ."[29] The medical examination and psychological assessment took eight minutes. Back in Langley, Jim Pavitt, the CIA's deputy director of operations, called Gus up to his office. "Pavitt said he wanted me to get the biggest, baddest guys and do whatever it takes to make him talk," Gus recalled.[30] "Yes, sir," he replied. As the Special Missions chief walked out, his deputy asked: "What are you going to do?" Gus said he replied: "He knows goddam well I'm not going to do anything illegal." But in Poland, the black site team felt the building pressure; a medic reported: "The requirements coming from home are really unbelievable in terms of breadth and detail."[31]

Approval to get started took twenty minutes. Mohammad was shifted to the interrogation room—where there were no cameras.[32] Mitchell, Jessen, and the third interrogator tag-teamed numerous standard and enhanced techniques, softening Mohammad up. Later, Mohammad gave them names: "Abu Captain," "Abu White," and "Abu Hanan," meaning the compassionate brother. Mitchell claimed "Abu Captain" and said the third interrogator was the Salt Pit–trained Wise acolyte, the Preacher.[33] Other sources indicated that Deuce Martinez spent many hours interrogating Mohammad.[34] Mohammad said "enormous men" dressed in black were also in the room, punching and slapping him, while Jessen did the official walling.[35] Mitchell ridiculed the terrified detainee. Whenever Jessen yanked Mohammad forward, his "naked potbelly swings out away from his body and bounces off Bruce's upper thighs."[36] Mitchell described Jessen's role-play avatar as "vintage Clint Eastwood."[37] As with Abu Zubaydah and bin al-Shibh, they homed in on weaknesses. Mitchell knew that Mohammad knew the CIA his sons, Hamza, eight, and Zaid, seven, who had been captured with Ramzi bin al-Shibh. Now, the CIA gave Mitchell permission to threaten they were going to kill Mohammad's boys, as long as the threats were "conditional."[38] Mitchell recalled: "I said something like, 'if there is another catastrophic attack on America and I find out you had information that could have prevented that attack and that another American child is killed I will cut your sons' throats.'"[39] He acknowledged it was distasteful but had no regrets. "I don't care if he's afraid of us killing his children."

Later, Mohammad accused Mitchell of sticking a photograph of his sons on the wall of his cell—two downcast boys sitting on a patterned couch, refusing to look at the CIA photographer.[40] Mitchell denied it. "That didn't happen," he insisted.[41] "We didn't have their picture. The entire crew would have been sent home if we had put up pictures." Mitchell was also accused of scrawling "50" on the wall, referring to the number of years they would keep interrogating him.[42] Mitchell denied this too, saying, "If we knew that person, they would have been sent home." He characterized his interactions with Mohammad as respectful. "If he was leaving stuff out I'd interject, 'Come on Mukh.'"[43] But cables reported Mohammad had been warned that the interrogations would "last forever" if he failed to cooperate.[44] Most of the allegations against Mitchell came from the Preacher.[45] Mitchell brushed them all aside, saying the Preacher made up allegations because he was jealous. "We were being paid more than other folks," Mitchell explained.[46]

By March 10, the interrogation room even more was crowded. Alfreda Bikowsky had flown in from Langley, accompanied by Jennifer Matthews. They were not going to miss out on the "Mukie" show, as Bikowsky referred to Mokhtar.[47] In addition, there were medics and several huge guards. Possibly McConnell and Martinez were there too. "We had a guard with a stopwatch and the physician had a stopwatch and a clicker," recalled Mitchell.[48] Before they got started, the team received a call from Gus, who conveyed a message from Jim Pavitt: "I want to know what he knows, and I want to know it fast."[49] The first day they subjected Mohammad to five sessions on the waterboard, a brutal initiation. The first session lasted thirty minutes, ten minutes longer than had been approved for Abu Zubaydah. In between pours, they bombarded Mohammad with questions. "What is the next target in the US?" "What is the plan?" "Who are the people?" "Who do you have in the US?" "Where are they?"[50] At the end of the day, he was left naked and in a "horizontal stress position," deprived of sleep.[51] This meant being stretched out, with arms and legs chained to opposite walls. Mitchell simply remembered the detainee snoring.[52]

Around five gallons of water had been used, thirty-eight pints more than the navy SERE-school limit.[53] At the end of the day, they debated how to "upgrade" his interrogation. A worried medic emailed DeMay, saying that the interrogators "felt that the [waterboard] was the big stick and that HQ was more or less demanding that it be used early and often."[54]

On March 12, the board was used "with an intensity far exceeding anything in the past," according to the medic. During five sessions spanning twenty-four hours, water was poured more than eighty times, with almost half the pours lasting between twenty and forty seconds. The medic interrupted multiple times and reported that Mohammad's "abdomen was somewhat distended, and he expressed water when the abdomen was pressed."[55] The detainee was ingesting and aspirating "a LOT of water," and they were effectively doing "a series of near drownings." Concerned about water intoxication, the medic requested that Mitchell and Jessen switch to saline. DeMay went to see Gus, telling him that the "extent of water board usage was both excessive and pointless."[56] In an attempt to rein in the process, DeMay cabled new guidelines, stating a maximum of three waterboard sessions in a twenty-four-hour period.[57] Counterterrorist Center lawyers overruled him, and Mitchell and Jessen pushed forward. The medic wrote to DeMay: "I am going the extra mile to try to handle this in a non-confrontational manner."[58]

Having quickly worked out the forty-second limit for a pour, Mohammad began pointing "upward with his two index fingers as the water pouring approached the established time limit."[59] Mitchell and Jessen described this as Mohammad deploying resistance-training and they adapted their technique by "dramatically [increasing] the water volume."[60] Someone held Mohammad's lips, "ultimately even creating a small reservoir of water directly over his mouth."[61] Mitchell later described this as "Goofy Duck lips" but said it was not his idea.[62] "I never held his lips," he said, before clarifying: "Holding his lips to me means grabbing him by the lips." Again, Mitchell blamed the Preacher. "He cupped his hands around the cloth, I moved my hands away, next time I look at the site manager, gesture what's up, he shrugs, gives a thumbs up. We do a couple more so we don't lead [Mohammad] to believe it's easy to stop. We came out, I said, 'what's going on?' They said, 'this is a change because he's able to defeat it.'"[63] "They" was never defined.

Various accounts of the day were sent home. The medic wrote: "Things are slowly evolving [from] OMS being viewed as . . . the limiting factor to the ones who are dedicated to . . . keeping everyone's butt out of trouble."[64]

A psychologist doing the assessments concluded: "There is no evidence that the subject is experiencing any profound or permanent psychological or emotional harm."[65] The cables noted that Mohammad "yelled and twisted while being secured onto the board" and "whimpered, moaned and appeared immensely exhausted at the end of the afternoon session."[66] In addition to waterboarding, Mohammad was also being "water doused" when he was in standing or horizontal sleep-deprivation positions.[67] It had been requested "as an additional EIT for KSM" and was approved with certain conditions: "KSM could not be placed naked on bare cement floor, but he had to be placed on a sheet or towel."[68] They did not want another Gul Rahman, but they also did not want Mohammad winning any respite. Mitchell described the in-between sessions as medically enforced "catnaps."[69]

Interrogators who doused another detainee in a similar fashion at the Salt Pit in April 2003 were reported for "possible violation of federal criminal law" to the US Attorney's Office, Eastern District of Virginia.[70] Water dousing was added as an authorized technique in January 2004, after the CIA decided to stop full-blown waterboarding, but the definitions often became blurred inside interrogation chambers. In Poland, no questions were asked, and when they strapped Mohammad back onto the proper board on March 15, they further tweaked their technique, using hands to create a one-inch-deep "pool" of water over his nose and mouth.[71] At one point, Jessen waited for Mohammad to open his mouth to speak before pouring.

When he was not undergoing water torture, Alfreda Bikowsky and Jennifer Matthews bombarded Mohammad with demands for information. He did not have anything in the works, he replied, explaining that post-9/11 he had been busy helping move Al Qaeda families out of Afghanistan.[72] The last operatives he tried to infiltrate into the United States were "shoe bomber" Richard Reid, a British Muslim convert with mental-health problems, who attempted to detonate explosives on a Miami-bound flight in December 2001, and "dirty bomber" Jose Padilla, who flew into Chicago in May 2002.[73] Both were in custody, but Reid's failed shoe bomb had pricked fear across the entire aviation industry, and Padilla's bucket bomb idea still fed the "one percent" fearmongers in Washington.

Mitchell and Jessen, who were conducting the "hard interrogation sessions," as opposed to the softer "debriefings" by the women, told Mohammad that "he was either stupid and incompetent as the chief of external operations of Al Qaeda or that he was lying."[74] The next time they put him on the board and asked about future plans, he replied. "I don't have any. I'm stupid."[75] When Jennifer Matthews told him that she knew everything about him and that he shouldn't lie to her, Mohammad sneered: "Then why are you here?" As with Abu Zubaydah, as his fear eased up, his resistance training began to show, Mitchell claimed. It was time to limit his "talk-time."[76]

After the team drastically stepped up the use of standing sleep deprivation, a "crack" finally formed in Mohammad's defenses.[77] As the CIA had implied with the sleeping pills story, the one thing Mohammad could not live without was sleep. For two days straight, Mohammad was chained to an overheard bar. He eventually fell asleep, hanging by his wrists, "resulting in open and bleeding wounds."[78] When told Mohammad still had scars almost seventeen years later, Mitchell shrugged. It was not unusual for handcuffs to "chafe." One day, Mohammad claimed, his head was banged against the wall "so hard it started to bleed."[79] Other detainees accused Mitchell of pointing to a stain on the walling wall in Poland and saying, "that's KSM's blood." He denied this. There were lots of stains on the burlap that covered the walling wall, he recalled; none of them were blood.[80] But Mitchell did admit to using fear with others. One day, when Mohammad was on the board, the team decided Ramzi bin al-Shibh should take a "walk-by."[81] According to the Preacher, who later complained, Mitchell wanted to plant the idea that bin al-Shibh's turn on the waterboard was coming.[82] "[Ramzi] was visibly upset," Mitchell recalled. "The Preacher took him into an alcove and he sat on his knee like a child. I walked by and said, 'maybe we are coming for you next.'"[83]

On March 21, the day after the United States went to war with Iraq, Mohammad endured his thirteenth waterboarding session. It was approved after Bikowsky misread intelligence from another CIA detainee about having seen African American converts at Al Qaeda training camps. She wrote in an email: "I love the Black American Muslim at AQ camps in Afghanuistan [sic]. . . . Mukie is going to be hatin' life on this one."[84] Extrapolating, she accused Mohammad of trying to make contact with African American converts in the United States. It was a farcical suggestion, but after numerous pours on the waterboard, Mohammad spluttered that he was "ready to talk."[85] He told them he had sent a British operative to Montana to recruit African American Muslim converts there. Even though practically no African American Muslims lived in Montana, this ridiculous story was reported as fact and triggered multiple inquiries. Mohammad was chained back up to an overhead bar and ordered to turn slowly, like shawarma on a spit, as they hosed him down.[86] Finally, he said, "Men break. . . . If I don't break tomorrow, it will be the next day."[87] Mitchell and Jessen told him: "Give the information we need . . . otherwise, it lasts forever." By nine o'clock that night, he had been sleep-deprived for 132 hours. His legs were swollen with edema, and he had abrasions on his wrists and head.[88] He was soft and pudgy, but evidently, he was mentally tough. Because there were "no indications of any profound and permanent emotional or psychological harm," according to the psychologist, Mitchell and Jessen kept going.[89] Tough upbringings and years at SERE school had taught them how to break an opponent's will.

————◆————

By the time Khalid Sheikh Mohammad's waterboarding ordeal came to an end, on March 24, 2003, he had been waterboarded over 180 times, more than twice as often as Abu Zubaydah, with most pours lasting twenty to forty seconds.[90] He had been put through standing sleep deprivation for almost seven days straight, had been fed a bare-bones diet, most of which dribbled down his legs as diarrhea, and had lost a third of his body weight.[91] Now, Mitchell and Jessen put him in Abu Zubaydah's wobbling cage behind the false wall. "I preferred it as there was no music and, as it was a cage structure instead of solid walls, the ventilation was better," Mohammad said.[92] Debriefers took over, but Mitchell and Jessen dropped by for regular "heart-to-heart" sessions to make sure he always knew they were still there.[93] Sometimes, Bikowsky and Matthews questioned him. At some stage Deuce Martinez was brought into the equation. He and Mohammad reportedly bonded over a shared belief in God, Martinez being a practicing Catholic, and Mohammad allegedly wrote poems for Martinez's wife.[94] Martinez refused to get involved in any rough stuff, although Mitchell and Jessen offered to get him "certified" in enhanced techniques.[95]

After Mohammad became "compliant," he was afforded "creature comforts," like a cup of tea, a snack, or a T-shirt.[96] One cable noted that he was relaxed, smiled "broadly," and seemed to "relish" talking to Bikowsky and Matthews.[97] The CIA recorded a "poignant moment" when a frog jumped out of a drain. Mitchell caught it and asked Mohammad if he wanted it removed. "No, no, let it stay."[98] According to the official CIA tally, Mohammad's revelations led to one thousand intelligence disseminations, but he was never allowed to get too comfortable, as Mitchell and Jessen regularly reappeared to explain "the facts of life" to him.[99] This was just a reprieve. If he were caught regressing or lying, they would "react vigorously."[100]

The CIA shared some of Mohammad's admissions with the FBI in a report entitled "Precious Truths, Surrounded by a Bodyguard of Lies."[101] Gus recalled that this led to a showdown. "We started getting a lot of good information, and I remember to this day that Jose called and said Mueller had rung and [the FBI] wants to get back in."[102] Rodriguez asked Gus to draft some notes "as to why this can't happen." Later, Gus was called up to deputy CIA director John McLaughlin's office and found him reading the notes to Mueller over the phone. "McLaughlin said, 'Well, we told liaison that only CIA people are authorized at the black sites.'" According to Gus, Mueller suggested, "Well, you can tell them they are CIA." McLaughlin apparently refused, according to Gus: "He said: 'These people are not stupid, and they can tell the difference.' It went on and on and finally I heard Mueller screaming, and John put down the phone." The FBI director had hung up on him. "John said, 'I don't care.' So we never did let them back in."

Years later, at his home in New England, Gus hung a framed retirement card on his wall, showing him catching a fish with Khalid Sheikh Mohammad's face superimposed on it. "You caught the big one," wrote his colleagues.[103] Officially, the CIA represented that Mohammad had made dozens of confessions either during or after enhanced interrogation, from masterminding 9/11 and the Bali bombings to planning to cut the cables on New York City suspension bridges, Godzilla style. Unsure of the validity of some of Mohammad's statements, Mueller asked for the FBI to have access to the detainee "in order to better understand CIA reporting indicating threats to U.S. cities."[104] Tenet agreed, but the CIA dragged its feet, and the FBI did not get to question Mohammad until he was turned over to US military custody three and a half years later.

Well before the FBI rerecorded Mohammad's confessions, internal CIA reporting revealed that he had recanted many statements. He fabricated information indicating that Jose Padilla and another suspected Al Qaeda operative were plotting together, because he "felt some pressure to produce information about operations in the United States in the initial phases of his interrogation."[105] On the day he expelled the most water, he said, he had projected a vague idea to crash planes into Heathrow and Canary Wharf in London as an active operation. He did the same with an Al Qaeda anthrax program. Suspicions that he was lying were even reported in live CIA cables. On March 18, when he "seemed to lose control" on the waterboard and appeared "somewhat frantic," the cable further stated that Mohammad "had been forced to lie, and made up stories," and that some of his reporting was "complete fabrication."[106] The greatest fiction was his plan to recruit African American converts in Montana. This was not among the thirty-one confessions officially listed when Mohammad was "interviewed" by an FBI "clean team" in 2007. His "confession" statement was partially released to the media by the Pentagon a year before he was charged.[107] Mohammad was only assigned a legal team after he was charged, and he told them he made up the Montana confession and many others just to get Mitchell and Jessen to stop enhanced interrogation.[108]

Pressed about false reporting, Mitchell argued, "The interrogators didn't make the distinction that things are true or false."[109] That was the job of debriefers. His goal was simply to get detainees talking, to "stop people jumping off the top of burning buildings and dying." A later investigation into information the CIA gave to the "White House, National Security Council, the Department of Justice, the Congress, the CIA Office of Inspector General, and the public" found that the information was "consistently inaccurate."[110]

Some of Khalid Sheikh Mohammad's "confessions" led to rewards, like being told he had a new son (his wife had been pregnant when he was captured). "Bruce was comforting KSM, who was in his arms like a child," Mitchell recalled.[111] Later, Mohammad recanted many of his stories. His most controversial "confession" concerned the beheading of *Wall Street Journal* reporter Daniel Pearl in January 2002. President Bush wrote that he had been motivated to authorize Abu Zubydah's enhanced interrogation after meeting Pearl's widow, even though Abu Zubaydah had zero connection to the journalist's death. Mohammad confessed in Poland in April 2003, shortly after Mitchell had delivered another stark reminder that they could go back to "hard times" any time he was perceived not to be cooperating. Mitchell told Mohammad that on a scale of 1 to 100 of compliance, he was "vacillating between 50 and 60."[112] Mohammad became distressed, according to a cable. "After a further quiet exchange of words," which was not recorded, "KSM said that he had something more to tell" and asked for a debriefer to witness it too, almost certainly Deuce Martinez.[113] "KSM spoke with some-what low volume and appeared increasingly solemn as his story unfolded," reported the cable.[114] He broke eye contact and looked down into his lap. He was the true murderer of Daniel Pearl. It was an astonishing moment, reflected Mitchell. "[KSM] was trying very hard to convince us he was work-ing with us."[115]

However, several key aspects of Mohammad's story did not stack up, and his death penalty lawyer, David Nevin, later produced a CIA document that stated: "[KSM] had been promised he would not be punished for the murder if he confessed so he felt he had nothing to lose."[116] He also had a lot to gain. When could he write to his family, Mohammad asked tentatively a few minutes after making the Pearl confession? He was told by Mitchell it was still "too early" and may "never be a possibility."[117] Mohammad still had "a considerable way to go to demonstrate that he could be consistently truthful." However, he was given a small reward. "At the end of the session, interrogator gave KSM a better than average dinner," although he was warned again that "things would not go well with him if another target [was] hit by Al Qaeda and KSM had not given a warning."[118]

To verify the Pearl confession, Mitchell said that he, the debriefer, and Mohammad reenacted the beheading, using a pillowcase stuffed with bags of sugar as a substitute for Pearl's head. They videotaped it, using the same angles as the real beheading footage. "Throughout the reenactment, KSM smiled and mugged for the camera," wrote Mitchell.[119] He recalled that Mo-hammad had "new scars and lost a lot of weight so he was worried his arms might not look the same."[120] But when the video of Mohammad's reenact-ment was shared with the FBI, which compared the "pattern of veins" and other features, news came back that Mohammad's arms and hands matched those that had wielded the knife.[121] According to Mitchell, the detainee re-torted: "See, I told you. I cut Daniel's throat with these blessed hands."[122] One of the black site guards commented: "That guy needs to die. Real bad!"[123] Mitchell and the CIA hailed the "confession" as evidence that enhanced interrogation worked, with Rizzo later characterizing Mohammad as the "proud personal butcher of the Wall Street Journal reporter Daniel Pearl."[124]

Other detainees detailed being goaded or tortured into telling lies by interrogators. Abu Zubaydah recalled that while he was in Poland, when he was asked to come up with a hypothetical plot in Australia, he suggested targets could include the Sydney Opera House. Like before, whenever he was conditioned, he would "create, fabricate and invent."[125] Shortly afterward, the Preacher and Albert El Gamil (who had served his suspension and was back in action) demanded Abu Zubaydah disclose his secret attack plans for Australia. When he said he did not have any, they threatened him with the waterboard. He then made things worse by saying "meow," like a cat, a reference to the old cat joke about Arab intelligence services being willing fools. "I'm not Al Qaeda, stupid." The Preacher and Gamil brought in Mitchell and Jessen, who also threatened to put Abu Zubaydah back on the waterboard.[126]

Ramzi bin al-Shibh reported a similar experience. When he was asked by an unidentified interrogator to give the Arabic word for "fission," headquarters was informed that he was talking about Al Qaeda's nuclear capability and approved more pressure.[127] Mitchell blamed Charlie Wise for this infraction. Another high-value detainee, Hambali, later reported giving "false information in an attempt to reduce the pressure on himself . . . and to give an account that was consistent with what [Hambali] assessed the questioners wanted to hear."[128]

Mitchell denied going too far, even with Khalid Sheikh Mohammad. Allegations that he stuck "a hose up KSM's butt" were completely untrue.[129] That was probably Charlie Wise, he said. "KSM spent 21 days under EITs," he recalled.[130] The rest of Mohammad's 1,287 days in CIA custody were, according to Mitchell, spent "rubbing his belly." While Mitchell was still at Stare Kiejkuty, his treatment of detainees was brought to the attention of senior officials in the Bush administration, who sought out Ari Fleischer, the White House press secretary. Stop telling reporters that the US is treating all detainees "humanely," John Bellinger requested of Fleischer.[131] Maybe enhanced interrogation techniques worked. Maybe not. Others would determine that later. But they were certainly not humane.

CHAPTER 16

"STRAWBERRY FIELDS FOREVER"

May 2003, CIA headquarters, Langley, Virginia

How to keep Abu Zubaydah and others "incommunicado" fell to Gus. The "endgame facility," as he called the place the detainees would be kept, needed to be well hidden, securely staffed by Americans, defendable, escape-proof, suicide-proof, outside US jurisdiction, and beyond "pesky little international obligations."[1] The host state would have no visitation rights or ability to shut it down. The CIA would need constant access. There was a lot to match up. Langley had only ever addressed the "disposition of detainees" in late 2001, long before Abu Zubaydah was captured, when Rizzo wrote a classified paper for George Tenet that was never disseminated. Abu Zubaydah's waterboarding team had raised the issue several times but never got an answer. Mitchell later said that he "wasn't particularly concerned" about Abu Zubaydah ever getting out but always suspected that what they had done to him in Thailand would "end up in court" someday.[2] By mid-2003, the CIA could no longer ignore the endgame issue. Many more detainees were enduring brutal treatment, the CIA was building new black sites in Romania and Morocco, and Abu Zubaydah was not the only one who needed to disappear. They could not shuffle broken men who could never be released, irrespective of guilt, around the world forever. For John Rizzo, who characterized the detainees as the "most despicable creatures on the planet," the greatest fear was one of them dying before they were prosecuted.[3] "I can't say that it was motivated by any real sense of human compassion," he later recalled.[4] "Rather, I was worried that if and when they started keeling over . . . not only would they never face justice, the interrogation tactics the

Agency had employed on them would inevitably be linked to their demise, no matter how attenuated or even specious those links were."

Gus started from zero. After making a "deep dive into the program for the big boys," including Tenet, McLaughlin, Pavitt, Rodriguez, and Krongard, he presented four options.[5] One was to "keep them in our custody forever." They discounted this on the grounds that "we should not be in the prison business." The second was "hand them to a third-party liaison." That would not work because the host government "could let them go" or give the International Committee of the Red Cross (ICRC) access. A third option was to try them by "military commissions" outside the US judicial system. That might suit someone like Khalid Sheikh Mohammad, who had admitted his role in 9/11, but not Abu Zubaydah, who denied practically everything the CIA threw at him.[6] A fourth option was "let them go," which was a nonstarter. Gus sat back. "I can't think of any other option," he said. Someone spoke up: "Well, there's always five." He looked at his papers. What was five? "Kill them." Silence was followed by nervous laughter. Gus said it was an off-color joke, made by, "I can't say who."[7]

The endgame was "a policy issue for the US Government rather than a CIA issue," determined Tenet.[8] Everyone involved in legitimizing Abu Zubaydah's enhanced interrogation would have to join in deciding where to hide the detritus. Tenet was not willing to let "torture" and fake WMDs define his entire government career. Some of those attending these meetings later professed regrets. John Brennan, who was there in his capacity as Krongard's deputy and became Obama's CIA director in 2013, recalled that when he first learned what they had done to Abu Zubaydah, he took himself out to the parking lot for a cigarette. "My God," he thought, "what are we doing?" Later, he chastised himself for not having done more to stop it.[9] Gus remembered differently. "[Brennan] was at all these five o'clock meetings about the program," he recalled. "He never raised an objection, ever."[10]

While the government debated where, Gus got on with how, and sometime during the summer of 2003, he sent a team to the only US federal super-max prison, ADX Florence, in Colorado. Known as "the Alcatraz of the Rockies," the ADX held the most dangerous, uncontrollable inmates in the federal prison system, including Khalid Sheikh Mohammad's nephew Ramzi Yousef and three East Africa embassy bombers.[11] It was a brutalist, silent space where prisoners were kept under 24/7 lockdown in soundproof poured-concrete cells. Beds were equipped with "strap-down" rings. For one hour a day, compliant prisoners were permitted to exercise alone in a concrete pit resembling an empty swimming pool. They were cut off from the world, pinned in place by motion detectors, cameras, pressure pads buried in the ground that would set off an alarm if anyone stepped on them, fourteen hundred remote-controlled steel doors, and a twelve-foot-high razor-wire perimeter fence. The ADX held twenty-two inmates designated as "terrorists" when Gus's team visited. They would later be joined by Ahmed Ressam, whose testimony had condemned Abu Zubaydah, "dirty bomber" Jose Padilla, "shoe bomber" Richard Reid, and "twentieth hijacker" Zacarias Moussaoui. The ADX staff reported that a third of the terrorist population had attempted suicide, twelve were on a hunger strike, many refused to use the recreation pit due to a prerequisite body search, and most showered in their underpants because of CCTV surveillance. They tried communicating by shouting down drainage holes. Because it was in the United States, ADX Florence did not provide a solution to the CIA's dilemma, but it gave Gus some ideas.

US Naval Station Guantánamo Bay was the obvious answer: a remote offshore corner of the world controlled by the US military beyond the United States and its laws, consisting of forty-five-square miles of pristine Caribbean frontage located around a large natural harbor in far southeastern Cuba. Seized during the Spanish-American War of 1898, it was transformed into America's first overseas military base in 1903, during Theodore Roosevelt's presidency, and leased from the Cubans for $2,000 per year (to be paid in gold coins). The lease was renegotiated in 1934, stating that both the US and Cuban governments had to consent to a termination. Washington had hung onto it ever since, keeping the Cubans out even through the Bay of Pigs fiasco.[12] An eighteen-hour bus ride from Havana, six hundred air miles from Key West, Florida, its waters patrolled by US naval warships and flying fish, it was home to banana rats, iguanas, and seven hundred War on Terror detainees. Under pressure from Dick Cheney, Donald Rumsfeld reluctantly agreed to let the CIA build a mini "Alcatraz" facility even more secure than the main Joint Task Force Guantánamo detention site, Camp Delta. Gus called his forever facility "Strawberry Fields," after the Beatles song.[13] It was located close to the southern shore of the naval station, near a half-moon of white coral and azure water that the Americans called Kittery Beach and that Christopher Columbus had sailed past in April 1494.[14]

While Gus drew up specifications and a budget (unlimited), Mitchell and Jessen began prepping for the big move. "With the AZ transition as our learning study, Bruce and Jim will also be able to lay out a general set of psychological, physical, medical, occupational, recreational and operational requirements," the CIA reported on May 28, 2003.[15] "Bruce and Jim are naturals for this task: they know AZ best and have the psychological expertise." Others argued that they were completely the wrong people. "There is just too much extraneous at play—with both AZ wanting to be friends, so as not to return to the former situation, and the psychologists wanting to be friends, so that bygones are bygones—to view even a correct assessment as valid," one staffer cautioned.[16] Using Mitchell and Jessen to ease the detainee into the idea that he was never getting out until he was put in his real coffin was an archetype of abuse. There was another problem. A CIA medic returning from a SERE course at Fort Bragg said a "senior SERE psychologist" had told him that Mitchell and Jessen were bragging about using the waterboard on War on Terror detainees. "I hope these folks are not promoting their importance among their colleagues by inappropriate disclosures," the email writer needled.[17]

Gus recommended that Mitchell and Jessen step back from the front line and take a more active role in training, saying he wanted to get "more bang for our buck."[18] The two "docs" agreed.[19] They wanted to focus on "strategic consulting." On June 13, 2003, they signed new contracts: $598,000 each to work on and support the live program; $90,500 more for Mitchell and $99,900 more for Jessen to rewrite training materials; and another $78,000 apiece to coach newly hired psychologists.[20] Not everyone was happy. A senior official, whose name was later redacted, sent an excoriating email, saying that their expertise in training people for real-world situations seemed to have "escaped me up until now."[21] Getting into the old schoolhouse psych argument of trainers not having appropriate experience to operate in the real world, the email writer continued, "We are not training personnel at risk of being wrapped up during military missions." These were real interrogations and real detainees. "Wholesale adoption of the Jim and Bruce show just isn't appropriate." It was time to explore "less invasive physical means," more "due diligence," and no more "dual role" practice. To make sure this happened, Terry DeMay was assigning a senior Medical Services psychologist to Gus's department.[22] The email writer was hitting his stride. Did the CIA appreciate that "any data collected by [Mitchell and Jessen] from detainees . . . will always be suspect"? A taint hung over everyone connected to them. It was time to loosen, not tighten, their stranglehold. "My greatest concern . . . is the likelihood of Jim and Bruce ignoring or interfering with our on-site psychologists when they are deployed," he continued. They believed "that their way is the only way," and they should be diverted before their "arrogance and narcissism evolve into unproductive conflict in the field." Everyone "read-in" had watched the pair's clashes with Ali Soufan, Scott Shumate, Charlie Wise, and the Preacher. The program dangled precariously. The media, human rights lawyers, and the CIA inspector general were all probing. Someday, someone would talk. The two men's time would be better spent helping new interrogators understand why high-value detainees, "like 'normal' human beings," did not always recall everything the intelligence "model" said they should.

"Teflon" Mitchell and Jessen returned to Poland, tasked to "prepare the [high-value terrorists] for the transition to the Endgame Facility at Guantánamo," and were advised that the process would be "extremely tricky."[23] The detainees were all relatively young and would be "confined for the rest of their natural lives." The two "docs" were also needed to assess two new detainees who were accused of playing major roles in 9/11 and who had been upgraded to high-value. Both were in a messy state, because they had spent the previous few weeks at the Salt Pit with Matthew Zirbel and Charlie Wise. The first was Khallad bin Attash, who came from a prominent Yemeni family with links to Osama bin Laden. According to his CIA biography, he had volunteered for jihad at fourteen, lost a leg and a brother while fighting in Afghanistan, joined forces with bin Laden, and was photographed at Al Qaeda's 9/11 planning summit in Kuala Lumpur, Malaysia, in January 2000. Describing him as "a warrior," Mitchell proclaimed "he was a jihadist and still in the fight." He also offered that bin Attash "didn't like women, probably because his mom dropped him off as a teenager at an Al Qaeda camp."[24] The CIA and FBI accused bin Attash of selecting and training 9/11 hijackers, asserted that Abu Zubaydah had helped him with passports and travel documents, and dubbed him "KSM's deputy."[25]

The second new high-value detainee was Ammar al-Baluchi, another member of Khalid Sheikh Mohammad's extended family. Westernized, fluent in English, and well traveled, he was accused of moving money to the hijackers from his base in Dubai. He had also allegedly sent flight-safety manuals to his uncle Khalid Sheikh Mohammad in Karachi and was at one point married to Aafia Siddiqui, a US-based Pakistani neuroscientist accused of joining Al Qaeda and wanted by the FBI for plotting attacks in the United States.[26]

By the summer of 2003, the Salt Pit was an "in-processing" factory, where Wise, Zirbel, and trainee interrogators sorted new detainees into low-, medium-, or high-value status. Those at the top end were sent on to Mitchell and Jessen in Poland for enhanced interrogation, while the "dark prison" kept the rest for "on-the-job training."[27] Gus did not like the abusive setup, but he had few choices, as detainees were still pouring in, and he was still short of trained interrogators. "We really counted on eight," he said.[28] Among the best were the "two gals," one of whom was Sharon. Female interrogators were particularly effective, "because the Muslim men won't put up with women poking them and touching them and looking at them in a way that is negative," Gus explained. Mitchell called Sharon a "tough girl."[29]

The Salt Pit was a perfect place to practice. A senior CIA officer who visited joked that it was an enhanced interrogation technique in its own right, and when Gus sent a team to visit, it was unable to come up with any suggestions to reduce the facility's "baseline conditions" because they were already rock-bottom.[30] Jessen had told Zirbel that detainees should be deprived "substantially" before interrogations, so "there's not much to take away," rather they could be rewarded for compliance.[31] In emails, Zirbel described having "3 or 4 rooms" where undocumented detainees could be hidden away. For a "few hundred bucks a month," he could use the rooms "for whoever I bring over—no questions asked." The arrangement housed "guys that shouldn't be in [the Salt Pit] for one reason or another but still need to be kept isolated and held in secret detention."[32] It was a human scrapyard.[33]

Later, when Mitchell was asked during a 9/11 pretrial hearing to describe the next generation of interrogators, a picture emerged of inexperienced contractors and officers holding different titles simultaneously and playing interchangeable roles. Sometimes they were "debriefers," other times "subject matter experts" or "targetters," or "psychologists" or "interrogators."[34] The entire interrogator-training program was a facade, according to Glenn

Carle—a CIA case officer who was "surged" into interrogating detainees at Temara and the Salt Pit in 2002 and 2003. "Anyone who had not gone through interrogator-training could still do the job as long as they were described as interviewers or debriefers," he recalled.[35] Asked to explain how certification worked, Mitchell suggested "qualified" and "trained" meant the same thing: "He's lowest level of interrogator allowed to interrogate under supervision 'in certification mode.'"[36] Having qualified in the classroom, they had to "amass a number of hours" practicing in the real world.

Some practiced on Khalid Sheikh Mohammad's former traveling companion Mustafa al-Hawsawi, who was "water doused" at the Salt Pit on April 6, 2003. A CIA "interviewer" who later debriefed al-Hawsawi said the technique was "just too close to the water board, and if it is continued may lead to problems for us."[37] Later, a photograph emerged from the Salt Pit showing a "water board device . . . surrounded by buckets, with a bottle of unknown pink solution (filled two thirds of the way to the top) and a watering can resting on the wooden beams of the water board."[38] On May 17, 2003, the focus switched to Khallad bin Attash.[39] At least seven people were in the room, including five new "qualified interrogators" seeking certification.[40] Reviewing their names, Mitchell said they were all Charlie Wise "acolytes," although further probing established that one of them was Bruce Jessen's protégé Matthew Zirbel.[41] The Preacher, who was now "certified," having helped Mitchell and Jessen waterboard Khalid Sheikh Mohammad, was also there for some sessions.

Despite Gul Rahman's death and the subsequent investigation, Tenet's new guidelines, and Gus's revamped training scheme, cables to headquarters hinted at numerous ongoing abuses at the Salt Pit. The trainee interrogators working on bin Attash joked that he was "left without a leg to stand on," after he was chained up and subjected to standing sleep deprivation for eleven hours, during which time his artificial leg was removed and his real leg gave way.[42] Edema formed around his ankle and crept up his thigh. Urged by a CIA medic to use a different technique, the interrogators launched a "kebab operation."[43] A room was decorated with rugs, books, a table with tablecloth, teapot, cans of soda, cups, and large plates of kebabs with bread. Bin Attash was dressed in loose clothes and given a blanket, but there was no record of whether he was allowed to eat the food. The following day he was stripped and subjected to standing sleep deprivation for two weeks, his only respite coming when the medic insisted he be moved into the horizontal sleep-deprivation position: stretched out like a medieval prisoner on a torture rack with his arms and leg chained to eyebolts embedded in opposite walls. Female interrogators were also present, which he found "highly humiliating in my naked state." He later claimed to have also been threatened with HIV shortly before a doctor gave him injections, and he was given "ice baths" in a cinched-up tarpaulin.[44] Abu Zubaydah later drew a graphic illustration of this un-authorized technique, which Mitchell described as "poor man's waterboarding."[45] According to Mitchell, it was approved as a "standard" technique in March 2003, meaning no headquarters authorization was needed.[46]

Wise, the Preacher, and four newly qualified interrogators moved from bin Attash to Ammar al-Baluchi. Wise used the broomstick technique on him, and after forty-eight hours of near constant walling by trainees, he passed out.[47] Al-Baluchi was later diagnosed with post-traumatic brain injury.[48] Asked whether he would have allowed trainee interrogators to practice on real de-tainees, Mitchell did not discount it, but he made strong efforts to distance himself from Wise's team. Shown a document that named the newly quali-fied interrogators practicing on al-Baluchi, Mitchell could identify only two of them. In 2003, he did not know all the trainees joining the enhanced program, he said, because Wise was "wanting to take over and move Dr. Jes-sen and I out."[49] Mitchell insisted that he took control of interrogator training only in 2005, after he and Jessen won a multimillion-dollar CIA contract, although official documents show they were actively involved in training at the same time as Wise.[50] A murky picture emerged during Mitchell's 9/11 pretrial hearing of a training program in Afghanistan that broke all the rules and an enhanced interrogation program in Poland run under strictly con-trolled conditions by Mitchell and Jessen.[51] Because several detainees were processed by the first regime before being moved to the second, everyone working in both programs was compromised. Interrogators and psycholo-gists also switched between the two CIA black sites, sometimes changing roles and titles. They also dispersed to the military, taking good and bad practices with them to Guantánamo, Bagram, and later Abu Ghraib. As the War on Terror rolled out across the globe, and the number of detainees not covered by the Geneva Conventions multiplied, it was inevitable that the CIA's legally approved template became distorted. Mitchell and Jessen were no longer in control of the monster they had created.

Khallad bin Attash recalled entering the Stare Kiejkuty villa after an eight-hour flight from Kabul. "I think I was detained underground as I had to walk down some steps," he said.[52] For the next month, nothing much happened. He was given solid food, a waste bucket, and a sleep mat, although loud music and "white torture" lights kept him awake 24/7. He had no idea Khalid Sheikh Mohammad was chained inside a cage behind a false wall at the end of the walkway, or that Abu Zubaydah was upstairs, or that Ramzi bin al-Shibh had occupied his cell until just a few hours before he arrived. The CIA had determined that bin al-Shibh and al-Nashiri were now compliant, and the same Gulfstream that had delivered bin Attash and al-Baluchi to Poland rendered bin al-Shibh and al-Nashiri to Temara, the Moroccan interrogation facility south of Rabat, were the CIA stabled some of its detainees, who complained that at night the corridors echoed with the sounds of people screaming.[53]

———·———

On June 21, 2003, another CIA detainee died in Afghanistan. This time it was at Forward Operating Base Asadabad in the northeast of the country. Dave Passaro, an untrained interrogator, had used unauthorized enhanced techniques on Abdul Wali, a twenty-eight-year-old Afghan, who had been accused of orchestrating rocket attacks against the American base.[54] Eyewitnesses stated that Passaro "severely beat" Wali with a "large metal flashlight," threw him against a wall, kicked him and jumped on his groin in an attempt to make him confess.[55] It is impossible to establish where Passaro "learned" his techniques, but at the very least he was likely to have met some of those who worked at the Salt Pit, as almost everyone working for the CIA in Afghanistan stayed at the Ariana Hotel in Kabul.[56] After two nights of beatings, Abdul Wali died, after repeatedly denying any involvement in the rocket attack. No autopsy was conducted, although shocking photographs showed his body covered in cuts and bruises. It was returned to his family the following day.[57] The CIA opened an investigation and found that Wali had no connection to the rocket attacks and was never registered as a detainee. Although the CIA introduced a rule after this incident to document all detainees (twenty-one months after the president had given the CIA lead authority to capture and detain War on Terror detainees), Passaro, a former paramilitary officer, was allowed to return to his civilian posting at Fort Bragg without censure, for the time being.[58]

Five days after Abdul Wali died, President Bush gave a speech to mark the United Nations' International Day in Support of Victims of Torture. Notorious human rights abusers were shielded "from the eyes of the world by staging elaborate deceptions," he said.[59] He described sadistic acts taking place behind closed doors in foreign countries, while the United States led the fight for democracy and the rule of law. Torture "anywhere" was an affront to human dignity "everywhere." He championed international laws and conventions that his own administration had sidestepped in order to legalize Abu Zubaydah's torture, even quoting the very words Jonathan Fredman focused on to avoid having any CIA employee prosecuted, to lament about "deliberately inflicting severe physical or mental pain or suffering." But since the president was not officially briefed about the CIA program, he could rightly claim not to know the CIA was doing such things. His words came on the back of a damning State Department human rights report that named and shamed countries for using techniques such as "suspension from bars by handcuffs, and threats against family members . . . [being] forced constantly to lie on hard floors [and] deprived of sleep."[60] No country was exempt from scrutiny, according to Secretary of State Colin Powell, who also had not been briefed, although some of those closest to him, including former chief of staff Larry Wilkerson, later claimed Powell had always known the gist of what was going on.[61]

Within hours of Bush's speech, a White House press secretary yet again assured the media that the treatment of all US-held detainees was "humane."[62] Knowing this to be untrue and worried about the CIA being exposed, George Tenet met Condoleezza Rice on July 29, 2003.[63] It was just over a year since he had been given policy approval for Abu Zubaydah's enhanced interrogation. Vice President Dick Cheney and Attorney General John Ashcroft also attended the meeting, along with Rice's chief attorney, John Bellinger, and Bush's chief attorney, Alberto Gonzales, all of them involved in the original approval process. Secretary Powell was not invited, an email noting that the White House was "extremely concerned Powell would blow his stack if he were to be briefed on what's been going on."[64] At the outset of the meeting, Ashcroft "forcefully reiterated the view" that the techniques being employed by the CIA "were and remain lawful."[65] Getting to the point, Cheney asked why the White House had told the media that the United States treated terror detainees "humanely." The press officers had "gone off script," and used out-of-date briefing notes, replied a deputy. Tenet commented that the word "humane" was "susceptible to misinterpretation." Bellinger suggested it was better to simply say that the United States was "complying with the law." Scott Muller, who had recently been appointed as CIA chief counsel, shunting compromised Rizzo sideways, distributed at the meeting a new briefing paper approved by Fredman.[66]

Authorized enhanced techniques did "not violate" the federal anti-torture statute or the Constitution, the paper stated. They did not "shock the conscience" in a manner contrary to the rights afforded by the Fifth and Fourteenth Amendments. The Eighth Amendment prohibition on cruel and unusual punishment was "inapplicable." Enhanced interrogation did not constitute "cruel, inhumane and degrading treatment or punishment" as defined by the UN Convention against Torture. Everyone who needed to be briefed in Congress had been kept up-to-date and fully informed.[67] Proper safeguards were in place. All prospective interrogators were psychologically prescreened and put through rigorous "training, qualification and certification." This was a systematic, legal, and scientific program. There was no mention of "Bodies," "Rawhide," "Slim Shady," "Goofy Duck lips," broomsticks, drills, guns, deaths, or kebab operations. There was no mention of official complaints that the CIA had actively impeded or avoided congressional oversight.[68] Detainee-specific, technique-specific, and interrogator-specific headquarters approvals had been requested and obtained for the thirteen high-value detainees who had been processed by this system, reported Muller. A medical officer was always present as was a psychologist. The CIA maintained the strictest guidelines about techniques, detention standards, and record keeping.

What about the death of a CIA detainee in Afghanistan, as reported in the *Washington Post* the previous weekend? asked Condoleezza Rice.[69] Scott Muller, a Princeton University graduate, former vice chair of the American Bar Association, and an adjunct professor at Georgetown University, was relatively new to the CIA's way of doing things, and he told Rice that two CIA detainees had died, although neither had involved authorized personnel or authorized techniques.[70] The CIA Office of the Inspector General was conducting a review of both deaths, he continued.

Turning to results, Muller listed "major threat info" obtained from five key high-value detainees, including Abu Zubaydah, who was described as a "Senior Al Qaeda Lieutenant," and Khalid Sheikh Mohammad, the 9/11 mastermind, who had confessed to multiple planned attacks, including on the US Capitol, towers, subways, trains, reservoirs, Jewish centers, and nuclear power plants. Muller told the attendees that half of all intelligence reports issued by the CIA since 9/11 had come as a result of enhanced interrogation. He also reported on the "cons" the CIA faced: public misperceptions about "humane treatment," multiple claims from the ICRC that the CIA was abusing "ghost prisoners" in secret locations, unfounded media attacks on legally approved US government detention policy, and the prospect of congressional inquiries as demanded by the likes of Bob Graham and John D. Rockefeller IV.[71] A slide titled "WITHOUT THIS CAPABILITY THEN . . . ?" was later redacted, although a subsequent congressional investigation stated the CIA repeatedly warned the National Security Council that "termination of this program will result in loss of life, possibly extensive." Mitchell's claim that Abu Zubaydah had recommended the waterboard should be used on every high-value detainee was cited.

Rice again interrupted the drumroll of positivity when Muller got to a slide stating Abu Zubaydah had been waterboarded 42 times and Mohammad 119 times. Other reporting had given tallies of 83 and 183. The state of the waterboarding tapes suggested the figure was even higher for Abu Zubaydah. What had caused the discrepancies? Muller explained that some of the sessions were for less than the permitted forty seconds. Yet again, the CIA was lying to the National Security Council by discounting shorter sessions.[72] Pushing ahead, Cheney stated that "KSM" was obviously a "tough customer," but the CIA was executing administration policy. Rice agreed. Tenet need not worry. The program was fully approved, including the "expanded use of various EITs, including multiple applications of the water board."[73] There was no requirement for a full principals meeting to ratify this decision, as Rumsfeld and his chief lawyer, Jim Haynes, were "clearly aware of the substance of the CIA program." However, someone did need to brief the president that the CIA was conducting interrogations that had been approved as lawful by the attorney general but "could be controversial."

A few days later, Rice called Bellinger. She was now of the view that national security principals Powell and Rumsfeld should both be fully briefed about the program.[74] Bellinger later reflected that combining forced nudity with "shackling a person in order to prevent sleep" could not be reasonably considered "humane treatment." He worried that "the world would find these acts particularly revolting." The legal opinion written by John Yoo and ratified by Jay Bybee for use on Abu Zubaydah was "inconsistent with traditional U.S. treaty practice" and "unlikely to be viewed as objective legal analysis."[75]

———————◆———————

Five weeks after Khallad bin Attash was rendered to Poland, psychologists deemed he was suitably "conditioned" for the next phase: enhanced interrogation. A team of men in black charged into his cell, stripped him, diapered him, chained him to an eyebolt in the ceiling, and shackled his one leg to the floor.[76] On July 18, the Preacher, who was back from the Salt Pit, wrote up a plan designed to "eliminate [any] sense of hope," and for the next ten days, bin Attash was blitzed by male and female interrogators.[77] To avoid having to ask for authorization, interrogators subjected him to seventy hours of standing sleep deprivation, two hours less than the "standard" maximum, allowed him four hours of sleep, then subjected him to another twenty-three hours.[78] In contrast to the Salt Pit, they did monitor for signs of edema. "My lower leg was examined on a daily basis by a doctor using a tape measure for signs of swelling," bin Attash recalled.[79] After a photograph taken on July 23 showed evidence of cellulitis and abrasions from a leg shackle, his medical condition was referred to headquarters.[80] The following day he was placed back in the standing sleep-deprivation posture, even though his leg was so extensively swollen that a medic examined him three times that day. Mitchell was at the black site but claimed not to have been involved. "I never dealt with this at all," he asserted. The Preacher was in charge.[81]

On July 25, the Preacher entered bin Attash's cell and ripped off his diaper. "A combination of the rest and solicitous medical care . . . has restored his arrogance," the team reported.[82] Bin Attash "now believes he knows the limits to which they can go, and he probably believes that apparent negative health conditions or sickness on his part will terminate any adverse conditions."[83] Like Gul Rahman, who had died while being conditioned, bin Attash was judged to be using complaints about his physical wellbeing as a resistance tool. Mitchell later characterized it as bin Attash "bringing jihad into the room."[84] On August 3, bin Attash was put in a cell next door to another detainee being "water doused" and making a lot of noise.[85] The Preacher warned bin Attash that enhanced interrogators were coming for him next, saying, "they had been busy lately and had had no time to spend with him, but they thought they would have time soon."[86] Mitchell denied even seeing bin Attash in Poland but could not say whether he observed the detainee's interrogations on CCTV, saying he would go and look at panels of videos and was not sure who was who to start with. Bin Attash "wasn't someone on my radar," he explained.[87]

Mitchell was overworked, and the black site was crowded. Stare Kiejkuty had been designed for two detainees, then retrofitted to take five, but inconsistent CIA records suggested that between eight and twelve were now held there, with compliant detainees locked up in bedrooms redesigned as "holding units" and rewarded with creature comforts. Abu Zubaydah recalled receiving a Koran, real food, a chemical toilet, and a small digital clock that Mitchell attached to his wall with Velcro. It was a life changer. For the first time in eighteen months, he knew the date, the day of the week, and what time to pray.[88] "Noncompliant" detainees occupied holding units in the basement and the cage. Even the cabin at the end of the garden was being used.

Because the global enhanced interrogation program was so busy, some high-value detainees still had to be processed at the Salt Pit.[89] In August 2003, Charlie Wise interrogated four of them, all picked up by General Tritot's Special Branch in Thailand.[90] The operation had started in December 2002, when the CIA asked Tritot to track Majid Khan, a Pakistani American who it alleged was delivering $50,000 from Khalid Sheikh Mohammad for Al Qaeda's Southeast Asian affiliate, Jemaah Islamiyah (JI).[91] After Khan was seized in Bangkok and sent to the Salt Pit, Tritot went after a man Khan had called from his hotel room, a Malaysian operative whose *kunya* was Zubair.[92] He was captured in Bangkok on June 8, 2003, and also sent to the Salt Pit, while Tritot went after Zubair's handlers. He caught up with them on August 11, 2003, in Ayutthaya, north of Bangkok. Hambali, the Indonesian-born JI chief, and his Malaysian assistant, Lillie, were rendered to the Salt Pit as the CIA announced it had broken up the most important Al Qaeda offshoot since 9/11, a cell responsible for the Bali bombings of October 2002 and more recent attacks.[93] A week earlier, a suicide bomber had attacked the JW Marriott Hotel in Jakarta, Indonesia, killing twelve people. The CIA alleged that Hambali was mastermind of the Jakarta and Bali attacks and had links to Khalid Sheikh Mohammad going back to 1995, when Mohammad and his nephew Ramzi Yousef lived in Manila and had tested out explosive devices to smuggle onto planes.[94]

At the Salt Pit, Majid Khan, Zubair, Hambali, and Lillie were all stripped, sheared, photographed naked, and cavity-searched, and then subjected to naked standing sleep deprivation.[95] Hambali was walled multiple times by multiple trainee interrogators. Majid Khan endured "ice baths."[96] All four were subjected to music 24/7. In all four cases, requests to use enhanced interrogation were sent to headquarters before the detainees actually arrived. There was no longer any need to prove resistance, just a probable connection to Al Qaeda. The CIA was most interested in Hambali, and Jessen flew over to the Salt Pit to conduct his enhanced interrogation, assisted by a staff psychologist whose name was later redacted from the records.[97] All four men were interrogated in English because there were no linguists available. Only Majid Khan, who had attended high school in Baltimore, understood the questions.[98]

No one at headquarters complained about the uniform nature of approval requests coming from the field, the use of music or unauthorized ice baths, or edema. But when Charlie Wise used the broomstick method on Zubair one day, Jessen flew into a rage and complained to Gus, who had no choice but to recall his chief of interrogations to Langley.[99] "I had said, 'Charlie, don't do that again,'" Gus recalled. "And he did it again. It was nothing serious, but it was not approved, and I said, 'that's it.' I retired him." Mitchell's latest "nemesis" was finally out of the picture, thanks to Jessen's keen eye. After a year in the job, Gus's cowboy handed back his staff blue badge and drove out of CIA headquarters for the last time in September 2003.

Wise, age fifty-three, died two weeks later. No agency colleagues attended his funeral. Jose Rodriguez recalled: "He was a pain in the ass. He got so angry he retired, went home and was having breakfast with his kids when he had a massive heart attack."[100] The untimely death was the best result the CIA could have hoped for, as the troublesome Wise could now be a scapegoat responsible for all the program's excesses.[101] Mitchell later characterized Wise's approach as: "Hurt them and don't stop until they tell you what you want to know. And then continue hurting them, because if they are lying, they will change their story." In a rare slip, he also recounted once telling Abu Zubaydah, "If you don't tell me what I need to know, I will hurt you some more."[102]

CHAPTER 17

"A Torture Ponzi Scheme"

September 22, 2003, Stare Kiejkuty, Poland

"Travel day" to the endgame facility arrived. Abu Zubaydah was told he was moving to a place that "would be much better in all aspects."[1] Pictures he drew of himself while in Poland showed a skinny, wild-haired Old Testament prophet.[2] Now, they sheared him for the first time in months, and he fought with the men in black as they taped him into an adult diaper. Trussed up—goggles, duct tape, foamies, earmuffs, harness, handcuffs, shackles, and chains—he was carried downstairs. He and others in what the CIA described as "debriefing mode" were going to Strawberry Fields, Gus's new facility at Guantánamo. The "noncompliants," who included Khalid Sheikh Mohammad, Khallad bin Attash, and Ammar al-Baluchi, were heading for more rigorous enhanced interrogation in Romania.[3] Having racked up $29 million, the Polish deal had run its course, but the Romanians were happy to accept huge CIA bribes.[4] Designed around the concept of disorientation—more cages built on truck tires—the Romanian facility was hidden in the basement of a government office in Bucharest and code-named Bright Light.[5]

Since many detainees were on the move, the CIA leased a stripped-down Boeing 737 that flew first to Kabul to pick up Mustafa al-Hawsawi and Ibn Sheikh al-Libi.[6] Al-Hawsawi was compliant, while al-Libi needed "debriefing" about his Al Qaeda and Saddam Hussein claims, another job on Mitchell and Jessen's never-ending to-do list.[7] The 737 flew on to Szymany, an airstrip designed for light aircraft. The Boeing's pilot had to execute an emergency maneuver to stop the plane from skidding off the end of the runway.[8] The airport did not have steps to reach the Boeing's door, so the crew rigged a solution. American guards heaved all the detainees aboard. Abu

Zubaydah recalled being chained on the floor sideways, with his hands cuffed behind his back.[9] Large plastic earmuffs prevented him from putting his head on its side, so he lay contorted, concentrating on the muffled sounds of his companions but not knowing that just a few feet away lay his brother emir from Khaldan, Ibn Sheikh al-Libi.[10] The next stop was Bucharest, where Mohammad, bin Attash, and al-Baluchi were off-loaded. Then, the plane flew on to Rabat, where Abd al-Rahim al-Nashiri and Ramzi bin al-Shibh boarded. The next flight was much longer. "I was destroyed and felt that was the end," Abu Zubaydah recalled. He counted time, which felt like "several lifetimes." By the time the plane landed in Cuba, on September 24, 2003, he had been in the air for thirty hours.[11] "This was the beginning of the end but not the end itself," he reflected.

Landing on the leeward side of Guantánamo Bay, each detainee was put in a separate vehicle and ferried to the windward side, where the main Camp Delta and the new CIA facility were located side by side. They could feel the warmth of the sun and the bump of waves but could not see the bright blue sky or the crystalline Caribbean Sea. Clanking off the ferry, Abu Zubaydah was driven for twenty minutes before the vehicle tires scrunched to a halt on gravel. He was manhandled out in silence. When the hood came off, he was back in the cold, chained and shackled, in a fiercely air-conditioned, windowless cell with a mesh inner door featuring a lockable flap that allowed guards to shackle a detainee without entering and a solid outer door with a glass viewing window that locked on the outside. It smelled of paint, dust, and the sea. Footage had aired on Pakistani TV channels of the first Guantánamo detainees arriving in orange jumpsuits before Abu Zubaydah was captured, and he suspected he might end up there too.[12] One month before he arrived, detainees had attempted a "mass suicide" after hearing that guards had wrapped a Koran in the Israeli flag.[13] More than 350 incidents of self-harm were registered that year by General Geoffrey Miller, the Joint Task Force Guantánamo commander, who wanted detainees to know the US military had "more teeth than they have ass, hoo-ah."[14] But Miller did not have authority over Strawberry Fields, which was hidden away from the rest of Camp Delta and was the exclusive domain of the CIA.

The Stare Kiejkuty villa went back to its previous decrepit state. Weeds grew over. Mildew crept over sticky carpets and up walls. The dank basement was locked up, with frogs and spiders ranging freely again. Abu Zubaydah's man cage disappeared into someone's private torture museum, while the stained burlap from Khalid Sheikh Mohammad's walling wall was burned. A couple that owned a farm just outside the perimeter turned their property into a homestay. Guests sleeping in featherbeds underneath the red-tiled eaves at Mazurskie Uroczysko did not know that the CIA had brought some of the "most dangerous men on the planet" to the verge of death just a few hundred yards away in an experiment that had already spread to the US military.[15]

———•———

The Pentagon's experiment with enhanced interrogation started shortly after Mitchell and Jessen delivered their seminal paper on Al Qaeda resistance to interrogation to the CIA in December 2001, with the CIA exploring the possibility of running some kind of joint detention and interrogation program with the Department of Defense. Jim Haynes, Rumsfeld's chief attorney, poked his head into his deputy's office in the middle of December, asking, "Where is the locus for interrogations expertise?"[16] Richard Shiffrin, the deputy general counsel for intelligence, whose office was behind vault-like metal security doors on the same corridor as the office of Rumsfeld, recalled: "It was early on, before Guantánamo even. We were starting to hold people at Bagram but not much else." Shiffrin, who described himself as a "super-user of sensitive information," was on a committee that oversaw special access programs (SAPs), including the advanced JPRA course at Fairchild, where Mitchell and Jessen had both worked.[17] Shiffrin told Haynes what he knew. Asked to get more details, Shiffrin called Dan Baumgartner, JPRA's chief of staff, who sent him an enthusiastic pitch. "Here's our spin on exploitation," wrote Baumgartner. "If you need experts to facilitate this process, we stand ready to assist. There are not many in DoD outside JPRA that have the level of expertise we do in exploitation and how to resist it."[18]

Shiffrin sensed he was being hustled.[19] Before meeting "exploitation" experts looking to win lucrative contracts, he needed assurance this was the right way to go. Being methodical, he wanted to know the history and the science. Had SERE techniques been properly tested, or was it just grown men role-playing torture in the wilds of Washington? Some methods, such as submerging students in vats of water for hours on end, sounded horrifying, like real torture. What exactly was learned helplessness, and was it to be avoided or embraced? Had instructors ever caused real psychological damage to students? Baumgartner, a paper shuffler based at JPRA headquarters in Fort Belvoir, Virginia, could not answer Shiffrin's questions.[20] "Whatever we have is out in Spokane. Eight hours away." Within days, three boxes of files arrived for Shiffrin: a selection of classified materials from the Fairchild library, including a manual, *Pre-Academic Laboratory (PREAL) Operating Instructions*, and papers by the original SERE course designer, Albert Biderman.[21] Shiffrin also received "excerpts from SERE instructor lesson plans . . . and a memo from a SERE psychologist assessing the long-term psychological effects of SERE resistance training on students and the effects of waterboarding," documents authored by Mitchell, Jessen, and their JPRA colleagues.

Baumgartner later testified that he sent the same material to the CIA at the same time.[22] By the spring of 2002, some of it had been shared with the National Security Council.[23] Mitchell and Jessen's Al Qaeda resistance-to-interrogation paper was also shared with JPRA and then dispatched by Jessen's commander, Randy Moulton, up the military chain of command to the Pentagon.[24] Haynes and Shiffrin surveyed the materials. "It was interesting stuff but not what we were looking for," said Shiffrin. They needed highly trained experts to suggest methods of detention and interrogation and to draw up training plans to certify real military interrogators, which was exactly what Jessen had done, aided by Chris Wirts and other SERE experts, before Abu Zubaydah was captured and the CIA decided to go it alone. After Shiffrin and Haynes received the SERE materials from Fairchild, Chris Wirts briefed the Pentagon on interrogation training and techniques. A few weeks later, he and Jessen drew up an interrogation plan for the Pentagon's new long-term detainee holding facility in Guantánamo Bay. Wirts also briefed the CIA.

Early in the War on Terror, the US Naval Station Guantánamo Bay was described as "America's Battle Lab."[25] But in reality, as soon as it opened in January 2002, it filled up with what the first Joint Task Force Guantánamo commander, General Michael Dunlavey, a reservist and judge from Pennsylvania, called "Mickey Mouse" detainees.[26] Because the CIA creamed off the best detainees in Afghanistan, many of those sent to Cuba were innocent victims of petty tribal jealousies or mistaken identity. Some were mentally unstable, while others were below the age of criminal responsibility. Guantánamo's interrogation policy descended into a farce, as a plethora of competing interrogation teams from the FBI, the CIA, and different military investigation units descended, many with little knowledge of Al Qaeda, the

Taliban, or the Arab world.[27] Some early sessions took place in the open-air compound of Camp X-Ray, the temporary detention facility where Guantánamo's first detainees were paraded. Most military interrogators were young reservists with no training—one had previously been managing a Dunkin' Donuts.[28] Linguists were in short supply. Detainees were ridiculed as "dirt farmers."[29] One, who arrived suffering from pneumonia, tuberculosis, frostbite, and dysentery, was nicknamed "Half-Dead Bob."[30] Another, who ate his own feces, was dubbed "Wild Bill."[31] Against this backdrop, Dunlavey was expected to fly up to the Pentagon weekly to brief Donald Rumsfeld on "intel successes" that were needed to pave the way to war in Iraq.[32]

Mark Fallon, deputy commander of the Criminal Investigation Task Force, a Pentagon agency created in February 2002 to interrogate War of Terror detainees, blamed Dunlavey for letting Guantánamo get out of control, saying the commander drove around with the Pointer Sisters blaring from his car windows and bragged he knew all about interrogations because he had served in "'Nam."[33] As Guantánamo interrogators began experimenting with methods they heard were being used with legal approval by the CIA, the JTF interrogations encompassed strobe lights, blaring music, female interrogators smearing fake menstrual blood, stress positions, and duct tape, recalled Fallon. "One guy even wore a full cowboy outfit."

During the first few months, Dunlavey's interrogators failed to produce any meaningful results, something he had to report to Rumsfeld weekly. Richard Shiffrin watched the impact. "[Rumsfeld] had a little outer suite," Shiffrin recalled.[34] "There would be a four-star there, and they don't get nervous generally. They'd be pacing, they'd go in and come out with a wet circle here," he recalled, pointing to his groin. Shiffrin, who like Rumsfeld was a Princeton graduate, stood up for himself, but as he listened to Dunlavey delivering meaningless downloads, he saw what the reservist general could not. "That's where the idea that we're failing came from," Shiffrin recalled. "Everyone was insisting we got to make it really rough in GTMO." Through Jim Haynes, Shiffrin knew the hard lobbying was coming from Vice President Dick Cheney's office, and he saw it up close when David Addington, Cheney's lawyer, attended a White House Situation Room discussion about killing Saddam Hussein. "They wanted to assassinate him," said Shiffrin, and were discussing a possible legal basis. "Most of us rational people were dubious and concerned," Shiffrin recalled. "There was this big guy sitting to my right [Addington], and all of a sudden his booming voice comes out calling us stupid. These are lawyers who meet regularly on covert action, sensitive matters. Not stupid. Anyway, so Addington was screaming at us to push it through." Since Haynes was Addington's protégé, Cheney must have known that the Pentagon would help the Iraq war materialize by making enhanced interrogation at Guantánamo legal.[35]

As the first anniversary of 9/11 approached and with nothing of significance obtained from Guantánamo despite Rumsfeld's characterization of detainees as "the most dangerous, best-trained and vicious killers on the face of the earth," Dunlavey came under intense pressure to ramp things up. He put together a team of psychologists and psychiatrists to assist military interrogators, something spelled out in Jessen and Wirts's classified paper, "Prisoner Handling Recommendations."[36] Dunlavey borrowed "psychs" from a combat-stress company that had just arrived in Cuba. One of them, Major John Leso, was so deeply alarmed at being reassigned to hostile Al Qaeda suspects he called up his old boss at the Walter Reed National Military Medical Center, military psychologist Larry James, to ask where he could get training.[37]

James called Morgan Banks, an Army psychologist and chief of the Directorate of Psychological Applications at Fort Bragg. Banks was a close friend of Mitchell's, and like Mitchell he was highly trained, with a psychology PhD from the University of Mississippi.[38] But unlike most of his SERE psych colleagues Banks also had real-world experience. Between November 2001 and March 2002, Banks had been deployed to Bagram, where he was involved in "supporting combat operations against Al Qaeda and Taliban fighters," advising the military on detainee handling and interrogation at the same time Mitchell was establishing a similar role at the CIA.[39] Noting that the last time the US had tested its interrogation capabilities was during World War Two, Banks found himself "dealing with a bunch of nineteen- and twenty-year-olds trying to interrogate Al Qaeda." Hearing that the situation at Guantánamo was not much better and that interrogators were drawing their ideas from the *Fox* television series *24*, where torture always worked, Banks invited Leso to Fort Bragg for SERE training. Designed by Wirts and Jessen, it began on September 16, 2002, five days after the first 9/11 anniversary. Leso brought along Major Paul Burney, a psychiatrist also redeployed into Dunlavey's interrogation support team, and four JTF trainee interrogators.

Like Leso, Burney was deeply worried, saying later that he was "hi-jacked" and told to establish a link between Al Qaeda and Iraq.[40] The more frustrated the Pentagon became, the more pressure it put on Dunlavey to use hard measures. Hosted by Banks, the Fort Bragg course was run by Gary Percival, Joe Witsch, and Terry Russell and assisted by a "CIA psychologist" whose name was redacted from the records. Chris Wirts said it was "similar in nature to what we did for the [CIA] on the last iteration," a reference to the two-day CIA interrogator training course in July 2002.[41] After four days of training, Leso and Burney returned to Guantánamo to draw up a SERE-based interrogation plan for the military's test case, Mohammed al-Qahtani, a twenty-one-year-old Saudi suspected of wanting to be a 9/11 hijacker. Having heard about a Guantánamo detainee with possible links to 9/11, George Tenet and the CIA were agitating to take custody of al-Qahtani as they had done with Ibn Sheikh al-Libi and Abu Zubaydah.[42] Donald Rumsfeld, who "did not do detainees," was under pressure to keep al-Qahtani and turn him quickly. The Pentagon passed this down the line to Guantánamo, with Burney recalling that there was "a lot of pressure to use more coercive techniques." If his and Leso's interrogation plan didn't include them, "it wasn't going to go very far."[43]

On September 25, 2002, shortly after Banks' course ended, the same top-level legal team that authorized Abu Zubaydah's enhanced interrogation made a whistle-stop visit to Guantánamo.[44] The party included Alberto Gonzales, David Addington, Jim Haynes, John Rizzo, and Michael Chertoff.[45] They had come after reviewing a shocking assessment by a senior CIA analyst who had interrogated a random sample at Guantánamo and concluded that at least a third of all Guantánamo detainees had no connection whatsoever to terrorism. A furious row between Addington and John Bellinger had ensued at the White House, with Addington dismissing Bellinger's demands for a review. "The President has determined that they are ALL enemy combat-ants," screamed Addington.[46] "We are not going to revisit it!" Enhanced inter-rogation was the way to get all detainees talking. The techniques had been given a different name—"counter-resistance techniques" (CRTs)—but were essentially the same EITs Mitchell and Jessen tested out on Abu Zubaydah. Mohammed al-Qahtani would be the US military's patient zero.

The case against al-Qahtani appeared compelling. On August 3, 2001, he had flown into Orlando, Florida, on a one-way ticket from Dubai. He had $2,800 in his pocket and a six-day visitor's visa, had no hotel reservation, and spoke no English. Drawing suspicion, he was sent back to the Middle East by immigration officials. After 9/11, he was captured in Afghanistan and arrived at Guantánamo among dozens of low-level detainees. Young and naive-looking, during initial interrogation he claimed to be a falconry hunter who got caught up in the Afghan war by mistake, a story that fell apart in July 2002 after the FBI matched his DNA to the Saudi national refused entry one month before 9/11. The FBI had already charted some hijackers' travels through Florida, where several had undergone flight training, worked out, and frequented lap-dancing clubs, including the lead hijacker, Mohamed Atta. In August 2002, Ali Soufan questioned al-Qahtani for two weeks, telling guards to cover their faces to increase his isolation.[47] When Soufan "hit a roadblock" and the young detainee stopped talking, he was put in Guantánamo's naval brig, away from the rest of the detainee population.[48]

However, al-Qahtani was not quite what he seemed. He had suffered traumatic brain injury during a childhood car accident, started showing psychiatric problems during his teens, and repeatedly ran away from home. One time, police found him sleeping in a dumpster in Riyadh. He was diagnosed with schizophrenia, medicated, and sent to a mental hospital in Mecca.[49] He then tried running away to the United States and later Afghanistan. Guards at Guantánamo noted that he talked to nonexistent people, but no one cared much about his mental state because the working theory was that al-Qahtani should have been on United Airlines flight 93, the plane that crashed into a field in Pennsylvania instead of its suspected target, the US Capitol. According to the FBI and CIA, Khalid Sheikh Mohammad had planned to have two pilots and three "muscle hijackers" on each of the four 9/11 flights.[50] But only two muscle hijackers had boarded United flight 93. Passengers and crew had grappled with them, causing the plane to crash. Even though Zacarias Moussaoui had already been indicted as the "twentieth hijacker" for conspiring to commit terrorism and "aircraft piracy," the Pentagon spun up a story that al-Qahtani was the hijacker who had got away.[51] After the FBI produced evidence that Mohamed Atta's phone card had been used to call Mustafa al-Hawsawi, who allegedly managed Khalid Sheikh Mohammad's finances, while al-Qahtani was being detained by US Immigration and Naturalization Service (INS) agents at Orlando airport, President Bush and Attorney General Ashcroft were briefed about his case.[52]

When Rizzo, Gonzales, Haynes, Addington, and Ashcroft's deputy Michael Chertoff arrived in Cuba in September 2002, Mark Fallon, who had interrogated al-Qahtani using rapport-building techniques, tried to get a word in. "I wanted to make sure the lawyers got the real story, before Dunlavey's plans for al-Qahtani were approved," he explained.[53] Due to limited resources, interrogation teams working for different government agencies had to share computer terminals. Fallon had worked out how to access JTF interrogation logs and had read of alarming plans to "kidnap" al-Qahtani from his cell and drive him around the naval station for hours before an Egyptian interrogator subjected him to enhanced interrogation, a "false flag" operation used to great effect several times by Albert El Gamil for the CIA. However, Fallon was pushed aside when the Washington lawyers arrived off the ferry. "Dunlavey blew right past me," Fallon recalled.[54] Courtesy buses were taking them down to where the metal hangar of the Expeditionary Legal Complex would one day be located. The US government envisaged some of those responsible for 9/11 being tried by military commission at Guantánamo to give an impression that justice would one day be served to those who had killed almost three thousand people.[55]

Fallon was told to wait in the office for a call that never came. Others who took the war-court tour later told Fallon they had heard Jim Haynes telling Dunlavey that he had full authority to make decisions about Guantánamo interrogation strategy as long as he remained in line with presidential orders.[56] Official reports of the visit suggested the request to use harsh techniques originated in Guantánamo not Washington. If things did not go to plan, Dunlavey would take the fall. "Major General Dunlavey did take Mr. Haynes and a few others aside for private conversations. It appeared that MG D was doing most, if not all, of the speaking at these side meetings."[57] Haynes "did not recall" anything about this discussion, and Addington said nothing at all.[58] However, both Dunlavey and his military lawyer, Diane Beaver, later insisted the impetus came from the Pentagon. Rumsfeld was "directly and regularly involved," Dunlavey insisted. On the day of the lawyers' visit, Addington was "definitely the guy in charge," recalled Beaver.[59] They were told to use whatever it took to make al-Qahtani confess.

A week after the top-flight lawyers' visit, Rizzo sent the Counterterrorist Center's chief lawyer Jonathan Fredman to Cuba.[60] For the past year, Fredman had been advising Jose Rodriguez on how to walk up to the legal chalk line, and he had led the Abu Zubaydah discussions with John Yoo at the Department of Justice. Now Fredman sat down with Beaver to advise her on obtaining legal protections and to listen to a briefing from Leso and Burney.[61] In recent days, al-Qahtani had been moved to Camp X-Ray (which was otherwise empty) and conditioned with blinding white light and Christina Aguilera's song "Dirrty" playing on endless repeat.[62] Seventeen counter-resistance techniques had been proposed, ranging from "mildly adverse approaches," such as threatening al-Qahtani that he would be at Guantánamo forever, to "Category III," which included subjecting him to hard takedowns and short-chaining on the floor and leaving him in the cold "until such time as the detainee begins to shiver"—like Gul Rahman. He could be isolated for considerable periods—like Abu Zubaydah. And he could be threatened with execution—like al-Nashiri. All aspects of the detainee's environment "should enhance capture shock, dislocate expectations, foster dependence, and support exploitation to the fullest extent possible."[63] These recommendations were almost identical to those compiled in Jessen's JPRA slideshow earlier in the year.[64]

According to meeting minutes that Fredman later disputed, he explained the legal rollout for Mitchell and Jessen's EITs. The CIA had "rallied" for the Geneva Conventions to be dispensed with and had got around the Convention against Torture because the definition of severe mental and physical pain had been "written vaguely." Since President Ronald Reagan, who signed it in 1988, had not agreed to the part that outlawed "cruel and unusual punishment," the CIA had "more license to use more controversial techniques." Only "significantly harsh techniques" had to be approved by the attorney general.[65] Everything else was done in-house. Beaver expressed concerns about having to "curb the harsher operations" whenever the ICRC was around.[66] Guantánamo was not the same as a CIA black site, and "they will be in and out, scrutinizing our operations," she warned. Were these techniques even safe? she asked. "If the detainee dies you're doing it wrong," Fredman replied, according to the minutes of the meeting.[67] "So far, the techniques we have addressed have not proven to produce these types of results."[68] Gul Rahman and Abdul Wali were then still alive. Referring to death threats made against a detainee (al-Nashiri) or his family (Abu Zubaydah and Khalid Sheikh Mohammad), Fredman said, "The threat of death is also subject to scrutiny and should be handled on a case by case basis."

Fredman gave advice on staffing and atmospherics gleaned from Mitchell and Jessen's experience. Techniques at the harshest end of the spectrum "must be performed by a highly trained individual."[69] Medical personnel needed to be present "to treat any possible accidents," as the backlash if someone died would be "severely detrimental." Video-recording was problematic, as footage looked "ugly." Asked about waterboarding, he said that if a well-trained individual performed it, "it can feel like you're drowning . . . but your body will not cease to function." Beaver noted it down as the "wet towel" technique. "We'll need documentation to protect us," she said. "Yes," agreed Fredman. "Everything must be approved and documented." The bottom line was that with legal cover in place, the United States could go further than many other countries. The CIA had used aggressive techniques on a "handful" of detainees since 9/11 and had found them "very helpful." According to the official record, the only detainee subjected to authorized enhanced interrogation at this point was Abu Zubaydah, but presumably Fredman was also referring to the Salt Pit, where unauthorized enhanced interrogation was taking place.

When minutes of the Fredman meeting were leaked, Mark Fallon reported his serious concerns. "This looks like the kind of stuff congressional hearings are made of," he warned Pentagon lawyers.[70] Some of Fredman's comments would "shock the conscience of any legal body." Someone needed to ask the CIA and the Pentagon "how history will look back at this." Fredman later attempted to distance himself, claiming his main reason for traveling to Guantánamo had been to see CIA officers stationed there. "I wanted to speak with them directly about the legal requirements applicable to them and their activities," he wrote.[71] During the course of his visit, Beaver had asked him for help, he said. Yet again, an impression was given that the request to use aggression on detainees had come not from the top but from "the dirt on the ground," as Beaver later characterized herself.[72] Fredman claimed the minutes contained "several serious misstatements of fact."[73] Quotes had been "paraphrased sloppily and poorly." He had "expressly warned that should a detainee die as a result of a violation, the responsible parties could be sentenced to capital punishment." But since his guidance was classified, it was impossible to verify his claim.

Nobody at the Pentagon listened to Fallon, and nobody could hear al-Qahtani, whose interrogation restarted the day Fredman arrived "on station," inside the overgrown sprawl of Camp X-Ray, which was located beyond the last housing units at the very end of Sherman Avenue. Beyond, lay a waste-disposal station and the Cuban border. No one heard the barking dogs or loud music. No one saw al-Qahtani hanging in the standing sleep-deprivation position or being taunted by a female naval ensign.[74] Still, he would not talk. After eight days, one of the FBI agents involved suggested: "I think we should consider leaving him alone, let him get healthy again and do something 'different.'"[75] Major Burney wrote to Morgan Banks: They did not know what they were doing. Could Banks help with more SERE training? "The answer is no, I do not know of anyone who could provide that training," Banks replied.[76] He was cutting connections.

The enhanced interrogation train was hurtling out of control at Guantánamo, but shortly after Fredman's visit, Burney and Leso passed on what they had been taught at Fort Bragg to a special missions unit (SMU) from Bagram. The visiting military team was told that the interrogation process was designed to cause "psychological/physical stress" and was based on "psychological deception leading to learned helplessness and increased compliance."[77] It was a recipe for disaster, because Bagram Collection Point already resembled the Salt Pit "dungeon." Built by the Soviets as an aircraft machine shop, it consisted of a long, squat concrete building with rusted metal sheets where the windows should have been. Inside, the US military had constructed wire pens that held upwards of fifty detainees. The CIA maintained a shadowy presence. Like the Salt Pit, Bagram suffered huge staffing problems: one of the reasons why Morgan Banks had gone there in November 2001.

Bagram's interrogators were mostly military intelligence (MI) officers or military police and had no interrogation experience. For many, it was their first foreign tour. Captain Carolyn Wood, a thirty-two-year-old MI officer, who had arrived to find no standard operating procedures, led them. One of her interrogation teams called itself "the Testosterone Gang." Damien Corsetti, a six-foot-tall, bearded specialist, who had the Italian word for "monster" tattooed on his belly, was "the king of torture."[78] They used dogs, "the screaming technique," Metallica's "Enter Sandman" playing at top volume, standing sleep deprivation, and the "peroneal strike," whereby a detainee was repeatedly kneed at the base of the thigh, a "pressure point control tactic" learned during training with police in New Jersey. "It drops 'em pretty good," said one interrogator.[79] It could also prove lethal if used on a detainee suffering from edema. After returning from Guantánamo, Wood's interrogation team added learned helplessness into the mix. "The brass knew. They saw them shackled, they saw them hooded and they said, 'Right on. Y'all are doing a great job,'" claimed Corsetti.[80]

When Dunlavey's request to use counter-resistance techniques on al-Qahtani reached the Pentagon, senior lawyers expressed concern. The army general counsel stated that threats to life and the wet towel treatment appeared to be "clear violations of the federal torture statute." The air force worried that some techniques "could be construed as torture." The navy was concerned that the ICRC might find out.[81] General Richard Myers, chairman of the Joint Chiefs of Staff, rejected Dunlavey's request, after his legal counsel concluded: "We do not believe the proposed plan to be legally sufficient."[82] This was not what Cheney, Rumsfeld, and their lawyers, Addington and Haynes, wanted to hear.

Dunlavey was relieved of his position almost immediately and replaced by Major General Geoffrey Miller, a regular soldier with a reputation for getting the job done.[83] He set Beaver to work improving her legal argument and began putting his stamp on Guantánamo. Military personnel were instructed to salute one other, exchanging the salutes "Honor bound!" and "Defend freedom!"[84] They were painted on oil drums lined up outside his office. Foreign intelligence agents were brought in to front "false flag" interrogations and began appearing in the commissary and on the beach.[85] Miller even persuaded Leso's mentor and former boss at Walter Reed, Larry James, to deploy to Guantánamo to advise on interrogation tactics. Morgan Banks flew down too.[86]

Miller pitched a revamped al-Qahtani plan to the Pentagon on November 21, the day after Gul Rahman died in Afghanistan. On November 27, Jim Haynes wrote up an action memo. Rumsfeld signed it five days later, adding a handwritten flourish at the bottom: "I stand for 8–10 hours a day. Why is standing limited to 4 hours?"[87] Al-Qahtani's official enhanced interrogation began two days later with a mock kidnapping. Once they got him to the interrogation room, Leso and Burney played a typical Mitchell-Jessen double act, advising interrogators and conducting psychological assessments to keep things going. Female guards participated in an exercise called "invasion of space by a female," straddling stripped naked and shorn al-Qahtani. They put a woman's thong on his head and made him wear a bra. Threatened with dogs, he was put on a leash and made to act like a dog. He was ordered to pick up trash while they called him "a pig." Leso advised interrogators to spin him on a swivel chair to "keep him awake and stop him from fixing his eyes on one spot."[88] One day his heart rate dropped so low that he had to undergo cardiac monitoring. The interrogators and psychologists were, in Fallon's opinion, "testing Seligman's theory on humans" to the very limit.[89] Over a fifty-one-day period, al-Qahtani was subjected to forty-eight days of near constant interrogation.[90] In 2008, the US government tried to charge him in the 9/11 attacks along with "KSM et al.," but the case against him was dismissed after the government's own prosecutor Susan Crawford ruled that he had been tortured.[91]

Using al-Qahtani's interrogation plan as a template, Miller instructed Colonel Ted Moss, the newly appointed commander of the Interrogation Control Element, to write up standard operating procedures for all interrogations.[92] Littered with typos, the document explained that techniques used in SERE schools "are appropriate for use in real world interrogations." The aim of the techniques was to "break real detainees in interrogation operations," although all tactics were "strictly non lethal."[93] It was critical that interrogators "do [sic] cross the line" when utilizing the techniques. If "watch officers" saw something illegal, they should shout out, "Stop wasting time with this pig." With an eye to the law, Moss noted: "This mission has legal and political issues that may lead to interrogators being called to testify, keeping the number of documents with interrogation information to a minimum can minimize certain legal issues."

Interrogation techniques approved by Donald Rumsfeld for use at Guantánamo would soon find their way to Bagram and Abu Ghraib. When Captain Carolyn Wood, who ran interrogation policy at Bagram and later at Abu Ghraib, was dispatched to Guantánamo in January 2003, her interrogator training included a PowerPoint about "aggressive techniques."[94] Mitchell's oft-stated concerns were coming true: people without appropriate training or any psychology qualifications were misrepresenting SERE and the theories upon which it was based, and passing their mistakes along the line. Fredman's recommendation that only "highly trained individuals" be allowed to perform techniques at the harshest end of the spectrum was being ignored. "You put these things together and you give the policy decision to do this and you have got torture," stated Larry Wilkerson, Colin Powell's chief of staff, who later investigated the Abu Ghraib scandal. "Really, really horrible mental torture in particular. I don't think [Rumsfeld] realizes this even today. He didn't have the experience of being in a prison guarding people who wanted to kill him. It's a different world."[95]

The day al-Qahtani's enhanced interrogation began at Guantánamo, a Bagram detainee died after spending hours subjected to standing sleep deprivation followed by repeated peroneal strikes. Six days later, another Bagram detainee died in similar circumstances. The first victim, a twenty-two-year-old taxi driver called Dilawar who was falsely accused of conducting a rocket attack, had his legs "pulpified" and looked like he had been run over by a truck.[96] A military coroner concluded that had he lived, his legs would have had to be amputated. One member of Wood's team summed up the situation: "Two prisoners dying within a week of each other. That's bad."[97]

———◆———

Alberto Mora, the US Navy's general counsel, had been inside the Pentagon when American Airlines flight 77 crashed into the building on 9/11.[98] He ran outside, just as Rumsfeld briefly emerged and helped an injured man on a stretcher to safety.[99] The next day, Mora was back at the Pentagon, listening to the president addressing America's top brass. "Over time, the American people will forget what happened here yesterday. But you won't forget and I won't forget," he said. As the administration rolled out its response, Mora noted that it was all based on fear and fury. The fear was that the next attack would come "tomorrow or that afternoon or in the next half hour," he recalled.[100] "Everybody was just gripped with a desire to try to find the intelligence, try to get a clue, get a hint and do whatever was required to stop the next attack from occurring." The fury came from a widely held sense of outrage at the "sheer inhumanity." Those who had planned it "should be treated as subhuman," Mora recalled people telling him.[101] However, he went along with the War on Terror, even the proposed invasion of Iraq, until December 18, 2002, when Mark Fallon and his boss told Mora about the abuse of Guantánamo detainees. Similar things were being reported at Bagram. Interrogation teams at both locations were using each other's practices to bolster and justify their own use of SERE tactics, recalled Fallon, who described it as "a torture Ponzi scheme."[102]

Mora went to see Jim Haynes, Rumsfeld's chief attorney. US personnel could face criminal prosecution, he warned. Haynes assured Mora that torture was not being committed or condoned at Guantánamo or anywhere else. Nevertheless, Mora asked him to investigate. "I thought that he'd instantaneously recognize it, and it would stop. I went on vacation." But while Mora enjoyed a family Christmas in Miami, Guantánamo's Interrogation Control Element chief, Ted Moss, supervised a training course run by two survival instructors from the US Navy SERE school in Brunswick, Maine.[103] Neither of them had any real-world interrogation experience or authorization to use the waterboard. After training, students were shown copies of the Manchester manual and were talked through Biderman's "Chart of Coercion": the table of measures designed to set a man against himself. Seligman's concept of learned helplessness was taught under the title "demonstrated omnipotence."[104] The visitors then supervised students using detainees as training props.

When Mora returned to work to find the abuses still going on, he became so vocal that Rumsfeld rescinded authorization to use enhanced techniques on military-held detainees.[105] But in March 2003, Jim Haynes obtained a legal opinion from John Yoo, who was now acting head at the Office of Legal Counsel at the Department of Justice.[106] It was even more shocking than the Yoo-Bybee memo. Techniques such as throwing "scalding water, corrosive acid or caustic substance" did not constitute torture.[107] "To put out or destroy an eye" was also exempt, as long as there was no specific intent to cause the detainee severe pain. Harsh techniques tested out on Abu Zubaydah—who had lost his eye in CIA custody—were soon back in use at Guantánamo, Bagram, and across the CIA black site network. About to be deployed in Iraq too, the Bush administration deemed them legal. Richard Shiffrin, who attended some of the National Security Council meetings to chart this second memo's progress, recalled being stunned. Yoo's work was, he said, "intellectually dishonest."[108]

In Cuba, General Miller already had his sights on another detainee, a Mauritanian called Mohamedou Ould Slahi, whose cousin was Osama bin Laden's personal spiritual advisor. He had arrived at Guantánamo in August 2002, and Miller was finessing a "special projects" interrogation involving a boat trip and mock drowning.[109]

CHAPTER 18

"A GREAT BIG TERRARIUM"

December 2003, Strawberry Fields, Guantánamo Bay, Cuba

One day during Abu Zubaydah's enhanced interrogation in Thailand, Jim Mitchell had suggested the CIA install "a great big terrarium" in George Tenet's office, so he could question the detainee whenever he liked. "They were spending so much time asking us to ask him what he thought about something, why not take the middleman out?" Mitchell recalled. "I was actually joking."[1]

Abu Zubaydah's new home resembled a viewing cage in a zoo. It was partitioned down the middle by a wire-mesh screen: one-half was for him to live in; the other half was for interrogators, who could come and go as they liked, and had a table and padded office chairs.[2] No more dank basements, unfamiliar food, and unsuitable billets in Afghan bars or Soviet-era bedrooms for his questioners. No more troublesome liaison partners or endless tours of the globe, glancing over one's shoulder for reporters or worse. This was bright, fresh, and airy, on American-controlled soil outside US jurisdiction, and "The Star-Spangled Banner" rang out across the station twice a day. Many of the guards had previously worked in the black sites. It wasn't as much fun as Thailand, but now they lived in trailers with views over the Caribbean, the snorkeling was out of this world, and Guantánamo's bars, McDonald's, and Subway sandwich shop were just down the road.

The CIA interrogators wore US military fatigues, but their wages were paid by Langley.[3] They knew the black site drill, and their familiar faces and voices served to remind the high-value detainees of the hard times. One function of this endgame facility was to "maintain" learned helplessness. Mitchell called it "compliance."[4] While studying brain function for the SERE school, Jessen had once concluded that long-term memory lasted thirty years.[5] Abu Zubaydah and his compatriots would never be allowed to forget what was done to them. The new facility was fitted with noise and temperature-control devices, just like the black sites.[6]

Upon Abu Zubaydah's arrival, guards in blue rubber gloves silently stripped, photographed and cavity-searched him, took a retinal scan of his one surviving eye, and then left him alone to explore his new forever home.[7] "There was a shower," he recalled, although it had no door, and access could be locked off.[8] "Soap as well." Small mercies made a huge impact. Special Missions chief Gus characterized Strawberry Fields as five-star. "They had reading material, they had dental, they had vision," he said.[9] Mitchell dubbed it the "terrorist think tank," a world-class repository of knowledge about Islamist extremism. The idea had come from observing Khalid Sheikh Mohammad, who had "a massive ego," according to Gus. "One of the program managers called me and said, 'Why don't we see if we can get him to teach?' We brought him in a whiteboard, tea, and Snickers. He couldn't shut up." Referring to Mohammad's short stature, Gus called him "little professor," the partner to Mitchell's "professor," Abu Zubaydah.[10] The CIA's previous derogatory names, like "Boo boo" and "Abu Butthead," were hushed up. For his compliance, Abu Zubaydah was rewarded with a magnetized watch to put on the mesh partition in his cell.[11] Apart from his CIA-era diary, which was still being withheld along with his Hani-era diaries, this became the "most important thing" in his tiny world.

Several weeks after he arrived, Abu Zubaydah was shackled through the flap in his inner door (which guards called the "bin hole"), then he was "extracted," hooded, and taken outside. Propelled along by guards at his elbows and shoulders, they entered a covered area, where they pulled off the hood. He spun around. "I saw the sun!" he exulted.[12] It was so bright, it took thirty minutes for his eye to adjust. He was in an open-air "rec yard" (recreation area) surrounded by "strong wire mesh." He could use it twice a day if he remained compliant and kept talking. There wasn't much, just a couple of basic exercise bikes. He could smell the ocean. Shrouded in high razor-wire fences and masked by miles of plastic netting that ripped up during hurricane season, Strawberry Fields sat at the southern end of Kittery Beach Road, a long ribbon of asphalt that led down from the naval station's undulating central hills via the Roosevelt command post to the Caribbean. The horseshoe of frothing surf and bone-white coral was tantalizingly close and accessible down rusting metal steps, but it was off-limits to everyone except CIA contractors and their JTF neighbors. To the west lay Camp Delta, which would eventually consist of multiple detention blocks of ascending security for compliant (dressed in white) and noncompliant (dressed in orange) detainees.[13]

Most of the time, however, Abu Zubaydah remained alone in his cell, trying to bring order to his fractured torture experiences and adapt to his multiple physical handicaps. Vomiting episodes were triggered by noises and smells pumped into his cell; his right hand and right leg went into spasms without warning; and he had a semipermanent headache that went away only if he drank coffee or repeatedly hit his head against the wall, which he knew made him look "like a crazy man."[14] He also continued suffering seizures (more than two hundred in one year) and he woke several times to find guards pulling him up off the floor.[15] On occasion, when he tried to speak, his tongue got so twisted up that "words wouldn't get out of my mouth."[16] For the first time in his life he stuttered. When they eventually gave him paper, he tried to write everything down but made so "many unforgivable spelling mistakes" it was unintelligible. He suffered constipation that could last two weeks, a condition he blamed on his compromised digestive system, the diapers, rendition flights, and the swiveling CCTV cameras.[17]

Proof of prolonged mental and physical harm, Yoo-Bybee had warned, would invalidate legal cover for enhanced interrogation. But Yoo-Bybee had determined that for mental pain or suffering to amount to torture, it had to "result in significant psychological harm of significant duration, e.g., lasting for months or even years," and Abu Zubaydah's post-traumatic symptoms were never diagnosed as PTSD because the only people allowed to see him were CIA employees.[18] His extensive physical scars were cited as evidence the CIA had "saved his life," which technically was true.[19] So torrid were his nightmares—in which he repeatedly drowned—that he feared falling asleep. Later, he drew pictures of a tiny Abu Zubaydah trapped inside a drinking water bottle, banging on the plastic with his fists in a futile bid to get out.[20]

In this near-permanent nervous, exhausted state, he became filled with a deep anger about Mitchell's threats. Knowing that his incarceration was forever, he tried to reconcile himself to the years ahead. He drew pictures of a man made of sand slowly dissolving in an hourglass and of his face with cell bars in front of and behind him, a state of permanent limbo. The only hope was God.[21] During one bout of insomnia he carved his name into the wall by his bed, "small and squiggly."[22] If this really was home, he would make his mark.

The CIA guards did not to speak except for "transactional orders," so he made the most of visits by "interrogators," "debriefers," and "interviewers."[23] No one outside the CIA was allowed access to the detainees, the US government constantly fearing the prospect of them gaining access to an attorney and filing a habeas petition.[24] Oblivious to the outside world, Abu Zubaydah tried to be helpful and told jokes to stave off thoughts about the "hard times." The Strawberry Fields base chief was a woman "like a man," called Jennifer. She was between fifty and sixty, "large, a Mormon," and was assisted by a Syrian American translator called Abbas, a former bodybuilder whose muscles had run to fat.[25] Familiar faces reappeared, including that of Gina Haspel, who turned up in December 2003 wearing a party dress. "It was a very long dress with a cut to mid-thigh," Abu Zubaydah recalled.[26] "Underneath, she wore some pants that don't match. Just to meet me and then take off and return to her party." He was less happy to see others. When the "bad doctor," a CIA medic he recognized from the waterboarding period, walked in, Abu Zubaydah was thrown into panic. Mitchell and Jessen were regulars. Mitchell said they "did calisthenics together" and played ball games, and he arranged for the detainee to receive testosterone supplements.[27] Mitchell implied that he and Abu Zubaydah were cemented together in mutual respect because of their intense shared experiences. But in Abu Zubaydah's mind, Mitchell would always be his torturer.[28]

Mitchell was at Strawberry Fields over Christmas in 2003, conducting detainee "maintenance." He preferred the term "morale visits," and recalled asking the men how they were feeling and whether they needed books, clothes, special food, or medication.[29] Some of them were exceptionally demanding, he recalled, especially Ramzi bin al-Shibh, who accused the CIA of trying to poison him and complained of constant noise and vibrations rocking his cell, as if he were still at the Salt Pit.[30] Mitchell ridiculed bin al-Shibh's paranoia, describing him as "crazy," and "nearly a constant pain in the ass," who complained about everything from "women interrogators" to "headgear." Mitchell thought about "giving him a special tinfoil hat to make it all go away."[31] But while Mitchell presented himself as providing vital aftercare, the detainees felt scarring bouts of terror whenever they saw him, or Jessen.

A CIA cable written shortly after Khalid Sheikh Mohammad's waterboarding ended showed how these feelings were deliberately engendered. Mohammad was told that "no matter how much progress he has made . . . his status will immediately reverse and if not corrected he will find himself in the same or worse conditions than those he has experienced here to fore."[32] Mitchell denied threatening detainees, saying there were no triggers, cues, or any intention to maintain learned helplessness.[33] "Normally I'd get sent to a place when someone was acting out," he explained.[34] Sometimes he was registered as a "debriefer" because he was "servicing the needs of the 9/11 Commission," although his presence was not broadcast. "Half the time I go anywhere they normally try to hide me from other people," he recalled.[35] "I'd give a throwaway name. Sometimes I said I was with Washington, sometimes with the CIA." Jessen would also drop by for "fireside chats." Sometimes their visits were not even registered. "We didn't date every entry." It was all benign and fuzzy. Later, Mitchell gave a more candid explanation of the fireside chat concept. "OK, the interrogation's over, well it's never really over, both you and I know it's not over because you can't really trust me. Then, we would talk."[36]

Mitchell also claimed he took time to gain a "more nuanced understanding" of the detainees' worldviews, although this was not evident in his written recollections. Abu Zubaydah's "brand of Islam," consisted of "slavery, crucifixion, beheading, burning, stoning, looting, hacking off limbs, blinding, throwing gays off tall places, raping captives as spoils of war."[37] Khalid Sheikh Mohammad, according to Mitchell, believed that killing innocent American men and women who were not actively fighting Islam was "permissible because they pay taxes that fund those who do." Killing babies and children was also permissible "because they bring comfort to infidels." But there were no references in CIA cables to either detainee saying such things. "Maybe there was a little hyperbole," Mitchell later conceded.[38]

Seventeen years later, Mitchell's and Jessen's roles at Strawberry Fields would come under much scrutiny. One CIA document recorded that both were present on December 10, 2003, for a full medical examination of Mustafa al-Hawsawi, who was recovering from months of abuse at the Salt Pit. His physical injuries included a prolapsed anus, tears inside his anal cavity, and hemorrhoids, the result of rectal examinations and worse. "[The government] wanted to know how he was doing emotionally," Mitchell recalled, adding it was the first time he had met al-Hawsawi, who was one of Charlie Wise's "mistakes," a reference to Wise's alleged abusive treatment, and therefore someone to avoid. Mitchell and Jessen's psychological assessment concluded: "No sign of profound or prolonged mental harm."[39] The CIA needed to keep these all-important conclusions up-to-date to maintain legal cover. No mention of al-Hawsawi's injuries appeared in their report. "I didn't really discuss his medical history with him," Mitchell explained. Neither did al-Hawsawi's experiences of illegal waterboarding and "water dousing" appear, even though CIA records showed he gave detailed descriptions to Mitchell.[40]

In January 2004, Mitchell and Jessen debriefed Ibn Sheikh al-Libi at Strawberry Fields. Mitchell met the Libyan detainee "many, many times" but did not conduct any enhanced interrogation.[41] His and Jessen's job was simply to reexamine the intelligence George Tenet had put forward to justify the Iraq war. The Egyptians had done a bad job on al-Libi, Mitchell argued. "After we got [al-Libi] back, Bruce and I had to sort through the retraction of that information," he said, suggesting the CIA was looking to backtrack from Secretary of State Colin Powell's United Nations Security Council speech. Al-Libi said that after the Egyptians tortured him, he "told them what he assessed they wanted to hear," which was WMDs in Iraq and a connection to Al Qaeda.[42] By the time the CIA reported this, the United States was bogged down in a war that would ultimately cost almost half a million lives, including almost forty-five hundred Americans. After debriefing al-Libi and reporting that the detainee had made up his previous stories, Mitchell and Jessen signed new CIA contracts worth $467,500 each.[43] The CIA kept quiet about another of al-Libi's claims: that Abu Zubaydah was "not a member of [Al Qaeda], was not a member of the Taliban," and that the Khaldan training camp was not associated with the same.[44]

Donald Rumsfeld kept up the official braggadocio that Guantánamo was working, saying, "We are keeping them off the street and out of the airlines and out of nuclear power plants and out of ports across this country and across other countries."[45] In truth, some Bush administration officials were having sleepless nights. Ever since the *Washington Post* had exposed the existence of secret CIA prisons in December 2002, the International Committee of the Red Cross had been demanding access.[46] "It was political," claimed Special Missions chief Gus. "We said, 'No, we don't have to give you access to anything because they are under our control and are being well taken care of, and you have no authority.'"[47] Because Bush had broken with the Geneva Conventions, Gus was within his rights, but the ICRC kept pushing. In July 2003, its president raised the issue with Colin Powell, who officially did not know anything so could not help.[48] In January 2004, the ICRC demanded access to detainees held "incommunicado for extensive periods of time, subjected to unacceptable conditions of internment, to ill treatment and torture, while deprived of any possible recourse."[49] According to the CIA, the ICRC had a "fairly complete list" of names, and on March 25, 2004, it followed through with an official request for access to Abu Zubaydah, Khalid Sheikh Mohammad, Ramzi bin al-Shibh, Mustafa al-Hawsawi, and Hambali.[50] The US Supreme Court had recently determined it would hear the cases of a number of Guantánamo detainees, consolidated as *Rasul v. Bush*, bringing them into US jurisdiction.[51] While that action did not apply to those who were not officially at Guantánamo, it was enough to send the CIA into a panic.

———•———

"They said it was a real emergency," recalled Abu Zubaydah.[52] The sun was setting over Cuba as the high-value detainees were flown out on March 27, 2004.[53] They landed in Morocco the next day. Abu Zubaydah realized he was not alone when guards broke the no-talking rule to discuss arranging detainees in different vehicles. He was back to the old hell of not knowing where he was going or what would happen when he got there. Gus recalled the rapid burn: "There were legal moves to give them the same rights as US citizens, so we moved them all out of there and never brought some of those guys back."[54] Strawberry Fields was turned over to Joint Task Force Guantánamo, which renamed it "Echo Special" and used it for segregating troublesome military detainees, one of whom hung himself from a pole in the rec yard.[55] Among those never going back was Ibn Sheikh al-Libi, who was returning to Temara for a second time. It was Abu Zubaydah's first time there, and according to human rights reports, the Moroccan intelligence officials were torturing suspects connected to a devastating mosque attack in Casablanca.[56] Beatings, asphyxiation, simulated drowning, psychological and sexual violence, throwing people off buildings, and subjecting prisoners to the "roast chicken" technique (shackling them to a "spit" and beating them) were just a few of their chosen methods.[57]

The CIA zeroed in on Morocco as an alternative location for an "end-game facility," paying $20 million to build a secret detention camp near Ain Aouda nature reserve, south of Rabat. Located on land belonging to the Alaouite royal family, it was patrolled by royal guards, and visitors had to pass the king's palace to reach it.[58] The CIA code-named it Bombay but in the end did not use it because it did not have "tenable" access to medical facilities.[59]

Fine sand blew in from the desert, coating everything at Temara. Occasionally, Abu Zubaydah was allowed to shower or visit a basic rec yard, which had an exercise bike and weights.[60] He never saw another detainee and was not subjected to any physical abuse, but at night, when the CIA and the FBI—which still had agents working in Temara, despite director Robert Mueller's pledge to pull out of the CIA program in June 2002—went back to their hotels, he heard screaming.[61] One day in the rec yard, he read a familiar name scribbled in the sand, "Khallad." He wondered if it was the Al Qaeda brother, Khallad bin Attash. Another name appeared, Hassan Ghul, Abu Zubaydah's former holiday-jihad fund-raising chief. He had not seen either of them since early 2002, after the Taliban surrendered and the Afghan Arabs scattered. It was the first hint that either of them had survived.

Bin Attash and Ghul had been rendered from Bucharest, where they were held with Khalid Sheikh Mohammad. There, they had all communicated using a similar trick near a shared shower room.[62] In Temara, when Abu Zubaydah saw the guards looking at the names, he quickly scrubbed them out with his foot. It was the last he ever heard of Hassan Ghul, who was later turned over to Pakistan's ISI, released with instructions to spy on Al Qaeda, went rogue instead, and was killed in a drone strike in Waziristan. Many years later, Abu Zubaydah would be reunited with bin Attash at Guantánamo. But his closest friend in jihad, Ibn Sheikh al-Libi, whose false intelligence was produced as a result of torture, would be permanently silenced. In April 2006, the CIA handed him over to his native Libya, where he had been sentenced in absentia for trying to overthrow the Gaddhafi regime. He died in Tripoli's Abu Salim prison in May 2009, the cause written up as suicide by hanging, although few believed it. Human Rights Watch researchers who tried to interview him two weeks earlier said he looked fit and well but refused to speak to them, other than asking why they had not come to visit when he had been incarcerated in American jails. Tortured into saying what the US government wanted to hear before it invaded Iraq and executed Saddam Hussein, al-Libi had signed his own death warrant. Far too many American lives had been lost in Iraq for the Bush administration to admit it had lied to the United Nations. Mike Scheuer, who had started the renditions program, had no regrets. "The goal was to protect America, and the rendered fighters delivered to Middle Eastern governments are now either dead or in places from which they cannot harm America," he told Congress. "Mission accomplished, as the saying goes."[63]

Jessen also turned up in Temara, asking Abu Zubaydah about the names scribbled in the sand. They had been written in Arabic and Abu Zubaydah refused to translate.[64] He would never rat on a brother. The Mormon interrogator who called herself Jennifer also reappeared, now as a base chief at the Moroccan facility. She tried to ingratiate herself, telling Abu Zubaydah she was sorry about his previous mistreatment, and attempted to enlist his support for an internal CIA investigation into interrogation abuses. He refused. Since the CIA had tortured him, and she worked for the CIA, how could he ever trust her?[65] He heard she left the CIA soon after, following a disagreement over religious beliefs, and she was replaced by a "very fat white American man who spoke Arabic with an Egyptian accent," and consumed Snickers bars, Pepsi and pizza. It was the Preacher. Abu Zubaydah, who had previously met him in Poland and called him "George," said he threatened a return to "hard times" and often worked in tandem with Albert El Gamil.[66] Also working in Temara was a "burly Hispanic American" who called himself "Iskander, or Alexander" and wore a saint's medal around his neck. Abu Zubaydah recalled having seen him previously in Thailand or Poland. "Iskander/Alexander," he said, "looked like a beach boy." Alexander bragged that he had tortured bin Attash, saying, "When I want to take the truth, I take it. I took it from Khallad and he cried."[67] According to his *curriculum vitae*, former CIA analyst Deuce Martinez, the former lead targeter on the Abu Zubaydah hunt in Pakistan, also worked as a contractor in the CIA program. Martinez's real first name was Alejandro, the latinized version of Alexander. Mitchell would not say whether Martinez questioned Abu Zubaydah in Temara or anywhere else. "Deuce Martinez is not an interrogator, he's an analyst," he snapped.[68] Jose Rodriguez was also vague about Martinez, saying only that a lot of "interrogating analysts" working for him post-9/11 were old Latin America hands.[69] Roger Aldrich, Mitchell's former boss, was more forthcoming, saying Martinez "knows the program very well, knows Jim and Bruce very well."[70]

April 26, 2004, Washington, DC

One month after the Strawberry Fields rapid burn, Larry Wilkerson was in his office when the secretary of state came in and shut the door. "We are going to see some really shocking pictures from a place called Abu Ghraib in Iraq, and once you have felt the full impact, I want you to investigate," said Powell.[71] He was talking about a prison that was notorious during the Saddam Hussein era for torture and executions. But these abusers were Americans. Two days after Powell's warning, the photographs flashed up on *60 Minutes*.[72] Some depicted reservist Charles "Chuck" Graner, a former corrections officer with a history of abusing Black prisoners and of domestic violence.[73] Graner had been called up to active duty and sent to Iraq with a traffic patrol in May 2003 but was redeployed into Abu Ghraib. His unit guarded Hard Site Tier 1-A, where the CIA operated a secret "Detention Elicitation Cell" to interrogate unregistered detainees, who were referred to as "ghost detainees."[74] In one image, Graner gave a thumbs-up over the body of a ghost detainee who had died during his CIA interrogation. Because the CIA had packed him in ice to smuggle him out, the guards had dubbed him "Iceman."[75]

As Wilkerson dug into the situation, a brutal picture emerged. Command of Abu Ghraib had been given to Brigadier General Janis Karpinski, a reservist with no experience in detention or interrogation.[76] To help her set up the facility, in August 2003 the Pentagon had deployed Captain Carolyn Wood, who had been awarded a Bronze Star for valor in spite of two detainees dying on her watch at Bagram.[77] Around the same time, military interrogators from Guantánamo's Interrogation Control Element, where Wood had been taught aggressive interrogation techniques, exchanged emails about the forthcoming plan in Iraq. "The gloves are coming off gentlemen regarding these detainees, [redacted] has made it clear that we want these individuals broken," read one.[78] A former Bagram interrogator recommended open-handed facial slaps, backhanded blows to the torso, confinement boxes, sleep deprivation, white noise, and the use of snakes. During later testimony,

Wood stated that she brought the "Bagram model" over to Abu Ghraib.[79] On August 31, 2003, General Geoffrey Miller, Guantánamo's "hoo-ah" commander, also arrived, accompanied by Diane Beaver, to help "GTMO-ize" the setup.[80] A few days later, the first Iraqi detainees were delivered.

While Miller was at Abu Ghraib, Bruce Jessen's former JPRA partner Chris Wirts sent a team of SERE-trained survival instructors to Camp Cropper, a detention site near Baghdad international airport, where the CIA kept detainees hidden from the ICRC.[81] Steven Kleinman, an old adversary of Mitchell and Jessen, led the team, assisted by Terry Russell, who had helped train Guantánamo interrogators at Fort Bragg as well as CIA interrogators bound for the Salt Pit. Their job was to train US military interrogators. Within a couple of days, Kleinman became worried after Russell and the third team member, Lenny Miller, who was also a SERE instructor, started using Camp Cropper detainees as training props. Kleinman watched as they took a hooded detainee into a shipping container, stripped him, and left him hanging in the standing sleep-deprivation position. Kleinman rang his commander, Randy Moulton, who had also been Jessen's commander. His colleagues were not only conducting real interrogations without authorization but also using tactics that did not comply with the Geneva Conventions. "They had never actually seen what I would describe as a real-world interrogation," Kleinman said.[82] Days later, Kleinman was ordered home, and his concerns were glossed over. He later accused the CIA of encouraging Mitchell and Jessen to develop an abusive program that infected the US military. The consequences, he said, would "last decades." He respected Mitchell and Jessen for their unblemished careers in SERE school but "despised what they did" for the CIA.[83]

While General Miller was at Abu Ghraib, interrogation procedures changed numerous times. In September 2003, Rumsfeld flew in and was photographed with a worried-looking Karpinski.[84] The message was clear: to win the war in Iraq the US military needed harsher interrogation, irrespective of the risks, and starting in October 2003, a number of "sadistic, blatant and wanton criminal abuses [were] inflicted on several detainees" in Hard Site Tier 1-A.[85] Wilkerson built a dossier "as tall as my ceiling" in which the prevailing message was that torture worked and that the CIA had the perfect model. "Everywhere I went I kept hearing 'Jack Bauer, Jack Bauer,'" he recalled, referencing a television character popular with CIA officers.[86] "Reputable people would look at me and say, 'Well, it works on 24.'" Like a virus, SERE techniques introduced to the CIA by Mitchell and Jessen, taught to CIA and US military interrogators on courses designed by Jessen and JPRA instructors, trialed on Abu Zubaydah and rolled out at Bagram, Guantánamo, and the Salt Pit, and swapped between CIA and military contractors over drinks at the Ariana Hotel in Kabul were passed on to abusive reservists in Abu Ghraib as Iraq drowned in blood.

Some of the worst things had happened after the "Iceman," whose real name was Manadel al-Jamadi, died in the shower stalls of Hard Site Tier 1-A on November 4, 2003. US Navy SEALs had broken five of his ribs during his capture. Without being checked over by a doctor, as stipulated in prison protocol, he was taken to the shower area, where his arms were cinched up behind him, strappado style. The CIA interrogator, a polygraph examiner named Mark Swanner, did not know about al-Jamadi's injuries and ordered the guards to pull him higher.[87] Al-Jamadi's arms were "almost literally coming out of his sockets. . . . I mean, that's how bad he was hanging," recalled a guard.[88] Shortly afterward, al-Jamadi, who was hooded, slumped forward, his full weight falling on his shackled wrists behind him. Accusing al-Jamadi of "playing possum," Swanner told the guards to reposition him, only to discover that he was dead.[89]

The CIA officer in charge of the secret Detention Elicitation Cell, David Martine, also a polygraph examiner, was asleep in Baghdad's secure Green Zone when he got a call around 4:30 A.M.[90] He later agreed the CIA had caused al-Jamadi's death but did not accept the cause to have been negligence.[91] The main fault lay with the SEALs who broke his ribs, he said, although he admitted his team took steps to conceal al-Jamadi's death. After packing the body in ice, they inserted a false IV drip in his arm, and the bloodied nylon bag that had been over his head was stashed in Martine's office. The "Iceman" was then smuggled out and buried in an unmarked grave.[92] But three days later, news of his death spread around the prison nevertheless.

On the night of November 7, 2003, Abu Ghraib detainees rioted. The main troublemakers were brought into Hard Site Tier 1-A. It was the night of Private Lynndie England's twenty-first birthday.[93] She was having an affair with Graner and got involved in the abuse after she came down to the tier to collect her birthday gift. Early in the evening, she was photographed cuddling with Graner. A few hours later, she was giving a thumbs-up behind a "dog pile" of naked detainees and holding a detainee on a leash. When these images were broadcast, England became the primary villain of the story—scapegoated because she was a woman.[94]

Larry Wilkerson blamed the CIA. "Step by step, I built a case that abusive practices introduced by the CIA for use in secret prisons were spread to Gitmo and then Abu Ghraib," he said.[95] An official inquiry reached a softer conclusion, reporting: "CIA detention and interrogation practices led to a loss of accountability, abuse, reduced interagency cooperation, and an unhealthy mystique that further poisoned the atmosphere at Abu Ghraib."[96] "It was clearly a policy decision to torture made by the highest levels in the US government, at a minimum, Dick Cheney," Wilkerson insisted.[97] "At a maximum, George W. Bush was in compliance."

In May 2004, Rumsfeld revisited Abu Ghraib and promised to bring the guilty to justice. He asked the Office of the Naval Inspector General to investigate the abuses, and Alberto Mora, who had been trying to block enhanced interrogation since December 2002, submitted a detailed memo.[98] "What happens when you give the green light for the use of brutality is that the word spreads through the system," Mora explained.[99] "It took the army a long time to try to control the torturers." In al-Jamadi's case, one member of the SEAL team that captured him was court-martialed but found not guilty.[100] Graner, England, and several other members of the prison team were convicted.[101] General Miller, who had "GTMO-ized" Abu Ghraib with tragic consequences, was promoted to run detainee operations across Iraq.[102] The CIA's role in al-Jamadi's death would not be probed until 2011, when federal prosecutor John Durham investigated two CIA deaths in custody, those of al-Jamadi and Gul Rahman. Durham recommended opening a full criminal investigation, but the Department of Justice concluded that no charges should be brought.[103] During questioning, the CIA interrogator Mark Swanner said: "I wish we had just killed [al-Jamadi], because then I could just say he deserved to die."[104] Martine was cleared of any wrongdoing but subsequently conceded: "If we crossed a line, I am part of that."[105]

The only CIA employee ever convicted for abusing a detainee was contractor Dave Passaro, who beat Abdul Wali to death at Forward Operating Base Asadabad in June 2003 and was suddenly indicted after the Abu Ghraib scandal broke. The CIA needed a fall guy to distract attention away from its mistakes at Abu Ghraib and the official enhanced interrogation program.

After serving his sentence, Passaro remained unapologetic. "Man, I wasn't hired to be nice to those terrorists," he said.[106] In their books cowritten with CIA spokesman Bill Harlow, James Mitchell and Jose Rodriguez each vehemently denied any connection to abuses committed at Guantánamo, Bagram, or Abu Ghraib. Mitchell recalled his "heart sank" and claimed critics "used the Abu Ghraib scandal like a club" against the CIA program.[107] When he and Jessen were later asked to make a presentation to Condoleezza Rice, who had replaced Colin Powell as Secretary of State in January 2005, she raised concerns that standing sleep deprivation "was reminiscent of images associated with Abu Ghraib." According to CIA records, "while she readily recognized that CIA had nothing to do with the Abu Ghraib scandal, she characterized the problem as 'something we all have to live with.' The problem is standing in shackles with arms tied to [a] ceiling bar."[108] Mitchell later blamed Chris Wirts for encouraging the military to use unauthorized techniques and leaking his and Jessen's names to the media. "Given the choice to use two bullets on Chris Wirts and KSM, I'd use both on Wirts," Mitchell said.[109] "He blamed Bruce for all the JPRA stuff that went wrong at GTMO. He ran that shit and then tried to blame Bruce." Mitchell wanted to "drive a stake through this little shit's heart."

However, behind the scenes, the CIA reacted swiftly after Abu Ghraib. Rodriguez ordered the Salt Pit closed and stripped out. By the time the contractors had finished, the only things left were paperwork and photographs, and at least one grave—that of Gul Rahman. Some images, taken for Gus so he could maintain standards across the program, showed a walling wall, an isolation cell, and an unauthorized waterboard.[110] Others showed naked detainees and close-ups of injuries, such as Khallad bin Attash's edema. The team connected to the Salt Pit dispersed. Rich Blee, the Kabul station chief, who had been unable to provide adequate facilities or training, was offered the Baghdad station at the start of the war against Saddam Hussein but opted to retire.[111] Matthew Zirbel, Jessen's protégé, lost his enhanced interrogation certification around the time Charlie Wise died, but the CIA kept him on the team. A recommendation to suspend him was quashed, and he received a bonus.[112] Later, he was posted to the CIA's Riyadh station.[113] Eventually, he saved enough to buy a lavish $1.3 million home in Great Falls, Virginia.[114] As Mitchell had done with his house, Zirbel filled his with Persian rugs and faux *Lawrence of Arabia*–style memorabilia. Gul Rahman remained where he had died, buried in an unmarked grave somewhere outside the Salt Pit perimeter. Rahman's family would not learn of his fate until 2010, when the Associated Press told them.[115]

Detainees who survived the Salt Pit were dispersed to other black sites. More than half of the ninety-six detainees officially processed by the CIA had passed through the "dark prison."[116] Thirty-nine detainees had been subjected to enhanced techniques.[117] Ghost detainees who had been held in Matthew Zirbel's secret cells remained forever undocumented, and a subsequent investigation found at least twenty-three detainees were never accounted for.[118] Some of those who were registered also disappeared, such as Abu Yasir al-Jaza'iri, an Algerian who Mitchell claimed was the last detainee he ever subjected to enhanced interrogation, although CIA interrogators employed by Mitchell, Jessen, and Associates used enhanced techniques until November 2007.[119] Jaza'iri was "bathed," stripped, walled, sleep-deprived, and strung up naked at the Salt Pit in 2003.[120] He was then rendered to Poland, where the Preacher accused Mitchell of punching him so hard he dropped to the floor.[121] Mitchell countered: "I slapped him open-handed and with my fingers spread across his left cheek."[122] He claimed he caught Jaza'iri on the way down so he didn't "hit his head." In September 2003, Jaza'iri was rendered to Strawberry Fields with Abu Zubaydah. He was then rendered back to Afghanistan, where another detainee last saw him in September 2006.[123] Jaza'iri told another detainee he had suffered permanent injuries due to torture. Soon after, he disappeared. Two detainees captured with Abu Zubaydah in Faisalabad also vanished: Noor al-Deen, who was only a teenager, and Omar Ghramesh were both rendered to Syria in May 2002 and vanished.[124] But while dead and missing detainees became CIA Inspector General John Helgerson's focus, Jose Rodriguez was fixated on destroying Abu Zubaydah's waterboarding tapes. "We knew that if the photos of CIA officers conducting authorized EITs ever got out . . . the propaganda damage to the image of America would be immense," he later wrote.[125]

CHAPTER 19

"EGO AND HYPOCRISY. NOTHING ELSE MATTERS"

The CIA managed to conceal Abu Zubaydah's waterboarding tapes for three years. When a judge in Virginia asked for any interrogation videos relevant to Zacarias Moussaoui, who was charged as a 9/11 conspirator, the agency argued that Abu Zubaydah was irrelevant, even though Moussaoui had trained at Khaldan.[1] A New York district court judge was blocked from seeing the tapes when the CIA argued in a Freedom of Information Act (FOIA) suit that all Abu Zubaydah–related material was still operational and therefore classified.[2] The agency also dodged an order to safeguard all evidence related to the mistreatment of detainees at Guantánamo Bay, because Abu Zubaydah's mistreatment had happened in Thailand.[3] But after Abu Ghraib, Rodriguez intensified the pressure on Scott Muller and John Rizzo, the latter of whom claimed he pushed back. "I was given consistent instructions not to destroy them until we had gotten approval from the White House and the Congress," Rizzo recalled. There was another problem. Several anti-Mitchell people already knew about the tapes.[4] One of them was Charles Morgan, who as a Yale researcher studying cortisol (stress-hormone) levels in SERE students had once dismissed Mitchell's data as "no good." A long-term critic of the SERE "cabal" controlling the CIA's interrogation program, Morgan now worked at the CIA, in the Office of the Chief Scientist. His boss was Mitchell's former boss, Kirk Hubbard. Morgan was not "read-in" to the enhanced interrogation program but he still had some idea about what was going on.[5] Mitchell and Jessen sometimes dropped by to see Hubbard, and Morgan noted the reverence and fear surrounding them. Mitchell noticed too. "I've had people stop me in the hall and say they did things I know that I did, that's how weird it is," he recalled.[6]

One day in 2005, a young medic from the Office of Medical Services came to Morgan's office and shut the door. "He was terrified," Morgan recalled. "He teared up and told me he had been working at the black sites and said, 'These people are worse than Nazis.' He wanted to know how to get out." Morgan advised him to concoct a marriage problem and ask for time off so he could avoid being redeployed. One Friday afternoon not long after, Morgan was the last to leave his office, a "sensitive compartmented information facility" with strictly controlled access. He locked up, but when he came back on Monday morning, a big box was sitting beside his desk. According to the log, no one had been in or out over the weekend. Only he had the keys, or so he thought. Flicking open the box, using a ruler rather than his fingers, he could see CDs related to numbered and dated interrogation sessions. "I asked my colleague, 'Are these what I think they might be?'" They both knew about the Abu Zubaydah tapes, as there had been a discussion about giving them to Morgan so he could analyze the effectiveness of waterboarding. Mitchell had put a stop to that, Morgan recalled. If these were copies, they could cause a scandal.

Morgan was worried. Exposing the material would cost him his career, maybe even his life. Scott Gewehr, a former researcher at RAND Corporation, who had worked as Hubbard's deputy, knew Morgan, and had been authorized to read documents connected to the program, had been killed in a bizarre traffic accident after turning against enhanced interrogation. Question marks still lingered over Charlie Wise's untimely death.[7] Morgan decided not to watch the Abu Zubaydah tapes and pushed the box out of his office with his foot.[8] An hour later it had vanished. But getting rid of the original tapes was not so easy.

The subject of their destruction had come up a few days after Abu Ghraib, when Scott Muller, the CIA's chief attorney, met White House lawyers, and the conversation turned to Charles Graner's and Lynndie England's shocking images. John Bellinger asked Muller to confirm that the CIA was not sitting on anything dangerous. Muller had to admit that the agency had something even worse—Abu Zubaydah's gruesome waterboarding videotapes.[9] David Addington, Cheney's legal counsel, was stunned. Almost a year earlier, he, Muller, Bellinger, Alberto Gonzales, and Jim Haynes had flown down to Guantánamo a second time to review the legality of detainee treatment and the CIA's "endgame facility" at Strawberry Fields. During the trip, Addington had asked Muller about rumors that there were tapes of Abu Zubaydah on the waterboard. "I told him that tapes were not being made," Muller reported back to Rizzo.[10] Now he had to admit that historically tapes had been made. Everyone at the meeting agreed: in the light of Abu Ghraib, the tapes could not now be destroyed.

While the legal elite sought solutions to Abu Ghraib, Jose Rodriguez "pestered" Scott Muller for permission to destroy the Abu Zubaydah tapes, accusing the CIA of foot-dragging.[11] Muller said no. Rodriguez turned to dependable John Rizzo, who would be irreversibly damaged by his association to enhanced interrogation.[12] But even Rizzo would not play ball. "The CIA will be accused of a cover-up," he warned. Before Rodriguez could make another move, John Helgerson, the CIA inspector general, wrote about the tapes in a damning review of the program that went to the Justice Department and the leadership of the House and Senate Intelligence Committees. It was a wake-up call to Congress that the CIA had until this point kept its secret interrogation program in the dark and had failed to inform Congress about the program.[13] Rodriguez was furious. Having borne the brunt of past congressional inquiries over Latin America, they were his worst nightmare. He hated the politicians who encouraged the CIA to take off the gloves but abrogated responsibility when human rights "assholes" got involved. "One of my biggest fantasies was the last time that I would do a briefing to both houses of Congress I would say, 'I had a great career, but you know what, fuck you, all of you,'" he later said.[14]

Rodriguez, who lived for the wilder operational side of agency work, characterized those who worked in the inspector general's office as failed case officers, but he could not ignore Helgerson's findings. The inspector general's team had visited all the black sites, watched all the tapes, reviewed thirty-eight thousand documents, and conducted one hundred interviews, and his report packed a punch.[15] Some of Mitchell's and Jessen's interrogation techniques appeared to violate international laws, as the Yoo-Bybee memo did not cover Article 16 of the Geneva Conventions that stated: "All prisoners of war shall be treated alike by the Detaining Power, without any adverse distinction based on race, nationality, religious belief or political opinions, or any other distinction founded on similar criteria."[16] Helgerson concluded:

"SERE waterboard experience is so different from the subsequent Agency usage as to make it almost irrelevant." Later, he described Mitchell's and Jessen's program as "guinea pig research on human beings."[17] In his report, Helgerson stated it had been impossible to determine the number of detainees in the program, and he warned about possible criminal prosecution. The agency faced "potentially serious long-term political and legal challenges as a result of its use of EITs and the inability of the US Government to decide what it will ultimately do with terrorists detained by the Agency," especially those, like Abu Zubaydah, "who cannot be prosecuted."[18] Helgerson delivered a stark ultimatum to George Tenet. "The [CIA director] should brief the President on the use of EITs and the fact that detainees have died."[19] Three years on from the instigation of the program, President Bush still did not officially know. Helgerson also ordered Scott Muller to obtain "a new formal legal opinion" that reflected actual practices. He gave Muller ten days to comply.[20]

———•———

While the seventh floor debated what, if anything, to tell the president, and Muller tried to cajole the Justice Department, the first major repercussions of America's uncompromising War on Terror, at the heart of which sat enhanced interrogation, were felt in Iraq when the decapitated body of Nick Berg, a missing American radio-tower repairman, was found on an overpass in Baghdad. Three days later, a video of his killing was published online. Berg was dressed in an orange jumpsuit, as a masked man, whom the CIA later identified as the Jordanian insurgent Abu Musab al-Zarqawi, severed Berg's head.[21] A statement said the killing was revenge for detainee abuse at Guantánamo and Abu Ghraib. Orange jumpsuits, which categorized noncompliant US detainees in an invisible prison system, now evoked horrific resistance staged by extremists. Berg's beheading set the tone for the systematic abduction, torture, and murder of hundreds of journalists, aid workers, and military contractors, many of whom were filmed as they were executed.

After Berg, Italian journalist Enzo Baldoni was kidnapped and killed in August 2004. Two months later, American civil engineers Eugene Armstrong and Jack Hensley were beheaded in Baghdad, along with their British colleague Kenneth Bigley. Margaret Hassan, the director of CARE International, was abducted in Baghdad in October 2004 and executed a month later. Salvatore Santoro, an Italian photojournalist, was reported kidnapped and killed in December 2004. American journalist Steven Vincent was kidnapped in Basra in August 2005, interrogated, and shot in the back. American electrician Ronald Alan Schultz was shot in the head in December 2005 after the US government refused to release Iraqi detainees. The body of Thomas Fox, a missionary from Christian Peacemakers, was found on a rubbish heap in March 2006. Four American security contractors, John Young, Joshua Munns, Paul Reuben, and Jonathon Cote, along with an Austrian named Bert Nussbaumer, were kidnapped and executed in November 2006. The practice carried over into the Syrian war, long after enhanced interrogation was over. American journalists James Foley and Stephen Sotloff, British aid workers David Haines and Alan Henning, American aid worker Peter Kassig, Japanese reporter Kenji Goto, and American human rights activist Kayla Mueller were just a few of those killed. Many appeared on camera dressed in orange, the color of Guantánamo.

In May 2004, while the *Dallas Morning News* published an image of Nick Berg's severed head, the *Washington Post* focused on the cause, reporting that the CIA had an interrogation site called "the Pit" in Kabul and another at Baghdad airport.[22] The newspaper connected the CIA program to abuses committed at Abu Ghraib and revealed that CIA employees were under investigation by the Justice Department and the CIA inspector general for the deaths of two detainees in Iraq and a third "who was being questioned by a CIA contract interrogator in Afghanistan." John Rizzo watched with horror as secrets spilled out. "All of us involved in the program could only look on, silent and helpless, as collectively we were being publicly portrayed as untethered, sadistic goons," he recalled.[23] Later, Mitchell railed against the media, describing reporters as "self-serving" and their product as "crap."[24] They were fueled by a "crack-like addiction" to "*schadenfreude*," he said. Mitchell was proud of what he had done for his country and later denied all accusations he was a torturer. "Just as killing a baby born live in Washington, DC, with a screwdriver is not murder but it's a euthanasia of an infant after a failed abortion, this ubiquitous use of the word 'torture' in a colloquial way is just as wrong," he reflected.[25] For one thing, detainees were unreliable witnesses. "When you ask Abu Zubaydah what was going on, it's like asking someone who's been in the audience of a magician show how the tricks are done. Sometimes they just don't know what happens behind the scenes. All they know is their experience."

Bill Harlow also came out fighting, putting forward "senior officials" to give statements. "We have put together a very professional, controlled, deliberate and legally rationalized approach to dealing with the Abu Zubaidas [sic] of the world," said one.[26] But behind the scenes, the program was turning into "quicksand" and the CIA was facing stark choices about how to limit the damage to a president facing reelection in November 2004.[27] In addition to Abu Ghraib, the deaths in custody, Helgerson's report, and the exposure of the Abu Zubaydah tapes, a less amenable team had taken over at the Office of Legal Counsel in the Justice Department and was lobbying to pull the legal rug out from under enhanced interrogation.

"At some point in a job like mine, you just give out," George Tenet reflected in *At the Center of the Storm*, the book he coauthored with Bill Harlow.[28] "Something comes along, some essential trigger, and that's it. You know you've hit the wall." Tenet's trigger was journalist Bob Woodward and his new book, *Plan of Attack*, which accused the CIA director of having told the president it was a "slam dunk" case that Iraq possessed WMDs. "Woodward's book had ignited a media bonfire, and I was the guy being burned at the stake," wrote Tenet. But there was more behind his resignation than just the false evidence given by Abu Zubaydah's friend Ibn Sheikh al-Libi to his Egyptian torturers. Tenet went to the White House on the evening of June 3, 2004. Only three people at the agency knew he was resigning, including Harlow.[29] When it was announced the following morning, Richard Shelby, a former chairman of the Senate Select Committee on Intelligence, who had complained about being improperly briefed about enhanced interrogation, described Tenet's departure as long overdue. "There were more failures of intelligence on his watch as director of the CIA than any other DCI in our history," he said.[30] Tenet addressed his staff at Langley, saying he would stay on until July 11, officially bowing out on his seventh anniversary as director. His teenage son John Michael was in the audience as Tenet choked back tears and said, "You've been a great son—and now I'm going to be a great dad."[31] Within hours, Jim Pavitt, the CIA's deputy director of operations, also announced he was leaving. Harlow tried to convince the media that Pavitt's retirement was unrelated but nobody believed him.[32]

Mitchell was more concerned by CIA Inspector General Helgerson. His report detailed abuses at the Salt Pit, concluded that Mitchell and Jessen's version of waterboarding verged on torture, and expounded on training programs that had gone wrong as well as the death of Gul Rahman, all of which was intertwined with references to "IC psychologists" and "psychologist/interrogators"—clear references to Mitchell and Jessen. Mitchell felt as if he and Jessen were being "perp-walked as war criminals" and that it was only a matter of time before the CIA officially made them scapegoats for a program the CIA had paid them to create.[33] He complained to Gus, who promised to smooth things over. "I wasn't comforted by the assurances of the chief of special missions," said Mitchell, who was glad he had worked to get "unmasked senior CIA officers" on the Abu Zubaydah waterboarding tapes.[34] They were his insurance policy, and some in the CIA, including Wise, had alleged he had made copies, which he vehemently denied. On June 16, less than two weeks after Tenet resigned, Mitchell and Jessen signed new nondisclosure agreements.[35]

Tenet expressed no regrets about enhanced interrogation, reflecting: "The average American said they were OK with using techniques that were used for a couple of hours on US military personnel. Nine out of ten people at the time said we understand you are in a tough place. We respect what you are doing."[36] The program was "disciplined and focused," and the techniques were applied in a "precisely monitored, measured way." He made no mention of ghost detainees, those who had vanished or died, the permanent injury done to Abu Zubaydah, al-Hawsawi, and others, or the proliferation of SERE-based techniques into the military. There was only a confident projection of the eight thousand–plus intelligence briefings derived from the program, and their results, from the thwarting of the ticking time bomb to the unveiling of Daniel Pearl's "real" killer to the assassination of Osama bin Laden.[37] Like Mitchell, Tenet characterized America's enemies as being "so full of hate they would murder thousands of our children without a thought." Singling out Abu Zubaydah, Tenet claimed enhanced interrogation had persuaded him to reveal "a mother lode" of information, just as Mitchell had once promised Ali Soufan. After Tenet left Langley, he carried around a large ring binder containing "all sorts of secrets about AZ and KSM."[38] The intelligence Abu Zubaydah gave up to the FBI before Mitchell got started was reduced to two or three "nuggets," while Tenet made only excuses for the forty-seven days Abu Zubaydah was left in isolation with his ticking time bomb as the CIA sought legal approval, and the time wasted on following up false information spun by a desperate man who was never Number Three in Al Qaeda were all worth it because countless American lives had been saved.[39]

After Tenet resigned, the original Yoo-Bybee memo was leaked, sending the "torture" story viral. The *New York Times* published details of "highly coercive interrogation methods" that included waterboarding and placing a noose around a detainee's neck.[40] On June 22, 2004, senior Bush administration lawyers held a press conference in which they fought back against widely reported links between the CIA program and Abu Ghraib. The memo was not connected to Iraq, claimed White House counsel Alberto Gonzales and Rumsfeld's chief lawyer, Jim Haynes. It had simply explored "the limits of the legal landscape," had never made it into the hands of soldiers in the field, and did not "reflect the policies that the administration ultimately adopted," said Gonzales.[41] Gonzales would be rewarded for his loyalty, becoming Bush's second attorney general, in January 2005.

Circulating ring binders filled with legal documents, Haynes sought to blame everything that went wrong at Guantánamo on former commander General Michael Dunlavey, later describing him as "an aggressive major general."[42] Washington had merely reacted to a request from below to interrogate "key people" at Guantánamo, including "a guy named al-Qahtani," Haynes said. Legal justification for al-Qahtani's interrogation had come not from the Justice Department but Lieutenant Colonel Diane Beaver, Dunlavey's judge advocate. From there, enhanced interrogation had spread to Abu Ghraib.

On June 24, 2004, the US Supreme Court ruled that Guantánamo detainees could challenge the legality of their detention though civil actions in US courts.[43] Although no high-value detainees were presently at Guantánamo, as they had been evacuated to Morocco, the widely held belief was that one day they would end up there, and the prospect of them speaking was too much for the CIA general counsel, Scott Muller. Several times he had warned senior cheerleaders for enhanced interrogation, including David Addington, that the CIA program appeared to conflict with the president's February 2002 memo entitled "Humane Treatment of al Qaeda and Taliban Detainees."[44] Muller had been told not to worry, but now he resigned, putting Rizzo back in the hot seat.[45] Days later, the Justice Department withdrew legal approval for the CIA program.

With ninety-two tapes still out in Thailand, and copies possibly in the United States too, Jose Rodriguez and several others were completely exposed. In his book with Bill Harlow, Rodriguez directed his fury at Yoo's successors. "The Department of Justice started to moonwalk away from us on the authorities they had previously provided regarding interrogation," he wrote.[46] Mitchell and Harlow's book contained similarly expressed concerns: "The Department of Justice showed signs of moonwalking away from some of its previous pronouncements about the program's legality."[47] Tenet also talked of "moonwalking," although he had just done so himself.[48] Rizzo also described it as "moonwalking" but he stayed to resolve the "festering situation."[49] Rodriguez did not appear in a group photograph of Tenet and his senior management team, taken on one of his last days in office, although John Rizzo, Jim Pavitt, and Bill Harlow were in the picture. In his book with Harlow, Tenet thanked Pavitt and acknowledged Harlow's central role. "Bill and I journeyed through the storm's center for seven years," he wrote. "He was by my side through the most difficult and trying times." Rodriguez was not even mentioned in Tenet's long list of acknowledgments. Neither was Rizzo.

On his very last day at Langley, Tenet sat at his desk contemplating a charred American flag on his wall that had been pulled from the rubble of the World Trade Center shortly after 9/11.[50] As the sun went down, he lit a cigar gifted by his friend King Abdullah of Jordan and walked alone around the deserted CIA compound (it was a Sunday). He was the second-longest serving CIA director in history, proud of what he had achieved. "Would I make that long journey again?" he asked himself. "Absolutely—in a heartbeat."[51]

——————◆——————

After awarding Tenet the Medal of Freedom, President Bush needed a trustworthy successor to steer the CIA through its rockiest period since the Latin American torture scandal and get him through the November election. An interrogation program that sat at the very center of War on Terror strategy had just been halted by the withdrawal of legal approval, and for the next two months, Tenet's deputy, John McLaughlin, occupied the lonely CIA director's chair while Bush's team approached potential candidates. Helping out was family friend Porter Goss, who had chaired the House Intelligence Committee. The leading Republican member of the Gang of Eight (congressmen and -women who received CIA briefings on classified intelligence matters), Goss had served as a clandestine officer himself in Latin America and Europe, and he lambasted the "finger pointers," who had accused Tenet and the CIA of sleepwalking into 9/11.[52]

Goss later claimed he had tried to quit politics for health reasons shortly after 9/11 but said Bush's team stopped him. "Cheney called me in, closed the door, and said 'I'm not opening it until you agree to stay,'" he recalled.[53] Cheney told him: "You're the only guy we got on the Hill." When Tenet called Goss to tell him was leaving the CIA in June 2004, Goss was even more reluctant to get involved. "All kinds of mischief was going on," he said. "The Hill was divided. Bush was cast as a warmonger. Dick Cheney was the devil incarnate. My ulcer was acting up. I had enough of this place, and I could hardly wait to get out." He wanted to get back to his island paradise, Sanibel, Florida, and put on his swim shorts. "I came up with some names and gave them to the White House. They came back at one point and said, 'Do you have any interest?' I said, 'No, I'm out of here.'" In late August 2004, Goss finally got off on vacation and was standing in his swim shorts in the kitchen when the phone rang. It was Andy Card, Bush's chief of staff. "He said, 'The president wants to have dinner with you tonight.'" Goss had a sinking feeling as he returned to Washington.

The White House looked deserted when he arrived at seven P.M. "The gate guard said, 'No, there's nobody here.'"[54] After persuading the guard to open up, Goss located Andy Card. They wandered around, trying every door and finding most locked. Goss did not want the job. "I was aware at that point that three or four much better candidates than myself had rejected it, so I knew there was a problem," he recalled. "And there was an election coming up." When they eventually took an elevator up to the residence and found Bush, they sat down to dinner, and the president got to the point. "He said, 'Hey, I really need somebody out there at least for the next couple of months.'" Goss replied: "Mr. President, if you want me, I will take it, but don't you have a better choice?" Bush did not. Goss was nonplussed. "Did I ever want to be director of CIA? No. Would I want to be CIA director today? No." Over dessert, Goss reluctantly agreed. "I said, 'OK,' and I got out there, and it was not a happy place." But he was a determined supporter of the EIT program. "Nobody gets to kill an American and get away with it."

Goss recalled opening his initial discussions about enhanced interrogation with, "Have you had any problems?" The answers went: "Yes, well, we have. Some techniques we taught were inappropriate. Some didn't seem to work. Some we changed. There's some location problems. Some of this and that. But by and large it's worked."[55] Regarding the fate of forever detainees who could never be prosecuted, he reflected: "I can't tell you if Abu Zubaydah deserves any justice or not, but what I can tell you is that he's become caught up in the complexity of the system. But that's because of his own choices. He is not an innocent man. But we don't let these people go because of justice; they have blood on their hands, they have killed Americans." A convivial, polished operator, Goss had no interest in re-prosecuting the CIA's "evidence." However, as he settled in at Langley, he discovered that the program had already restarted.

On July 22, acting CIA director McLaughlin had made the first of a series of requests to the attorney general for approval of the use of enhanced techniques on specific new high-value detainees. John Ashcroft signed the first letter, and Dan Levin, acting assistant attorney general, signed the rest.[56] Levin had previously been chief of staff to FBI director Robert Mueller and, in the spring and summer of 2002, had been a party to the original approval process for Abu Zubaydah.[57] On August 2, 2004, when Rizzo asked Levin for permission to reintroduce the waterboard, Levin insisted on first experiencing it himself. Rizzo called Jonathan Fredman, who insisted that a lawyer from the Counterterrorist Center (CTC) come along too.[58]

Mitchell did the waterboarding in the basement of an abandoned military base near Langley used for training CIA interrogators, with a "senior CTC officer" standing in for Jessen, who was not available. "Are you sure you want to do this?" Mitchell recalled asking the CTC lawyer, who went first. "It's an ugly experience."[59] She nodded but commented "that sucked" when it was over and she was drying her hair. No record was kept of whether the waterboarding application was SERE-style or "AZ"-style. When it was Levin's turn, Mitchell did not feel so "creeped out." After all, the Justice Department had moonwalked away from the program just a few weeks earlier. Levin "took it well. He was stoic." Mitchell could not remember the assistant attorney general's exact words but they were something like: "It was terrifying. I felt like I was going to drown." But in Levin's opinion, the threat of imminent death was legal.

Soon after, Levin was asked to produce a new, overarching opinion to support a program with the ultimate goal to "create a state of learned helplessness" in high-value detainees.[60] Levin signed it on December 30, 2004, after adding an ameliorating opening statement that began, "torture is abhorrent both to American law and values and to international norms." His wording was similar to that inserted into the upgraded KUBARK manual that Charlie Wise had used in Honduras. Waterboarding was also now redefined as "water dousing." The CIA program was back on track, and so was Jose Rodriguez, who had been promoted to head of the National Clandestine Service. Gina Haspel, Rodriguez's chief of staff, went with him to the seventh-floor executive suite. Now that he was among what he described as "the big boys," Rodriguez intended to outsource the entire interrogation program and fix the "tape albatross."[61] His new boss, Porter Goss reflected: "There's only two words you need for your coverage in Washington: ego and hypocrisy. Nothing else matters."[62]

The situation turned critical in November 2005, when Mike Winograd, the Bangkok station chief, announced he was leaving his post.[63] It was Rodriguez's last chance to act before someone not connected to the Abu Zubaydah videotapes inherited the codes to the safe. Rodriguez did not want those tapes brought back to the United States. They needed to be destroyed in situ. Rizzo was also growing increasingly worried about efforts by Senator Carl Levin, chairman of the Senate Armed Services Committee, to establish an independent 9/11 Commission–style inquiry into the CIA's mistreatment of War on Terror detainees. "I think I need to be the skunk at the party again and see if the Director is willing to let us try one more time to get the right people downtown on board with the notion of our destroying the tapes," Rizzo wrote.[64] When Goss said no, Rodriguez went solo and ordered Haspel to ask the Counterterrorist Center's legal department two simple questions: Was destruction of the tapes legal? Did Rodriguez as head of the National Clandestine Service have the authority to make the decision?[65] Rodriguez claimed the lawyers, Robert Eatinger and Steven Hermes, said yes to both.[66] They worked for Jonathan Fredman, who had been instrumental in obtaining legal cover for Abu Zubaydah's enhanced interrogation and whose face was probably on the tapes.

Working fast, Rodriguez cited a "memorandum for the record" from February 2003 that suggested when the CIA had briefed the Senate Select

Committee on Intelligence about the tapes, the vice chairman, Senator Pat Roberts, had not objected to the CIA's intention to destroy them.[67] Rodriguez then contacted the CIA inspector general who said his inquiries into abuse allegations were complete so he did not have any further use for the tapes.[68] Next, Rodriguez ordered Winograd, who had almost been sacked for removing the tapes from the black site, to make an official request to destroy them, using language drafted by headquarters. "The instructions basically were: 'Ask us in this way and we will say yes,'" Rodriguez recalled. A draft was shared with Rizzo.[69] The following day, Winograd's official request duly arrived from Bangkok. "The language was just right, of course," recalled Rodriguez, who asked Haspel to prepare a cable granting permission. The last two tapes showed waterboarding sessions of al-Nashiri while Haspel had been base chief in Thailand, meaning she was also compromised. Rodriguez read Haspel's draft cable twice on November 8, 2005, and then pressed send. He did not inform Rizzo because he was just getting rid of some "ugly visuals that could put the lives of my people at risk."[70] Winograd used an industrial shredder, the kind that could "chew through hundreds of pounds of material in a single hour," Rodriguez recalled, with five spinning and two stationary steel blades that could chop up DVDs, CDs, cell phones, and credit cards. By the following morning, Abu Zubaydah's footage had been reduced to "confetti." The CIA's greatest "existential threat" was vacuumed into heavy-duty trash bags.[71] The "tapes albatross" was gone forever, or so Rodriguez thought.

The repercussions were wide-ranging. "I was beside myself," Rizzo said.[72] "I was told in the immediate aftermath when I was blowing a gasket, 'Oh, your lawyers signed off on this.'" He dug out the relevant cables and found no lawyers' names on them. "In my entire career at CIA, I know because I've been on thousands of such cables myself, if a lawyer has approved of what you're doing, you make sure you get his name on the bottom of that cable, and their names were not on it." He recalled confronting Rodriguez: "I made clear, I thought, that you, Mr. Rodriguez, do not have the authority to destroy these tapes."[73] But it did not really matter what Rizzo said afterward because the tapes were gone.

No record of Haspel's discussion with Fredman's department was ever produced, and the heat fell on Porter Goss. "It was a very unpleasant moment," he recalled.[74] He was even more furious when news that the CIA had destroyed the waterboarding tapes leaked. "I made every senior member of the CIA take a polygraph, including me, and sure enough someone admitted doing it," he said, without revealing the guilty party. "I said, 'This is highly sensitive classified information that you are sworn to protect. You are fired.'"[75]

Mitchell claimed to be surprised but grateful. "No dithering, no effort to cover his own ass," he said of Rodriguez.[76] But Mitchell was seemingly now without a safety net. The Justice Department launched an independent inquiry into the tapes' destruction, led by federal prosecutor John Durham, and considered criminal charges against Rodriguez and Haspel, while the FBI questioned Mitchell.[77] "They asked me if I had any personal copies of the tapes," he recalled, referencing the accusation by Charlie Wise that he had either copied or stolen tapes in Thailand.[78] "Nicely done, I thought. That rascal was dead, and he was still making trouble for me."

CHAPTER 20

"THEY ARE LIARS, LIARS, LIARS!"

Mitchell's public shaming began in July 2005, a few days after he sat in the parking lot at Langley with the car windows rolled up, waiting for a call from the *New Yorker*.[1] He had always suspected this day would come, and the CIA had made sure contractors were first in line for the reckoning. As Mitchell listened to reporter Jane Mayer's probing questions, he suspected her primary source was Ali Soufan, who had recently retired from the FBI. "Soufan's involvement in a program that lasted seven years was only a few short weeks, but he made a career out of it," Mitchell gibed. "The FBI lost and never got over it."[2] Now that Soufan was heading into the private security sector, he wanted the world to know all about Mitchell and his crazy pseudo-science. Because of Mitchell's self-confessed tendency to "shoot my mouth off accidentally," the CIA insisted on having a senior official chaperone him through Mayer's questions, and he sat in the passenger seat.[3] "He authorized everything I said," Mitchell recalled.[4] Asked by Mayer if he conducted secret interrogations for the CIA, Mitchell glanced at his companion. "If that was true, I couldn't say anything about it," he replied, explaining that he was a private contractor and bound by a nondisclosure agreement. Had he "tried to reverse-engineer" SERE techniques to use on War on Terror detainees at Guantánamo? He was not willing to confirm or deny anything but did not "have anything to hide."[5] "Following the vagueness" was what Mitchell had called it whenever Abu Zubaydah had skirted around something he wanted to conceal.[6]

Mayer's article, headlined "The Experiment," got deep into tactics that read like a revenge tragedy: mock drowning, mock rape, Koran "trashing," fake menstrual blood, and detainees being driven mad by the sound of crying babies and Yoko Ono.[7] She cited Abu Ghraib and quoted a "senior counter-terrorism officer," who accused Mitchell of wanting to treat Al Qaeda suspects "like the dogs in a classic behavioral-psychology experiment." Martin Seligman, who was still framing his association as nonexistent, was referenced but not quoted.[8] Mayer named Mohammed al-Qahtani as a victim of experimental interrogation practices at Guantánamo but did not identify Abu Zubaydah or Ali Soufan.

The article was full of damaging revelations, including a vivid description of the first press tour of Guantánamo on July 6, 2005. Opening up the detention camp to the media was a high-risk strategy, and the journalists, Mayer included, had been carefully corralled—though one snafu ("situation normal all fucked up") would occur. A beaming Colonel Mike Bumgarner, commander of the guard force, told the visiting journalists: "I'd be proud to let the media see anything in this camp." Detainees got honey-glazed chicken and lemon-baked fish. "It's like a big family." He did not mention that he had his staff salute him serenaded by the reggae song "Bad Boys" ("What you gonna do when they come for you?") or that he called the naval station "ground zero" or that he believed "there is not a trustworthy son of a bitch in the entire bunch" of detainees.[9]

The media toured Camp Five, a facility for compliant detainees. Strawberry Fields, the black site built by Special Missions chief Gus, had been renamed Echo II and was used for "noncompliants," so it was off-limits, as was Penny Lane, a second black site Gus had built in a grassy dip hidden from view.[10] The CIA had designed it for detainees who had been "rolled up by mistake," Gus explained.[11] "We were going to train them to come into the US, and we were going to set them up in certain locations where there was a big Muslim community to feed back to us what some of their guys were doing." It never happened. "I think they are still in Gitmo." By the time the media arrived, Penny Lane was better known as "Camp No" because if anyone asked, "No, it didn't exist." Instead of housing innocent detainees, some of Guantánamo's most troublesome characters were held there—like British Saudi Shaker Aamer—and subjected to extra-forceful interrogations.[12] Many were on hunger strike and every day they were strapped to a force-feeding chair that resembled a medieval torture device. Shortly after the media departed, three detainees died on the same night at Camp No, and their deaths were covered up.[13]

During the tour, a few setups could be photographed, such as "a tour cell," American flags, McDonald's, and General Miller's slogan, "Honor Bound—Defend Freedom."[14] However, when the journalists passed a caged rec yard, the snafu occurred. A detainee wearing the orange uniform of a "noncompliant" yelled out, "They are liars," and military escorts rushed everyone along. The detainee grabbed his chance. "No sleep!" he yelled. "No food! No medicine! No doctor! Everybody sick here! They are liars, liars, liars!" One military escort quipped, "His English is pretty good." Bumgarner tried to get the tour back on track by talking about the Manchester manual. "They are trained to make false accusations," he said. "It's part of their P.R."[15]

The "Gitmo" tour did nothing to dampen public interest in government-sponsored torture, as the international media exposed ever more shocking details about enhanced interrogation, detainee abuse, and deaths.[16] Mitchell later complained that his program was "gutted," and he chiefly blamed Inspector General Helgerson and "that asshole" Ali Soufan.[17] When the *Washington Post* published an editorial entitled "Central Torture Agency?" Langley did its best to put Mitchell and Jessen in the frame.[18] "You know what the agency's response was to my being outed by Jane Mayer?" he griped. "'So what? Everyone gets outed.'"[19]

The CIA had more serious problems with which to contend. One overview reported that "Problems on the Hill" had escalated since Abu Ghraib and the inspector general's report.[20] Senators took to the floor of Congress to demand the CIA stay "within the bounds of our laws," and politicians on both sides of the House demanded the right to inspect black sites. After several powerful Republican senators, foremost among them John McCain, supported efforts to introduce legislation to limit the Bush administration's continued ability to sidestep the Geneva Conventions, the CIA suspended enhanced techniques for a second time. The program appeared to be running into a brick wall, and a conscious decision was made at Langley to create more deniability of official responsibility for mistakes. Gus described it as outsourcing "all the cats and dogs," from interrogators to psychologists, from building contractors to black site architects and guards. Mitchell and Jessen were interested, as long as the price was right.

As a CIA contractor, Mitchell had earned $1,459,601.43. Jessen had earned $1,204,550.42.[21] They already had a company, Mitchell, Jessen and Associates (MJA), formed in Delaware in September 2004.[22] MJA went operational in early 2005. Gus drew up the paperwork to bring them in, with input from Jose Rodriguez and Gina Haspel. "The office of admin said, 'You can't just do this, you got to put this out to bid."[23] Gus sought a solution. "I just happened to run into Gina in the hall and told her, and she went through the roof, and she told Jose, who said, 'Hell no, we are not going out to bid; we are going to hire these guys.'"

Mitchell, Jessen and Associates opened offices in downtown Spokane in March 2005 and was doing business with Langley by the summer.[24] Besides Mitchell and Jessen, there were five other owners, including Joseph Matarazzo and Roger Aldrich.[25] A staunch Mitchell loyalist, after being rewarded with a share in MJA, Matarazzo was habitually accused of helping run the CIA program. Mitchell later tried to soften the blow, saying Matarazzo had known nothing and done nothing to support it. "I regret any misery and grief that merely knowing me has brought him," he wrote in his book, even though Matarazzo owned shares in two of Mitchell's companies, the other being Knowledge Works, which started out facilitating "continuing education" programs for psychologists on temporary duty-yonder contracts and later became a vehicle for MJA's training programs, according to Mitchell.[26]

Aldrich, Mitchell and Jessen's mentor and former boss, was happy to talk business. He had resigned as dean of the JPRA academy in February 2004 after learning that Chris Wirts had sent three of his staff, Steven Kleinman, Terry Russell, and Lenny Miller, to Iraq without his knowledge. "I decided it was time to put my papers in and move on down the road," he said.[27] "Jim rang me and said, 'Rog, Bruce and I are forming a company, and we'd like you to be our director of training.'" The CIA was offering a two-year contract, with three one-year options to extend.[28] Mitchell owned 26 percent, and Jessen had 25 percent, according to Aldrich, who took a share of the remaining 49 percent. The full five-year contract was worth in excess of $180 million, and the new business partners set about hiring and training interrogators, psychologists, and guards.[29]

With the company based in Spokane, finding the right kind of people was easy, said Aldrich, who immediately brought over "six or seven" people from the JPRA academy, but not Kleinman. Denny Keller, a white-bearded SERE survival instructor who worked for MJA as an interrogator until 2007, said, "[It] was fun. I was on the road 270 days a year."[30] Dozens of SERE trainers Mitchell had once lambasted as "lunks" expressed an interest, except Bob Dussault, who was not invited to the party.[31] Chris Wirts was also left out. "We were wholly, 100 percent in support of the agency," recalled Aldrich, handling everything from training interrogators to supplying guards for black sites.

According to Mitchell's *bête noire* Charles Morgan, who also was not invited to join MJA, Mitchell and Jessen recruited psychologists through the American Psychological Association. At the 2005 annual conference in Hawaii, Morgan recalled being heckled by protestors dressed as Abu Ghraib detainees, standing on boxes wearing black hoods, with fake electrocution wires attached to their fingers. When he got past them, he spotted Mitchell and Jessen sitting inside a recruitment booth that listed clients, including the CIA.[32] It was like a psychologist's version of Blackwater, the private security company founded by Erik Prince, surrogate son to the CIA's former executive director Buzzy Krongard.[33]

Many of those MJA employed simply resigned from the CIA and went back in on larger contracts, with Mitchell recalling, "We had to pay our senior security guys the same as Blackwater—$250 an hour, or $2000 a day—that was common, they were in a combat zone, all jocked up."[34] Kirk Hubbard became "contracts manager," liaising with his agency successor. Charles Morgan recalled him leaving: "He said there had been a death in the family."[35] In June 2005, Hubbard wrote to CIA colleagues, saying he had moved to Montana and was happily sitting in the fresh air on his porch doing some consulting work for MJA.[36] Others who switched over included CIA analyst turned interrogator Deuce Martinez, Mitchell's "tough girl" interrogator Sharon, psychologist Judy Philipson, and former Salt Pit warden Matthew Zirbel.[37] Gus, who retired from the CIA in July 2005, said he was "reemployed by Jose as a contractor for special projects."[38] Mitchell later said the mystery interrogator he called "the Preacher" continued to work in the program until it closed in 2009, suggesting that the Preacher was also employed by MJA.[39] To keep everyone happy, the company organized day trips, including one to Lake Coeur d'Alene, Idaho. A group shot taken aboard a cruiser showed a sea of smiling faces: guards, black site building contractors, interrogators, debriefers, interviewers, and psychologists. The Idaho farm boy and the "little shit" from Tennessee had come a long way through flirting with notoriety.

On April 8, 2006, Porter Goss finally briefed President Bush about the special program and told him that detainees had died.[40] He did not mention waterboarding, as it had been discontinued, but regardless, Bush expressed discomfort with the "image of a detainee, chained to the ceiling, clothed in a diaper, and forced to go to the bathroom on himself."[41] Four days later, Mitchell's contractor performance report listed his recent ratings as "exceptional" and noted that he had been awarded the Agency Seal Medallion for running a program that "had produced what is universally considered within the US government to be some of the most important intelligence ever gained regarding the War on Terrorism."[42] Another medal was awarded by the Office of Technical Service and showed a wizard in a pointed hat.

———•———

Goggles, duct tape, foamies, earmuffs, handcuffs, shackles, chains, a cavity search, and a diaper: Abu Zubaydah was on the move again. In February 2005, after eleven months at Temara, Morocco, he was rendered to a new black site in Lithuania. Earlier, President Bush had secured the country's support by pledging to back its efforts to join NATO.[43] Romania (where Khalid Sheikh Mohammad was still being held) and Lithuania both joined NATO in March 2004. Thailand was also rewarded for its quiet and timely assistance. During a visit to Bangkok in October 2003, President Bush thanked General Tritot personally, calling him "my hero."[44] As well as facilitating the first CIA black site, Tritot had also led a highly secretive "sabotage operation" to weaken Iraq shortly before the United States went to war in March 2003. During Saddam Hussein's time, every Iraqi embassy communicated with Baghdad via a special "enigma machine," explained Tritot. It scrambled messages that only those with the appropriate codes could read. Inventing another good story, Tritot had temporarily closed down the Iraqi embassy in Bangkok and searched it, despite historic rules and conventions forbidding this type of action. While inside, he'd stolen the "enigma" codes, which enabled Washington to eavesdrop on Saddam's secret communications and his proposed battle formations. Thailand became a major non-NATO ally in 2003, and General Tritot received a signed photograph of himself with the US president.[45]

In Lithuania, the CIA had purchased an equestrian center surrounded by thick forest in Antaviliai, a well-to-do hamlet fifteen miles outside Vilnius. "The facilities must be as small and as inconspicuous as possible," read

Gus's now standard spec.[46] "Special security measures" (such as man cages) should be used to make up for "architectural shortcomings." After screening off a large paddock area behind the stable block, Gus's contractors excavated "large amounts of earth" before erecting a large metal warehouse with multiple air vents but no windows.[47] Inside, prefabricated interrogation pods were submerged into a concrete base. There was "white noise in the walkways," and each cell was illuminated 24/7 with two seventeen-watt T8 fluorescent tube light bulbs. Detainees were sheared for the purpose of "removing hair in which a detainee might hide small items that might be used against his interrogators." Contractors and staff were housed in the stable block, which was linked to the interrogation center via a sally port. Detainees, who included Abu Zubaydah and later Khalid Sheikh Mohammad and Mustafa al-Hawsawi, were reportedly delivered to the site in oblong transfer boxes that resembled coffins and were declared on immigration forms as "cargo."[48] Basic needs like food and medical treatment were overlooked, Abu Zubaydah recalled years later. "For one meal I was given only ketchup," he said. "For another, one piece of square bread."[49]

John Rizzo, who inspected two black sites in 2005, recalled arriving in an "unmarked, unremarkable van" that whisked him "an underground garage through an entrance tucked into the back of the building."[50] Once inside, "our waiting escorts took us through a number of locked security-coded doors and down some twisting hallways to the command center." Because there were no windows, it was "hard to tell if we were now above ground level or still underground." The atmosphere was "claustrophobic." On a bank of TV monitors in the command center, Rizzo saw Abu Zubaydah, Khalid Sheikh Mohammad, and others sleeping, eating, or praying. When he was escorted into the cell block itself—"through another set of hallways and through more locked doors"—the bright lights and deafening music hit him. This was life, 24/7, for the CIA's forever prisoners.

Rizzo felt no sympathy, but one day, Bruce Jessen turned up alone in Abu Zubaydah's Lithuanian cell and launched into an extraordinary speech. "I am truly very sorry for what I did because after we captured those responsible for 9/11, we discovered that we did all of these things to you, the wrong person," Abu Zubaydah recalled him saying.[51] Blaming the CIA for this misinformation, Jessen continued: "Our hands were never tied, as the most important thing was to get information from you in any way." Astounded by this out-of-the-blue mea culpa, Abu Zubaydah quizzed him. "On what basis did you believe I was Number Three in Al Qaeda?" Why were they so sure he knew about future terrorist operations? Jessen's reply stunned him. The CIA had read these things in "newspapers and books" and then heard the same from "Pakistani and Arab intelligence." Abu Zubaydah could barely believe what he was hearing. He had made jokes about foolish Arab intelligence agencies, and he had meowed like a cat, but he never actually thought the CIA would swallow unsubstantiated stories without verification. As for Pakistan, everyone knew the ISI would say anything to get paid. Surely the world's superpower had better intelligence-gathering and analytical capabilities than that?

"You, the CIA and FBI before you . . . do you really count on these sources?" Abu Zubaydah asked, incredulous. "They sometimes don't have any leads and so they follow the wrong leads," Jessen replied, adding that it wasn't his job to question sourcing. "Our job is extracting information—from you." Abu Zubaydah saw Jessen welling up. "He got up and left the room, returning only after he had washed his face." There would be no such speech from Mitchell, reported Aldrich, who knew because they had had a few spats. "Bruce will take a few days and will apologize, but Jim—I have never ever heard Jim apologize about anything."[52]

———◆———

Goggles, duct tape, foamies, earmuffs, handcuffs, shackles, chains, another cavity search, and a diaper: After months in Lithuania, during which time his body weight dropped forty pounds, Abu Zubaydah was on the move yet again. In November 2005, after the *Washington Post* reported that the CIA was holding detainees at black sites in eastern Europe, the Lithuanian government demanded the CIA close up Antaviliai.[53] The CIA clung on for another four months, but during that time, when Mustafa al-Hawsawi suffered a medical emergency, the Lithuanians refused CIA requests to treat him at a local hospital.[54] The furor over enhanced interrogation was growing, the CIA was running out of willing liaison partners, and several Western powers were incriminated in the program, including Britain, whose security services had asked Abu Zubaydah questions in the knowledge that he was being subjected to enhanced interrogation.[55] Now, Abu Zubaydah was rendered to Afghanistan, one of the only places left in the world where the CIA could still do whatever it wanted. The Salt Pit had been replaced by a new black site code-named Fernando.[56] Abu Zubaydah and other high-value detainees were fattened up with better food, as the CIA revived its "endgame" discussions, got together with the Departments of Justice and Defense about prosecutions, and put pressure on Defense Secretary Donald Rumsfeld, who was resisting demands to readmit the CIA's detainees to Guantánamo.[57]

By the summer of 2006, the entire outsourced enhanced interrogation program was under review. In addition to debating whether to prosecute via military commissions at Guantánamo or in federal courts inside the United States, senior administration lawyers worked on establishing immunity from prosecution for all those connected to the official program and made sure detainees had no legal recourse. Most meetings took place in assembly hall one of the Department of Justice Building, a room used for the trial of eight Nazi saboteurs in 1942, according to a plaque on the wall. "We envisaged swift justice just like we had achieved with the Nazi saboteurs who were captured in June 1942 and executed in August 1942," said Colonel Morris Davis, the government's chief prosecutor.[58] "Growing up, I had a reverential view of the Nuremberg war trials and wanted to get it right this time too." Davis "believed the narrative that the CIA's high-value detainees were all of one type: the worst of the worst. It wasn't until much later I found out they had been tortured, at which point I resigned and started calling for war crimes charges." When Mitchell and Jessen briefed the lawyers, Davis was surprised. "I was expecting Rambo and instead saw someone who looked like an aging uncle," he recalled of Mitchell. "I was struck by how ordinary they were."

However, war crimes charges against Americans were not part of the US government's agenda. Back in 2003, several CIA officers had told the CIA inspector general they were worried about prosecution. One expressed concerns that he and others would "wind up on some 'wanted list' to appear before the World Court for war crimes."[59] To make sure that could never happen, the Detainee Treatment Act signed by Bush on December 30, 2005, granted immunity to government agents and military personnel from civil and criminal action for using interrogation techniques that "were officially authorized and determined to be lawful at the time they were conducted." An amendment permitted the Pentagon lawyers to consider evidence obtained through torture and strengthened the prohibition of habeas corpus rights for detainees too. Soon after, the Military Commissions Act created a new legal defense against lawsuits for misconduct arising from the "detention and inter-rogation of aliens" between September 11, 2001, and December 30, 2005, and provided "legal protections that ensure our military and intelligence personnel will not have to fear lawsuits filed by terrorists simply for doing their jobs," according to the president.[60] All costs associated with any attempted civil action or criminal prosecution would be borne by the government.[61] The only hitch was that immunity was good only within the United States.[62]

"It was time to bring the CIA's detention program out of the shadows," said Jose Rodriguez.[63] It was also time to bring other responsible govern-ment agencies into the equation. On August 31, 2006 detainee-shy Donald Rumsfeld finally signed a memorandum authorizing the transfer of the four-teen high-value detainees to Guantánamo, although the CIA retained crucial handholds. "These individuals are unlawful enemy combatants (ECs) en-gaged in an armed conflict against the United States and under the laws of war, may be detained until the cessation of hostilities," it read.[64] Only the president could determine when that war was over. Military commissions over which the Pentagon had total authority would process those who could be prosecuted. Colonel Davis, whose job was to build cases against them, stated: "The CIA controlled the process."

President Bush announced the transfer on September 6, 2006, surrounded by those who had lost loved ones on 9/11, suggesting justice was being sought for the families, although the government's real focus was self-preservation. Bush described Abu Zubaydah as "a senior terrorist leader and a trusted as-sociate of Osama bin Laden," even though the CIA had produced an intel-ligence assessment just weeks earlier stating that Abu Zubaydah "had been rejected by Al Qaeda" and acknowledging that the CIA had "miscast Abu Zubaydah as a 'senior Al Qaeda lieutenant.'"[65] President Bush's Abu Zubay-dah was "defiant and evasive," had stopped talking, and "had received train-ing on how to resist interrogation," necessitating an "alternative set of procedures," which had been "designed to be safe, to comply with our laws, our Constitution and our treaty obligations." The president did not mention the four high-value detainees who were being repatriated to their own coun-tries because they had produced nothing. The CIA called this process "return[ing] the empties."[66]

ABC News described those heading for Cuba as "the veritable 'crown jewels.'"[67] In Riyadh, this news was the first confirmation Malika and Muhammad Abu Zubaydah had that their errant son "Hani" was alive. Hesham, still living in Portland because US immigration had been unable to deport a stateless Palestinian without a country, kept his head down, as Bush declared: "I want to be absolutely clear with our people and the world: The United States does not torture. It's against our laws and it's against our values. I have not authorized it, and I will not authorize it." Since the president had never attended any meetings to discuss Abu Zubaydah's enhanced interrogation and the official program was all but over, technically he was telling the truth.

————◆————

The fourteen high-value detainees were already in Cuba, having landed at Leeward Point airfield the day before Bush's press conference. "You have arrived to Naval Station Guantánamo Bay," announced the Camp 7 commander, as MJA contractors carried the detainees down the ramp while the C-17's engines were still running.[68] "You are under the custody of the Department of Defense," he declared, even though their new home was built by the CIA and was a CIA endgame facility, and the CIA retained "operational control."[69] Mitchell had "prepared the detainees for the journey" and "was probably" on the plane with them.[70]

Everyone was role-playing. The commander addressing them was not a soldier but a corrections officer employed by MJA and dressed up in a generic military uniform.[71] "Our detention operations are consistent with Geneva Convention Common Article 3," he told the detainees, the US Supreme Court having ruled three months earlier in a landmark case, *Hamdan v. Rumsfeld*, that Guantánamo detainees had to be afforded these protections. Nevertheless, several months would pass before the ICRC was allowed to meet the new arrivals, and it was even longer before they could consult a lawyer or send a message home. After the ferry crossing to the windward side, Abu Zubaydah and the others were placed in man-size dog cages inside windowless paddy wagons, which took off along Sherman Avenue and then up into the hills behind the Navy Lodge. Joint Task Force Guantánamo code for high-value detainee movement was "delivering a pizza."[72]

Camp Seven lay beyond a yellow gate with a sign warning "no photography." It was surrounded by munitions bunkers disguised as hillocks, near Camp No (where three detainees had died), and policed by contractors also dressed as soldiers, with fake name patches but no rank.[73] Some were "just back from Afghanistan." Others were former police or corrections officers. Their official title was Task Force Platinum. Mitchell and Jessen made several visits to "provide guidance to Agency debriefers on the handling of the [high-value detainees] we had transferred there." Although it "was a DoD base, the actually [*sic*] facility was CIA, funded by CIA dollars," many of which were earned by MJA.[74]

FBI special agent Fred Humphries, who had extracted condemning evidence about Abu Zubaydah from the millennium-plot bomber Ahmed Ressam, was waiting to "in-process" the detainees. "[AZ] came walking in; he had the whole garb on," Humphries recalled.[75] "There was a step off the truck into the area where we were doing the DNA and fingerprinting." The detainees were still hooded. "Most others came out wobbling, hesitant, even KSM." But not Abu Zubaydah. "He literally walked out of the back of the van not knowing where he was walking to. He could have been walking to a ten-foot bridge. It was amazing." When Abu Zubaydah's hood was removed, Humphries was surprised by how good he looked. "He had an impeccable mustache." The FBI agent had alopecia. "Of course, he only had one eye and one testicle," he added, as if engaging in a sartorial face-off.

"In-processing" included stripping, shaving, cavity searches, retinal scans, weighing, and photographing the detainees naked. To ensure they saw only Americans, they were processed one by one, and it took all night, recalled the Camp Seven commander.[76] They were showered and given medical and psychological checkups, an orange uniform, a Koran, prayer beads, "two types of shoe," and an internment security number (ISN). The weakest detainee, Mustafa al-Hawsawi (10011), was in-processed first, while the toughest, Khalid Sheikh Mohammad, was left until last, becoming "10024." Abu Zubaydah was somewhere in the middle, and would henceforth be addressed as "10016." Listless, self-absorbed, sex-obsessed Hani 1, who he now called "Hani the free," only existed in volume one of his old diary, which he had not seen since the night he was captured.

Task Force Platinum had spent a month in rehearsal and had strict instructions: no talking beyond "transactional" necessities; no names, only ISNs; no communication or visual sighting between detainees; no eyeglasses or books, except the Koran; no paper or pens; no socks; hoods and shackles (to a tightness of two fingers) whenever moving about; and no lawyers until they confessed to their crimes.[77] The rules were set by the CIA, approved by the Pentagon, and enforced by the Joint Task Force commander, Rear Admiral Harry Harris, who supervised the Naval Station and who four months earlier had pronounced the suspicious deaths at Camp No to have been a triple suicide, and "an act of asymmetrical warfare." The men had been found hanging, with rags stuffed down their throats, which some called "dry-boarding," and hinted at a connection to Mitchell.[78] To make sure any US mistreatment was covered up, the bodies were repatriated with their throat organs carved out.[79]

Guantánamo was shaping up as a grim hospice where high-value detainees would die before they were tried. They were re-hooded, re-shackled, and split between two blocks (or tiers), Alpha and Bravo. Each prefabricated cell had the same familiar features: an inner mesh door with a "bin hole" for safe shackling and food delivery, a bench-like bed, a metal toilet, a shower, and a solid outer door with an observation window. The detainees would live in total isolation, under bright lights, while white noise played in the walkways. "Big fans" blasted the cells with freezing cold air and black site-like noise.[80] Although the commander described the rec yard as "state-of-the art," exercise machines were basic and access was limited to "compliant" detainees. To prevent any communication, at least one cell remained vacant between each detainee and the next. To avoid more "suicides" and provide evidence in case of untimely death, there was 24/7 in-cell CCTV and a "visual search" of each cell every ten minutes. All aspects of detainee activity—from "meal refusals" to "acts of non-compliance," every cough and splutter, stool movement, involuntary medicalization, "forced cell extraction," sob, scream, or "threat of self harm"—were logged in the computerized Detainee Information Management System. But the guards were not always vigilant, and former Baltimore student Majid Khan, Abu Zubaydah's nearest neighbor, had to holler for help whenever he heard him thump on the floor in the grips of another seizure.[81] Abu Zubaydah usually awoke to find vomit-splattered military boots around his head and a nurse holding a rag soaked in ammonia against his nostrils.[82]

Four days after arriving at Camp 7, Abu Zubaydah could barely believe it when the guards gave him a notebook and prison pen. Immediately he restarted his diary, writing: "I rushed to write to you." Now aged thirty-five, he addressed himself as "Hani 3," and described himself as just having entered the second circle of hell, the "injustice circle" in which America, having kept him for "four years, five months and a whole week," in the first circle of hell ("integration and torturing"), now intended to keep him incommunicado for the rest of his life, breaking all its false claims of "defending human rights, justice and democracy."[83]

However, it would be done in keeping with the "laws of war" setup, so Abu Zubaydah was allowed to speak to the International Committee of the Red Cross shortly after Ramadan in late October 2006.[84] He was brought out in a paddy wagon to Echo II, which had previously functioned as Strawberry Fields. He was not forewarned or told whom he was meeting. The Camp Seven commander and a military prosecutor came too. But, for the first time in more than four years, he was allowed to talk to a human being outside the CIA program, and he did not hold back. He described how he had been "slammed directly against a hard concrete wall" and "suffocated with water." The ICRC reported: "Mr Abu Zubaydah also believed that his interrogation was a form of experimentation."[85] Mitchell and Jessen had told him he was the first, as he recalled, so "no rules applied." Usually, there had been three interrogators, Mitchell and Jessen, who beat him and asked questions, and a third who only ever asked questions: the Hispanic man, who wore a saint's medal and called himself Alexander or Iskander.

After all fourteen high-value detainees described their mistreatment, John Rizzo received an alarming ICRC report.[86] The CIA had committed "torture." Twelve detainees had been subjected to "systematic physical and/ or psychological ill treatment" that induced "severe physical and mental pain and suffering" and resulted in "depersonalization and dehumanization." Even health personnel had participated in "suffocation by water," which the ICRC regarded as a "gross breach of medical ethics." The US government needed to establish a review process that allowed detainees to challenge their "continued internment." Rizzo's "pesky little international obligations" had finally caught up with the Bush administration, although Donald Rumsfeld had previously done his best to undermine detainee stories, saying they were "trained to lie, they're trained to say they were tortured, and the minute we release them or the minute they get a lawyer, very frequently they'll go out and they will announce they've been tortured."[87] Since Pentagon lawyers had already warned that anything the detainees had said to the CIA would be inadmissible in a military commission, if anyone was going to be charged, all fourteen needed to be re-interrogated by another government agency as quickly as possible.[88]

Colonel Davis, the chief prosecutor, knew he had a problem. "On my first day in office, September 2005, my deputy laid it out over the course of an hour: some of these folks had been tortured."[89] Once again, the FBI was asked to assist, and less than a month after the last ICRC interview was conducted in December 2006, each detainee was brought back down to Echo II without explanation or warning. The Camp Seven commander watched the interviewing of the detainees and later said Colonel Robert Swann, a US military prosecutor, was also there, "reading a book most of the time."[90] Colonel Davis said he, Swann, and other government attorneys sat in another room and watched on CCTV with the sound turned off.[91] "We didn't want to be disqualified as witnesses," he recalled, "but others watched and listened." Davis said before getting started, they asked the detainees what they most wanted to eat, then sent staff out to the Navy Exchange for fresh eggs and to McDonald's for lattes, burgers, fries, and apple pies.

Each detainee was "debriefed" by an FBI "clean team" consisting of two or three special agents. As far as Davis knew, none had any prior association to the CIA program. However, it was inevitable that the FBI's most knowledgeable agents had brushed up against the CIA program, and clean-team members included Steve Gaudin, who had interrogated Abu Zubaydah in Thailand, and Mike Butsch, who had identified Ramzi bin al-Shibh on the asphalt at Karachi airport and accompanied him to the Salt Pit.[92]

Several detainees appeared reluctant to participate in Davis's new "voluntary interview" process, including bin al-Shibh, who was already complaining about noise, smells, temperature manipulation, and vibrations in his cell. Shortly before being brought out of Camp Seven to be questioned by Butsch and two other FBI agents, bin al-Shibh smashed a CCTV camera in his cell, was subjected to a "forced cell extraction," and was forcibly shaved and given antipsychotic sedatives.[93] He refused to come out of Camp Seven on the second day, though the FBI subsequently claimed to have received a note from him saying, "My tongue is sharp athough flawlessly [sic], and I'm not affected by anything." an unlikely occurrence given that he did not have access to a pen or paper.[94] Further compromising the process, the clean teams wrote up their interviews as a "letterhead memorandum on a CIA laptop" and were instructed to record any claims of CIA mistreatment separately.[95] A few days after his FBI debriefing, bin al-Shibh was given an "involuntary injection of psychotropic medications."[96] He and four others were charged with the 9/11 attacks a year later, in February 2008, sealing their fates.[97] Khallad bin Attash, who was among those charged, was "clean-teamed" by Steve Gaudin, who also took Abd al-Rahim al-Nashiri's statement before he was charged as mastermind of the USS *Cole* attack.[98] Robert McFadden, from the Naval Criminal Investigative Service, assisted Gaudin in both these interviews. A co-leader of the investigation into the USS *Cole*, McFadden later referred to al-Nashiri as "Abu Charles Manson" and described him as a "natural-born killer."[99]

----◆----

After Colonel Davis got what the US government needed to bring charges, the Department of Defense responded to the ICRC's demand that detainees be afforded a right to challenge their ongoing internment. But justice would be served Guantánamo style.[100] In March 2007, Abu Zubaydah, who was "clean-teamed" by the FBI on February 7, 2007, but was not charged with anything, attended an "enemy combatant" status review tribunal in an air-conditioned trailer parked on gravel adjacent to Camp Seven.[101] Inside the trailer, the tribunal president sat on a high-backed office chair flanked by two deputies and framed by a large American flag. Seven of the eight officials wore military uniforms. Abu Zubaydah sat on a white plastic chair in baggy prison scrubs, handcuffed, with his feet shackled to the floor. He was allowed a "language analyst" (the only civilian) and a "personal representative" (an air force colonel) but not a lawyer. There was exculpatory evidence, but under tribunal rules he was not allowed to see it, and it was never released.[102] The substance of the case against him—that relied heavily on coerced statements given by other Guantánamo detainees—would be considered in a classified session after he was delivered back to his isolation cell.[103]

The unclassified evidence consisted of eleven points, six related to accusations made by Ahmed Ressam. One further allegation came from an unidentified FBI source, three more relied upon Abu Zubaydah's pre-capture diary, and the government falsely claimed that his group had fired weapons during their capture in Faisalabad, strengthening the government's case that he was an "enemy belligerent."[104] In a transcript of the unclassified portion of this hearing, the CIA's claim about him being Number Three in Al Qaeda was gone (the sole source having redacted his statement back in July 2002). There was no suggestion that the US government still considered him to have been a senior lieutenant to Osama bin Laden or a 9/11 planner or privy to Al Qaeda's future attack plans. Just months earlier, a CIA intelligence assessment had noted that its previous belief that Khaldan was an Al Qaeda–affiliated camp had been misconceived.[105] Abu Zubaydah was also no longer held responsible for the Manchester manual, which in CIA training materials provided by Mitchell and Jessen in 2005 was now attributed to an "unknown author."[106]

During this tribunal and many years later, Abu Zubaydah's story never changed. He had met Ressam, the man whose testimony had condemned him, only twice in his life.[107] He had simply given Ressam shelter at the House of Martyrs on his way in and out of Khaldan in 1998 and 1999. Abu Zubaydah recalled being distracted at the time by his dispute with Osama bin Laden over Khaldan and said there was no discussion with Ressam about any plots or conspiracies. "I felt obligated to assist him especially if he cannot speak Urdu or English, and he is afraid the Pakistanis may trick him to steal his money and belongings," Abu Zubaydah later explained.[108] He did admit that while Ressam was at Khaldan, he had studied Ressam's passport (a standard procedure). He also admitted that when Ressam returned from Afghanistan, he asked if he could get more passports. He did not say they were for his Swedish wife and unborn child.

Years later, Abu Zubaydah reflected on the Ressam allegations: "After he trained (studied) a little bit in Khaldan, he left us and joined the Algerian group. He believed, up until he departed to Canada, that we and Al Qaeda are one, but that is not true."[109] After Ressam left, Abu Zubaydah "started to hear in news and read in the newspapers that this person was attempting a terrorist operation in Jordan! This weak loner—who is without a group—comes and attempts to fight the entire country of Jordan!!" He noted: "My name began to be linked with him as a funder or associate and with many untrue things, when all I did was receive him as a guest."[110] Mitchell later described Abu Zubaydah's pleas of innocence as his "lawyer's position."[111]

Ressam had many reasons to condemn Abu Zubaydah. A primary factor was self-preservation. Found guilty of plotting a terrorist attack against Los

Angeles International Airport in a trial during which France's chief counterterrorism-investigating magistrate, Jean-Louis Bruguiere, gave crucial testimony, Ressam was convicted in April 2001 and faced 130 years in jail.[112] Ressam was also convicted in absentia in France for conspiring to commit terrorist attacks there, winning Bruguiere plaudits at home too. Bruguiere also helped the Jordanian GID connect Ressam to the Jordanian millennium plot. King Abdullah, who Bruguiere briefed personally, thanked him and the Jordanian intelligence operatives who brought in the evidence that led to six convictions, including a death sentence in absentia for Abu Zubaydah in September 2000.[113]

"Ressam cooperated because he was trying to whittle away some time," explained Fred Humphries, who interrogated him almost daily from May to December 2001, while sentencing was held up.[114] All Ressam's allegations about Abu Zubaydah were made during this period. Later, it was alleged that Ressam had been offered "inducements or promises of favorable treatment," and was possibly "subjected to torture, coercion or coercive conditions of confinement."[115] However, Ressam stopped fabricating accusations against Abu Zubaydah in 2002, and in 2003 he recanted his prior testimony. Later, it was alleged Ressam "suffered from a mental illness or instability."[116] By then, the CIA had what it needed, since Abu Zubaydah had also "confessed." Ressam was eventually sentenced to twenty-two years in July 2005, still denying everything he had said about others. The US government complained his sentence was too lenient, and on October 24, 2012, after a third resentencing, Ressam was delivered to the twilight world of ADX Florence to serve out thirty-seven years. Later, Jose Rodriguez conceded that Ressam's "evidence" might have been inflated. "Maybe there's an exaggeration there, I don't know," he said.[117] "I wasn't there for Ressam, but the reason we were focusing on AZ was because of his participation in the millennium plotting, including this case." Mitchell never questioned Ressam's claims, as he and Humphries worked closely on Abu Zubaydah's alleged crimes.

What Abu Zubaydah heard at his 2007 Guantánamo tribunal was that aside from Ressam, the US government was reliant on an unidentified FBI source, who alleged that Abu Zubaydah had traveled to Saudi Arabia in 1996 to give Osama bin Laden $600,000 in cash. The tribunal also cited Abu Zubaydah's diary, in which analysts had highlighted careless and foolish comments expressing a desire to assist Osama bin Laden in waging war against America after 9/11.

In preparation for his 2007 tribunal, Abu Zubaydah requested documents to show that he had supported "defensive" not "offensive" jihad. His focus was Israel, not America.[118] The tribunal president (a US Air Force colonel) refused the documents on the basis that "the definition of an enemy combatant does not distinguish between offensive or defensive actions. Only the fact that the person was a part of the enemy force is relevant."[119] A prepared statement read by Abu Zubaydah's personal representative addressed multiple issues: his disagreements with Osama bin Laden; a flat-out rejection that he had authored the Manchester manual; his assertion that Khaldan was not an Al Qaeda camp; his denial of involvement in Ahmed Ressam's millennium plot and of Al Qaeda membership. None of the brothers in Faisalabad had had guns, Abu Zubaydah asserted. One had managed to grab a fruit knife but he was shot dead. He noted that his diary entries showed he was in Karachi and Peshawar when the unidentified FBI source claimed he had gone to Saudi Arabia with a suitcase full of dollars. Bin Laden was also not in Saudi Arabia in 1996, since the king had expelled him years before.

When the tribunal panel questioned Abu Zubaydah directly, he cut a pathetic figure. He apologized for stuttering and explained that seizures impaired his speech. Over the past eighteen days he had fainted daily, which he later blamed on the "big fan" making an incessant loud noise outside his cell, triggering memories of the hard times.[120] He chose to speak in English but frequently cross-referenced his speech with his "language analyst"; it was clear from an audio recording of the tribunal that his English-language skills would have been wholly insufficient to take on the superlative verbal trickster Mitchell, who falsely claimed Abu Zubaydah spoke "excellent English."[121] Abu Zubaydah's voice was unrecognizable as that of the confident young ideologue on the old Afghan videotape. Struggling to take off his left shoe to show that he wore a cotton prayer cap on his foot because it was permanently cold and socks were banned, he said: "This leg, it is nothing, nearly die now."

When the tribunal president suggested Abu Zubaydah had worked for Al Qaeda after 9/11, volunteering as a soldier, raising money, and providing fake passports to forces fighting Americans, he denied it, even though there was some reference to sourcing weapons in his old diary.[122] He was simply helping the families of *mujahideen* who had got caught up in the race to escape Afghanistan, he replied. "I am not here to lie to you, or cheat you, or lie to myself," he said. "I not try to . . . escape from something I do or done." So much of the case against him was based on misunderstanding, he said, as he again tried to tell his version of the Ahmed Ressam story. "He thinks I am big relations and controls all camps." This was not true. Khaldan was like a "supermarket." Brothers shopped for what they needed and went on their way. Yes, he had asked Ressam to send him Canadian passports but for his own personal use, as he was desperate to get out of Pakistan, not for attacks against America. "Myself, I want to marry but what will happen to my child or even my wife if she wants to travel to her country?" he explained, alluding to his Swedish wife. "So I tell him please, I need this real passport, same what you have."

His first meeting with Osama bin Laden was not until August 2000, after Khaldan had been closed at bin Laden's insistence, he said. "Bin Laden come. He says enemy is America. We say . . . this is not allowed in Islam; same killing the civilians, killing the old mens or womens [*sic*]; not allowed to kill the woman's child. I never believed in killing civilians." He told bin Laden the same. "I told him, if it's only war—he wants to make only war . . . you not care about what is not allowed in Islam." No one outside bin Laden's tight inner circle had known 9/11 was coming, Abu Zubaydah explained. "The big groups they was angry from bin Laden, why you not tell us about this big operation?" Asked why he had made a video championing 9/11, he said everyone was compelled to rally around bin Laden after the United States declared war. "I was angry from bin Laden but it is not good, appropriate time. So everybody, we were ready. What you want us to do in Afghanistan, oh bin Laden?"

Regarding his CIA treatment, he was allowed to make a statement, but because talking about it brought on seizures, or vomiting, his personal representative read it. Afterward, the tribunal president addressed him directly, asking for more details. Large sections of an audio recording of his reply were redacted, but a written transcript was later reviewed and some of the redactions were removed. "They put one cloth in my mouth, and they put water, water, water. Last point before I die they stand [the gurney]. They make like this (breathing noises) again and again . . . and I tell him, 'if you

military custody. After learning about Mitchell and Jessen, Levin swung his attention to investigating connections between the military and CIA interrogation programs, and in May 2007, Mitchell was ordered to supply all "personal records" and MJA files to the committee. Mitchell called up Gina Haspel, who contacted Jonathan Fredman, who argued for national security privilege. Nevertheless, the committee won access to the documents, and Mitchell and Jessen were compelled to testify in classified hearings.[136] Mitchell was not worried, as he had retired from the military before becoming involved in enhanced interrogation. But Jessen, he said, was in a "slightly different position," because "he had worked on a few minor issues on the edges of the activities the SASC was investigating," like drawing up training materials and advising on detention setups.[137] Mitchell's only concession to there being any connection was that "military units seeking SERE-related interrogation techniques might have rubbed up against the CIA in passing."[138] Probably at the Ariana Hotel in Kabul.

No one employed in the CIA program was ever convicted. Jose Rodriguez had a brief brush with the law, after what began in 2008 as John Durham's inquiry into the CIA destruction of the tapes expanded into a full-blown "hot wash" of the entire program.[139] Not wanting to hang around, Rodriguez retired, handed his blue staff badge to a security guard, and walked out to his car. "I drove home to a very uncertain future," he recalled.[140] On November 9, 2010, the fifth anniversary of the tapes' destruction, the very last day that legal charges could be brought under the statute of limitations, he learned he was off the hook.[141] After he published his version of what happened, *Hard Measures*, coauthored by Bill Harlow, and "went on TV three or four times in one week," Rodriguez left Washington for good, buying the villa next door to Ric Prado in Saint Augustine, Florida.[142] He had no regrets about the waterboard. "Am I morally worried by it? No way. Not a problem," he asserted.[143]

In retirement, Rodriguez, Prado, and Cofer Black bought matching Corvettes. Prado and Rodriguez also had Harleys (Black's wife would not let him have one), and Rodriguez had a thirty-foot sea-fishing boat named *Shaken Not Stirred*. A large marlin he caught hung above his fireplace. Prado, who had "two puppies" in the military, continued to work as a CIA contractor for many years, often with his friend Erik Prince.[144] He sometimes rode over to Tampa to see Billy Waugh, who celebrated his eighty-eighth birthday by jumping out of a helicopter while strapped to a former Miss Tennessee who, he noted, had a "fifty-one-inch chest."[145] Waugh was a ten-minute drive from Mitchell, who counted Ahmed Ressam's French-speaking FBI interrogator, Fred Humphries, who lived in Tampa, as a near neighbor. One of Porter Goss's several beach retreats lay a little farther south, on Sanibel Island.[146] Even Hesham Abu Zubaidah ended up in Florida, living a three-hour drive away from his brother's former interrogator, although he never got his green card but remained under permanent risk of deportation if a country could ever be persuaded to take him.

George Tenet went home to compose his book with Bill Harlow, happy that his days of being a "human piñata" were over.[147] "Listen, I'm at peace," he said, with Harlow present, at the Chevy Chase Club in Maryland on an icy morning in November 2018. "In my own mind this is not something I think about." He did not trust any media. "There isn't a single journalist on the planet who took our side." And he was not changing tack now. "I don't need or want the next young jihadi to find out where I live and go blow me and my family up." Everyone involved in the program was right to be worried. Jennifer Matthews of the AZ Task Force had been killed alongside six CIA officers and contractors in a suicide bomb blast at Camp Chapman, Afghanistan, in December 2009.[148]

Scott Shumate left the CIA in May 2003 and became a director of behavioral science at the Pentagon, before launching a private consultancy.[149] Ali Soufan made his name as a high-profile security consultant and commentator, and in 2018, his character (played by Tahar Rahim) starred in the Hulu drama series *The Looming Tower*, about the road to 9/11. In one scene, two characters based on Alfreda Bikowsky and Mike Scheuer got hot and flustered about Al Qaeda and each other in a parking lot. In real life, Scheuer expressed no regrets that mistakes had been made over some detainees. "They are not Americans," he said. "I really don't care. I never got paid, sir, to be a citizen of the world."[150] Tenet was unhappy that his character in *The Looming Tower* was played by Alec Baldwin ("Alec has his problems") and was shown bribing the Saudi ambassador.[151] John Rizzo was also disappointed when he was portrayed in a 2019 Steven Soderbergh film about CIA torture by "someone who had previously played Tony Soprano's dad."[152]

In 2010, Professor Martin Seligman won a $31 million sole-source Pentagon contract for his Positive Psychology Center at the University of Pennsylvania. According to critics, it was given for "assistance provided to the government with its counter-terrorism efforts."[153] Seligman denied this connection. Years later, Mitchell spun a rumor that the professor had written to Rumsfeld shortly after 9/11, offering instruction in learned helplessness. "I saw it myself," Mitchell claimed, although he could not put his hand on a copy.[154]

Others, farther afield, were also enabled by the CIA program. In Thailand, Prime Minister Thaksin Shinawatra launched a "war on drugs" that made liberal use of CIA-style interrogation practices, and Washington sent military trainers to assist. More than two thousand people were killed.[155] In 2016, the new Filipino president, Rodrigo Duterte, launched an even more brutal war on drugs with torture techniques inspired by the United States. As many as seven thousand people were killed. Narendra Modi, Indian's prime minister since 2014, used the US government model to justify widespread torture and detention of Muslims and other minorities, particularly in Indian-administered Kashmir.[156] "CIA practices inspired torturers worldwide," said Parvez Imroz, Kashmir's preeminent human rights lawyer.[157]

———————•———————

In December 2014, the US Senate Select Committee on Intelligence published a scathing summary of a six-year-long investigation into enhanced interrogation. It tore into CIA claims that it had acted legally, professionally, and in good faith; had prevented countless terrorism plots; and had gained intelligence that enabled the agency to "capture or kill the entire AQ senior command with the exception of Zawahiri."[158] Seven of the thirty-nine detainees subjected to enhanced interrogation produced "no intelligence," while multiple detainees who did speak had "fabricated information, resulting in faulty intelligence." The report accused the CIA of unprofessionalism, lying about safety and effectiveness, inventing imaginary plots, brutality, murder, and cover-up. "The Committee reviewed 20 of the most frequent and prominent examples of purported counterterrorism successes that the CIA has attributed to the use of its enhanced interrogation techniques, and found them to be wrong in fundamental respects," it concluded. Yoo-Bybee's "golden shield" was a legal travesty. Jose Rodriguez's "silver bullet" was a sham. "There was no evidence that the water board produced time-perishable information which otherwise would have been unobtainable."

John Brennan, who was appointed CIA director in 2013, wrote a brutally honest response to the committee. The CIA had been "unprepared and lacked

core competencies" after 9/11, which had resulted in "significant lapses," ranging from employing "unauthorized, improvised techniques including mock
executions and 'hard takedowns,'" to authorizing enhanced techniques that
were not properly analyzed, were "inappropriate," and "fell short of Agency
tradecraft." Tearing into Mitchell and Jessen, Brennan admitted the CIA
had allowed a conflict of interest in letting contractors play dual roles as psychologists assessing their own interrogation and had made "inaccurate,
imprecise" representations about the agency's expertise and abilities to other
government departments. Brennan, who as the CIA's deputy executive director had been at many of the seventh-floor meetings where Abu Zubaydah's
guilt, mistreatment, and endgame options had been discussed, concluded
that enhanced interrogation had impaired "our ability to continue to play a
leadership role in the world."[159]

George Tenet was furious. "You all took it as gospel truth," he said.
"Nobody gave a shit that this [Senate committee report] was one of the most
dishonest things that ever happened."[160] Bill Harlow produced an extensive
response, *Rebuttal: The CIA Responds to the Senate Intelligence Committee's Study
of Its Detention and Interrogation Program*, which was largely ignored. It
began with supportive essays from Tenet, John Rizzo, Jose Rodriguez, John
McLaughlin, Porter Goss, Michael Hayden, and Michael Morell, who until
Brennan took over had served as President Obama's acting CIA director.
Tenet argued the Senate committee had totally failed to account for the "living hell" he and his officials had lived through after 9/11 and claimed that
politicians who had failed to listen to the CIA's Al Qaeda warnings and then
lobbied to go harder after 9/11 were the same people now backpedaling. Citing the biblical quotation engraved in the marble lobby at Langley, "And ye
shall know the truth, and the truth shall set you free," he accused the committee of stitching together an after-the-fact fabricated mosaic of untruths.[161]
Harlow et al. rejected the committee's primary conclusion that nothing had
been gained from the program; sought to spread around the blame, asserting
"this was a Presidential program"; and noted that the CIA inspector general
had conducted "nearly 60 investigations" related to it.[162] However, even Harlow et al. had to concede that contractors had imposed brutal conditions,
used unapproved techniques, were rarely held accountable, were enabled by
a flawed legal rationale, and used the waterboard too hard. One significant

lesson for the future was never again to listen to experts selling their own wares.

After *Rebuttal*, Mitchell, who was furious, was allowed to defend himself on Fox News, appearing angry and red-eyed on Megyn Kelly's program in December 2014 and later, several times, on Sean Hannity's show. To counter Mitchell's "full-blown, full-tilt, bozo wild person" act, as described by Roger Aldrich, Morell and Harlow published a book written in Morell's trademark calm, reasonable guy tone. However, the Senate committee then produced a fifty-four-page fact-checking response that accused Morell of making multiple "inaccurate and misleading assertions."[163] Harlow pushed back, publishing *Enhanced Interrogation* with Mitchell in December 2016. Although it contained classified information—such as Mitchell's retelling of how Abu Zubaydah lost his eye—and partially identified some CIA staffers, including Scott Shumate, the book sailed through the CIA's Publications Review Board, although a self-aggrandizing subtitle, "Architect of the CIA Interrogation Program" was dropped on legal advice.[164] Harlow et al. also launched CIA Saved Lives, a website "created by former CIA officials with hundreds of years of combined service."[165]

When Mitchell was not on television or signing books with his "Arabic-style" signature and a doodled cat, he went canoeing with Kathy, ice climbed with Jessen, and exchanged emails with Rodriguez and other like-minded friends of the program, including Rob O'Neill, the US Navy SEAL who claimed to have killed Osama bin Laden. Occasionally, Mitchell went to CIA and military reunions at the Bad Monkey bar in Tampa, where he was treated like a hero and downed a nonalcoholic drink. The bar was run by Dave Scott, a retired US Air Force major general formerly based in Afghanistan. Naked female torsos fashioned from bullets adorned the walls. Genuine 105mm howitzer shells had been adapted into craft-beer pumps. A plaque received by General Scott on his retirement read: "With Respect and Admiration from Your Friends at CIA, July 2009." In one corner was a sign for the Talibar, the CIA's former watering hole at the Ariana Hotel in Kabul.[166] During one of many visits we made to Mitchell's home before the Guantánamo hearing of January 2020, he briefly opened a cupboard in his office containing a large plastic storage box. "Oh, that's stuff you are not allowed to see," he quipped, shutting it again.[167] On another visit, he admitted the CIA had put another \$10 million into his legal fund. The CIA still has Mitchell and Jessen. But as rumors persist that copies of an Abu Zubaydah video still exist, maybe Mitchell has the CIA too.

———•———

While Mitchell seized every opportunity to enhance his reputation, Jessen hid away, living in a large, wooded compound near Hangman Valley golf course outside Spokane; aggressive guard dogs kept strangers out. Jessen's only companion was his wife, Sharon, and his only regular visitors were his grown daughters. "Bruce tends to turn inwards, becomes like Eeyore," Roger Aldrich explained.[168] Jessen never got over the fact that Khalid Sheikh Mohammad had warned him that the US government would one day turn on them, said Aldrich. Mitchell had brushed aside "KSM's wagging finger," but after Michael Hayden exposed their names in 2007, "Mitchell and Jessen" or "Jim and Bruce" were the only unredacted names in declassified CIA documents.[169] At every new turn in the scandal, the CIA always had a document ready to condemn them, not the agency, said Mitchell.[170] Only the tapes could save them. But officially they had been destroyed. "Now, I'm afraid Bruce is like, 'I'm just going to stay in my house with my wife and have my kids visit, and I don't want to deal with anybody,'" said Aldrich.[171] "There was a time when if we'd seen each other we would have run up and hugged, 'How you doing? It's great to see you,'" he continued. "To see that change and not to be able to say, 'What's going on, talk to me about it,' it's very sad." Aldridge blamed the CIA. "When you've served your purpose, you are an empty pop can, recycle, maybe, otherwise garbage. It's nothing personal."

Jessen was not the only person thrown in the trash. Mohammed al-Qahtani, who was made to bark like a dog and wear women's underwear, remains uncharged at Guantánamo, with his lawyer describing his treatment as "a war crime."[172] Majid Khan, one of five detainees fed rectally, who once tried to chew through veins in his arm to kill himself, is still there too, charged with being an Al Qaeda courier, to which he has pleaded guilty. In May 2021, he did a deal with the Pentagon-appointed judge not to raise the issue of CIA torture in return for a possible reduction in his sentencing.[173] Sharon, who once interrogated Khan, said: "We always wondered about the endgame for all of them. They were interesting because of what they knew, not because of their crimes."[174]

Abd al-Rahim al-Nashiri, who Mitchell and Jessen waterboarded in Thailand when Gina Haspel was the black site chief, was also charged, with the USS *Cole* attacks. His trial is on hold, although his military lawyers successfully obtained a psychiatric assessment that he was suffering from PTSD, which invalidates the legal authority to subject him to enhanced interrogation.[175] Outside Guantánamo, Jose Padilla is still locked up at ADX Florence. At one stage, Rumsfeld's deputy general counsel Richard Shiffrin took pity and tried to get Padilla freed by setting up a meeting with his mother, who lives in Miami. "He was a schmo," Shiffrin said. "I was not worried about him being a terrorist. If he gave us some useful information, I would have been willing to give him his freedom. I had hoped his mother could persuade him to talk to us. But his lawyer screwed it up by advising the mother against speaking to me."[176] Instead, Padilla was convicted of terrorism, and his sentence was extended by seven years in 2014. Ahmed Ressam is on the same block although they never see each other.

CHAPTER 21

"BAD GUYS BECOME GOOD GUYS AND VICE VERSA"[1]

January 21, 2020, Guantánamo Bay, Cuba

Hearing days started early for "KSM et al.," with five windowless paddy wagons emerging from Camp Seven while stars were still in the sky.[2] Inside each one, a detainee sat shackled, carrying his chosen war-court attire. As they made their way through two checkpoints and the now rusting yellow Camp Seven gate, the Expeditionary Legal Complex at Camp Justice switched to "operational" mode. SkyWatch Frontier mobile surveillance towers rose like waking dinosaurs. Stadium lighting flared off media tents, concertina wire, crash barriers, and twelve-foot-tall chain link fences. Joint Task Force Guantánamo guards chased banana rats out. When the paddy wagons reached the end of Sherman Avenue and wove through the Camp Justice barriers, the "movement guys" snapped on rubber gloves. They would guard the detainees in five holding cells lined up in a high-security compound to the left of the war court until it was time to enter. Here, the defendants could pray, have breakfast, read, snooze, get changed, or watch the live feed as government geeks tweaked the courtroom and the "white noise" panic button was tested. Physical body-cavity searches were no longer conducted, but detainees were still processed before entering the war court by a Boss II body-scanning device, a nonlethal electric chair.

At 8:30 A.M., observers filed into court via a canvas tunnel the US military called "the red carpet," passing warning notices about smart glasses, Fitbits, and open-toed sandals. Bowls of candy sat at the end of the processing table as a reward for compliance. "Welcome to court," declared a chirpy guard who was still in diapers on 9/11. Inside the viewing gallery, observers lined up in preassigned seats behind triple panes of glass, between which mold bloomed. Security staff monitored the gallery via CCTV, watching for any evidence of illicit communication between those inside and outside the courtroom. For the Mitchell hearing, 9/11 "victim family members" chose to pull a curtain, separating themselves from the media. Beyond the glass, many elements of the court would appear to be standard. Judge Shane Cohen, a US Air Force colonel, wore a black robe over his dress uniform and was flanked by American flags and the witness stand. Five long defense-team tables sat in front of him, ordered according to the severity of their client's charges. The detainees had padded office chairs at the far end of their team's table with shackling rings beneath their feet. The main accused, Khalid Sheikh Mohammad would sit closest to the judge.

However, some things were unique. Because this was a national security court, there was a forty-second delay on the sound shared with the gallery and the remote access channel, allowing Judge Cohen, the Pentagon, and the CIA to invoke "national security privilege" and mute audio. Observers would still see them deliberating but would only hear CIA white noise until the issue was resolved. Likewise, classified material was always displayed on monitors shielded from the gallery. Although a military jury will eventually decide on whether to sentence the 9/11 five to death, for now the jury box remained empty.

The defense and prosecution lawyers were identifiable by their attire. A female prosecutor wore a pencil skirt and a sleeveless petrol-blue satin blouse. General Mark Martins, the chief prosecutor, sported eight rows of ribbons on his dress blues. On the defense side, almost every woman wore a hijab. Some, like Cheryl Bormann, who represents Khallad bin Attash, also wore a black abaya, hers studded with rhinestones. Another accessorized her abaya with black patent-leather Manolo Blahniks with six-inch heels. In 2017, one family member, who lost a firefighter nephew on 9/11 and her husband, a policeman, in 2008, when he died of complications from inhaling toxic fumes at Ground Zero, described the non-Muslim defense teams' choice of Islamic dress as "an insult to all American women." Bormann said she simply wanted her client to feel "comfortable."[3]

At ten A.M., Judge Cohen took his seat beneath a row of military seals. "All rise." Martins, ramrod straight, introduced his team, including a squat, grumpy-looking defense counsel, Robert Swann, who sat in on most of the January 2007 FBI clean-team interrogations. At the start of every session, Swann gruffly informed the accused of their rights. Jim Harrington, Ramzi bin al-Shibh's retiring lawyer, called him "Angry Bird" and once gave him an *Angry Birds Movie* poster signed by Camp Seven detainees.[4] Sitting at the back were Mitchell and Jessen's civilian lawyers.[5] There was no official CIA presence apart from the unacknowledged live feed facility to Langley.

The "movement guys" delivered the defendants one by one via a recessed side entrance to the left of the viewing gallery. Whenever the wooden doors opened and sunlight flooded in, the observers drew a collective breath and leaned forward. A dozen guards filed in to form a human corridor before a shackled detainee walked in with rubber-gloved hands on his shoulders and forearms. A phalanx of gum-chewing guards would remain seated next to detainees throughout this hearing. Cohen was informed that Khalid Sheikh Mohammad and Khallad bin Attash were running late for Mitchell's opening day because both were finishing "PT sessions." Cohen was not pleased at the obvious snub.

First in was defendant number four, Ammar al-Baluchi, who the judge called Mr. Ali (his given name) and his learned counsel, James Connell, called Mr. al-Baluchi (his chosen name). According to the CIA, al-Baluchi was inspired by his cousin (Ramzi Yousef), recruited into jihad by his uncle (Khalid Sheikh Mohammad), and was conspiring with his wife (Aafia Siddiqui) to attack America again when he was caught. Aafia Siddiqui is serving an eighty-six-year sentence in a psychiatric prison ward at Fort Worth, Texas, for allegedly trying to kill US military officers after she was captured in Afghanistan in 2008.[6] Now age forty-three and smiling broadly, al-Baluchi was dressed in a Sindhi prayer cap, a checkered Harry Potter–style scarf, and a white Pakistani *shalwar kameez*. He greeted male members of his team with handshakes, and while the courtroom settled, he got into a deep discussion with Stephen Xenakis, a retired military psychiatrist who is helping the detainees deal with undiagnosed PTSD.[7]

Next in was defendant number five, Mustafa al-Hawsawi, fifty-two, all in white, tiny like a sparrow. Financial information found on his laptop and pursued by the FBI showed that Mohamed Atta sent unspent cash back to al-Hawsawi before 9/11.[8] He sat with his face shielded by a large white *ghutra* (Saudi scarf), and clutching prayer beads. Later, when asked whether he recognized al-Hawsawi, Mitchell narrowed his eyes and replied: "I can't really see because he's got a lot of stuff on his head." Al-Hawsawi requested painkillers and did not show up to the following hearing.

Ramzi bin al-Shibh, forty-eight, defendant number three, entered next, his famous buck-toothed profile wrapped in multiple scarves. A close friend of Mohamed Atta, a would-be hijacker, and a companion of Khalid Sheikh Mohammad, he had confirmed his role in 9/11 in the *Al Jazeera* interview of 2002.[9] He nonchalantly threw his sunglasses to one of the guards, flipped a green prayer rug over the back of his chair, draped a Palestinian flag across a courtroom evidence monitor, and kicked off his shoes. Later, when his lawyer, Jim Harrington, was questioning Mitchell, bin al-Shibh slumped in his chair. After the judge noted that bin al-Shibh had been recommended for a full psychological evaluation and an MRI scan, Harrington asked Mitchell what he had known about his client's background when he interrogated him. "We were only interested in his terror activities not what he did in his teenage years," sneered Mitchell. "Do you know what country he's from?" asked Harrington. "Don't know if I'm aware now," Mitchell fired back with a shrug. In his world, Arabs were all the same and the "Arab mind" was as foreign to him today as it ever had been.

Defendant number two, Khallad bin Attash, forty-two, eventually showed up, dressed in a long-sleeved khaki military jacket, white *shalwar*, and a salmon-pink scarf. Accused of being involved in multiple plots, the man "left without a leg to stand on" and then subjected to a "kebab operation" took his seat without fanfare. A few minutes later, the double doors swung back and a human corridor formed for defendant number one. A tiny pair of white-stockinged feet barely touched the floor as Khalid Sheikh Mohammad was physically propelled into the war court by guards, including a woman. Smartly dressed 9/11 "victim family members" rushed to the front of the gallery. The fifty-five-year-old 9/11 mastermind was barely recognizable as the disheveled man photographed in his nightwear after his capture in 2003. These days, he dyes his long beard bright orange with henna, and on Mitchell's first day he wore a dramatic black-and-white-striped Pashtun turban.

At 11:02 A.M., witness Jim Mitchell entered in a crumpled suit, because clothes mattered nothing to him. He said later he had been sleeping in his trailer while he waited for Mohammad to turn up. A welcoming General

Martins took his oath. Mitchell looked over to the detainees with a wry smile. He was where he was, and they were where they should be, his expression seemed to suggest. But the proceedings did not say this. Quite the opposite. This session, like everything else, was simply a placeholder for a trial that likely would never even begin let alone conclude. Everyone, from the relatives of those murdered on 9/11 to the detained men tortured to those accused of war crimes, remained a very long way from justice.

Before Mitchell began speaking, bin Attash talked vigorously to a male attorney. Bin al-Shibh tightened his *ghutra*. Al-Baluchi fell silent. Al-Hawsawi gripped his prayer beads. After a few moments, Khalid Sheikh Mohammad coolly glanced up from his red notebook and caught Mitchell's eye. Mitchell hesitated, then winked. Later, he claimed Mohammad smiled at him. "So did bin Attash," he said. "The only one giving me the stink-eye is Ramzi."[10]

The prosecution handed Mitchell a "top-secret" booklet of "unique functional identifier" codes that would be used in place of real names to protect the identities of those who had once engaged in torture. Mitchell said he might need a gentle reminder not to wave it around. "I'm an old guy and a little bit slow," he gibed. Defense attorney James Connell, who called Mitchell as a witness, stepped up to the podium and thanked him for showing up. Mitchell regarded him with scorn. "I did it for the victims and families, not for you." Connell tried again. When did "Dr. Mitchell" first learn he would be testifying in a military commission? "I suspected from the beginning I would eventually end up here," Mitchell derided.

Mitchell remained on the witness stand for eight days, batting away almost every accusation effortlessly. A thunderous-looking Bruce Jessen gave evidence for only a few hours. Alka Pradhan, who questioned him, did not get very far beyond Jessen's assurances that he was never returning to Cuba. His main agenda was putting distance between this hearing and his last visit to Guantánamo. "I don't recognize these guys anymore," he said, glancing at the defendants. "They've all grown up . . ."

One witness who was mentioned throughout the two-week hearing but never appeared was Abu Zubaydah, Mitchell's patient zero. The closest he ever got to the war court was on June 5, 2016, when he agreed to be a witness for one of the other Camp Seven brothers. "I went but I didn't enter," he said. "I remained by the court door."[11] In January 2020, while everyone else converged on the Expeditionary Legal Complex, he remained hidden away in Camp Seven, waiting for the nightly lowdown from Khalid Sheikh Mohammad. A more lenient and recently appointed Camp Seven commander had loosened isolation rules and the detainees were now allowed to pray, eat, and exercise together. But Abu Zubaydah was still reminded of his forever prisoner status twice a day, every day, when "The Star-Spangled Banner" was broadcast across the naval station and into his cell. According to the CIA narrative, America had won its War on Terror and he was guilty. His entire CIA experience and near death had been entirely legal as long as the CIA still controlled the Guantánamo circus, and he would never get a chance to state otherwise.

In some ways, it did not matter whether Mitchell lied under oath, because Abu Zubaydah had heard it all before. Still imprisoned and still incommunicado, he suspected he was never getting out until he was in his real coffin. What did matter were his memories, many of which were newly recorded in the thirteenth volume of his diary. It took him more than twenty years to write about certain things, like his Swedish ex-wife, her pregnancy, the raid that ended their marriage, and her red handkerchief. After he was allowed legal representation, he had learned she had never remarried, or had children, and was still out there somewhere, waiting for him. He contemplated his unborn son, who would be a young man by now. Had he lived, he suspected he, too, would have been falsely accused of carrying out terrorist attacks to avenge his father, and of being Number Three in Al Qaeda or Da'esh.

He wrote it all down in his diary, which would also simply become a memory one day. "Also myself will be just a memory. . . . One day. . . . And now. . . . I escaped with you or thru you from my bad reality. . . . For a lovely period of time, I was writing to you and (*ruminate*) the memories."

He put his memories aside. "Let me back to reality. . . . And open my eyes; (sorry it's one eye) on the walls of my cell in the camp 7 in *GTMO*, and leave you packing your (bags and belongings) in order to be ready to travel over time to take the position of (Hani 5 who [is] 60 years) because I will reach to you shortly, and take your place."[12]

CAST LIST

DETAINEES

Zayn-al-Abidin Muhammad Hussein Abu Zubaydah, age fifty-one, the CIA's first "high-value detainee." Still incarcerated without charges at Guantánamo Bay detention camp more than twenty years after the attacks of September 11, 2001, he was waterboarded at least eighty-three times at a CIA black site, and disputes almost all the allegations the CIA leveled at him.

Khalid Sheikh Mohammad, fifty-eight, self-declared mastermind of the 9/11 attacks. He was waterboarded at least 183 times by Jim Mitchell and Bruce Jessen (see "CIA," below), and made more than thirty confessions, many of which he has since recanted.

Ibn Sheikh al-Libi, the *emir* of Khaldan, the oldest *mujahideen* training camp in Afghanistan. A close associate of Abu Zubaydah, al-Libi was sent by the CIA to Egypt in a coffin to be tortured. As a result, he gave up false information about Saddam Hussein working with Al Qaeda to produce weapons of mass destruction.

Mohammed al-Qahtani, forty-two, a Saudi detainee who became the subject of a US military enhanced interrogation experiment that lasted forty-eight days at Guantánamo in 2002. US government prosecutors later refused to charge him, saying his treatment amounted to torture.

Gul Rahman, a CIA detainee who died at age thirty-four at the "Salt Pit," a CIA black site in Kabul, Afghanistan, in November 2002, where unauthorized enhanced interrogation was used. Mitchell and Jessen had interrogated him a week earlier but were not there when he died. Nevertheless, they were later sued by Rahman's family, and the US government settled the case for an undisclosed sum in 2017.

CIA

Dr. James "Jim" Mitchell, seventy, retired US Air Force psychologist and architect of the CIA's "enhanced interrogation" program. His company earned in excess of $80 million, after he and Bruce Jessen reverse engineered mock-torture techniques taught in US military survival schools and turned them into a "weapon" to deploy against Al Qaeda.

Dr. John "Bruce" Jessen, seventy-two, Mitchell's "best buddy" and enhanced interrogation partner, who conducted the "pours" during waterboarding. Like Mitchell, he sought written assurances that Abu Zubaydah would remain "incommunicado" for the rest of his life. Jessen also developed harsh interrogation training materials that were used by the US military on detainees held at Guantánamo; Bagram, Afghanistan; and Abu Ghraib, Iraq.

Scott Shumate, sixty-five, chief operational psychologist at the CIA's Counterterrorist Center. He condemned the CIA's proposed techniques, which included subjecting Abu Zubaydah to a "mock burial," as gratuitous, ineffective, and sadistic. An early member of the Abu Zubaydah's interrogation team, he later concluded that torture produced false intelligence because it encouraged people to lie.

"Adil," fifties, a senior undercover officer of Egyptian origin who was Abu Zubaydah's first "primary interrogator." He later withdrew from the program because he "did not like doing it."

"Bryan," sixties, a polygraph expert and an aficionado of the Reid technique, a rapport-building method of interrogation favored by the FBI. He helped interrogate Abu Zubaydah before enhanced techniques were introduced.

George Tenet, sixty-nine, director of the Central Intelligence Agency from 1997 to July 2004. He led the charge for enhanced interrogation, stating that Abu Zubaydah was "Number Three" in Al Qaeda and a 9/11 planner and financier, who was trained to resist traditional interrogation methods and was withholding vital information about a "second wave" of attacks on the United States.

Bill Harlow, seventy-one, Tenet's director of public affairs. Harlow later authored books with Mitchell, Tenet, Jose Rodriguez, and Michael Morell, in which enhanced interrogation was described as a major success story that led to more than eight thousand intelligence reports and prevented more attacks on the United States.

Michael Morell, sixty-three, Tenet's executive assistant in 1998–99, who became President George W. Bush's daily intelligence briefer in 2001 and was with Bush at a school in Sarasota, Florida, when he learned of the 9/11 attacks. Over the following months, Morell and Tenet briefed the president daily about the "second wave."

Jose Rodriguez, seventy-three, director of the CIA's Counterterrorist Center from May 2002 to November 2004, and an advocate for the psychological state of "learned helplessness" that Mitchell promoted. Rodriguez was later investigated for illegally destroying videotapes showing Abu Zubaydah being waterboarded.

"Gus," seventies, a pseudonym for the chief of the CIA's Renditions, Detention, and Interrogation Group that ran the secret CIA black site network and supervised the recruitment of interrogators, who obtained "on-the-job training" and "certification" by practicing on real detainees.

Gina Haspel, sixty, a temporary black site base chief in Thailand, who interrogated Abu Zubaydah and witnessed the waterboarding of a second detainee, Abd al-Rahim al-Nashiri. She later became chief of staff to Jose Rodriguez and was investigated for assisting him in destroying Abu Zubaydah's waterboarding tapes. She served as President Donald Trump's CIA director from 2018 to 2021.

Marty Martin, seventies, CIA station chief in Amman, Jordan, during the so-called millennium plot of 1999, who returned to the United States post-9/11 to lead the "worldwide hunt for Al Qaeda." He accused Abu Zubaydah of masterminding a plan to attack American and Israeli targets across Jordan and in the United States during millennium celebrations, and of being a senior lieutenant to Osama bin Laden.

Michael Scheuer, seventy, the founder of Alec Station, a CIA unit targeting Osama bin Laden. From 1995 onward, Scheuer and his team of predominantly female targeters led the CIA's attempts to interdict Al Qaeda. Post-9/11, his team was accused of having hidden information that could have prevented the attacks.

Alfreda Bikowsky, fifty-six, a senior Alec Station official and a major figure behind the CIA's "Zubaydah Biography," produced to justify enhanced interrogation. She was accused of hiding intelligence from the FBI pre-9/11, misinterpreting intelligence post-9/11, and encouraging Mitchell and Jessen to go harder on Abu Zubaydah to the point he almost died.

Jennifer Matthews led the AZ (Abu Zubaydah) Task Force, a dedicated unit formed in February 2002 to hunt him down. After he was captured, Matthews and her team worked at the black site in Thailand, feeding questions to interrogators. A Jordanian suicide bomber killed Matthews, age forty-five, and six other CIA personnel at Camp Chapman, Afghanistan, in December 2009.

Albert El Gamil, seventies, an Egyptian-born Coptic Christian CIA interrogator. He rendered Ibn Sheikh al-Libi to Cairo, interrogated Gul Rahman at the Salt Pit, and threatened detainee Abd al-Rahim al-Nashiri with a handgun and a power drill. After receiving a one-year reprimand and a five-day suspension, Gamil, who was untrained, returned to CIA work and threatened to put Abu Zubaydah back on the waterboard.

Charlie Wise, a former marine, who trained in the US military's Survival, Evasion, Resistance, Escape (SERE) program. Wise became the CIA's "chief of interrogations" in November 2002, putting him in direct competition with Mitchell and Jessen. Mitchell accused Wise of abusing detainees, while Wise accused Mitchell of stealing copies of Abu Zubaydah's waterboarding tapes. Wise was fired and died two weeks later, aged fifty-two. Mitchell was exonerated.

"The Preacher," sixties, Mitchell's pseudonym for an overweight, Southern Baptist, Charlie Wise–trained interrogator with an appetite for Snickers bars, pizza, and Pepsi. The Preacher helped waterboard Khalid Sheikh Mohammad and later he also interrogated Abu Zubaydah. He also made multiple complaints about Mitchell to the CIA inspector general.

Alejandro "Deuce" Martinez, fifty-four, a CIA Latin America Division analyst brought into the Counterterrorist Center post-9/11 and put on the hunt for Abu Zubaydah. He interrogated Abu Zubaydah and Khalid Sheikh Mohammad and later worked for Mitchell, Jessen and Associates (MJA), a company formed in 2004 to run the CIA's enhanced interrogation program.

Matthew Zirbel, forties, a first-tour CIA officer who ran a CIA black site in Kabul, Afghanistan, a place that was known as the "Salt Pit," where detainees, including Gul Rahman, were strung up naked in darkness for days at a time. Jessen described the Salt Pit as "nasty, but safe," and he recommended Zirbel as an enhanced interrogator.

FBI

Ali Soufan, fifty-one, a Lebanese American special agent who interrogated Abu Zubaydah before Mitchell and the CIA team arrived in Thailand. Soufan flew home in late May 2002 after making an official complaint that Mitchell's techniques were "borderline torture." After retiring from the FBI in 2006, he became one of Mitchell's primary critics.

Stephen Gaudin, fifties, a former army captain, who was Soufan's interrogation partner on Abu Zubaydah and continued working alongside Mitchell in Thailand after Soufan's departure. He was pulled off the case in July 2002, when FBI director Robert Mueller decided to sever official FBI connections to enhanced interrogation.

LAWYERS

John Rizzo, CIA acting general counsel at the time of Abu Zubaydah's capture, who persuaded the Department of Justice, the attorney general, and the National Security Council to provide legal approval for enhanced interrogation. He was closely assisted by the Counterterrorist Center's chief attorney, Jonathan Fredman, whose wife, Judy Philipson, an operational psychologist in the CIA's Office of Technical Service, recommended Mitchell. He died in August 2021 age seventy-four.

John Yoo, fifty-four, a Department of Justice lawyer, who wrote the controversial August 1, 2002, "torture memo" that legalized waterboarding. Yoo also wrote a legal opinion that enabled President Bush to drop Geneva Conventions rights for War on Terror detainees and another opinion stating that it was not torture to "put out or destroy an eye."

David Addington, sixty-five, Vice President Dick Cheney's "chief counsel and alter ego," who had previously worked at the CIA. He was a key figure in making enhanced interrogation legal, working closely with Jim Haynes, chief counsel to Defense Secretary Donald Rumsfeld; John Bellinger, chief counsel to National Security Advisor Condoleezza Rice; Alberto Gonzales, chief counsel to President Bush; and John Ashcroft, Bush's first attorney general.

OTHER

Roger Aldrich, seventy-four, Mitchell's friend and former working partner at the US Air Force SERE school and the Personnel Recovery Academy, located at Fairchild Air Force Base in Spokane, Washington. Aldrich hired Mitchell in 1988 and, along with Bruce Jessen, chief psychologist at the academy, taught Mitchell everything he knew about survival training. In 2005, Mitchell appointed Aldrich as head of training at MJA.

Joseph Matarazzo, ninety-six, a former president of the American Psychological Association (APA) and member of the Professional Standards Advisory Board at the CIA's Office of Technical Service. Matarazzo was a champion of Mitchell and SERE. He later held shares in two companies Mitchell set up to run his CIA contracts, MJA and Knowledge Works.

Martin Seligman, seventy-nine, a former APA president and the author of "learned helplessness," a psychological state that the CIA wanted to engineer in Abu Zubaydah so he would give up everything he knew about future Al Qaeda attacks. After speaking to Seligman several times, the CIA misrepresented his theory to senior administration lawyers, saying that when harsh conditions were discontinued Abu Zubaydah would make a full recovery.

General Tritot Ronnaritivichai, seventy-two, the chief of Thai Special Branch, the country's domestic intelligence agency, who worked with CIA's Bangkok station chief, Michael Winograd, to set up the CIA's first black site—in a property that he owned. General Tritot also delivered the alleged Southeast Asian Al Qaeda cell to the CIA: Hambali, Zubair, and Lillie. President Bush described Tritot as "my hero."

ACKNOWLEDGMENTS

First and foremost: thank you to Jim and Kathy Mitchell for being welcoming hosts to their home in Florida. While they will certainly not agree with many of the conclusions reached in this book, we hope they will agree that we have told their story fairly.

Many thanks to Roger Aldrich for a generous and spirited information download in Spokane, and to the late John Rizzo for taking a punt, and agreeing to speak frankly. Thanks also to those who overcame their reluctance to speak, including Jose Rodriguez, Ric Prado, and George Tenet, and thank you to Bill Harlow for hearing us out and facilitating. Thanks to Scott Shumate for the good company and apocryphal stories, and to Glenn Carle and John Kiriakou for some salutary lessons about falling foul of the official CIA narrative. Thanks to Mike Scheuer for his acerbic but revealing conversations about leading Alec Station and the work of the Counterterrorist Center post 9/11, and to Rolf Mowatt-Larsson for a discussion about Al Qaeda's nuclear capabilities. Thanks also to the many at the CIA who talked but wished to remain anonymous.

Thanks to Billy Waugh for illuminating his life's exploits—from eight purple hearts and his baseball bat "CIA interrogation tool," to spying on Osama bin Laden and Carlos the Jackal. Thanks to Buzzy Krongard for welcoming us to his incredible home, chauffeuring us in one of his spectacular cars, and putting us in touch with Erik Prince, who was also engaging. Thanks to John McLaughlin for an early introduction to the politics of the EIT program, and also to Michael Morell for his bird's-eye view of how 9/11 transformed George W. Bush's presidency. Thanks to Porter Goss for a fascinating discussion about ego and hypocrisy. David Petraeus and Zalmay Khalilzad provided views into the wars in Afghanistan and Iraq, on US detention and interrogation policy, and America's place in the world.

Thanks to "Gus," Scott Fales, Butch Stoddard, Kirk Hubbard, Morgan Banks, Denny Keller, and "Sharon," who would not have spoken if Jim

Mitchell had not made the introductions. Jim has many loyal friends and we hope there will be no bad feelings in trying to balance how they saw their roles against how others did. Thanks to Bob Dussault, Steven Kleinman, and Chris Wirts for their inputs regarding JPRA. Thanks to Larry Wilkerson, Alberto Mora, and Richard Shiffrin for their insights into the Pentagon's interest in enhanced interrogation. Thanks to Jerry Ogrisseg for an alternative view of SERE techniques, and to Susan Brandon and Charles "Andy" Morgan for an informed view about science and practitioners.

In Thailand, thanks to Thai Special Branch chief General Tritot Ronnaritivichai, former prime minister and supreme commander of the Royal Thai Armed Forces, General Chavalit Yongchaiyudh, and Assistant Police Commissioner General Attachai Doungamporn. Thanks also to Paddy Brown, Suchada "Nikki" Phoissat, and Dominic Faulder. Thanks also to our old friends Yongyut and Sukanya Thavikulwat, who we first met when we rented their house in Chiang Mai in 2002, not knowing that just down the road Jim Mitchell and Bruce Jessen were subjecting Abu Zubaydah to enhanced interrogation.

From the FBI, thanks to Jack Cloonan, Jennifer Hale Keenan, Dan Coleman, Mark Rossini, Fred Humphries, and Ali Soufan. Thanks to Robert McFadden and Mark Fallon for the NCIS view of abuses committed at Guantánamo, Bagram, and Abu Ghraib. Thanks to Ron Flesvig and Shawn Eklund, generous Office of Military Commission hosts during the game-changing 9/11 pretrial hearing of January 2020; to Carol Rosenberg, Terry McDermott, Julian Borger, John Ryan, and Margot Williams for their insightful reporting; and to Janet Hamlin for her war court drawings.

A very special thanks to Lieutenant Colonel Chantell Higgins and Praxedes Kennedy for their assistance in telling Abu Zubaydah's story, and to Paul Bless for his hospitality. Thanks to Mark Denbeaux, Joe Margulies, David Nevin, Jim Harrington, Cheryl Bormann, Walter Ruiz, Alka Pradhan, and Jay Connell for their legal inputs, and to Stephen Xenakis. Thanks to Hina Shamsie and Dror Ladin at the ACLU, and to Lisa Magarrell and the Open Society Foundations for the first grant that got *The Forever Prisoner* research rolling in February 2017. A special thanks to David Schultz, Charles Crain, and the team at Yale Law School's Media Freedom & Access Clinic, without whom many of the CIA documents used in this book would have remained classified.

In France, thanks to Jean-Louis Bruguiere for an illuminating discussion about Ahmed Ressem and Abu Zubaydah, and thanks to Zaina and Omar bin Laden for their recollections of life for the bin Laden family post-9/11. In the UK, thanks to Moazzam Begg, Hider Hanani, Abdullah Anas, Ghareeb Iskander, Abdel Bari Atwan, and former Pakistan High Commissioner Wajid Shamsul Hassan.

In Florida, thanks to Hesham Abu Zubaidah for his childhood stories, photographs, and recollections of his older brother. We hope that one day he will achieve his dream of becoming a US citizen. In Riyadh, thanks to Dr. Maher Abu Zubaydah for his support in our telling of the story of his brother, Zayn-al-Abidin. In Mauritania, thanks to Mohamedou Ould Slahi for some enlightening discussions about life during and after incarceration.

Many thanks to Alex Gibney for investigating enhanced interrogation with us for the groundbreaking HBO film *Forever Prisoner*, and to journalist-lawyer Ray Bonner for his insights, and to the whole Jigsaw Productions team, especially Erin Edeiken, Tess Ranahan, Mahak Jiwani, and Gabriele Alcalde. Via Alex Gibney, thanks also to Dan Jones for a window into the work of the Senate Select Committee on Intelligence and the seminal "CIA Torture" report. Thanks to Peter Bergen and his wife Tresha Mabile for being generous hosts in Washington, DC, and sharing insights.

In Amman, many thanks to Dr. Marwan Shehadeh for always being a generous and willing collaborator. Thanks to Abu Qatada for sharing his memories of Abu Zubaydah, to Abu Muhammad al-Maqdisi for talking us through his story of jihad, to Huthaifa Azzam for his memories of his father, Abdullah Azzam, the post–Soviet war jihad scene, and the rise of Osama bin Laden, and thanks also to his late mother, Samira Mohyeddin, for her food and recollections of life in Peshawar. Thanks also to Alex Strick van Linschoten and Saba Imtiaz, and also to Abu Zubaydah's old friend from Irbid, Abdullah Jafar.

In Pakistan, thanks always to Rahimullah Yusufzai, and his family, for generous help in Peshawar, to Inspector General Syed Kaleem Imam in Islamabad, and to Dr. Tajik Sohail Habib for his assistance in Faisalabad. Thanks also to General Masood Aslam, General Ehsan ul-Haq, Lieutenant General Javed Alam Khan, Tariq Parvez, Khalid Qureshi, and the late Asad Munir.

Special thanks to our editor, George Gibson, and the team at Grove Atlantic, especially managing editor Julia Berner-Tobin and assistant editor Emily Burns. Thanks to Eric Rayman for the legal handrails, and to co-pyeditor Amy Hughes for finessing the manuscript. Finally, thanks to our agent David Godwin, and all those who have worked with us on this and other projects, especially Heather Godwin, Philippa Sitters, and Kirsty McLachlan.

Lastly, thank you to Abu Zubaydah for sharing his incredible story. He will not agree with everything we have concluded in this book, but we have attempted to paint the most complete and accurate picture possible of a man who in 2002 was deemed by the CIA to remain incommunicado for the rest of his life.

NOTES

INTRODUCTION

1. Author visit to Guantánamo Bay for 9/11 pretrial hearing, Jan. 18–31, 2020.
2. Pretrial hearing transcripts can be viewed via the Office of Military Commissions website, www
.mc.mil; see also Carol Rosenberg, "At War: Bracing for a Busy Year at Guantánamo's War
Court," *New York Times Magazine*, Jan. 10, 2020.
3. Author interviews with 9/11 defense attorneys including James Connell and Alka Pradhan
(Ammar al Baluchi), Cheryl Bormann (Khallad bin Attash), and Jim Harrington (Ramzi bin
al-Shibh), Jan. 18–31, 2020.
4. Daniel Jones, who led the Senate investigation into "CIA" torture, was given 6.3 million documents by the CIA; see Alex Gibney (dir.), *Forever Prisoner* (HBO Films/Jigsaw Productions),
documentary, 2021.
5. US Senate Select Committee on Intelligence, *Report of the Senate Select Committee on Intelligence
Committee Study of the Central Intelligence Agency's Detention and Interrogation Program* (hereafter,
SSCI report), US Senate, 113th Congress, 2d Session, S. Report 113–288, Dec. 9, 2014, www
.intelligence.senate.gov/sites/default/files/publications/CRPT-113srpt288.pdf. The SSCI report
found evidence that at least 119 detainees passed through the CIA program while the CIA asserted the number was no more than 98, p. 14; during one congressional testimony in 2006, CIA
director Michael Hayden said "96," while in a second testimony given in 2007, he said "97," SSCI
report, pp. 216–217.
6. Ibid., see p. 172 onward for a full examination of the CIA's claims.
7. For one example, federal prosecutor John Durham's 2010 inquiry into the destruction of Abu
Zubaydah's waterboarding tapes resulted in no charges. See Mark Mazzetti and Charlie Savage,
"No Criminal Charges Sought over CIA Tapes," *New York Times*, Nov. 9, 2010.
8. For example see George Tenet and Bill Harlow, *At the Center of the Storm: My Years at the CIA*
(New York: HarperCollins, 2007), and Jose Rodriguez and Bill Harlow, *Hard Measures: How
Aggressive CIA Actions after 9/11 Saved American Lives* (New York: Threshold Editions, 2012).
9. Scott Shane, "Ex-Officer Is First from CIA to Face Prison for a Leak," *New York Times*, Jan. 5,
2013.
10. Mitchell produced a memoir, *Enhanced Interrogation: Inside the Minds and Motives of the Islamic
Terrorists Trying to Destroy America* (New York: Crown Books, 2016), cowritten by the CIA's former
chief spokesman Bill Harlow and cleared by the CIA's Publications Review Board.
11. "'Incommunicado' Forever: Gitmo Detainee's Case Stalled for 2,477 Days and Counting," *Pro-
Publica*, May 12, 2015.
12. Abu Zubaydah correspondence, author archive; for "not Hollywood innocent," see Joseph Margulies, "The Innocence of Abu Zubaydah," *The New York Review*, Sept. 28, 2018.
13. Brigadier General Mark S. Martins, American Academy of Arts and Sciences, updated
Nov. 2016, www.amacad.org/person/mark-s-martins.
14. Author interviews with Mitchell, Land O' Lakes, FL, Feb. 2017, Aug. 2017, Nov. 2017, Feb. 2018,
May 2018, July 2018 (twice), Sept. 2018, Nov. 2018, Feb. 2019, Mar. 2019, June 2019 (twice);
Washington, DC, Dec. 2019; Guantánamo Bay, Cuba, Jan. 2020; plus multiple telephone interviews
and email exchanges, 2017–21.

15. Ibid.; in 2015, Mitchell was deposed in *Salim v. Mitchell*, in which he was sued for damages by two former black site detainees and the family of a third detainee who died. He was accompanied by CIA lawyers. Salim v. Mitchell (E.D. Wash., 2017), James Mitchell Deposition Transcript, Jan. 16, 2017, ACLU-RDI 6807; during his 9/11 pretrial testimony Mitchell told the judge: "It is possible I may shoot my mouth off accidentally."

16. "Accountability for Torture: Why a Criminal Investigation Is Necessary," American Civil Liberties Union (ACLU), www.aclu.org/sites/default/files/field_document/accountabilityfortorture-whyacriminalinvestigationisnecessary.pdf.

17. "Factsheet: Military Commissions," Center for Constitutional Rights, Oct. 17, 2007, updated Jan. 11, 2010, bit.ly/2VXFnYR.

18. Author telephone interview with Colonel Morris Davis, chief Guantánamo prosecutor 2005–7, Mar. 2021.

19. Steve Vladeck, "It's Time to Admit That the Military Commissions Have Failed," Lawfare, Apr. 16, 2019. For Ghailani see Benjamin Weiser, "Detainee Acquitted on Most Counts in '98 Bombings," *New York Times*, Nov. 17, 2010.

20. "The Guantánamo Trials," Human Rights Watch, www.hrw.org/guantanamo-trials.

21. Carol Rosenberg, "The 9/11 Trial: Why Is It Taking So Long?" *New York Times*, April 17, 2020.

22. Author interview with Pradhan.

23. Carol Rosenberg, "The Strange Case of the CIA Interpreter and the 9/11 Trial," *New York Times*, Aug. 14, 2019.

24. Author interviews with Lieutenant Colonel Chantell Higgins, lead military counsel for Abu Zubaydah, Washington, DC, Nov. 2018–end 2020.

25. Ibid.

26. Carol Rosenberg, "Military Judge in 9/11 Trial at Guantánamo Is Retiring," *New York Times*, Mar. 25, 2020.

27. Sacha Pfeiffer, "New 9/11 Judge at Guantánamo Quits after Two Weeks," *KPBS (NPR)*, Oct. 2, 2020.

28. Carol Rosenberg, "Lawyers Press Case That 9/11 Confessions to FBI Are Tainted," *New York Times*, July 29, 2019.

29. Author interview with Harrington.

30. Author interview with Pradhan.

31. Author interviews with Mitchell. Major sources obtained via the FOIA (foia.gov) are documents released to the ACLU in preparation for *Salim v. Mitchell*, 2015–17; the National Security Archive and documents released to Ray Bonner et al., courtesy of the Media Freedom and Access Clinic at Yale University in preparation for Alex Gibney (dir.), *Forever Prisoner* (HBO Films), documentary film, 2021. ACLU and NSA documents can be obtained by searching by FOIA reference number on the ACLU and NSA websites. Releases to Ray Bonner are not yet publicly available.

32. Khalid Sheikh Mohammad statement to the International Committee of the Red Cross (ICRC), see "Khalid Sheikh Mohammed," The Rendition Project, www.therenditionproject.org.uk/prisoners/khaled-sheikh-mohammed.html.

33. For the original case brought, see Amy Roe, "ACLU Sues Psychologists Who Designed and Ran the CIA Torture Program," ACLU Washington, Oct. 13, 2015; for the settlement, see "CIA Torture Psychologists Settle Lawsuit," ACLU Washington, Aug. 17, 2007.

34. Carol Rosenberg, "The Cost of Running Guantánamo Bay: $13 Million per Prisoner," *New York Times*, Sept. 16, 2019.

35. For figures see Scott Horton, "The Guantánamo 'Suicides,'" *Harper's Magazine*, Mar. 2010.

36. Sgt. David McLean, "Columbus' Journey to Guantánamo Bay," Joint Task Force Guantánamo Public Affairs, Oct. 14, 2009, www.dvidshub.net/news/printable/40103.

37. Johanna McGeary, "Confessions of a Terrorist," *Time*, Aug. 31, 2003.

38. Abu Zubaydah drawings, author archive.

39. Abu Zubaydah statement to Combatant Status Review Tribunal (hereafter, Abu Zubaydah CSRT transcript, Mar. 2007), Mar. 27, 2007, 15-L-1645_CSRT Transcript ISN 10016_27-mar-07.pdf.

40. Abu Zubaydah wrote about these dreams in his diary, Vol. 1, pp. 44–45. According to Abu Zubaydah, he wrote Vols. 1–6 prior to capture, Vols. 7, 8, and 9, while in CIA detention, and Vols. 10 and 11 after being transferred to Guantánamo in Sept. 2006. He is currently working on Vol. 13. All volumes, excepting 13, are currently with the US government, although photocopies of the English translation of Vols. 1–6 were obtained by Jason Leopold in 2012 and published by *Al Jazeera*. Vols. 7 to 12 remain unavailable, but Abu Zubaydah has replicated some entries from this period.

41. Abu Zubaydah drawings.

42. Memo from Jay Bybee, assistant attorney general, to Alberto Gonzalez, White House counsel, Aug. 1, 2002 (hereafter, Yoo-Bybee memo).

43. Multiple references to what he shouted out in CIA cables, for example FOIA to Ray Bonner C06644662 and C06631188, Mar. 5, 2018.

44. Author interviews with Mitchell.

45. Cable dated Aug. 15, 2002, and FOIA to Salim v Mitchell C06541507, June 10, 2016.

46. Martin Seligman invented the learned helplessness theory during the 1960s; Seligman, "Learned Helplessness," *Annual Review of Medicine* 23 (1972): 407–12, ppc.sas.upenn.edu/sites/default/files /learnedhelplessness.pdf.

47. Author interviews with Hesham Abu Zubaidah, 2017–21; family photographs, author archive; Abu Zubaydah diary, Vol. 13. Hesham spells his surname differently to distance himself from his brother.

48. For Vol. 1–6, see "The Abu Zubaydah Diaries," *Al Jazeera America*, america.aljazeera.com/articles /abu-zubaydah-diaries.html.

49. Author photographic archive, interviews with Hesham Abu Zubaidah, and Abu Zubaydah correspondence.

50. Abu Zubaydah correspondence, also author interviews with Higgins.

51. The CIA's "Zubaydah Biography" is referenced in an extensive psychological assessment conducted before government lawyers gave legal approval to use enhanced techniques on him, ACLU-RDI 4560 p. 1–6, DOJ OLC 001033-38.

52. Zayn-al-Abidin Muhammad Husayn (ISN#10016) v. Lloyd Austin et al., United States District Court for the District of Columbia, Case 1:08-cv-01360-UNA, May 24, 2021.

53. Abu Zubaydah correspondence; see also Abu Zubaydah CSRT transcript, Mar. 2007.

54. Abu Zubaydah correspondence.

55. "Abu Zubaydah," The Rendition Project, www.therenditionproject.org.uk/prisoners/zubaydah .html.

56. Abu Zubaydah correspondence. In one cable reporting the interrogation of Abd al-Rahim al-Nashiri, Mitchell was quoted warning that Nashiri was "headed for the inner ring of hell," see FOIA to NSA, C06665566, 2018/07/31.

57. Author telephone interview with Maher Abu Zubaydah, May 2021.

58. Ibid.; see also Jason Leopold, "*The Other Abu Zubaidah: From Hopeful Immigrant to FBI Informant; A Truthout Reader*," Kindle, June 6, 2012.

59. Abu Zubaydah described his injuries in correspondence with the author; Abu Zubaydah CSRT transcript, Mar. 2007; Office of Medical Services report into his treatment, Summary and Reflections of Chief of Medical Services on OMS Participation in the RDI Program, C06541727, 2018/08/14 (hereafter OMS report), https://www.aclu.org/report/summary-and-reflections-chief -medical-services-oms-participation-rdi-program.

60. Abu Zubaydah CSRT transcript, Mar. 2007.

61. Abu Zubaydah correspondence.

62. Ibid.

63. Ibid.; author interviews with Higgins.

64. Author interview with Harrington.

65. Abu Zubaydah correspondence.

66. Abu Zubaydah diary.

67. "If The Detainee Dies You're Doing It Wrong," *McClatchy Newspapers*, June 17, 2008.

68. Author interviews with John Rizzo, Washington, DC, Oct. 2018, Mar. 2019, June 2019, telephone interview Mar. 2021.

69. Author interviews with Mitchell.

70. Author interviews with Roger Aldrich, Mitchell's former boss at the US Air Force SERE school, Spokane, WA, Mar. 2019, June 2019.

71. Bruce Jessen testimony to 9/11 pretrial, Jan. 31, 2020, mc.mil.

72. Author copies of Mitchell's citations.

73. Tenet and Harlow, *At the Center of the Storm*, p. xix.

74. Author interviews with Rizzo.

75. Tenet and Harlow, *At the Center of the Storm*, p. 173.

76. Author interviews with Mitchell.

77. Ibid.

78. Report to the Special Committee of the Board of Directors of the American Psychological Association, *Independent Review Relating to APA Ethics Guidelines, National Security Interrogations, and Torture* (hereafter, APA report), Sept. 4, 2015, p. 45.

79. Mitchell, Jessen and Associates, see Hunter Walker, "These 7 Men Owned the Company Linked to CIA Torture," *Business Insider*, Dec. 11, 2014, also, author interviews with Mitchell and Aldrich; for "slovenly mistake," see Office of Professional Responsibility, Department of Justice, "Investigation into the Office of Legal Counsel's Memoranda Concerning Issues Relating to the Central Intelligence Agency's Use of 'Enhanced Interrogation Techniques' on Suspected Terrorists" (hereafter, OPR report), July 29, 2009, p. 9.

80. Author interviews with Jose Rodriguez, St. Augustine, FL, July and Oct., 2018; see also Central Intelligence Agency Office of the Inspector General, *Special Review: Counterterrorism Detention and Interrogation Activities (September 2001–October 2003)*, (hereafter, OIG report), 2003-7123-IG, May 7, 2004, CIA-OIG, ACLU-RDI 4611.

81. Author interviews with Mitchell.

82. Author interview with Morell, Washington, DC, Oct. 2018.

83. All these allegations were made by defense attorneys during Mitchell's testimony at 9/11 pretrial, Jan. 2020, see mc.mil.

84. Tim Weiner, "CIA Taught, Then Dropped, Mental Torture in Latin America," *New York Times*, Jan. 29, 1997. See also opening page of KUBARK updated manual, *Human Resource Exploitation Training Manual 1983*, nsarchive2.gwu.edu//NSAEBB/NSAEBB27/docs/doc02.pdf.

85. SSCI report, p. 144.

86. SSCI report, p. xxv.

87. The link between CIA and military enhanced interrogation techniques was made by Alberto Mora, Navy general counsel on 9/11, author interviews with Mora, Feb. 2019 and June 2019; also by Larry Wilkerson, chief of staff to Secretary Colin Powell, author interviews, June 2019, and by Mark Fallon, deputy commander of the Navy's Criminal Intelligence Task Force, author interviews, June 2019.

88. SSCI report, p. xxv.

89. "Lithuania and Romania Complicit in CIA Torture—European Court," *BBC News*, May 31, 2018, www.bbc.co.uk/news/world-europe-44313905.

90. AFP, "Guantánamo Detainee to File Complaint with UN Agency," *France24*, April 30, 2021.

91. FOIA to Salim v. Mitchell, C06541507, 2016/06/10.

CHAPTER 1: "*MAI PEN RAI*"

1. Author interview with John Kiriakou, Washington, DC, Dec. 2019, plus multiple telephone interviews, 2019–21.

2. Author interview with neighbor, Shafiq Ghani, Faisalabad, Pakistan, 2014.

3. Author telephone interview with Jennifer Hale Keenan, the FBI's assistant legal attache in Pakistan from 2001–3, June 2021. Keenan coordinated all the Abu Zubaydah–related raids, the questioning of suspects, and the processing of evidence from a safe house in Lahore.

4. Author interviews with Kiriakou; also author interview with a Punjab police official who was on the raid, Faisalabad, Pakistan, May 2015.

5. 9/11 Commission, "The 9/11 Commission Report," July 22, 2004, p. 255.

6. For the President Only, "Bin Ladin Determined to Strike in US," Aug. 6. 2001, www.fas.org /irp/cia/product/pdb080601.pdf. This memo was written by Barbara Sude of Alec Station.

7. For an example of contemporaneous media reporting see Johanna McGeary; see also Romesh Ratnesar and Massimo Calabresi, "Can We Stop the Next Attack?," Time, Mar. 11, 2002.

8. Author interview with Keenan.

9. Abu Zubaydah confirmed in correspondence that his weight when he was captured was two hundred pounds.

10. Author interview with Keenan; for copies of evidence photographs see the unnumbered plates section in John Kiriakou and Michael Ruby, The Reluctant Spy: My Secret Life in the CIA's War on Terror (New York: Skyhorse Publishing, 2012).

11. FOIA to Ray Bonner, 17cv9378-349 to 351, June 8, 2018.

12. Scott Shane, "Inside a 9/11 Mastermind's Interrogation," New York Times, June 22, 2008.

13. Rodriguez and Harlow, Hard Measures, p. 176; Special Agents Chris Reiman and Dave Franco, who were on the Shahbaz Cottage raid, recalled that Kiriakou was not with them, but Keenan recalled that Kiriakou was the CIA's deputy team leader in Faisalabad.

14. Author interviews with Kiriakou.

15. Author interviews with Hesham Abu Zubaidah.

16. Robert Grenier, 88 Days to Kandahar: A CIA Diary (New York: Simon and Schuster, 2015), pp. 331–32; also author telephone interview with Grenier, Mar. 2015.

17. Author interviews with senior counterterrorism officers in Pakistan's Inter-Services Intelligence (ISI); the figure was said to be $10 million, and the ISI used the money to build a new headquarters in Islamabad.

18. Author interview with Ghani.

19. Ibid.

20. Author interview with Alvin Bernard "Buzzy" Krongard, Lutherville, MD, Nov. 2018; and with Rodriguez.

21. Author interviews with Rizzo; for skunk see SSCI report, p. 444.

22. Martin quotes from his interview in Greg Barker (dir.), Manhunt: The Search for Bin Laden (documentary), HBO Films, 2013; for Cajun patois, see Tenet and Harlow, At the Center of the Storm, p. 252.

23. Author interview with Mark Rossini, New York City, June 2019; for circulation of Geneva Conventions memo, see SSCI report, p. 22.

24. Author interview with Morell.

25. Ibid.

26. Author interviews with Rizzo, Rodriguez, and Krongard; see also Hard Measures, p. 49.

27. One example of a TOSR can be found at FOIA to Ray Bonner, C06867074, 2021/02/26.

28. Author interview with George Tenet, Chevy Chase, MD, Nov. 2018.

29. For Matthews background, see Warrick, The Triple Agent, p. 103, and Ian Shapira, "For CIA Family a Deadly Suicide Bombing Leads to Painful Divisions," Washington Post, Jan. 28, 2012. For Grenier email, see Rodriguez and Harlow, Hard Measures, p. 49.

30. John Rizzo, Company Man (New York: Scribner, 2014), p. 182.

31. George W. Bush, Decision Points (New York: Crown, 2010).

32. Ratnesar and Calabresi, "Can We Stop the Next Attack?"

33. For a definition of "disposition," see OIG report, pp. 4–5.

34. Cheney to Tim Russert, Meet the Press, NBC, Sept. 16, 2001.

35. Daniel Jones, leading investigator in the Senate "CIA Torture" investigation, said the CIA was extremely possessive of high-value detainees, see Alex Gibney (dir.), *Forever Prisoner*, HBO Films (documentary), 2021.

36. For the most unredacted copy of Mitchell's Al Qaeda resistance paper see FOIA to Ray Bonner, C05330712, 2021/03/26.

37. In an email exchange with the authors in November 2020 Mitchell said the techniques listed in his report but later redacted were the same as those listed in the *Pre-Academic Laboratory (PREAL) Operating Instructions* (hereafter, *PREAL Operating Instructions*), Department of Defense, Joint Personnel Recovery Agency, May 7, 2002, info.publicintelligence.net/DoD -PREAL.pdf.

38. Author interviews with Rodriguez and Mitchell.

39. Tenet and Harlow, *At the Center of the Storm*, p. 241.

40. Nicholas Schou, "How the CIA Hoodwinked Hollywood," *Atlantic*, July 14, 2016.

41. Author interviews with Rizzo.

42. For Rizzo's early discussions with Department of Justice lawyers, see OPR report, pp. 41–42.

43. Author interviews with Mitchell.

44. FOIA to Ray Bonner, C006630774, 2018/03/05.

45. SSCI report, p. 18.

46. Ibid.

47. Author interview with Morell.

48. For "Number Three" assertion see OMS report, p. 6; for quote see *Company Man*, p. 194.

49. OIG report, p. 12; OPR report, pp. 40–43.

50. Rizzo, *Company Man*, p. 189.

51. Ibid., p. 225.

52. Author interview with Tenet.

53. SSCI report, p. 19; see also OPR report, pp. 31–32, for references to early CIA memos on the subject of interrogation and the law.

54. Rizzo, *Company Man*, p. 190.

55. Author interviews with Kiriakou.

56. OMS report, p. 7, states one bullet; FOIA release to Ray Bonner C06745537, 2019/01/25 mentions two bullets; see also C06745538, 2019/01/28; Rizzo, *Company Man*, says three bullets, p. 3; Rodriguez, *Hard Measures*, says one bullet, p. 54.

57. Author interview with Grenier; multiple author interviews with Brigadier Azmat, Rawalpindi, Pakistan, 2018–20.

58. Author interviews with Rodriguez and Krongard.

59. Author interview with Krongard.

60. Author interview with Keenan.

61. Author interviews with Kiriakou.

62. Author archive.

63. Author interview with Keenan.

64. For a transcript of his words see FOIA to Ray Bonner, Case 1:08-cv-01360-UNA, Document 474-2, Filed 03/29/17, pp. 648–55.

65. Abu Zubaydah Diary, Vol. 6.

66. Ibid., p. 85.

67. Abu Zubaydah later contested this was done by the FBI or CIA; see Zayn-al-Abidin Muhammad Husayn (ISN#10016) v. Lloyd Austin et al., United States District Court for the District of Columbia, Case 1:08-cv-01360-UNA, May 24, 2021.

68. Rodriguez and Harlow, *Hard Measures*, p. 77.

69. Author interviews with Kiriakou. This evidence never materialized and has never been corroborated.

70. Author interviews with Kiriakou.

71. Zayn-al-Abidin Muhammad Husayn (ISN#10016) v. Lloyd Austin et al., United States District Court for the District of Columbia, Case 1:08-cv-01360-UNA, May 24, 2021.

72. Author interview with Keenan.

73. Bill Harlow (ed.), *Rebuttal: The CIA Responds to the Senate Intelligence Committee's Study of Its Detention and Interrogation Program* (Annapolis, MD: Naval Institute Press, 2015), pp. 304–5.

74. SSCI report, p. 11.

75. Grenier, *88 Days to Kandahar*, p. 333.

76. Rodriguez and Harlow, *Hard Measures*, pp. 107–8.

77. Author telephone interview with Mike Scheuer, Oct. 2018.

78. Author telephone interview with McFadden, Feb. 2021.

79. Author interview with Ric Prado, Saint Augustine, FL, Oct. 2018, and interview with Scheuer.

80. Quote from Prado, author interview; clashing with FBI and "Crazy Mike" from Jack Cloonan, author interview, Long Neck, DE, Dec. 2019, plus multiple telephone interviews, 2018–21.

81. Author interview with Prado.

82. Author interview with Rossini.

83. Author interview with Tenet.

84. Rory O'Connor and Ray Nowosielski, "Insiders Voice Doubts about CIA's 9/11 Story," *Salon*, Oct. 14, 2011.

85. Jeff Stein, "The Inside Information That Could Have Stopped 9/11," *Newsweek*, Jan. 14. 2015.

86. Warrick, *The Triple Agent*; also Shapira, "For CIA Family a Deadly Suicide Bombing Leads to Painful Divisions."

87. Scheuer statement in *Extraordinary Rendition in U.S. Counterterrorism Policy: The Impact on Transatlantic Relations*, Joint Hearing Before the Subcommittee on International Organizations, Human Rights, and Oversight and the Subcommittee on Europe of the Committee on Foreign Affairs, House of Representatives, 110th Congress, 1st session, Apr. 17, 2007, Serial No. 110–28.

88. Author interview with Cynthia Storer, Coastal Carolina University, SC, Sept. 2014.

89. Author interview with Morell.

90. Tim Golden, Stephen Engelberg, and Daniel DeFraia, "A Prisoner in Gina Haspel's Black Site," *ProPublica*, May 7, 2018.

91. Scheuer statement to *Extraordinary Rendition in U.S. Counterterrorism Policy*, Committee on Foreign Affairs, Apr. 17, 2007, Serial No. 110–28.

92. Author interview with Tenet.

93. "Abu Zubaydah was a guy who just ran a guesthouse but the CIA's chief analyst claimed he was superior even to bin Laden," author telephone interview with Cloonan, Feb. 2021.

94. "Twelve feet tall" from Ali Soufan, *The Black Banners: The Inside Story of 9/11 and the War against al-Qaeda* (New York: W. W. Norton, 2011), p. 542.

95. Quote from Barker, *Manhunt*; for Martin confirmed as head of Alec Station, see Tenet and Harlow, *At the Center of the Storm*, p. 232.

96. Author interview with Tenet.

97. Author interview with General Tritot, Ronnaritivichai, Bangkok, Thailand, Aug. 2019.

98. Author interview with Krongard.

99. Author interview with General Tritot.

100. Author interview with Chavalit Yongchaiyudh, Bangkok, Thailand, Aug. 2019.

101. Author interview with General Tritot.

102. SSCI report, p. 23.

103. Author telephone interview with Scheuer.

104. Later, it would also become known as "Location 3" or "Detention Site Green."

105. OMS report, pp. 87–88.

106. OMS report, pp. 6–7.

107. Author interview with Rodriguez; see also OIG report, pp. 9–10.
108. Tenet and Harlow, *At the Center of the Storm*, p. 241; author interview with Krongard.
109. Soufan, *The Black Banners*, p. 490.
110. Ibid.
111. Ibid.
112. Chuck Frahm told them this on the drive to Dulles; see US Department of Justice, Office of the Inspector General, *A Review of the FBI's Involvement in and Observations of Detainee Interrogations in Guantánamo Bay, Afghanistan, and Iraq* (hereafter, FBI report), rev. ed., Oct. 2009, p. 68, www.oversight.gov/sites/default/files/oig-reports/s0910.pdf.
113. Adam Goldman, "The Hidden History of the CIA's Prison in Poland," *Washington Post*, Jan. 23, 2014.
114. Gibney, *The Forever Prisoner*.
115. FBI report, pp. 318–21.
116. The officer was Tom Hale. See Kiriakou and Ruby, *The Reluctant Spy*, photographic credits in unnumbered plates section.
117. Soufan, *The Black Banners*, pp. 195–98; Soufan called Martin "Alvin" and Gamil "Fred."
118. Soufan, *The Black Banners*, p. 197.
119. Barker, *Manhunt*.
120. Soufan, *The Black Banners*, chapter 20.
121. SSCI report, p. 23.
122. SSCI report, p. 24.
123. Rodriguez and Harlow, *Hard Measures*, p. 55; and author interview with General Tritot.

CHAPTER 2: "I AM THE HEAD MOTHERFUCKER-IN-CHARGE"

1. Soufan, *The Black Banners*, p. 492.
2. OMS report, pp, 7–8.
3. Abu Zubaydah diary, Vol. 1.
4. Author interview with General Tritot; he said Abu Zubaydah asked about the planes and where he was.
5. Abu Zubaydah correspondence.
6. Bob Woodward, *Bush at War* (New York: Simon and Schuster, 2002).
7. Unclassified testimony of Cofer Black to Congress, Sept. 26, 2002, www.fas.org/irp/congress/2002_hr/092602black.html.
8. OPR report, p. 42.
9. Legal chalk line from Michael Hayden, *Playing to the Edge: American Intelligence in the Age of Terror* (New York, Penguin Press, 2016).
10. "Text: Vice President Cheney on NBC's 'Meet the Press,'" *Washington Post*, Sept. 16, 2001.
11. Author interview with Tenet.
12. Author interview with Prado; author interview with Billy Waugh, Lutz, FL, Nov. 2018. Waugh was based in Khartoum with Black.
13. FOIA to Ray Bonner, C06257473, 2021/02/26.
14. Author interview with Prado.
15. Author interviews with Rizzo.
16. Frank Foley, "Why It's So Rare to Hear an Apology for Torture," *BBC News*, Dec. 12, 2014, https://www.bbc.co.uk/news/magazine-30435652.
17. Philippe Sands, *The Torture Team* (London: Penguin, 2008).
18. Author interviews with Mora.
19. John Yoo and his colleague Robert Delahunty delivered memos that discussed war crimes to Alberto Gonzales on Nov. 30, 2001, and a more refined memo to Department of Defense counsel William Haynes on Jan. 9, 2002; see www.aclu.org/other/memo-john-yoo-and-robert-delahunty-regarding-treaties-and-laws-applicable-captured-persons.

20. SSCI report, p. 11.
21. OIG report, p. 1.
22. "Transcript of President Bush's address," *CNN*, Sept. 21, 2001.
23. OIG report, p. 12, states that Rizzo's department, the Office of General Council, "researched, analyzed and wrote 'draft' papers on multiple legal issues" between September 17, 2001 and November 7, 2001.
24. Author interview with Prado.
25. Prado said this was "a few days after 9/11"; author interview.
26. Rodriguez and Harlow, *Hard Measures*, chapter two.
27. Author interviews with Rodriguez.
28. Author interview with Prado.
29. Author interviews with Rodriguez.
30. Rodriguez and Harlow, *Hard Measures*, pp. 28 and 158–64.
31. Unclassified testimony of Cofer Black to Congress, Sept. 26, 2002.
32. Author interview with Prado.
33. Rodriguez and Harlow, *Harsh Measures*, p. 164.
34. Author interviews with Rodriguez.
35. Author interview with Tenet.
36. Author telephone interview with Glenn Carle, Feb. 2021. Carle was one of hundreds of case officers with no counterterrorism experience who were "surged" into the Counterterrorism Center post-9/11; for more see, Glenn Carle, *The Interrogator: An Education* (London: Hachette, 2011).
37. Rodriguez and Harlow, *Hard Measures*, pp. 30–37.
38. Author interviews with Rodriguez.
39. Gary Berntsen and Ralph Pezzullo, *Jawbreaker* (New York: Crown Publishing, 2005).
40. Woodward, *Bush at War*.
41. Author interview with Prado.
42. Author interview with Waugh.
43. Ibid.
44. Author interview with Prado.
45. FBI report.
46. Tim Russert, "Meet the Press," *NBC*, Sept. 16, 2001.
47. Scheuer statement to *Extraordinary Rendition in U.S. Counterterrorism Policy*, Committee on Foreign Affairs, Apr. 17, 2007, Serial No. 110–28.
48. Author interviews with "Gus," Concord, NH, Feb. 2019, also telephone interview with Gus, Oct. 2018; also interview with Mark Rossini; see also Soufan, *The Black Banners*, p. 195.
49. Author interviews with Rossini and Gus.
50. Author interviews with Rodriguez.
51. Barker, *Manhunt*.
52. Author interview with Krongard.
53. Author telephone interview with Porter Goss, July 2018; and interview, Washington DC, Oct. 2018.
54. Eric Schmidt and Erik Eckholm, "A Nation Challenged: The Hunted," *New York Times*, Jan. 6. 2002.
55. "Ibn Sheikh al-Libi," The Rendition Project, www.therenditionproject.org.uk/prisoners/ibn-sheikh -al-libi.html.
56. The two hijackers were Majed Moqed and Satam al-Suqami.
57. Author interview with Fincher's superior at the FBI, Jack Cloonan, who talked to him on the phone during this standoff.
58. OIG report, p. 99.
59. Author interviews with Cloonan.
60. Ibid.

61. Ibid., Gamil has never agreed to an interview. See also James Risen, *State of War: The Secret History of the CIA and the Bush Administration* (New York: Scribner, 2006).

62. Author interviews with Cloonan; see also Report of the Select Committee on Intelligence on Post War Findings about Iraq's WMD Programs and Links to Terrorism and How They Compare with Prewar Assessments, 109th Congress, 2nd Session, Sept. 8, 2006, www.therenditionproject .org.uk/documents/RDI/060908-SSCI-Iraq-WMD-Terrorism-Report.pdf.

63. In Jan. 2004, after being put into CIA custody, al-Libi was "debriefed" by Mitchell and Jessen. Author interviews with Mitchell. See also SSCI report, p. 141.

64. Author interviews with Moazzam Begg, a former Guantánamo detainee and outreach director at CAGE, a British charity that campaigns for the release of War on Terror detainees and investigates the fates of those who went missing, 2019–2021; see also, Alex Gibney (dir.), *Taxi to the Dark Side* (Discovery Channel, Jigsaw Productions), documentary film, 2007.

65. Tenet and Harlow, *At the Center of the Storm*, p. 269.

66. Author interviews with Mitchell.

67. "Ibn Sheikh al-Libi," The Rendition Project, www.therenditionproject.org.uk/prisoners/ibn -sheikh-al-libi.html.

68. Author interview with Tenet.

69. Woodward, *Bush at War.*

70. "List of 'Ghost Prisoners' Possibly in CIA Custody," *Human Rights Watch*, Nov. 30 2005, www .hrw.org/news/2005/11/30/list-ghost-prisoners-possibly-cia-custody.

71. SSCI report, p. 22.

72. Tenet and Harlow, *At the Center of the Storm*, p. 354.

73. Rodriguez and Harlow, *Hard Measures*, p. 52.

74. Tenet and Harlow, *At the Center of the Storm*, p. 240.

75. Rodriguez and Harlow, *Hard Measures*, pp. 45–48; see also Rodriguez interview in Barker, *Manhunt.*

76. Author interviews with Gus.

77. Author interviews with Mitchell.

78. Abu Zubaydah diary, vol. 6, p. 91.

79. Ibid, p. 84.

80. Rodriguez and Harlow, *Hard Measures*, p. 32

81. Author interviews with Rodriguez.

82. OIG report, p. 13.

83. Ibid., also author interviews with Rizzo.

84. Rodriguez deposition to Salim v. Mitchell, Mar. 7, 2017, see https://www.aclu.org/sites/default /files/field_document/205-2._exhibit_b.pdf.

85. Soufan, *The Black Banners*, pp. 491–92.

86. FBI cable 17cv9378-345 to 348, FOIA to Ray Bonner, May 15, 2018.

87. Gaudin describes his limited Arabic skills and past investigations during testimony to the al-Nashiri pretrial at Guantánamo in Nov. 2017; see www.mc.mil/Portals/0/pdfs/alNashiri2/Al%20 Nashiri%20II%20(TRANS3Nov2017).pdf.

88. FBI cable, 17cv9378-345 to 348, FOIA to Ray Bonner, May 15, 2018.

89. Rodriguez and Harlow, *Hard Measures*, p. 56.

90. Both Chuck Frahm and John Rizzo claimed this but later downplayed Tenet's anger, Gibney, *The Forever Prisoner.*

91. Author interview with Bob Dussault, former deputy director of JPRA, who also bid for the CIA interrogation contract and said he was told that this was Tenet's order, June 2019, Seattle, WA.

92. Soufan, *The Black Banners*, pp. 494–95.

93. Author interview with Tenet.

94. Author interviews with Rizzo.

95. SSCI report, pp. 22–26.

96. Ibid.

97. OIG report, p. 13, states that the recommendation to use SERE techniques originated with Mitchell and Jessen.
98. Author interviews with Rodriguez.
99. Ibid.
100. Soufan, *The Black Banners*, pp. 499–500.
101. OMS report, pp. 7–8.
102. Jose Rodriguez describes this promise in Rodriguez and Harlow, *Hard Measures*, p. 54; also, author interviews, Concord, NH, Feb. 2019.
103. Soufan, *The Black Banners*, p. 500, Ali Soufan asserts this order came directly from Tenet's office; see also Gibney, *The Forever Prisoner.*
104. Author interview with General Tritot.

CHAPTER 3: "HANI 1"

1. Abu Zubaydah explains his method in the opening pages of his diary, Vol. 1, and in Vol. 13.
2. Abu Zubaydah diary, Vol. 1, p. 7.
3. Abu Zubaydah diary, Vol. 1, p. 19.
4. Ibid.
5. Author interviews with Hesham Abu Zubaidah; Ben White, "The Jordan Valley's Forgotten Palestinians," *The Electronic Intifada*, May 30, 2008.
6. White, "The Jordan Valley's Forgotten Palestinians"; and Palestinian Localities Study, Jericho Governate, "Az Zubeidat Village Profile," The Applied Rserach Institute—Jerusalem, 2012, vprofile.arij.org/jericho/pdfs/vprofile/Az%20Zubeidat_en_Final.pdf.
7. Author interviews with Hesham Abu Zubaidah.
8. Abu Zubaydah correspondence.
9. Peter Beinart, "A Jewish Case for Palestinian Refugee Return," *Guardian*, May 18, 2021.
10. Author photographic archive.
11. A ground-floor apartment in al-Salam building opposite the al-Hijaz bus stop in Shumaisi, Abu Zubaydah diary, Vol. 1.
12. Abu Zubaydah diary, Vol. 1, p. 15.
13. Ibid., p. 19.
14. Abu Zubaydah diary, Vol. 1.
15. Ibid., p. 16.
16. Author interviews with Hesham Abu Zubaidah.
17. Ibid.
18. Abu Zubaydah diary, Vol. 1, p. 22.
19. Ibid., pp. 44–45.
20. Author interviews with Hesham Abu Zubaidah.
21. OMS report, pp. 7–8, see also *The Black Banners*, pp. 500–501.
22. Author interview General Tritot, 2019. See also Soufan, *The Black Banners*, pp. 500–501.
23. OMS report, pp. 7–8.
24. SSCI report, p. 27.
25. Author interview with General Tritot.
26. Author interviews with Hesham Abu Zubaidah; FOIA to Ray Bonner, FBI cables, 17cv9378-1, and 17cv9378-6, June 4, 2018.
27. Author email exchange with Hubbard, 2017; author interviews with Mitchell, 2017–20; see also, M. Gregg Bloche, M.D., *The Hippocratic Myth: Why Doctors Are Under Pressure to Ration Care, Practice Politics, and Compromise Their Promise to Heal* (New York: Palgrave Macmillan, 2011).
28. Author interviews with Marwan Shehadah, journalist, author, and expert in jihadist publications, Amman, Jordan, 2014–21; and with Mitchell.
29. "How to Deal with the Interrogator: A Field Manual," *Free Arab Voice*, 2005.
30. See FOIA to Ray Bonner, C06867065, 2021/02/26.

31. Author interview with Babar Ahmad, London, Oct. 2019.

32. *The Al Qaeda Manual*, Part 1, UK/BM-1 Translation, Department of Justice, October 8, 2002, www.justice.gov/sites/default/files/ag/legacy/2002/10/08/manualpart1_1.pdf.

33. Author interviews with Cloonan, who handled Ali Mohamed after he immigrated to America and who worked on the embassy investigation in which Mohamed was implicated.

34. Deborah Feyerick and Phil Hirschkorn, "Jury Convicts Four on All Charges in Embassy Bombings," *CNN*, May 29, 2001.

35. Multiple references in declassified CIA cables.

36. Mitchell said in an email exchange with the author that his countermeasures were based on the techniques laid out in the *PREAL Operating Instructions*.

37. Rodriguez deposition to Salim v. Mitchell, p. 40.

38. Author interviews with Rodriguez.

39. Author interviews with Aldrich and Dussault.

40. Kevin Weeks and Phyllis Karas, *Brutal: The Untold Story of My Life Inside Whitey Bulger's Irish Mob* (New York: HarperCollins, 2007), pp. 83–84.

41. Stephen Kinzer, *The Poisoner in Chief* (New York: Henry Holt, 2019).

42. *KUBARK Counterintelligence Interrogation*, CIA, July 1963; it can be accessed via www.nsarchive2 .gwu.

43. Terry Gross, "The CIA's Secret Quest for Mind Control: Torture, LSD and a 'Poisoner in Chief,'" *Fresh Air*, NPR, Sept. 9, 2019.

44. For a copy of the *Human Resource Exploitation Training Manual*—1983, see Thomas Blanton, "Prisoner Abuse: Patterns from the Past, National Security Archive Electronic Briefing Books No 122," *The National Security Archive*, Feb. 25, 2014.

45. Tim Weiner, "C.I.A. Taught, Then Dropped, Mental Torture in Latin America," *New York Times*, Jan. 29, 1997.

46. Gary Cohn, Ginger Thompson, and Mark Matthews, "Torture Was Taught by CIA," *Baltimore Sun*, Jan. 27, 1997; see also SSCI report, p. 19.

47. SSCI report, p. 26.

48. Mitchell shared his annual performance reports the author.

49. APA report; author interviews with Mitchell.

50. This contract was signed on August 8, 2001, see FOIA to Salim v. Mitchell #000032-36, 07/01/2016,

51. Philipson had "worked on interrogations before," APA report, pp. 157–58; author email correspondence with Hubbard, 2017–18.

52. For references to McConnell see APA report, p. 157–58, OMS report, p. 11, and *The Dark Side*, p. 163.

53. *PREAL Operating Instructions*.

54. Ben Taub, "The Spy Who Came Home," *New Yorker*, April 30, 2018.

55. Author interview with Prado.

56. Robert Beckhusen, "Top CIA Spy Accused of Being a Mafia Hitman," *Wired*, June 27, 2012.

57. Author interviews with Mitchell and Aldrich; also *PREAL Operating Instructions*.

58. The pilot was Frank Schwable, see Jane Mayer, *The Dark Side* (New York: Doubleday, 2008), pp. 158–59.

59. Albert D. Biderman and Herbert Zimmer, *The Manipulation of Human Behavior* (New York: John Wiley and Sons, 1961).

60. Bruce Jessen to 9/11 pretrial, Jan. 31, 2020, mc.mil.

61. Author interview with Charles Morgan, New Haven, CT, June 2019, see also deposition of Charles Morgan to Salim v. Mitchell, Apr. 27, 2017, www.aclu.org/legal-document/salim-v-mitchell -exhibit-k-3.

62. Author interviews with Scott Shumate, Mar. 2019, June 2019, Dec. 2019, and Jan. 2020, Reston, VA; also deposition of Morgan (ibid.).

63. OMS did see the CIA's preparatory materials for the EIT program until spring 2003, OMS report, pp. 16, 80, 87–88.

64. Author interviews with Susan Brandon, New York, Dec. 2019 and Jan. 2021.

65. Author interview with Morgan.

66. Author email exchange with Hubbard; see also APA report.

67. Maria Konnikova, "The Real Lessons of the Stanford Prison Experiment," *New Yorker*, June 12, 2015.

68. Emails from Kirk Hubbard, December 2017; also author interviews with Brandon.

69. APA report, p. 2.

70. Author interviews with Brandon.

71. SSCI report, p. 17.

72. OPR report, p. 31; OIG report, p. 12.

73. SSCI report, p. 19.

74. OIG report, p. 12; SSCI report, p. 19; author interviews with Rizzo.

75. For the President Only, "Bin Ladin Determined to Strike in US," Aug. 6. 2001, www.fas.org /irp/cia/product/pdb080601.pdf.

76. Author interviews with Mitchell.

77. Ibid.

78. Ibid.

79. FOIA to Salim v. Mitchell, #000037-42, July 1, 2016.

80. Author interviews with Mitchell.

81. For "$16,000," FOIA to Salim v. Mitchell, #000037-42, 07/01/2016; quotes from Jessen 9/11 pretrial testimony.

82. FOIA to Ray Bonner, C05330712, Mar. 26, 2021.

83. FOIA to Ray Bonner, C06867065, Mar. 26, 2021.

84. "Jordan: Slander Charge Signals Chill," *Human Rights Watch*, Dec. 22, 2004, www.hrw.org/news /2004/12/22/jordan-slander-charge-signals-chill.

85. Glenn Kessler and Scott Wilson, "Slander Case Seen as Test of Free Dissent," *Seattle Times*, Jan. 28, 2005.

86. Ibrahim Alloush, "Ali Hattar Arrested on His Arrival to Amman Airport Monday," *Free Arab Voice*, Mar. 19, 2001; also "Anti-Normalization Activist Arrested on Return to Amman," *Al-bawaba*, Mar. 20, 2001.

87. Author email exchange with Mitchell, Nov. 2019.

88. *PREAL Operating Instructions.*

89. Author interview with Shiffrin, Tarpon Springs, FL, June 2019; and telephone interview, Feb. 2021.

90. Author interview with Morgan.

91. Mitchell testimony to 9/11 pretrial.

92. Martin Seligman, *The Hope Circuit* (Boston: Nicholas Brealey Publishing, 2018), pp. 295–310; for details of his home, see Stacey Burling, "The Power of a Positive Thinker," *Philadelphia Inquirer*, May 30, 2010.

93. Martin Seligman, "The Hoffman Report, the Central Intelligence Agency, and the Defense of the Nation: A Personal Review," *Health Psychology Open* 5, no. 2 (July–Dec 2018): 2055102918796192.

94. Martin Seligman and Steve Maier, "Failure to Escape Traumatic Shock," *Journal of Experimental Psychology* 74 (1967): 1–9; also Seligman, "Learned Helplessness," *Annual Review of Medicine* 23 (1972): 407–12.

95. Author interviews with Brandon.

96. Seligman, *The Hope Circuit*, pp. 295–310.

97. Ibid., p. 297.

98. Feb. 1, 2002; see SSCI report, p. 20. The CIA had "rallied" for the Geneva Conventions to be dispensed with, Fredman said during a counter-resistance strategy meeting on Oct. 2, 2002, at Guantánamo Bay, Cuba, *Inquiry into the Treatment of Detainees in U.S.: Custody Report of the*

Committee on Armed Services, US Senate, 110th Congress, 2nd session, Nov. 20, 2008 (hereafter, SASC report), p. 3.

99. SSCI report, p. 20.
100. "Humane Treatment of Taliban and Al Qaeda Detainees," The White House, Washington, Feb. 7, 2002, www.pegc.us/archive/White_House/bush_memo_20020207_ed.pdf.
101. Mayer, *The Dark Side*, p. 194.
102. Author emails with Seligman; also, Seligman, *The Hope Circuit*, pp. 298–99.
103. Author interviews with Mitchell.
104. SASC report, pp. 11, 15, 184; author telephone interview Chris Wirts, Feb. 2021.
105. Author interviews with Shiffrin.
106. Jessen testimony to 9/11 pretrial; this paper was delivered on Feb. 28, 2002.
107. SASC report, pp. 11, 15.
108. Author interview with Wirts.
109. SASC report, pp. 8–10; the official request for the slide presentations came from the Defense Intelligence Agency (DIA), which handled military intelligence.
110. SASC report, pp. 8–11.
111. Ibid., pp. 10–11.
112. SASC report, pp. 25–26.
113. Jessen 9/11 pretrial testimony.
114. SASC report, p. 7.
115. Jessen 9/11 pretrial testimony.
116. Author interview with Steven Kleinman, Washington, DC, June 2019.
117. SASC report, p. xiv.
118. Author interviews with Mitchell and Wirts.
119. APA report, pp. 163–64; for Vogt see Associated Press, "CIA to Testify on Destruction of Interrogation Tapes," *NPR*, Dec. 20, 2007.
120. Seligman, *The Hope Circuit*, pp. 299–302.
121. Ibid., p. 301.
122. Ibid.
123. Hubbard email to author Dec. 23, 2017.
124. OPR report, p. 37.
125. OPR report, p. 42; Mitchell differentiated between acute and profound learned helplessness, saying in his *Salim v. Mitchell* deposition that "it's so unlikely as to be impossible" that those subjected to EITs, in the way the program intended, would suffer from long term physical or psychological harm.
126. Morgan deposition to Salim v. Mitchell, Apr. 27, 2017.
127. OPR report, p. 37.
128. Rizzo denies this. See OPR report, pp. 37–42.
129. OPR report, p. 197.
130. Dan Jones, *Intercepted Podcast*.
131. Tenet and Harlow, *At the Center of the Storm*, p. 242; OPR report, p. 37.
132. OPR report, pp. 37–39.
133. OMS report, pp. 80, 88.
134. Gibney, *The Forever Prisoner*.
135. Author interviews with Shumate.
136. "Suggestions for Japanese Interpreters Based on Work in the Field," by Sherwood F. Moran, Major, USMC, Division Intelligence Section, Headquarters, First Marine Division, Fleet Marine Force, San Francisco, CA, 168/292 July 17, 1943.
137. Author interviews with Shumate; see also Stephen Budiansky, "Truth Extraction," *Atlantic*, June 2005.
138. Author interviews with Shumate.

139. SSCI report, p. 26.
140. Rodriguez deposition to Salim v. Mitchell.
141. Ibid.
142. Author interviews with Mitchell.
143. Abu Zubaydah correspondence.
144. SSCI report, p. 26.
145. FOIA to Ray Bonner, C06656059, Feb. 22, 2020.
146. FOIA to Ray Bonner, C067545394, Jan. 25, 2019.
147. Mitchell and Harlow, *Enhanced Interrogation*, p. 11; Soufan, *The Black Banners*, p. 163; this view is shared by Cloonan, who was Ali Mohamed's FBI handler, author interviews with Cloonon.
148. Author interviews with Cloonan
149. FOIA to Ray Bonner, C06745465, 2018/11/19, and C06745463, 2019/01/25.

CHAPTER 4: "DISGRACE IN THEIR FACE"

1. FOIA to Ray Bonner, C06656059, Feb. 25, 2020; in an interview with the author Mitchell said this meeting was unrelated to Abu Zubaydah's interrogation.
2. Author interviews with Mitchell.
3. Quoted in Husain v. Poland, 2014, www.reprieve.org.uk/wp-content/uploads/2015/04/2014_07 _24_PUB-ECHR-judgement-ABU-ZUBAYDAH-v-POLAND.pdf.
4. Mitchell and Harlow, *Enhanced Interrogation*, p. 9; also author interviews with Mitchell.
5. Mitchell and Harlow, *Enhanced Interrogation*, p. 9.
6. Ibid., p.10.
7. Seligman, *The Hope Circuit*, p. 301.
8. Author interviews with Mitchell and his unpublished stories from childhood.
9. Author interviews with Mitchell.
10. Ibid.
11. Ibid., also Mitchell's unpublished stories from childhood.
12. Ibid.
13. Ibid.
14. Ibid.
15. Author interviews with Mitchell.
16. Ibid.
17. Ibid.
18. Mitchell's unpublished stories from childhood; also author interviews with Mitchell.
19. Author interviews with Mitchell.
20. Ibid.
21. Author interviews with Mitchell.
22. Ibid.
23. Mitchell certificates and citations.
24. Author interview with Kleinman.
25. Author interviews with Mitchell.
26. Anonymous (1946). "Current Comment: Psychiatric Examination of Rudolf Hess," *Journal of the American Medical Association* 130, no. 790, doi:10.1001/jama.1946.02870120036012.
27. Author interviews with Aldrich.
28. Ibid.
29. Ibid.
30. *PREAL Operating Instructions.*
31. Morgan deposition to Salim v. Mitchell.
32. Author interviews with Aldrich.
33. Ibid.

34. Ibid.
35. For "stickler," author interviews with Kleinman.
36. Author interviews with Aldrich.
37. Ibid.
38. Author interviews with Mitchell.
39. Author telephone interview with Butch Stoddard, Don Hutchings's stepbrother, Apr. 2018.
40. Author interviews with Mitchell.
41. Mitchell performance reports, author archive.
42. Tim Wilkerson and Scott Fales. Author interview with Scott Fales, Fredericksburg, VA, July 2018.
43. Author interviews with Mitchell.
44. Mitchell performance reports, author archive.
45. Author interviews with Aldrich.
46. Author interviews with Mitchell.
47. Ibid.
48. Adrian Levy and Cathy Scott-Clark, *The Meadow* (London: HarperCollins, 2012).
49. Author interviews with Mitchell.
50. Levy and Scott-Clark, *The Meadow*.
51. Author interviews with Mitchell.
52. Ibid.
53. Author interviews with Rodriguez.
54. Ibid., also author with interviews Mitchell, author interviews with Harlow, 2018–2019, Washington, DC; also Mitchell and Harlow, *Enhanced Interrogation*, pp. 12–15.
55. Rodriguez and Harlow, *Hard Measures*, p. 164.
56. Mitchell and Harlow, *Enhanced Interrogation*, p. 12.
57. AP, "Anti-terror Raids Yield Bonanza for U.S. Intelligence," *Washington Post*, Apr. 3, 2002.
58. The CIA's assessment of Abu Zubaydah was reproduced in his psychological assessment: ACLU-RDI 4560 p. 1–6, DOJ OLC 001033-38.
59. 9/11 Commission Report, p. 175.
60. FOIA to Ray Bonner, C06745465, 2018/11/19, and C06745463, 2019/01/25.
61. Rodriguez and Harlow, *Hard Measures*, p. 59.
62. Mitchell and Harlow, *Enhanced Interrogation*, p. 13; also Mitchell to 9/11 pretrial.
63. OPR report, pp. 40–42.
64. OPR report, p. 197.
65. Author interviews with Rodriguez.
66. Rodriguez deposition to Salim v. Mitchell.
67. Mitchell to 9/11 pretrial.
68. Ibid.
69. Author interviews with Rizzo.
70. During his meeting with Dianne Beaver on Oct. 2, 2002, Jonathan Fredman allegedly told her that the CIA "makes the call internally on most of the types of techniques," Counter Resistance Strategy Meeting Minutes, see Index of Documents, "The origins of aggressive interrogation techniques," Senate Armed Services Committee inquiry into the treatment of detainees in U.S. custody, Nov. 20, 2008 (hereafter SASC report Index), http://hrlibrary.umn.edu/OathBetrayed /SASC-08.pdf, pp. 14–17.
71. Mitchell to 9/11 pretrial.
72. Mitchell and Harlow, *Enhanced Interrogation*, p. 15.
73. Author interviews with Mitchell.
74. Author interviews with Shumate; also OMS report, pp. 87–88; also OIG report, p. 35.
75. Mitchell to 9/11 pretrial.
76. Author interviews with Mitchell.
77. Four times, OMS report, p. 30; $3,000 a day, interviews with Mitchell; quote from contract document, see FOIA to Salim v. Mitchell, #000048, July 1, 2016.

78. FOIA to Salim v. Mitchell, #001101, Sept. 2, 2016.

79. FOIA to Salim v. Mitchell, #001923, Apr. 11, 2017.

80. "The Al Qaeda Manual," Department of Justice, Oct. 8, 2002; for the most unredacted copy of Mitchell's Al Qaeda resistance paper see FOIA to Ray Bonner, C05330712, 2021/03/26.

81. Soufan, *The Black Banners*, pp. 163–64.

82. Soufan interview, see Gibney, *The Forever Prisoner*; at the beginning of Vol. 6 of Abu Zubaydah's diary he writes extensively about his dislike for this group.

83. Hugh Dellios, "Palestinian-American Khalil Deek Stands Trial This Month," *The Chicago Tribune*, Mar. 5, 2000.

84. See the start of Vol. 6 of Abu Zubaydah's diary for evidence of this.

85. Author interview with McFadden, Feb. 2021.

86. Harlow, *Rebuttal*.

87. FOIA to Ray Bonner, C06745483, 2019/01/25.

88. Rizzo, *Company Man*, p. 185–86.

89. Author interviews with Rizzo.

90. Author interviews with Mitchell.

91. Gibney, *The Forever Prisoner*.

92. OPR report, pp. 185–86.

93. OPR report, p. 39.

Chapter 5: "The Hell with Chris de Burgh"

1. Author interviews with Shumate.

2. Mitchell and Harlow, *Enhanced Interrogation*, p. 21.

3. Author interviews with Mitchell.

4. Mitchell's unpublished childhood memoir.

5. Scott Shumate and Randy Borum, "Psychological Support to Defense Counterintelligence Operations," *Military Psychology* 18, no. 4 (2006): 283–96.

6. Ibid.

7. Mitchell to 9/11 pretrial and author interview.

8. Author interviews with Shumate.

9. FOIA to Salim v. Mitchell, #001779, Sept. 20, 2016.

10. As described but not named by McFadden and Gus, author interviews.

11. Author interviews with Shumate.

12. SSCI report, p. 87.

13. Author email exchange with Hubbard.

14. Author interviews with Shumate.

15. Ibid.

16. OMS report, p. 8.

17. Soufan, *The Black Banners*, p. 514.

18. Gibney, *The Forever Prisoner*.

19. Author interviews with Shumate.

20. Ibid.

21. Soufan, *The Black Banners*, chapter fifteen; and Gibney, *The Forever Prisoner*.

22. Satam al-Suqami (American Airlines 11) and Majed Moqed (American Airlines 77).

23. Soufan, *The Black Banners*, p. 488.

24. Levy and Scott-Clark, *The Exile* (New York: Bloomsbury, 2017).

25. Mitchell and Harlow, *Enhanced Interrogation*, p. 23.

26. Author interviews with Mitchell.

27. FOIA to Salim v. Mitchell, #001999-2000, 12/20/2016.

28. Abu Zubaydah correspondence.

29. Ibid.

30. Ibid.
31. OMS report, p. 8.
32. Abu Zubaydah correspondence.
33. Ibid.
34. Ibid.
35. Ibid.
36. Dexter Filkins, "How Did Abu Zubaydah Lose His Eye?," *New Yorker*, June 9, 2015.
37. Abu Zubaydah correspondence.
38. Ibid.
39. FOIA to Ray Bonner, 17cv9378-18, 27, and 34, 05/15/2018.
40. The 9/11 Commission Report, pp. 174–82.
41. Judith Miller, "Dissecting a Terror Plot from Boston to Amman," *New York Times*, Jan. 15, 2001; for FBI take, see FOIA to Ray Bonner, 17cv9378-8, 05/16/2018.
42. The 9/11 Commission Report, pp. 174–75.
43. Ibid., p. 175.
44. Tenet and Harlow, *At the Center of the Storm*, pp. 125–26.
45. The 9/11 Commission Report, p. 176.
46. Craig Pyes, "Canada Add Details on Algerians' Suspected Bomb Plot," *New York Times*, Jan. 21, 2000.
47. United States of America v. Ahmed Ressam, United States District Court, Western District of Washington at Seattle, Case No. 99-547M, Complaint for Violation USC, Title 18, Sections 842(a) (3) (A) and 1001, before David E. Wilson, United States Magistrate Judge United States Courthouse, 1010 Fifth Avenue, Seattle, Washington.
48. Author interview with FBI Special Agent Fred Humphries, Land O'Lakes, FL, Oct. 2018.
49. Zayn-al-Abidin Muhammad Husayn (ISN#10016) v. Lloyd Austin et al., United States District Court for the District of Columbia, Case 1:08-cv-01360-UNA, May 24, 2021.
50. The 9/11 Commission Report, pp. 176–80.
51. Author interview with Hanani, see also Sean O'Neill, "'Architect of Terror' Held in British Jail Cell," *Telegraph*, Jan. 9, 2003.
52. Abu Zubaydah diary.
53. Hugh Dellios, "Palestinian-American Khalil Deek Stands Trial This Month," *The Chicago Tribune*, Mar. 5, 2000.
54. Miller, "Dissecting a Terror Plot from Boston to Amman."
55. Ibid.
56. Phil Reeves, "Six Muslim Militants Sentenced to Death for Plotting to Attack Tourists in Jordan," *Independent*, Sept. 9, 2000.
57. Nick Schou, "Where Is Missing OCS Terrorist?" *OC Weekly*, June 15, 2006.
58. Miller, "Dissecting a Terror Plot from Boston to Amman."
59. Abu Zubaydah correspondence.
60. Ron Suskind, *The One Percent Doctrine* (New York, Simon and Schuster, 2006), p. 62.
61. Abu Zubaydah correspondence.
62. Tenet and Harlow, *At the Center of the Storm*, p. 243.
63. Abu Zubaydah diary, Vol. 6.
64. Author interviews with Mitchell.
65. Abu Zubaydah correspondence.
66. Ibid.
67. Abu Zubaydah diary, Vol. 13.
68. Photocopies of the original Arabic diary.
69. Abu Zubaydah diary, Vol. 1, p. 12.
70. Ibid.
71. Ibid.
72. Abu Zubaydah correspondence.

73. Ibid.

74. Abu Zubaydah diary, Vol. 13.

75. Ibid.

76. Abu Zubaydah diary, Vol. 1, p. 15.

77. Ibid., Vol. 1, p. 27.

78. Ibid, Vol. 1.

79. Author interview Abdullah Anas, London, 2015; see also Abdullah Anas, *To The Mountains* (Oxford: Oxford University Press, 2019).

80. Abu Zubaydah correspondence.

81. Abu Zubaydah diary, Vol. 1, p. 22.

82. Ibid., p. 34.

83. Ibid., p. 37.

84. Benjamin Weiser, "Bombing Suspect Threatened His Interrogators, They Testify," *New York Times*, Dec. 13, 2000.

85. Abu Zubaydah correspondence.

86. Ibid.

87. Al-Adel had already obtained sanctuary in Iran. Author interviews with Mahfouz Ibn El Waleed, Nouckchott, Mauritania, Dec. 2014, Jan. 2015, June 2015.

88. According to Abu Zubaydah interview notes written by Gaudin and Soufan in April 2002 and sent to CIA and FBI headquarters, FOIA to Ray Bonner, FBI(21-cv-2166)-94 - 164, Nov 19, 2021.

89. Steve Gaudin interview, Alex Gibney (dir.), *The Forever Prisoner*, HBO Films (documentary), 2021.

90. Ali Soufan interview, Alex Gibney (dir.), *The Forever Prisoner*, HBO Films (documentary), 2021.

91. Abu Zubaydah correspondence.

92. Soufan, *The Black Banners*, p. 529.

93. Yosri Fouda and Nick Fielding, *Masterminds of Terror* (London: Random House, 2011); quote from Abu Zubaydah diary, Vol. 1, p. 9.

94. Soufan, *The Black Banners*, pp. 507–8.

95. Ibid.

96. Abu Zubaydah correspondence.

97. Ibid.

98. Mitchell to 9/11 pretrial.

99. FOIA to Ray Bonner, C06745509, 2019/01/25.

100. Ibid.

101. Author interviews with Mitchell.

102. Author interviews with Mitchell and Tenet.

103. Mitchell to 9/11 pretrial.

104. *PREAL Operating Instructions*.

105. Soufan, *The Black Banners*, p. 515; Mitchell disputed this was his plan during an interview with the author.

106. *KUBARK Counterintelligence Interrogation*, July 1963.

107. Mitchell to 9/11 pretrial.

108. Author interviews with Mitchell.

109. Soufan, *The Black Banners*, p. 517.

110. Jessen to 9/11 pretrail.

111. Author interviews with Mitchell.

112. *PREAL Operating Instructions*.

113. Author interviews with Mitchell; also FOIA to Ray Bonner, C06745492, 2018/11/19.

114. Author interviews with Shumate.

115. Author interviews with Mitchell.

116. FOIA to Salim v. Mitchell, #001999-2000, 12/20/2016.

117. Author interviews with Mitchell. For more on the cell environment, see FOIA to Ray Bonner, C06745492, 2018/11/19.

118. FOIA to Salim v. Mitchell, #001999-0012000, 12/20/2016.
119. FOIA to Salim v. Mitchell, #001782, 12/20/2016.
120. Author interviews with Rizzo.
121. FOIA to Salim v. Mitchell, #001782, 12/20/2016.
122. FOIA to Ray Bonner, C06745496, 2019/01/29.
123. Author interviews with Mitchell.
124. Rodriguez, *Hard Measures*, p. 55.
125. Author interviews with Mitchell.
126. Author interviews with Rodriguez.

CHAPTER 6: "OH MY GOD, I CAN BE HORRIBLE"

1. SSCI report, p. 27.
2. Soufan's missing cables are explored in Gibney, *The Forever Prisoner*.
3. FOIA to Ray Bonner, C06745393, 2019/01/25.
4. FOIA to Ray Bonner, C06745496, 2019/01/29.
5. Author interviews with Mitchell and Aldrich.
6. FOIA to Salim v. Mitchell, C06656126 and C06745516 on 2018/08/02.
7. Ibid.
8. Abu Zubaydah diary, Vol. 1, p. 25; Abu Zubaydah correspondence.
9. FOIA to Ray Bonner, C06656123, 2018/08/02.
10. Ibid.
11. FOIA to Ray Bonner, C06745508, 2019/01/25; "bare bones" quote from SSCI report, p. 111.
12. FOIA to Ray Bonner, C06656126, 2018/08/02.
13. Ibid.
14. FOIA to Ray Bonner, C06656128, 2018/08/02.
15. Author interviews with Mitchell; see also FOIA to Ray Bonner, C06644730, 2018/08/02.
16. Rizzo, *Company Man*, pp. 224, 270.
17. Mayer, *The Dark Side*, p. 188.
18. Ibid, p. 197; author interviews with Larry Wilkerson.
19. Author interview with Morell.
20. OPR report, pp. 39–42.
21. Ibid.; see also FOIA to Ray Bonner, C06745496, 2019/01/29.
22. *PREAL Operating Instructions*; also Jessen to 9/11 pretrial.
23. OPR report, p. 42.
24. Ibid.
25. Author interviews with Mitchell.
26. FOIA to Ray Bonner, C06745496, 2019/01/29.
27. Author interviews with Aldrich.
28. Author interviews with Shumate.
29. FOIA to Salim v. Mitchell, C00656129, 2018/08/02.
30. Abu Zubaydah correspondence.
31. For an explanation of how "conditioning factors" were deployed, see FOIA to Salim v. Mitchell, #002001-5, 12/20/2016.
32. Abu Zubaydah diary, Vol. 1, p. 11.
33. Abu Zubaydah statement recorded by his lawyer Amanda Jacobsen, Aug. 31, 2011, Guantánamo Bay, Cuba (hereafter Abu Zubaydah to Jacobsen).
34. *PREAL Operating Instructions*; for "firmly roust," see FOIA to Ray Bonner, C06745496, 2019/01/29.
35. Author interviews with Mitchell.
36. FOIA to Ray Bonner, C06656129, 2018/08/02; for Soufan's reactions, see Soufan, *The Black Banners*, pp. 545–46.

37. Soufan, *The Black Banners*, chapter twenty-one.

38. Author interview with Morgan; also Morgan deposition to Salim v. Mitchell, 2017.

39. Abu Zubaydah to Jacobsen.

40. FOIA to Ray Bonner, C06745513, 2019/01/30.

41. Ibid.

42. Author interviews with Mitchell.

43. Ibid.

44. Open Society Justice Initiative, *Globalizing Torture; CIA Secret Detention and Extraordinary Rendition* (New York: Open Society Foundations, 2013), p. 38, www.justiceinitiative.org/uploads/655bbd41-082b-4df3-940c-18a3bd9ed956/globalizing-torture-20120205.pdf.

45. See Abu Zubaydah diary, Vol. 6, p. 28, for a description of how he cared for the brothers. At least seven were captured with him. Six ended up in GTMO: Noor Uthman Mohamad, Khalid Hubayshi, Jabran al Qahtani, Ghassan al Sharbi, Sufyian Barhoumi, and Abdul Zahir. The last three are still at GTMO. According to Clive Stafford Smith, former GTMO detainee Ahmed al-Darbi was possibly in the group too; he was released in 2018. Author interview with Stafford Smith, London, Dec. 2016. Syrian Noor al-Deen, who was still a teenager at the time of the Faisalabad raid, was rendered to Temara and then to Syria in May 2002, after which he disappeared. Another man detained with Abu Zubaydah, Omar Ghramesh, was also rendered to Syria in May 2002, and subsequently disappeared. See Ibid., pp. 38–41.

46. FOIA to Salim v. Mitchell, #002017.

47. SSCI report, p. 49.

48. Abu Zubaydah to Jacobsen.

49. FOIA to Salim v. Mitchell, #001777, 12/20/2016.

50. FOIA to Ray Bonner, C06656129, 2018/08/02.

51. FOIA to Salim v. Mitchell, #001777, 12/20/2016; see also Soufan, *The Black Banners*, chapter twenty-one.

52. Jamie Tarabay, "The Case against Abu Zubaydah," *Al Jazeera*, Nov. 7, 2013.

53. Author interviews with Jamaal Ismail, Islamabad, Pakistan, 2012–14.

54. Author interview with Abdullah Anas, London, 2015, and multiple interviews with Huthaifa Azzam, Amman, Jordan, 2015/16.

55. Author interview with Jean-Louis Bruguiere, Villeneuve-sur-Lot, France, Aug. 2020.

56. Abu Zubaydah diary, Vol. 1, p. 36.

57. Ibid., p. 38.

58. Ibid., p. 47.

59. Author interviews with Hesham Abu Zubaidah.

60. Abu Zubaydah diary, Vol. 1.

61. Ibid.

62. Abu Zubaydah correspondence.

63. FOIA to Ray Bonner, C06745508 and C06745510, 2019/01/25.

64. FOIA to Ray Bonner, C06257473, 2021/02/26.

65. Author interviews with Mitchell, also Mitchell and Harlow, *Enhanced Interrogation*, p. 262.

66. Author interviews with Mitchell.

67. FOIA to Ray Bonner, C06745508, 2019/01/25.

68. Author interviews with Mitchell.

69. Ibid., also author interviews with Shumate.

70. Author interviews with Mitchell.

71. Ibid.

72. Ibid.

73. Ibid.

74. Mayer, *The Dark Side*, p. 168; Mitchell's training packages talked of "the Arab mind."

75. https://independent.academia.edu/NORVELLDeAtkine/CurriculumVitae.

76. Author interviews with Shumate.

77. Abu Zubaydah to Jacobsen.

78. Author interviews with Mitchell.

79. Abu Zubaydah to Jacobsen.

80. Author interviews with Mitchell.

81. OMS report, p. 13.

82. Abu Zubaydah diary.

83. Abu Zubaydah to Jacobsen.

84. Ibid.

85. OMS report, p. 9.

86. FOIA to Ray Bonner, C06656133, 2018/08/02.

87. He entered custody at 200 pounds, by now he was down to 150 pounds. FOIA to Ray Bonner, C06656133, 2018/08/02. Other cables discuss what to do about his weight loss, see C06745518, 2019/01/25.

88. APA Hoffman report, p.160.

89. Joseph Matarazzo, "The American Psychological Association's Hoffman Report Allegations of My Association with the 'CIA Torture' Program," *Health Psychology Open*, Sept. 3, 2018.

90. Mitchell to 9/11 pretrial.

91. Author interviews with Mitchell.

92. Abu Zubaydah to Jacobsen.

93. FOIA to Ray Bonner, C06745508, 2019/01/25.

94. FOIA to Ray Bonner, C06745511, 2019/01/25.

95. Abu Zubaydah to Jacobsen.

96. FOIA to Ray Bonner, C06745492, 2018/11/19.

97. For "gonna have to pay," see Abu Zubaydah to Jacobsen; for rectal, see FOIA to Ray Bonner, C06745512, 2019/01/25, and SSCI report, p. 100.

98. SSCI report, p. xiii.

99. Author interviews with Mitchell.

100. FOIA to Salim v. Mitchell, #001777-8, 12/20/2016.

101. Soufan, *The Black Banners*, p. 523.

102. Abu Zubaydah diary, Vol. 13.

103. Ibid.

104. Soufan, *The Black Banners*, p. 550.

105. Abu Zubaydah diary, Vol. 13.

106. FOIA to Ray Bonner, C06745492, 2018/11/19.

107. FOIA to Ray Bonner, C06656133, 2018/08/02.

108. Soufan, *The Black Banners*, p. 525.

109. Ibid., pp. 526–27.

110. Ibid., also author interviews with Shumate.

111. Soufan, *The Black Banners*, p. 545.

Chapter 7: "A Full-Size American Refrigerator, Only Taller"

1. Soufan, *The Black Banners*, pp. 543–44.

2. Author interviews with Mitchell.

3. Author interviews with Jose Rodriguez.

4. FOIA to Ray Bonner, C06745492, 2018/11/19.

5. Author interviews with Shumate.

6. FOIA to Ray Bonner, C06745506, 2019/01/03.

7. Author interviews with Mitchell; see *PREAL Operating Instructions*; FOIA to Ray Bonner, C06630774, 2018/03/05; and Mitchell to 9/11 pretrial.

8. FOIA to Ray Bonner, C06257473, 2021/02/26.

9. Mitchell to 9/11 pretrial.

10. Richard E. Mezo, "Why It Was Called Water Torture," *Washington Post*, Feb. 10, 2008.

11. OMS report, "upright," p. 11, "reclining," p. 12.
12. FOIA to Salim v. Mitchell, #002015 and #001766, Apr. 11, 2017.
13. OMS report, p. 18.
14. FOIA to Ray Bonner, C06745492, 2018/11/19.
15. Abu Zubaydah drawings, author archive.
16. FOIA to Salim v. Mitchell, #001659.
17. Author interviews with Mitchell.
18. OPR report, pp. 37–42.
19. FOIA to Salim v. Mitchell, #000475, 08/13/2016.
20. Counter Resistance Strategy Meeting Minutes, SASC report Index, pp. 14–17.
21. FOIA to Salim v. Mitchell, #002171, May 18, 2017.
22. FOIA to Salim v. Mitchell, #002015-18, May 18, 2017.
23. After the Apr. 16 National Security Council meeting, John Yoo began the first of four drafts of the memo that would formally be issued on Aug. 1, 2002; see OPR report, pp. 37–42.
24. Soufan, *The Black Banners*, p. 536.
25. Abu Zubaydah to Jacobsen.
26. FOIA to Ray Bonner, C06745492, Nov. 19, 2018; Abu Zubaydah to Jacobsen.
27. FOIA to Ray Bonner, C06745520, 2019/01/25.
28. Mitchell and Harlow, *Enhanced Interrogation*, p. 285.
29. Adrian Levy and Cathy Scott-Clark, *Deception* (New York: Walker Books, 2005).
30. Author interview Ralph Mowatt-Larssen, Herndon, VA, Dec. 2019.
31. FOIA to Ray Bonner, C06745517, 2019/01/25.
32. FOIA to Ray Bonner, 17cv9378-17 and 17cv9378-32, 5/15/2018.
33. The Justice Department disagreed in June 2004 and released "Summary of Jose Padilla's Activities," fas.org/irp/news/2004/06/padilla060104.pdf.
34. FOIA to Ray Bonner, C067455560, 2018/11/19.
35. FOIA to Ray Bonner, C06745571, 2018/11/19, see also Tenet and Harlow, *At the Center of the Storm*, pp. 233, 264.
36. Mohamed et al v. Jeppesen Dataplan, Inc. CSS Decl. (Dec 2007) pdf; see https://www.therendition project.org.uk/pdf/PDF%20319%20%5BMohamed%20et%20al%20v.%20Jeppesen%20Dataplan%2C%20Inc.%20-%20CSS%20Decl.%20(Dec%202007)%5D.pdf.
37. Husayn (Zubaydah) v. The Foreign and Commonwealth Office, The Home Office, the Attorney General, [2021] EWHC 331 (QB), Feb. 19, 2021.
38. Author interviews with Rodriguez and Bruguiere.
39. FOIA to Ray Bonner, C06745517, 2019/01/25.
40. Abu Zubaydah correspondence.
41. FOIA to Ray Bonner, C06745517, 2019/01/25.
42. FOIA to Ray Bonner, C06745506, 2019/01/03. See also Salim v. Mitchell, #001111, 09/20/2016, for Mitchell signing off on the wording.
43. Author interviews with Mitchell.
44. Mayer, *The Dark Side*, p. 175.
45. Abu Zubaydah diary, Vol. 13.
46. OMS report, p. 9.
47. Abu Zubaydah CSRT transcript, Mar. 2007.
48. FOIA to Salim v. Mitchell, #002144-7, Apr. 11, 2017.
49. FOIA to Ray Bonner, C06745517, 2019/01/25.
50. FOIA to Ray Bonner, C06745519, 2019/01/25.
51. Author interviews with Mitchell.
52. FOIA to Ray Bonner, C06745521, 2019/01/25.
53. Ibid.
54. FOIA to Ray Bonner, C06745520, 2019/01/25.
55. FOIA to Salim v. Mitchell, C06644730, 2018/08/02.
56. FOIA to Salim v. Mitchell, #001821, Apr. 11, 2017.

57. Author interview with Dussault.
58. Ibid.
59. Dated Apr. 17, 2002, author archive, from Dussault.
60. SASC report, p. xiii.
61. Ibid., p. 14.
62. Ibid., p. 15.
63. Ibid.
64. Ibid., p. 16.
65. Author interviews with Aldrich.
66. Author interview with Dussault.
67. Ibid.
68. Author interviews with Mitchell.
69. For details of the government's case against Padilla, see www.justice.gov/osg/brief/padilla-v -hanft-opposition-0.
70. James Risen and Philip Shenon, "U.S. Says It Halted Qaeda Plot to Use Radioactive Bomb," *New York Times,* June 10, 2002.
71. FOIA to Ray Bonner, C06745537, 2019/01/25.
72. Risen and Shenon, "U.S. Says It Halted Qaeda Plot."
73. Soufan, *The Black Banners,* p. 535.
74. For NSC see the OPR report; for ticking time bomb, see OPR report, p. 210.
75. Soufan, *The Black Banners,* p. 535.
76. Harlow, *Rebuttal,* pp. 21–22.
77. Ibid., p. 20.
78. Soufan, *The Black Banners,* pp. 539–41
79. Author interviews with Mitchell.
80. FOIA to Salim v. Mitchell, #002166-8, Apr. 11, 2017.
81. FOIA to Salim v. Mitchell, #001589/90, 12/20/2016.
82. FOIA to Salim v. Mitchell, #000007-10, 5/20/2016.
83. FOIA to Salim v. Mitchell, #000009, #000007, and #000048, 7/10/2016.
84. FOIA to Salim v. Mitchell, #001915-22, 12/20/2016.
85. FOIA to Salim v. Mitchell, #002173, 01/13/2017; www.thetorturedatabase.org/files/foia_subsite /al-qaida_resistance_slides_part1.pdf.
86. FOIA to Ray Bonner, C06745523, 2019/01/25.
87. Author interviews with Mitchell.
88. Author interviews with Aldrich and Mitchell.
89. Abu Zubaydah to Jacobsen and his statement to *ICRC Report on the Treatment of "Fourteen 'High Value Detainees' in" CIA Custody,* International Committee of the Red Cross, Washington, Feb. 14, 2007 (hereafter Abu Zubaydah to ICRC), https://www.therenditionproject.org.uk/documents /general.html.
90. Abu Zubaydah to Jacobsen.
91. Mitchell to 9/11 pretrial.
92. FOIA to Ray Bonner, C06745470, 2018/11/19.
93. Author interviews with Mitchell.
94. FOIA to Ray Bonner, C06745523-24, 2019/01/25.
95. Ibid.
96. FOIA to Ray Bonner, 17cv9378-26, 05/15/2018, and C06745523-24, 2019/01/25.
97. FOIA to Ray Bonner, C06745524, Jan. 25, 2019.
98. FOIA to Ray Bonner, C06745523-24, Jan. 25, 2019.
99. Abu Zubaydah correspondence.
100. Ibid.
101. Author interviews with Mitchell.
102. Ibid.
103. FOIA to Ray Bonner, C06745518, 2019/01/25.

104. FOIA to Ray Bonner, C06745519, 2019/01/25.

105. FOIA to Ray Bonner, C06745521 and C06745522, 2019/01/25.

106. FOIA to Ray Bonner, C06644730, 2018/08/02.

107. FOIA to Ray Bonner, C06745552, 2018/11/19.

108. FOIA to Ray Bonner, C06745492, 2018/11/19.

109. Abu Zubaydah correspondence.

110. Soufan, *The Black Banners*, pp. 537–38.

111. Abu Zubaydah correspondence; FOIA to Ray Bonner, 17cv9378-31, 5/15/2018.

112. FOIA to Ray Bonner, C06745556, 2018/11/19.

113. FOIA to Ray Bonner, C06754558, 2018/11/19.

114. Author interviews with Mitchell.

115. Ibid.

116. Soufan, *The Black Banners*, pp. 551–53.

117. Mitchell and Harlow, *Enhanced Interrogation*, p. 37.

118. Soufan, *The Black Banners*, pp. 552–55.

119. FBI report, p. 68.

120. Ibid., p. 69.

121. Mitchell and Harlow, *Enhanced Interrogation*, p. 33.

122. Mitchell claimed in interviews with the author that he returned to the US only for two days and that he had polygraph tests on June 11 and 12, 2002. Official records suggest there were also meetings at CIA headquarters on June 4 and 10, 2002. FOIA to Salim v. Mitchell, #001642, Apr. 11, 2017.

123. Chris Whipple, "The Attacks Will Be Spectacular," *Politico Magazine*, Nov. 12, 2015, www.politico.com/magazine/story/2015/11/cia-directors-documentary-911-bush-213353.

124. SSCI report, p. 30.

125. Author interviews with Mitchell.

126. Ibid.

127. Ibid.

128. FOIA to Ray Bonner, C06618328, 2020/02/25.

129. Mitchell to 9/11 pretrial.

130. Ibid., also author interviews with Mitchell.

131. "Mini experience" from Morgan deposition to Salim v. Mitchell, 2017; see the Yoo-Bybee legal opinion, which mentions the interrogation is expected to last thirty days.

132. Morgan deposition to Salim v. Mitchell, 2017, see also his expert report to the same case.

133. Quote from author interviews with Rodriguez; for isolation, see OPR report, p. 210.

134. FOIA to Salim v. Mitchell, #001642, Apr. 11, 2017.

135. Mitchell to 9/11 pretrial.

136. Jessen to 9/11 pretrial.

137. Mitchell and Harlow, *Enhanced Interrogation*, pp. 44–45.

138. Author interviews with Aldrich.

139. Jessen to 9/11 pretrial.

140. Mitchell to 9/11 pretrial; author interviews with Mitchell.

141. Mitchell to 9/11 pretrial.

142. FOIA to Salim v. Mitchell, #001667-001671, Apr. 11, 2017.

Chapter 8: "Controlled Death"

1. Abu Zubaydah to Jacobsen.

2. FOIA to Salim v. Mitchell, #001667-#001671, Apr. 11, 2017; for "anodyne note," see OPR report, p. 42.

3. Author interviews with Mitchell.

4. FOIA to Salim v. Mitchell, #001667-#001671, Apr. 11, 2017.

5. Ibid.

6. FOIA to Salim v. Mitchell, #001811-2, 2/20/2016.

7. Abu Zubaydah diary, Vol. 1, p. 11.

8. FOIA to Salim v. Mitchell, #001811-2, 2/20/2016.

9. Mitchell to 9/11 pretrial.

10. FOIA to Salim v. Mitchell, #001642, Apr. 11, 2017.

11. Ibid.

12. Abu Zubaydah correspondence.

13. Abu Zubaydah correspondence.

14. Abu Zubaydah diary, Vol. 2.

15. Ibid.

16. Ibid.

17. Abu Zubaydah correspondence.

18. Ibid.

19. Joseph P. Fried, "The Terror Conspiracy: The Overview; Sheik and 9 Followers Guilty of a Conspiracy of Terrorism," *New York Times*, Oct. 5, 1995.

20. Author interviews Abu Qatada, Amman, 2014–18; for Muntasir see Tracey McVeigh, "'Recruiter' of UK Jihadis: I Regret Opening the Way to Isis," *Guardian*, June 13, 2015.

21. Author interview with Bruguiere.

22. Abu Zubaydah correspondence.

23. Thomas Sancton, "Anatomy of a Hijack," *Time*, June 24, 2001.

24. Abu Zubaydah correspondence and diary.

25. Author interview with Bruguiere.

26. Author interview with Aimen Dean, London, 2019.

27. Author interview with Hanani.

28. Author interview with Dean.

29. Ibid.; author interviews with Begg.

30. Abu Zubaydah correspondence.

31. Abu Zubaydah diary, Vol. 2.

32. Abu Zubaydah correspondence.

33. Abu Zubaydah CSRT transcript, Mar. 2007.

34. Abu Zubaydah correspondence.

35. Alex Strick van Linschoten and Felix Kuehn, *An Enemy We Created: The Myth of the Taliban–Al-Qaeda Merger, 1970–2010* (London: Hurst Publishers, 2012).

36. Author interview with Hanani.

37. Author interview with Bruguiere.

38. Author interviews with Abu Muhammad al-Maqdisi, Amman, Jordan, 2016–19; Joas Wagemakers, *A Quietist Jihadi* (Cambridge: Cambridge University Press, 2013).

39. Author interview with Bruguiere.

40. Author interview with Hanani, London, Oct. 2019.

41. Abu Zubaydah correspondence.

42. Abu Zubaydah diary.

43. Author interviews with Hesham Abu Zubaidah.

44. Abu Zubaydah diary and Abu Zubaydah CSRT transcript, Mar. 2007.

45. Abu Zubaydah correspondence.

46. Author interview with Omar Nashiri, Dussseldorf, 2016; he stayed at the House of Martyrs and trained at Khaldan.

47. Author interview with Dean.

48. Ibid.; also Aimen Dean, *Nine Lives* (London: Simon and Schuster, 2018).

49. Abu Zubaydah diary.

50. Ibid.

51. Author interview with Safwat Ghayur, Islamabad, Pakistan, 2009.

52. Author interviews with Mitchell, see also Mitchell and Harlow, *Enhanced Interrogation*, pp. 50–51.
53. Author interviews with Rizzo.
54. Author interviews with Mitchell.
55. Author interviews with Rizzo.
56. OPR report, p. 197.
57. www.politifact.com/factchecks/2015/jan/12/bobby-scott/bobby-scott-after-wwii-us-executed -japanese-war-cr/ and www.abcnews.go.com/WNT/Investigation/story?id=1356870.
58. US v. Lee, 744 F.2d 1124 (1984).
59. In an interview with the author Mitchell said this was "early June."
60. Mitchell to 9/11 pretrial.
61. Ibid.
62. FOIA to Salim v. Mitchell, #001656-62, 12/20/2016, see also FOIA to Ray Bonner, C06666234, 2018/08/02.
63. Mitchell to 9/11 pretrial.
64. Ibid.
65. FOIA to Salim v. Mitchell, #001926, 12/20/2016.
66. Mitchell and Harlow, *Enhanced Interrogation*, p. 53.
67. "Devil's lake," Abu Zubaydah diary, Vol. 5, p. 13.
68. For an example of drowning dreams, see Abu Zubaydah diary, Vol. pp. 44–45.
69. FOIA to Salim v. Mitchell, #001656-62, 12/20/2016, see also FOIA to Ray Bonner, C06666234, 2018/08/02.
70. Waterboarding instruction booklet on display in the Torture Section of the International Spy Museum, Washington, DC.
71. FASO Detachment Brunswick Instruction 3305.C (Jan. 1, 1998), see SASC report, p. 98.
72. FOIA to Ray Bonner, C06745538, 2019/01/28.
73. FOIA to Salim v. Mitchell, #001158-61, Apr. 12, 2017.
74. Revised FOIA to Ray Bonner, C06745506, 2019/11/06.
75. Author interview with Morgan.
76. APA report, p. 125.
77. Mitchell and Harlow, *Enhanced Interrogation*, p. 52.
78. Author interview with Denny Keller, Spokane, WA, Mar. 2019.
79. FOIA to Ray Bonner, C06745506, 2019/01/03.
80. Abu Zubaydah correspondence.
81. FOIA to National Security Archive, C06606424, 2017/11/29.
82. Ibid.
83. OPR report, pp. 191–92.
84. Ibid., pp. 193–96.
85. Jessen deposition to Salim v. Mitchell, 01/20/17, www.aclu.org/legal-document/salim-v -mitchell-exhibit-2-3.
86. SASC report, pp. 21–22; also author telephone interview with Chris Wirts, Feb. 2021.
87. Interview with Gary Percival, www.soundcloud.com/user-52299767/episode-9b-dr-gary -percival.
88. SASC report, pp. 20–21.
89. Ibid.
90. Ibid., p. 23.
91. Ibid., pp. 21–22.
92. Ibid., p. 21.
93. Ibid.
94. FASO Detachment Brunswick Instruction 3305.C (Jan. 1, 1998), see SASC report, p. 98.
95. Author interview with Wirts.
96. FOIA to Salim v. Mitchell, #001111, 09/20/2016.

97. OIG report, p. 21.
98. SASC report, p. 27.
99. Testimony of Malcolm Nance to the SASC, 2007; Leonard Doyle, "Waterboarding Is Torture—I Did It Myself," *Independent*, Nov. 1, 2007.
100. www.smallwarsjournal.com/blog/waterboarding-is-torture-period-links-updated-9.
101. "House Panel Gets Earful on Waterboarding," *CBS News*, Nov. 8, 2007.
102. SASC report, p. 22.
103. Ibid.
104. FOIA to Ray Bonner, C06745506, 2019/01/03.
105. Ibid.
106. Ibid. See also Salim v. Mitchell, #001111, 09/20/2016, for mock burial.
107. FOIA to Salim v. Mitchell, #001656-62, 12/20/2016, see also FOIA to Ray Bonner, C06666234, 2018/08/02.
108. Ibid.
109. Ibid., for size of wound and blister details see FOIA to Salim v. Mitchell, #002116, 12/20/2016.
110. Ibid., FOIA to National Security Archive, C06606424, 2017/11/29.
111. FOIA to Salim v. Mitchell, #001158-61, Apr. 12, 2017; FOIA to Ray Bonner, C06606424, 2017/11/29.
112. FOIA to Salim v. Mitchell, #001158-61, Apr. 12, 2017; FOIA to Ray Bonner, C06745506, 2019/01/03.
113. July 13th from OPR report, p. 65; for Tenet and Rice July 17th meeting, see FOIA to Salim v. Mitchell, #001761, Dec. 20, 2016.
114. FOIA to Ray Bonner, C06745506, 2019/01/03.
115. Mitchell to 9/11 pretrial.
116. Steve Gaudin interview, Alex Gibney (dir.), *The Forever Prisoner*, HBO Films (documentary), 2021.
117. Mike Butsch and Adam Drucker testimony to 9/11 pretrial, Oct. and Nov. 2019.
118. FOIA to Salim v. Mitchell, #000020, 5/20/2016, #000049, 07/01/2016, #000086, 07/01/2016; FOIA to Ray Bonner, C06630774, 2018/03/05.
119. They flew out on July 9, 2002. See Salim v. Mitchell, #001846. For quote, see Jessen to 9/11 pretrial.
120. Abu Zubaydah to Jacobsen.

CHAPTER 9: "BOO BOO"

1. "Worse even," Abu Zubaydah correspondence; "brotherhood," Abu Zubaydah Waziristan video, author archive.
2. This investigation was carried out in the early 1990s by Ali Mohamed, author interviews with Jack Cloonon.
3. Cathy Scott-Clark and Adrian Levy, *The Exile* (New York: Bloomsbury Publishing, 2017).
4. "Transcript: Bin Laden Determined to Strike in US," *CNN*, Apr. 10, 2004.
5. Al Qaeda called 9/11 the "Planes Operation" and the USS *Cole* attack the "Boats Operation"; see testimony of Stephen Gaudin to al-Nashiri pretrial, Nov. 2017; also author interviews with Mahfouz Ibn El Waleed, Nouckchott, Mauritania, Dec. 2014, Jan. 2015, June 2015.
6. Author interviews with al-Maqdisi.
7. Simon Reeve, *The New Jackals: Ramzi Yousef, Osama bin Laden and the Future of Terrorism* (Boston: Northeastern University Press, 1998).
8. Blond hair, author interview with Begg; quotes from Abu Zubaydah diary.
9. Bruguiere linked them, author interview; quotes from Abu Zubaydah diary.
10. Abu Zubaydah diary.
11. Ibid.
12. United States of America v. Usama bin Laden, Indictment: web.archive.org/web/20120906010435/http://cns.miis.edu/reports/pdfs/binladen/indict.pdf.
13. Author interview with Dean, see also Dean, *Nine Lives*.

14. Author interview with Bruguiere.
15. Author interviews with Dean and Bruguiere.
16. Author interviews with Begg; also Moazzam Begg, *Enemy Combatant* (London: Simon and Schuster UK, 2007).
17. Abu Zubaydah diary, Vol. 13.
18. Abu Zubaydah diary, Vol. 5.
19. Abu Zubaydah diary, Vol. 13.
20. Ibid.
21. Abu Zubaydah diary, Vol. 5.
22. Author interviews with Hesham Abu Zubaidah.
23. Abu Zubaydah diary, Vols. 5, 13.
24. Ibid.; author interviews with Hesham Abu Zubaidah.
25. Abu Zubaydah diary, Vol. 5.
26. Abu Zubaydah diary, Vol. 5, p. 15.
27. Bin Laden refused to help, Abu Zubaydah CSRT transcript, Mar. 2007.
28. Peter Bergen, *The Osama Bin Laden I Know* (New York: Free Press, 2006).
29. Abu Zubaydah CSRT transcript, Mar. 2007.
30. Abu Zubaydah uses this phrase in his diary, see for example Vol. 6, p. 10.
31. Author interviews with Begg; also Abu Zubaydah correspondence.
32. Abu Zubaydah correspondence.
33. Ibid.
34. Mitchell and Harlow, *Enhanced Interrogation*, p. 78.
35. Ibid.
36. Scott-Clark and Levy, *The Exile*.
37. Abu Zubaydah claimed he asked for his money back but did not receive it, author interviews with Higgins.
38. Mark Fineman, Bob Drogin, and Josh Meyer, "Camps Are Rubble But Their Threat Remains," *Los Angeles Times*, Dec. 18, 2001.
39. Abu Zubaydah diary, Vol. 6, pp. 12–96.
40. Author interviews with Higgins.
41. www.justice.gov/archives/ag/indictment-zacarias-moussaoui.
42. SSCI report, p. 410; Harlow, *Rebuttal*, pp. 304–5.
43. OPR report, p. 57.
44. Ibid.
45. Ibid.
46. FOIA to Ray Bonner, C06745540, 2018/11/19; SSCI report, p. 33; see also SSCI report, pp. 17–18.
47. Rizzo, *Company Man*, p. 191.
48. FOIA to Salim v. Mitchell, #001162, 09/26/2016, see also C06745463; for "no information," see SSCI report, p. 410.
49. FOIA to Salim v. Mitchell, #001760-65, 12/20/2016.
50. FOIA to Salim v. Mitchell, #001158-61, Apr. 12, 2017.
51. Rizzo, *Company Man*, p. 192.
52. Ibid.
53. Declination from OPR report, pp. 198–99; incommunicado from FOIA to Salim v. Mitchell, C06541507, 2016/06/10.
54. Mitchell to 9/11 pretrial, GTMO.
55. Author interviews with Mitchell.
56. FASO Detachment Brunswick Instruction 3305.C (Jan. 1, 1998), SASC report p. 98.
57. Author interviews with Mitchell, see also Mitchell and Harlow, *Enhanced Interrogation*, p. 68.
58. Abu Zubaydah drawings.
59. FOIA to Salim v Mitchell, #002115, 12/20/2016.

60. OMS report, p. 14.
61. Mitchell and Harlow, *Enhanced Interrogation*, p. 57.
62. Mitchell to 9/11 pretrial.
63. FOIA to Salim v. Mitchell, #001651, 12/20/2016.
64. SSCI report, p. 34.
65. Mitchell and Harlow, *Enhanced Interrogation*, p. 62.
66. Spencer Ackerman, "Declassified CIA File: Detainee Would Probably Have Cooperated before Torture," *Guardian*, June 14, 2016.
67. SSCI report, p. 34.
68. Author interview with General Tritot.
69. Author interviews with Rizzo.
70. FOIA to Salim v. Mitchell, #000475, 08/13/2016, see also Salim v. Mitchell, #001763, Dec. 20, 2016.
71. FOIA to Salim v. Mitchell, #001761, Dec. 20, 2016.
72. FOIA to Ray Bonner, C06666188, 2018/08/02; see also Tenet and Harlow, *At the Center of the Storm*, pp. 239, 242–43, 256–57.
73. FOIA to Ray Bonner, C06666188, 2018/08/02.
74. FOIA to Salim v. Mitchell, #001809, 12/20/2016.
75. Statement read out during Jessen testimony to 9/11 pretrial.
76. FOIA to Ray Bonner, C06666189, 2018/08/02.
77. FOIA to Salim v. Mitchell, C06541507, 2016/06/10; also SSCI report, pp. 34–55.
78. FOIA to Ray Bonner, C06630774, 2018/03/05.
79. OPR report, pp. 54–55.
80. Morgan deposition to Salim v. Mitchell.
81. FOIA to Ray Bonner, C06677032, 2018/08/02; for "not aware" see FOIA to Ray Bonner, C06630774, 2018/03/05.
82. Author telephone interview with Ogrisseg, July 2019, and Jerald Ogrisseg, Memorandum for JPRA, July 24, 2002, see SASC report Index, pp. 10–11, http://hrlibrary.umn.edu/OathBetrayed /SASC-08.pdf.
83. Ogrisseg, Memorandum for JPRA.
84. ACLU-RDI 4560, DOJ OLC 001033-8.
85. Ibid.; for "no physical harm," see OIG report, p. 21.
86. FOIA to Ray Bonner, C06745463, 2019/01/25; see also ACLU-RDI 4560, DOJ OLC 001034-8.
87. FOIA to Ray Bonner, C06745463, 2019/01/25.
88. FOIA to Salim v. Mitchell, #001163, 06/09/2017.
89. ACLU-RDI 4560 DOJ OLC 001033.
90. FOIA to Salim v. Mitchell, #001839, 06/09/2017.
91. FOIA to Ray Bonner, C06630774, 2018/03/05.
92. OPR report, pp. 56–58.
93. Author interview with Tenet.
94. FOIA to Ray Bonner, C06745532, 2019/01/25.
95. OPR report, p. 54.
96. OPR report, pp. 56–60.
97. OPR report, p. 57.
98. Rizzo, *Company Man*, p. 194.
99. OPR report, p. 61.
100. Ibid.
101. SSCI report, p. 38.
102. Ibid.
103. Author interviews with Rizzo.

104. FOIA to Salim v. Mitchell, C06541525, 2016/06/10; SSCI report, pp. 38–39.
105. Bush, *Decision Points* (New York: Crown Publishing, 2010).
106. Author interviews with Rizzo.
107. Chris Whipple, "What the CIA Knew before 9/11: New Details," *Politico*, Nov. 13, 2015.
108. Yoo-Bybee memo.
109. Author interviews with Ogrisseg and Wirts.
110. OMS report, p. 41.
111. Ibid., see also APA Hoffman report, 2015, see also author emails with Kirk Hubbard.
112. Author interviews with Rodriguez.

CHAPTER 10: "FULL-BLOWN, FULL-TILT, BOZO WILD PERSON"

1. For nutrition reference see FOIA to Salim v Mitchell, #001653, 12/20/2016; also Abu Zubaydah to Jacobsen.
2. Abu Zubaydah to Jacobsen.
3. Ibid.
4. Author interviews with Mitchell.
5. FOIA to Salim v. Mitchell, #001163, 09/26/2016; "complete helplessness," see FOIA to Salim v. Mitchell, #002020, Apr. 11, 2017; also FOIA to Salim v Mitchell, #002344, 02/21/2017.
6. Author interviews with Mitchell.
7. Mitchell and Harlow, *Enhanced Interrogation*, p. 63.
8. Ibid.
9. Abu Zubaydah diary, Vol. 13; during his 9/11 pretrial testimony, Mitchell said he had never used or heard of short-chaining until KSM in Mar. 2003.
10. Abu Zubaydah to Jacobsen.
11. Mitchell and Harlow, *Enhanced Interrogation*, p. 66.
12. Mitchell to 9/11 pretrial.
13. Author interviews with Mitchell.
14. Author interviews with Aldrich.
15. Mitchell and Harlow, *Enhanced Interrogation*, p. 64.
16. Abu Zubaydah to Jacobsen.
17. FOIA to Salim v. Mitchell, #001755-59, 12/20/2016.
18. Abu Zubaydah to Jacobsen.
19. Abu Zubaydah correspondence.
20. FOIA to Salim v. Mitchell, #001755-59, 12/20/2016.
21. Abu Zubaydah to Jacobsen.
22. Author interviews with Mitchell.
23. FOIA to Salim v. Mitchell, #001755-59, 12/20/2016; Abu Zubaydah to Jacobsen; for neck collar reference, see FOIA to Ray Bonner, C06644662, 2018/03/05.
24. Cable dated Aug. 15, 2002, and FOIA to Salim v. Mitchell, C06541507, 2016/06/10.
25. Abu Zubaydah to Jacobsen; FOIA to Ray Bonner, C06631188, 2018/03/05; also C06779678 and C06779681, 2018/12/19.
26. Abu Zubaydah to Jacobsen.
27. SSCI report, p. 41.
28. *PREAL Operating Instructions.*
29. Mitchell testimony to 9/11 pretrial.
30. Abu Zubaydah diary, Vol. 13.
31. Abu Zubaydah to Jacobsen.
32. Abu Zubaydah diary, Vol. 13.
33. Abu Zubaydah to Jacobsen.
34. Author interviews with Mitchell.

35. Ibid.

36. FOIA to Salim v. Mitchell, #001755-59, 12/20/2016.

37. Abu Zubaydah drawings; Abu Zubaydah to Jacobsen.

38. Abu Zubaydah diary, Vol. 13.

39. Ibid.

40. Yoo-Bybee memo.

41. As described by Joseph Margulies, attorney for Abu Zubaydah, in this Brief in Opposition, Feb. 11, 2021, www.supremecourt.gov/DocketPDF/20/20-827/168704/20210211112338780_20 -827_Brief%20in%20Opposition.pdf

42. Abu Zubaydah to Jacobsen; also Abu Zubaydah CSRT transcript, Mar. 2007.

43. Ibid.

44. FOIA to Salim v. Mitchell, #001755-59, 12/20/2016.

45. Ibid.

46. Ibid.

47. Abu Zubaydah diary, Vol. 13.

48. Ibid.

49. Abu Zubaydah correspondence.

50. Abu Zubaydah to Jacobsen.

51. Abu Zubaydah's drawings.

52. FOIA to Salim v. Mitchell, #001760-65, 12/20/2016.

53. In correspondence written in 2021, Abu Zubaydah states that specialists have only ever diagnosed "pseudo-seizures."

54. Mitchell to 9/11 pretrial.

55. Abu Zubaydah to the ICRC.

56. Author interviews with Mitchell, Aldrich, and former CIA officers whose names cannot be disclosed; also Shane, "Inside a Terrorist Mastermind's Interrogation": also Abu Zubaydah recalls meeting Hispanic "Iskander/Alexander" in Lithuania and possibly Thailand, too, author interviews with Higgins.

57. Mitchell to 9/11 pretrial.

58. Abu Zubaydah to Jacobsen

59. Abu Zubaydah diary, Vol. 1.

60. Abu Zubaydah to ICRC.

61. Mitchell and Harlow, *Enhanced Interrogation*, p. 69.

62. Ibid.

63. Mitchell to 9/11 pretrial.

64. SSCI report, p. 41.

65. Author interviews with Mitchell.

66. FOIA to Ray Bonner, C06644662, 2018/03/05.

67. Author interviews with Mitchell and *PREAL Operating Instructions*.

68. SSCI report, p. 494.

69. Mitchell to 9/11 pretrial.

70. FOIA to Salim v. Mitchell, #001755-59, 12/20/2016.

71. Gibney, *The Forever Prisoner*.

72. FOIA to Salim v. Mitchell, #001755-59, 12/20/2016; also FOIA to Ray Bonner, C06631237, 2018/03/05.

73. FOIA to Ray Bonner, C06779676, 2018/12/19.

74. Abu Zubaydah to Jacobsen.

75. FOIA to Ray Bonner, C06631237, 2018/03/05.

76. Mitchell and Harlow, *Enhanced Interrogation*, p. 67.

77. FOIA to Ray Bonner, C06631231, 2018/03/05.

78. Author interviews with Mitchell, see also FOIA to Ray Bonner, C06779679, 2018/12/19.

79. Abu Zubaydah drawings.
80. Abu Zubaydah to Jacobsen.
81. OMS report, p. 29.
82. FOIA to Ray Bonner, C06631231, 2018/03/05.
83. FOIA to Ray Bonner, C06779672, 2018/12/19.
84. FOIA to Ray Bonner, C06779674, 2018/12/19.
85. FOIA to Ray Bonner, C06779676, 2018/12/19.
86. Ibid.
87. Ibid.
88. Author interview with Morgan.
89. Abu Zubaydah correspondence, see also FOIA to Ray Bonner, C06631187, 2018/03/05.
90. Mitchell to 9/11 pretrial.
91. FOIA to Ray Bonner, C06631188 and C06644662, 2018/03/05.
92. Author interviews with Mitchell.
93. Abu Zubaydah to Jacobsen.
94. FOIA to Salim v. Mitchell, #001949, 12/20/2016.
95. FOIA to Ray Bonner, C06644662, 2018/03/05.
96. FOIA to Ray Bonner, C06779680, 2018/12/19; see also FOIA to Salim v. Mitchell, #002340-42, 02/21/2017.
97. FOIA to Salim v. Mitchell, #001760-65, 12/20/2016.
98. For example, FOIA to Ray Bonner, C06631187 and C06631188, 2018/03/05; also C06644725, 2018/03/05.
99. FOIA to Ray Bonner, C06745463, 2019/01/25; also ACLU-RDI 4560, DOJ OLC 001034-8.
100. Author interviews with Mitchell; see Ian Shapira, "For CIA Family a Deadly Suicide Bombing Leads to Painful Divisions," and Warrick, *The Triple Agent*, p. 23–24, 199–200.
101. FOIA to Salim v. Mitchell, #002356, 02/21/2017.
102. FOIA to Salim v. Mitchell, #001161, 09/26/2016; also Yoo-Bybee memo.
103. FOIA to Ray Bonner, C06644723 and C06656590, 2018/03/05.
104. Abu Zubaydah to Jacobsen.
105. FOIA to Ray Bonner, C06644723 and C06656590, 2018/03/05.
106. Abu Zubaydah to Jacobsen.
107. FOIA to Salim v. Mitchell, #001945, 12/20/2016.
108. Mitchell unpublished childhood memoir.
109. Mitchell to 9/11 pretrial.
110. Ibid.
111. Mitchell and Harlow, *Enhanced Interrogation*, p. 263.
112. FOIA to Ray Bonner, C06666295, 2018/08/02.
113. FOIA to Ray Bonner, C06644723, 2018/03/05; for other revelations see Salim v. Mitchell, #001949, 12/20/2016.
114. FOIA to Ray Bonner, C06644724, 2018/03/05.
115. FOIA to Salim v. Mitchell, #002343, 02/21/2017, also C06666295, 2018/08/02, and C06656590, 2018/03/05.
116. Author interviews with Mitchell.
117. Mitchell unpublished childhood memoir.
118. FOIA to Ray Bonner, C06644724, 2018/03/05.
119. Author interviews with Mitchell.
120. Ibid.
121. Ibid.
122. Ibid.
123. Mitchell and Harlow, *Enhanced Interrogation*, p. 76.

124. Mitchell to 9/11 pretrial.
125. Rodriguez declaration to Salim v. Mitchell, www.aclu.org/legal-document/salim-v-mitchell -declaration-jose-rodriguez.
126. Author interviews with Mitchell, and Mitchell and Harlow, *Enhanced Interrogation*, pp. 77–78.
127. Abu Zubaydah CSRT transcript, Mar. 2007.
128. Abu Zubaydah diary, Vol. 6, pp. 12–96.
129. Abu Zubaydah CSRT transcript, Mar. 2007.
130. FOIA to Ray Bonner, C06644724, 2018/03/05.
131. Ibid.
132. SSCI report, p.45.
133. FOIA to Ray Bonner, C06666275, 2018/08/02.
134. FOIA to Ray Bonner, C06666297, 2018/08/02.
135. FOIA to Salim v. Mitchell, #002340-42, 02/21/2017.
136. Author interviews with Mitchell.
137. Mitchell to 9/11 pretrial.
138. Mitchell and Harlow, *Enhanced Interrogation*, p. 73.
139. Ibid.
140. Author interviews with Mitchell.
141. FOIA to Salim v. Mitchell, #002340-42, 02/21/2017.
142. FOIA to Salim v. Mitchell, #002345, 02/21/2017.
143. FOIA to Ray Bonner, C06644727, 2018/03/05.
144. SSCI report, p. 43.
145. FOIA to Salim v. Mitchell, #002340-42, 02/21/2017.
146. SSCI report, p. 43.
147. FOIA to Salim v. Mitchell, #002343, 02/21/2017.
148. Ibid.
149. Author interviews with Mitchell.
150. FOIA to Ray Bonner, C06644726, 2018/03/05.
151. Ibid.
152. Ibid.
153. See Abu Zubaydah diary, Vol. 1, p. 45, where he writes this supplication.
154. Abu Zubaydah diary, Vol. 13.

CHAPTER 11: "LOST IN SPACE"

1. Mitchell to 9/11 pretrial.
2. FOIA to Salim v. Mitchell, #002348, 02/21/2017.
3. Ibid.
4. SSCI report, p. 45.
5. Ibid.
6. Author interviews with Mitchell.
7. SSCI report, p. 45.
8. FOIA to Salim v. Mitchell, 002350-55, 02/21/2017.
9. Author interview with Scheuer.
10. Author interviews with Mitchell, and Mitchell to 9/11 pretrial.
11. Mitchell to 9/11 pretrial.
12. OMS report, p. 42.
13. OMS report, p. 42; also OIG report, p. 90.
14. Author interviews with Mitchell.
15. Ibid.
16. Mitchell to 9/11 pretrial.

17. Ibid.
18. Ibid.
19. Ibid.
20. Abu Zubaydah to Jacobsen.
21. FOIA to Salim v. Mitchell, 002350-55, 02/21/2017.
22. FOIA to Salim v. Mitchell #002350-55, 02/21/2017.
23. Ibid.
24. Author interview with Gus.
25. FOIA to Salim v. Mitchell, #002356, 02/21/2017. In interviews with the authors, Mitchell said he and Jessen did not want to keep going for thirty days.
26. Author interviews with Gus.
27. OMS report, p. 19, "all decisions on technique [were] left to those at site."
28. Mitchell to 9/11 pretrial.
29. FOIA to Ray Bonner, C06781437 and C06644728, 2018/12/19.
30. Ibid.
31. SSCI report, p. xii.
32. Mitchell and Harlow, *Enhanced Interrogation*, p. 69.
33. Ibid.
34. Abu Zubaydah to Jacobsen; also author interviews with Higgins.
35. Author interviews with Aldrich.
36. Gibney, *The Forever Prisoner*.
37. OMS report, p. 19.
38. OMS report, pp. 80, 87–88.
39. Author email exchanges with Hubbard.
40. Author interviews with Mitchell; for "unprofessional" see CIA OIG report, p. 35.
41. OMS report, p. 39.
42. Ibid., p. 24.
43. Ibid.
44. Ibid., p. 25.
45. Ibid., p. 37.
46. Ibid., p. 39.
47. OIG report, p. 21.
48. Abu Zubaydah CSRT transcript, Mar. 2007.
49. OIG report, p. 37.
50. OMS report, p. 41.
51. "Not qualified" from SASC report, p. 22; "long retired" from Chris Wirts, who organized the CIA training sessions in June and July 2002, author telephone interview.
52. Harlow, *Rebuttal*, pp. 53–54.
53. Ibid., p. 44.
54. FOIA to Salim v. Mitchell, 002366-68, 02/21/2017.
55. Author interviews with Mitchell.
56. Ibid.
57. Ibid.
58. Mitchell to 9/11 pretrial.
59. Abu Zubaydah to Jacobsen.
60. Ibid.
61. FOIA to Salim v. Mitchell, 002366-68, 02/21/2017.
62. Mitchell to 9/11 pretrial.
63. Ibid.
64. Author interview with Scheuer.
65. They married in 2014.

66. Abu Zubaydah to Jacobsen.
67. Ibid.
68. FOIA to Salim v. Mitchell, #002366-68, 02/21/2017.
69. Abu Zubaydah to Jacobsen.
70. FOIA to Salim v. Mitchell, #002369-71, 02/21/2017; also C06656738, 2018/03/05.
71. Author interviews with Higgins.
72. FOIA to Salim v. Mitchell, #002369-71, 02/21/2017.
73. FOIA to Ray Bonner, C06631189, 2018/03/05.
74. FOIA to Salim v. Mitchell, #002379-81, 02/21/2017.
75. Ibid.
76. Ibid.
77. Mitchell to 9/11 pretrial.
78. Abu Zubaydah correspondence.
79. Author interviews with Higgins.
80. Mitchell to 9/11 pretrial.
81. FOIA to Salim v. Mitchell, 002379-81, 02/21/2017.
82. Abu Zubaydah to Jacobsen.
83. Ibid.
84. Mitchell and Harlow, *Enhanced Interrogation*, p. 75.
85. Author interviews with Mitchell; also Mitchell to 9/11 pretrial.
86. "Softie," author interviews with Mitchell; "dog food commercials," Mitchell to 9/11 pretrial.
87. Mitchell to 9/11 pretrial.
88. Mitchell and Harlow, *Enhanced Interrogation*, p. 75.
89. FOIA to Salim v. Mitchell, 002379-81, 02/21/2017; OIG report, p. 96.
90. OIG report, p. 21.
91. http://www.aclu.org/files/assets/ReVaughn04152010Release_DurhamDocs_20100510.pdf.
92. Abu Zubaydah correspondence.
93. Mitchell to 9/11 pretrial.
94. Author interviews with Mitchell.
95. OMS report, p. 41.
96. SSCI report.
97. "Slovenly mistake" was a comment made by Michael Mukasey to investigators from the Department of Justice Office of Professional Responsibility, see OPR report, p. 9.
98. Enhanced Interrogation, p. 264; "silver bullet," see OMS report, p. 42.
99. FOIA to Salim v. Mitchell, #002020-23, Apr. 11, 2017.
100. FOIA to Salim v. Mitchell, #002382-4, 02/21/2017.
101. FOIA to Salim v. Mitchell, #002385, 02/21/2017.
102. Abu Zubaydah to Jacobsen.
103. FOIA to Salim v. Mitchell, #002020-23, Apr. 11, 2017.
104. Mitchell to 9/11 pretrial.
105. Author interview with Dussault.
106. FOIA to Salim v. Mitchell, #002388-90, 02/21/2017.
107. Author interviews with Mitchell.
108. SSCI report, p. 45.
109. FOIA to Salim v. Mitchell, #000030, 07/01/2016 and #000013, 5/20/2016.
110. FOIA to Salim v. Mitchell, #000092 and 000050, 07/01/2016.
111. The OIG report was delivered in 2004 and the OMS report in 2007.
112. Author interviews with Gus.
113. OIG report, p. 83.
114. OIG report, p. 85.
115. Author telephone interview with "Sharon," Feb. 2019.

116. Author interviews with Mitchell.
117. Ibid.
118. Author interviews with Gus.
119. Mike Butsch to 9/11 pretrial.
120. Fouda and Fielding, *Masterminds of Terror*.
121. Jason Burke, "Brutal Gun-Battle That Crushed 9/11 Terrorist," *Guardian*, Sept. 15, 2002.
122. Ibid.
123. Mike Butsch to 9/11 pretrial.
124. Ibid.
125. Ibid.
126. FOIA to Salim v. Mitchell, #000054, 07/01/2016.
127. FOIA to Salim v. Mitchell, #000005 and 000003, 5/20/2016 and 000094, 07/01/2016.
128. Author interviews with Mitchell; SSCI report, p. 75.
129. Mike Butsch to 9/11 pretrial. On the tarmac were Butsch, Aaron Zebley, Ray Holcomb, Ali Soufan, Debbie Manchas, and Rich Kolko. Interrogating the sons were Jennifer Keenan and Dan Cudmore; small boxes, see Scott-Clark and Levy, *The Exile*.

CHAPTER 12: "ON-THE-JOB TRAINING"

1. Author interviews with Mitchell.
2. For tricks, see FOIA to Salim v. Mitchell, #001052, Sept. 2, 2016.
3. Sept. 18, 2002, email cited in Jessen deposition to Salim v. Mitchell.
4. www.therenditionproject.org.uk/prisoners/binalshibh; Butsch to 9/11 pretrial; also Mitchell to 9/11 pretrial (James Connell: "Less than two months after that [he was captured Sept. 11] Ali Soufan interrogated RBS naked chained to floor and sleep deprived at Cobalt"); also author interview with Harrington; also OIG report, p. 74.
5. Rizzo, *Company Man*, p. 211.
6. FOIA to Ray Bonner, C06644763, 2020/02/25.
7. FOIA to Salim v. Mitchell, #002581-2, Apr. 12, 2017.
8. Author interview with Gus.
9. Ibid.
10. Tom Scotney, "Infamous Handcuff Manufacturer to Leave Birmingham," *Birmingham Post*, June 18, 2008.
11. Hubbard email to APA, see Hoffman report, www.psychcentral.com/blog/wp-content/uploads/2015/07/APA-FINAL-Report-7.2.15.pdf; also FOIA to Salim v. Mitchell, #001916, 12/20/2016.
12. Author interviews with Gus.
13. Ibid.
14. SSCI report, p. xxvi.
15. Author interviews with Gus.
16. Ibid.
17. OIG report, p. 55.
18. OIG report, pp. 48–49.
19. See depositions of Suleiman Abdullah Salim and Mohamed Ahmed Ben Soud, who were both interrogated in the Dark Prison, www.aclu-wa.org/cases/salim-et-al-v-mitchell-et-al-0.
20. Author interview with Carle.
21. Mitchell to 9/11 pretrial; FOIA to Salim v. Mitchell, #001916, 12/20/2016.
22. FOIA release to Ray Bonner, C06644763, 2020/02/25.
23. FOIA to Salim v. Mitchell, #001915-22, 12/20/2016.
24. Author interviews with Mitchell.
25. Author interviews with Gus.

26. SSCI report, p. 19.
27. Author interviews with Mitchell.
28. SSCI report, p. 19.
29. *KUBARK Counterintelligence Interrogation*, July 1963.
30. Author interviews with Gus.
31. Wirts stated in an author interview that he never met Wise.
32. SASC report, pp. 91–94.
33. Jessen to 9/11 pretrial.
34. OIG report, p. 67.
35. OIG report, p. 32.
36. The Guantánamo course, which took place at Fort Bragg, was entitled "Counter Measures to Defeat Al Qaeda Resistance Contingency Training Based on Recently Obtained Al Qa'eda Documents," see also Jessen to 9/11 pretrial.
37. SASC report, p. 45.
38. FOIA release to Ray Bonner, C06644763, 2020/02/25.
39. FOIA to Salim v. Mitchell, #001081-97, May 22, 2017 and #001591, 12/20/2016.
40. SASC report, pp. 21–22.
41. Author interviews with Mitchell.
42. Author interviews with Gus.
43. SSCI report, p. 58.
44. "Get to Know Our Deputy Director," CIA, Mar. 27, 2018, https://www.cia.gov/stories/story/get-to-know-our-deputy-director/.
45. Tim Golden, Stephen Engelberg, and Daniel Defraia, "A Prisoner in Gina Haspel's Black Site," *ProPublica*, May 7, 2018.
46. FOIA to Salim v. Mitchell, #002581-2, Apr. 12, 2017.
47. FOIA to Jason Leopold, C06666321, 2017/12/01.
48. SSCI report, p. 47.
49. Author interviews with Higgins.
50. Mitchell and Harlow, *Enhanced Interrogation*, p. 78.
51. Ibid.; plus FOIA to Salim v. Mitchell, #001066 and #001047-53, 9/2/2016.
52. Author interviews with Higgins.
53. Ibid.
54. Ongoing claim in the Queen's Bench Division of the High Court of Justice, London against the Foreign and Commonwealth Office, Home Office and Attorney General.
55. Ibid.; for Aamer see Phil Hirschkorn, "11 Years in Guantánamo without Trial or Charges," *CBS News*, May 31, 2013.
56. Author interviews with Begg; also Soufan, *The Black Banners*, p. 515.
57. Abu Zubaydah to Jacobsen.
58. Ibid.
59. Ibid.
60. Mitchell and Harlow, *Enhanced Interrogation*, p. 81–82.
61. Author interview with McFadden.
62. The CIA's determination to keep other government agencies away from all high-value detainees was discussed by Daniel Jones in his interview with Alex Gibney, Gibney, *The Forever Prisoner.*
63. According to an undated and unsigned CIA document, "Legal Principles Applicable to CIA Detention and Interrogation of Captured Al Qaeda Personnel," see OIG report, p. 22.
64. Mitchell and Harlow, *Enhanced Interrogation*, p. 85.
65. Author interviews with Gus.
66. Mitchell to 9/11 pretrial.
67. Brian Ross and Richard Esposito, "CIA's Harsh Interrogation Techniques Described," *ABC News*, Mar. 14, 2008.

68. Depositions of Salim and Ben Soud, Salim v. Mitchell, Mohamed Ahmed Ben Soud Deposition Transcript, Vol. 1, Jan. 31, 2017, ACLU-RDI 6810.

69. Author interviews with Mitchell.

70. Ridha al-Najjar, FOIA to Salim v. Mitchell, #001081-97, May 22, 2017; also SSCI report, pp. 53–54, Khalid Sheikh Mohammad also described himself being chained with his feet barely touching the floor, Mohammad testimony to the ICRC (hereafter, Mohammad to ICRC); also Zirbel's statement to the OIG, FOIA to Salim v. Mitchell, #001081-001097, May 22, 2017 (hereafter Zirbel statement).

71. SSCI report, pp. 50, 54.

72. Ibid., p. 50.

73. SSCI report, p. 50.

74. OIG report, p. 52.

75. Jessen to 9/11 pretrial.

76. OIG report, pp. 48–66.

77. FOIA to Salim v. Mitchell, #001081-97, May 22, 2017.

78. As described by Sean Naylor in *Not a Good Day to Die* (New York: Penguin, 2005); and Mitchell in Mitchell and Harlow, *Enhanced Interrogation*, pp. 93–94.

79. Center for Constitutional Rights, "Former CIA Detainee Majid Khan's Torture Finally Public," June 2, 2015.

80. SSCI report, p. 100.

81. OIG report, p. 57.

82. OIG report, p. 52, Zirbel statement, SSCI report, p. 70, for "mock execution" see Albert El Gamil statement, OIG report, p. 71.

83. Blankets, etc, OIG report, p. 51; "creature comforts," Zirbel statement.

84. Jessen to 9/11 pretrial, "masks" Zirbel statement.

85. SSCI report, p. 57, the OIG report, p. 48, notes the Kabul Station proposed the creation of the Salt Pit in April 2002, while headquarters approved the funding in June 2002.

86. Mitchell and Harlow, *Enhanced Interrogation*, pp. 91–92.

87. Ray Nowosielski and John Duffy, *The Watchdogs Didn't Bark* (New York: Simon and Schuster, 2020).

88. Glenn Carle's book, *The Interrogator*, has a description of the frenetic activity at the Kabul Station.

89. SSCI report, pp. 52–53.

90. John Durham inquiry.

91. Jessen to 9/11 pretrial.

92. FOIA to Salim v. Mitchell, #001081-97, May 22, 2017.

93. For a timeline, see FOIA to Salim v. Mitchell, #001048, Sept. 2, 2016; for quotes see FOIA to Salim v. Mitchell, #001081-97, May 22, 2017.

94. Mitchell to 9/11 pretrial.

95. Mitchell and Harlow, *Enhanced Interrogation*, pp. 93–94.

96. Ibid.

97. Ibid., p. 102.

98. Ibid.

99. Mitchell to 9/11 pretrial.

100. Mitchell and Harlow, *Enhanced Interrogation*, p. 86.

101. Ibid., p. 85.

102. Ibid., p. 88.

103. Author interview with Ghairat Baheer, who was arrested with Gul Rahman, Islamabad, Pakistan, 2015.

104. FOIA to Salim v. Mitchell, #001081-97, May 22, 2017.

105. Ibid.

106. FOIA to Salim v. Mitchell, #001047-53, 9/2/2016.

107. OIG report, p. 73.

108. Water heater not working FOIA to Salim v. Mitchell, #001081-97, May 22, 2017; also OIG report, p. 75.

109. OIG report, p. 74.

110. OIG report, pp. 73–74.

111. Jessen to 9/11 pretrial.

112. FOIA to Salim v. Mitchell, #001075-77, 9/2/2016.

113. OIG report, p. 75.

114. FOIA to Salim v. Mitchell, #001072-74, 9/2/2016.

115. Author interviews with Mitchell.

116. FOIA to Salim v. Mitchell, #001061-63, 9/2/2016, also #001865-70, 12/20/2016.

117. FOIA to Salim v. Mitchell, #001054 and #001072-74, 9/2/2016.

118. FOIA to Salim v. Mitchell, #001865-70, 12/20/2016; also OMS report, p. 33.

119. Author interviews with Mitchell; Mitchell to 9/11 pretrial.

120. SSCI report, p. 58, the two techniques were "finger press" and "abdominal slap"; also SASC report, pp. 91–94.

121. Author interview with Wirts.

122. Mitchell to 9/11 pretrial.

123. According to the OIG report, p. 32, two of the sixteen attendees were "independent contractor/ psychologists . . . certified by CTC/RDG as interrogators." They were certified "based on their experience as SERE instructors and their interrogations of Abu Zubaydah and al-Nashiri."

124. SASC report, p. 93.

125. Ibid., p. 93.

126. Ibid., p. 93.

127. Ibid., p. 94.

128. FOIA to Salim v. Mitchel, #001892, May 22, 2017; the OIG report claims they were among the sixteen selected candidates for the course, p. 32.

129. FOIA to Salim v. Mitchel, #001892, May 22, 2017.

130. *PREAL Operating Instructions.*

131. FOIA to Salim v. Mitchell, #001892, May 22, 2017.

132. FOIA to Salim v. Mitchell, #001061-3, 9/2/2016.

133. Ibid.

134. FOIA to Salim v. Mitchell, #001081-97, May 22, 2017.

135. OMS report, p. 34.

136. OIG report, pp. 1, 68.

137. OIG report, p. 68.

138. Mitchell and Harlow, *Enhanced Interrogation*, pp. 90–92.

139. Mitchell to 9/11 pretrial.

140. OIG report, p. 68.

141. FOIA to Salim v. Mitchell, #001061-3, 9/2/2016.

142. OIG report, p. 6.

143. OIG report, pp. 1, 68.

CHAPTER 13: "ALLAH WILL LOOK INTO THEIR HEARTS AND KNOW"

1. Mitchell and Harlow, *Enhanced Interrogation*, pp. 95–97.

2. Ibid.

3. FOIA to Salim v. Mitchell, #001929, 12/20/2016 and #000959-62, 08/31/2016; also FOIA to National Security Archive, C06238939, 2014/09/11.

4. FOIA to Salim v. Mitchell, #000959-62, 08/31/2016, see also FOIA to National Security Archive, C06238939, 2014/09/11.

5. OIG report, p. 90.
6. The date of al-Nashiri's arrival in Thailand is confirmed in the OIG report, p. 35.
7. FOIA to National Security Archive (NSA), C06665557, 2018/07/31.
8. FOIA to NSA, C06665565, 2018/06/26.
9. Mitchell and Harlow, *Enhanced Interrogation*, pp. 86–87.
10. Adam Goldman, "The Hidden History of the CIA's Prison in Poland," *Washington Post*, Jan. 23, 2014.
11. Author interview with McFadden.
12. FOIA to NSA, C06665564, 2018/07/31.
13. Ibid.; and C06665566, 2018/07/31.
14. FOIA to NSA, C06665564, 2018/07/31.
15. FOIA to NSA, C06665565, 2018/06/26.
16. FOIA to NSA, C06718444, 2018/02/28.
17. FOIA to NSA, C06665564, 2018/07/31.
18. Ibid.
19. Mitchell and Harlow, *Enhanced Interrogation*, p. 97.
20. FOIA to NSA, C06665564, 2018/07/31.
21. SSCI report, p. 67.
22. FOIA to NSA, C06665565, 2018/06/26.
23. Ibid.
24. Rodriguez and Harlow, *Hard Measures*, p. 119; also author interviews with Harlow, Rodriguez, Mitchell, and Gus.
25. As produced by David Nevin, counsel for Khalid Sheikh Mohammad, at 9/11 pretrial Jan. 2020.
26. Author interviews with Mitchell and General Tritot.
27. Mitchell to 9/11 pretrial.
28. Author interviews with Gus.
29. Goldman, "The Hidden History of the CIA's Prison in Poland."
30. Ibid.
31. Affidavit of Józef Pinior to the European Court of Human Rights Abu Zubaydah v. Poland, www .statewatch.org/media/documents/news/2013/nov/cia-echr-husayn-poland.pdf, para 78.
32. Author interviews with Gus.
33. Mitchell and Harlow, *Enhanced Interrogation*, p. 106; affidavit of Jozef Pinior.
34. Affidavit of Józef Pinior.
35. Spec of black sites, Case 2:15-cv-00286-JLQ Document 176-9, Filed 05/22/17.
36. SSCI report, p. 62.
37. Affidavit of Józef Pinior.
38. The cage was made in Pruszków.
39. Abu Zubaydah drawings.
40. Author interviews with Gus.
41. Mitchell stated in his 9/11 pretrial testimony that they stopped conducting EITs several days before the move, but the OIG report stated they continued until the day of the move, December 4, 2002, OIG report, p. 4.
42. FOIA to NSA, C06665566, 2018/07/31.
43. Ibid.
44. Ibid.
45. Ibid.
46. Author interviews with Mitchell and Rodriguez; also OIG report, p. 37; for an inventory of the tapes see http://www.aclu.org/files/assets/cia_release20100415_p10-18.pdf.
47. According to Dan Jones, who was allowed to read Tenet's and Rodriguez's statements to the CIA inspector general, Gibney, *The Forever Prisoner*.

48. Ibid.

49. Mitchell to 9/11 pretrial.

50. http://www.aclu.org/files/assets/cia_release20100415_p10-18.pdf.

51. Author interviews with Gus.

52. http://www.aclu.org/files/assets/cia_release20100415_p10-18.pdf.

53. http://www.aclu.org/files/assets/cia_release20100415_p10-18.pdf.

54. Douglas Cox, "Burn after Viewing: The CIA's Destruction of the Abu Zubaydah Tapes and the Law of Federal Records," *Journal of National Security Law & Policy* 5, no. 131, June 15, 2011.

55. http://www.aclu.org/files/assets/cia_release20100415_p10-18.pdf.

56. Author interviews with Mitchell.

57. Author interviews with Mitchell.

58. Ibid.; for Rodriguez's account see *Hard Measures*, pp. 184–85.

59. Ibid.

60. Author interviews with Rizzo.

61. OIG report, pp. 36–37.

62. Abu Zubaydah to Jacobsen.

63. This scar can be seen on Abu Zubaydah's earliest detainee photograph, first published by WikiLeaks in 2011.

64. Ibid.

65. Ibid.

66. OIG report, p. 60.

67. Mitchell to 9/11 pretrial.

68. See "body cavity check (BCC)," section 9.3, of *PREAL Operating Instructions*.

69. Tailfin number N63MU; "Abu Zubaydah," The Rendition Project, www.therenditionproject.org.uk/prisoners/zubaydah.html.

70. Abu Zubaydah to Jacobsen.

71. www.statewatch.org/media/documents/news/2013/nov/cia-echr-husayn-poland.pdf.

72. Author visit to the facility, 2020.

73. Abu Zubaydah to Jacobsen, and drawings.

74. Charlie Wise made an official complaint; author interviews with Mitchell; in *Enhanced Interrogation*, Mitchell describes this allegation as "false rumors," p. 108.

75. Author interviews with Mitchell.

76. Author interviews with Gus.

77. OIG report, p. 68.

78. Jessen to 9/11 pretrial.

79. FOIA to Salim v. Mitchell, #001081-97, May 22, 2017.

80. Jessen to 9/11 pretrial.

81. OIG report, p. 23.

82. Tim Golden, "In U.S. Report, Brutal Details of 2 Afghan Inmates' Deaths," *New York Times*, May 20, 2005.

83. Mitchell and Harlow, *Enhanced Interrogation*, p. 105.

84. Ibid.

85. Ibid.

86. Mitchell's unpublished childhood memoir.

87. Author interviews with Gus.

88. Mitchell to 9/11 pretrial.

89. Ibid.

90. Mitchell and Harlow, *Enhanced Interrogation*, pp. 112–15.

91. OIG report, pp. 43, 73.

92. Mitchell and Harlow, *Enhanced Interrogation*, p. 115.

93. Mitchell to 9/11 pretrial.

94. Abu Zubaydah drawings.
95. Abu Zubaydah correspondence.
96. Mitchell to 9/11 pretrial.
97. Abu Zubaydah CSRT transcript, Mar. 2007.
98. SSCI report, p. 68.
99. Author interviews with Gus.
100. OIG report, p. 44.
101. SSCI report, p. 68.
102. Sealy's cable was dated December 23, 2002, according to the OIG report, p. 84.
103. Author interviews with Gus, also SSCI report, pp. 66–68.
104. SSCI report, p. 69.
105. Ibid.
106. Dana Priest and Barton Gellman, "U.S. Decries Abuse but Defends Interrogations," *Washington Post*, Dec. 26, 2002.
107. OIG report, p. 70.
108. OIG report, p. 71.
109. OIG report, p. 42.
110. SSCI report, p. 69.
111. OIG report, p. 1.
112. Author interviews with Gus, SSCI report, p. 70.
113. OIG report, p. 71; suspension, SSCI report, p. 70.
114. Author interviews with Higgins.

CHAPTER 14: "ZAPPING THE DOG FOR POOPING ON THE RUG"

1. Author interviews with Mitchell and Gus.
2. Jessen to 9/11 pretrial.
3. OIG report, p. 2.
4. APA report; also, author interviews with Brandon, Shumate, and Mitchell.
5. Matarazzo response to APA, www.opa.org/assets/docs/APA/matarazzo%20response%20to%20apa.pdf.
6. Mitchell to 9/11 pretrial.
7. Author interviews with Gus.
8. Ibid.
9. Ibid.
10. Mitchell to 9/11 pretrial.
11. FOIA to Salim v. Mitchell, #001591-93, 12/20/2016, and #001891-/2, 12/20/2016.
12. Mitchell to 9/11 pretrial.
13. Mitchell and Harlow, *Enhanced Interrogation*, p. 133.
14. Mitchell to 9/11 pretrial.
15. Ibid.
16. Author interview with Sharon.
17. FOIA to Salim v. Mitchell, #001610-15, 12/20/2016.
18. Author interviews with Gus.
19. Author interview with Sharon.
20. Author interviews with Aldrich.
21. *PREAL Operating Instructions.*
22. Author interview with Sharon.
23. Mitchell to 9/11 pretrial.
24. SSCI report, p. 71.
25. Ibid.

26. Jessen to 9/11 pretrial.
27. SSCI report, p. 71.
28. Author interviews with Mitchell, SSCI report, p. 71.
29. OIG report, p. 35.
30. OMS report, pp. 29–31.
31. SSCI report, p. 65.
32. Mitchell to 9/11 pretrial.
33. OIG report, p. 40.
34. Harlow, *Rebuttal.*
35. SSCI report, p. 71.
36. Author interviews with Mitchell.
37. FOIA to Salim v. Mitchell, #001170-74 and #001477-51, 09/26/2016.
38. OIG report, pp. 6–7.
39. OIG report, p. 103.
40. OMS report, pp. 38–45
41. Douglas Cox, *Burn after Viewing.*
42. SSCI report, p. 59.
43. SSCI report, p. xiii.
44. OIG report, pp. 28–29.
45. www.hrw.org/reports/2004/usa0604/2.htm.
46. Mitchell and Harlow, *Enhanced Interrogation*, p. 135.
47. FOIA to Salim v. Mitchell, #001047-001053, Sept. 2, 2016.
48. Lawrence E. Hinkle and Harold G. Wolff, "The Methods of Interrogation and Indoctrination Used by the Communist State Police," *Bulletin of the New York Academy of Medicine* 33, no. 9 (Sept. 1957): 600–615, www.ncbi.nlm.nih.gov/pmc/articles/PMC1806200/.
49. Author interview with Connell.
50. Author interviews with al-Maqdisi.
51. Amnesty International, *Morocco/Western Sahara: Torture in the "Anti-terrorism" Campaign—the Case of Témara Detention Centre*, p. 5, https://www.amnesty.org/download/Documents/100000/mde 290042004en.pdf.
52. Mike Busch to 9/11 pretrial; author telephone interview with Carle, who interrogated another detainee, Haji Pacha Wazir, at Temara in fall 2002.
53. Statement of Ibn Sheikh al-Libi to the ICRC.
54. SSCI report, p. 76.
55. OIG report, p. 23.
56. Abu Zubaydah to Jacobsen, also author interviews with Higgins.
57. SSCI report, pp. 77–78.
58. Ibid.
59. Mitchell to 9/11 pretrial.
60. According to the OIG report, p. 76, water dousing was first used at the Salt Pit in early 2003.
61. Four conditioning techniques used—sleep deprivation not beyond 72 hours, continual light or darkness, loud music, and white noise—were deemed as "standard techniques" and therefore did not need headquarters' approval, OIG report p. 40.
62. SSCI report, p. 77.
63. SSCI report, p. 76; "cookie-cutter," see Rizzo, *Company Man*, pp. 193–94.
64. Author interview with Harrington; "delivery of liquids" from OMS draft guidelines.
65. SSCI report, p. 80; Abu Zubaydah correspondence.
66. Author interviews with Aldrich.
67. Author interview with Harrington, see also SSCI report, p. 429.
68. Claim made by Harrington during Mitchell testimony to 9/11 pretrial. Reply from Mitchell.
69. This document was read out during Mitchell to 9/11 pretrial.

70. Mitchell to 9/11 pretrial.

71. SSCI report, p. 78.

72. Author interview with Sharon.

73. SSCI report, p. 78.

74. Ibid.

75. Author interviews with Harlow and Tenet, Maryland; see dedication to Harlow in Tenet and Harlow, *At the Center of the Storm*, p. 519.

76. Ian Cobain and Richard Norton-Taylor, "CIA Used False Heathrow Terror Plot Confession to Justify Waterboarding," *Guardian*, Dec. 9, 2014.

77. Sarah Left, "Tanks Guard Heathrow," *Guardian*, Feb. 12, 2003.

78. SSCI report, p. 79.

79. SSCI report, p. 80.

80. SSCI report, p. 422.

81. SSCI report, p. 80.

82. Ibid.

83. SSCI report, p. 76.

84. Ibid.

85. Mitchell to 9/11 pretrial.

86. Ibid.

87. "Ibn Sheikh al-Libi," The Rendition Project, www.therenditionproject.org.uk/prisoners/ibn-sheikh-al-libi.html.

88. "Full Text of Colin Powell's Speech," *Guardian*, Feb. 5, 2003.

89. Author interviews with Wilkerson.

90. Douglas Jehl, "Report Warns Bush Team about Intelligence Doubts," *New York Times*, Nov. 6, 2005.

91. Author interviews with Wilkerson.

92. "Iraq and al-Qaida: Interpreting a Murky Relationship," June 21, 2002, www.fas.org/irp/congress/2005_cr/CIAreport.062102.pdf.

93. Author interviews with Wilkerson.

94. Ibid.

95. Ibid.

96. Tenet and Harlow, *At the Center of the Storm*, pp. 341, 369.

CHAPTER 15: "MEOW"

1. Author interview with Porter Goss, Washington, DC, Oct. 2018.

2. Barker, *Manhunt*.

3. Author interviews with Harlow, see also Tenet and Harlow, *At the Center of the Storm*, pp. 251–52.

4. Tenet and Harlow, *At the Center of the Storm*, pp. 251–52; nephew of Abu Muntasir, from author interviews with Jamal Ismail, Islamabad, 2014–15.

5. Shane, "Inside a 9/11 Terrorist's Interrogation."

6. SSCI report, pp. 73–75.

7. "Khalid Sheikh Mohammed," The Rendition Project, www.therenditionproject.org.uk/prisoners/khaled-sheikh-mohammed.html.

8. SSCI report, pp. 83–84.

9. Author interviews with Mitchell, see also Mitchell to 9/11 pretrial.

10. Mitchell to 9/11 pretrial.

11. Author interview with Connell.

12. SSCI report, p. 81.

13. Mitchell phrase, author interviews with Mitchell, see also SSCI report.

14. Mohammad to ICRC.
15. SSCI report, p. 82.
16. Mohammad to ICRC.
17. SSCI report, p. 84.
18. Goldman, "The Hidden History of the CIA's Prison in Poland."
19. "Mustafa al-Hawsawi," The Rendition Project, www.therenditionproject.org.uk/prisoners /hawsawi.html.
20. Mitchell to 9/11 pretrial.
21. Mohammad to ICRC.
22. This Roger Aldrich's phrase for hooding; author interviews with Aldrich.
23. Mitchell and Harlow, *Enhanced Interrogation*, p. 146.
24. Author interviews with Mitchell.
25. Author interviews with Aldrich, see also SERE training materials cited in SASC report, pp. xiii, xiv, 4.
26. Mohammad to ICRC.
27. Ibid.
28. OMS report, p. 39.
29. Ibid.
30. Author interviews with Gus.
31. SSCI report, p. 84.
32. Author interviews with Gus.
33. Mitchell to 9/11 pretrial.
34. Shane, "Inside a 9/11 Terrorist's Interrogation."
35. Mohammad to ICRC.
36. Mitchell and Harlow, *Enhanced Interrogation*, p. 147.
37. Ibid.
38. Mitchell to 9/11 pretrial.
39. Ibid.
40. Carol Rosenberg, "Chains, Shackles and Threats: Testimony on Torture Takes a Dramatic Turn," *New York Times*, Jan. 28. 2020.
41. Mitchell to 9/11 pretrial.
42. Nevin, to 9/11 pretrial.
43. Author interviews with Mitchell.
44. Mitchell to 9/11 pretrial and FOIA to NSA, C06669362, 2017/12/27.
45. The Preacher's classified statement to the John Durham inquiry was cited by Cheryl Bormann (Khallad bin Attash) during Mitchell to 9/11 pretrial.
46. Mitchell to 9/11 pretrial.
47. For example, see FOIA to NSA, C06672307 and C06669362, 2017/12/27; "It's not supposed to be entertainment," one of Bikowsky's superiors allegedly told her.
48. Mitchell to 9/11 pretrial.
49. Pavitt statement to Office of the CIA Inspector General (OIG), SSCI report, p. 85.
50. FOIA to NSA, C06672303, 2017/12/27.
51. Ibid.
52. Author interviews with Mitchell.
53. OIG report, p. 45.
54. SSCI report, p. 85.
55. SSCI report, p. 86.
56. Ibid.
57. FOIA to NSA, C06672310, 2017/12/27; between April and September 2003 OMS issued four versions of guidelines, although CTC Legal insisted they be marked as "draft" only, OIG report, pp. 25, 31.

58. SSCI report, p. 472.
59. FOIA to NSA, C06672307, 2017/12/27.
60. Ibid.
61. Nevin to 9/11 pretrial.
62. Mitchell to 9/11 pretrial.
63. Ibid., see also FOIA to NSA, C06672307, 2017/12/27.
64. SSCI report, p. 87.
65. FOIA to NSA, C06672310, 2017/12/27.
66. Ibid.
67. For example see FOIA to NSA, C06672307 and C06669362, 2017/12/27.
68. Ibid.
69. Author interviews with Mitchell.
70. The detainee was Abu Hazim, a Libyan, the US attorney later concluded there was "insufficient evidence" to warrant a criminal prosecution; see also FOIA to Salim v. Mitchell, C05959918, 2016/06/10.
71. SSCI report, p. 88.
72. FOIA to NSA, C06676662, 2017/12/27.
73. Ibid.
74. Ibid.
75. Ibid.
76. FOIA to NSA, C06669354, 2017/12/27.
77. Ibid.
78. Nevin to 9/11 pretrial; also FOIA to NSA, C06718741, 2018/03/28.
79. Mohammad to ICRC.
80. Mitchell to 9/11 pretrial.
81. Ibid.
82. Classified statement to John Durham inquiry, referred to by Harrington during 9/11 pretrial.
83. Mitchell to 9/11 pretrial.
84. SSCI report, p. 91.
85. Ibid.
86. FOIA to NSA, C06669362, 2017/12/27.
87. Ibid.
88. FOIA to NSA, C06718741, 2018/03/28.
89. Ibid.; FOIA to NSA, C06669361, 2017/12/27.
90. OIG report, pp. 45–46.
91. Nevin to 9/11 pretrial.
92. Mohammad to ICRC.
93. Nevin to 9/11 pretrial; also FOIA to NSA, C06669361, 2017/12/27, and C06718718, 2018/03/28.
94. Shane, "Inside a 9/11 Mastermind's Interrogation."
95. Ibid.
96. FOIA to NSA, C06669361, 2017/12/27.
97. FOIA to NSA, C06718741, 2018/03/28.
98. Ibid.
99. On one thousand disseminations, see FOIA to Ray Bonner, C06257473, 2021/02/26; for "facts of life," see FOIA to NSA, C06718741, 2018/03/28.
100. FOIA to NSA, C06718718, 2018/03/28.
101. Michael V. Hayden, "Factual Errors and Other Problems in "Playing to the Edge: American Intelligence in the Age of Terror," SSCI, Mar. 2016.
102. Author interviews with Gus.
103. Ibid.
104. SSCI report, p. 93.

105. SSCI report, p. 85.
106. FOIA to NSA, C06669354, 2017/12/27.
107. "I Don't Like to Kill Children," *New York Times*, Mar. 15, 2007.
108. Nevin to 9/11 pretrial.
109. Mitchell to 9/11 pretrial.
110. SSCI report, main conclusion #9.
111. Mitchell and Harlow, *Enhanced Interrogation*, pp. 205–6.
112. FOIA to NSA, C06718676, 2018/03/28.
113. Ibid., also FOIA to NSA, C06718673, 2018/03/28, see also Shane, "Inside a 9/11 Mastermind's Interrogation."
114. FOIA to NSA, C06718673, 2018/03/28.
115. Mitchell to 9/11 pretrial.
116. Nevin read this cable to Mitchell testimony to 9/11 pretrial hearing.
117. FOIA to NSA, C06718676, 2018/03/28.
118. Nevin read this cable to Mitchell during 9/11 pretrial hearing.
119. Mitchell and Harlow, *Enhanced Interrogation*, pp. 166–68.
120. Mitchell to 9/11 pretrial.
121. Mitchell and Harlow, *Enhanced Interrogation*, p. 168.
122. Ibid.
123. Ibid.
124. Rizzo, *Company Man*, p. 194.
125. Abu Zubaydah correspondence.
126. Ibid.
127. Connell to Mitchell 9/11 pretrial.
128. Hambali, see SSCI report, pp. 108–9.
129. Mitchell and Harlow, *Enhanced Interrogation*, p. 281.
130. Mitchell to 9/11 pretrial.
131. Evan Perez and Stephen Collinson, "CIA Feared for Future of Interrogation Program, Report Shows," *CNN*, Dec. 11, 2014, www.edition.cnn.com/2014/12/11/politics/us-torture-bush/index.html.

CHAPTER 16: "STRAWBERRY FIELDS FOREVER"

1. Author interviews with Gus; Dror Ladin "In Secret Email, CIA's Chief Lawyer Mocked 'Pesky Little International Obligations,'" ACLU, July 21, 2016.
2. Mitchell to 9/11 pretrial.
3. Rizzo, *Company Man*, p. 226.
4. Ibid., p. 255.
5. Author interviews with Gus.
6. Abu Zubaydah correspondence.
7. Author interviews with Gus.
8. OIG report, p. 97.
9. John O. Brennan, *Undaunted: My Fight against America's Enemies at Home and Abroad* (New York: Celadon Books, 2020).
10. Author interviews with Gus.
11. Ibid.; also OMS report, p. 51, and Mark Binelli, "Inside America's Toughest Federal Prison," *New York Times Magazine*, Mar. 26, 2015.
12. www.cnic.navy.mil/regions/cnrse/installations/ns_Guantánamo_bay/about/history.html.
13. Author interviews with Gus.
14. www.cnic.navy.mil/regions/cnrse/installations/ns_Guantánamo_bay/about/history.html.
15. FOIA to Ray Bonner, C06630637, 2018/03/05.
16. FOIA to Salim v. Mitchell, #001106-08, 09/20/2016.

17. Ibid.
18. FOIA to Ray Bonner, C06630637, 2018/03/05.
19. FOIA to Salim v. Mitchell, #001102-05, 09/20/2016.
20. FOIA to Salim v. Mitchell, #000061-119, 07/01/2016.
21. FOIA to Salim v. Mitchell, #001102-05, 09/20/2016.
22. FOIA to Salim v. Mitchell, #001594, 12/20/2016.
23. FOIA to Salim v. Mitchell, #001102-05, 09/20/2016.
24. Mitchell to 9/11 pretrial.
25. Abu Zubaydah involvement was claimed by Ali Soufan; for "KSM's deputy" see Scott Muller briefing to Rice, Cheney et al., FOIA to Salim v. Mitchell, #000959-62, 08/31/2016; also FOIA to NSA, C06238939, 2014/09/11.
26. www.aclu.org/other/ammar-al-baluchi-csrt-transcript en.wikisource.org/wiki/CSRT_Summary _of_Evidence_memo_for_Walid_Bin_Attash. Note his given name is Walid but he calls himself Khallad.
27. Accusation made by defense teams at the 9/11 pretrial hearing, Jan. 2020.
28. Author interviews with Gus.
29. Author interviews with Mitchell.
30. An "enhanced technique," SSCI report, p. 4; "baseline conditions," p. 60.
31. Zirbel statement, FOIA to Salim v. Mitchell, #001081-001097, May 22, 2017.
32. SSCI report, p. 61.
33. The Constitution Project Task Force on Detainee Treatment, Apr. 2013, see also Khallad bin Attash to the ICRC.
34. Mitchell to 9/11 pretrial.
35. Author interview with Carle.
36. Mitchell to 9/11 pretrial.
37. Cable read out by Walter Ruiz (learned counsel for al-Hawsawi) during Mitchell to 9/11 pretrial.
38. The photograph is classified but was shown to the war court during Mitchell to 9/11 pretrial, see also SSCI report, p. 51.
39. SSCI report, p. 244.
40. According to Bormann, Mitchell to 9/11 pretrial.
41. Mitchell to 9/11 pretrial; they were referred to as X3L, LQ3, PU2, QY7, and Z2C (Matthew Zirbel), and were assisted by PG6 (a physician) and JP2 (a psychologist).
42. Classified cable read out by Bormann during Mitchell to 9/11 pretrial.
43. Ibid.
44. Khallad bin Attash to the ICRC.
45. Abu Zubaydah drawings; Mitchell to 9/11 pretrial.
46. Mitchell to 9/11 pretrial, see also OIG report, p. 76.
47. Allegations made during Mitchell to 9/11 pretrial.
48. Author interview with Connell.
49. Mitchell to 9/11 pretrial.
50. Mitchell, Jessen & Associates was formed in Mar. 2004 and signed a contract with the CIA in Mar. 2005, but Mitchell and Jessen were already conducted training in 2003, see FOIA to Ray Bonner, C06867088, 2020/10/30.
51. Connell to 9/11 pretrial.
52. Bin Attash to the ICRC.
53. "Ramzi bin al-Shibh," The Rendition Project, www.therenditionproject.org.uk/prisoners /binalshibh.html.
54. "Court Upholds CIA Contractor's Detainee Abuse Conviction," AFP, Aug. 12, 2009.
55. OIG report, pp. 78–79.
56. Mitchell and Harlow, *Enhanced Interrogation*, p. 93.

57. OIG report, p. 79.

58. For paramilitary see OIG report, p. 79; PBS NewsHour, "Convicted Former CIA Contracter Speaks Out about Prisoner Interrogation," Apr. 20, 2015, www.pbs.org/newshour/show/convicted -former-cia-contractor-speaks-prisoner-interrogation; Passaro was not charged until after the Abu Ghraib scandal.

59. OIG report, pp. 93–94.

60. Ibid.

61. Author interviews with Wilkerson.

62. Peter Slevin, "U.S. Pledges to Avoid Torture," *Washington Post*, June 27, 2003.

63. FOIA to NSA, C06238939, 2014/09/11.

64. SSCI report, p. 119.

65. FOIA to NSA, C06238939, 2014/09/11.

66. For the briefing paper see FOIA to Salim v. Mitchell, #000959-62, 08/31/2016; also FOIA to NSA, C06238939, 2014/09/11.

67. The Executive Branch had been briefed in the spring and summer of 2002, and updated during the winter, spring, and summer of 2003. Congress had been briefed during the summer and fall of 2002 with Porter Goss, Nancy Pelosi, Bob Graham and Richard Shelby attending. Goss, Jane Harman, Pat Roberts, and John Rockefeller had come to an update meeting in the winter of 2002.

68. SSCI report, pp. xiv–xv.

69. FOIA to NSA, C06238939, 2014/09/11.

70. From CIA biography: Scott W. Muller, General Counsel, Office of General Counsel, Office of the Director of Intelligence, Jan. 11, 2005, declassified, Nov. 6, 2009, https://www.cia.gov /readingroom/docs/DOC_0005459067.pdf.

71. SSCI report, pp. xiv–xv.

72. SSCI report, pp. xv–xvi.

73. According to a Memorandum for the Record written by Muller, OIG report, p. 24.

74. FOIA to NSA, C06238939, 2014/09/11.

75. Ladin, "In Secret Email, CIA's Chief Lawyer Mocked 'Pesky Little International Obligations.'"

76. Bin Attash to ICRC.

77. Cable read out during Mitchell testimony to 9/11 pretrial.

78. SSCI report, p. 117.

79. Bin Attash to ICRC.

80. The classified photograph was displayed to the war court only during Mitchell to 9/11 pretrial.

81. Mitchell to 9/11 pretrial.

82. Cable read out during Mitchell testimony to 9/11 pretrial.

83. Ibid.

84. Mitchell to 9/11 pretrial.

85. Cable read out during Mitchell testimony to 9/11 pretrial.

86. Ibid.

87. Mitchell to 9/11 pretrial.

88. Abu Zubaydah correspondence.

89. OIG report, pp. 4–5.

90. Author interview with General Tritot.

91. Ibid., also "Majid Khan," The Rendition Project, www.therenditionproject.org.uk/prisoners/majid -khan.html.

92. Ibid., also "Zubair," The Rendition Project, www.therenditionproject.org.uk/prisoners/zubair.html.

93. Ibid., also "Lillie," The Rendition Project, www.therenditionproject.org.uk/prisoners/lillie.html.

94. They lived in Manila planning the Bojinka plot, see Terry McDermott and Josh Mayer, *The Hunt for KSM* (New York: Little, Brown and Company, 2012).

95. Ibid., also "Hambali," The Rendition Project, www.therenditionproject.org.uk/prisoners /hambali.html.
96. SSCI report, p. 96.
97. SSCI report, p. 108; also Mitchell to 9/11 pretrial.
98. SSCI report, p. 109.
99. Author interviews with Gus; also SSCI report, p. 117.
100. Author interviews with Rodriguez.
101. Multiple examples of this during Mitchell to 9/11 pretrial.
102. Author interviews with Mitchell.

CHAPTER 17: "A TORTURE PONZI SCHEME"

1. Abu Zubaydah to Jacobsen.
2. Abu Zubaydah drawings.
3. Author interviews with Gus; also "Walid bin Attash," The Rendition Project, www.therendition project.org.uk/prisoners/walid-binattash.html.
4. In the SSCI report, the Romanian facility was identified as Detention Site Black, pp. 97–98.
5. Spencer Ackerman, "Go Deep inside a Secret CIA Torture Prisoner," Wired, Dec. 8, 2011.
6. Tailfin number N313P; see "Ammar al-Baluci," The Rendition Project, www.therenditionproject .org.uk/prisoners/ammar-albaluchi.html.
7. Author interviews with Mitchell; they interrogated Ibn Sheikh al-Libi in Jan. 2004.
8. www.hudoc.echr.coe.int/fre#{%22itemid%22:[%22001-183687%22]}.
9. Abu Zubaydah correspondence.
10. "Ibn Sheikh al-Libi," The Rendition Project, www.therenditionproject.org.uk/prisoners/ibn-sheikh -al-libi.html.
11. Abu Zubaydah correspondence.
12. Author interviews with Higgins.
13. Scott Horton, "The Guanatanmo Suicides: A Camp Delta Sergeant Blows the Whistle," Harper's Magazine, Mar. 2010, www.harpers.org/archive/2010/03/the-Guantánamo-suicides/.
14. For "hoo-ah" see Mark Fallon, Unjustifiable Means (New York: Simon and Schuster, 2017); for "350" see Horton, "The Guanatanmo Suicides."
15. www.mazurskieuroczysko.pl/, quote from Mitchell and Harlow, Enhanced Interrogation, p. 126.
16. Author interviews with Shiffrin.
17. PREAL Operating Instructions makes reference to this course as a special access program.
18. Jeff Kaye, "Expanding the Investigation into CIA Torture," Shadowproof, Aug. 14, 2009.
19. Author interviews with Shiffrin.
20. Paper shuffler from author interview with Wirts.
21. PREAL Operating Instructions.
22. SASC report, xiv–xv.
23. This claim was made by Alka Pradhan during Jessen testimony to 9/11 pretrial.
24. SASC report, p. 7.
25. Ibid., p. 38.
26. Greg Miller, "Many Held at Guantánamo Not Likely Terrorists," Los Angeles Times, Dec. 22, 2002.
27. Fallon, Unjustifiable Means; they ranged from Army CID, the Army's recently created Criminal Investigation Task Force (CITF), to interrogators from Joint Task Force-170, a military intelligence task force created in Feb. 2002 to process incoming GTMO detainees.
28. Tim Golden and Don van Natta Jr., "The Reach of War: U.S. Said to Overstate the Value of Guantánamo Detainees," New York Times, June 21, 2004.
29. Fallon, Unjustifiable Means.

30. Christopher Cooper, "Detention Plan in Guantánamo, Prisoners Languish in Sea of Red Tape Inmates Waiting to Be Freed Are Caught in Uncertainty; Improvising Along the Way," *The Wall Street Journal*, Jan. 26, 2005.

31. Golden and van Natta Jr., "The Reach of War."

32. Fallon, *Unjustifiable Means*.

33. Author interviews with Mark Fallon, Washington, DC, June 2019.

34. Author interviews with Shiffrin.

35. Philippe Sands, *The Torture Team* (London: Penguin, 2008).

36. SASC report, pp. 11–12.

37. James, Larry, *Fixing Hell* (New York: Grand Central Publishing, 2014).

38. Author telephone interview Morgan Banks, Mar. 2020.

39. www.propublica.org/article/tortured-profession-psychologists-warned-of-abusive-interrogations -505, see also www.salon.com/2007/06/21/cia_sere/, also Jane Mayer, "The Experiment," *New Yorker*, July 11, 2005.

40. SASC report, p. 39.

41. Ibid., p. 44.

42. Mayer, *The Dark Side*, pp. 194–96.

43. SASC report, pp. 39–44.

44. The visit was on Sept. 25, 2002, see SASC report, pp. xvi–xvii.

45. Author interviews with Rizzo; also Philippe Sands, "The Green Light," *Vanity Fair*, Apr. 2, 2008.

46. Mayer, *The Dark Side*, pp. 182–86.

47. FBI report, p. 81.

48. Author interviews with Fallon.

49. Center for Constitutional Rights, Mohammed al-Qahtani, Oct. 8, 2020, https://ccrjustice.org /mohammed-al-qahtani.

50. Philip Shenon, "Panel Says a Deported Saudi Was Likely '20th' Hijacker," *New York Times*, Jan. 27, 2004.

51. www.justice.gov/archives/ag/indictment-zacarias-moussaoui.

52. Ibid., see also Laura Sullivan, "Sept. 11 Hijacker Raised Suspicions at Border," *Baltimore Sun*, Jan. 27, 2004; also FBI report, pp. 80–82.

53. Author interviews with Fallon.

54. Fallon, *Unjustifiable Means*.

55. Carol Rosenberg, "When It Comes to Guantánamo, Trump Is Truly the Builder in Chief," *Miami Herald*, Mar. 28, 2018.

56. Author interviews with Fallon.

57. SASC report Index.

58. SASC report, p. xviii.

59. Sands, "The Green Light."

60. SASC report, p. xvii, also author interviews with Fallon.

61. Fredman statement to SASC, copy embedded at www.propublica.org/article/tortured-profession -psychologists-warned-of-abusive-interrogations-505.

62. Danny Gallagher, "Six Song to Torture and Intimidate," *The Wall Street Journal*, July 21, 2009.

63. SASC report , p. 52.

64. Jessen to 9/11 pretrial.

65. Fredman statement to SASC.

66. Fallon, *Unjustifiable Means*.

67. Joby Warrick, "CIA Played Larger Role in Advising Pentagon," *Washington Post*, June 18, 2008.

68. Fredman statement to SASC.

69. Ibid.

70. Author interviews with Fallon.

71. Fredman statement to SASC.

72. Sands, "The Green Light."

73. Fredman statement to SASC.
74. Author interviews with Fallon; also SASC report, p. 90.
75. SASC report, p. 61.
76. Ibid., p. 57.
77. Ibid., p. 151.
78. Jennifer Turner, "The Monster of Bagram," ACLU, May 7, 2010, www.aclu.org/blog/national -security/detention/monster-bagram.
79. Alex Gibney, "Killing Wussification," *Atlantic*, May 21, 2009.
80. Ibid.
81. Ibid.
82. Ibid.
83. Fallon, *Unjustifiable Means*.
84. Ibid.
85. Author interviews with Fallon.
86. Mayer, "The Experiment."
87. David S. Cloud, "Concern Led to Revisions, Rumsfeld Says," *New York Times*, Feb. 22, 2006.
88. Spencer Ackerman, "US Psychology Body Declines to Rebuke Member in Guantánamo Torture Case," *Guardian*, Jan. 22, 2014.
89. Author interviews with Fallon.
90. Interrogation Log Detainee 63, obtained by *Time*, http://content.time.com/time/2006/log/log .pdf.
91. William Glaberson, "Detainee Was Tortured, a Bush Official Confirms," *New York Times*, Jan. 14, 2009
92. SASC report, pp. 74–75; also SASC report Index.
93. SASC, pp. 97–98; also SASC report Index.
94. Wood statement to SASC, reported by Gibney, "Killing Wussification."
95. Author interviews with Wilkerson.
96. According to a subsequent coroner's report, see Gibney, "Killing Wussification"; also Gibney, *Taxi to the Dark Side*.
97. Gibney, "Killing Wussification."
98. Author interviews with Mora.
99. Andrew Cockburn, "Rumsfeld," *New York Times*, Mar. 25. 2007.
100. Author interviews with Mora.
101. Ibid.
102. Author interviews with Fallon.
103. SASC report, pp. 103–5.
104. Ibid., p. 103.
105. Author interviews with Mora.
106. Jeffrey Rosen, "Conscience of a Conservative," *New York Times Magazine*, Sept. 9, 2007.
107. U.S. Department of Justice, Office of Legal Counsel, Memorandum for William J. Haynes II, General Counsel of the Department of Defense, Re: Military Interrogation of Alien Unlawful Combatants Held Outside the United States, Mar. 14, 2003, p. 30, https://www.aclu.org/sites /default/files/pdfs/safefree/yoo_army_torture_memo.pdf.
108. Author interviews with Shiffrin.
109. Mohamedou Salahi and Larry Siems, *Guantánamo Diary* (New York: Little, Brown and Company, 2015).

CHAPTER 18: "A GREAT BIG TERRARIUM"

1. Author interviews with Mitchell.
2. Ibid.; and author interviews with defense teams from Military Commissions Defense Organization (MCDO).

3. Mitchell to 9/11 pretrial.
4. According to CIA briefing papers produced as late as 2005; for "compliance," see Mitchell to 9/11 pretrial.
5. Jessen to 9/11 pretrial.
6. Allegation made by multiple detainees, including Abu Zubaydah and Ramzi bin al-Shibh, author interviews Higgins, Harrington, Connell, and Pradhan.
7. Testimony of Camp 7 commander, Nov. 1, 2019, 9/11 pretrial; for transcript see www.mc.mil. Standard Operating Procedures, described to author by FBI Special Agent Fred Humphries who "in-processed" the high-value detainees in Sept. 2006.
8. Abu Zubaydah to Jacobsen.
9. Author interviews with Gus.
10. Author interviews with Mitchell; the OMS report, p. 41, refers to Abu Zubaydah as "the professor."
11. Author interviews with Mitchell and Higgins.
12. Abu Zubaydah to Jacobsen.
13. Author visit to Guantánamo Bay, Jan. 2020.
14. Abu Zubaydah to Jacobsen.
15. Author interviews with Abu Zubaydah's *habeas* lawyers, Joe Margulies, Amman, Jordan, 2015, and Mark Denbeaux, New Jersey, 2017–18, London, 2018.
16. Abu Zubaydah to Jacobsen.
17. Abu Zubaydah to ICRC.
18. OIG report, p. 19.
19. Author interviews Mitchell; Mitchell to 9/11 pretrial.
20. Abu Zubaydah drawings.
21. Abu Zubaydah correspondence.
22. Author interviews Higgins.
23. Camp 7 commander testimony and Mitchell to 9/11 pretrial.
24. SSCI report, p. 151.
25. Abu Zubaydah correspondence.
26. Ibid.
27. Author interviews with Mitchell.
28. Abu Zubaydah correspondence.
29. Mitchell to 9/11 pretrial.
30. Author interviews with Harrington.
31. Mitchell to 9/11 pretrial.
32. Read out during Mitchell during 9/11 pretrial.
33. See his report written in 2005: FOIA to Salim v. Mitchell, #002285-302, 2/14/2017.
34. Mitchell to 9/11 pretrial.
35. Ibid.
36. Author interviews with Mitchell.
37. Mitchell and Harlow, *Enhanced Interrogation*, pp. 178–83.
38. Mitchell to 9/11 pretrial.
39. Read out by Ruiz during Mitchell to 9/11 pretrial.
40. CIA reports read out during Mitchell 9/11 pretrial.
41. Author interviews with Mitchell.
42. "Libya/US Investigate Death of Former CIA Prisoner," Human Rights Watch, May 11, 2009.
43. FOIA to Salim v. Mitchell, #000120, 07/01/2016.
44. Zayn-al-Abidin Muhammad Husayn (ISN#10016) v. Lloyd Austin et al., United States District Court for the District of Columbia, Case 1:08-cv-01360-UNA, May 24, 2021.
45. Golden and van Natta Jr., "The Reach of War."
46. ICRC report.
47. Author interviews with Gus.
48. ICRC report.

49. Ibid.
50. Ibid.
51. Center for Constitutional Rights, Rasul v. Bush, www.ccrjustice.org/home/what-we-do/our-cases /rasul-v-bush.
52. Abu Zubaydah to Jacobsen.
53. Tailfin number N85VM; see "Abu Zubaydah," The Rendition Project, www.therenditionproject .org.uk/prisoners/zubaydah.html; see also Matt Apuzzo and Adam Goldman, "CIA Flight Carried Secret from Gitmo," AP, Aug. 7, 2010.
54. Author interviews with Gus.
55. Horton, "The Guantánamo 'Suicides.'"
56. Amnesty International, *Morocco: Getting Away with Torture*, Jan. 12. 2018.
57. Ibid.
58. www.justiceinitiative.org/uploads/655bbd41-082b-4df3-940c-18a3bd9ed956/globalizing-torture -20120205.pdf, p.97.
59. Author interviews with Gus, see also SSCI report, pp. 155–56.
60. Abu Zubaydah correspondence.
61. Ali Soufan and Mike Butsch were both there with Ramzi bin al-Shibh, see Butsch testimony to 9/11 pretrial, Nov. 6, 2019.
62. Scott-Clark and Levy, *The Exile*.
63. Scheuer statement to *Extraordinary Rendition in U.S. Counterterrorism Policy*, Committee on Foreign Affairs, Apr. 17, 2007, Serial No. 110–28.
64. Abu Zubaydah correspondence.
65. Ibid.
66. Ibid.
67. Ibid.
68. Author interviews with Mitchell, who added that "[Martinez] does state on his resume that he worked for us."
69. Author interviews with Rodriguez.
70. Author interviews with Aldrich.
71. Author interviews with Wilkerson.
72. Dan Rather, "Abuse at Abu Ghraib," *CBS News*, May 5, 2004, www.cbsnews.com/news/abuse-at -abu-ghraib/.
73. David Finkel and Christian Davenport, "Records Paint Dark Portrait of Guard," *Washington Post*, June 5, 2004.
74. Jeff Stein and Adam Zagorin, "A Former CIA Interrogator on Death, Torture and the Dark Side," *Newsweek*, Oct. 7, 2015.
75. Adam Zagorin, "Haunted by the Iceman," *Time*, Nov. 14, 2005.
76. Seymour M. Hersh, "Torture at Abu Ghraib," *New Yorker*, May 10, 2004.
77. See *Fay Report*, "Investigation of 205th Military Intelligence Brigade's Activities in Abu Ghraib Detention Facility," Aug. 23, 2004, ACLU-RDI 4999, p. 68; also Gibney, "Killing Wussification."
78. SASC report Index.
79. Wood's testimony was reported in Gibney, *Taxi to the Dark Side*.
80. SASC report, p. 191.
81. Author interviews with Kleinman, see also SASC report, pp. 170–71.
82. Author interviews with Kleinman.
83. Ibid.
84. AP photo, archive.boston.com/news/world/middleeast/gallery/iraq_abuse?pg=3.
85. Seymour M. Hersh, "The General's Report," *New Yorker*, June 18, 2007.
86. Author interviews with Wilkerson.
87. For background on Swanner, see Jane Mayer, "A Deadly Interrogation," *New Yorker*, Nov. 7, 2005.
88. Inteview with Tony Diaz, former military policeman, on *NPR Morning Edition*, see "Documents Shed Light on Abu Ghraib Death," NPR, Oct. 28, 2005.

89. Ibid.
90. Stein and Zagorin, "A Former CIA Interrogator on Death, Torture and the Dark Side."
91. Ibid.
92. Ibid.
93. Emma Brockes, "What Happens in War Happens," *Guardian*, Jan. 3, 2009.
94. Hersh, "Torture at Abu Ghraib."
95. Author interviews with Wilkerson.
96. Fay Report.
97. Author interviews with Wilkerson.
98. Author interviews with Mora.
99. Ibid.
100. "The Death of an Iraqi Prisoner," *All Things Considered*, NPR, Oct. 27, 2005.
101. David Dishneau, "Abu Ghraib Abuse Ringleader Freed Early from Military Prison," AP, Aug. 7, 2011.
102. Mayer, "A Deadly Interrogation."
103. Mark Thompson, "Haunted by Homicide: Federal Grand Jury Investigates War Crimes and Torture in Death of 'the Iceman' at Abu Ghraib," June 13, 2011, https://voxverax.blogspot.com /2011/06/haunted-by-homicide-federal-grand-jury.html; also AP, "US Justice Department Rules Out Prosecutions Over CIA Prison Deaths," *Guardian*, Aug. 31, 2012.
104. Stein and Zagorin, "A Former CIA Interrogator on Death, Torture and the Dark Side."
105. Ibid.
106. www.pbs.org/newshour/show/convicted-former-cia-contractor-speaks-prisoner-interrogation.
107. Author interviews with Mitchell and Rodriguez, also Mitchell and Harlow, *Enhanced Interrogation*, p. 233; and Rodriguez and Harlow, *Hard Measures*, p. 189.
108. The meeting was June 2007, see Mitchell and Harlow, *Enhanced Interrogation*, pp. 237–38.
109. Author interviews with Mitchell.
110. Produced in the war court during Mitchell to 9/11 pretrial.
111. Nowosielski and Duffy, "The Watchdogs Didn't Bark."
112. SSCI report, p. 117.
113. Author interview with Jeff Gorman, Cocoa Beach, FL, July 2017.
114. Ken Silverstein, "The Charmed Life of a CIA Torturer," *The Intercept*, Dec. 15, 2014.
115. Adam Goldman and Kathy Gannon, "Death Shed Light on CIA 'Salt-Pit' Near Kabul," AP, Mar. 28, 2010.
116. SSCI report, p. 10.
117. SSCI report, p. xv.
118. SSCI report, p. 8, notes investigators found evidence that at least 119 detainees went through the program, compared to the official CIA tally of 96.
119. SSCI report, p. xxv.
120. "Abu Yasir al-Jazairi," The Rendition Project, www.therenditionproject.org.uk/prisoners/jazairi .html.
121. Referenced during Mitchell to 9/11 pretrial.
122. Mitchell and Harlow, *Enhanced Interrogation*, pp. 194–95.
123. "Abu Yasir al-Jazairi," The Rendition project.
124. www.justiceinitiative.org/uploads/655bbd41-082b-4df3-940c-18a3bd9ed956/globalizing-torture -20120205.pdf, pp. 38–41.
125. Rodriguez and Harlow, *Hard Measures*, p. 189.

CHAPTER 19: "EGO AND HYPOCRISY. NOTHING ELSE MATTERS"

1. Mark Mazzetti and Scott Shane, "C.I.A. Destroyed Tapes as Judge Sought Interrogation Data," *New York Times*, Feb. 7. 2008.
2. Dan Eggen and Joby Warrick, "CIA Destroyed Videos Showing Interrogations: Harsh Techniques Seen in 2002 Tapes," *Washington Post*, Dec. 7, 2007.

3. Scott Shane and Mark Mazzetti, "Tapes by CIA Lived and Died to Save Image," *New York Times*, Dec. 30, 2007, see also SSCI report, p. 252.

4. Author interviews with Rizzo.

5. Author interviews with Morgan.

6. Author interviews with Mitchell.

7. James Risen, *Pay Any Price* (New York: Houghton, Mifflin Harcourt, 2014).

8. Author interviews with Morgan.

9. Shane and Mazzetti, "Tapes by CIA Lived and Died to Save Image."

10. SSCI report, pp. 451–52.

11. Rodriguez and Harlow, *Hard Measures*, p. 190.

12. Efforts to appoint Rizzo as General Counsel in 2007 were abandoned after the Senate Select Committee on Intelligence objected on the grounds of his role in the EIT program.

13. OIG report, p. 9; see also discussion about oversight in Harlow, *Rebuttal*.

14. Author interviews with Rodriguez.

15. OIG report; also Speigel International, "The Agency Went Over Bounds and Outside the Rules, Aug. 31, 2009.

16. Ibid.; see also Harlow, *Rebuttal*, for reference to Helgerson's finding that Article 16 of the Convention against Torture was not covered by Yoo-Bybee.

17. SSCI report, p. 126.

18. OIG report, p. 8.

19. Ibid., p. 9.

20. Ibid., p. 107.

21. Brian Whitaker and Luke Harding, "American Beheaded in Revenge for Torture," *Guardian*, May 12, 2004.

22. Dana Priest and Joe Stephens, "Secret World of US Interrogation," *Washington Post*, May 11, 2004.

23. Rizzo, *Company Man*, p. 233.

24. Mitchell and Harlow, *Enhanced Interrogation*, pp. 290–91.

25. Author interviews with Mitchell.

26. Priest and Stephens, "Secret World of US Interrogation."

27. Rizzo, *Company Man*, p. 245.

28. Tenet and Harlow, *At the Center of the Storm*, p. 477.

29. Ibid., pp. 483–84.

30. www.shelby.senate.gov/public/index.cfm/newsreleases?ID=EFE1A508-26AE-47EF-8A6A-484EB6A61366.

31. Tenet and Harlow, *At the Center of the Storm*, p. 486.

32. "CIA Covert Operations Chief Retiring," *CNN*, June 4, 2004.

33. Author interviews Mitchell, also Mitchell to 9/11 pretrial.

34. Mitchell and Harlow, *Enhanced Interrogation*, pp. 483–84.

35. FOIA to Salim v. Mitchell, #000001-2 and 000011-12, 5/20/2016.

36. Author interview with Tenet.

37. FOIA to Ray Bonner, C06257473, 2021/02/26.

38. Author interview with Tenet.

39. FOIA to Ray Bonner, C06257473, 2021/02/26.

40. David Johnston and Don van Natta, "Threats and Responses: The Interrogations; Account of Plot Sets Off Debate Over Credibility," *New York Times,* June 17, 2004.

41. Sands, "The Green Light."

42. Ibid.

43. Linda Greenhouse, "The Supreme Court: Detainees; Access to Courts," *New York Times*, June 29, 2004.

44. Shane and Mazzetti, "Tapes by CIA Lived and Died to Save Image."

45. A. John Radson, "Sed Quis Custodiet Ipsos Custodes: The CIA's Office of General Counsel?" *The Journal of National Security Law and Policy* 2, no. 201, www.jnslp.com/wp-content/uploads/2010/08/01_Radsan-Master-09_11_08.pdf.

46. Rodriguez and Harlow, *Hard Measures*, p. 128.

47. Mitchell and Harlow, *Enhanced Interrogation*, p. 231.

48. Author interview with Tenet.

49. Rizzo, *Company Man*, p. 213.

50. Tenet and Harlow, *At the Center of the Storm*, p. 487.

51. Ibid, p. 506.

52. Author interview with Goss.

53. Ibid.

54. Ibid.

55. Ibid.

56. FOIA to Salim v. Mitchell, #000487-8, #000489-90, #000200-1, and #000198-9, 08/31/2016.

57. The OPR report noted that Levin attended National Security Council meetings about Abu Zubaydah with Jonathan Fredman, John Rizzo, John Yoo, Michael Chertoff, and John Bellinger, among others.

58. This was probably Elizabeth Vogt, who went to see Martin Seligman with Kirk Hubbard and Judy Philipson in early April 2002.

59. Mitchell and Harlow, *Enhanced Interrogation*, p. 250.

60. FOIA to Salim v. Mitchell, #000491-510, 08/31/2016.

61. Rodriguez and Harlow, *Hard Measures*, p. 191.

62. Author interview with Goss.

63. Author interviews with Gus.

64. Letter dated Oct. 31, 2005, SSCI report, pp. 443–44.

65. Rodriguez and Harlow, *Hard Measures*, p. 192.

66. Mark Mazzetti, "Grand Jury Inquiry on Destruction of CIA Tapes," *New York Times*, July 2, 2009; the congressional panel asked to speak to Hermes, Eatinger, plus two other CTC lawyers, Elizabeth Vogt and John McPherson.

67. FOIA to Ray Bonner, C06257473, 2021/02/26.

68. Douglas Cox, *Burn after Viewing*.

69. Rodriguez and Harlow, *Hard Measures*, p. 193; author interviews with Rizzo and Rodriguez.

70. Rodriguez and Harlow, *Hard Measures*, pp. 193–94.

71. Daniel Jones, lead senate investigator into "CIA Torture" read the statements that Tenet and Rodriguez gave to Helgerson where they described the tapes as an existential threat, Gibney, *The Forever Prisoner*.

72. Author interviews with Rizzo.

73. Ibid.

74. Author interview with Goss.

75. Ibid.

76. Mitchell and Harlow, *Enhanced Interrogation*, p. 266.

77. Author interviews with Mitchell, see also www.justice.gov/opa/pr/department-justice-statement-investigation-destruction-videotapes-cia-personnel.

78. Mitchell and Harlow, *Enhanced Interrogation*, pp. 266–67.

CHAPTER 20: "THEY ARE LIARS, LIARS, LIARS!"

1. Author interviews with Mitchell.

2. Ibid.

3. Ibid.

4. Ibid.

5. Mayer, "The Experiment."

6. Author interviews with Mitchell.

7. Mayer, "The Experiment."

8. Seligman, "The Hoffman Report, the Central Intelligence Agency, and the Defense of the Nation."
9. Horton, "The Guantánamo 'Suicides.'"
10. AP, "CIA Turned Guantánamo Inmates into Double Agents, Ex-officials Claim," *Guardian*, Nov. 26. 2013.
11. Author interviews with Gus.
12. Joseph Hickman, *Murder at Camp Delta: A Staff Sergeant's Pursuit of the Truth about Guantánamo Bay* (London: Simon and Schuster, 2015).
13. Horton, "The Guantánamo 'Suicides.'"
14. Ben Wederman, "CNN Tours Gitmo Prison Camp," CNN, July 7, 2005.
15. Mayer, "The Experiment."
16. Many relevant articles are cited in this CIA overview of the program, FOIA to Ray Bonner, C06257473, 2021/02/26.
17. Author interviews with Mitchell.
18. Jeffrey Smith, "Central Torture Agency?" *The Washington Post*, Nov. 9, 2005.
19. Author interviews with Mitchell.
20. FOIA to Ray Bonner, C06257473, 2021/02/26.
21. FOIA to Salim v. Mitchell, #001906, 12/20/2016.
22. Walker, "These 7 Men Owned the Company Linked to CIA Torture."
23. Author interviews with Gus.
24. Author interviews with Aldrich.
25. Ibid., the other three owners were David Ayers, Randall Spivey, and James Sporleder.
26. Author interviews with Mitchell.
27. Author interviews with Aldrich.
28. FOIA to Jason Leopold, C06640010, 2019/05/14.
29. FOIA to Ray Bonner, C06644659, 2020/02/25.
30. Author interview with Keller.
31. Author interviews with Mitchell.
32. Author interview with Morgan.
33. Author interview with Krongard.
34. Author interview with Mitchell.
35. Author interview with Morgan.
36. Author interview with a former colleague of Hubbard, who wishes to remain anonymous.
37. Author interviews with Sharon, Morgan, Mitchell, Aldrich, Gus, Rodriguez; for Martinez see also Scott Shane, "Ex-Officer Is First from C.I.A. to Face Prison for a Leak," *New York Times*, Jan. 5, 2013.
38. Author interviews with Gus.
39. Mitchell to 9/11 pretrial.
40. Author interview with Goss.
41. Eyder Peralta, "Torture Report: A Close Look at When and What President Bush Knew," *NPR*, Dec. 16, 2014.
42. Mitchell shared his file of citations and awards with the author.
43. The Lithuanians sold the black site to Elite LLC, a company based in Delaware, in Mar. 2004.
44. Author interview with General Tritot.
45. Author copy of photograph.
46. Case 2:15-cv-00286-JLQ Document 176-9, Filed 05/22/17.
47. Matthew Cole and Brian Ross, "Exclusive: CIA Secret 'Torture' Prison Found at Fancy Horseback Riding Academy," *ABC News*, Nov. 18, 2009.
48. "Site Violet: How Lithuania Helped Run a Secret CIA Prison," Bureau of Investigative Journalism, Oct. 10, 2016.
49. Abu Zubaydah to Jacobsen.

50. Rizzo, *Company Man*, pp. 219–22.
51. Abu Zubaydah correspondence.
52. Author interviews with Aldrich.
53. Dana Priest, "CIA Holds Terror Suspects in Secret Prisons," *Washington Post*, Nov. 2, 2005; also "Site Violet: How Lithuania Helped Run a Secret CIA Prison," Bureau of Investigative Journalism.
54. SSCI report, pp. 153–54.
55. Poland and Lithuania were successfully sued by Abu Zubaydah for damages under EU human rights legislation. In 2020, Abu Zubaydah's lawyers issued proceedings against the United Kingdom. In 2021, Abu Zubaydah's lawyers requested the United Nations to intervene in his case.
56. Goldman, "The Hidden History of the CIA's Prison in Poland."
57. SSCI report, pp. 153–54.
58. Author interview with Davis.
59. OIG report, p. 94.
60. Sands, "The Green Light"; also www.aclu.org/sites/default/files/field_document/accountabilityfor torture-whyacriminalinvestigationisnecessary.pdf.
61. OMS report, pp. 82–83.
62. OIG report, p. 95.
63. Rodriguez and Harlow, *Hard Measures*, p. 196.
64. FOIA C06541712, 2016/06/10, see https://www.cia.gov/readingroom/document/6541712.
65. For text of speech, see "President Bush's Speech on Terrorism," *New York Times*, Sept. 6, 2006; for CIA error acknowledgment, see SSCI report, p. 430.
66. Michael Hayden quote, see p. 22 of C06257473, 2021/02/26.
67. Jonathan Karl, "High-Value Detainees Transferred to Guantánamo," *ABC News*, Sept. 6, 2006.
68. 1st Camp 7 commander to 9/11 pretrial.
69. SSCI report, p. 160.
70. Author interviews with Mitchell.
71. 1st Camp 7 commander to 9/11 pretrial.
72. Horton, "The Guantánamo 'Suicides.'"
73. 1st Camp 7 commander to 9/11 pretrial.
74. Because the program was cut short when the Obama administration took over in Jan. 2009, the five-year contract period shortened to three years. MJA was paid in excess of $80 million. See FOIA to Ray Bonner, C06644659, 2020/02/25; and FOIA to Jason Leopold, C06640010, 2019/05/14.
75. Author interview with Humphries.
76. 1st Camp 7 commander to 9/11 pretrial.
77. Ibid.
78. Mitchell said during an interview with the authors that Scott Horton emailed him and accused him of dry-boarding the three dead detainees. Mitchell denied this, saying he was in the US at the time the deaths occurred. Horton removed Mitchell's name from his subsequent article; see also Mitchell and Harlow, *Enhanced Interrogation*, pp. 288–89.
79. Horton, "The Guantánamo 'Suicides.'"
80. Author interviews with Higgins; other detainees also complained about huge fans, see Mansoor Adayfi, "Taking Marriage Class at Guantánamo," *New York Times*, July 27, 2018.
81. Author interviews with defense teams.
82. Abu Zubaydah correspondence.
83. Ibid.
84. 1st Camp 7 commander to 9/11 pretrial.
85. Abu Zubaydah to ICRC.
86. Ibid.
87. June 21, 2005, Rumsfeld on *Tony Snow Show*.
88. SASC report Index.

89. Author interview with Davis; the deputy was Stuart Couch, who later switched sides and represented Mohamedou Ould Salahi.

90. 1st Camp 7 commander to 9/11 pretrial; for more on Swann see Jess Bravin, "The Conscience of a Colonel," *Wall Street Journal*, Mar. 31, 2007.

91. Author interview with Davis.

92. 1st Camp 7 commander to 9/11 pretrial.

93. Allegations made by Harrington during testimony of Mike Butsch and 1st Camp 7 commander, Nov. 2019.

94. Author interview with Harrington.

95. Allegations made by Harrington.

96. Allegation made by Harrington.

97. For the original charge sheet see www.web.archive.org/web/20101109025708/http://www.defense .gov/news/commissionsCo-conspirators.html.

98. See Gaudin testimony to al-Nashiri pretrial, Nov. 2017, www.mc.mil/Portals/0/pdfs/alNashiri2 /Al%20Nashiri%20II%20(TRANS3Nov2017).PDF.

99. Author interview with McFadden.

100. The first Guantánamo chief prosecutor, Colonel Fred Borch, resigned in Aug. 2005 after three prosecutors complained that he had rigged the system against providing due process to the detainee. Colonel Davis replaced him after a brief interlude with Robert Swann acting as intermediary prosecutor, author interview with Davis.

101. Date of clean-team interview from Zayn-al-Abidin Muhammad Husayn (ISN#10016) v. Lloyd Austin et al., United States District Court for the District of Columbia, Case 1:08-cv-01360-UNA, May 24, 2021; see also Abu Zubaydah CSRT transcript, Mar. 2007.

102. Leigh Sales, "Leaked Emails Claim Guantánamo Trials Rigged," Australian Broadcasting Corporation, Aug. 1, 2005.

103. Author interviews with Denbeaux and Margulies; some of these detainees are identified in Zayn-al-Abidin Muhammad Husayn (ISN#10016) v. Lloyd Austin et al., United States District Court for the District of Columbia, Case 1:08-cv-01360-UNA, May 24, 2021.

104. Tenet describes Abu Zubaydah's capture as a "gunfight," see Tenet and Harlow, *At the Center of the Storm*, p. 240.

105. SSCI report, p. 21.

106. FOIA to Ray Bonner, C06867633, 2020/12/17.

107. Abu Zubaydah correspondence.

108. Ibid.

109. Ibid.

110. Ibid.

111. Author interviews with Mitchell.

112. Author interview with Bruguiere.

113. Phil Reeves, "Six Muslim Militants Sentenced to Death for Plotting to Attack Tourists in Jordan," *Independent*, Sept. 19, 2000.

114. Author interview with Humphries.

115. Zayn-al-Abidin Muhammad Husayn (ISN#10016) v. Lloyd Austin et al., United States District Court for the District of Columbia, Case 1:08-cv-01360-UNA, May 24, 2021.

116. Ibid.

117. Author interviews with Rodriguez.

118. Author interviews with Higgins.

119. Abu Zubaydah CSRT transcript, Mar. 2007.

120. Author interviews with Higgins.

121. www.media.miamiherald.com/smedia/2008/04/16/18/AZ.source.prod_affiliate.56.mp3; Mitchell quote from Mitchell and Harlow, *Enhanced Interrogation*, p. 59.

122. Abu Zubaydah diary, Vol. 6.

123. Author message exchange with Zaina and Omar bin Laden, Apr. 2021.

124. See Abu Zubaydah's JTF-GTMO Detainee Assessment, Nov. 11, 2008; also author interviews with Rizzo.
125. Jason Leopold, "Guantánamo Parole Board Says Abu Zubaydah Will Be a 'Forever Prisoner,'" *VICE News*, Oct. 27, 2016.
126. Author interviews with Higgins.
127. Abu Zubaydah correspondence.
128. Abu Zubaydah's diary.
129. On August 12, 2015, he noted in his diary that his weight was 146 pounds.
130. Abu Zubaydah correspondence.
131. Author interviews with Aldrich.
132. Ibid.
133. Author interview with Connell.
134. Author interviews with Mitchell.
135. Ibid.
136. Mitchell and Harlow, *Enhanced Interrogation*, pp. 255–57.
137. Ibid, p. 256.
138. Ibid. p. 260.
139. Author interviews with Mitchell.
140. Rodriguez and Harlow, *Hard Measures*, p. 210.
141. Ibid.
142. Author interviews with Rodriguez and Prado.
143. Author interviews with Rodriguez.
144. Author interview with Erik Prince, Dulles, VA, Nov. 2018.
145. Author interview with Waugh.
146. Author interview with Goss.
147. Author interviews with Tenet and Harlow.
148. Shapira, "For CIA Family a Deadly Suicide Bombing Leads to Painful Divisions."
149. Valutare LLC, see www.cybersecuritysymposium.uncc.edu/speaker/scott-shumate.
150. Scheuer statement to Extraordinary Rendition in U.S. Counterterrorism Policy, Committee on Foreign Affairs, Apr. 17, 2007, Serial no. 110–28.
151. Author interview with Tenet.
152. Author interviews with Rizzo.
153. Mark Benjamin, "'War on Terror' Psychologist Gets Giant No-Bid Contract," *Salon*, Oct. 14, 2010.
154. Author interviews with Mitchell.
155. www.hrw.org/reports/2004/thailand0704/4.htm.
156. Amnesty International, "More Than 7,000 Killed in Philippines in Six Months, as President Encourages Murder," May 18, 2020; Amnesty International, "India: Prime Minister Modi Must End Lockdown in Jammu and Kashmir," Aug. 15, 2019.
157. Author telephone interview with Imroz, 2021.
158. "Capture or kill" quote from Jose Rodriguez, author interview, Oct. 2018.
159. Harlow, *Rebuttal*, pp. 42–47.
160. Author interview with Tenet.
161. Harlow, *Rebuttal*, pp. 2–6.
162. Ibid., for presidential see p. 71, for investigations see p. 72.
163. www.feinstein.senate.gov/public/_cache/files/e/3/e369f4a2-6993-43d2-aa99-23c15075dd4d/78 FA199F8373DAFA360335AA07372B80.fact-check---response-morell-and-harlow-book-6-2 -15.pdf.
164. Mitchell to 9/11 pretrial, see also FOIA to Ray Bonner, C06775587, 2020/02/25; for "Architect" see Rodriguez to Salim v. Mitchell.
165. www.ciasavedlives.com.
166. Bad Monkey, www.badmonkeyybor.com.
167. Author interviews with Mitchell.

168. Author interviews with Aldrich.

169. Mitchell and Harlow, *Enhanced Interrogation*, p. 188.

170. Author interviews with Mitchell, also Mitchell to 9/11 pretrial.

171. Author interviews with Aldrich.

172. Elena Schor, "US Drops Charges against 9/11 Suspect Detained at Guantánamo," *Guardian*, May 14, 2008.

173. Carol Rosenberg and Julian E. Barnes, "CIA Detainee Agrees to Drop Call for CIA Testimony," *New York Times*, May 14, 2021.

174. Author interview with Sharon.

175. Author telephone interview with Brian Mizier, counsel to Abd al-Rahim al-Nashiri, May 2020.

176. Author interviews with Shiffrin, see also the government case against Padilla, www.justice.gov /osg/brief/padilla-v-hanft-opposition-0.

CHAPTER 21: "BAD GUYS BECOME GOOD GUYS AND VICE VERSA"

1. Author interviews with Mitchell.

2. Author interviews with defense teams for the 9/11 accused.

3. Carol Rosenberg, "Inside America's War Court: Clothing and Culture at Guantánamo Bay," *New York Times*, Dec. 27, 2019.

4. Author interview with Harrington.

5. Their names were Hank Schuelke and Brian Paszamant.

6. Salman Masood and Carlotta Gall, "U.S. Sees a Terror Threat; Pakistanis See a Heroine, *New York Times*, Mar. 5, 2010.

7. Author interviews with Mizier, Stephen Xenakis, and Connell, Jan. 2020, Guantánamo Bay, Cuba.

8. Adam Drucker to 9/11 pretrial.

9. Fouda and Fielding, *Masterminds of Terror*.

10. Author interviews with Mitchell.

11. Abu Zubaydah diary, Vol. 13.

12. Ibid.

INDEX